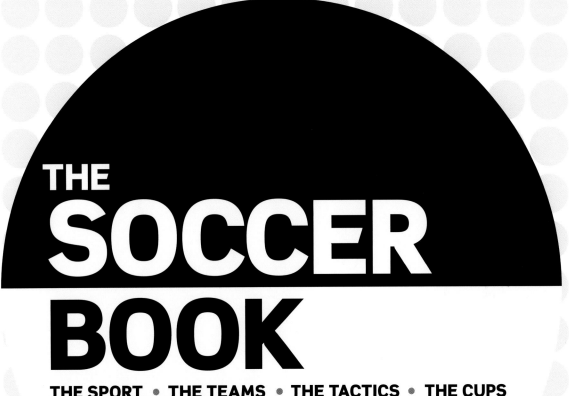

THE
SOCCER
BOOK

THE SPORT • THE TEAMS • THE TACTICS • THE CUPS

**LONDON, NEW YORK,
MUNICH, MELBOURNE, AND DELHI**

Writers David Goldblatt, Johnny Acton

Senior Editor Conor Kilgallon
Senior Art Editor Michael Duffy

Editors Bob Bridle, Chris Hawkes, Chris Stone
Designers Katie Eke, Brian Flynn,
Phil Gamble, Jillian Burr
Editorial Assistant Rory Thomas
Researcher Neil Mason

Illustrators Mike Garland, Mark Walker
Production Editor Tony Phipps
Production Controller Imogen Boase

Managing Editor Stephanie Farrow
Managing Art Editor Lee Griffiths

Discover more at
www.dk.com

Publisher Jonathan Metcalf
Art Director Bryn Walls

US Editor Jenny Siklós

Produced with assistance from
Cooling Brown

First American Edition, 2009

Published in the United States by
DK Publishing
375 Hudson Street
New York, New York 10014

09 10 11 12   10 9 8 7 6 5 4 3 2 1

TD411—August 2009

Published in Great Britain by
Dorling Kindersley Limited.

A catalog record for this book is available from the
Library of Congress

ISBN 978-0-7566-5098-8

DK books are available at special discounts when
purchased in bulk for sales promotions, premiums,
fund-raising, or educational use. For details,
contact: DK Publishing Special Markets, 375
Hudson Street, New York, New York 10014 or
SpecialSales@dk.com.

Printed and bound in China by
Hung Hing Offset Printing

CONTENTS

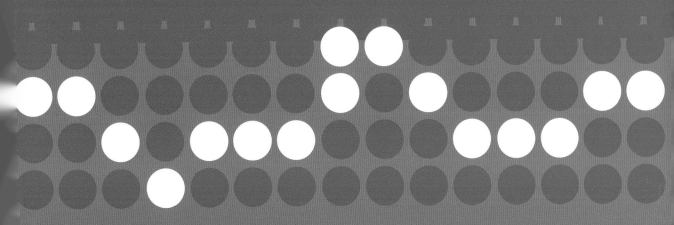

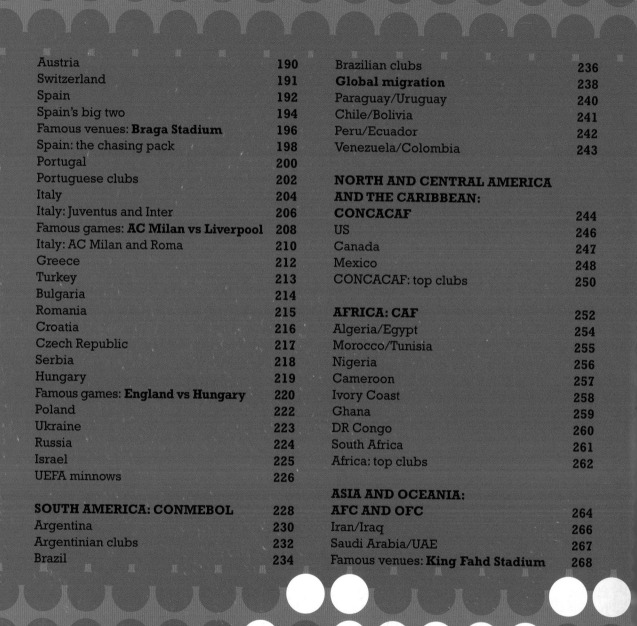

6. THE COMPETITIONS

7. THE RECORDS

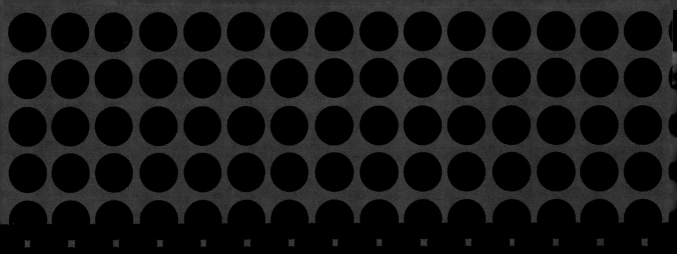

INTRODUCTION

Soccer is the most popular sport in the world. From Greenland to the Andes, people just can't seem to resist kicking a leather ball around or watching others doing the same. The figures are staggering. Approximately 250 million people play the game regularly. If players made up a nation, it would be the fourth most populous on earth. Meanwhile, the cumulative television audience for the 2002 World Cup final was estimated at 1.3 billion, a quarter of the total human population.

You could almost say that soccer is the universal language. If you found yourself in the middle of a strange country with no knowledge of the local tongue, you would still be able to strike up a conversation by using a few hand gestures accompanied by the names of some prominent players. Place one hand at chest level while saying "Pele," then raise it with the word "Maradona" and you'll quickly start making friends.

Soccer brings people together and gives them a sense of identity. It is a never-ending soap opera which provides a timeline to our lives and a source of endless debate. All aspects of human existence are here: heroes and villains, love and loathing, power, politics, and money. Like life itself, the game provides moments of sublime beauty and others of crushing disappointment.

The Soccer Book celebrates this amazing diversity in full, from the relative merits of zonal and man-marking to the most amusing bleacher chants. Within its pages you will learn how to bend the ball like Beckham, meet the dog who found the World Cup hidden in a suburban garden, and discover how a Madagascan league game could possibly have finished 149–0. The one thing this book cannot do is provide an ultimate explanation of why people are so fascinated by soccer. Still, there's no harm in looking at some of the theories.

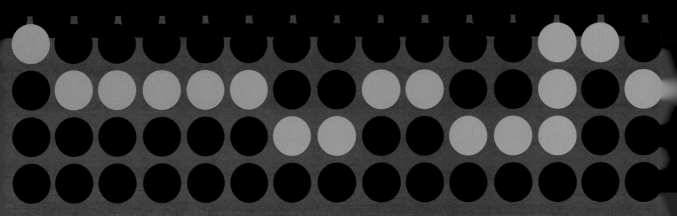

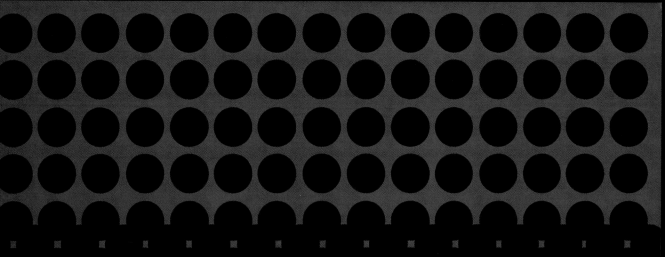

Some have claimed that the game is a surrogate for hunting—on which, of course, our ancestors depended for their survival. According to this view, a goal is equivalent to a kill, which would certainly explain the sense of importance surrounding the game. Another possibility is that soccer is a kind of ritualized warfare. After all, the sport is couched in military language (such as campaigns, tactics, and captains) and it may be no accident that its popularity has coincided with an era in which young men have been less regularly engaged in battle than in the past.

Both these theories have their merits but perhaps another, simpler explanation needs to be added. Our history can be seen as the story of an increasing split between our physical selves and our minds. Soccer works the other way around. By uniting the brain with the parts of the body at the opposite extremity (the feet), it temporarily heals the split. When we play the game or identify with others who are doing so, we become whole again. And, of course, it is not just men who feel this way. The women's game is extremely popular—for every reference to a "he" in this book, a "she" can and should just as easily be substituted.

Maybe even this is to overcomplicate things. We planned to write this book without using soccer's most famous and clichéd quotation but in the end we might as well admit defeat. "Some people believe football [soccer] is a matter of life and death," the great Liverpool manager Bill Shankly once said. "I am very disappointed with that attitude. I can assure you it is much, much more important than that." No one has better captured the irrational depth of passion aroused by twenty-two men chasing a ball.

David Goldblatt

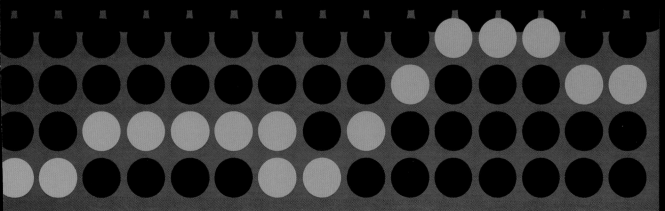

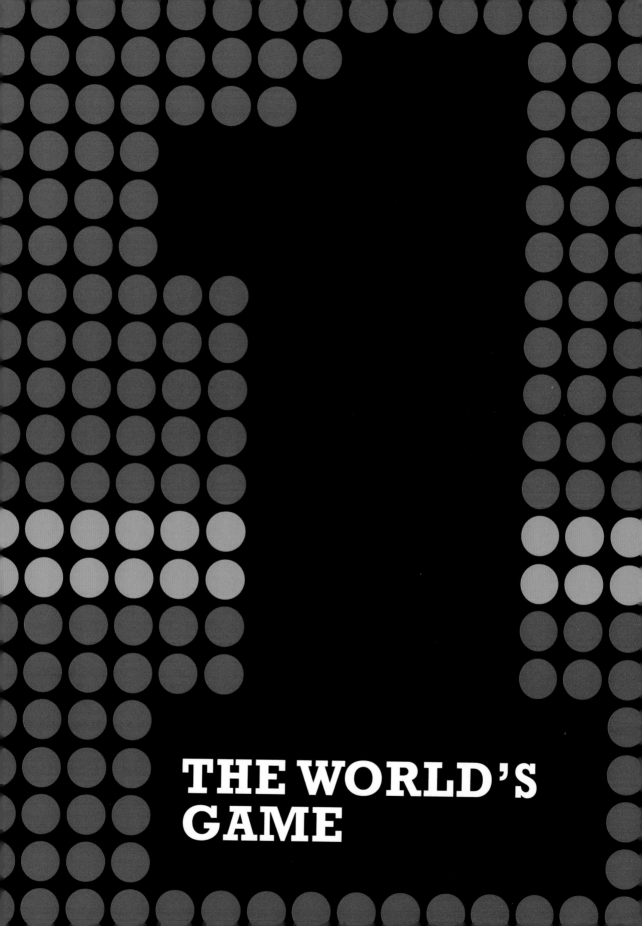

THE WORLD'S
GAME

ANCIENT BALL GAMES

Humanity has been kicking spherical objects for as long as they've both been around, but more formal ball games are no more than 4,000 years old at the most—the age of the oldest ball ever discovered. As with most good ideas, a lot of people had the same thought in different parts of the world, and each of them created their own distinct ancient ball game.

HISTORIC RELATIONS

Of all the ancient ball games, *cuju*, from China, in its oldest form, was the closest to modern soccer, with two teams moving a ball toward a fixed goal. But it was in Mesoamerica that a ball game acquired the kind of importance that soccer has today. For 3,000 years the "ball game," as it was known, was a pastime, a spectator sport, a passion, and a ritual. Soccer as we know it today descends from the variety of riotous folk-soccer games played in medieval England.

THE WORLD'S FIRST MASS-APPEAL BALL GAME

Although the exact rules of the Mesoamerican ball game are not known, the sport's widespread popularity is not in doubt: ball courts have been found as far north as Arizona in the United States and as far south as Nicaragua in Central America. The main aim appears to have been to keep the solid rubber ball in play. The game was an integral part of society—it is thought that children played the game recreationally.

SOCCER FOR THE MASSES

English folk soccer, also known as "mob football," involved huge numbers of people (often the population of a village divided into two sides, based on who lived where) and few, if any, rules. Games were usually linked to special events in the calendar, such as saints' days. The sport was not universally popular, though: English kings Edward II, Henry V, Edward IV, Henry VII, and Henry VIII all issued edicts against the noisy, rough game.

KEMARI
The game was enormously popular in Japan between the 10th and 16th centuries.

A ROUND BALL AND A SQUARE WALL.
JUST LIKE THE YIN AND YANG

LI YU (50–136ce) ON THE CHINESE GAME OF *CUJU*

EVOLUTION OF THE MODERN GAME

From Central America to the Roman Empire, history is littered with various types of ball game.

1500bce The first rubber ball is made in Mesoamerica

1200bce The first major olemec ball courts emerge in Mesoamerica

350bce First written evidence of *harpastum* in Roman Empire

200bce *Cuju* first formalized in the Han Dynasty, China

-1500bce   -1250bce   -1000bce   -750bce   -500bce   -250bce

SOCCER'S ORIGINS

The origins of soccer can be found in every corner of the globe. Civilizations throughout history have all invented games that are played with balls, and every one of them can be considered as an ancient forerunner to the modern game.

CURIOUS DISCOVERIES

During the 1930s, Costa Rican banana plantation workers started to uncover enormous stone spheres hidden in the jungle. They weighed up to 16 tons and date to between 200BCE and 1500CE. No one knows their purpose, but they attest to the human fascination with spherical objects.

East Coast Americas
Seventeenth-century colonial reports mention mass games of *Passuckquakkkohowog* in the region. The word translates as "those who gather to play soccer"

England and Scotland
From the 11th century, there are numerous references to both urban and rural forms of soccer

Greco-Roman World
Ball games were a minor affair in the Greco-Roman world. A raucous, rugbylike game called *harpastum* appears to have been played among the Roman legions at various points

China
Cuju was first formalized under the Han Dynasty (206BCE–220CE). By 1000CE, the game had split into a courtly version and a popular version, but had died out by the 18th century

Celtic Periphery
Different versions of folk soccer were played throughout the area. In Cornwall, it was known as "hurling;" in South Wales, "knappen." In Ireland, the authorities attempted to ban it; and in Brittany the game was called *la soule*.

Japan
The Japanese game of *kemari* was played with four players. An umpire counted passes and awarded points for the most stylish tricks and flicks.

Mesoamerica
The "ball game" was at the center of religious and everyday life for the Aztecs, the Maya, and for societies as far north as Arizona for 3,000 years

Northern Italy
Calcio was a game played in medieval Florence before its disappearance in the 18th century. It was primarily a courtly game with fixed rules.

Southeast Asia
Rattan balls were first made in Southeast Asia in the first millennium CE. Games of many kinds evolved in the region, but tended to exclude the use of hands.

KEY
- 1500–750BCE
- 750–0BCE
- 0–1250CE
- 1250–1750CE

Ethiopia
Ganna has been played on the high plains of Ethiopia for over a millennium. It is a form of mass-participation field hockey and is often played by whole communities.

Australasia
Marn grook was played among the Aboriginal Australians. The game involved kicking and running with the ball and is considered a forerunner to Australian Rules football.

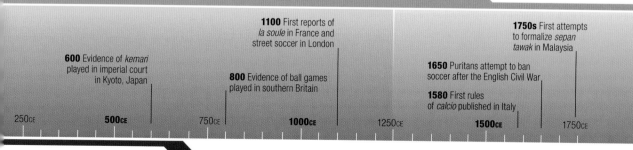

1100 First reports of *la soule* in France and street soccer in London

1750s First attempts to formalize *sepan tawak* in Malaysia

600 Evidence of *kemari* played in imperial court in Kyoto, Japan

800 Evidence of ball games played in southern Britain

1650 Puritans attempt to ban soccer after the English Civil War

1580 First rules of *calcio* published in Italy

250CE   500CE   750CE   1000CE   1250CE   1500CE   1750CE

FROM FOLK TO ASSOCIATION

Soccer was transformed from a dying folk ritual in the British countryside to the world's most popular and commercialized sport in just a century. It was nurtured in England's elite universities and private schools before bursting out into the cities of Victorian Britain. Along the way the game acquired field markings, 11 players per side, and forbade the use of hands.

FOLK SOCCER

By the early 19th century, folk soccer was dying. Increasingly the authorities feared the drunken mob and the impact their games would have on property and land. In 1835, the new Highways Act gave magistrates the power to ban street soccer, which they did. By the 1860s, the game had been taken into the private schools, where it underwent a transformation and emerged as what we now call "association soccer."

THE PRIVATE SCHOOLS AND SOCCER

Reformers in private schools in the early 19th century resolved to create muscular Christian gentleman fit in mind and body to run the British Empire —and what better way to enforce this than through the regular playing of soccer. Aside from physical activity, this new breed of schoolmaster hoped to teach their charges discipline, teamwork, fair play, and courage.

THE ETON FIELD GAME
A cross between soccer and rugby, the rules for this traditional game were documented for the first time in 1815.

YEAR	SOCCER FIRSTS
1857	The first dedicated soccer club, Sheffield FC, is established.
1870	Specified goalkeepers are used for the first time.
1872	First FA Cup final; first international.
1873	Players could be sent off for a serious offense for the first time.
1877	Match length fixed at 90 minutes.
1878	Referees use whistles for the first time.
1880	Crowds pay an admission fee to watch matches for the first time.
1881	The FA rule book states the need for referees to officiate matches.
1882	Crossbars for goalposts are introduced.
1887	The center-mark and center-circle are first used.
1888	The first season of the Football League is played in England.
1898	Linesmen introduced for first time.
1909	Goalkeepers first required to wear a different colored uniform.

PRIVATE SCHOOL GAMES

Played since the mid-18th century, the Eton Field Game has no offside rule and is closer to rugby than soccer (see left). Harrow Football, played with a large flat-bottomed ball, saw the first use of the defensive wall for free-kicks. Winchester Football, a six-, ten-, or 15-a-side game played on a long, narrow field, places an emphasis on kicking.

MAKING OF THE MODERN GAME

1846
Cambridge Rules drawn up at Cambridge University

1863
FA founded; FA rules first published

1872
First official international, England vs Scotland, ends 0–0 in Glasgow; the first FA Cup final sees Wanderers beat Royal Engineers 1–0

1840   1850   1860   1870   1880

ESTABLISHING THE RULES

In November 1863, members of 12 London clubs met to agree on an accepted set of rules. They decided that there would be no carrying of the ball with the hands, and no hacking (kicking an opponent's shins). Those who disagreed created rugby union; those who agreed wrote the rules of association soccer and created its governing body, the Football Association.

1863 RULES

Field: maximum dimensions of 200 x 100 yards (180 x 90 m); goalposts should be 8 yards (7.32 m) apart, with no tape or crossbar.

Coin toss determines ends; kick-off to be taken from center-mark.

Teams change ends after every goal.

Goal scored if the ball is kicked between the two posts (at whatever height).

Throw-ins to be taken by player who first touches the ball after it has gone out of play; from the restart, the ball is not in play until it has touched the ground.

When a player kicks the ball, any member of his team who is in front of him is offside.

No running with the ball in the hands.

No hands to throw or pass the ball.

No tripping, hacking, or holding.

THE SPREAD OF SOCCER

As the first generation of players left the private schools and elite universities, they took soccer into the world with them. Once the rules had been set down, the game quickly spread to the middle and working classes. Throughout the 1880s, fierce competition between clubs saw under-the-counter payments to the best players. Through gritted teeth, the FA legalized professionalism in 1885.

THE EARLY SOCCER MAP

Association soccer grew out of traditional folk soccer (games of which are still played in some locations today) and evolved further in English private schools and universities.

CLUBS INVOLVED IN THE FORMATION OF THE ENGLISH FA IN 1863

Barnes
Blackheath (later withdrew)
Blackheath School
Charterhouse
Crusaders
Crystal Palace
Forest
Kensington School
No Names of Kilburn
Percival House
Surbiton
The War Office

KEY
- Major private schools
- Surviving folk-soccer venues
- Major universities

WILLIAM McGREGOR
A director at Aston Villa FC, the Scot is regarded as the founder of the Football League—the first organized soccer league in the world—in 1888.

1883 Blackburn Olympic beat Old Etonians in the FA Cup final—the first working-class team to win it

1885 FA legalizes professionalism in English soccer

1888 Football League created: Preston North End are the first champions

1892 Second Division created

1880 1890 1900

THE GLOBAL GAME

In just over a century, the professional game reached every continent and culture in the world. Soccer was traveling almost as soon as it was invented, through the many tentacles and connections of the formal British Empire (to South Africa, for example) and the huge network of British traders, sailors, miners, merchants, bankers, and teachers who traveled the globe in search of business in the late 1800s.

THE GREAT ENTERTAINER

Soccer's mass appeal can be explained because it is one of the simplest, most flexible games ever invented. It can be played on a variety of surfaces, by many different body types, and requires several skills rather than one. It needs almost no equipment, can be played without referees, and is an extraordinary and unpredictable game to watch. It demands a unique combination of individual skills and teamwork, and goals scored are both rare and special. Above all, anyone can beat anyone else on their day.

CHARLES MILLER

The son of a rich coffee merchant, Charles William Miller (left) is considered the father of soccer in Brazil. Sent off to school in England in 1884 (aged ten), he returned to São Paulo in 1894 bringing with him two soccer balls and a set of rules. The following year, he arranged a soccer match between gas, bank, and railroad workers in the city. It was the first ever organized soccer match played in Brazil.

EARLY SOCCER HOTSPOTS

In the late 19th and early 20th centuries, soccer took off in key cities, ports, and coastal regions around the world. These became beachheads from which the game would steadily expand to reach the provincial cities, countryside, and peripheries of every nation in the world.

Eastern United States
Despite the already established popularity of other sports in the United States in the 1880s and 1890s, new waves of working-class British immigrants established a thriving soccer culture in the years before World War I

Mexico City
Soccer's popularity exploded in Mexico City at the turn of the 20th century as British expatriates formed clubs all over the city. The first league was contested in 1903

Rio de Janeiro-São Paulo (Brazil)
Brazil's two biggest cities were the first home of soccer in the country. Men such as Charles Miller (see left) were important figures in soccer's development in the region

Rio Plata
With over 40,000 Britons in Buenos Aires in the 1870s and more in Montevideo, soccer established itself quickly on the Rio Plata. Buenos Aires had established a city league by 1891 and Montevideo followed a year later

MAKING OF THE MODERN GAME

1900
First Olympic soccer tournament in Paris—Great Britain wins the gold medal

1904
Fédération Internationale de Football Association (FIFA) is established in Paris

1920s
Soccer becomes the sport of the working class all over Europe

1930
The first World Cup is played in Montevideo, Uruguay—the hosts become first world champions

MID-1930s
Shift to professionalism in continental Europe and Latin America

1900   1910   1920   1930   1940   1950

SOCCER... IS DIRECTED AT PEOPLE WITH **ADVANCED CULTIVATED IDEAS**

BASQUE SPECTATOR AT AN EARLY SOCCER MATCH, CA.1903

DIVISION AMONG THE RANKS

Not everyone was in favor of the game spreading to foreign parts. F.W. Campbell of Blackheath resigned from the infant FA when the practice of hacking was outlawed. "If you do away with [it], I will be bound to bring over a lot of Frenchmen who would beat you with a week's practice," he warned.

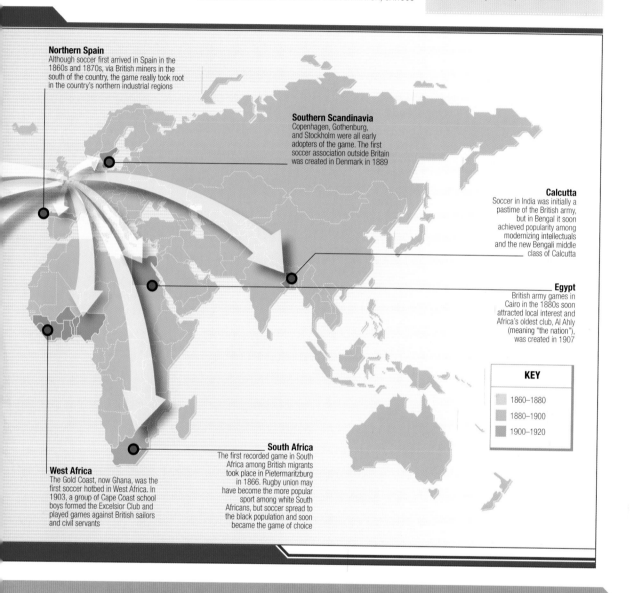

Northern Spain
Although soccer first arrived in Spain in the 1860s and 1870s, via British miners in the south of the country, the game really took root in the country's northern industrial regions

Southern Scandinavia
Copenhagen, Gothenburg, and Stockholm were all early adopters of the game. The first soccer association outside Britain was created in Denmark in 1889

Calcutta
Soccer in India was initially a pastime of the British army, but in Bengal it soon achieved popularity among modernizing intellectuals and the new Bengali middle class of Calcutta

Egypt
British army games in Cairo in the 1880s soon attracted local interest and Africa's oldest club, Al Ahly (meaning "the nation"), was created in 1907

KEY

	1860–1880
	1880–1900
	1900–1920

West Africa
The Gold Coast, now Ghana, was the first soccer hotbed in West Africa. In 1903, a group of Cape Coast school boys formed the Excelsior Club and played games against British sailors and civil servants

South Africa
The first recorded game in South Africa among British migrants took place in Pietermaritzburg in 1866. Rugby union may have become the more popular sport among white South Africans, but soccer spread to the black population and soon became the game of choice

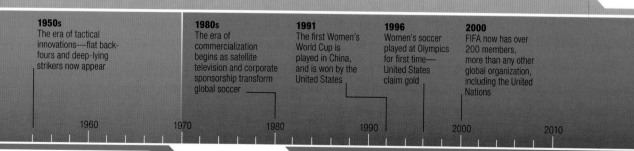

1950s
The era of tactical innovations—flat back-fours and deep-lying strikers now appear

1980s
The era of commercialization begins as satellite television and corporate sponsorship transform global soccer

1991
The first Women's World Cup is played in China, and is won by the United States

1996
Women's soccer played at Olympics for first time— United States claim gold

2000
FIFA now has over 200 members, more than any other global organization, including the United Nations

1960   1970   1980   1990   2000   2010

INTO THE 20TH CENTURY

It was only at the turn of the 20th century that soccer fields began to take on their modern form, and not until the 1920s that the rules finally settled down. The game achieved immediate and widespread popularity, and was soon transformed into the biggest mass-entertainment sport in Victorian Britain. It did not take long before the rules and innovations spread around the world and formed the basis of what we now know as a global game.

STRANGE EARLY RULES

The game's original laws allowed several unusual practices that would now be unthinkable. Players could catch the ball if it reached them on the full toss. Even more odd, if an attacker managed to touch the ball behind the opponent's goal line, his side was awarded a free-kick 15 yards (13.7 m) from goal.

THE EVOLUTION OF THE SOCCER FIELD

The FA's first rulebook in 1863 contained no field markings. In fact, it would take until 1882 for the sidelines and goal lines to become compulsory. By then, the size of the field had shrunk and a steady series of rule changes and innovations turned the blank, muddy fields of the 1860s into the modern markings that are used all over the world today.

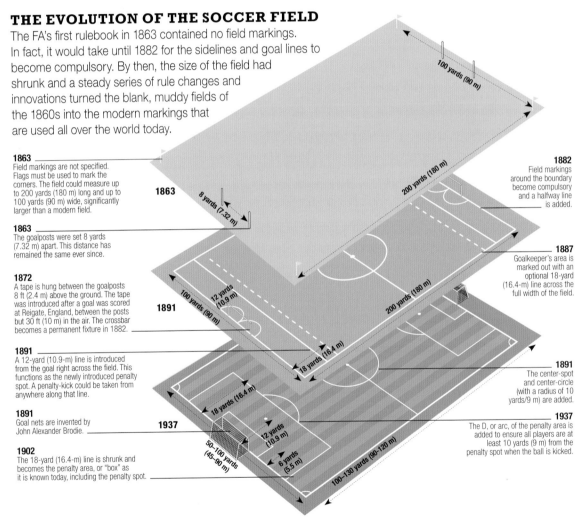

1863
Field markings are not specified. Flags must be used to mark the corners. The field could measure up to 200 yards (180 m) long and up to 100 yards (90 m) wide, significantly larger than a modern field.

1863
The goalposts were set 8 yards (7.32 m) apart. This distance has remained the same ever since.

1872
A tape is hung between the goalposts 8 ft (2.4 m) above the ground. The tape was introduced after a goal was scored at Reigate, England, between the posts but 30 ft (10 m) in the air. The crossbar becomes a permanent fixture in 1882.

1891
A 12-yard (10.9-m) line is introduced from the goal right across the field. This functions as the newly introduced penalty spot. A penalty-kick could be taken from anywhere along that line.

1891
Goal nets are invented by John Alexander Brodie.

1902
The 18-yard (16.4-m) line is shrunk and becomes the penalty area, or "box" as it is known today, including the penalty spot.

1882
Field markings around the boundary become compulsory and a halfway line is added.

1887
Goalkeeper's area is marked out with an optional 18-yard (16.4-m) line across the full width of the field.

1891
The center-spot and center-circle (with a radius of 10 yards/9 m) are added.

1937
The D, or arc, of the penalty area is added to ensure all players are at least 10 yards (9 m) from the penalty spot when the ball is kicked.

THE ONLY THING THAT HASN'T CHANGED IS... THE SHAPE OF THE BALL

FORMER MANCHESTER UNITED AND SCOTLAND FORWARD **DENIS LAW**

HISTORY OF THE OFFSIDE RULE

Soccer had been plagued by the offside issue from its very earliest private school forms—the perennial problem of how to stop players from hanging around the goal. The offside rule (see pp.66–67) was designed to prevent this, and has undergone two subtle revisions since its inception in 1863.

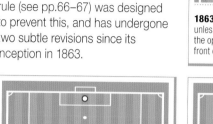

1863 A player is offside unless three players of the opposing side are in front of him

- ● Attacking team
- ● Defensive team
- ○ Offside player
- – – Pass

1925 A player is now deemed offside unless two opponents are in front of him when he gets the ball

- ● Attacking team
- ● Defensive team
- ○ Offside player
- – – Pass

1990 A player is onside if he is level—rather than just behind—the second-to-last opponent

- ● Attacking team
- ● Defensive team
- ○ Offside player
- – – Pass

HOW SOCCER BECAME A SPECTATOR SPORT

Crowds had gathered to watch kickabouts since the 1850s, but in Victorian Britain, the crowds began to boom in the 1870s and 1880s. The working week was getting shorter, wages were increasing and, as professionalism arrived in 1885, the quality of play and the size of stadiums began to grow. Large numbers of fans from the north of England began to make FA Cup final day in London a vast pilgrimage, and in just 30 years, attendance at the match had grown more than 50-fold. This was mirrored around the world where soccer fever quickly caught on.

RISE IN POPULARITY

FA Cup final attendances 1872–1901

1872	1892	1897	1901
2,000	**25,000**	**65,891**	**114,815**

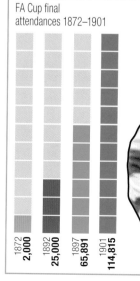

TOP 5: DERBIES

Derbies are the big, tension-filled games between two local rivals—usually from the same city. The term is derived from either the folk-soccer game played in Ashbourne, Derbyshire, or from the often-chaotic games of street soccer played in the city of Derby.

GALATASARAY vs FENERBAHÇE
Istanbul's biggest derby pits Galatasaray, from the European side of the city, against Fenerbahçe, the biggest team on the Asian side of the Bosphorus. The geographical divide is heightened by a social one: Galatasaray grew out of one the most elite schools in the city, while Fener has always been the people's club.

RIVER PLATE vs BOCA JUNIORS
El Superclásico is the biggest derby in Buenos Aires, a city full of intense local rivalries. It pitches the upmarket, uptown River Plate against the low-down, downtown Boca. The rivalry is as much about style as social origins.

OLYMPIAKOS vs PANATHANAIKOS
Known in Greece as the "Derby of the Eternal Enemies," the game pits Olympiakos (from the working-class port zone of Piraeus) against Panathinaikos (from the well-heeled central districts of Athens). The result often determines the outcome of the Greek league.

PARTISAN vs RED STAR
The two clubs were founded within six months and one-third of a mile (500 m) of each other in central Belgrade. Partizan were the team of the Yugoslav army; Red Star the team of the police and Communist party. The game has become even more intense since the break-up of Yugoslavia in 1992.

CELTIC vs RANGERS
The "Old Firm" play out the oldest derby in the world. Passions are always high, but have been regularly inflamed by the state of community relations in Glasgow between Protestants and Catholics, and especially by the political conflicts that took place in Ireland.

MO JOHNSTON
The striker (who played for Celtic between 1984 and 1987) fueled passions in 1989 when he turned down a chance to rejoin his former team and signed for the club's archrivals, Rangers.

FUTSAL (FUTEBOL DE SALÃO)

Futsal is FIFA's official form of indoor five-a-side soccer. Invented in Uruguay—and perfected in Brazil—in the first half of the 20th century, it uses a small, heavy ball that ensures a frenetic, high-speed game in which touch, control, and indeed love, of the ball are the keys to success. It is the fastest-growing variant of soccer in the world.

FUTEBOL DE SALÃO

Juan Carlos Cerianio, who worked at Uruguay's Montevideo YMCA in the 1930s, was the first person to think systematically about playing soccer on a basketball court—which every YMCA possessed, as they had invented basketball in the first place. However, as a standard soccer ball was too large and bouncy for the game to be played on the polished, hardwood floors, something smaller and more controllable was required before the game could really take off.

MAKING ITS MARK

The new ball was perfected and the first rules of what was then called *Futebol de Salão* ("drawing-room soccer") were created at Brazil's São Paulo YMCA in 1936. The ball was weighted with a mixture of cork, horsehair, and sawdust, and then reduced in size. In Brazil, the game's first nickname was "sport of the heavy ball," though in the end the compressed Futsal—an abbreviation of *Futebol de Salão*—won out.

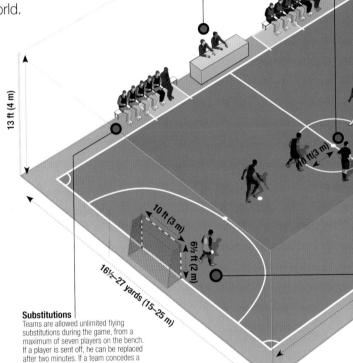

Timekeeper and third referee
A timekeeper and a third referee sit outside the playing area on the same side of the field as the substitute zone. The timekeeper monitors time; the third referee keeps a record of a team's number of fouls

Officials
Futsal is played with two referees on the field. The first referee has the final say, the second referee assists

13 ft (4 m)

10 ft (3 m)

10 ft (3 m)

6½ ft (2 m)

16½–27 yards (15–25 m)

Substitutions
Teams are allowed unlimited flying substitutions during the game, from a maximum of seven players on the bench. If a player is sent off, he can be replaced after two minutes. If a team concedes a goal while down to four players, it can immediately bring on a fifth

THE RULES

1. Number 3 or 4 ball with reduced bounce.
2. Five players.
3. Unlimited flying substitutions.
4. Smaller-sized goal: 10 x 6½ ft (3 x 2 m).
5. Ball kicked into play.
6. Referee and an assistant, plus a third referee and a timekeeper.
7. Running clock.
8. 24-minute halves.
9. One time-out per team per half.
10. No offsides.
11. Goalkeeper throws ball back into play.
12. Four-second rule to put ball back into play.
13. Five-foul limit.
14. Defending team not allowed to form a wall for free-kicks.
15. Player sent off can be substituted after two minutes.
16. Corners taken from corner arc.
17. No slide tackles are allowed.

THE SKILLS

BALL TOUCHES

A statistical study comparing Futsal to indoor-arena soccer with walls showed that players are 210 percent more likely to touch the ball in Futsal.

BALL CONTROL

Playing in such a limited space and under constant pressure, Futsal demands improved ball-control skills and a calm temperament.

SPEEDY PLAY

With fewer stoppages than in the 11-a-side game, the four-second re-start rule, and smaller spaces to cover, players must learn to play and think faster; there is nowhere to hide on a Futsal court.

SUPPORT PLAY

Without a wall to bounce the ball off, players must make supporting runs when their teammates have the ball.

GETTING ORGANIZED

Rules were not systemized in Brazil until the 1980s and until that time bizarre variants of the game existed across the country (see below). In 1988 FIFA took co-responsibility for the sport, alongside the International Futsal Federation, and the first FIFA Futsal World Cup was held in the Netherlands the following year.

EQUIPMENT

A major factor in Futsal's increasing popularity is that it does not require much equipment to play, simply a specialized indoor ball (with a reduced bounce) and rubber-soled, non-marking sports shoes.

24½–25 in (62–64 cm) circumference

Rubber soles
Molded soles aid a player's control and movement during a match.

THE BALL
The ball must be of a circumference of between 24½–25 in (62–64 cm) and weigh between 14–15½ oz (400–440 g) at a pressure of 0.4–0.6 atmospheres.

BOOTS
The only types of footwear permitted in Futsal are canvas or soft-leather sports shoes with soles made of rubber or a similar material.

The goal
The goalposts must be 10 ft (3 m) apart, and the lower edge of the crossbar must be 6½ ft (2 m) above the ground. The lower part of the net is attached to the goal frame's curved tubing, creating a depth of 31½ in (80 cm) at the top and 3½ ft (1 m) at the bottom

Five fouls and the second penalty spot
Teams are allowed five fouls that result in free-kicks. If a player commits a team's sixth foul, the free-kick becomes a penalty taken from the second penalty spot

Ceilings
Many Futsal arenas are indoors and the ceiling must be at least 13 ft (4 m) high. If a player kicks the ball and it hits the ceiling, then play is re-started with a kick-in for the opposing side

Kick-in
If a ball crosses the touchline or goal line, it is kicked back in to play. Players must be 16½ ft (5 m) away from the ball when it is kicked back into play

Indirect free-kicks
Goalkeepers concede a free-kick if they control a back pass from one of their own players with their hands or if they control the ball for more than four seconds in their own half

(6 m) radius

3 ft (10 m)

7–46 yards (25–42 m)

BIZARRE BEGINNINGS

Unusual rules existed in the early days of Futsal in Brazil. In some states, players who had a hand on the floor could not play the ball. Consequently, players would fall in absurd ways to keep their hands off the floor, resulting in a huge increase in fractures.

FALCÃO

Alessandro Rosa Vieira, better known as Falcão, is the world's leading Futsal player. He has scored more than 150 goals for Brazil and starred at the 2004 and 2008 Futsal World Cups.

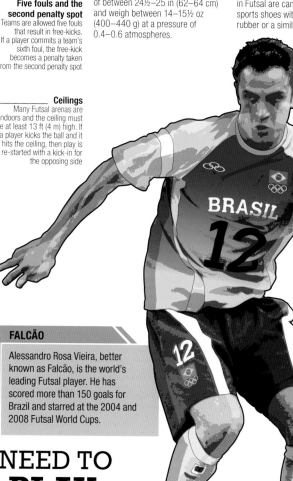

IN FUTSAL YOU NEED TO **THINK AND PLAY QUICK,** SO IT IS EASIER FOR YOU WHEN YOU PLAY OUTDOOR SOCCER

PELÉ

BEACH SOCCER

People have been playing with a ball on the beach for many years, but it wasn't until the 1920s, in Rio de Janeiro, that the game acquired informal rules and new evolving styles of play. Mayor Henrique Dodsworth tried to ban the game from the beaches at that time, but received a petition containing 50,000 signatures complaining about his proposed actions. The rules were formalized in 1992 in an attempt to make it suitable for television.

MADE FOR TV

Beach soccer, in its new version, was designed for television. The three periods, 12 minutes in length, provide perfectly timed, regular advertising breaks without the need to introduce time-outs. The creation of temporary, closed mini-stadiums removed the problems of overcrowding and spectator intrusion. The main appeal, however, is that beach soccer delivers relentless shots on goals and high-scoring games.

THE FIELD

The playing surface must be level, composed of sand, and free of any stones, pebbles, or any other objects that could cause injury to players. In international competitions, the sand used must be fine (rather than coarse) and at least 15¾ in (40 cm) deep.

Officials
Beach soccer has two referees on the field, and one off it who is charged with keeping the team benches under control

Halfway line
Two red flags on opposite sides of the field represent the halfway line

10 yards (9 m)

30 yards (28 m)

40 yards (37 m)

The goal
Must be 18 ft (5.5 m) across and 7 ft (2.2 m) high. There are no field markings between the goalposts

Penalty area
The penalty area is within 29½ ft (9 m) of the goals and is marked by four yellow flags

THE RULES

1. Five-a-side.

2. Unlimited substitutions.

3. No shoes allowed.

4. Coin toss determines choice of ends.

5. Goalkeepers must throw the ball back into play rather than kick it.

6. There are three periods of 12 minutes with a three-minute break between each period.

7. No draw. In the event of a tie, three minutes of extra-time is followed by sudden-death penalties.

8. No offside rule.

9. Defenders are not allowed to form a wall for free-kicks; all defending players must be at least 16 ft (5 m) away when the kick is taken.

10. No kicking sand in anyone's face.

11. Free-kicks to be taken by the person who was fouled.

12. Balls that cross sidelines can be put back into play either as a throw-in or a kick-in.

13. Yellow card awarded for serious fouls.

14. Blue card awarded after second yellow-card offense. Recipient is suspended for two minutes and cannot be replaced.

15. Red card awarded for very serious fouls or for a third yellow-card offense. A team can replace dismissed player after two minutes.

OLD HABITS DIE HARD

Some traditions from the 11-a-side game carry over to beach soccer. At the 2006 Beach Soccer World Cup, held in Rio de Janeiro, Brazil, Uruguay came back from 1–0 down to beat Argentina 2–1 and knock them out of the competition. The game, already fractious, descended into a vast melée of players and officials fighting after the Uruguayans celebrated their second goal.

ON SAND YOU CAN NEVER BE SURE OF ANYTHING

ERIC CANTONA

EQUIPMENT

In keeping with its informal nature, the emphasis in beach soccer has always been on keeping the game and equipment simple and cheap. Players wear neither shoes nor socks, field markings are minimal, and no walls or sideboards are allowed around the field.

30 Average time in seconds between every shot on goal in a beach soccer match

12 Number of Beach Soccer World Championship titles won by Brazil —the most won by any nation

9.4 Average number of goals per game at the 2003 Beach Soccer World Championships—the highest average in the tournament's history

ERIC CANTONA
Eric Cantona (above) is one of an increasing number of professional soccer stars to have moved from the 11-a-side game to beach soccer. After retiring from Manchester United in 1997, Cantona was a key figure in building the French national beach soccer team.

Beach ball
The ball's soft polyurethane (PU) cover is forgiving on a player's bare feet

Soccadelic
BEACH SOCCER

26¾–27½ in (68–70 cm) circumference

BALL
The ball is the same size as those used in the 11-a-side game, with a circumference between 26¾–27½ in (68–70 cm), but beach soccer balls are much lighter.

Shin protection
A high-density shield provides durable protection for the shins

SHINGUARDS
Players may wear adapted shinguards for protection: ankle supports, giving support to a player's ankles, are also permitted.

SKILLS

Sand is a very difficult surface on which to run and over which to pass a ball. On the other hand, it is much nicer to fall on than either grass or concrete. Given this, and the small, intense space and time in which the game is played, beach soccer uses all the skills of 11-a-side soccer, but favors some over others.

TOUCH
Touch is everything in any version of soccer, but in beach soccer, a player needs to practice the kind of touch and control that enables him to pluck the ball out of the air, because that's where it will be a lot of the time.

KEEP IT UP
The ball is harder to control and slower to move in the sand, so a player tries to keep the ball in the air and not on the ground. Chips and flicks are much more effective than long, slide-rule passes along the ground.

VOLLEYING
With small goals and crowded penalty areas, a shot needs to be accurate and fast if a player wants to score. Anyone who can volley a pass, or flick the ball up and volley it themselves, is going to do well.

HEADING
With so many balls coming in the air, a player has to use his head, not just for scoring, but as another form of passing.

ACCELERATION
The sand saps much of the power from a player's legs and can prevent him from accelerating away from an opponent. If a player can develop both the strength and balance to overcome this, he will have a real edge over his opponents.

OVERHEAD KICK
A rare but spectacular feature of the 11-a-side game, the overhead kick is commonplace in beach soccer.

INDOOR/STREET SOCCER

Indoor soccer takes a number of different forms, but what distinguishes these forms from the official indoor variant—Futsal (see pp.22–23)—is that they use walls and boards instead of touchlines. The ball can be played directly off the wall, which eliminates the need for throw-ins, goal-kicks, and corners, and so produces a very fast-paced game.

INDOOR SOCCER

In Britain, the main form of indoor soccer is five-a-side, which is played both informally and in organized leagues around the country. In the United States and in Spain, the game is usually played with six players. All the different leagues in the world play slightly different rules and versions of the game, but they have many similar features.

The crease
Some versions of indoor soccer enforce a special zone inside the goalkeeper's box called the "crease." No player may shoot from inside the crease unless the player was already in possession of the ball when he entered it. If a defender enters the crease, a penalty is awarded to the opposition

MASTERS SOCCER

Masters soccer is an indoor competition open to retired professional players over the age of 35, who play in six-a-side teams representing their old clubs. The field is 66 x 33 yards (60 x 30 m), there is no offside, and the games consist of two eight-minute halves. The format is particularly popular in the UK, where recent winners have included Wolverhampton Wanderers, Leicester City, and Glasgow Rangers. There is also an international version of the Masters tournament, which was won by the Netherlands in 2006.

The team
Five or six, one of whom is the goalkeeper. Substitute players are permitted

Walls
Walls or boards—at least 6 ft (1.8 m) high in the US version of the game—surround the field

The ball
For games that are played on hardwood, the ball is generally covered with suede

5 yards (4.6 m)
30 yards (27.4 m)
8 yards (7.3 m)
50 yards (45.7 m)

The field
Most indoor soccer is played on artificial turf. The game can also be played on hardwood basketball courts

INDOOR SOCCER RULES

Indoor soccer rules vary around the world, but these are among the most commonly found ones.

1. Most professional indoor soccer games play four quarters of 15 minutes, with overtime for draws. Amateur leagues tend to play two 25-minute halves with no overtime.

2. If the ball flies over the walls or touches the ceiling, play is stopped and the opposing team is awarded a free-kick at the point of the infringement.

3. Standard contact rules as used in the 11-a-side game.

4. There is no offside in indoor soccer.

5. No headers allowed.

6. The ball is not allowed to go above head height. If it does, the opposition is awarded a free-kick at the point of the infringement.

7. Some versions of the game rule that the ball may not cross three lines without touching the ground. The lines are evenly spaced along the length of the field, one of them being the exact center.

INDOOR LEAGUES

SPAIN:
Campeonato Nacional de Liga de Fútbol Indoor
UNITED KINGDOM:
Netbusters Soccer Leagues
UNITED STATES AND MEXICO:
National Indoor Soccer League
UNITED STATES, CANADA, AND MEXICO:
Professional Arena Soccer League
UNITED STATES:
Xtreme Soccer League

STREET SOCCER

Soccer has always been a game of the city, and where there isn't grass, the street has served as a field. Coats function as goalposts, a goalmouth is chalked on a wall, and rules are invented as a match progresses. Generations of players have honed their ball skills in these tight, crowded spaces.

STREET SOCCER RULES AND VARIANTS

Street soccer is played with the minimum of rules and accommodates any number of players. No one plays offside because there are no officials and there are no time limits unless agreed. When team numbers are uneven, rules evolve or are invented to deal with the situation.

TAKING SOCCER OFF THE STREETS

One explanation often put forward for the supposed decline in standards in English soccer is the gradual disappearance of street soccer. Local regulations, the installation of speed bumps, and a general increase in intolerance have all taken their toll on this traditional form of the game.

EVERYTHING I EVER ACHIEVED IN SOCCER IS DUE TO **PLAYING SOCCER ON THE STREETS** WITH MY FRIENDS

THREE-TIME WORLD PLAYER OF THE YEAR **ZINÉDINE ZIDANE**

WORLD CHAMPIONSHIPS

In 2006, the first World Street Soccer Championships were held in Germany. The street soccer initiative brought teams from all over the world to compete. Mathare Youth Sports Association, from Nairobi in Kenya, were the tournament's first winners.

STREET GAMES

Children playing soccer in the street is a common sight. Any spare piece of flat ground will serve as a field.

STREET VARIATIONS

CUBBIES

Also known as "Wembley Doubles." One player goes in the game's only goal. Any number of other players must try to score and stop other players from doing so.

60 SECONDS

Played with one goalkeeper and at least two other players. The goalkeeper kicks the ball out, then others have to cooperate to score with a volley within 60 seconds.

21

One player goes in goal; three or more others try to score goals from volleys or headers. Points are awarded for the manner in which goals are scored.

FOUR NETS

The game is played with multiple goals and multiple teams, often four. Teams have to score a set number of goals into one of the opposing team's nets.

GOL PARA MI

A three-player game in which a goal is set up against a fence or wall. One player starts as goalkeeper, but can't use his hands. Shots have to be at waist height or below.

MUNICH

Played one on one. Players have two touches to score in their opponent's goal from within their own half. Players may not enter their own penalty area or their opponent's half.

THREE AND IN

A game played with any number of players, one of whom is the goalkeeper. When an outfield player scores three goals, he changes positions with the goalkeeper.

HEADERS AND VOLLEYS

A game played with a minimum of three players, one of whom is the goalkeeper. Players can only score goals with either a header or a volley.

POINTS

The goalkeeper awards points out of five for each goal scored, typically five for an outstanding attempt, such as an overhead kick. The first player to score 20 points wins.

TEN SHOTS

A two-player game. Each player takes it in turns to take ten shots against the other player, who goes in goal. The winner is the player who scores the most goals out of ten.

SHOOTIES

A game played with a minimum of two players. Each player is only allowed in his own half and is only allowed one touch of the ball before shooting.

FREESTYLE SOCCER

Freestyle soccer is essentially juggling with a ball in as creative a fashion as possible. As in the real game, any part of the body can be used except the hands and arms. At the highest level, freestyle is like a cross between break-dancing and gymnastics, with a sprinkling of martial arts and a soccer ball thrown into the mix. Originally a street art, freestyle soccer is rapidly becoming a legitimate sport in its own right.

FREESTYLE SOCCER'S ORIGINS

People have been juggling with balls without using their hands for millennia. During the Heian Period (794–1185ce), for instance, a ritualized form of the game, called *kemari* (see p.15), was extremely popular at the Japanese imperial court. Since then, almost every child has tried to develop clever solo tricks to impress their friends. Freestyle in its modern form, however, owes its popularity to two things: the advertising industry and video-sharing on the Internet. Both have propelled the sport into the limelight and are a constant source of inspiration and fun.

UNOFFICIAL WORLD CHAMPIONSHIPS

Although the sport is not yet organized by a universally recognized international body, several self-proclaimed freestyle world championships have taken place and have spawned numerous freestyle stars. Previously unheard-of players, such as Mr. Woo (see far right), John Farnworth, Nam the Man, and Arnaud Garnier, have starred in one of these tournaments and have gone on to feature in a number of television ads.

US PRESIDENT PLAYS *KEMARI*

During a state visit to Japan in 1992, George Bush Sr. noticed a game of *kemari* in progress at the old Imperial Palace in Kyoto. He decided to join in, despite not being dressed in the required traditional costume. When he further violated the game's etiquette by heading the ball, the president of Japan, Hirotada Kohno, joined the American president to ensure that any ensuing embarrassment would be diffused.

IMPRESSING THE JUDGES
Style and an impressive array of tricks mark out a stand-out freestyle soccer performance.

> YOU NEED TO HAVE A STRONG WILL, PUT IN THE TIME AND THE EFFORT, AND REMEMBER... THERE ARE **NO SHORTCUTS**
>
> MR. WOO

THE JUDGES' BRIEF

MARKS OUT OF TEN

According to the World Freestyle Football Association (WFFA), established in 2005, performers should be given marks out of ten in the following categories:

1. Control: demonstrating and maintaining ball control using various parts of the body.

2. Transitions: moving fluidly from one trick to the next.

3. Use of both feet.

4. Use of entire body, except hands.

5. Combinations: including consistently completing the same move twice or more.

6. Sticks: stalling the ball on different parts of the body.

7. Variety of tricks.

8. Level of difficulty.

9. Creativity: originality and imagination shown in performance, using crowd reaction as a guide.

10. Blotto: pushing the envelope of the sport to new levels.

IN THE HANDS OF THE GODS

Freestyle soccer hit the silver screen in 2007 with the release of *In the Hands of the Gods*. The much-acclaimed documentary follows five British freestylers from varied backgrounds as they attempt to use their skills to raise enough money to track down their idol, Diego Maradona—the player considered by many to be the father of the freestyle soccer movement. In a journey that changes their lives forever, the five finally track down the Argentine star at his home in Buenos Aires.

5:6:30
Duration in hours, minutes, and seconds, of Mr. Woo's record for head-juggling the ball

644
Year of first written reference to *kemari*, the ancient Japanese ancestor of freestyle soccer

MR WOO
One of the stars of freestyle soccer, Mr Woo has appeared in numerous ads and holds several world records.

MADE FOR TV

For several years, a leading sports equipment manufacturer has had a policy of using top soccer players in its ads. The ad that really catapulted freestyle soccer into public consciousness featured the Brazil squad for the 1998 World Cup performing tricks around an airport. Players subsequently filmed doing incredible things with soccer balls have included Ronaldinho, Edgar Davids, Wayne Rooney, and Cristiano Ronaldo.

BREAKING INTO THE BIG TIME

The commercials have also made stars of previously unknown performers. In addition, several competitions have been organized in the UK and elsewhere, notably in 2001 and 2003. Recently, one company has teamed up with Google to create a freestyle-oriented networking site called *Juga Bonito*. Several other prominent brands have used freestyle soccer players in their ads.

MAJOR FREESTYLE TOURNAMENTS

Rules may not have been standardized, and the sport may lack an official governing body, but there have been several self-proclaimed freestyle world championships over the years.

MASTERS OF THE GAME I

An organization called "Masters of the Game" held a tournament at the Amsterdam Arena, Netherlands, in 2003. It was won by South Korea's Mr. Woo (above).

MASTERS OF THE GAME II

The second Masters of the Game world championship was held in 2006 and was won by the UK's John Farnworth.

KOMBALL KONTEST

The Komball Kontest held in France in 2008 introduced a new format for freestyle competitions. Sixteen participants performed individually in front of three judges, with the best eight progressing to a knockout phase. Ireland's Nam "the Man" Nguyen was crowned European soccer freestyle champion.

RED BULL STREET STYLE

In 2008, the Red Bull Street Style world finals were held in São Paulo, Brazil. A panel judged the participants on ball control, technique, style, and their ability to synchronize their movements with background music.

PARALYMPIC SOCCER

Paralympic soccer describes variants of association soccer that have been adapted for people with disabilities. Games played by the deaf have perhaps the longest history. Two versions, played by the visually impaired and those with cerebral palsy, have become paralympic sports. Amputee soccer has grown hugely, especially in Africa, whereas in the richer nations of the global north, power wheelchair soccer has prospered.

FIRST WORLD CROWN

Spain hosted and won the first Blind Futsal World Cup in 2005, beating France 1–0 in the final. Seven teams—all from Europe —competed, and the biggest win went to Italy, who beat Russia 5–0 to take fifth place.

SOCCER FIVE-A-SIDE

Soccer five-a-side was first developed in Spain in the 1980s. World championships were first held in 1998 and it became a paralympic sport in 2004. The sport is governed by the International Blind Sports Association (IBSA). Each side has four outfield players, a sighted goalkeeper, and sighted guides.

3–4 ft (1–1.2 m)

16½ ft (5 m)

19½ ft (6 m)

6 ft (2 m)

19½–24 yards (18–22 m)

Kickboards
Kickboards at a height of 3¼–4 ft (1–1.2 m) run along the length of the touchline

Substitutions
Substitutions may be made through a door in the kickboard located in front of the timekeeper's table

EYE PADS
Every player on the field, bar the goalkeeper, has to wear a blindfold.

THE RULES

1. Field is surrounded by boards.
2. Two 25-minute halves.
3. Teams are allowed to use sighted goalkeepers and guides.
4. The four outfield players must wear blindfolds.
5. No offside.
6. Unlimited substitutions.
7. A player who has committed five fouls during a match may take no further part in the game.
8. If a player is sent off, he may be replaced after a period of five minutes.
9. Teams are allowed one time-out (of one minute) per half.
10. Teams must field at least two B2 category players (see right) at all times.

ELEGIBILITY

B1 Totally or almost blind.

B2 Partially sighted—able to recognize the shape of a hand up to visual acuity of 2/60.

B3 Able to recognize the shape of a hand up to visual acuity from between 2/60 to 6/60.

SEVEN-A-SIDE SOCCER

This version of soccer is designed for players with cerebral palsy and other neurological disorders, especially those resulting from a stroke and other kinds of brain injury. The Cerebral Palsy International Sports and Recreation Association govern the sport. International competitions began in 1978 and it became an Olympic sport in 1984.

DEAF SOCCER

Deaf soccer is played to standard FIFA rules, and has grown out of the organized communities of deaf people all over the world. Scotland boasts the oldest deaf soccer club in the world, Glasgow Deaf Athletic Football Club, which was founded in 1871. Leagues and cup competitions for deaf people have been running for many years all over the world.

THE RULES

1. Field: 41½–46 yards (38–42 m) by 19½–24 yards (18–22 m).
2. Ball rolled into play from throw-ins with one hand.
3. Two 30-minute halves.
4. At least one C5 or C6 player (see below) at all times.
5. No more than two C8 players (see below) at the same time.

ELIGIBILITY

C5 Athletes with difficulties when walking or running, but not when standing or kicking a ball.

C6 Athletes with control and coordination problems of upper limbs.

C7 Athletes with hemiplegia (i.e. suffering from paralysis on one side of the body).

C8 Minimally disabled athletes.

Officials
Matches are officiated by three officials (two on opposite sides of the field and one who oversees substitutions) and a timekeeper

DEAF AND PROFESSIONAL

Deafness is only a minor hurdle for a player, and several deaf players have gone on to enjoy a successful career in the professional game. Former deaf players include Cliff Bastin (Arsenal and England) and Rodney Marsh (QPR, Manchester City, Fulham, and England).

OTHER VERSIONS

Ingenuity and imagination mean that the loss of a limb or being restricted to a wheelchair are no barriers when it comes to playing soccer. Confirming the all-inclusive spirit of the game, soccer for amputees and wheelchair soccer are becoming more popular year after year.

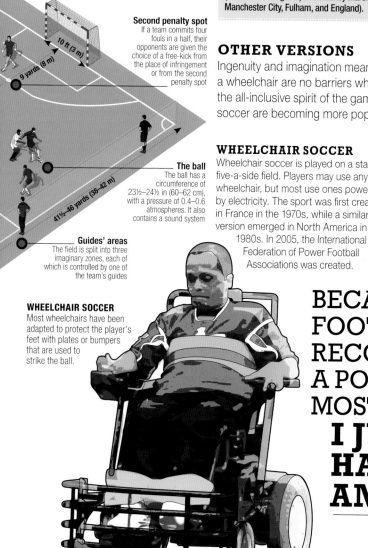

Second penalty spot
If a team commits four fouls in a half, their opponents are given the choice of a free-kick from the place of infringement or from the second penalty spot

10 ft (3 m)

9 yards (8 m)

The ball
The ball has a circumference of 23½–24½ in (60–62 cm), with a pressure of 0.4–0.6 atmospheres. It also contains a sound system

41½–46 yards (38–42 m)

Guides' areas
The field is split into three imaginary zones, each of which is controlled by one of the team's guides

WHEELCHAIR SOCCER
Most wheelchairs have been adapted to protect the player's feet with plates or bumpers that are used to strike the ball.

WHEELCHAIR SOCCER

Wheelchair soccer is played on a standard five-a-side field. Players may use any wheelchair, but most use ones powered by electricity. The sport was first created in France in the 1970s, while a similar version emerged in North America in the 1980s. In 2005, the International Federation of Power Football Associations was created.

SOCCER FOR AMPUTEES

Officially, an amputee is someone who is "abbreviated" at least at the wrist or ankle. Outfielders may have two hands, but only one foot. Goalkeepers may have two legs, but only one hand. The game is played without prostheses and always on metal crutches. Player's crutches may touch the ball incidentally, but they can't be used to pass or shoot.

BECAUSE OF FOOTBALL, PEOPLE RECOGNIZE US IN A POSITIVE WAY. MOST OF ALL, I JUST FEEL HAPPY WHEN I AM PLAYING.

JIMMY HARRISON
FIRST CAPTAIN OF LIBERIA'S NATIONAL TEAM, 2006

THE WORLD'S GAME

GRASSROOTS SOCCER

Soccer has to be played before it can be watched or followed. At the base of every healthy soccer culture is a vigorous network of clubs, players, and coaches who do it for the love of the game. In the developed world, the challenge is to get players away from their game consoles and out onto the field. In the developing world, players are plentiful—it's fields and equipment that are in short supply.

THE SOCCER HIERARCHY

International soccer and professional club soccer are the tip of an enormous hierarchy of playing, organizing, and coaching that makes a soccer culture. Without a huge base of youth and recreational soccer, the professional game can't hope to recruit the playing and administrative talent of the next generation or secure a wide base of fans and enthusiasts.

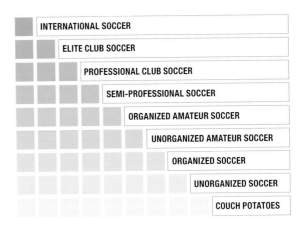

INTERNATIONAL SOCCER									
	ELITE CLUB SOCCER								
		PROFESSIONAL CLUB SOCCER							
			SEMI-PROFESSIONAL SOCCER						
				ORGANIZED AMATEUR SOCCER					
					UNORGANIZED AMATEUR SOCCER				
						ORGANIZED SOCCER			
							UNORGANIZED SOCCER		
								COUCH POTATOES	

SOCCER MOMS

The term "soccer moms" first came into use in the United States in the 1990s as a stereotype of suburban, middle-class women who spend a lot of time ferrying their kids to soccer practices.

GRASSROOTS SOCCER IS FOR ALL AGES, GENDERS, SIZES, SHAPES, LEVELS OF SKILL, NATIONALITIES, FAITHS, RACES... EVERYONE!

JÜRGEN KLINSMANN,
FORMER GERMAN SOCCER PLAYER AND MANAGER

HACKNEY MARSHES

Hackney Marshes is an area of wetland in East London and is considered the San Siro of grassroots soccer. Matches have been played there since the 19th century and the area contains more than 80 soccer fields.

SOCCER CRAZY

Soccer is plagued by overcompetitive and demanding parents who rage on the sideline screaming at opponents and abusing referees—and that is before the game has even started. In 2008, in Wiltshire, England, a father drove his Range Rover onto the field in protest at a referee's decision, and refused to back it off unless the decision was reversed.

PLAYERS OF TOMORROW
Youth soccer has proved hugely successful in recent years and that success is dependent on a whole army of parents, coaches, and caregivers.

WORLD GRASSROOTS CUPS

The two biggest grassroots youth tournaments in world soccer are the Norway Cup and the Swedish Gothia Cup. The Norway Cup was started in 1974 and in recent years more than 1,500 youth teams from over 40 nations have competed. The Gothia Cup, held in Gothenburg, Sweden, surpassed this in 2007, when 34,200 players and team leaders from 1,585 teams and 65 nations participated.

THE BIG KICKABOUT

Manaus is the largest city in the great Brazilian Amazon basin—it is also home to the Big Kickabout, Amazonia's gargantuan grassroots soccer tournament that involves more than 500 soccer teams from all over Brazil. Uniquely among such events, each team also includes a beauty queen, who takes part in a parallel pageant. Teams that get knocked out in the early rounds of the soccer tournament are reinstated if their beauty queen is successful on the catwalk.

GLOBAL INITIATIVE

Launched in 2002, streetfootballworld is a global non-governmental organization that networks the world's grassroots soccer projects. Connecting leagues, teams, and players on six continents, streetfootballworld channels money and expertise to soccer projects that are linked to social development, education, and environmental programs. The first Street Football World Championship was held in Germany in 2006.

WAYNE ROONEY

The Manchester United and England striker's career started on the streets and playing fields of his native Liverpool. He was already playing and starring in adult soccer aged 12.

34,300
The number of boys' sides playing in English grassroots soccer in the 2007–08 season

2006
The year of the inaugural Street Football World Championship, in Berlin, Germany, in which 24 teams competed

88
Number of full-size fields that are marked out at Hackney Marshes, the spiritual home of grassroots soccer in London, England

GOTHIA CUP STARS

Several now high-profile players have featured in the Gothia Cup over the years. Here are a selection of them:

PLAYER	COUNTRY	YEAR
Alan SHEARER	England	1985
Xabi ALONSO	Spain	1987
Andrea PIRLO	Italy	1990
E. ADEBAYOR	Togo	1999
Ze ROBERTO	Brazil	1993, '94
Kieron DYER	England	1988

SOCCER BENEFITS

A healthy grassroots structure sends a constant stream of new playing and coaching talent to the elite game, and sustains the interest and enthusiasm of its future fan base.

POSITIVE INFLUENCE

The benefits of playing soccer, for individuals and for society, are numerous. They can split into three main categories: health benefits, social benefits, and personal benefits.

HEALTH BENEFITS

Healthier, fitter players mean smaller medical bills and a happier population.

SOCIAL BENEFITS

Soccer clubs and networks of soccer organizations create personal and institutional connections that bind neighborhoods together.

PERSONAL BENEFITS

Playing soccer builds friendships, personal skills, communication skills, self-confidence, and wellbeing.

WATCHING THE GAME

Soccer is nothing without its crowds. For over a century, they have paid the players' wages, filled the stadiums with atmosphere, and served as both a chorus and commentary on the game. Nothing is sadder than a match played behind closed doors to empty stands. Crowds have changed in many ways over the years, but the energy and passion they bring has not diminished.

MUSICAL INSTRUMENTS

Music has played a major part in creating a charged atmosphere in stadiums for many years. Rapid Vienna had their own fans orchestra in the 1920s, African stadiums pulsate to the beat of drums, and the England team is followed by a brass band who hammer out the theme tune to *The Great Escape*.

FOLLOWING THE TEAM
Rosettes and rattles were the way to show support for a team in the early 1920s.

SOCCER FAN HISTORY

Vast crowds first started to gather in Britain's industrial cities in the mid-1880s. The first "break club"—drinking parties of fans going to away games—was created in Glasgow around this time. The crowds that came to the grounds found their home on the terraces, which became a natural breeding ground for communal banter. Later, chanting and singing started, capable of creating a cauldron of noise.

> WHEN **THE CROWD SURGES,** A MAN CAN BE **LIFTED OFF THE GROUND...** AS IF BY SOME SOFT-SIDE CRANE

ARTHUR HOPCRAFT DESCRIBING A SCENE ON THE KOP AT ANFIELD FROM THE 1950s IN HIS BOOK *THE FOOTBALL MAN: PEOPLE AND PASSIONS IN SOCCER*

THE CHANGING FACE OF SOCCER

What was once akin to a mass gathering at a factory gate has become more like a day out at a shopping mall. Following the mass introduction of all-seater stadiums after the Hillsborough disaster in 1989, it is now no longer possible to stand through a game at many top league matches around the world. Some things don't change, though: the ubiquitous poor-quality half-time snack still remains the fans' food of choice.

OLD STADIUMS

SEATS: Nearly all standing on concrete bleachers

CROWD CONTROL: No monitoring and few police

CONDITIONS: Most fans exposed to all weathers; few facilities such as bathrooms at the stadiums

FOOD: Generally bad and almost always unhealthy

ADS: Hand-painted billboards

DEMOGRAPHIC: Overwhelmingly blue collar

GENDER: Almost 100 percent men

MUSIC: No music, no announcements, and no PA system

MODERN STADIUMS

SEATS: All-seater

CROWD CONTROL: Highly organized by ushers; widespread use of CCTV cameras

CONDITIONS: Most fans under roofs; many more facilities

FOOD: Still bad and unhealthy

ADS: Video screens and advertising hoardings

DEMOGRAPHIC: Much more diverse mix of class and background

GENDER: 10–15 percent women

MUSIC: Relentless advertising and cheesy announcements

ATTENDANCES

As more countries create professional leagues and the popularity of the game continues to grow, global attendances at soccer matches is steadily rising. The best-attended leagues are in Europe—the Premier League in England, the Bundesliga in Germany, and La Liga in Spain. All attract more than 11 million fans a season. In recent years, the Championship—England's second-level league—has become the fourth most attended league in the world, ahead of Serie A in Italy and Ligue 1 in France.

TICKET PRICES

In the early days of professional soccer in Europe and Latin America, ticket prices were kept low—on a par with a trip to the musical hall or to the movies. With an overwhelmingly working-class clientele, there was no sense in pricing customers out of the market—though stopping people from jumping the turnstiles or climbing over walls to get into the stadium was much trickier.

14.8 Total attendance (in millions) at the English Premier League in the 2007–08 season—the world's most-attended league

39,076 Average attendance figure in Germany's Bundesliga—the world's highest

4.31 Total attendance (in millions) at England's Football League One—the best-attended third-level league in the world

TICKET PRICE EXPLOSION

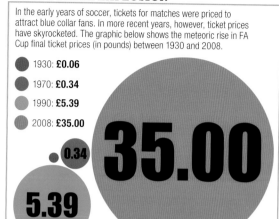

In the early years of soccer, tickets for matches were priced to attract blue collar fans. In more recent years, however, ticket prices have skyrocketed. The graphic below shows the meteoric rise in FA Cup final ticket prices (in pounds) between 1930 and 2008.

- 1930: £0.06
- 1970: £0.34
- 1990: £5.39
- 2008: £35.00

0.34

35.00

5.39

SOCCER AS A CARNIVAL

Sometimes the crowd can be the best thing about soccer. Fans have been making a carnival of the game for over a century. Homemade rosettes, hats, and banners started appearing in the 1920s. Pioneered by fans of the Danish national team, face paint arrived in the 1980s, while fans of the Dutch national team have filled stadiums with their unbroken banks of orange shirts for a number of years.

MODERN FANS
Replica shirts, baseball caps, and team scarves are a must for the modern soccer supporter.

THE MEXICAN WAVE

The origins of the Mexican wave, produced by fans standing and sitting in order around the stadium, is disputed. Some say Frank Zappa started it at a rock festival in 1969, others say it started at ice hockey rinks, but it reached a global public at the 1986 World Cup in Mexico.

FAN CULTURE

Before the arrival of professional soccer in the 1880s, England already had three national magazines devoted to sports that covered soccer. Fans today can follow soccer in innumerable ways—through radio, TV, cellphone Internet coverage, newspapers, magazines, and an ever-growing number of books. In addition, there are fantasy soccer leagues, the pools and betting, computer games, board games, and a mountain of other soccer-themed memorabilia.

BRAZIL'S NO.1 FAN

Claudio Riberio is Brazil's No.1 professional fan. At Brazil's World Cup games, cameras always hover on his huge afro and energetic dancing. He has attended every World Cup since 1978 and claims never to leave the country with valid tickets for the matches, but always manages to find his way into every stadium.

NEWSPAPERS

Despite the rise of the Internet, some soccer cultures still require their daily fix in print. In Italy, the biggest-selling national newspaper by far—*La Gazzetta dello Sport* (with a daily circulation in excess of 400,000 copies)—is devoted to sports, and in particular, soccer. Italy is not alone: Portugal has three dailies focused on soccer, Spain has four, and Greece, incredibly, has nine.

THE NATURAL STATE OF THE SOCCER FAN IS ...BITTER DISAPPOINTMENT

AUTHOR AND ARSENAL FAN **NICK HORNBY**

CIRCULATION OF SPORTS NEWSPAPERS

- Gazetta dello Sport, Italy: **436,000**
- Corriere della Serra, Italy: **677,000**
- Marca, Spain: **2,100,000**
- El País, Spain: **2,300,000**

436,000　677,000　**2,100,000**　**2,300,000**

RADIO

The BBC aired the first-ever live radio broadcast of a soccer match in 1927—a league game between Arsenal and Sheffield United. The first broadcasters attempted to give listeners a sense of the game with one person commentating on the flow of play while a second voice announced which numbered square of the field (divided into eight in a useful diagram in the famous UK listings magazine, the *Radio Times*) the ball was in.

ARY BORROSO

Ary Borroso was the leading soccer announcer on Brazilian radio in the 1940s and '50s. Moonlighting from his day job as one of the country's great composers, his accounts of games would be accompanied by him playing the harmonica and hysterical partisan support for his club Flamengo. He was the first to report live from the field, interviewing players before, during, and after games.

FANZINES

In the 1970s and '80s, a new generation of soccer fans and writers emerged in Britain. Taking their cue from the DIY ethos of punk, they began to make their own magazines and to say things that official material and a staid press could never say.

FOLLOWING THE GAME

ELECTRONIC	PRINT MEDIA		MERCHANDISE		GAMES	
Club websites	Newspapers	Yearbooks	Club credit cards	Mugs/Glasses	Table foosball	Soccer pools
Television	Fanzines	Trivia/Quiz Books	Club shirts	T-Shirts	Subbutteo	Spot the ball
Videos	Club magazines		Bed linen	Bags/ Backpacks	Computer games	Fantasy soccer
DVDs	Books		Pyjamas	Posters	Board games	
Cellphone text alerts	Encyclopedias		Towels	Calenders		
Soccer-related music	Biographies		Baby clothes	Mouse mats		
				Soft toys		

TELEVISION

Although experiments began before World War II, matches were not televised live until the 1950s—parts of the 1954 World Cup were broadcast live across Europe. Resistance among traditionalists was fierce, who feared that no one would come to games if it could be seen live on television, but their fears were largely unfounded.

TV AUDIENCE FOR WORLD CUPS

- 1986—13.5 billion
- 1990—26.6 billion
- 1994—32.1 billion
- 1998—24.7 billion
- 2002—28.8 billion
- 2006—26.2 billion

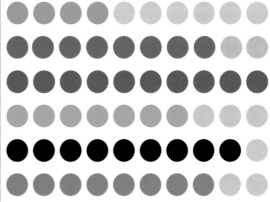

FULL-TIME PASSION
Following a favorite team has become a 24-hour-a-day pastime for many soccer fans.

THE MEMORABILIA INDUSTRY

Although fans have been collecting soccer memorabilia for a long time, it is only since the 1980s that prices for old programs, shirts, medals, and balls have begun to climb. Soccer programs have certainly proved to be a good investment.

THE INTERNET

The Internet is steadily accommodating soccer fans' insatiable desire for chat, argument, information, and replays. The blog has proved the best format for online soccer, offering everyone the chance to have their say. More darkly, many hooligan firms have used the Internet to arrange fights away from the police.

FANTASY SOCCER

Fantasy soccer is a parallel soccer universe in which fans can create imaginary teams from real league players and score points in their own league according to their players' performances with their actual clubs. It was first invented in the United States. The massive rise in computing power and the collection of soccer statisitics has seen fantasy soccer become immensely popular. The majority of newspapers now run fantasy leagues.

91,750 The price paid at auction for Geoff Hurst's 1966 World Cup final shirt (in pounds)

478,000 The oldest surviving FA Cup, first awarded in 1896, when Sheffield Wednesday beat Wolverhampton Wanderers at the Crystal Palace (in pounds)

225,841 The price paid at auction for Pelé's 1970 World Cup final shirt—a world record (in dollars)

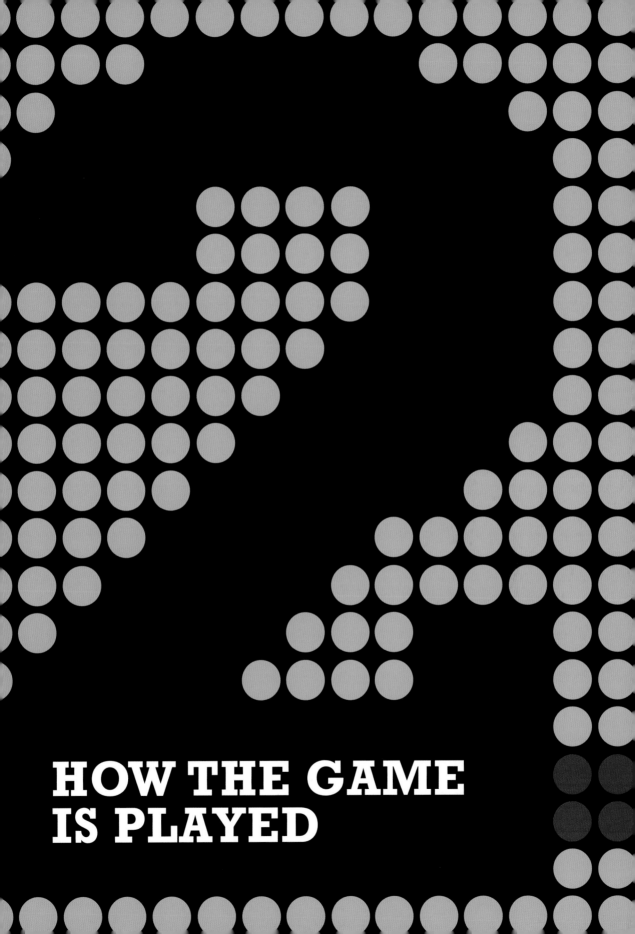

HOW THE GAME
IS PLAYED

THE FIELD

Professional soccer is played on a flat grass or artificial turf field, the markings of which must be in a set position. However, the overall area of the field may vary. The playing area must be rectangular—the length of the sideline must be greater than the length of the goal line.

PLAYING SURFACE

Outside of the professional game, soccer can be played on any flat surface—such as sand, hard-packed mud, or synthetic materials—but natural turf is the most desirable. However, turf needs people to maintain it, using tractors, rollers, forks, and sprinklers. But whatever the surface, anyone can play social soccer: all that is needed are two teams, a ball, two goals, and an even surface.

THE FIELD OF PLAY

The outer extremes of the field are delineated by the sidelines and goal lines: if the ball wholly crosses the sideline, it is out of play; if the ball crosses the goal line between the goal posts a goal is scored. If part of the ball is on the line, it is still in play.

Penalty spot
The penalty spot is located 12 yd (11 m) from the goal line. Penalty kicks are taken from here

Goal area
Also known as the six-yard box, goal kicks are taken from anywhere inside this area

Technical area
Both teams have a technical area that extends 3 ft (1 m) either side of the dugout. One person at a time is allowed to shout instructions from here

Penalty area
Also known as the 18-yard box, the goalkeeper can handle the ball anywhere inside this area. Fouls committed in this area result in a penalty kick

Field labels: 18 yd (16.5 m) · 10 yd (9.15 m) · 12 yd (11 m) · 10 yd (9.15 m) · 6 yd (5.5 m) · 6 yd (5.5 m) · 100–130 yd (90–120 m) · 50–100 yd (45–90 m) · 10 yd (9.15 m) · 4¾ in (12 cm)

SIZE MATTERS

Barcelona's Nou Camp stadium has one of the largest fields in the world. It measures 115 yd x 78 yd (105 m x 72 m). Opened in 1957, the stadium can hold nearly 99,000.

FIELD DIMENSIONS

The Laws of the Game published by FIFA (see pp.62–63) state that the position of the field markings within the playing area is unchangeable. There is, however, a degree of flexibility regarding the length of these lines and the overall dimensions of the field. The permitted range of field size varies depending on whether matches are being played in domestic or international competitions (see right). The line markings must be 4¾ in (12 cm) in width.

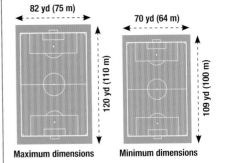

DOMESTIC GAMES
100 yd (90 m) · 131 yd (120 m) — **Maximum dimensions**
49 yd (45 m) · 98 yd (90 m) — **Minimum dimensions**

For domestic games, the overall size of the field can range between the measurements shown above, as long as the field does not become square.

INTERNATIONAL GAMES
82 yd (75 m) · 120 yd (110 m) — **Maximum dimensions**
70 yd (64 m) · 109 yd (100 m) — **Minimum dimensions**

For international games, the dimensions of the field can vary within allowed parameters, although the range is narrower than it is for domestic matches.

24,428
The weight in tons (22,161 tonnes) of stone, gravel, sand, and soil that is used to create a typical professional soccer field.

23
The distance in miles (37 km) of undersoil heating pipes at Manchester United's Old Trafford stadium.

1
The number of time capsules buried at Wembley stadium.

528
The distance in yards (0.6 km) of white lines on a typical playing surface.

1
The optimum length in inches (25 mm) of the blades of grass.

PLAYING SURFACES

According to the Laws of the Game (see pp.62–63), official matches may be played on either natural or manmade surfaces. Artificial fields must meet the requirements set out by FIFA and the surface must be green.

NATURAL PLAYING SURFACES

Grass is the most natural form of playing surface. At the highest level, grass fields are regularly watered and forked to improve drainage and get air to the roots. Typically, fields will be re-turfed at least once a season to maintain high standards. Many feature undersoil heating to prevent frost damage.

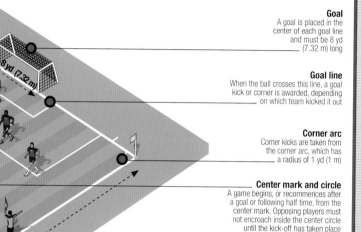

Goal
A goal is placed in the center of each goal line and must be 8 yd (7.32 m) long

8 yd (7.32 m)

Goal line
When the ball crosses this line, a goal kick or corner is awarded, depending on which team kicked it out

Corner arc
Corner kicks are taken from the corner arc, which has a radius of 1 yd (1 m)

Center mark and circle
A game begins, or recommences after a goal or following half time, from the center mark. Opposing players must not encroach inside the center circle until the kick-off has taken place

Halfway line
This line divides the playing area into two equal halves

Sideline
If the ball wholly crosses this line, a throw-in is awarded to whichever team did not put the ball out of play

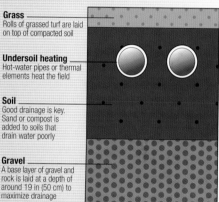

Grass
Rolls of grassed turf are laid on top of compacted soil

Undersoil heating
Hot-water pipes or thermal elements heat the field

Soil
Good drainage is key. Sand or compost is added to soils that drain water poorly

Gravel
A base layer of gravel and rock is laid at a depth of around 19 in (50 cm) to maximize drainage

IMPERFECT FIELD?

English team Yeovil Town's former field at Huish was famous in the game for its alarmingly sloping field. There was a difference in height of approximately 6 ft (1.8 m) from one side to the other. The site of the old field, which is located in the center of the town, is now home to a supermarket.

ARTIFICAL PLAYING SURFACES

Artificial, or synthetic, surfaces have existed since 1965 when AstroTurf™ was used in the Astrodome in Houston, Texas. In soccer, the surface was initially popular in the 1980s, before falling out of favor. In recent years, FIFA has expressed renewed interest in artificial fields following technological advances.

Field weave
The "grass blades," which are made of polyethylene, are approximately 2 in (5 cm) long, and are mixed with short springlike fibers that keep the blades upright

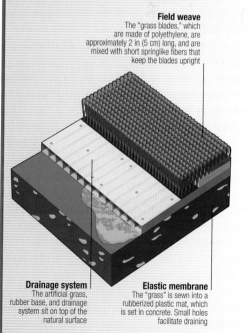

Drainage system
The artificial grass, rubber base, and drainage system sit on top of the natural surface

Elastic membrane
The "grass" is sewn into a rubberized plastic mat, which is set in concrete. Small holes facilitate draining

TOP 5: MOST UNUSUAL FIELDS

Every field is unique, but the following are among the most unusual in the world.

ESTADIO HERNANDO SILES
Bolivia's national stadium is 2⅓ miles (3.6 km) above sea level. In May 2007, following complaints that competing at this altitude left many players gasping for breath, FIFA banned international matches more than 1¾ miles (2.75 km) above sea level. After protests from affected nations, FIFA backed down.

MARINA BAY PLATFORM
Having decided to demolish Singapore's National Stadium, the island state's authorities chose to build a giant floating field anchored in Marina Bay. The first competitive matches were played on the platform in February 2009.

ADIDAS FOOTBALL PARK
In 2001, a field was opened on the roof of the Tokyu Toyoko department store in Tokyo's Shibuya district. Approximately 500 teams have since registered to play futsal there— 130 ft (40 m) above the space-strapped metropolis.

MOUNT SAJAMA
In 2001, two 20-minute halves of soccer were played on the flat summit of South America's second highest mountain— 4 miles (6.5 km) above sea level.

GRYTVIKEN
The world's most southerly permanent soccer field is located at Grytviken on the island of South Georgia in the South Atlantic Ocean (latitude 54.3 degrees south). Founded by Victorian whalers, it is still used by British Antarctic Survey staff.

DEFENDERS

Defenders are responsible for preventing the attacking team from scoring and for winning back possession of the ball so that a counter-attack can be mounted. While every player on the field must contribute to these two tasks, responsibility lies most heavily with the defenders. They can be categorized as either "central" (see opposite) or "wide" (see pp.44–43).

THE DEFENDER'S ROLE

As well as taking individual initiative when required, the defender must work together with his team, using a variety of skills and tactics. He must force the attacking team to make mistakes by marking opponents closely, intercepting their passes, and gaining possession of the ball. Defensive strategies may involve "zonal defending" or "man-to-man marking" (see pp.90–93).

SKILLS REQUIRED

The defender must be a highly skilled player who is able to bring the ball out of defense in a controlled way before making accurate passes to teammates who are better placed to set up attacking moves. An ability to accurately anticipate threats is important, as is possessing the necessary levels of concentration to focus on the task in hand. Courage and excellent technical ability combine in the defender to produce a player willing to make last-ditch tackles in front of the goal mouth. Strength and precision will also enable the player to deal effectively with one-on-one attacks wherever they happen to occur on the field.

THE ULTIMATE PRICE

When defenders make mistakes, a goal often results. One such mistake was made by Andrés Escobar, a defender for Colombia in the 1994 World Cup. His own goal, which knocked his team out of the tournament, cost him his life—he was gunned down on his return to Colombia.

ROBERTO AYALA

Ayala is regarded as one of the best central defenders in the game. He has captained Argentina more times than any other player.

Defensive pressure
The player being marked is under constant pressure from the defending player

MARKING

When a defender closely shadows the movements of an attacker, this is known as marking. The defender may be able to intercept the ball, or an attacker may be dissuaded from passing to a marked teammate.

Quick work
Defenders need fast reflexes to intercept well

INTERCEPTING

When a defender intercepts an attacker's pass, this is often the result of the pressure applied by the defending team as a whole, through persistent marking and closing down the available space.

Battle for possession
The defender launches a feet-first slide toward the ball; he must take the ball and not the player

TACKLING

Using the feet to take the ball away from a player is known as tackling. The sliding tackle (above) can be highly effective, but the defender's timing must be perfect, and there is a risk of conceding a foul.

FIELD PERFORMANCE

Defenders must be able to tackle. On average, they make more interceptions per game than any other player:

- Interceptions made by a player per game—**15**
- Interceptions made by a defender per game—**20**

15   20

CENTRAL DEFENDERS

The role of central defender, which includes the positions center back and sweeper (see below), requires constant alertness and great physical strength. The ability to anticipate danger before it materializes—and take effective preventative action—is often fundamental to a team's success.

CENTER BACK

The center back—sometimes known as center half (see box, p.45)—is a team's last line of defense. Success or failure often rests on the player's ability to tackle effectively and win the ball. A center back needs to be tall, as it is vital that he can win the ball when it is in the air. He should also be powerful, fearless, decisive, and willing to make all-or-nothing tackles.

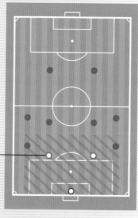

On patrol
The center backs are responsible for patrolling the area in front of the goal mouth

RIO FERDINAND
The England center back has great composure and passing ability, as well as the skills needed to bring the ball out of defense.

CENTER BACK'S DOMAIN
Playing in a central position, a team typically places two center backs in front of the goalkeeper. They mark the most advanced attacking forwards, aiming to bring the ball away from the penalty area.

STRIKERS WIN YOU GAMES, BUT DEFENDERS WIN YOU... CHAMPIONSHIPS

JOHN GREGORY
ASTON VILLA MANAGER, 1998–2002

THE SWEEPER

As the name suggests, the role of the sweeper is to "sweep up" the ball if the attacking team breaks through the defensive line. Unlike his other colleagues in defense, the sweeper does not mark a specific attacker. Instead he remains "fluid" and is free to roam around the goal mouth, closing down any gaps in defense. An ability to anticipate play is especially important, as the sweeper must predict attacks from any quarter.

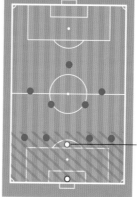

Roaming
The sweeper roams laterally in front of the goal, but can advance upfield

GAETANO SCIREA

A real gentleman of soccer, Gaetano Scirea was one of the greatest defenders in the history of the game. The Italy and Juventus player was famed for his grace, style, and sportsmanship. He was equally adept at initiating attacks and snuffing out danger, and won every available soccer honor.

THE SWEEPER'S DOMAIN
The sweeper is usually positioned behind the center backs. As he has no marking duties, he may travel a long way forward when his team is in possession.

WIDE DEFENDERS

The standard four-man defense consists of two center backs (see p.43) in the middle of the field and two fullbacks to the side. A further wide defender, the wingback, will regularly advance a long way down the flanks. All wide defenders are expected to prevent the opposing team from launching attacks down the flanks, and to join in with their own team's attacks.

FULLBACK

The main responsibility of the fullback is to stay wide and prevent the attacking team from developing attacks down the flanks. He must be quick, and will usually mark a designated forward. He should also join in with attacking play.

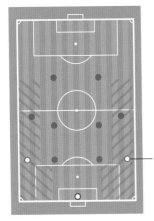

Forward run
One of the fullbacks may decide to advance up the field during attacks

FULLBACK'S DOMAIN
The fullback operates on either the right- or left-hand side of the field and defends the flanks. When one fullback goes on a forward run, the other "tucks in" to support the central defenders.

OLYMPIC PERFORMANCE

One of the world's fastest players is diminutive Iranian rightback Hossein Kaebi. He claims to be able to run 330 ft (100 m) in less than 10 seconds which, if true, would make him a contender for an Olympic medal.

PUTTING THE BOOT IN

The England and Leeds United center half Jack Charlton was introduced to the tougher side of the game from the start. At his 1953 debut, he asked his manager, Raich Carter, what tactics he should use. Carter replied: "See how fast their center forward can limp."

WINGBACK

The wingback is a cross between the fullback (see left) and the winger (see p.55). He must defend like a fullback, preventing attackers from reaching the goal line, while charging forward like a winger when his team is in possession.

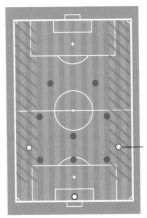

Upfield
The wingback has an attacking role and ranges up the field

WINGBACK'S DOMAIN
The wingback operates on either the right- or left-hand side of the field, but further upfield than the fullback. He is responsible for both defending and attacking along the flanks.

CAFU

Brazilian soccer teams have a long tradition of using wingbacks. Cafu (aka Marcos Evangelista de Moraes) is a prime example. Famous for his overlapping runs, he is one of the few players to have appeared in four World Cup tournaments.

TOP 5: OWN GOALS

The first official own goal was scored by Gersham Cox of Aston Villa in 1888. Since then, countless balls have been knocked into the wrong net by a succession of shame-faced players. The following are five of the most notorious own goals.

GARY MABBUT
Although Gary Mabbut had already scored a defining goal for Tottenham Hotspur against Coventry in the 1987 Cup Final, he left his "best" attempt at goal to last. Having taken the game into extra time, he placed a ball over the head of his own keeper and handed the cup to Coventry.

DELFI GELI
In the 2001 UEFA Cup Final, tiny Spanish team Alaves came from behind three times to level the score against Liverpool. With 117 minutes gone, Alaves player Delfi Geli tried to clear a cross, but instead scored a match-winning, golden goal for Liverpool.

STAN VAN DEN BUYS
The hapless Van Der Buys holds the unique record in professional soccer of having scored the most own goals in a single game. Playing for Belgian team Germinal Ekeren in 1995, he put three balls past his own goalkeeper, handing a 3–2 victory to Anderlecht.

BARBADOS VS GRENADA
Barbados was 2–0 up against Grenada in the 1994 Shell Caribbean Cup and needed a two-goal advantage to qualify. When Grenada scored a late goal, Barbados exploited a rule stating that the match must go to extra time in the event of a tie by equalizing with an own goal.

MADAGASCAR CHAMPIONSHIP
During the 2002 Madagascar Championship, reigning champions Stade Olympique protested against a questionable penalty decision by scoring an own goal from the kick off—and repeated the process for 90 minutes. The final score was Stade Olympique 0, AS Adema 149.

THE "BACK FOUR"

The members of a standard four-man defense are known as the "back four." This unit consists of two fullbacks (see left) and two central defenders (see p.43), or two fullbacks, one central defender, and one sweeper (see p.43). The back four must work together as a coordinated unit. For example, a "flat" formation provides defensive cover across the whole width of the field.

BACK FOUR AS A UNIT

Good attacking invariably begins with a solid defense. A strong back four should be well organized, committed, and focused. The unit must contain a mix of talented players who are able to work together to wrong-foot the attacking team. At the highest level of the game, the pressure to perform effectively can be immense—especially given that an attacker who outwits the back four will almost certainly score.

CARLOS PUYOL
Spanish defender Carlos Puyol was awarded the "Best European Rightback" award by UEFA in 2002.

1 The number of clubs Franco Baresi played for during his 20-year career (AC Milan).

-3 Jamie Carragher's net goal total for Liverpool (four goals, seven own goals).

108 The number of games ASEC Abidjan went unbeaten between 1989 and 1994.

15 The number of goals conceded by Chelsea's defense during the 2004–05 Premiership season.

MISLEADING POSITION NAMES

In the early 20th century, when the standard formation was 2-3-5, the two players at the back were known as "fullbacks" and the three players in front were called "half-backs" or "halves." As tactics grew more cautious over time, the central of the three halves was moved back into defense, pushing the fullbacks out to the sides. Although the name doesn't make much sense today, center backs are often still called "center halves."

THE GOALKEEPER IS THE JEWEL IN THE CROWN AND GETTING AT HIM SHOULD BE... ALMOST IMPOSSIBLE!

GEORGE GRAHAM, ON THE IMPORTANCE OF A TIGHT DEFENSE
MANAGER, LEEDS UNITED, 1997

STAR DEFENDERS

BEST BACK FOURS

Successful teams are invariably built on solid defenses. The following back fours provided the greatest defensive support in the history of the game.

BRAZIL (1958)
While center backs Hilderado Bellini and Orlando, and fullbacks Nilton Santos and Djalma Santos may not have invented the phenomenon of the "back four," they were the first to perfect it. This formidable unit helped propel Brazil to victory at the 1958 World Cup.

LEEDS UNITED (1960s–70s)
Jack Charlton, Norman Hunter, Terry Cooper, and Paul Reaney didn't exactly have a delicate touch when it came to tackling, but they were highly effective. The Leeds team of the late 1960s and early '70s owed much of its success to this hard-as-nails back four.

AC MILAN (1980s–90s)
Sweeper Franco Baresi, center back Alessandro Costacurta, and fullbacks Mauro Tassotti and Paulo Maldini formed one of the greatest back fours of all time at AC Milan during the 1980s and '90s. They won three European Cup and Champions League titles.

AFC AJAX (1995)
Center backs Frank Rijkaard and Danny Blind, and fullbacks Frank de Boer and Michael Reizeger oozed talent. They were the Amsterdam team's formidable back four in the Champions League winning side of 1995.

MIDFIELDERS

As the name implies, midfielders play in the middle of the field between the defenders (see pp.42–45) and the forwards (see pp.50–53). Depending on the formation being used (see pp.86–89), there can be three, four, or five in a team. Their precise roles will vary accordingly, but they can usually be categorized as either "central" or "wide."

THE MIDFIELDER'S ROLE

The midfielder has an all-around view of the game and his role is to both anticipate and exploit as many attacking opportunities as possible. He must be actively involved in both defense and attack, which involves gaining and retaining possession of the ball, feeding it to the forwards, and making attempts at goal himself.

SKILLS REQUIRED

The midfielder must have excellent fitness as he is required to cover the whole field, alternating between defense and attack as play dictates. Above all, he needs to be a good all-rounder. To fulfil his defensive duties, he needs to be an excellent tackler who is able to win aerial battles in the center of the field. Meanwhile, the attacking aspects of his role require him to be equally adept at tackling, passing, dribbling, and shooting. As well as possessing excellent technical ability, a good midfielder needs creativity and vision. Setting up goal-scoring opportunities is a major part of the midfielder's job and, without these attributes, he is unlikely to do so very often.

Timing
A well-timed sliding tackle is an effective way to gain the ball

TACKLING

As part of his defensive duties, the midfielder must be an accomplished tackler. Much of the technique in tackling comes from pressuring the opponent before seizing the ball.

Types of pass
The midfielder must be equally at home making both short and long passes

PASSING

The midfielder passes the ball more often than other players on the field. Top-class performers, for example, may make 50 or more passes during a match, with a success rate above 80 percent.

Moving up
Dribbling is the main way for a wide midfielder to move upfield

DRIBBLING

The wide midfielder in particular needs good dribbling skills in order to get himself into positions from which he can deliver effective crosses into the opponent's penalty area.

MAGNUS FORCE

The technique behind adding curve to a shot (as perfected by midfielder David Beckham) has its roots in science. In 1853, a German physicist called Heinrich Magnus showed (with his Magnus Theory) how a ball kicked to the right of center will spin in a counterclockwise direction and curl to the left.

LIAM BRADY
Former Irish midfielder Liam Brady—a player for Arsenal, Juventus, and Republic of Ireland in the 1970s and '80s—had great technical ability.

AVERAGE DISTANCE COVERED PER MATCH

- Midfielders— **7½** miles (12 km)
- Forwards— **7** miles (11.25 km)
- Defenders— **6¼** miles (10 km)

6¼   **7**   **7½**

CENTRAL MIDFIELDER—BOX-TO-BOX

The central midfielder, as typified by the box-to-box midfielder, is the hardest-working player on the field. He must work to create and exploit attacking possibilities—such as identifying and passing the ball to forwards who are running into space—while also ensuring that he meets his defensive responsibilities. Technical skills such as dribbling and passing must become second nature, so that he can distribute the ball effectively to teammates. When he is not setting up offensive attacks or engineering plays, he drops back into defense to pressurize the attacking team.

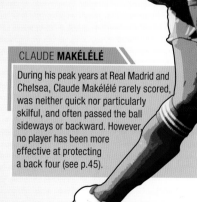

BRYAN ROBSON
As one of Manchester United's most well-known midfielders, Bryan Robson remains the longest-serving captain in club history (1982–94).

ARCHETYPAL MIDFIELDER

The box-to-box player is the archetypal midfielder. He is actively involved in every part of the game, running from one penalty area to the other in an attempt to dominate play. He typically has incredible stamina and impeccable technical ability. The mold for the role was set by the great Alfred Di Stefano of Argentina and Real Madrid in the 1950s. Recent greats have included Rubén Baraja and Bryan Robson.

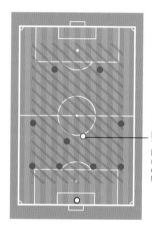

End to end
The box-to-box midfielder races from one end of the field to the other.

BOX-TO-BOX PLAYER'S DOMAIN

The box-to-box midfielder covers the whole length of the center of the field. When on the offensive, he races up to the opposition's penalty area; when on the defensive, he races back to his own penalty area.

Defense
The holding midfielder is responsible for preventing the attacking team from reaching the defenders

CENTRAL MIDFIELDER— HOLDING

Primarily a defensive role, the holding midfielder is stationed between the other midfielders and the full- and wingbacks (see p.45). He is responsible for repelling attacking players who have made it through the midfield.

HOLDING MIDFIELDER'S DOMAIN

The holding midfielder operates further back down the field than the box-to-box midfielder. He "holds back" attacking players by intercepting passes with hard tackling and shrewd positioning.

WHY PUT ANOTHER LAYER OF GOLD PAINT ON THE BENTLEY **WHEN YOU ARE LOSING THE ENTIRE ENGINE?**

ZINÉDINE ZIDANE
ON DAVID BECKHAM REPLACING CLAUDE MAKÉLÉLÉ AT REAL MADRID, 2003

CLAUDE MAKÉLÉLÉ

During his peak years at Real Madrid and Chelsea, Claude Makélélé rarely scored, was neither quick nor particularly skilful, and often passed the ball sideways or backward. However, no player has been more effective at protecting a back four (see p.45).

CENTRAL MIDFIELDER—PLAYMAKER

The playmaker is a midfielder who is responsible for setting up attacking plays for the forwards (see pp.50–53), usually from a central position. To do this effectively, he must have great passing ability and vision. A playmaker can be described as either "advanced" or "withdrawn" (see below).

ADVANCED PLAYMAKER

The advanced playmaker makes himself available for passes and can turn defensive moves into attacking ones by using short, incisive passes. He usually has very little time in which to make decisions, and very little space in which to make passes.

WITHDRAWN PLAYMAKER

The withdrawn playmaker usually plays alongside a holding midfielder (see p.47). While the holding midfielder concentrates on defensive duties, the withdrawn playmaker takes advantage of this support to launch long, decisive passes.

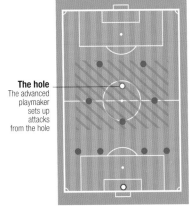

The hole
The advanced playmaker sets up attacks from the hole

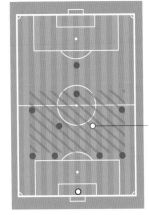

Defensive
The withdrawn playmaker sets up attacks from further down the field

ADVANCED PLAYMAKER'S DOMAIN
The advanced playmaker plays in the "hole"— an area between midfield and the opposing line of defense. In occupying this position, he is hard for the attacking team to mark.

WITHDRAWN PLAYMAKER'S DOMAIN
Despite being relatively deep-lying, the withdrawn playmaker must set up attacks. He makes long balls either through the middle (into the path of a running center forward, for example) or to a wide player.

FERNANDO GAGO
The highly skilled Fernando Gago of Real Madrid typifies the role of the withdrawn playmaker.

KAKÁ
Kaká of Brazil and AC Milan epitomizes the role of the attacking midfielder. His skill has secured his place as one of the highest-paid players in the world.

CENTRAL MIDFIELDER—ATTACKING

Midfielders with particularly attacking instincts are often deployed relatively far upfield. Known as attacking central midfielders, these players often produce excellent shots, contribute several goals during a season, and have the potential to be a team's star player. The attacking central midfielder must have great vision and technical ability, including faultless passing and shooting skills.

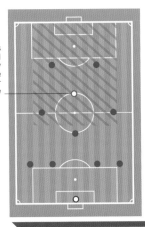

Great shooters
Attacking central midfielders usually play upfield and are renowned for their shooting ability

ATTACKING CENTRAL MIDFIELDER'S DOMAIN
With a talent for bursting into the attacking team's penalty area at exactly the right moment (either with or without the ball), attacking central midfielders are positioned in an advanced position. They often form the front point of a four-man diamond in a 4-4-2 formation (see p.88).

WIDE MIDFIELDERS

The wide midfield player is an attacking midfielder. However, in contrast to the attacking central midfielder (see left), he focuses on one particular side of the field. The extent to which the wide midfielder is restricted to patrolling the touchline varies. He is often required to be relatively flexible in his movements, for example, rather than just sticking to the flanks.

TRADITIONAL WINGERS

Prior to the mid-1960s, wingers were attacking players who rarely helped with defense. Stationed toward the touchline, they stretched the attacking team's defense and provided an outlet for their own defenders. Their main duty was to take the ball past the attacking team's fullback and deliver crosses into the penalty area. England's Stanley Matthews (1915–2000) was one of the all-time greats.

MODERN WIDE MIDFIELDER

In recent years, the role of wide midfielder has become very fluid. This is the result of increasing tactical sophistication, as well as a desire to confuse the opposition. The rise of the wingback (see p.45) also means that the modern winger must provide defensive cover when the wingback is upfield.

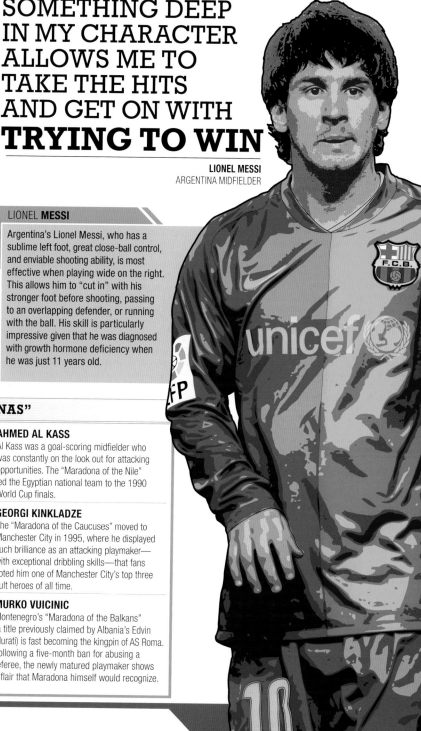

SOMETHING DEEP IN MY CHARACTER ALLOWS ME TO TAKE THE HITS AND GET ON WITH TRYING TO WIN

LIONEL MESSI
ARGENTINA MIDFIELDER

In attack
The modern wide midfielder stays wide to stretch the attacking team's defense

MODERN WIDE MIDFIELDER'S DOMAIN
Active in both defense and offense, the modern wide midfielder provides defensive cover by tracking back and moving in toward the middle to help maintain a tight defensive unit.

LIONEL **MESSI**

Argentina's Lionel Messi, who has a sublime left foot, great close-ball control, and enviable shooting ability, is most effective when playing wide on the right. This allows him to "cut in" with his stronger foot before shooting, passing to an overlapping defender, or running with the ball. His skill is particularly impressive given that he was diagnosed with growth hormone deficiency when he was just 11 years old.

TOP FIVE "NEW MARADONAS"

Exceptionally talented players (usually midfielders or forwards) are often favorably compared to Argentina's Diego Maradona. The following global players have been associated with the legendary midfielder.

GEORGI HAGI

An erratic but undoubtedly brilliant playmaker, Romania's greatest player was a star of Spanish, Italian, and Turkish soccer. The defining moment for the "Maradona of the Carpathians" came with his goal against Colombia in the 1994 World Cup.

SAEED OWAIRAN

Already a national hero for taking Saudi Arabia to its first World Cup finals in 1994, Owairan proceeded to dribble the ball for 70 yd (64 m) against Belgium before scoring and taking the team into the knock-out phases. It earned him the nickname "Maradona of the Arabs."

AHMED AL KASS

Al Kass was a goal-scoring midfielder who was constantly on the look out for attacking opportunities. The "Maradona of the Nile" led the Egyptian national team to the 1990 World Cup finals.

GEORGI KINKLADZE

The "Maradona of the Caucuses" moved to Manchester City in 1995, where he displayed such brilliance as an attacking playmaker— with exceptional dribbling skills—that fans voted him one of Manchester City's top three cult heroes of all time.

MURKO VUICINIC

Montenegro's "Maradona of the Balkans" (a title previously claimed by Albania's Edvin Murati) is fast becoming the kingpin of AS Roma. Following a five-month ban for abusing a referee, the newly matured playmaker shows a flair that Maradona himself would recognize.

HOW THE GAME IS PLAYED

FORWARDS

Forwards, or strikers, are positioned furthest forward on a team, closest to the opponent's goal. These players come in all shapes and sizes, from small and agile to large and powerful, but they all have one essential job: to score goals. As the principal goal scorers, forwards are often a team's most celebrated—and expensive—players.

THE FORWARD'S ROLE

As well as taking advantage of goal-scoring opportunities, forwards are also expected to set up goals for other forwards and sometimes for attacking midfielders and playmakers (see pp.46–49). Forwards may also aim to keep possession of the ball until other players can move forward and join the attack. The most common formation (4-4-2) makes use of two forwards.

SKILLS REQUIRED

There are many different ways to score a goal and, consequently, many different types of forward. However, certain mental and physical characteristics are common for all. Forwards must have pace (at least over short distances), show great courage, and have an instinctive eye for goal. Excellent shooting ability is a pre-requisite, but heading, crossing, and passing skills are also vital in order to engineer goal-scoring opportunities and out-maneuver defenders while advancing up the field.

Forceful shot
A powerful swing of the kicking leg produces a strong shot

Firm strike
Headers should come from the center of the forehead

SHOOTING
As the ball will arrive to the forward at a variety of speeds and angles, there are many shooting techniques. However, the most common method is a low, hard shot struck off the instep of the boot.

HEADING
Used for passing, shooting, or controlling the ball, heading is a versatile and important skill—not just for the forward, but for all players. It allows the player to reach high balls.

GEORGE WEAH
The Liberian forward was named FIFA World Player of the Year in 1995.

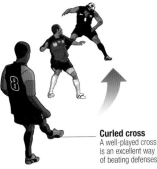

Curled cross
A well-played cross is an excellent way of beating defenses

Swift pass
The forward uses the inside of his foot to make a quick, decisive pass

CROSSING
The cross pass, in which the ball is quickly moved from the edge of the field to the center, is used to deliver the ball toward players in attacking positions. Well-hit crosses are hard to defend against.

PASSING
A well-executed pass consists of three elements: the correct amount of power, appropriate direction, and good timing. A forward will use the inside of his foot for making swift, short passes.

LIGHTNING FAST

Forwards must be quick. Over short distances, many can run almost as fast as 100m sprinters:

Forwards—**9.7m per second**

100m sprinter—**10.1m per second**

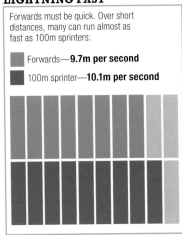

CENTER FORWARD

With the aim of scoring as many goals as possible, the center forward is a tall, powerful player who fights his way to the ball before his opponents. Also known as a "target man," the center forward usually operates near the goal, where he waits to "receive" the ball from teammates in midfield or defense. He often scores from corners and crosses, using his height and strength to head the ball, or shield it from other players while they turn and shoot.

SKILLS REQUIRED

The center forward must have superior strength and excellent heading ability. He must be an accurate shooter, and have the necessary ball control to retain possession of the ball while waiting for other players to enter the game and provide support. The center forward often plays with his back to the goal so must be able to control the ball, often with a defender at his back, while looking to bring teammates into play.

ALAN SHEARER

Famed for celebrating goals with a simple flat-palmed raise of the arm, Shearer scored a hat-trick on his full league debut for Southampton in 1988 and never looked back. He is living proof that old-style center forwards still have a place.

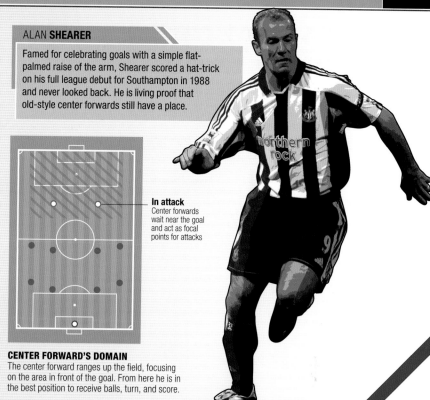

In attack
Center forwards wait near the goal and act as focal points for attacks

CENTER FORWARD'S DOMAIN
The center forward ranges up the field, focusing on the area in front of the goal. From here he is in the best position to receive balls, turn, and score.

WITHDRAWN STRIKER

The withdrawn striker has a similar role to the advanced playmaker midfielder (see p.48) in that he plays between midfield and the opponent's defense, aiming to set up attacks. However, the withdrawn striker typically has just one player from his team in front of him, while advanced playmakers have two. Many of the greatest players in the game's history have been withdrawn strikers.

ROOM TO ROAM

Exceptionally talented players, such as Diego Maradona and Zinédine Zidane, flourished in this position because it allowed them the freedom to roam the field and express their creative instincts. The withdrawn striker must be aware of the positions of both teammates and opponents and be able to instinctively time his runs so that players can pass to him. The withdrawn striker is an excellent passer of the ball and must be able to turn quickly and accelerate.

GIANFRANCO ZOLA
Zola spent his formative years as understudy to Diego Maradona at Napoli—and the master's influence showed. In 2003, Chelsea fans voted the Sardinian their greatest ever player.

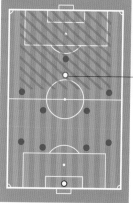

Set ups
The withdrawn striker retains possession, sets up attacks, or shoots, from his position in the "hole"

WITHDRAWN STRIKER'S DOMAIN
The withdrawn striker exploits the space between the midfield and the opponent's defense (the "hole"). He holds up the ball, passes, and shoots.

TELEPATHY EXPERIMENT

In the 1970s, Liverpool forwards Kevin Keegan and John Toshack developed such an intrinsic partnership that many people thought they were telepathic. To test the theory, a local TV station invited them into the studio to guess the shape drawn on a card by the other player. They guessed correctly every time. Only later did Toshack confess that they could see the shapes reflected in the cameras.

THE "OFF-THE-SHOULDER" STRIKER

A forward who specializes in timing his runs so that he is only just onside when the ball is played forward to him is known as an "off-the-shoulder" striker. This is because he stays directly parallel with the opposing team's last defender, only moving off the shoulder at the last possible moment.

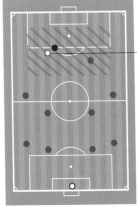

Offside danger
The striker hangs "off-the-shoulder" of the opponent's deepest-lying defender (shown in blue)

PATIENCE REQUIRED

As the off-the-shoulder striker is often ruled offside (correctly or otherwise), patience is a key requirement. Patience is also required of the fans, as the technique employed by these forwards can be frustrating to watch. However, when it works, the tactic can be highly effective, as it offers the striker a crucial head start over the defenders. AC Milan's Pippo Inzaghi is one of the greatest off-the-shoulder strikers.

THIERRY HENRY

Henry played as a forward in his youth but began his professional career as a winger (see p.49). Under the tutelage of Arsène Wenger at Arsenal he evolved into a mixture of both. His trademark approach is to drift to the left before cutting in and shooting. He frequently plays "off-the-shoulder."

OFF-THE-SHOULDER STRIKER'S DOMAIN
The off-the-shoulder striker positions himself alongside the opposing team's last man (the last defender before the goalkeeper). From this position he is well placed to break through on goal.

THE "POACHER"

The poacher is a penalty-box opportunist who either quickly finds space to shoot, or who picks up loose balls and toe-pokes them into the goal. While he may not always look like a conventional player, the poacher is one of the most effective types of striker. He has a geat goal-scoring ability and possesses excellent "off-the ball" movements, which allow him to shake off defenders and gain enough space to shoot. Rarely scoring from outside the penalty area, the poacher is renowned for his powerful and accurate close-range finishes.

GERD MÜLLER
Müller was the ultimate opportunist striker, playing for West Germany and Bayern Munich in the 1960s and '70s.

QUICK REACTIONS

While the poacher doesn't have to be particularly strong or skilful, or even have great pace over more than short distances, he does have to possess extremely quick reactions. Above all, he needs to hone the knack of being in the right place at the right time. He is usually found working in and around the opponent's penalty area hoping to snatch goals.

UNCONVENTIONAL PLAYER

Gerd Müller was once memorably described as "short, squat, awkward-looking, and not notably fast." Nevertheless, his extraordinary acceleration over short distances and unparalleled eye for goal made him one of the greatest strikers of all time.

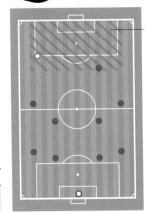

Penalty area
The poacher occupies the penalty area of the opposing team, where he aims to score opportunistic goals

THE POACHER'S DOMAIN
The poacher is an extremely forward-lying striker, focusing his attentions on the opponent's penalty area. He looks to exploit any goal-scoring opportunities that present themselves.

UNCLASSIFIABLE STRIKERS

Not all strikers can be neatly pigeonholed. In fact, it can be a positive advantage to a team that they can't. While the defending team can use a tall defender to mark a conventional target man, it will struggle to defend against a forward who defies categorization. For this reason, some of the greatest strikers have been mavericks with playing styles all of their own.

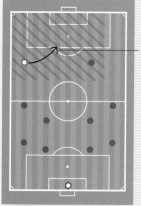

Cutting In
One frequently used ploy is for the unclassifiable striker to "cut in" from the wing before shooting

UNCLASSIFIABLE STRIKER'S DOMAIN
While by definition it is difficult to place the unclassifiable striker, he often receives the ball on the wing before "cutting in" toward the center of the field and unleashing a shot.

VERSATILITY REQUIRED
A striker who can vary his role during the course of a game is rare but invaluable. Dutch star Robin Van Persie is a prime example. He is tall, quick, and capable of shooting from any angle and distance—attributes that allow him to play with equal effectiveness on the left wing, in the "hole," or as a target man. By moving between these positions, he is able to shake off his markers and create scoring opportunities for himself.

SUPERSTAR SCORER
Sometimes a forward can be too versatile for his own good. Manchester United's Wayne Rooney, for example, is so adaptable that manager Sir Alex Ferguson has played him as a main striker, a support striker, and on both wings, making it difficult for him to make any one position his own.

ROBIN VAN PERSIE
Netherlands and Arsenal forward Robin van Persie is a creative and "unclassifiafiable" striker.

STRIKING PARTNERSHIPS

Strikers often work in pairs to form effective partnerships. The best duos consist of players with differing styles, much like the partnerships between central defenders (see p.45). One well-tested formula places a tall, powerful player with a smaller, more agile one. The larger player wins headers and sets up goals for his partner, or tries to retain the ball to bring him more into play.

GREAT PAIRINGS
The greatest striking partnerships, however, are based on far more than just complementary playing styles—the players must instinctively know what the other will do in any given situation. This can be achieved by experience, but there is another more elusive ingredient—the pair must "click." Equally, partnerships that look great on paper may fail to come off in reality.

THE TIGER
Born in Brazil in 1892, Arthur Friedenreich is thought to have scored 1,329 goals in his career. Known as "The Tiger" he was the first black soccer superstar. Playing at a time when soccer was the preserve of the white middle classes, Friedenreich spent a lot of time making himself look white by flattening his naturally curly hair with brilliantine.

I LOVE TO SCORE GOALS AFTER PASSING ALL THE DEFENDERS AS WELL AS THE KEEPER. THIS IS NOT MY SPECIALTY...
BUT MY HABIT!

RONALDO
BRAZIL STRIKER, 2003

STAR STRIKERS

STRIKING PARTNERSHIPS

ROMARIO AND BEBETO
The front two in Brazil's 1994 World Cup-winning team are the exception that proves the rule that duos with differing styles are best. Both were small, quick, and mobile, making opponents feel they were seeing double.

SHEARER AND SHERINGHAM
The striking duo who played up front for England in the mid-1990s represented the classic pairing of a "target" man (Alan Shearer) and a more cerebral "touch" player (Teddy Sheringham).

MORIENTES AND RAUL
Between 1997 and 2005, Morientes formed a powerful partnership with his close friend Raul at Real Madrid. In a typical finish, Morientes would win the ball in the air and Raul would then slam it into the net.

BERGKAMP AND HENRY
With his intelligent play and silky-smooth passing ability, Dennis Bergkamp was the perfect foil for goal-scorer Thierry Henry, his great striking partner at Arsenal from 1997–2006.

GOALKEEPERS

The goalkeeper is the last line of defense between attacking players and the goal. As such, the position carries great responsibility—the outcome of a match can depend more on the goalkeeper than any other player. Each team must have a goalkeeper on the field at all times. If he or she is injured or sent off, a substitute must be used. If no substitutes are available, another outfield player must assume the role.

THE GOALKEEPER'S ROLE

Goalkeeping is the most specialized role in soccer. While inside his own penalty area, the goalkeeper is the only player on the team who is allowed to touch the ball with any part of the body—including the hands. He must defend his team's goal, prevent the opposition from scoring, and organize the defenders. The role requires courage, quick reactions, and the ability to concentrate for the entirety of a match.

ESSENTIAL SKILLS

The essential skills of a goalkeeper include saving, clearing, marshalling the defense, and distributing the ball. As well as being a "safe pair of hands," the goalkeeper must show strength of character. If an outfield player makes a mistake, for example, a teammate may be able to salvage the situation; if a goalkeeper errs, the consequences are usually a confidence-shattering goal. Therefore he must be strong enough to deal with any flack.

Diving save
Quick reactions and a willingness to dive are important skills for the goalkeeper

SAVING
Keeping the ball out of the net is the goalkeeper's number-one priority. He must stop and block any shots at goal as well as use his height advantage to pluck high crosses out of the air.

Punched out
A well-placed punch will clear the ball away

CLEARING
Goalkeepers need to get the ball away from danger areas quickly, whether with their feet or via a punch. They must make sure that their clearance doesn't offer the ball back to the opposition.

Organization skills
The goalkeeper is instrumental in organizing the defense and relaying advice

MARSHALLING
Goalkeepers are in charge of the goal area and must tell their defenders exactly where they want them. This is particularly important during free kicks, when the goalkeeper organizes the wall.

Quick pass
The keeper quickly decides which player is best placed to receive the ball

DISTRIBUTION
Once the ball is safely in the goalkeeper's hands, he must make good use of it. He looks to see which of his teammates are available and punts or throws the ball to them as quickly as possible.

"GOLO!"

Gordon Banks' miraculous clearance of a downward header from Pelé in the 1970 World Cup is often cited as the greatest save in history. The England goalkeeper heard the great Brazilian shout "golo!" as soon as he made contact. However, Banks managed to reach the ball and flick it over the crossbar with one finger and a roll of his hand.

STAR GOALKEEPERS

A World Cup penalty shootout is one of the most stressful situations for the goalkeeper. See right for the top three highest goal-savers in the tournament.

Some goalkeepers are as adept at scoring goals as they are at saving them. See far right for the most prolific goal-scorers in the game.

BEST WORLD CUP PENALTY SAVERS

SERGIO GOYCOECHEA has saved **5** penalty shootout goals for Argentina.

CLAUDIO TAFFAREL of Brazil has also saved **5**, although **2** went over the crossbar.

HARALD SCHUMACHER of West Germany is in third place with **4** shootout saves.

BEST GOAL-SCORING GOALKEEPERS

NAME	FROM/TO	GOALS
Rogério CENI	1990–present	83
José Luis CHILAVERT	1982–2004	68
Jorge CAMPOS	1988–2004	38
René HIGUITA	1985–2009	33
Hans-Joerg BUTT	1994–present	26
Peter SCHMEICHEL	1981–2003	11

RENÉ **HIGUITA**

Colombian goalkeeper René Higuita is famous for his "scorpion kick" (pictured). During a friendly match at Wembley in 1995, England midfielder Jamie Redknapp tried to lob the ball over his head. However, Higuita allowed the ball to float over his head and then turned himself into a human scorpion and kicked it back into play with his heels.

TOP 5: ECCENTRIC GOALKEEPERS

Like drummers in rock groups, goalkeepers are well-known for their eccentric behavior—both on and off the field. Perhaps their unique position on the field and the amount of character they must show is the reason behind this phenomenon. The following five goalkeepers are among the most eccentric:

FABIAN BARTHEZ

The former Marseilles, Manchester United, and France goalkeeper was as energetic and unpredictable as a bouncing rubber ball. His eccentric antics included taunting dribbles and step-overs, and attempts to psyche out opposing strikers.

BRUCE GROBBELAAR

Having served in the Rhodesian bush war, the Liverpool goalkeeper was fearless—if not always inclined to take the game seriously. During a penalty shoot-out against Juventus at the 1984 European Cup final, he put Francesco Graziani off his shot by wobbling his legs like spaghetti.

OLIVER KAHN

Former Germany goalkeeper Oliver Kahn was notorious for arguing with anyone and everyone, from rival goalkeepers and players, to managers and even his own teammates. Not surprisingly, he earned a number of nicknames, which included "Genghis Kahn" and "Kung-fu Kahn."

JORGE CAMPOS

Known for his flamboyant, multi-colored shirts (which he designed himself), the Mexican goalkeeper spent as much time out of his area as in it. At club level he would frequently start between the posts and finish the game as a striker—a position in which he excelled. Campos was talented enough to win 130 caps for his country.

JOSÉ LUIS CHILAVERT

The former goalkeeper for Paraguay was renowned for his incredible skill at taking free-kicks—and for his hotheadedness. His fiery temper led to him being sent off for brawling with Colombia's Tino Asprilla and banned for spitting at Brazil's Roberto Carlos. He was also imprisoned for falsifying club documents.

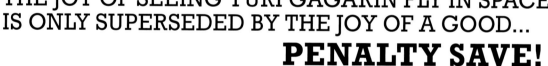

THE JOY OF SEEING YURI GAGARIN FLY IN SPACE IS ONLY SUPERSEDED BY THE JOY OF A GOOD... # PENALTY SAVE!

PAT JENNINGS' HANDS
The success of the former Northern Ireland goalkeeper, who played from 1964–86, was due in part to his large hand span, which enabled him to make spectacular one-handed catches.

LEV YASHIN
USSR GOALKEEPER, 1954–67

GIANLUIGI BUFFON
Consistent, commanding, and unflappable, Buffon is one of the best shot-stoppers in the game. In 2001, Juventus paid Parma €52 million (over $80 million) for his signature, a fee that remains the world record for a goalkeeper.

THE OFFICIALS

In professional matches, the game is controlled by four officials: the referee (see below), two assistant referees, and the fourth official (see pp.58–59). The referee has full authority and, aided by the other officials, is tasked with enforcing the 17 Laws of the Game (see pp.62–63).

RISE OF THE REFEREE

During the early days of association soccer, these "men and women in black" were absent. Instead, teams relied on a spirit of fair play and good sportsmanship. As disputes began to escalate during the 1860s and '70s, however, umpires were introduced. But it wasn't until 1881 that an objective and authoritative official, known as the referee, first appeared.

PIERLUIGI COLLINA

Collina became the leading referee in global soccer, setting new standards for authoritativeness, even-handedness, and tact in this often impossibly complex task. For example, in his refereeing career (1988–2005) he was unique among referees for his willingness to apologize to managers for any mistakes made during the match.

LEADING LIGHT

As the referee's standing grew during the 20th century, influential figures began to emerge. English referee Stanley Rous, for example, was one of the leading referees of the 1930s. In addition to instigating the diagonal system of control (see right), he drafted the 1938 rewrite of the rules, which remain substantially unchanged today. He also championed the provision of referee training by FIFA for all of its new members.

THE REFEREE'S HAND SIGNALS

Referees use a variety of hand signals, which are employed to indicate decisions to the players. The referee also blows a whistle to stop play before making the appropriate signal. A short, quick whistle usually indicates a less-serious offense, while more-serious fouls elicit harder blasts. If the attacking team has a foul commited against one of its players, the referee may signal an advantage in the attacking team's favor without blowing his whistle.

IT'S A KNOCKOUT

Concetto Lo Bello (1924–91) is one of the most famous Italian referees in the history of the game. Known as "the prince," he was noted for his immaculate dress, a carefully manicured moustache, and such vigorous hand signals that, on numerous occasions, he knocked players to the ground when signaling for a free-kick.

YELLOW CARD
A yellow card is held up, above the head, to the player being cautioned.

RED CARD
A red card is held up, above the head, to the player being sent off.

DIRECT FREE-KICK
The referee blows the whistle and points in the direction of the kick.

INDIRECT FREE-KICK
A hand is held up until the taker and a teammate have touched the ball.

ADVANTAGE
The referee extends both arms to indicate that play can continue.

PENALTY KICK
The referee points to the appropriate penalty mark.

GOAL KICK
The referee points to the appropriate part of the goal area.

CORNER KICK
The referee points to the appropriate corner arc.

OFFICIALS' EQUIPMENT

The referee and the assistant referees (see p.58) make use of several different pieces of equipment. These are all designed to help the referee enforce the Laws of the Game effectively.

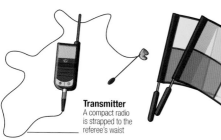

Transmitter
A compact radio is strapped to the referee's waist

EARPIECE AND RADIO SET
In all top-flight matches, referees and their assistants communicate by using a small radio set.

ASSISTANT'S FLAGS
Flags are used by the assistant referees to signal to the referee (see p.58 for assistant's signals).

TIMEPIECE
Referees need at least one timepiece—a wrist watch and stopwatch.

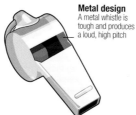

Metal design
A metal whistle is tough and produces a loud, high pitch

Needle
A built-in needle fits directly into the valve of the ball

CARDS AND NOTEBOOK
The referee may decide to penalize players by issuing yellow or red cards. Incidents are recorded in a notebook.

WHISTLE
The referee blows his whistle to start play, stop or delay play due to a foul or injury, and to end each half.

PRESSURE GAUGE
A pressure gauge is used to check that the ball is correctly inflated.

REFEREEING SYSTEMS

Early matches were played without the referee being on the field. From the late 1890s, however, it became clear that a coordinated and more mobile approach to refereeing was needed. Several systems of patrolling the field have since been developed.

LINEAR SYSTEM
The referee patrols one side of the field only, while one or two assistants move along the opposite sideline. The side views afforded are helpful, but the referee is in danger of obstructing wing play.

DIAGONAL SYSTEM
This is the most common system in modern soccer. The referee patrols a diagonal area between two opposing corner flags, while the assistant referees stand on opposite sides. This system means that two people should see any incident on the field.

ZIGZAG-PATH SYSTEM
In lower leagues in which the referee officiates alone, he may choose to move in a steady zigzag path, following a line between the teams' penalty arcs. The refereee will, however, have to change positions for corners and penalty kicks.

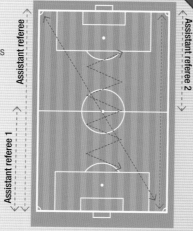

Assistant referee 1

Assistant referee

Assistant referee 2

KEY

<----> Linear system
<----> Diagonal system
<----> Zigzag-path system

CHECK LIST

CHECK LIST

REFEREE'S DUTIES

The match is controlled by the referee, who has full authority to enforce the rules for the match to which he has been appointed. His main duties are:

ENFORCE THE RULES
The referee's principal responsibility is to enforce the rules to his appointed match as set out in the Laws of the Game.

CONTROL THE MATCH
The referee must control the match in cooperation with the assistant referees and, for official matches, the fourth official.

CHECK EQUIPMENT
He must ensure that the ball and the players' equipment meet the requirements of the Laws of the Game.

TIMEKEEP AND MAINTAIN RECORDS
The referee must act as the timekeeper for the match, and keep a record of any substitutions and offenses.

STOP PLAY WHEN NECESSARY
The referee must stop, suspend, or abandon the match for any infringements of the Laws of the Game, or because of any other outside interference.

ENSURE PLAYER SAFETY
The referee must stop the match if a player is seriously injured, ensuring that he is removed from the field of play.

REFEREE'S FITNESS

Officials must have very high levels of fitness. In elite matches, for example, the referee can cover up to 8 miles (13km) during a game—more than the players themselves. FIFA tests its international referees for the following:

AVERAGE RUNNING SPEED
Candidates run six 44-yd (40-m) sprints, with a maximum recovery time of 90 seconds between each sprint. The average time of the runs is then calculated. Male referees must complete the distance in 6.2 seconds or less; female referees must run it in 6.6 seconds.

HIGH-INTENSITY RUNNING
Male referees must cover 164 yd (150 m) in 30 seconds or less, followed by 35 seconds of recovery time during which they must walk 55 yd (50 m). This distance is repeated to count as one lap. Referees must complete 10 laps. Female referees are allowed 35 seconds to complete the run sections and 40 seconds to complete the walks.

ASSISTANT REFEREE

The assistant referee is responsible for helping the referee to officiate a match. In professional games, two assistants patrol each touchline. They each take responsibility for half of the field, standing diagonally across from each other (see "Refereeing systems", p.57). The assistants officiate in situations in which the referee is not in a position to make the best decision. While their expertise is often crucial, their role is purely advisory.

THE GENDER AGENDA

The role of "linesman" was added to the Laws of the Game (see pp.62–63) in 1891—at a time when the officials were always male. It wasn't until 1996 that the term was dropped in favor of the gender-neutral "assistant referee."

THE ROLE OF THE ASSISTANTS

The more senior of the two assistants usually oversees the side of the field that contains the technical areas, so that he or she can help supervise substitutions. Typical duties for either assistant include signaling for offside and determining which team should be awarded a throw-in.

FLAG SIGNALS

The flag is the assistant's most important piece of equipment, as flag signals are the standard form of communication with a referee (although a buzzer system is sometimes also used). The distinctive red and yellow checkered design of the flag has been proven to be the most eye-catching color combination over a long distance. The following signals (see right) are most commonly used during a match.

BEST BEHAVIOR

The referee has the power to relieve an assistant of his or her duties—and make a report to the appropriate authorities—if an assistant acts in an improper way.

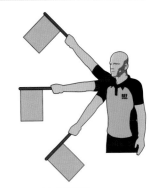

OFFSIDE
The flag is held above the head to signal for an offside offense.

OFFSIDE POSITION
A high flag is used for far offside, a horizontal flag for middle offside, and a low flag for near offside.

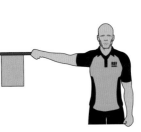

FLAG CARRYING
The assistant referee carries the flag unfurled so that any signals can be clearly seen.

THROW-IN
A flag is held out to one side, pointing in the direction of play of the team awarded the throw.

SUBSTITUTION
A flag is held above the head with both hands to indicate a substitution.

OTHER SIGNALS

As well as using flag signals and a buzzer system, the assistant referees employ a variety of other forms of communication. Discrete hand signals, for example, let the referee know that a close ball has not gone out of play or that no offense has been committed. In return, the referee can use hand signals to inform an assistant the direction in which a throw-in should be taken if he or she is unsure.

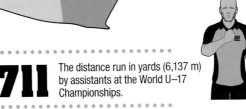

6,711 The distance run in yards (6,137 m) by assistants at the World U–17 Championships.

20 The percentage of the distance run by assistant referees (see above) at speeds of 8 mph (13 kph) or faster.

CALLING TIME
A clenched fist on the chest means 45 minutes have elapsed in the half.

NO OFFENSE
The assistant referee shows a lowered palm to indicate that no offense has been committed.

FOURTH OFFICIAL

The fourth official assists the referee with administrative duties before and after the game, helps with assessing players' equipment, and may be called on to replace another match official (see below). The fourth official is also responsible for setting and holding up electronic display boards, acts as another pair of eyes for the referee, and keeps an extra set of records.

THE FOURTH OFFICAL AS SUBSTITUTE

The fourth official may replace the assistant referee or referee if one of the other officials can't continue. If an assistant is injured, for example, the fourth official replaces him or her automatically. If the referee is unable to continue, the fourth official may replace him directly, or an assistant may replace the referee, with the fourth official taking the vacant assistant's position.

NO IFS, ANDS, OR BUTTS

During the 2006 World Cup final it was the fourth official, Luis Medina Cantalejo, who spotted Zidane's infamous head butt—not referee Horacio Elizondo. As a result, Zidane was sent off. The French coach Raymond Domenech argued that Cantalejo had seen the incident on a replay and not as it happened, which would have broken FIFA rules. However, FIFA insisted that Cantalejo had not breached the rules and the decision stood.

THE REFEREE HAS GOT ME THE SACK (FIRED)... # THANK HIM FOR THAT!

GRAHAM TAYLOR
ENGLAND MANAGER, 1993

SUPPORTING ROLE
Among other duties, the fourth official must hold up a display board to indicate any time added on at the end of each half.

ASSISTANT REFEREE

The assistant referee assists with (rather than insists on) refereeing decisions. His or her duties include:

SIGNALING FOR OUT OF PLAY
The assistant referee signals to the referee when the ball leaves the field of play.

SIGNALING FOR RESTARTS
The assistant indicates which side is entitled to a goal-kick, corner-kick, or throw-in.

SIGNALING FOR OFFSIDE
The assistant referee signals when a player is in an offside position.

SIGNALING FOR SUBSTITUTIONS
The assistant referee signals when a substitution has been requested.

SIGNALING FOR MISCONDUCT
The assistant signals when misconduct occurs out of the referee's field of vision.

MONITORING THE GOALKEEPER
The assistant monitors the goalkeeper during penalty-kicks, signaling if he moves off his line before the kick.

FOURTH OFFICIAL

The fourth official is responsible for the following duties during the course of a professional match:

ASSISTING WITH RECORD KEEPING
The fourth official keeps a duplicate set of records.

CHECKING PLAYERS' EQUIPMENT
The fourth official helps the referee check that the players' equipment meets the requirements set out in the rules.

OVERSEEING SUBSTITUTIONS
The fourth official ensures that substitutions are conducted in an orderly manner.

DISPLAYING INFORMATION
The fourth offical uses numbered boards or electronic displays to inform the referee of any substitution, and to show the amount of time added on at the end of each half (having been advised by the referee).

MAINTAINING CONTROL
He or she maintains control in the teams' technical areas, intervening in situations in which coaches, bench personnel, or substitutes become argumentative.

ACTING AS AN INTERMEDIARY
The fourth official acts as the contact point between the match officials and any non-participants, such as stadium managers, broadcast crews, and ball retrievers.

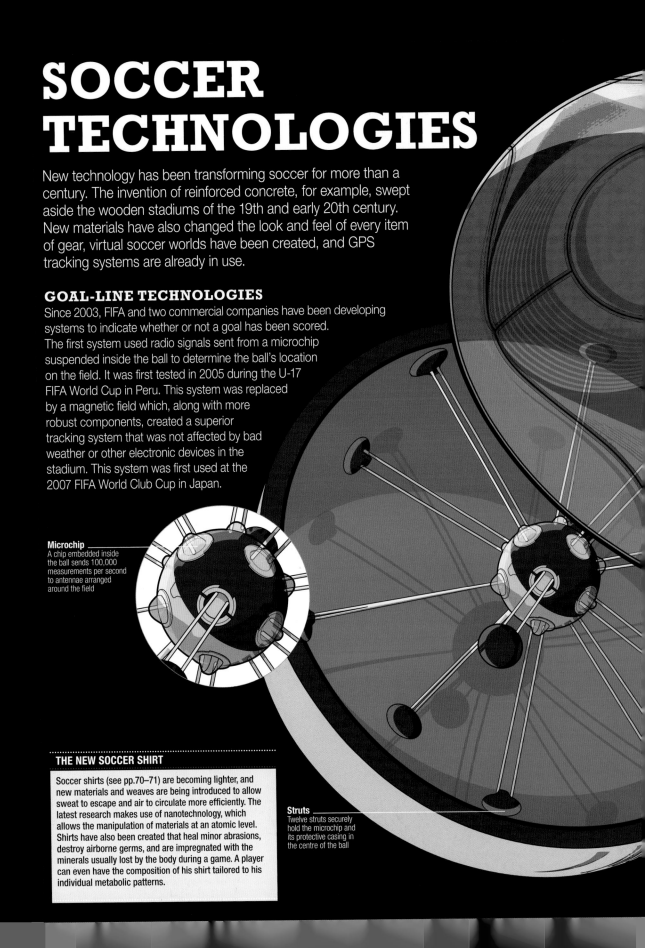

SOCCER TECHNOLOGIES

New technology has been transforming soccer for more than a century. The invention of reinforced concrete, for example, swept aside the wooden stadiums of the 19th and early 20th century. New materials have also changed the look and feel of every item of gear, virtual soccer worlds have been created, and GPS tracking systems are already in use.

GOAL-LINE TECHNOLOGIES

Since 2003, FIFA and two commercial companies have been developing systems to indicate whether or not a goal has been scored. The first system used radio signals sent from a microchip suspended inside the ball to determine the ball's location on the field. It was first tested in 2005 during the U-17 FIFA World Cup in Peru. This system was replaced by a magnetic field which, along with more robust components, created a superior tracking system that was not affected by bad weather or other electronic devices in the stadium. This system was first used at the 2007 FIFA World Club Cup in Japan.

Microchip
A chip embedded inside the ball sends 100,000 measurements per second to antennae arranged around the field

THE NEW SOCCER SHIRT

Soccer shirts (see pp.70–71) are becoming lighter, and new materials and weaves are being introduced to allow sweat to escape and air to circulate more efficiently. The latest research makes use of nanotechnology, which allows the manipulation of materials at an atomic level. Shirts have also been created that heal minor abrasions, destroy airborne germs, and are impregnated with the minerals usually lost by the body during a game. A player can even have the composition of his shirt tailored to his individual metabolic patterns.

Struts
Twelve struts securely hold the microchip and its protective casing in the centre of the ball

BRAVE NEW WORLD

PROZONE ET AL

For years, barely any statistics about player and team performance were gathered—the flow of play was just too complex, frenetic, and unpredictable to create systems of record-keeping that could match baseball's box scores or cricket's complex multi-layered scorecards. New computing technologies, movement sensors, and GPS positioning systems have now been combined to create systems such as Prozone, which can track every player's actions and movements throughout a game.

GREEN IS THE COLOR

Soccer is not neglecting its environmental obligations. Future stadiums are designed, built, and maintained with energy conservation in mind. They incorporate facilities for recycling water and food waste, and even generate their own energy—through solar panels located on their large roofs, for example. In addition, artificial turf may become an increasingly familiar sight in soccer stadiums where water is scarce.

IPOD COACHING

In the gap between the end of extra time and the start of the penalty shootout at the end of the 2009 English League Cup final, Manchester United's goalkeeper Ben Foster watched footage of his opponents taking penalties on a coach's iPod. It seemed to help, as Foster made a brilliant save from Jamie O'Hara's spot kick, delivering the cup to United.

GAMES AND SIMULATIONS

Computer software companies have been quick to produce soccer simulation games. Many rapidly achieved cult status, offering fans the tantalizing prospect of taking Bristol Rovers to the Champion's League final, for example, from the comfort of their bedroom. As computing power and connectivity has increased, online multi-player games have created entire virtual soccer worlds.

57 The percentage of fans who think goal-line technology is the most important recent technological development to be made in soccer

68 The percentage of fans who would welcome the broadcasting of match officials' comments—as is currently the case with football and international rugby

82 The percentage of fans who think that technology, such as goal-line cameras, would considerably improve their enjoyment of the game

1966 WORLD CUP FINAL—DID THE BALL CROSS THE LINE?

With 12 minutes of extra time played and the score at 2–2, England's Geoff Hurst sent a thundering shot into the German goal. The ball bounced down from the crossbar and was cleared by a German defender. The referee was unsure if the ball had crossed the line, but the ruling linesman, Tofik Bakhramov, rushed over and, in the heat of the moment, ruled the shot a goal. Controversy has reigned ever since.

THE RULES

The Laws of the Game were devised by the FA in 1863, when there were just 13 rules. As a testament to the game's simplicity, there are still only 17 laws in place today. The offside rules (see pp.66–67) have proved to be the most complex to create and administer, having been overhauled three times in the rulebook's history.

THE INTERNATIONAL FA BOARD

Founded in 1886 by the football associations of England, Scotland, Wales, and Ireland, the International Football Association Board (IFAB) is the game's ultimate rulemaking body. The board now includes four members from outside the UK, as nominated by FIFA, and meets annually to decide potential rule changes. Its decisions are binding for all national football and soccer associations worldwide.

ROBERTO TROTTA
Former Argentina defender Roberto Trotta holds the dubious honor of receiving the most red cards. He was sent off a record-breaking 17 times during his career.

LAWS OF THE GAME

1. FIELD OF PLAY

The field (see pp.40–41) must be a rectangle, marked with touchlines, goal lines and areas, a halfway line, a center circle, penalty areas, spots, and arcs, corner arcs, and flag posts. It must be between 100–131 yd (90–120 m) long and between 49–98 yd (45–90 m) wide. For international soccer, the limits are 109–120 yd (100–110 m) and 70–82 yd (64–75 m) respectively.

2. THE BALL

The ball (see pp.76–77) must be made of approved materials. At the start of the game, it must have a diameter of 27–28 in (68–70 cm), weigh between 14–16 oz (410–450 g), and have an internal pressure of between 0.6 and 1.1 atmospheres at sea level. It can only be changed by the referee. If it bursts during a game, play is stopped and restarted with a new drop ball.

3. NUMBER OF PLAYERS

A match consists of two teams of not more than 11 players, each including a goalkeeper. An outfield player may swap with the goalkeeper during a stoppage of play. Teams must have at least seven players to begin or continue a match. In official competitions, a maximum of three player substitutions may be made.

4. PLAYERS' EQUIPMENT

Compulsory equipment for players are a shirt, shorts, socks, shin pads, and soccer boots (see pp.70–73). Goalkeepers must wear a uniform that distinguishes them from their own team, their opponents, and the officials. Headgear is permitted if it does not present a threat to other players. Most forms of jewelry are not permitted.

5. THE REFEREE

The referee (see pp.56–57) is the final arbiter and interpreter of the rules. He decides whether a game can go ahead or not, and may stop play if a player requires medical treatment. He cautions players (yellow card), sends them off (red card), and is responsible for timekeeping, record-keeping, and ensuring that all match equipment and uniforms are correct.

6. ASSISTANT REFEREES

The assistant referees (see pp.58–59)—formerly called linesmen—support the referee, primarily by signaling for corner kicks, throw-ins, and offside infringements. They must also bring the referee's attention to any other fouls or infringements that the referee may not have seen. However, the referee's word is always final.

7. DURATION OF MATCH

There are two equal halves of 45 minutes of play. Additional time may be added—at the discretion of the referee—for injuries, substitutions, and time-wasting. Time can also be added to allow a penalty to be taken at the end of normal time. Rules covering extra time are made by national football and soccer associations and confederations.

8. START/RESTART OF PLAY

A coin is tossed before the start of play; the winners choose ends for the first half and the losers kick off. The other team kicks off in the second half. The kick-off is taken from the center spot and the ball must move into the oppositions' half. All players must be in their own half, and the opposition must be at least 10 yd (9.15 m) away from the ball. The ball must be touched by a second player before the first player can touch it again.

9. BALL IN AND OUT OF PLAY

The ball is in play when it is inside the field of play and the referee has not stopped play. The ball is out of play when it has completely crossed the sidelines or the goal lines, whether in the air or on the ground. If the ball rebounds off a goalpost, crossbar, corner flagpost, or the referee or one of the assistant referees, and remains in the field of play, it is still in play.

ENFORCING THE RULES

The Laws of the Game are enforced by the referee (see pp.56–57), who has the final say in any match disputes. Since 1992, FIFA has stipulated that all referees in international matches must speak English. The referee may be helped by two assistant referees and a fourth official (see pp.58–59). The fourth official is increasingly used in international matches and the leading leagues, primarily to assist the referee with administrative duties.

VARIATIONS IN THE RULES

The Laws of the Game are simple enough to apply to every level of the game. However, there are minor variations between leagues. For example, while the names of substitutes must always be submitted to the referee before kick-off, in lower leagues, the teams can decide between themselves how many substitutions may be made; in FIFA competitions, the maximum is three.

BALL BOY SCORES

Law 5 states that the referee's decision is final—no matter how bizarre. In 2008, when a striker for Brazil's Santacruzense missed an attempted equalizer against Sorocaba, no one could have predicted what happened next. When the referee's back was turned, a ball boy decided to nudge the ball over the goal line. To everyone's amazement, the goal was allowed.

10. METHOD OF SCORING

A goal is scored when the ball has completely crossed the goal line between the goalposts and under the crossbar, provided that no other infringements have taken place. The team with the most goals wins. If both teams score the same number of goals, or if no goals are scored at all, the match is a draw.

11. OFFSIDE

A player is offside (see pp.66–67), at the moment a ball is passed forward, when he is: in the opponents' half of the field; is closer to the opponents' goal line than the ball; and there are fewer than two defenders (including the goalkeeper) closer to the goal line than the attacking player. When a player is called offside, the opposition is awarded a free-kick.

12. FOULS AND MISCONDUCT

A foul (see pp.68–69) has been committed if a player: trips, kicks, pushes, or charges another player recklessly; strikes, attempts to strike, or spits at an opponent; makes a tackle but connects with the player before the ball; deliberately handles the ball (goalkeepers in their area excepted); or obstructs an opponent or prevents them from releasing the ball.

13. FREE-KICKS

Free-kicks (see pp.64–65, 138–39) restart play after a foul or infringement and are usually taken from the place from which the offense was committed. Free-kicks can be "direct," in which the taker may score directly, or "indirect," in which the taker and a second player from the same team must touch the ball before a goal can be scored.

14. PENALTY-KICK

A penalty-kick (see pp.64, 140–41) is awarded for a foul committed by a defending player in his or her own penalty area. The kick is taken from the penalty spot and all other players—except for the goalkeeper and taker—must be at least 10 yd (9.15 m) from the spot. The taker may touch the ball if it rebounds from the goalkeeper, but not if it rebounds from the post or crossbar.

15. THE THROW-IN

A throw-in (see pp.64, 138–39) is awarded when the ball has crossed the touchline and an opposition player was the last to touch it. The throw is taken from the point from which the ball crossed the line. The taker must have both feet on the ground, use two hands, throw the ball from behind and over the head, and be facing the field of play.

16. GOAL-KICK

A goal-kick (see pp.142–45) is awarded to the defending team when the ball crosses its goal line, a goal has not been scored, and the last player to touch it was from the opposition. Any player may take the goal kick, placing the ball anywhere in the goal area. The kick must send the ball out of the penalty area or be retaken. The taker may not touch the ball again until it has been touched by a second player.

17. CORNER-KICK

A corner (see pp.64, 136–37) is awarded to the attacking team when the opposition is last to touch the ball and the ball crosses the goal line without a goal being scored. A corner is also awarded if the ball enters the goal from a throw-in or indirect free-kick. The attacking team restarts play by placing the ball in the corner arc closest to where it crossed the goal line.

SEEING RED
Law 5 says that the referee's decision is always final.

USING SET PIECES

A set piece is a predetermined, fixed move used to restart play when the referee is forced to halt the game temporarily. There are three occasions when the normally free-flowing game of soccer is stopped: following an infringement, such as a foul or offside; when the ball goes out of play; and following a player injury or other interruption, such as a burst ball.

TYPES OF SET PIECE

There are six different types of set piece: goal-kicks, free-kicks, throw-ins, penalty-kicks, corner-kicks, and drop-balls. Free-kicks can be either "direct," in which the taker can score a goal without another player touching the ball, or "indirect," in which a second player must first touch the ball. In either situation, every member of the opposing team must be at least 10 yd (9.15 m) from the ball at the moment the kick is taken.

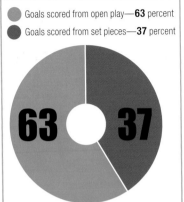

WORLD CUP 2006 GOALS

- ● Goals scored from open play—**63** percent
- ● Goals scored from set pieces—**37** percent

63   **37**

HIGH STAKES

Many goals are scored from set pieces (see box, right). As a result, teams spend a lot of time practicing how to attack (and defend) from set pieces. A defending team, for example, will adopt positions and patterns of movement designed to stop an easy goal. If a free-kick is awarded near the goal, the defenders will set up a line of players (called a wall) in front of the kicker to try to block the ball.

IN THE SPOT LIGHT

Almost 120 years after William McCrum invented the penalty-kick, a memorial was erected in his home town to celebrate his contribution to soccer. The bust and plinth sits in the small town of Milford in County Armagh, Northern Ireland. McCrum invented the set piece as the ultimate sanction after witnessing violent play.

Goal area
A goal-kick is taken from inside the goal area

GOAL-KICK
A goal-kick is awarded to a defending team when the ball completely crosses the goal line—either on the ground or in the air—having been kicked by an opposing player without a goal being scored.

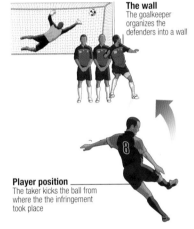

The wall
The goalkeeper organizes the defenders into a wall

Player position
The taker kicks the ball from where the the infringement took place

FREE-KICK
Direct free-kicks are awarded for serious offenses, such as kicking, tripping, or pushing, while indirect free-kicks are awarded for less serious offenses, such as obstruction or offside (see right).

Correct technique
The thrower must face the field of play and have both feet on the ground

THROW-IN
A throw-in is awarded against the team that last touches the ball before it crosses the touchline. It is made with both feet on or behind the touchline, and both hands moving from behind the taker's head.

Great expectations
There can be huge pressure on the taker of a penalty-kick, especially during a penalty shootout (see pp.140–41)

PENALTY-KICK
A penalty is awarded for any offense committed inside the penalty area that would otherwise be punished by a direct free-kick had it taken place outside the penalty area.

Scoring opportunity
Many goals are scored from corners, often as a result of headers

Testing time
The keeper must decide whether to defend from the goal line or advance to try and clear the ball

CORNER-KICK
A corner-kick is awarded when the whole of the ball crosses the goal line (either on the ground or in the air) having last been touched by a member of the defending team, including the goalkeeper.

SET PIECE ETIQUETTE

If a player is injured, the team in possession is expected to kick the ball into touch. The other side should then return it from the resulting set piece. During an English FA Cup tie in 1999, Sheffield United's goalkeeper kicked the ball out of play so that an injured teammate could receive treatment. But instead of returning the ball, Arsenal midfielder Ray Parlour initiated a move that led to the winning goal. The match was eventually replayed.

DROP-BALL

A drop-ball is played when a game needs to be restarted following an incident not covered in the rules, such as a serious player injury. The ball is not awarded to either team. Instead, a player from one team stands across from a player from the other team and the referee drops the ball between them.

THE "BANANA SHOT"

LEGENDARY FREE-KICK

In 1997, Roberto Carlos (see below) scored from an incredible direct free-kick. He hit the ball so far to the right of the French wall that a ballboy between the corner flag and the goalpost ducked. Miraculously, the ball swerved in and landed in the goal. Carlos' "banana shot" has entered soccer folklore.

With a shot that seemed to defy the laws of physics, Carlos swerved the ball around the wall.

- ● Roberto Carlos (Brazil)
- ● Defending team (France)
- — Trajectory of ball

ROBERTO **CARLOS**

Brazilian wingback (see p.44) Roberto Carlos is renowned for his trademark free-kicks. His seemingly impossible "banana shot" (see above) is legendary. Carlos has played for the Brazil national team in three World Cup tournaments, helping the South American team to reach the final in 1998 and to win in 2002. He was named as one of the top 125 greatest living players by Pelé in 2004.

OFFENSES

DIRECT FREE-KICKS

Direct free-kicks are usually awarded for relatively serious offenses (see pp.68–69). The most common are:

KICKING AND TRIPPING
It is an offense for a player to kick or trip—or attempt to kick or trip—an opponent.

JUMPING OR CHARGING
It is an offense for a player to jump or charge at an opponent.

STRIKING AND PUSHING
It is an offense for a player to strike, push, hold, or spit at an opponent.

MAKING CONTACT
It is an offense for a player to touch an opponent before touching the ball when making a tackle.

HANDLING THE BALL
It is an offense for a player to deliberately handle the ball (except for the goalkeeper in his area).

INDIRECT FREE-KICKS

Indirect free-kicks are usually awarded for less serious offenses than direct free-kicks. The most common are:

OBSTRUCTION
It is an offense for a player to deliberately impede the progress of an opponent.

DANGEROUS PLAY
It is an offense to make an attempt to kick the ball when an opponent is attempting to head it, for example.

IMPEDING THE GOALKEEPER
It is an offense to prevent the goalkeeper from releasing the ball.

TOUCHING THE BALL TWICE
It is an offense to touch the ball twice at a set piece without an intervening touch from another player.

OFFSIDE
If a player is offside (see pp.66–67), an indirect free-kick is given to the opposition.

THE OFFSIDE RULE

Offside is the most contentious and frequently misunderstood rule in soccer, as decisions often rest on an official's individual interpretation of the law. It is also the most frequently revised rule, as minor changes to the regulations can have dramatic effects on the character of matches.

KEY

- ● Attacking team
- ● Defending team
- ○ Goalkeeper
- - - Pass
- — Player movement

WHAT IS THE RULE?

A player is ruled offside at the moment the ball is passed forward by one of his teammates if: he is in the opponent's half of the field; he is closer to the opponent's goal line than the ball; there are fewer than two defenders (including the goalkeeper) closer to the goal line than himself. Only the head, body, and legs are taken into consideration (not the arms). A player is still onside if he is level with the second defender from the goal line or if he receives the ball directly from a throw-in, corner, or goal-kick.

THE DEVIL'S IN THE DETAIL

The situation is complicated, however, by the stipulation that a player in an offside position is only deemed to be committing an offense if he is "active." In 2005, FIFA expanded on the rule by defining an active player as one who is: interfering with play—meaning that he has played a ball passed or touched by a teammate; interfering with an opponent—meaning that he has obstructed the movement or line of vision of an opponent, or distracted them with a gesture or movement; gaining an advantage—meaning that he has used his offside position to benefit from a rebound off a post, crossbar, or an opponent.

OFFSIDE
In this situation, Player A is offside because there is only one defender —the goalkeeper (1)—between him and the goal line when Player B passes the ball. An indirect free-kick would be awarded for this offense.

Offside
Player A is in an offside position

Passing forwards
Player B passes the ball to Player A, who is offside

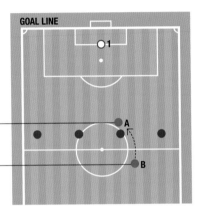

GOAL LINE

ONSIDE
In the scenario shown here, Player A is not offside. This is because when Player B passed the ball, there were two defenders between Player A and the goal line.

Two defenders
Both the goalkeeper (1) and another defender (2) are between Player A and the goal line

Onside
Player A is in an onside position

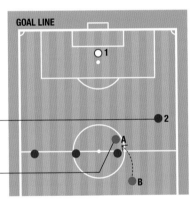

GOAL LINE

OFFSIDE OR NOT?

The offside rule has various nuances that often make rulings very subjective. There are, for example, many situations in which a player is in an offside position but is not deemed to be violating the offside rule. The following scenaros (right) illustrate some of the peculiarities of the rule.

KEY

- ● Attacking team
- ● Defending team
- ○ Goalkeeper
- - - Pass
- — Player movement

SCENARIO ONE

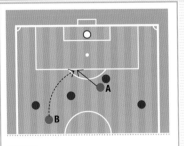

ONSIDE
In this example, Player A is in an offside position when he receives the ball but was onside when it was played forward by his teammate. He is therefore onside.

SCENARIO TWO

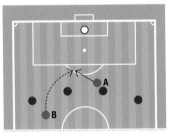

OFFSIDE
In this example, Player A, who is receiving the ball, was in an offside position when the ball was played forward by Player B. He is therefore offside.

HISTORY OF THE OFFSIDE RULE

The offside law was introduced to prevent "goal hanging," which usually results in a game degenerating into a series of long kicks from one end of the field to the other. The FA's first set of rules in 1896 stated: "When a player has kicked the ball, anyone of the same side who is nearer to the opponents' goal line is out of play." Three years later, forward passes were permitted, as long as there were three opponents between the receiver and the goal line. In 1925, this number was reduced to two. The most significant recent change came in 1990, when attackers were ruled onside if they were level with the second-to-last opponent.

MOST FREQUENT OFFSIDE OFFENDERS

English Premiership players with the highest average number of offside decisions given against them per match in 2007–08:

Emmanuel Adebayor—**1.83**
(Togo and Arsenal)

Marcus Bent—**1.74**
(England and Wigan)

Nicolas Anelka—**1.56**
(France and Chelsea)

Dimitar Berbatov—**1.25**
(Bulgaria and Man Utd)

FILIPPO **INZAGHI**

Italy and AC Milan forward Filippo Inzaghi is a predatory goal-scorer with a reputation for playing "off-the-shoulder" (see p.52). Manchester United manager Sir Alex Ferguson once joked that he was "born in an offside position." The World Cup-winning player was Italy's top goal-scorer during the qualifying rounds of the 2002 World Cup and Euro 2004.

IF A PLAYER ISN'T INTERFERING WITH PLAY OR SEEKING TO GAIN AN ADVANTAGE...
HE SHOULD BE!

BILL SHANKLY, LIVERPOOL MANAGER, 1960s–70s
ON "ACTIVE" PLAYERS IN OFFSIDE DECISIONS

SCENARIO THREE

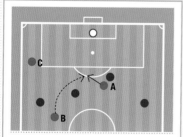

ONSIDE
In this example, Player C on the left wing is in an offside position. However, as he is not interfering with the play between Players A and B, he is deemed to be onside.

SCENARIO FOUR

OFFSIDE
In this example, Player A receives the ball in an onside position but was offside at the moment it was passed forward by Player B. Therefore, Player A is offside.

SCENARIO FIVE

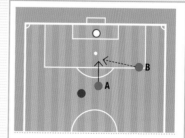

ONSIDE
In this example, despite the fact that Player A receives the ball in an offside position, he is actually onside. This is because he was behind the ball at the moment that it was played.

FOULS AND INFRINGEMENTS

When the FA's Laws of the Game (see pp.62–63) were first drawn up in 1863, one team decided to withdraw from the association because its favored habit of hacking (forcing the foot into an opponent's ankle) was about to be outlawed. Since then, a host of other offenses have been written into the rulebook as fouls, and referees, equipped with red and yellow cards, have been employed to enforce them.

UNRULY RULINGS

In a game between Curitiba and Santos in Brazil in 2003, Curitiba striker Jaba displayed his skill with a flamboyant show of close-ball control. The Santos players thought Jaba was mocking them and, incensed, physically attacked him. But instead of the Santos players being booked for their behavior, Jaba was cautioned for provoking his opponents.

CRIME AND PUNISHMENT

A foul is an act or offense committed by a player who is deemed by the referee to have contravened Law 12 of the Laws of the Game. This includes kicking, tripping, or striking an opponent, connecting with a player before connecting with the ball when tackling, and deliberately handling the ball. Yellow and red cards are used to punish serious fouls (see right), while, for lesser fouls, free-kicks are awarded to the opposing side.

> ## I'M COMMITTING WICKED FOULS... GOING FOR HIGH BALLS I USE MY ELBOW...
> # OR I'M DEAD
>
> **THIERRY HENRY**
> FRANCE STRIKER, 2000

DIRECT AND INDIRECT FREE-KICKS

A direct free-kick is awarded to the opposing team when a player commits a dangerous or "penal" foul, such as charging at an opponent with excessive force or performing a high tackle. A goal may be scored directly from this type of free-kick (see pp.64–65). An indirect free-kick is awarded to the opposing team when a player commits a foul other than a dangerous or penal foul, or infringes technical requirements. A goal cannot be scored directly from this type of free-kick (a second player must first touch the ball). See below for some typical fouls.

Blocking play
It is a foul for a player to use his body to block another player

OBSTRUCTION
If a player is positioned between the ball and an opponent and makes no attempt to play the ball, this is known as obstruction.

Dangerous play
High tackles are considered to be dangerous play

HIGH TACKLE
Whether attempting to play the ball or not, tackles made with "high feet" have become increasingly less acceptable in soccer.

Impeded
It is a foul for a player to hold back an opponent

HOLDING
Pulling on a player's shirt to slow him down in an attempt to gain possession of the ball contravenes the Laws of the Game.

Intentional trip
A player who deliberately trips up an opponent is committing a foul

TRIPPING
Tripping has long been an offense, but the referee must be sharp-eyed to see if there really has been contact between the players.

Dangerous tackle
A sliding tackle can be a serious offense if not executed properly

SLIDING TACKLE
A sliding tackle, in which the attacking player fails to gain possession of the ball, is considered to be a serious foul.

CRUNCH TIME
In 1987, Vinnie Jones was photographed grabbing midfielder Paul Gascoigne—by the crotch.

TOP 5: BAD BOYS

Soccer has always attracted players who are happy to flout the rules—no matter how dangerous their behavior. Here are five of the "best" bad boys.

PAULO MONTERO
Uruguay's reputation for nurturing hard men is neatly embodied in Paulo Montero. While at Juventus, he received a record 16 red cards.

HARALD SCHUMACHER
Schumacher's moment of infamy came in the 1982 World Cup Semi-final when he smashed into advancing French player Patrick Battiston. The Frenchman lost a number of teeth in the attack, but Schumacher wasn't booked.

ANDONI GOIKOETXEA
Dubbed "The butcher from Bilbao," Goiko was a ruthless defender who achieved notoriety for a dangerous tackle on Diego Maradona that resulted in a broken ankle for the Argentinian midfielder.

"CHOPPER" HARRIS
Ron "Chopper" Harris acquired his infamous nickname during 17 bone-crunching seasons at Chelsea between 1963 and 1980.

FRANK BARSON
A player for Barnsley, Aston Villa, and Manchester United between 1911 and 1935, Barson's tackles and barging of goalkeepers produced a strong reaction among rival fans. For his own safety, he was often escorted out by the local police.

HARALD SCHUMACHER
Schumacher injured Patrick Battiston at the 1982 World Cup by colliding into him.

THE CARD SYSTEM

In addition to awarding free-kicks, the referee can penalize an individual player by issuing him with either a yellow or red card. A yellow card (or caution) is issued for serious offenses or dissent. A red card is issued for very serious or violent offenses and results in the player being sent off immediately. If a player receives two yellow cards in the same game, he will also be sent off.

CARD HISTORY

A system of colored cards was first developed by English referee Ken Aston following the 1966 World Cup. He was inspired by stop lights, and the red and yellow cards were tried out at the 1968 Olympic Games and the 1970 World Cup. They became compulsory in 1982.

OFFENSES

A player is shown a yellow card for relatively serious offenses, such as those listed (see right). A player is shown a red card for very serious offenses, including those listed here (see far right). A player who has been dismissed may not remain on or in the vicinity of the field of play or the technical area.

YELLOW CARD OFFENSES

Dissent by word or action

Persistent infringement of the rules

Delaying the restart of play, and deliberate time-wasting

Making a poorly timed, dangerous tackle

Entering or leaving the field without the referee's permission

Unsporting behavior

RED CARD OFFENSES

Serious foul play

Violent conduct, or using offensive language

Spitting at an opponent or other person

Denying the opposing team a goal or potential chance at a goal by deliberately handling the ball (does not apply to a goalkeeper inside his own penalty area)

Receiving two cautions in the same match

SHIRTS, SHORTS, AND SOCKS

For official games, it is compusory for players to wear a shirt or jersey (with sleeves), shorts, and socks. Shin pads and boots must also be worn (see pp.72–73). All the players on a team (except for the goalkeeper, who wears his own distinguishing shirt) must wear matching uniforms. While shirts may feature stripes, hoops, or other patterned designs, shorts are usually one color, sometimes with a stripe down the sides. Undergarments may be worn for added comfort and protection, but they must be the same main color as the shirt or shorts.

HOME AND AWAY

The first clash of kits in the world came in 1890 when Sunderland played Wolverhampton Wanderers (both teams wore red and white stripes at the time). Sunderland was the home team and, in accordance with the rules of the English league, was required to change uniform. In 1921, however, the rules were reversed, with the away team required to change (although both teams had to change in FA Cup games played at a neutral ground).

REFEREE'S DECISION

A player who is not wearing the correct uniform will be asked to leave the field by the referee and may only return when the referee has confirmed that his uniform is correct. No uniform was specified in the first set of rules in 1863, when players could wear whatever they liked.

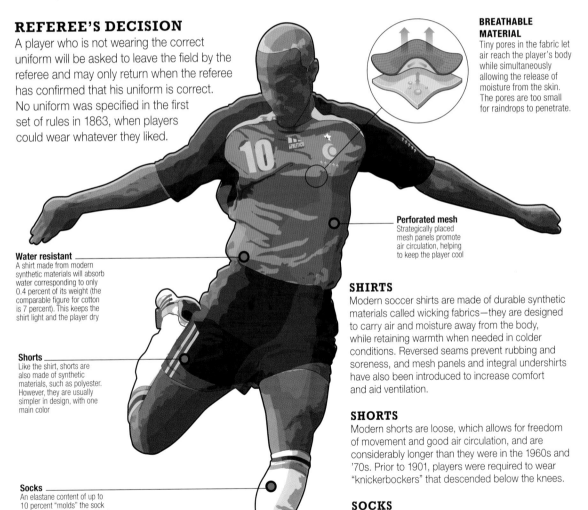

BREATHABLE MATERIAL
Tiny pores in the fabric let air reach the player's body while simultaneously allowing the release of moisture from the skin. The pores are too small for raindrops to penetrate.

Perforated mesh
Strategically placed mesh panels promote air circulation, helping to keep the player cool

Water resistant
A shirt made from modern synthetic materials will absorb water corresponding to only 0.4 percent of its weight (the comparable figure for cotton is 7 percent). This keeps the shirt light and the player dry

Shorts
Like the shirt, shorts are also made of synthetic materials, such as polyester. However, they are usually simpler in design, with one main color

Socks
An elastane content of up to 10 percent "molds" the sock to the body, while padded foot-beds ensure comfort

SHIRTS

Modern soccer shirts are made of durable synthetic materials called wicking fabrics—they are designed to carry air and moisture away from the body, while retaining warmth when needed in colder conditions. Reversed seams prevent rubbing and soreness, and mesh panels and integral undershirts have also been introduced to increase comfort and aid ventilation.

SHORTS

Modern shorts are loose, which allows for freedom of movement and good air circulation, and are considerably longer than they were in the 1960s and '70s. Prior to 1901, players were required to wear "knickerbockers" that descended below the knees.

SOCKS

Socks are an integral part of the uniform and must entirely cover the shin pad (see p.73). Teams first had to register the color of their socks in the 1930s. Prior to this, players could choose their own, which would often result in a lack of color coordination across the team.

GOALKEEPER'S SHIRT

As the only player who is allowed to handle the ball, it is important that the goalkeeper is easily indentifiable. For this reason, in 1909 goalkeepers could wear white, scarlet, or blue shirts. In 1912, the green shirt was introduced as an option and quickly became the most popular choice. Then, in the 1970s, regulations were relaxed, allowing manufacturers to experiment with designs.

SHIRT NUMBERS

Shirt numbers were first used in 1928 to help referees and the crowd identify players. They corresponded to fixed playing positions, with the center forward (see p.51), for example, always allocated the number nine. As formations have evolved, however, this practice has become rare. Today "squad" numbers are used, with individual players being designated a number for the whole season.

MICHAEL BALLACK
The talented midfielder is shown playing for Germany, whose uniform is typical of modern design.

SQUAD NUMBERS

The relaxation of the rules relating shirt numbers to playing positions has led some players to choose unique squad numbers for themselves. When Inter Milan signed the Brazilian striker Ronaldo, giving him Chilean forward Ivan Zamorano's number-nine shirt, Zamorano was allocated the number 18 shirt. However, because he liked to think of himself as a "number nine," he inserted a plus sign between the two digits (1+8=9).

HISTORICAL NUMBERING SYSTEM
This "classic" numbering system was based on the positions in the 2-3-5 formation (see p.86) that was dominant when shirt numbers were first introduced.

A HISTORY OF KIT

In 1891, the English league called for all clubs to register their shirt colors and, by the early 20th century, most of the biggest soccer clubs from Europe and Latin America had decided on their current uniform design. However, while shirt colors and designs may have remained largely unchanged since the early days of soccer, the materials used, the cut, and the details of those early shirts would be almost unrecognizable to the modern player.

SOCK TAGS AND SMILEY FACES

In 1961, Leeds United manager Don Revie changed the color of his team's uniform from blue to all white, in emulation of Real Madrid, whose success he hoped to copy. In 1973, he tried another tack and introduced numbered sock tags to the Yorkshire team to soften its hard-man image. In another attempt to update the team's image, he changed the badge so that the letters "LU" formed a smiley face.

1890s
Early shirts were heavy, long-sleeved, woollen jerseys. Some had no collar while others had a laced crew neck. Long shorts were standard.

1930s
Typically made from cotton, shirts became lighter with a more generous cut. Most had a player number and collars were popular.

1960s
With the introduction of the first synthetic materials, shirts became even lighter. V-necks and short sleeves were common.

1970s
Manufacturer's logos started to take up more space on shirts. Club emblems were redesigned as logos and shorts became very short.

1980s–90s
Sponsorship logos became widespread. Shadow stripes and pinstripes appeared, as did players' names on the backs of shirts.

2000s
Shorts are very light and skin-tight lycra shirts with piping and trim have been introduced. Sales of replica uniforms have exploded.

BOOTS AND PROTECTIVE GEAR

Players need comfortable, lightweight, and durable footwear that grips the playing surface. In addition, players need some protective gear. Shin pads, which are made from plastic, are worn to protect the shins, and must be covered entirely by socks. Goalkeepers can wear protective headgear and gloves that provide grip and hand protection when catching the ball.

FIT FOR A KING

Despite issuing a series of laws that banned the playing of soccer in England—it was blamed for inciting riots—King Henry VIII (1491–1547) owned a pair of soccer boots. In an inventory of the king's wardrobe made after his death, there is an entry for a pair of boots made from sturdy Spanish leather.

SOCCER BOOTS

The soccer boot should be flexible enough to maximize performance but sturdy enough to reduce the risk of injury. On grass, players wear studded boots (see right for types of studs); on artificial turf, players wear athletic shoes with rubber pimples on the sole.

TECHNOLOGICAL DEVELOPMENTS

While innovations in modern soccer boot design may appear to be limited to a profusion of often garish colors and logos, there have in fact been a number of significant technological developments. These have had wide-ranging implications for performance and play.

SCREW-IN STUDS
Detachable studs are used for wet conditions. Different lengths of stud can be fitted.

FIXED STUDS
Boots with fixed or "molded" studs are used for standard turf conditions.

BLADED STUDS
Boots with fixed "blades" provide a stable base on firm natural turf that is too hard for studs.

MODERN SOCCER BOOTS
Modern boots are extremely light and flexible and are made from an array of synthetic fabrics and plastics. Kangaroo leather, which is markedly stronger, lighter, and more supple than other leathers, is widely used in boot manufacture.

Specialized material
Synthetic materials reduce water absorption, which helps keeps the boot light

Outer coatings
An outer coating on some boots increases the level of friction for kicking

Elasticated tongue
An elasticated tongue covers the laces for a larger kicking area

Heel stiffener
A molded, reinforced heel stiffener supports the heel and protects against injuries

Pre-molded insole
The insoles can be pre-molded to the player's feet for a perfect fit

SOLE BRIDGE
A microfiber bridge links the studs at the front and back of the boot, which provides extra stability and flexibility.

A HISTORY OF THE BOOT

While the FA made no comment about balls or shirts in its first set of rules, it had strict rules about the use of boots (see quote below). By the 1880s, specialized boots were being made to supply both the professional and burgeoning amateur markets. With only minor developments, these early boots were the industry standard until the appearance of the low-cut design in the 1950s.

ALL WHITE ON THE NIGHT

In the early 1970s, Alan Ball (who had been the youngest player on England's 1966 World Cup-winning side) wanted to be the first player to wear white soccer boots. He daubed his black Adidas boots with paint, but the moment was short-lived as rain washed them clean.

Thick leather
The earliest boots were made from thick, stiff leather that offered little "give"

Fewer eyelets
In the 1930s, soccer boots were being laced using fewer eyelets

Conical stud
This popular boot from the late 1970s featured fixed conical-shaped studs

EARLY BOOT—1880s
The first specially designed boots were produced in small batches in the 1880s. Individual styles varied, but all boots had built-in studs, full ankle protection, and extra toe coverings.

CLASSIC BOOT—1930s
Although the basic boot design inherited from the 1800s had changed very little, by the 1930s the tops and tongue were often left loose. Lighter leather and synthetic materials were used.

BOOTS FROM 1954 ONWARD
Boots cut below the ankle were first manufactured in 1954, creating the distinct profile of all modern soccer boots. Screw-in studs (see p.72) were also pioneered at this time.

PROTECTIVE GEAR

Shin pads, which are designed to prevent fractures to the tibia resulting from rough tackles, were made compulsory by FIFA in 1990. Goalkeepers can, and always do, wear protective gloves (see below, right). Players are permitted to wear protective headgear as long as it doesn't jeopardize the safety of other players.

NO ONE WEARING PROJECTING NAILS ...IS ALLOWED
TO PLAY!

LAW 13
FA RULES, 1863

SHIN PADS

Pads are made from plastic polymers and fiberglass and protect the shins from other players' tackles. They strap to the shin, under the sock. The first shin pads are thought to have been invented in 1874 in England by Sam Widdowson, who played soccer for Nottingham Forest and cricket for Nottinghamshire.

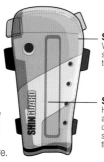

Straps
Velcro straps secure the pad tightly to the leg

Shell
High-impact and anatomically designed outer shell protects the shin

GOALKEEPER'S GLOVES

All players may wear gloves, although up until the 1970s, few chose to do so. Gloves are now universally worn by goalkeepers to increase grip on the ball and protect the hands. They are made from strong synthetic materials and are segmented to aid flexibility. Protectors prevent the fingers from bending backward.

HEADGEAR

Protective headgear is designed to cushion the head from collisions with other players, the ground, or the goalposts. Protective headgear is almost always worn by goalkeepers.

Flexible cap
Soccer headgear is flexible but tough enough to prevent injuries

PALM PROTECTION
The palm area of the glove is made from material designed to enhance grip and protection.

SHIRTS AND HAIRCUTS

The humble soccer shirt has come a long way since the heavy wooll jerseys and thick cotton smocks of the 19th century. For almost a century, a narrow range of colors, designs, and motifs was used. Over the last few decades, however, manufacturers have been pursuing ever more complex—and colorful—designs in an effort to innovate and sell more shirts. The results have not always been edifying.

BRAZIL'S WHITE UNIFORM

Brazil played the 1950 World Cup final in a white uniform, but the result was disastrous. Beaten 2–1 at home by Uruguay, the shirt has never been worn since. The now iconic yellow and green shirt was first used in 1958 after a national competiton was held to design a new uniform.

VOCABULARY OF THE SOCCER SHIRT

Although in recent years manufacturers have experimented with the range of colors and the complexity of designs used in their soccer shirts, for much of the last century, there were surprisingly few visual devices in use. Many of these designs were drawn from the language of European heraldry. Here are some of the most popular shirt designs.

CHECKERS
Checkered shirts are a useful strategy for confusing the opposition. The Croatian team's colors appear on Croatia's national coat of arms.

TEAMS: Croatia and Boavista

HORIZONTAL STRIPES
Two colors are the norm, but some teams, such as Rio's Flamengo, have three.

TEAMS: Celtic, Flamengo, Queens Park Rangers, and Sporting Lisbon

SASH
Rarely found in Europe, Latin American teams have a fondness for the cross-body sash shirt. The simple, bold design certainly adds panache.

TEAMS: Peru, Vasco de Gama, Rayo Vallecano, and River Plate

VERTICAL STRIPES
When soccer shirts were first made, the cheapest available material had vertically striped patterns (often the offcuts from material for mattresses).

TEAMS: Argentina, Athletic Bilbao, Internazionale, Juventus, Milan, Newcastle, Sunderland

HALF-AND-HALF
A favorite among English private schools, other clubs around the world that use the motif often have a strong English connection.

TEAMS: Barcelona, Basel, Blackburn Rovers, Cagliari, Genoa, Grasshopper, and Newell's Old Boys

CONTRASTING ARMS
The style was made popular by Herbert Chapman's Arsenal in the 1920s and '30s, although Aston Villa and West Ham were already sporting the look.

TEAMS: Arsenal, Aston Villa, Rapid Vienna, Stade de Reims, and West Ham

CENTRAL STRIPE
Amsterdam club Ajax considers itself unique in many ways, and few other clubs have followed its distinctive centrally striped shirt.

TEAMS: Ajax, Deportivo Pasto, Paris Saint-Germain, and Velez Sarsfield

SOCCER PLAYERS' HAIRCUTS

Players' relationship with fashion has always been ambiguous—the game has provided some of the best- and worst-dressed men in the world. While some sports, such as baseball, revel in a variety of beards and moustaches, soccer is a showcase for the talents of the world's hairdressers. Here are some of the most notable experiments in hair design (it isn't called the "beautiful game" for nothing).

DYED AND TIED
Nigerian defender Taribo West was renowned for his colorful dreadlocks, pigtails, and bunches.

THE COMBOVER
Now rarely seen, this style harks back to a time when men were men and a combover could hide the baldest patch.

WEIRD-LOOKING SHIRTS

Not only can the imagination run wild but—as with these extraordinary shirts—it can also turn nasty. Feast your eyes on the world's strangest shirts.

STAR DESIGNS

It is common for successful clubs and nations to remind everyone of their past successes. Three Italian clubs, for example, wear a star for every 10 league championships thay have won. All the World Cup-winners also wear gold or silver stars for each trophy won.

MEXICO
Jorge Campos, Mexico's goalkeeper for much of the 1990s, was renowned for his frequent bizarre and psychedelic adventures in shirt design.

MANCHESTER UNITED
Gray was the color of Manchester United's change shirt in 1995–96. Unfortunately, on the five occasions they played in it, they lost four matches and tied the fifth.

COLORADO CARIBOUS
In 1978, the caribous lasted just one season in the North American Soccer League. With a unique leather-fringed shirt, it was just like the Wild West on the field.

CAMEROON 2004
Cameroon unveiled the first one-piece soccer uniform at the African Nations Cup in 2004. It was banned by FIFA, who then deducted six points after Cameroon continued to wear it.

INTERNAZIONALE
In 2007, Internazionale wore a change shirt in white with a red cross—the symbol of Milan. But opponents in the Muslim world took exception to the design, feeling it was redolent of the crusades.

ATHLETIC BILBAO
Bilbao has reinvented itself as the home of the critically acclaimed Guggenheim art museum. A similar reinvention of the club's shirt has been less well-received.

ODD COUPLES

Some of the most unikely teams in world soccer are united by their shirts. The distance betwen Juventus, the superstars of Italian soccer, and Notts County, forever mired at the bottom of the English league, is huge—but the teams are still connected. Here are five of soccer's oddest couples.

JUVENTUS AND NOTTS COUNTY
In 1903, one of the English members of Juventus arranged for a new shirt to be sent from Nottingham. It must have come from Notts County's tailors.

BLACKBURN ROVERS AND GRASSHOPPERS
English biology student Tom Griffiths gave the Zurich team its zoological title and the same shirt as his home team—Blackburn Rovers.

BARCELONA AND BASEL FC
The itinerant Swiss-born founding member of Barcelona didn't just take soccer to Barcelona, he also took his home club's shirt.

BOCA JUNIORS AND SWEDEN
The founders of Boca are said to have waited by the harbor in Buenos Aires and taken the colors of the first ship that entered port—it was Swedish.

ATHLETIC BILBAO AND SUNDERLAND
Red and white stripes arrived in the Basque country in the 1890s when English workers at the port showed the locals how to play their game.

THE MULLET
Often emulated but never bettered, England's Chris Waddle was the king of the mullet cut.

THE DISPLACED EYEBROW
Ronaldo stepped out for Brazil at the 2002 World Cup with a single strip of hair across the front of his head.

THE PERM
In the 1970s and early '80s, Kevin Keegan's "poodle" perm was an iconic addition to the England team.

LONG HAIR AND HEAD BAND
For many long-haired players, the humble head band is the accessory of choice on the pitch.

THE BALL

Modern soccer balls consist of an outer covering of synthetic leather panels stitched together to form a spherical surface. Real leather, which was used until the 1980s, often absorbed water, making the ball heavy (see box, far right). Inside the outer layer is the air bladder, which is usually made from latex or butyl. Between the bladder and the outer cover is an inner lining, which gives the ball its bounce.

FIFA REQUIREMENTS

According to the Laws of the Game (see pp.62–63), the ball must be spherical, made from leather or other suitable materials, and have a circumference of 27–28 in (68.5–71 cm). At the start of the match, the ball should weigh 14½–16 oz (410–450 g) and be inflated to a pressure of 8½ lb sq in (600–1,100 g/sq cm). These requirements were set in 1872 and have remained largely unchanged ever since.

WHAT'S IN A NAME?

Brazilian soccer commentator Washington Rodríguez has said: "In Brazil, you can call the ball anything except the ball." In fact, there are more than 30 synonyms for the ball in Brazilian Portuguese. Five are women's names and others include: baby, balloon, bladder, chestnut, capricious one, sphere, infidel, demon, doll, and pellet plum.

LABORATORY TESTING

A ball's level of bounce, its ability to swerve through the air, its level of air-retention, and its overall longevity can all be altered by its design. Recent developments in the use of synthetic materials and production techniques, for example, have produced balls that maximize the transfer of energy from the kicker to the ball and are flight-accurate. FIFA-approved balls are all laboratory-tested for balance, bounce, shape, trajectory, velocity, and water absorption.

THE VALVE

In professional soccer balls, the valve is silicone-treated to prevent air loss and to aid the smooth insertion of the inflating needle.

SOCCER BALL CONSTRUCTION

There are four main components of a ball: the outer cover, the stitching, the inner lining, and the bladder. The quality of the materials used for each of these elements can affect how it behaves.

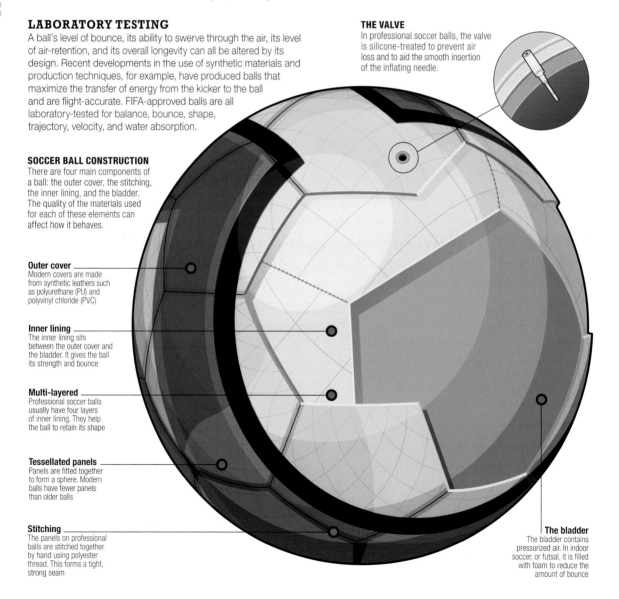

Outer cover
Modern covers are made from synthetic leathers such as polyurethane (PU) and polyvinyl chloride (PVC)

Inner lining
The inner lining sits between the outer cover and the bladder. It gives the ball its strength and bounce

Multi-layered
Professional soccer balls usually have four layers of inner lining. They help the ball to retain its shape

Tessellated panels
Panels are fitted together to form a sphere. Modern balls have fewer panels than older balls

Stitching
The panels on professional balls are stitched together by hand using polyester thread. This forms a tight, strong seam

The bladder
The bladder contains pressurized air. In indoor soccer, or futsal, it is filled with foam to reduce the amount of bounce

BALL DIMENSIONS

Soccer balls for official match use come in a range of standard sizes, depending on the type of soccer being played and the respective age of the players. These variations include professional soccer, indoor soccer or futsal, children's leagues, and beach soccer (see pp.22–27).

27–28 in (68.5–71 cm)

SIZE 5 BALL
This is the international standard ball for professional competitions, from the older child to adult age ranges.

25–26 in (63.5–66 cm)

SIZE 4 BALL
This is the standard size for futsal (see pp.22–23). It weighs 14–15½ oz (400–440 g).

23–24 in (58.5–61 cm)

SIZE 3 BALL
The smallest official ball, this is normally used for games for under 8 year olds. It weighs between 11–12 oz (310–340 g).

27–28 in (68.5–71 cm)

BEACH SOCCER BALL
The ball used in official beach soccer matches is a size 5 (see above), but is lighter at 14–15½ oz (400–440 g).

A HISTORY OF THE BALL

Medieval soccer was played using a ball stuffed with an inflated pig's bladder. Unsurprisingly, these balls lacked bounce, or bounced irregularly, and were prone to collapsing. In 1836, Charles Goodyear patented vulcanized (cured) rubber and, in 1855, designed and made the first balls with vulcanized-rubber bladders. This provided the ball with a consistent bounce—a key development.

SOCCER INJURIES
A coroner's report into the death of England striker Jeff Astle—a prolific header of the ball who died of a brain disease in 2002—suggested that he suffered from long-term damage caused by heading old-style leather balls that would grow heavy when wet.

Glued seams
Rubber panels (shaped like a modern basketball), were glued together at the seams

Interlocking panels
Seven or eight interlocking leather panels helped the ball retain its shape

Multi-sectioned panels
Balls from this period had heavy leather covers comprising six panels of three sections each

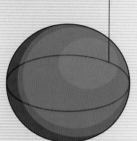 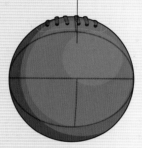 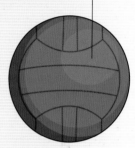

1850s BALL
Goodyear's invention meant that the dimensions of the ball could be set, rather than depending on the size and shape of the pig's bladder.

1880s BALL
The first mass-produced ball arrived after the founding of the English Football League in 1888. Its cover was made from cow leather.

1920s BALL
By the 1920s, the soccer ball's bladder was made from stronger rubber than its predecessors, so could be inflated to a higher pressure.

Waterproofing
Synthetic paints and other non-porous materials were used to stop water absorption

Hexagonal panels
The buckyball consists of 20 hexagonal and 12 pentagonal panels fitted together

Thermal bonding
Replacing stitching with thermal bonding creates a more aerodynamic surface

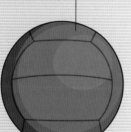  

1940s–50s BALL
The introduction of a carcass, made from strong cloth and placed between the bladder and outer cover, increased strength.

1970s "BUCKYBALL"
The buckyball (named after inventor Richard Buckminster Fuller) marked a new era in ball design. Its black panels helped players detect swerve.

21ST CENTURY BALL
Manufacturers have reduced the number of panels and have replaced stitching with thermal bonding for a smoother surface.

THE GOALKEEPER LIKES THE BALL BEST. EVERYONE ELSE KICKS IT. ONLY THE... KEEPER HUGS IT!

POMPIA
BRAZILIAN GOALKEEPER

THE GOAL

Soccer would be nothing without goals, so great importance is placed on the design of these structures. They must be safe and reliable, and must not obscure the spectators' view. They also need to be durable. Nets, for example, used to be made of string and had to be taken down between matches to prevent them from rotting. Today they are made from weatherproof synthetic fibers.

BARBECUE OF REVENGE

When Brazil lost the 1950 World Cup Final at home in front of a record-breaking crowd and having been 1–0 up against Uruguay, angry fans looked for a scapegoat. They chose their goalkeeper, Barbosa. Still shunned by the 1994 World Cup squad at their training camp, Barbosa is said, in Brazilian popular legend, to have burned the goalposts at the Maracana stadium and enjoyed a "barbecue of revenge" on the embers.

GOAL REQUIREMENTS

The Laws of the Game (see pp.62–63) state that a goal must be placed on the center of each goal line and consist of two upright posts joined at the top by a crossbar. It should be placed equidistant from the corner flagposts and may be made of wood, metal, or other approved material. The posts and crossbar must be white, and the goal should be securely anchored.

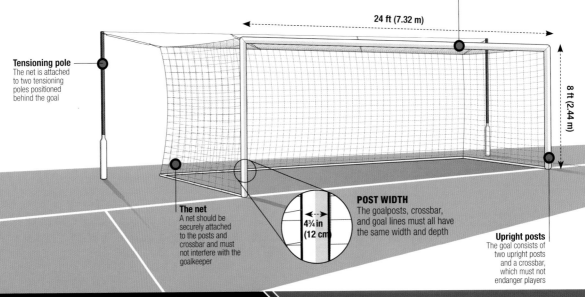

Crossbar
The crossbar must be the same width and color as the upright posts

24 ft (7.32 m)

8 ft (2.44 m)

Tensioning pole
The net is attached to two tensioning poles positioned behind the goal

The net
A net should be securely attached to the posts and crossbar and must not interfere with the goalkeeper

4¾ in (12 cm)

POST WIDTH
The goalposts, crossbar, and goal lines must all have the same width and depth

Upright posts
The goal consists of two upright posts and a crossbar, which must not endanger players

A HISTORY OF THE GOAL

Despite the obvious importance of the goal to soccer, the FA's first set of rules in 1863 was surprisingly vague about its size and construction. The posts were the first elements to be introduced, although their dimensions and shape could vary. There was also no mention of the crossbar, which meant that a goal was permitted at any height as long as the ball passed between the posts.

RAISING THE BAR

In 1888, London team Swifts were disqualified from the FA Cup when opponents Crewe Alexandra complained about one of the crossbars. Crewe claimed the bar was 2 in (5 cm) lower at one end—below the required height.

1860s GOAL
Early goals consisted of two vertical posts with no crossbar, which led to contentious goals from high balls.

1870s GOAL
A form of crossbar was introduced in the 1870s, when tape was hung between the tops of the posts.

1880s GOAL
In 1882, all soccer teams were required to replace the flimsy tape with a sturdier crossbar.

1890s GOAL
The net was introduced to avoid the need to retrieve the ball after a goal was scored.

DIFFERENT GOAL SIZES

The required dimensions of the goal vary depending on the type of soccer being played. In five-a-side, for example, the ball must not go above head height, so the goal is low. Equally, in beach soccer, the goal is slightly smaller than it is for professional matches because the sand makes it difficult for the goalkeeper to cover large distances quickly.

SIZE MATTERS
Clubs occasionally still make mistakes when setting up their goalposts. In 1998, for example, one of the crossbars at Real Mallorca's old ground—the Luis Sitjer Stadium—was found to be significantly lower than the other.

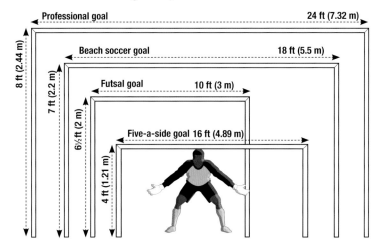

Professional goal — 24 ft (7.32 m)
8 ft (2.44 m)
Beach soccer goal — 18 ft (5.5 m)
7 ft (2.2 m)
Futsal goal — 10 ft (3 m)
6½ ft (2 m)
Five-a-side goal 16 ft (4.89 m)
4 ft (1.21 m)

750 The number of nets made each year by inmates of Durham prison, England; many are sold to top clubs

13 The distance in feet (4 m) that the nets at Real Zaragoza's La Romareda stadium extend back from the goal line

75 The delay in minutes during Real Madrid's European Cup Semi-final against Borussia Dortmund in 1998, when the crowd damaged the posts

4 Diameter in inches (10 cm) of a professional goalpost with round posts and crossbar

CROSSBAR AND POST PROFILE

Early posts and crossbars, which were usually made from wood (often Douglas fir), were typically either round or square in profile. This was largely because these were the easiest shapes for manufacturers to produce. In 1922, John Claude Perkins of the Standard Goals Company in Nottingham, England, patented a goal frame with a much stronger elliptical profile. He also reinforced his crossbars with metal rods drilled through the core, which helped prevent them from sagging in the middle. Elliptical posts are now standard in top-flight games.

ELLIPTICAL
Most modern goals have this profile, which offers strength and reasonably predictable rebounds.

CIRCULAR
The major drawback with this shape was that the ball might bounce off in any direction.

SQUARE
Some Scottish clubs retained square posts long after they had been abandoned elsewhere.

RECTANGULAR
The sharp edges of these posts and crossbars posed an injury threat now considered unacceptable.

HOW THE NET IS HUNG

Several net-hanging systems have been developed over the years. There are two main considerations for the design of these systems: the tension of the net should be such that it is clear when a goal has been scored; and the ball should not rebound off, or become lodged in, the back stanchion.

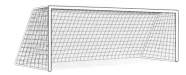

BALL-AND-SOCKET SYSTEM
In the 1970s, net extensions were plugged into "female" sockets that screwed into the posts and crossbar.

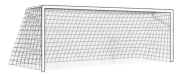

EXTRUSION SYSTEM
In the 1980s, triangular brackets projecting back from the corners of the goal were used to tighten the net.

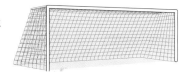

NET-TENSIONING SYSTEM
In the 1990s, goal nets were clipped onto fixed aluminum mounts that functioned in a similar way to curtain rails.

IN (AND OUT) OF THE NET
The "net pocket" was invented by a civil engineer from Liverpool called John Brodie. It was patented in 1889 for goals used in soccer, lacrosse, and other games. Early nets were occasionally strung so tautly that the ball would rebound. In 1909, for example, West Bromwich Albion missed out on promotion after a referee disallowed a goal, thinking that the ball had hit the crossbar—it had in fact rebounded off the net.

SING WHEN YOU'RE WINNING

Soccer is nothing without the crowd—is there any silence grimmer than that of a game played behind closed doors? Soccer crowds have been offering commentary, shouting criticism, and singing for over a century, drawing on their distinct popular cultures, from the Edwardian music hall and Brazilian carnival, to Viennese polka bands and Nigerian highlife. Football crowds have fused a love of music and rhyme to produce some memorable chants, many of which have inspired the players themselves (see pp.208–09).

FLARES
Although they are banned from all stadiums, fans cannot resist the theatrical swirl of the smoke bomb and the pyrotechnic magic of fireworks and big naval flares.

SOLO ARTISTES
Some people can sing well and some people are completely tone-deaf and together they provide the essential catalyst for singing—striking up the first bar alone, unperturbed by the thought that no one might join in.

CHANT ENTREPRENEURS
The poets of the terrace compose their odes in the shower and test them out in the stands. Wit and bravery are required, but the buzz these chant entrepreneurs experience when the chorus picks up their words keeps the songs coming.

DRUMMERS
In Mediterranean countries and across Latin America, singing is often well orchestrated. Most groups will have at least one drummer to keep time and a network of chant leaders, equipped with megaphones, who are strategically positioned throughout the bleachers.

BRASS BANDS
African soccer crowds, especially those in Nigeria, have specialized in the use of horns and brass instruments. Brass bands and instruments are also popular in central and northern Europe, while in Brazil they play sambas.

THE CHORUS
When the mood takes them and the song is right, the crowd provides the volume during the chorus, although some crowds and stands are notoriously hard to get going. At some clubs, calls between groups of fans across the field form a key component of the singing. Call and response also shapes the interaction between home and away fans.

SCARVES AND FLAGS
As well as singing, Spanish fans like to take off their scarves and wave them around their heads at moments of excellence on the field. Huge flags are also passed around the crowd like blankets before the game in stadiums around the world.

SUPPORTING ACTORS
Long-standing groups of season-ticket holders and boys who practice in the pubs and bars before the game form key parts of the singing crowd. They lend real weight to songs on their second and third lines and keep a tune going when the rest of the crowd is flagging.

SECOND IN COMMAND
Chant entrepreneurs (see left) often have acolytes and friends who lend their support to new chants.

TOP 5: SOCCER ANTHEMS

YOU'LL NEVER WALK ALONE (LIVERPOOL, ENGLAND)
The gold standard of collective solidarity in song, this was originally a tune from the Rodgers and Hammerstein musical *Carousel*. Gerry and the Pacemakers took it to number one in the UK charts in 1963, and it was quickly adopted by their fellow Liverpudlians in the Kop at Anfield.

LA ROMA NON SI DISCUTE, SI AMA (ROMA, ITALY)
The anthem of the club, which translates as "Roma is not to be questioned, it is to be loved," was penned by local singer Antonello Venditti.

HORTO MAGIKO (PANATHINAIKOS, GREECE)
Titled "Magic Weed," the song is a hypnotic dirge of praise that was first sung by the fans of Panathinaikos and notionally refers to the club's emblem, the shamrock.

CANT DEL BARÇA (BARCELONA, SPAIN)
Translated as "Song of Barcelona," this is the official hymn of FC Barcelona, commissioned in 1974 to celebrate the club's 75th anniversary. It was given its official debut that year before a game between Barca and East Germany.

I'M FOREVER BLOWING BUBBLES (WEST HAM, ENGLAND)
Originally a song in a Broadway musical and then a huge hit in the British music hall, this song was introduced to West Ham United in the 1920s by former player and manger Billie Paytner. It is the perfect anthem for a club whose aspirations invariably exceed performance. The song is often accompanied by mass bubble-blowing.

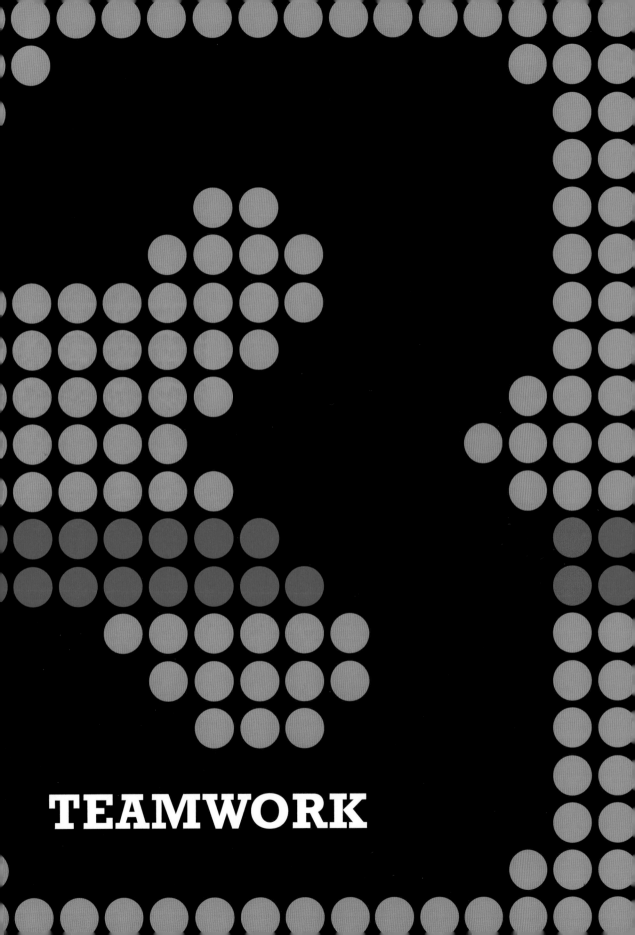

TEAMWORK

TEAMWORK: KEY CONCEPTS

There are many commonly used strategies in soccer, but certain principles can be applied to them all. Every player needs to have a grasp of these fundamentals if they are to succeed on the field. For a lucky few, it is a process that comes instinctively; for everyone else, a little theory, coupled with plenty of hard work on the training ground, is invaluable.

THE TEAM IS EVERYTHING

There is no "I" in "team." Individual brilliance is useless unless it is harnessed for the good of the team. Whenever a player is on the field, he needs to bear five things in mind: find some space so that teammates can pass to him; offer his teammates support whenever they are on the ball; guard possession of the ball; move to a new position after he has made a pass; and keep his teammates informed of his intentions.

SUPPORT

Players must always look to support their colleagues. This may involve joining them in attack, running back to help out in defense, or filling in for a teammate who has abandoned his usual playing position after joining an attack. Forwards should always follow up shots looking for rebounds off the goalkeeper.

COMMUNICATION

Communication on the field is vital. A player in possession of the ball isn't always aware of his teammates' intentions. Therefore it is essential they let him know where they are, where they are heading, and where they want the ball to be played. A player can make his teammate aware of his intentions by using one of a number of calls.

EMPTY SPACES AND SILENCES ARE AS IMPORTANT AS THOSE THAT ARE FILLED

FORMER INTER MILAN MANAGER **HELENIO HERRERA**

PLAYER CALLS

In theory, a player is allowed to shout out anything as long as he isn't deliberately attempting to deceive the opposition. In practice, referees will award an indirect free-kick against a player if he calls out ambiguous phrases like "leave it!" or "mine!"

GLOBAL STYLES

The way soccer should be played is a much-discussed topic, and the answer given varies from country to country. The descriptions below are generalizations, but they certainly have some validity.

Central American
Mexico (1986)
Crashed out of the World Cup on penalties without losing a game

ROY KEANE
The midfielder was an ultimate team player during his distinguished career with Nottingham Forest, Manchester United, Celtic, and the Republic of Ireland.

CENTRAL AMERICAN

Players (type): Clever, but sometimes excessive, dribblers

Characteristics: Ball tends to be moved around the field in a series of short passes; all players have good one-on-one skills; tempo of matches is often slow

Success: Mexico are the primary representatives of this style

USE OF SPACE

When children play soccer, they all tend to follow the ball. Then they realize they will be more useful to their team if they get away from the pack and find some space. The history of soccer can be seen as a process of gradual enlightenment when it comes to space; today, it is given the importance it deserves.

POSSESSION

In soccer, possession is nine-tenths of the law. Barring own-goals, no one can score against you if they don't have the ball. Chasing the play also tires and frustrates opponents. Possession soccer has developed into a fully fledged tactic, and one that is related to the "pass-and-move" philosophy (see right). It is particularly popular in Latin countries, not least because the patient approach makes excellent sense in a hot climate.

PASS AND MOVE

The pass-and-move philosophy is based on the idea that if a player is static, it is easy for opponents to pick him up. The great Liverpool teams of the 1970s and early '80s were masters of pass-and-move soccer, exhausting opponents and keeping possession with constantly shifting triangles.

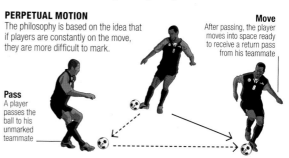

PERPETUAL MOTION
The philosophy is based on the idea that if players are constantly on the move, they are more difficult to mark.

Move
After passing, the player moves into space ready to receive a return pass from his teammate

Pass
A player passes the ball to his unmarked teammate

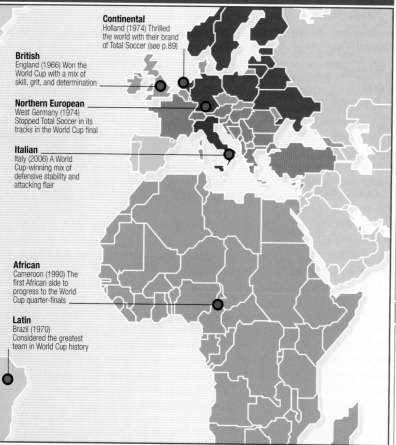

Continental
Holland (1974) Thrilled the world with their brand of Total Soccer (see p.89)

British
England (1966) Won the World Cup with a mix of skill, grit, and determination

Northern European
West Germany (1974) Stopped Total Soccer in its tracks in the World Cup final

Italian
Italy (2006) A World Cup-winning mix of defensive stability and attacking flair

African
Cameroon (1990) The first African side to progress to the World Cup quarter-finals

Latin
Brazil (1970) Considered the greatest team in World Cup history

NORTHERN EUROPEAN

Players (type): Aggressive, fast-paced, hardworking, and highly organized
Characteristics: Direct game with forceful, although sometimes predictable, attacks; defenses are typically hard to break down
Success: Germany remain the ultimate standard-bearers for the Northern European style of play

BRITISH

Players (type): Physical, athletic, fast tempo, and direct
Characteristics: Attacks are set up quickly with few touches on the ball; the game plan is based on substance over style
Success: Despite success at club level, the national teams flatter to deceive on the world stage

CONTINENTAL

Players (type): A combination of the Latin and Northern European games
Characteristics: All players are comfortable on the ball; emphasis is on creativity combined with composure and team coordination
Success: Holland and France are the style's leading representatives

LATIN

Players (type): Confident with the ball, good dribblers, and creative
Characteristics: The Latin game style has a possession-oriented character suited to the hot, draining climates in which matches are typically played
Success: Brazil, Argentina, Spain, and Portugal are among the world's best teams

AFRICAN

Players (type): Athletic, physical
Characteristics: Touch-and-move soccer similar to the Latin style; emphasis is on stylish attacking soccer and displays of individual skill
Success: African teams continue to threaten to reach the latter stages of the World Cup

ITALIAN

Players (type): Skilful, inventive, cautious
Characteristics: Reluctance to commit too many players forward in attack due to great emphasis on defense
Success: Italian clubs continue to feature in the latter stages off all major European competitions; the national side is a regular contender at major championships

FORMATIONS

The formation of a team is determined by the positions allocated to players and their relationship to each other. Managers select formations with two main aims: to neutralize the opposition, and to exploit its weaknesses. Formations are listed in numbers, with the defenders listed first and the strikers listed last (goalkeepers are never listed). The following are some of the most influential formations in soccer's formative years.

HERBERT CHAPMAN

English manager Herbert Chapman (below) redefined the role of manager and pioneered the use of organized tactics. His best achievement was to perfect the W-M (see right), which dominated soccer for a generation and brought him English league titles at Huddersfield and Arsenal.

1-2-7

In soccer's earliest days, forward passes were not permitted. Players could pass the ball sideways or backward, although this was seen as contrary to the spirit of the game. Instead, players moved up the field using a kind of charge-dribble, with several teammates in attendance.

2-3-5 (THE PYRAMID)

In 1866, the rules were changed to allow forward passing (provided there were at least three opponents between the player receiving the ball and the goal). This put more pressure on defenses and, by the 1880s, the standard formation had evolved into the more defensive 2-3-5.

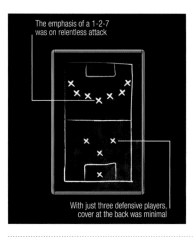

The emphasis of a 1-2-7 was on relentless attack

With just three defensive players, cover at the back was minimal

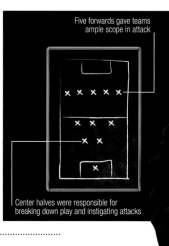

Five forwards gave teams ample scope in attack

Center halves were responsible for breaking down play and instigating attacks

THE DEATH OF THE 1-2-7

In 1872, Queen's Park, representing Scotland, lined up against a much bigger and stronger England team at Hampden Park. Realizing they would have little chance if they played dribble-and-charge soccer, Queen's Park decided to adopt a 2-2-6 formation and attempted to pass the ball around their opponents. It was deemed a success, as they held out for a famous 0–0 tie.

DEVELOPMENT OF FORMATIONS

The way teams have lined up on a field has changed radically throughout the game's history.

1889
Preston North End win the English league and FA Cup playing a 2-3-5

1934
Vittorio Pozzo's Italy win the World Cup with a 2-3-2-3 formation, known as *il metodo* ("the method")

1867
Offside rule first introduced

1872
Royal Engineers win the FA Cup with a 1-2-7 formation

1925
Changes in the offside rule give birth to the W-M

1860   1870   1880   1900 1920   1930   1940

3-2-2-3 (W-M)

The offside rule (see pp.66–67) was amended in 1925 to encourage more attacking soccer. A player receiving the ball was now onside provided there were two opponents ahead of him. To deal with the increased attacking threat, Herbert Chapman (see left) developed the 3-2-2-3 (or W-M) formation.

3-2-3-2 (M-U)

In November 1953, Hungary (the reigning Olympic soccer champions) lined up against England at Wembley in a revolutionary M-U formation. They gave their hosts, who were playing a rigid W-M, a soccer lesson, and went on to win the match 6–3—it was England's first-ever defeat at Wembley.

4-2-4

Developed to reinforce the defense without sacrificing attacking play, the 4-2-4 exploded onto the international scene with Brazil's victory at the 1958 World Cup. On paper, it looks as though it would leave a team light in midfield; in practice, it operates as a 3-3-4 when in possession and a 4-3-3 in defense.

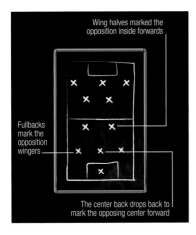

Wing halves marked the opposition inside forwards

Fullbacks mark the opposition wingers

The center back drops back to mark the opposing center forward

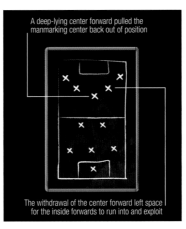

A deep-lying center forward pulled the manmarking center back out of position

The withdrawal of the center forward left space for the inside forwards to run into and exploit

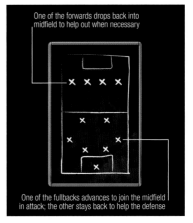

One of the forwards drops back into midfield to help out when necessary

One of the fullbacks advances to join the midfield in attack; the other stays back to help the defense

OTHER FORMATIONS

Several theories on how to play the game abounded throughout Europe in the 1920s and '30s—the following are among the most famous of those systems.

DANUBIAN SCHOOL

A modification of the pyramid (2-3-5) formation, utilized by the Austrians, Czechs, and Hungarians in the 1920s, this formation relied on short passing and individual skills. It reached its peak in the early 1930s with the Austrian national side, who finished fourth in the 1934 World Cup.

IL METODO ("THE METHOD")

Devised by Vittorio Pozzo, coach of the Italian national side in the 1930s, il metodo was a derivation of the Danubian School. Pozzo, seeking to gain midfield dominance, pulled back two of the forwards to just in front of midfield to create a 2-3-2-3 formation. It was a huge success: Italy won back-to-back World Cups using this formation in 1934 and 1938, and Pozzo remains the only manager to have won two successive World Cups.

THE DIAGONAL

During the 1940s, Brazil manager Flávio Costa developed a curiously lopsided system known as the diagonal. It was similar to the W-M, except that the two left-sided midfielders were stationed further forward than their equivalents on the right. Costa enjoyed considerable success with the system, but abandoned it halfway through the 1950 World Cup campaign in favor of a conventional W-M. Many blamed his decision for Brazil's sensational loss to Uruguay in the final match that cost them the trophy. The defeat is considered the darkest day in Brazilian sporting history.

IT WAS LIKE PLAYING
PEOPLE FROM
OUTER SPACE

ENGLAND'S **SYD OWEN** AFTER A 7–1 DEFEAT AGAINST HUNGARY IN 1954

1953
Hungary expose the weaknesses in the W-M by playing an innovative M-U formation

1958
Brazil win the World Cup playing 4-2-4

1966
England's "wingless wonders" win the World Cup with a midfield diamond

1970
Ajax win the first of three consecutive European Cups playing "Total Soccer"

1990
AC Milan deploy the definitive modern 4-4-2

2009
The dominant contemporary formations are fluid variants of 4-5-1 and 4-2-3-1, even 4-6-0

1850   1860   1870   1980   1990   2000   2010

TEAMWORK

MODERN FORMATIONS

During the first 100 years of soccer's existence, only a handful of formations were regularly used. There also tended to be just one used in a given era. Since the 1960s, the tactical side of the game has been blown wide open. Flexibility has become the watchword, with the team increasingly tailored to the opposition and to the way a match is panning out.

ARRIGO SACCHI

Although he never played professional soccer, Arrigo Sacchi managed the great AC Milan side of the early 1990s. His success came through perfecting the 4-4-2. The formation can leave big gaps between the ranks, but Sacchi solved the problem by making his players move up and down the field as a packed unit.

4-4-2

The basic modern formation, the 4-4-2, places a burden on midfielders: one of the central pair must go up and support attacks, while the other drops back. Wide players help out in defense and attack, creating a temporary 4-2-4. The two strikers work in tandem and need to have a good understanding of each other.

One striker can drop deep to create a 4-4-1-1

Wide players provide cover in defense and extra options in attack

3-5-2/5-3-2

The difference between 3-5-2 and 5-3-2 is one of emphasis, with the former being more attack-oriented than the latter since it has more midfielders. In either variant, the key men are the wide players, usually described as wingers, who are expected to help out with both attack and defense.

Hardworking wingers give this formation width

Bank of three midfielders adds defensive cover

Three central defenders, one of whom drops back

OTHER MODERN FORMATIONS

While the majority of formations have been adopted as standard throughout the soccer world, others—such as *catenaccio* and "Total Soccer"—have become synonymous with a particular team or nation.

CATENACCIO (1-4-3-2)

Catenaccio, which means "door bolt" in Italian, relied on a *libero*, or sweeper (see p.43) stationed in front of the goalkeeper to counter the risk of an opposing forward breaking through the main line of defense. It was fundamentally a defensive system, but by forcing opponents to commit extra players forward, it left them vulnerable to rapid counter-attacks.

THE BIRTH OF *CATENACCIO*

Catenaccio first became popular in Italy in the late 1940s. Gipo Viani, the Salernitana manager, claimed to have invented the formation after seeing fishermen using two nets, with a reserve net placed behind the main net to pick up any fish that had managed to evade it.

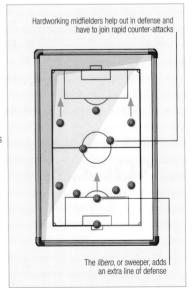

Hardworking midfielders help out in defense and have to join rapid counter-attacks

The *libero*, or sweeper, adds an extra line of defense

4-3-3

Essentially a more defensive version of the 4-2-4, the 4-3-3 was first pioneered by Brazil at the 1962 World Cup. The three midfielders could be staggered in various ways and tended to move across the field as a unit. Few teams now start with this system, but many adopt it late on in a match if they're chasing a game.

4-5-1

This is essentially a defensive formation, with a packed midfield and a lone striker left to fend for himself, or hold the ball up, until support arrives, usually from the wide players. English team Chelsea used this system to great effect during their back-to-back Premier League title successes in 2005 and 2006.

4-2-3-1

4-2-3-1 was arguably the dominant formation either side of the millennium. It revolves around the midfield, with two of the central players in holding roles and the other one concentrating on attack. France beat Brazil 3–0 in the 1998 World Cup final using this formation. It is popular in continental Europe.

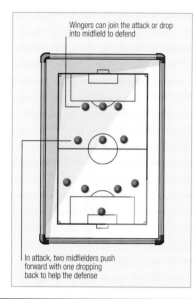

Wingers can join the attack or drop into midfield to defend

In attack, two midfielders push forward with one dropping back to help the defense

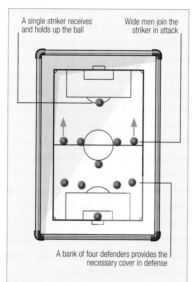

A single striker receives and holds up the ball

Wide men join the striker in attack

A bank of four defenders provides the necessary cover in defense

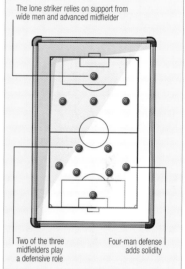

The lone striker relies on support from wide men and advanced midfielder

Two of the three midfielders play a defensive role

Four-man defense adds solidity

TOTAL SOCCER

Rinus Michels, manager of the great Ajax and Netherlands teams of the early 1970s, gave his players unprecedented freedom to express themselves on the field and adapt to the circumstances of a game. In Total Soccer, outfield players had no fixed positions, although the team did have a structure (a variant of 4-3-3); each player had to be prepared to occupy any position as the need arose. Although they thrilled, and influenced, a generation of fans, the Dutch ultimately failed in their attempt to win the World Cup, losing 2–1 to West Germany in the 1974 final.

THE TRUTH IS ... SOCCER MAKES ITSELF ON THE FIELD

FORMER NETHERLANDS MANAGER **RINUS MICHELS**

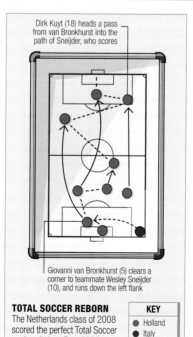

Dirk Kuyt (18) heads a pass from van Bronkhurst into the path of Sneijder, who scores

Giovanni van Bronkhurst (5) clears a corner to teammate Wesley Sneijder (10), and runs down the left flank

TOTAL SOCCER REBORN

The Netherlands class of 2008 scored the perfect Total Soccer goal, vs Italy at Euro 2008, turning defense into instant attack in the blink of an eye.

KEY	
●	Holland
●	Italy
- -	Pass
—	Player movement

VARIATIONS

THE DIAMOND

Alf Ramsey's "wingless wonders," England, won the 1966 World Cup with this formation, one that gives a side great solidity in midfield, with the fullbacks providing the width in attack. AC Milan won the Champions League in 2007 playing with the same system.

THE CHRISTMAS TREE

Named after its pointed shape, the 4-3-2-1 formation is a more attacking adaptation of 4-3-3, with two players playing behind a lone striker ("in the hole"). Terry Venables's England side used the Christmas Tree formation to great effect at Euro '96.

THE FUTURE: 4-6-0

At a 2003 coaching conference in Rio de Janeiro, former Brazil manager Carlos Alberto Parreira declared the 4-6-0 to be the formation of the future. His prediction seems to be coming true: Manchester United won the 2008 Champions League playing with no dedicated striker. Instead, they relied on attacking midfielders bursting forward as opportunities arose.

TEAMWORK

DEFENSIVE STRATEGIES

Defenders, like all other players, need to master the basic skills of the game, like passing and ball control, but in some departments—notably tackling—they have to be considerably better than average. Individual technical ability, though, is only part of the story. Defenders also need to address how they are going to work together as a unit.

DEFENDING AS A UNIT

A good defense provides the foundation for every great team, and if a defense wants to become impenetrable, it needs to become a coherent unit. That means working together to regain possession of the ball, holding a tight defensive line, claiming responsibility for marking attacking players, and disrupting the opposing side's organization as much as possible.

THE OFFSIDE TRAP

Holding a good defensive line is a deterrent in itself, but the offside trap takes matters a stage further. It involves all the defenders stepping forward just before an opponent passes the ball to a forward-running striker, thus playing him offside at the moment the ball is struck (see pp.66–67). It is a high-risk strategy, but can be particularly effective if performed properly. The Arsenal back four of the late 1980s and early '90s were masters of the offside trap, raising their arms simultaneously to alert the referee's assistant as they stepped forward in unison. The move was famously reenacted in the 1997 film *The Full Monty*.

HOLDING THE LINE

Defenders tend to form a line across the field exactly parallel to the goal line, particularly when the opposition has possession of the ball. This line serves two very important functions. It increases the chances of catching opposing forwards offside, unless one of them makes a well-timed run and is found by his teammate. It also dictates how far up the field the team as a whole plays. Midfielders should base themselves a certain distance ahead of the defensive line, and the same is true of forwards in relation to the midfielders.

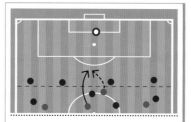

HIGH DEFENSIVE LINE
Danger of opponents breaking offside trap with a well-timed through-ball

● Attacking team
● Defensive team
-- Pass
— Player movement

LOW DEFENSIVE LINE
Danger of allowing opposition players to get too close to goal

● Attacking team
● Defensive team
-- Pass
— Player movement

MARKING

Marking is about preventing the ball from being passed easily from one opposing team member to another. Marking an opponent, whether from set-pieces or in open play, is one of the defender's most important tasks. Clearly, if several defenders decide to mark one opponent at the same time, they will leave other opponents dangerously unmarked. Therefore a system has to be worked out. There are two options when it comes to a team's marking strategy: they can use either zonal marking or man-to-man marking.

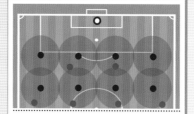

ZONAL MARKING
Players occupy an area of the field and do not directly mark an opponent

● Attacking team
● Defensive team

MAN-TO-MAN
Each player marks a single opponent

● Attacking team
● Defensive team

ZONAL MARKING

Zonal marking was developed in the 1950s to deal with the problem of playing against a team using withdrawn strikers. In zonal marking, defenders are responsible for specific areas of the field rather than particular opponents.

MAN-TO-MAN MARKING

Man-to-man marking is simple: a defender is allocated an opponent and has to stick to him no matter where he runs. The system's advantage is its clarity. The disadvantage is that it allows crafty attacking players to pull defenders out of position.

FOOTBALL IS A SIMPLE GAME BASED ON THE GIVING AND TAKING OF PASSES... IT IS TERRIBLY SIMPLE

FORMER LIVERPOOL MANAGER **BILL SHANKLY**

GREAT DEFENSIVE PARTNERSHIPS

Most formations pair two central defenders together at the back and their partnership is one of the most important on the field. It helps if they are not too similar in playing style (so they can offer more than one skill) and there are various theories about the ideal combination.

THE PERFECT MIX

One tried-and-tested formula is a ball-winner plus a ball-player, with the former doing most of the tackling and the latter picking up the ball and passing (such as Italy's Fabio Cannavaro and Alessandro Nesta). The most important ingredient is mutual understanding.

NESTA AND CANNAVARO

Cannavaro's positional sense and superb reading of the game broke up opposition attacks. Nesta, supremely quick and elegant on the ball, picked up the pieces and instigated new attacks.

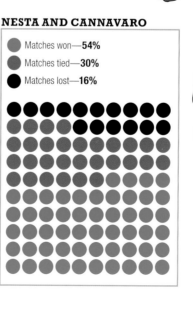

517 Number of minutes Italy goalkeeper Walter Zenga and his defense went without conceding a goal at the 1990 World Cup—a tournament record

14 Most goals conceded in one tournament by a team that has gone on to win the World Cup— West Germany in 1954

Successful teams are invariably built on the foundations of a great defensive partnership. Here are five of the finest:

BARESI AND COSTACURTA (AC MILAN)
The pair played together for so long at the heart of AC Milan's defense they instinctively knew where the other would be. When Baresi retired, Paolo Maldini stepped effortlessly into his shoes.

HANSEN AND LAWRENSON (LIVERPOOL)
The cornerstone of the great Liverpool team of the early 1980s. Lawrenson was the quicker, Hansen the more stylish, but both had the priceless ability to bring the ball out of defense.

ADAMS AND KEOWN (ARSENAL)
The Arsenal center-backs were formidable to begin with, but got even better with age. Born in the same year, they won a league and FA Cup double aged 31, and another in 2002 aged 35.

FERDINAND AND VIDIC (MAN UTD)
Manchester United's center-backs are an excellent example of how well contrasting styles can work together. Ferdinand epitomizes silky composure; Vidic is all about hustle and bustle.

CHARLTON AND MOORE (ENGLAND)
Jack Charlton's no-nonsense style gelled perfectly with Bobby Moore's more cultured approach to defending during England's World Cup-winning campaign in 1966.

NESTA AND CANNAVARO

- Matches won—**54%**
- Matches tied—**30%**
- Matches lost—**16%**

THE BEREZUTSKY TWINS

Understanding is arguably the most important component of a defensive partnership and no two people understand each other better than identical twins. Aleksei and Vasili Berezutsky of CSKA Moscow and Russia are living proof that such a formula can work at the highest level of the sport. Born 20 minutes apart, on June 20, 1982, Aleksei is the younger brother, and is also half an inch (1 cm) shorter. The pair have played together at the heart of the CSKA defense since 2002, and for the national side since 2003.

DEFENDING FROM THE FRONT

It's not just defenders who need to defend. Forwards today are expected to help out even when their side does not have the ball, putting pressure on the opposing defenders, and doing the same to the goalkeeper when he receives a back pass. The purpose of this is to force a defensive error. If forwards achieve this, they stand a good chance of being in a goal-scoring position.

CONDENSING PLAY

When the attacking team has possession of the ball, the defending team can make life difficult for them by quickly filling the gaps between players. Condensing the play in this way makes the field appear smaller, denies the attacking team room in which to operate efficiently, and increases the chances of forcing them to make a mistake. It is a major weapon to use when trying to regain possession of the ball.

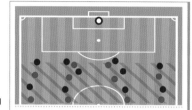

CONDENSING PLAY
Team B condenses the play, putting pressure on attacking Team A

- Attacking team A
- Defensive team B
- Action area

SHIELDING

Shielding the ball involves a player positioning his body between an opponent and the ball without actually obstructing the opponent. It is a useful skill and one that can be used all over the field, from a lone striker holding the ball up, to a defender shielding the ball from an attacker to ensure that it goes out of play for a goal-kick or a throw-in.

PROTECTION
When a defender places his body between the ball and an opponent, it is known as "shielding."

Shielded ball
Facing away from the attacker, the defender protects the ball

Ball skills
Close control is essential when shielding

TOP 5: HARDMEN

Defensive hardmen are there to terrify opponents. A type of anti-strategy, it can be very effective. The notion of having a hardman in the team is not a new one, but the following players can be viewed as being among the toughest players the game of soccer has ever seen.

CLAUDIO GENTILE

Gentile—which means "gentle" in Italian—was an inappropriate last name for one of the toughest defenders of all time. "Soccer is not for ballerinas," the Juventus hardman said, after famously kicking a young Diego Maradona into submission at the 1982 World Cup. Remarkably, despite his hardman reputation, he never received a red card.

TOMMY SMITH

According to Bill Shankly, the man they called the "Anfield Iron" wasn't born, he was "quarried." Smith, who enjoyed a 16-year career with Liverpool, once handed opposing striker Jimmy Greaves a piece of paper before a match. It was the lunch menu from the Liverpool Infirmary.

STUART PEARCE

Known as "Psycho," the giant-thighed England fullback used to listen to the Sex Pistols to get himself into the right mood for matches. Pearce (right) once tried to run off a broken leg, and when Basile Boli head-butted him at Euro '92, it was the Frenchman who came off worse.

SHEPHERDING

Just as a shepherd uses a dog to move and control his flock without touching them, when a defender "shepherds" an attacker, he is attempting to maneuver the attacker away from danger zones, without ever actually trying to take the ball from him. The two main purposes of shepherding are to channel attacking players away from the goal and to force them to play the ball with their weaker foot.

SHEPHERDING I
The defender shepherds a left-footed striker onto his weaker right foot

● Attacking team
● Defensive team
— Player movement
▨ Danger zone

SHEPHERDING II
The defender prevents the winger from getting in a cross

● Attacking team
● Defensive team
— Player movement
▨ Danger zone

IF I WANTED TO BE AN INDIVIDUAL, I WOULD HAVE TAKEN UP TENNIS

FORMER HOLLAND CAPTAIN **RUUD GULLIT**

DOUBLING UP

If an opponent becomes isolated, the defenders can improve their chances of dispossessing him by "doubling up"—putting two defenders on one forward. Defenders need to be careful: if two of them are attending to one forward, it means other forwards are likely to be left unguarded.

DOUBLING UP
Player C runs back to assist player B against opponent player A

● Attacking team
● Defensive team
— Player movement

BOBBY MOORE
Possessing an ability to read the game as it unfolded before him, few defenders played with as much effortless grace as England's 1966 World Cup-winning captain.

RONALD KOEMAN
After the Netherlands beat hosts West Germany in the semi-final of Euro '88, Koeman swapped his shirt with German midfielder Olaf Thon, then rudely pretended to wipe his backside with it. The great Dutch defender had a shot like a cannonball as well as a bone-crunching tackle.

DUNGA
Brazilians are not known for their hard tackling, but the captain of the 1994 World Cup-winning team played like a naval destroyer and also looked particularly scary. Capped 91 times, he added much-needed strength to Brazil's traditionally attacking style of play.

WORLD CUP—GOALS CONCEDED PER MATCH

Republic of Ireland—**0.77**
Croatia—**0.85**
England—**0.85**
Italy—**0.90**
Brazil—**0.91**
Netherlands—**1.06**
Spain—**1.06**

0   25   50   75   100

■ Games played   ■ Goals conceded

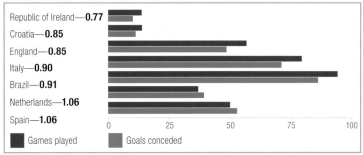

HOW TO FIX A SOCCER MATCH

If you think "what you see is what get," think again. Since 2000, over 30 countries have seen criminal investigations into allegations of match fixing at soccer games. From China to South Africa, Italy to Portugal, and Brazil to England, there is evidence (and plenty of rumors) to suggest that games are being fixed. Governing bodies, soccer associations, and the police are all handing out severe penalties to convicted offenders.

WHAT YOU SEE IS WHAT YOU GET?

If it takes two to tango, it often takes a lot more people to fix a soccer match. The fixers—the people with the money and power—tend to be club bosses, big-time gamblers, organized criminals, or all three. If they can get past the sentries of the media and the soccer authorities, there are a variety of ways that a match-fixer—intent on breaking the law—can ensure that officials, coaches, and players see things their way.

CASH, GIFTS, AND INCENTIVES
Money, particularly good old-fashioned cash, is the most usual means of influence. Incentives might include cars, expensive watches, vacations, and very soft loans.

THE DIRECTORS
If they are not directly involved in a betting scam, directors fix matches for a variety of reasons. They can bribe other teams to lose to avoid relegation, for example, or ask other teams to "go easy" on them in order to save their own players' energies for bigger matches to come.

BLACKMAIL
Simply produce some incriminating evidence about a key official and blackmail him.

THE GAMBLERS
Big-money gamblers and bookmakers actually prefer certainty to chance. The global soccer betting markets are growing fast, especially in East and Southeast Asia.

VIOLENCE
There may be direct threats to the person or indirect threats to their families. Officials and players who have crossed the fixers have faced kidnappings and attacks.

THE ORGANIZED CRIMINALS
Both gamblers and bookmakers are tied to networks of organized crime, so match-fixing is on the rise. Fixes include attempts to guarantee wins and defeats but, as the betting market becomes more complex, fixes also turn on arranging corners, throws, and the number and timing of goals.

DIRECT INTERVENTION
Simply stop the match. In some betting markets, games abandoned at half time stand as the final result. One way of ensuring your winnings, if the scoreline is right at half time, is to simply turn off the floodlights.

THESE PEOPLE MIGHT TRY TO FIX A MATCH... **BY USING THESE METHODS...**

30,000

The value of the loan in dollars (£20,000) made by Anderlecht's president to the referee in charge of their UEFA cup tie with Nottingham Forest in 1984

2
The number of games UEFA is certain were fixed between 2004 and 2009: a 2004 UEFA Cup match and a 2007 Intertoto Cup match

10
The length of prison sentence given to Chinese referee Gong Jianping by a Beijing court in 2001 for accepting bribes

2005
The year a huge match-fixing scandal rocked Brazil—eleven matches were declared null and void

THE MEDIA
The media can't fix a match, but they can make sure that nobody talks about it too much once it has been played. In many countries, much of the press is in thrall to the most powerful clubs, officials, and individuals.

THE REGULATORS
From the smallest associations to FIFA and the regional confederations, soccer bureaucracies have only begun to scratch the surface of the match-fixing problems. In countries where many of the most senior officials are involved in these practices, any form of regulation and investigation is obstructed and watered down.

TOP 5: MATCH FIXES

OLYMPIQUE MARSEILLES
Bernard Tapie, the flamboyant businessman, politician, and president of Olympique Marseilles, saw his team win a French league and European Cup double in 1993. It turned out that he had payed a small team called Valencienne to go easy against Marseilles in a league game before his side's big matches. Marseilles was stripped of its French title and Tapie served six months in jail.

MOGGIOPOLY
"Moggiopoly" wasn't just one fix, it was a system of fixes that affected almost the whole of Italian soccer. It centered around Luciano Moggi, the general manager at Juventus, and included players, agents, referees, and officials. Moggi's networks of pressure, influence, and power shaped Italian soccer in Juventus' favor for a decade. When the case was exposed in 2006, Juventus was relegated to serie B and stripped of its 2006 title.

AC ALLIANSSI
In 2005, tiny Finnish first division team AC Allianssi lost its first game under new ownership 8–0. Unlike most games in the Finnish first division, over €500,000 ($600,000) was staked on this one. New owner Ye Zheyun didn't take any chances that his new club would lose: the goalkeeper was sent to Belgium for non-existent training; six new players, all of whom were injured and unfit, had been brought into play; and, just for good measure, players wore short studs on their boots—highly inappropriate for the rain-drenched field.

WEST GERMANY VS AUSTRIA
West Germany and Austria played each other in the final game of their group at the 1982 World Cup. A 0–0 draw was all that was needed to see both teams safely through to the next round—at the expense of Algeria. The least competitive game in World Cup history was disgracefully played out and Algeria went home.

MANCHESTER UNITED VS LIVERPOOL
In spring 1915, relegation-threatened Manchester United beat Liverpool 2–0. Players on both sides visibly abused a Liverpool player (who wasn't in on the fix) after he almost scored when the match was standing at 2–0. The players, fearing the economic consequences of the coming suspension of professional soccer due to World War I, had organized a tiny betting coup among themselves. The ruse, however, was obvious.

THE OFFICIALS
Want things to go your way? Go straight to the top and the men and women in black

THE ASSISTANT REFEREES
The assistants aren't much use by themselves, but they can make a very helpful addition to the team if the referee is already on-board. The assistant referees can give those offside decisions real authenticity.

THE REFEREE
Score looking lopsided? How about a penalty. Wrong side on form? Simply disallow that goal. The referee is the most important man to "get" if you want to fix a game. He is in total control of the match and, with so much resting on a few key decisions, a referee who knows what he is doing can fix almost any game.

THE TEAM
They are paid to play, but the players can also be paid to play badly if the price is right.

THE COACH
With the coach in your pocket, you can be sure that the weakest team gets picked, or that injured players get their chance to fail.

GOALKEEPER
The goalkeeper can be a great asset if you want to lose the game, but he is less useful if you're trying to win.

DEFENDERS
With so many close decisions and penalty chances, center backs make great targets for the fixers.

MIDFIELDERS
Best bought in groups, a lackluster midfield shirking a tackle and misplacing passes can easily produce a draw—and any wrong-doing is hard to spot.

STRIKERS
Strikers are only useful if you need someone to keep on missing shots set up by an incorruptible midfield.

TO TRY TO INFLUENCE THESE GROUPS

SET PIECES

Set pieces are free-kicks, corners, and throw-ins. About 30 percent of goals are scored directly or indirectly from set piece situations, so they are extremely important for both the attacking and defending side. Modern teams spend hours on the training ground practicing, creating, and honing set piece routines, from both an attacking and defensive point of view.

CORNERS: THE ATTACKING TEAM

A corner provides an attacking team with a fantastic opportunity to create a goal-scoring chance. Numerous moves have been devised over the years—some more innovative than others—all of which fall into one of three categories: a short corner, a near-post corner, or a far-post corner.

SHORT CORNERS

Unlike a standard corner, no attempt is made to cross the ball directly into the penalty area; instead the corner-taker makes a short pass to a teammate, moves into an onside position, receives the ball back, and only then delivers his cross. The aim is to confuse the defenders' plans.

NEAR-POST CORNERS

A near-post corner is played to the goal post closest to the taker. It is good because it eliminates the goalkeeper, since the ball does not reach him. An attacking player is stationed on the near post. Usually tall, he flicks the ball on with his head, hoping an incoming teammate will pick it up and score.

SHORT CORNERS
Player B comes short, giving player A the option of using a short corner

● Attacking team
● Defensive team
- - Pass/cross
— Player movement

NEAR-POST CORNER
Player B flicks the ball on, hoping to find an onrushing teammate

● Attacking team
● Defensive team
- - Pass/cross
— Player movement

FAR-POST CORNERS

A far-post corner is played to the goal post furthest away from the taker. The aim is to bypass the goalkeeper. The ball is struck with pace and the plan is for a teammate to escape his marker, meet the ball, and score.

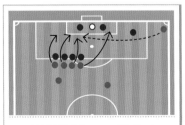

FAR-POST CORNER
Forwards try to avoid their markers to meet the deeper corner

● Attacking team
● Defensive team
- - Pass/cross
— Player movement

WHAT SHOULD THE GOALKEEPER DO?

A goalkeeper has two main choices: to come and meet the ball (either by catching or punching it) or to stay on his goal line and hope to make a save. It requires excellent judgment to decide what to do in the heat of the moment.

THE DEFENSIVE WALL

The number of players in a wall depends on the area of the field from which a free-kick is taken. It will range from between one player to five.

CORNERS: THE DEFENDING TEAM

Although a defending team has no idea what kind of corner an attacking side will deliver, it should always follow certain principles—such as adopting a marking strategy (be it zonal or man-to-man marking) and putting a man on the inside of each of the goal posts.

MARKING

Tactics vary depending on whether a team uses zonal or man-to-man marking, but the basic principle is to stick to your man and stay goal-side of him. If a defender lets the attacker get in front of him, the latter will have a chance to direct a header on goal.

GUARDING THE POSTS

The defending team should place one man on each post. As the ball comes in, they need to position themselves on the goal line, just inside the post they are guarding. If they do this, they will be ready to clear any goal attempts heading for the inside of their posts.

FREE-KICKS: THE DEFENDING TEAM

Because free-kicks provide an opponent with an ideal opportunity to shoot on goal, it is vital that defenses are organized to deal with the impending threat. Every defender needs to be on his guard. Marking (be it zonal or man-to-man) needs to be tight, and then a wall needs to be created that directly blocks the route to goal.

DEFENSIVE WALLS

If a free-kick is given in a scoring position, the defending team will set up a wall. The goalkeeper is in charge of positioning the wall, which may have as many as five members or as few as one, depending on how close to goal the free-kick is. The goalkeeper needs to ensure that one side of the goal is covered, leaving him free to concentrate on the other side.

ANTICIPATING FREE-KICKS

Defenders need to be alert to quickly taken free-kicks or ones delivered to an unmarked opponent. If the free-kick is indirect, a player should be nominated to close the ball down as soon as it has been touched by an opponent.

THROW-INS

The defending team needs to mark every opponent, including the thrower. The thrower's teammates should move around, looking to escape the attentions of their markers. Long throws (see p.139) can provide a dangerous attacking option.

IT'S AMAZING... JUST **HOW MANY GOALS** COME FROM SET PIECES

CELTIC MANAGER **GORDON STRACHAN**

SET PIECE SUCCESS
A cleverly worked free-kick resulted in a Argentinian goal for Javier Zanetti in his country's clash against England at the 1998 World Cup in France.

FREE-KICKS: THE ATTACKING TEAM

Some free-kicks awarded in advanced positions invite crosses, in which case—because the ball is crossed into the box—the tactics for both sides are similar to those in the corners section (see left). Others provide opportunities for a direct shot on goal.

REHEARSED FREE-KICKS

Rehearsed free-kicks can take various forms, from simple taps to the side to complex passing routines, but all have the same intention: to catch an opponent unawares. A classic example of a perfectly executed free-kick was given by Argentina in their second-round clash against England at the 1998 World Cup (see right). In a move honed on the training ground, Gabriel Batistuta made a dummy run, Javier Zanetti peeled into space from behind the defensive wall, was found by Juan Sebastián Verón, shot, and scored.

Zanetti

Veron   Batistuta

FREE-KICK TRICKS
Javier Zanetti positioned himself behind England's defensive wall

● Argentina
● England
- - Pass/shot
— Player run

ATTACKING STRATEGIES

There are three main choices when it comes to attacking play. How many strikers do you employ? Do you try to get into a scoring position via the sides of the field ("the flanks") or through the middle? And do you seek to get there through intricate or direct passing? The answers depend on the strength of your team, the weaknesses of the opposition, and the way the game is unfolding.

THROUGH THE MIDDLE: THE LONG-BALL GAME

The long-ball game involves getting the ball from the defenders to the forwards as quickly as possible. This entails passing the ball two-thirds of the length of the field or more in the air, and for this reason, the approach is also known as "route-one soccer."

IDEAL REQUIREMENTS

The long-ball game works best with a tall forward (the "target man"), who is likely to win the long aerial balls, or with wingers stationed near the sidelines ready to receive long passes. Teams resort to the long-ball game to get the ball rapidly out of defense to minimize the risk of losing possession in a dangerous area, and to get the ball up to the forwards before the defending team has had a chance to organize its defense.

ROUTE-ONE PERFECTION
There is nothing attractive or particularly skilful about the long-ball game and it is usually not pretty to watch, but there are exceptions, such as Dennis Bergkamp's exquisite 89th-minute, match-winning goal for the Netherlands against Argentina in the 1998 World Cup quarter-finals.

KEY
- ● Holland
- ● Argentina
- -- Pass
- — Player movement

ONE STRIKER OR TWO?

In the modern game, teams are unlikely to use more than two forwards through fear of leaving themselves too vulnerable in other parts of the field. The question then becomes whether you play with one, two, or conceivably with no strikers at all. This is a matter of formation (see pp.90–93), and will have an important impact on a team's attacking strategy. Typically a team plays with two strikers, one of whom features in a more advanced position (called a center forward—see pp.50–53). The second striker plays in a slightly deeper role—often called "playing in the hole"—and will act as a link between the midfielders and the center forward.

INTRICATE PASSING/BUILD-UP PLAY

Well-marshaled defenders can render the long-ball game ineffective by packing the defense with extra players to leave attacking forwards hopelessly outnumbered. When teams face such a defense, they have to rely on intricate passing to break through. It helps if they have players who are skilful enough to pass the ball accurately and quickly in confined spaces.

PLAYER MOVEMENT
Static players are easy for defenders to mark. Successful intricate passing depends on attackers moving around and the player in possession of the ball anticipating his teammates' movements. The passer should also move into space as soon as he has played the ball to provide teammates with another passing option.

ELEMENT OF SURPRISE
Tricks, such as back-heels, are invaluable in and around the penalty area. They are almost impossible for defenders to anticipate and so can buy the attackers time and space. Ideally, all attackers will be alert to their teammates' tricks, but even if they aren't, they may still find themselves in a position to capitalize on them.

FOOTBALL TACTICS ARE RAPIDLY BECOMING AS **COMPLICATED** AS THE CHEMICAL FORMULA FOR **SPLITTING THE ATOM**

FORMER TOTTENHAM HOTSPUR AND ENGLAND CENTER FORWARD **JIMMY GREAVES**

CHARLES REEP: THE LONG-BALL GAME

The guru of the long-ball game was Charles Reep. The former RAF wing commander first became convinced of the merits of route-one soccer in the 1930s and, after World War II, began to analyze matches to discover what strategies actually led to goals. After studying 578 games between 1953 and 1967, he figured he had discovered several "laws" (see numbers below).

BIG-NAME FOLLOWERS

Reep's theories were extremely influential on a generation of managers, particularly in the UK. Graham Taylor was one notable disciple. Another was Norway boss Egil Olsen, who was still turning to Reep for advice when Reep was over 90 years old.

FALLING OUT OF FASHION

Reep's ideas on the game have fallen out of fashion in recent years. The Latin/Continental-style passing game has tended to win out in the end, with the emphasis in the modern era placed on skilful, technical players.

60 Percentage of goals resulting from regaining possession in the final third of the field

12.3 Optimum distance in yards (11.2 m) for a successful shot on goal

80 Percentage of goals that resulted from a sequence of three passes or less

1 Number of goals scored from every ten shots taken on goal

SLIDE-RULE PASSES

A slide-rule pass is a pass that has been weighted so precisely that it arrives at the feet of a forward-running attacker at the exact moment he arrives in the desired position. It is a vital tool for breaking even the most stubborn of defenses, and can be used for beating offside traps and for finding players making overlapping runs. If a slide-rule pass is to work, however, the player receiving the ball will need to time his run to perfection.

SLIDE-RULE PASS
The forward takes the ball in his stride and shoots on goal

● Attacking team
● Defensive team
- - Pass
— Player movement

PAUL SCHOLES
The Manchester United attacking midfielder is one of the neatest passers in modern soccer.

ALEXANDER HLEB
A master of the intricate pass, the Barcelona attacking midfielder thrives in the final third of the field.

THE ONE-TWO

The one-two is an excellent way to get past a defender who is standing between the attacker (who has the ball) and the goal. It needs two attackers, one of them stationary and one running with the ball. The running attacker passes to his stationary teammate, continues to run forward past the defender, then receives the ball back from the stationary teammate. Also known as the "wall pass," the one-two is particularly effective around the edge of the penalty area.

INNOVATIVE IDEAS

Former Liverpool manager Bill Shankly introduced several unusual training methods to get the best out of his players. To increase their passing accuracy, he had an artificial goal painted on a convenient brick wall and split into eight segments, which he would then order his players to hit on demand.

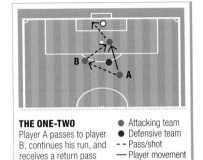

THE ONE-TWO
Player A passes to player B, continues his run, and receives a return pass

● Attacking team
● Defensive team
- - Pass/shot
— Player movement

PRESSING

The pressing game involves never giving an opponent a moment's rest when their team has the ball, thereby pressurizing them into making an error. In the modern game, all players are expected to press, including the forwards, who are expected to harry an opponent's goalkeeper and central defenders. This tactic requires great energy.

PROBING

If a team is comfortable in possession, there is no need to rush into an all-out attack. Instead, the attacking team can "probe" their opponents' defense, passing the ball between themselves until a clear shooting opportunity presents itself. The longer the move, the more tired and frustrated the defending team will become.

THE PERFECT GOAL

Argentina's second goal in their 6–0 thrashing of Serbia at the 2006 World Cup was a masterclass on patient build-up play. It had almost everything—one-touch passing, a neat one-two, superb movement, and support. The move began with Javier Mascherano tackling an opponent deep in his own half. It ended, 24 passes later, with Esteban Cambiasso slamming the ball high into the Serbian net.

The move begins when Javier Mascherano intercepts a misplaced Serbian pass and feeds the ball to teammate Maxi Rodríguez

KEY

● Argentina
● Serbia
→ Player movement
-→ Ball movement
⇢ Player with ball

Leftback Juan Pablo Sorín gets the ball in an advanced position on the left-wing

Hernán Crespo backheels the ball into the path of the onrushing Cambiasso

USING THE FLANKS

The alternative to playing the ball through the middle is to use wide players who have pace, dribbling skills, the ability to run past defenders to the goal line, and put in accurate crosses.

USING WINGERS
Player A beats the defender and delivers a dangerous cross

- Attacking team
- Defensive team
- -- Pass/shot
- — Player movement

SWITCHING THE ATTACK

If one side of the field looks a better attacking proposition, the team in possession can "switch the play," i.e. change the focus to a less well-defended area of the field.

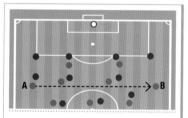

SWITCHING THE PLAY
Player A plays a cross-field pass to player B on the opposite flank

- Attacking team
- Defensive team
- -- Pass

STRETCHING PLAY

Just as teams condense play when their opponents have the ball (see p.92), they seek to stretch the play in attack by increasing the distance between their players to create more time and space.

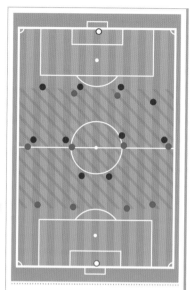

STRETCHING PLAY
The attacking team increases the distance between its players

- Attacking team
- Defensive team
- Action area

COUNTER-ATTACKING

An instant switch from defense to attack, the counter-attack can place an opponent's defense under huge pressure. To work, one or two counter-attacking players must stay upfield during an opposition attack.

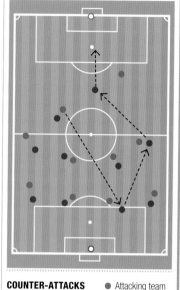

COUNTER-ATTACKS
An intercepted pass in defense can lead to an instant attack

- Attacking team
- Defensive team
- -- Pass
- — Player movement

BENEFITS OF FIVE-A-SIDE SOCCER

Arsène Wenger and Bill Shankly are just two of the managers who use five-a-side soccer in training sessions, to develop ball skills and close control.

MASCHERANO, RODRÍGUEZ, SORÍN, RIQUELME, SORÍN

MASCHERANO, RODRÍGUEZ, AYALA, CAMBIASSO, MASCHERANO, RODRÍGUEZ, SORÍN, RODRÍGUEZ, CAMBIASSO, RIQUELME, MASCHERANO, SORÍN, SAVIOLA, RIQUELME, SAVIOLA, CAMBIASSO, CRESPO, CAMBIASSO...GOAL!

AN ARGENTINIAN ANNOUNCER DESCRIBES THE 24-PASS GOAL AT THE 2006 WORLD CUP

Esteban Cambiasso
Argentina's midfielder celebrates scoring one of the greatest goals in World Cup history.

MANAGERS AND COACHES

The language of soccer is packed with military terminology. A season is often described as a "campaign," and an individual game as a "battle." In this spirit, a soccer team can be compared to an army. If the players are the troops, operating under a captain, the coach is the drill sergeant and the manager is the general.

A QUESTION OF TERMINOLOGY

In this book, when we use the word "coach" we are referring to the person who runs training and fitness sessions. The "manager," on the other hand, is the person in overall charge of team affairs, who has to decide everything from tactics to the buying and selling of players.

THE MANAGER

RESPONSIBILITIES

The 21st-century soccer manager has to juggle a bewildering number of tasks. The following are just a handful of them.

TEAM AND PLAYERS
Team selection
Motivating the players
Deciding on formations
Making substitutions
Giving team talks

BEHIND THE SCENES
Signing new players
Maintaining player discipline
Overseeing player development
Setting coaching policy
Scouting for new players

RUNNING THE CLUB
Appointing ancillary staff
Delegating responsibilities
Attending board meetings
Setting coaching policy
Scouting for new players

IN THE SPOTLIGHT
Dealing with the media
Preparing program notes
Helping club sponsors
Attending club functions
Appearing on club's TV channel

THE MODERN MANAGER

The role of the modern soccer manager was defined by three key figures in the late 1920s and early 1930s: the Englishman Herbert Chapman at Arsenal; Vittorio Pozzo, coach of the Italian national team; and Hugo Meisel, coach of Austrian Wien and Austria. Prior to their arrival, boardroom directors had picked squads and handled transfers and contracts, while players had determined tactics.

A NEW DIRECTION

With the arrival of professionalism in the early 20th century, all three of these managers carved out a new zone of control within their respective soccer clubs. Chapman added showmanship to the mix, inviting film stars to Highbury and calling for floodlit games; Pozzo and Meisel created new levels of tactical sophistication in their squads. All three also possessed another key ingredient: an aura of almost magical, charismatic authority.

A MANAGER HAS A RESPONSIBILITY TO **CREATE A TEAM** AND **USE HIS IDEAS** TO ACHIEVE THAT

REPUBLIC OF IRELAND MANAGER **GIOVANNI TRAPATTONI**

ARSÈNE WENGER
A rarity in the modern game, Arsenal's manager has been at the helm of the North London club for over a decade.

THE GREAT MANAGERS

A number of managers have achieved unparalleled success in the game, but here are perhaps the ten best managers ever to have taken charge of a team.

HERBERT CHAPMAN

The man who invented and personified the idea of the modern, autocratic, media-savvy manager, he won titles with Huddersfield and Arsenal.

SIR ALEX FERGUSON

Ferguson took his grit and cunning to Aberdeen and led them to the top of Scottish soccer. He then headed south and transformed Manchester United into England's dominant club.

BÉLA GUTTMANN

The Hungarian is the only coach to have won the European Cup and the Copa Libertadores (see pp.350–51)—with Benfica and Peñarol respectively—and was a key figure in bringing tactical innovations to Latin America.

HELENIO HERRERA

The man they called "The Magician" conjured up titles and trophies at Barcelona and Inter Milan with his mix of lock-tight defense and surreal motivational techniques.

RINUS MICHELS

"Iron" Rinus brought discipline and coherence to Dutch soccer, turned Ajax into a global force with his Total Soccer (see p.89), and coached the Dutch national side to Euro '88 success.

BOB PAISLEY

Twenty years in the famous Liverpool "boot room" before he became the club's manager, Bob Paisley may have appeared avuncular, but he ruled Anfield with a rod of iron and won six league titles and three European Cups.

BILL SHANKLY

Shankly's Liverpool teams delighted, his words inspired, and his memory is treasured. No other coach has been hoisted into and across the Kop in scenes of jubilation.

VITTORIO POZZO

Pozzo brought modern soccer management to Italy and defined its role there. He enjoyed success with Torino, but two World Cup wins and an Olympic gold for Italy are hard to beat.

BRIAN CLOUGH

Erratic and volcanic, Clough was also magnificent and inspirational. To take a small club like Nottingham Forest to two consecutive European Cup wins was a feat unparalleled in soccer management anywhere.

GIOVANNI TRAPATTONI

In the excruciating hothouse of Italian soccer, one man stays cool: Trapattoni (right) won it all with Juventus in the 1980s and again with Bayern Munich in the 1990s.

THE MANAGERIAL MERRY-GO-ROUND

The job of a top-flight soccer manager is one of the least secure in the world. Even the most talented boss can face being fired after a string of bad results or if there is the slightest hint of him losing the confidence of the players, known as "losing the dressing room."

MANAGERIAL MADNESS

There is no hotter seat in world sports than that of the soccer manager. The graphic on the right shows how many managers lost their job in the top five divisions of European soccer—Italy, Spain, England, Germany, and France—in the 2007–08 season. They reveal just how tenuous a manager's position can be, and that this phenomenon is not isolated to one particular country.

MANAGER CHANGES IN 2007–08

- Serie A (Italy)—26
- La Liga (Spain)—14
- Premier League (England)—12
- Bundesliga (Germany)—6
- La Ligue (France)—5

SHORTEST MANAGERIAL REIGN

On May 17, 2007, Torquay United announced that Leroy Rosenior would be joining the club for a second stint as head coach (he had led "The Gulls" to promotion to League One in 2004). Moments later, news emerged that the club had changed ownership, and that the new owners had appointed their own manager. Officially, Rosenior's second stint as Torquay manager lasted ten minutes—it is thought to be the shortest managerial reign in soccer history.

1 Number of managers to have won back-to-back World Cups—Italy's Vittorio Pozzo

6 Number of Italian managers to have won the European Cup—the most of any nation

45 Total number of managerial changes in all four divisions of top-flight English soccer during the 2007–08—out of a total of 92 clubs

MANAGEMENT STYLES

Managers and coaches come in every shape, size, and emotional disposition. At one end of the spectrum you find the icemen —coaches who barely flinch when their side has scored a goal—and at the other end of the scale are the fire-breathers and ecstatic shamans who patrol their technical zones as if they were in an endless war dance.

The Intimidator
(e.g. Alex Ferguson, right) Revitalizes a sluggish team performance with an inspirational, but terrifying, head-to-head, half-time tongue-lashing.

The Disciplinarian
(e.g. Fabio Capello) Runs his team with a rod of iron. There is no room in his team for the pampered star—the rules are the same for every player.

The Motivator
(e.g. Bill Shankly) Gives players the belief that they are on top of their game and that they are capable of beating any team in the world.

The Philosopher
(e.g. Arsène Wenger) Maintains an unflinching belief in how the game should be played. The emphasis is always on style over substance.

The Tinkerer
(e.g. Claudio Ranieri) Cannot stop himself from making numerous changes to his teams between and during matches. Some interpret this as indecisiveness, others as admirable flexibility.

THE HAIRDRYER TREATMENT

The former Manchester United striker Mark Hughes came up with the phrase "hairdryer treatment" to describe the tongue-lashings dished out by Alex Ferguson in his half-time team talks.

The Ranter
(e.g. Nereo Rocco) Communicates an all-consuming passion for the game to every one of the players, who invariably live in fear of him.

The Charismatic
(e.g. Brian Clough) Demands exacting standards from the players; constantly keeps his players, club officials, and the media on their toes.

The Mind-games Expert
(e.g. Jose Mourinho) Takes the pressure off his own team by making himself, and the opposing side, the center of the media spotlight.

The Wheeler-dealer
(e.g. Harry Redknapp) Forges a team in his own image, and at limited cost, by making a series of shrewd acquisitions in the transfer market.

The Innovator
(e.g. Vittorio Pozzo) Seeks to surprise the opposition by utilizing specific, and unusual, tactics that have been honed on the training ground.

The Father Figure
(e.g. Bobby Robson) Provides a comforting arm around the shoulder in the bad times and words of wisdom when things are going well.

The Tactician
(e.g. Rafa Benitez) More likely to scribble notes in his notepad when his side scores a goal than to celebrate with his players.

The Iceman
(e.g. Sven-Goran Eriksson, left) Remains unflappable under any circumstances, whether his team is 5–0 up in a crunch clash or about to crash out of a major tournament.

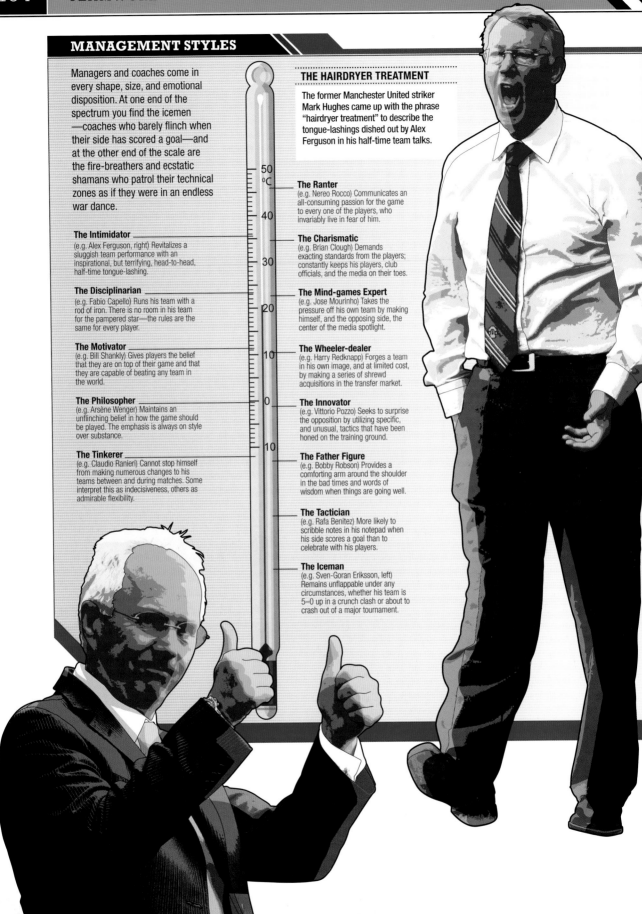

MOTIVATIONAL TECHNIQUES

Managers have used numerous techniques to try to encourage and cajole the players under their charge, from screaming and shouting at their players while marching up and down the sideline, to a more placid approach. Whichever technique is used, the intention is the same: to get the players to perform to the best of their ability on the field.

MOTIVATION THE ARSENAL WAY

In September 2008, the *Guardian* newspaper in England obtained a copy of a motivational handout prepared by Arsenal manager Arsène Wenger for his players to take away and digest before big matches. The text of the handout is printed below.

BIZARRE MOTIVATIONAL TECHNIQUES

Many managers have been known to use a number of unusual techniques to get the best out of their players; others have simply crossed the boundaries of normality. Former Nottingham Forest manager Brian Clough used to order his players to run through stinging nettles. Most bizarre of all, however, was Giovanni Trapattoni. The former Juventus manager was famously eccentric on the sideline, gesticulating frantically, and even showering his players with holy water.

OUR TEAM BECOMES STRONGER BY:
DISPLAYING A POSITIVE ATTITUDE ON AND OFF THE FIELD
EVERYONE MAKING THE RIGHT DECISIONS FOR THE TEAM
HAVE AN UNSHAKEABLE BELIEF THAT WE CAN ACHIEVE OUR TARGET
BELIEVE IN THE STRENGTH OF THE TEAM
ALWAYS WANT MORE—ALWAYS GIVE MORE
FOCUS ON OUR COMMUNICATION
BE DEMANDING WITH YOURSELF
BE FRESH AND PREPARED TO WIN
FOCUS ON BEING MENTALLY STRONGER AND ALWAYS KEEP GOING UNTIL THE END
WHEN WE PLAY AWAY FROM HOME, BELIEVE IN OUR IDENTITY AND PLAY THE SOCCER WE LOVE TO PLAY AT HOME
STICK TOGETHER
STAY GROUNDED AND HUMBLE AS A PLAYER AND A PERSON
SHOW THE DESIRE TO WIN IN ALL THAT YOU DO
ENJOY AND CONTRIBUTE TO ALL THAT IS SPECIAL ABOUT BEING IN A TEAM

IF I HAD AN ARGUMENT WITH A PLAYER WE WOULD... TALK ABOUT IT... AND THEN DECIDE **I WAS RIGHT!**

FORMER NOTTINGHAM FOREST MANAGER **BRIAN CLOUGH**

TOP 5: MANAGER SPEAK

Modern managers are exposed to extreme pressures and often say things they should not.

JOSE MOURINHO
While manager of Chelsea, Mourinho offered this recipe for success: "If you have no eggs, you have no omelet. And it depends upon the quality of the eggs. Some are more expensive than others and some give you better omelets. So when the class-one eggs are in [UK supermarket] Waitrose and you cannot go there, you have a problem."

GIOVANNI TRAPATTONI
The Italian criticized his own players on television, accusing them of being as weak as "empty bottles." But he surpassed himself later: "We can't behave like crocodiles and cry over spilt milk and broken eggs."

JAVIER CLEMENTE
When one journalist tried to validate his opinion by saying he'd "seen a lot of soccer," the much-traveled Spanish manager cut him down with the following observation: "The cows at Lezama [Athletic Bilbao's training ground in the country] watch soccer every day, and they haven't got a... clue."

JOEL SALDANHA
The former journalist became Brazil's manager prior to the 1970 World Cup. When Brazil's military president, General Medici, said he didn't like Saldanha's selections, Saldanha replied: "I don't chose the president's ministry... he can't choose my front line." He was promptly fired.

KEVIN KEEGAN
Keegan (below) fired off a tirade at Manchester United's Alex Ferguson's mind games in the climax to the 1995–96 Premier League season: "But I'll tell ya—you can tell him now if you're watching it—we're still fighting for this title, and... and I tell you honestly, I'd love it if we beat them, just love it!"

3,000,000
Average salary (in sterling) of an English Premier League manager in 2008–09

2
Number of men to have won World Cup as both a player and manager—Mario Zagallo (with Brazil) and Franz Beckenbauer (with Germany)

THE ANATOMY OF A CLUB

Since Sheffield FC was established in northern England in 1857, the club has been at the center of soccer cultures all over the world. But clubs come in many shapes and sizes, and methods of ownership have changed, too. In England, clubs moved from being private organizations to private limited companies. Socio clubs emerged in southern Europe and Latin America. In communist societies, state organizations and trade unions ran teams.

TYPES OF CLUB OWNERSHIP

A soccer club is no longer solely represented by 11 players taking to a field up to twice a week wearing a familiar kit; the modern club extends far beyond the confines of the sidelines. It is a business, a potential vehicle for political advancement, and in some cases even a rich man's toy. Clubs have evolved in various ways in different parts of the world.

PRIVATE LIMITED COMPANIES

The standard form of professional soccer club in Britain, with one or many private shareholders. For many years directors were not allowed to take anything but a tiny profit out of the club. In recent years, these restrictions have been lifted and most clubs are run as medium-sized private businesses.

THE SOCIO MODEL

In Latin America and southern Europe, the original sports/social clubs out of which so many teams grew left a legacy in which all members have an annual vote for the elected officers of the club's board. The club itself can neither be bought nor sold.

FC UNITED OF MANCHESTER

When American tycoon Malcolm Glazer acquired a controlling interest in Manchester United in May 2005, supporters who opposed the takeover decided to form their own club. FC United entered the tenth tier of English soccer in the fall of 2005.

I LOVE THIS SPORT, I LOVE THIS LEAGUE. **WHY DON'T I GET MY OWN TEAM?**

CHELSEA OWNER **ROMAN ABRAMOVICH**

OTHER TYPES OF CLUB

In France and Germany, soccer clubs are owned and controlled by the original amateur sports associations out of which they grew. In the US, Australia, and Mexico, clubs are operated on a franchise basis. A recent innovation has been the e-club (such as Ebbsfleet United in England) where anyone can buy a stake in the club.

WORLD'S RICHEST CLUBS

- Real Madrid—**$480**
- Man Utd—**$430**
- Barcelona—**$396**
- Chelsea—**$387**
- Arsenal—**$360**
- AC Milan—**$310**
- Bayern Munich—**$305**
- Liverpool—**$270**
- Inter—**$266**
- Roma—**$216**

TOP 5: TYCOONS AND TYRANTS

Money and power just can't keep away from the game and soccer associations and soccer clubs have been owned, run, embarrassed, and even ruined by business tycoons and political tyrants. Here are five of the biggest and baddest tycoons and tyrants in the history of the game, some of whom have made Genghis Khan seem like a benign dictator.

JOAO HAVELANGE (Brazil, FIFA)
The Sun King of global soccer, Havelange started in the Brazilian bus business and ran the Brazilian FA in its golden era before destroying Sir Stanley Rous in FIFA's 1974 presidential election. A master of power politics, Havelange revolutionized, expanded, and commercialized both FIFA and the World Cup—but he would brook no opposition. He is known to have blanked Rupert Murdoch and compared himself to the Pope.

IVAN KHOSA (South Africa, Orlando Pirates)
The "Iron Duke" made his money and his reputation in the townships of South Africa under apartheid, running a whole variety of "business interests." Now a commanding, controversial, and headline-grabbing figure in the whole of the African soccer scene, he has run his club, Orlando Pirates (from the Free State province in South Africa), and its budget with the same single-mindedness he devoted to his businesses.

WHO'S IN CHARGE?

The power structures and lines of command in soccer clubs are an endless source of intrigue. The relationships between presidents, coaches, technical directors, and directors of soccer serve to create as much friction as they do cooperation and have generated as many newspaper headlines in recent years as the action on the field.

PRESIDENT, PRIME MINISTER, AND PUNDIT

Italian prime minister Silvio Berlusconi bought AC Milan in 1986. Never one to keep away from the television cameras, he was often seen bemoaning his manager Carlo Ancelotti's tactics. The manager's insistence on playing 4-3-2-1 was a constant source of anguish for Berlusconi, who believes that soccer is a game requiring two strikers.

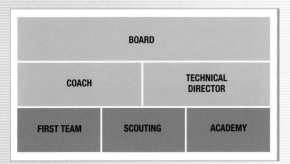

TRADITIONAL SET-UP
The classic set-up that hinges on an all-powerful manager who takes charge of all aspects of the first team, scouting, and youth development.

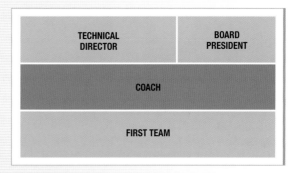

ALL-POWERFUL TECHNICAL DIRECTOR
Increasingly common in Europe, the technical director has total control of the club's transfer policy. The coach can ask for certain players, but has to make do with what he is given by the technical director.

CLASSIC CONTINENTAL
In this set-up, the club is run by the board, the technical director (who is responsible for dealings on the transfer market), and the coach (who is responsible for first-team affairs).

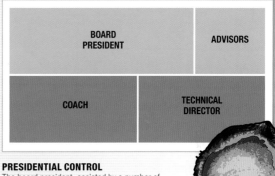

PRESIDENTIAL CONTROL
The board president, assisted by a number of advisors, calls all the shots, from team selection to transfer policy. The coach answers to only one person: the board president.

LEVANTI BERIA
(USSR, Dynamo Moscow)
The man who ran the KGB under Stalin and a key figure in the purges and the Gulag (the government agency that administered the penal labor camps in the USSR), Beria brought his own style of terror-based management to the KGB's very own soccer team—Dynamo Moscow.

ROMAN ABRAMOVICH
(England, Chelsea)
After making millions in oil and aluminum, the Russian turned his attention to soccer. He bought Chelsea in June 2003, spent big money and, although managers have come and gone (five in six years), trophies soon followed. Chelsea are now one of Europe's most feared teams.

JESUS GIL Y GIL
(Spain, Atlético Madrid)
A building magnate who was imprisoned after a hotel he made collapsed on its residents and who was wanted in courts across Spain on corruption charges, Gil (right) didn't care. He kept Atlético Madrid in the headlines for two decades.

INDIVIDUAL SKILLS

ANATOMY OF A PLAYER

Like dancers and singers, soccer players' bodies are their instruments, their means of performance and expression. Although professionals are generally getting taller and increasingly more fit, the game still offers space for a variety of physiques and specialisms. Above all, the game still demands the secret soccer biology of "guts" and "heart."

EDGAR DAVIDS

The hard-tackling Dutch international is best remembered for protective goggles, worn following an operation on his right eye for glaucoma in 1999. He required permission from FIFA to wear the glasses and to use eyewash which contained a banned substance.

KEY REQUIREMENTS

Although the size and shape of players does vary, there are certain anatomical requirements that all top level players have in common. As soccer players use their legs and feet more than anything else, strong lower-body muscles—the calf, thigh muscles (quadriceps), and hamstrings—are the most important. Upper-body strength is also key, in order to facilitate both powerful running and resisting tackles from opposing players.

BODY STRENGTH
A soccer player's leg muscles do much of the work (and are most prone to injury), but a strong neck, spine, chest, abdominals, and deltoids are all important.

CHANGING SHAPE

Soccer players are changing shape. One study looked at the height, weight, and body mass index (BMI) of players in the top English division between 1974 and 2004. Over those 40 years, players on average got taller and leaner—and the top six teams in the league each season consistently had more of these kinds of players.

Eyes
Players need to read the game and judge speeds and distances

Deltoids
Built by bench presses and weight lifting, these muscles power the arms and are useful for cushioning high balls

Chest muscles
Players need this large area of muscle, just one of three glutei muscles, to run and pass

Abdominals
Core inner-body strength is a prerequisite of the balance and posture required for top level soccer

AVERAGE HEIGHTS

Average heights of European professional players by position.

- Forwards—**5FT 10IN**
- Midfielders—**5FT 9IN**
- Defenders—**6FT**
- Goalkeepers—**6FT 2IN**

Quadriceps
The four muscles at the front of the thigh are the player's engine room, essential for running and kicking

70,000,000 The total cost in dollars (£47.8 million) to insure David Beckham's feet

66 Percentage of daily calorific intake burned in a match

23.3 Average Body Mass Index of Premiership players 2003–04

6ft 1in
Average height (185.8cm) of Europe's tallest team in 2006, the Slovakian club FC Košice

5ft 10in
Average height (177.7cm) of Europe's shortest team in 2006, Bulgarian club FK Vihren Sandanski

Groin
Take much of the muscle stress caused by shooting, so pre-match stretching is vital

Ankles
Must be strong to cope with the stress of constant changes of direction

HIGHS AND LOWS

Soccer does not favor one body type or one kind of player but, because it demands such a complex range and mixture of skills, it can accommodate all shapes and sizes. Many different physical makeups have played at the top level, from towering strikers and center backs to tiny midfield terriers.

THE LONG...

6ft 10in (2.08m) Kristof van Hout (Belgium)

6ft 9in (2.05m) Yang Changpeng (China)

6ft 8in (2.04m) Tor Hogne Aarøy (Norway)

...AND THE SHORT

5ft 3in (1.60m) Brian Flynn (Wales)

5ft 2in (1.58m) Élton Jose Xavier Gomes (Brazil)

5ft 1in (1.55m) Jafal Rashed (Qatar)

6ft 7in (2.01m)

5ft 5in (1.65m)

6ft 4in (1.93m)

5ft 8in (1.73m)

PETER CROUCH
Tall, gangly, but surprisingly mobile and a regular for England

DIEGO MARADONA
His low center of gravity gave him amazing balance

FATTY FOULKES
At his peak in the 1920s Foulkes weighed 280 lbs (127 kg)

PELÉ
The perfect player, a balance of height, speed, and power

Neck muscles
The key to powerful heading, players need to work specifically on these muscles to strengthen them

Spine
Liable to take a lot of stress in a match, as a player braces and stretches for every turn

Hamstrings
Give flexibility to the knee and hip and allow the leg to stretch. These are easily torn, so players need them to be long, supple, and tough

Calves
Raise the heel when running, walking, and jumping. The calf muscles are very prone to cramps

Achilles heel
Has to take all the strain of soccer's bursts of speed, stop and start motion, and sharp turns

THE PERFECT PLAYER?

Despite 150 years of top-flight soccer, the perfect player has yet to grace the field. Hypothetically, however, it would be rewarding to create the perfect identikit player by fusing together the best physical attributes of some of the game's greats.

PART	WHO AND WHY?
BRAIN	Johan Cruyff—dubbed "Pythagoras in Boots;" no player ever saw the angles and spaces of a game more quickly.
HANDS	Pat Jennings—huge, long-fingered, and reliable, the Northern Ireland keeper even scored a goal in 1967.
UPPER BODY	Christian Vieri—the powerful chest of the Italian striker gives him the strength to out-jump and out-muscle defenders.
THIGHS	Ronald Koeman—very muscular upper legs, so the Dutch player delivered shots and free-kicks with great force.
RIGHT FOOT	David Beckham—a foot that can caress and coax the ball as well as slam it is the perfect tool.
LEFT FOOT	Maradona—the Argentinian scored the "Goal of the Century" with his left foot and produced many other magical moments.

GARRINCHA

The brilliant Brazilian midfielder who won two World Cups in 1958 and 1962 was born with several disabilities. His spine was abnormally shaped, his right leg curved inward, and his left leg was bent and 2 in (6 cm) shorter than the right leg. Yet, from early on, he demonstrated complete mastery of the ball and developed a fierce shot.

MIND OF A PLAYER

Soccer players are often portrayed as stupid, possibly by people who are jealous of the wealth and adulation they receive. In fact, top players do not lack intelligence. Soccer demands a wide range of cognitive and creative skills including imagination, spatial awareness, and speed of thought. All great players need to demonstrate high levels of creativity and application.

MENTAL TRAINING

Many of the most important mental attributes of a top-class player are instinctive, such as spatial awareness and quick reactions. Various training methods are used to enhance these qualities. One of the most effective is a board on which are mounted several lights that switch on and off at random. The player's task is to touch them as soon as they come on. Performances are timed and compared to assess improvement.

PSYCHOLOGY

Natural abilities are only half the story. Big clubs routinely employ the services of sports psychologists to get their players in the optimum mental condition. Techniques regularly employed include visualization, relaxation, and positive thinking exercises. Players capable of calm and rational thought on the field are prized assets for any team.

CLEVER KEEPER

The Algerian-born French author and philosopher Albert Camus (1913–60) was a highly promising goalkeeper until his career was ruined by tuberculosis at the age of 17.

ALBERT CAMUS
The French novelist played for Racing Universitaire Algerois, which won four trophies during the 1930s.

SOCRATES

A player with a name like Socrates should have a powerful brain. The former Brazil captain holds two doctorates, in medicine and philosophy. Socrates was also blessed with a great ability to read the game and make astute passes.

YOU'RE BOOKED

Soccer attracts the literary mind. Alongside Albert Camus, these are our leading lights of literary soccer:

VLADIMIR NABOKOV (RUSSIA/US)

Before becaming a novelist, Nabokov learned goalkeeping skills at the Tenishev School in Saint Petersburg, Russia. He mused about the "blessing of the ball hugged to one's chest."

ORHAN PAMUK (TURKEY)

"Soccer is faster than words," Pamuk said in 2008, meaning that literature struggles to keep up with the visual medium of sport.

NAGUIB MAHFOUZ (EGYPT)

As a child, Mahfouz played street soccer in Cairo's Abbassiya section on land also used to stage Islamic festivals.

EDUARDO GALEANO (URUGUAY)

Galeano has said that he reserves for the page what he could not, as an "irredeemable klutz", manage on the field.

BARRY HINES (ENGLAND)

Hines brings a soccer player's awareness to his writing. He played for Barnsley, England, in the 1950s.

MAD, BAD, OR JUST PLAIN CRAZY?

For all the efforts of managers and psychologists to mold the personality of their players, once they walk onto the field, their emotions can sometimes take over. Soccer has had its fair share of unpredictable characters over the years, from George Best to Zinédine Zidane.

OFF THE RAILS

Some of the best players in the history of the game have gone spectacularly off the rails. George Best abandoned Manchester United for the bottle, Paul Gascoigne descended into a spiral of self-harm, and Diego Maradona shot a reporter with an air gun. Certainly madness and genius are closely related, although the pressure to perform and obsessive media attention players are subjected to are a contributing factor.

GEORGE BEST
He was the best player of his generation, but psychologically flawed.

I SPENT MOST OF MY MONEY ON BOOZE, BIRDS, AND FAST CARS; THE REST I JUST... SQUANDERED

FORMER MANCHESTER UNITED STAR, **GEORGE BEST**

LIMBIC LOSS

Certain players have found it hard to control their aggression during games. The career of French legend Zinédine Zidane ended in disgrace after the midfielder headbutted Italian defender Marco Materazzi during the 2006 World Cup final. The scientific explanation for these lapses lies with the limbic system—the area of the brain that controls emotions. Yoga and relaxation techniques can help keep this under control.

THE RED MIST

In 1995, Manchester United's Eric Cantona was sent off in an away game against Crystal Palace. As he was walking off the field, he suddenly launched himself into the crowd, flooring Palace fan Matthew Simmons with a spectacular kung fu kick. Mr. Simmons' claim that he had merely shouted "An early bath for you, Cantona" seems unlikely.

FASTEST SENDINGS OFF

3 SECONDS—Chippenham Town striker David Pratt was sent off for a wild tackle in an English minor league game in 2008.

10 SECONDS—Bologna's Giuseppe Lorenzo hit an opponent in a 1990 Italian league game.

13 SECONDS—Sheffield Wednesday keeper Kevin Pressman was sent off in 2000.

TOP 5: LUCKY CHARMS

Superstition plays a significant role in the mental make-up of many players. Here are five of the most famous characters through the years.

CARLITO ROCHA
The President of Rio Club Botofogo in the 1940s and '50s owned a dog called Biriba. One day the dog ran onto the field during a match and Botofogo scored in the ensuing disruption. From then on, Biriba was permanently on the bench and regularly used to disrupt games.

IVORY COAST
Before the 1984 African Cup of Nations, the Ivory Coast squad was joined at its hotel by over 150 healers and witch doctors. Each player was invited to "say his wishes privately into the ear of a living pigeon."

JOHN TERRY
Chelsea and England's captain has more pre-game superstitions than any other player in the English game. These range from listening to the same CD in his car to tying tape around his socks three times.

SERGIO GOYCOCHEA
The former Argentina goalkeeper believes, "If you have any natural human urges, you have to go (urinate) on the field." He relieved himself ahead of the 1990 World Cup semi-final against Italy and made two spectacular saves.

DON REVIE
The former Leeds United manager wore the same blue suit for every match, touched a bus stop before each home game, and sincerely believed that the club's stadium, Elland Road, had been cursed by Gypsies.

MARTIAL LAW
Manchester United's Eric Cantona took the law into his own hands at Selhurst Park (see left).

WARMING UP

Every game of soccer should start with a warm up. Soccer's twists and turns and its demand for fast accelerating movements will quickly pull or damage cold muscles and stiff joints and tendons. Similarly, the body's metabolism works best if it is gradually coaxed into life, by systematically raising the heart rate and body temperature of the player.

RUNNING LATE

In 2006, Spartak Moscow were stuck in traffic on the way to a match against Internazionale. With time running short, the team had to warm up by jogging through the streets to the nearest metro station and received their team talk in a packed commuter carriage.

THE ROUTINE

There are four stages to the typical warm up routine used by professional teams—jogging and gentle stretches, static stretches, dynamic stretches, and footwork and agility. The session is always followed by a warm down.

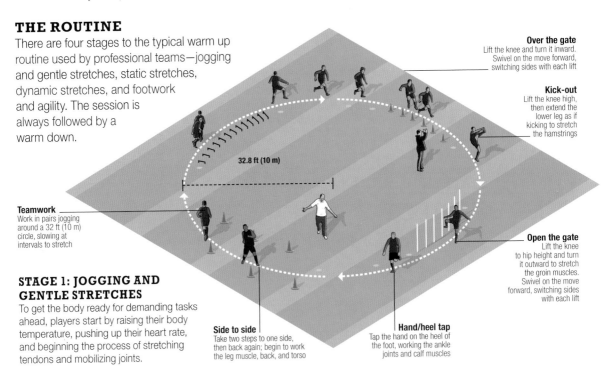

Over the gate
Lift the knee and turn it inward. Swivel on the move forward, switching sides with each lift

Kick-out
Lift the knee high, then extend the lower leg as if kicking to stretch the hamstrings

32.8 ft (10 m)

Teamwork
Work in pairs jogging around a 32 ft (10 m) circle, slowing at intervals to stretch

Open the gate
Lift the knee to hip height and turn it outward to stretch the groin muscles. Swivel on the move forward, switching sides with each lift

STAGE 1: JOGGING AND GENTLE STRETCHES

To get the body ready for demanding tasks ahead, players start by raising their body temperature, pushing up their heart rate, and beginning the process of stretching tendons and mobilizing joints.

Side to side
Take two steps to one side, then back again; begin to work the leg muscle, back, and torso

Hand/heel tap
Tap the hand on the heel of the foot, working the ankle joints and calf muscles

STAGE 2: STATIC STRETCHES

The body is warm, but the big muscle groups are not yet ready for a full work out. The key muscles in the leg need extra work. The quadriceps in the front of the thigh and the hamstrings in the back of the leg need stretching before running, while groins, calves, and ankles are prone to damage if used when cold.

SPIRITUAL SOCCER

Yoga, the ancient Indian art of stretching, breathing, and meditation has been used by several famous players to help them recover from injury and to prolong their careers. Practitioners have included Manchester United winger Ryan Giggs and England goalkeeper David James.

Both legs
Repeat the stretch to work both legs

Keep straight
The back should be straight

Tight muscles
Feel the muscles of the front leg tighten

Knee bend
Knee should not be bent beyond the ankle

QUAD STRETCH
Hold the heel against the buttock for at least 30 seconds. Use a wall to aid balance.

CALF STRETCH
Stand with the back foot flat on the floor and transfer weight to the front foot. Hold for about 10 seconds.

HAMSTRING STRETCH
Extend one leg in front with the foot flexed. Bend the other knee and lean forward slightly.

GROIN STRETCH
Good for inner thigh and groin muscles—should be held for 10–20 seconds.

STAGE 3: DYNAMIC STRETCHES

Players pick up the pace and combine aerobic work (which raises the activity rate of the heart and lungs) with full muscle stretches. Players work in pairs, moving through a series of routines that push their heart rates upward. Each player uses his partner for balance during the moves. The intention is also to raise the body's temperature by approximately 2°F (1°C).

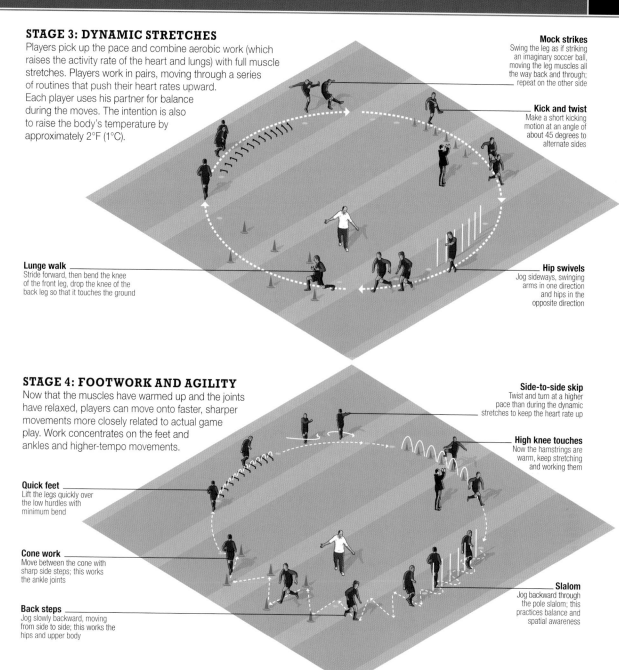

Mock strikes
Swing the leg as if striking an imaginary soccer ball, moving the leg muscles all the way back and through; repeat on the other side

Kick and twist
Make a short kicking motion at an angle of about 45 degrees to alternate sides

Hip swivels
Jog sideways, swinging arms in one direction and hips in the opposite direction

Lunge walk
Stride forward, then bend the knee of the front leg, drop the knee of the back leg so that it touches the ground

STAGE 4: FOOTWORK AND AGILITY

Now that the muscles have warmed up and the joints have relaxed, players can move onto faster, sharper movements more closely related to actual game play. Work concentrates on the feet and ankles and higher-tempo movements.

Quick feet
Lift the legs quickly over the low hurdles with minimum bend

Cone work
Move between the cone with sharp side steps; this works the ankle joints

Back steps
Jog slowly backward, moving from side to side; this works the hips and upper body

Side-to-side skip
Twist and turn at a higher pace than during the dynamic stretches to keep the heart rate up

High knee touches
Now the hamstrings are warm, keep stretching and working them

Slalom
Jog backward through the pole slalom; this practices balance and spatial awareness

THE WARM DOWN

At the end of training, players need to lower their heart rate and body temperature steadily, and allow the body to disperse the build-up of lactic acid that forms in well-worked muscles. Soreness and stiffness will last for longer, otherwise. Players repeat many of the gentle stretches but at a steadily lower pace. They then repeat long static and dynamic stretching of all the key muscle groups.

WARM-DOWN ROUTINE		
STAGE ONE GENTLE MOVEMENTS	STAGE TWO STATIC STRETCHES	STAGE THREE DYNAMIC STRETCHES
OVER THE GATE	QUADS	MOCK STRIKES
OPEN THE GATE	HAMSTRINGS	KICK AND TWIST
HAND TAP	CALVES	HIP SWIVELS
KICK-OUT	GROIN	LUNGE WALK
SIDE STEP		

TRAINING

Top teams spend a great deal of time practicing with the ball. Some of this is devoted to rehearsing set pieces (see pp.64–65), but a major part of the average training session is given over to honing basic ball skills, so that they become instinctive.

BALLWORK

A good training session encompasses a variety of skills, exercises all the key muscle groups, and encourages teamwork. The drills below represent only some of the infinite choices available to coaches.

POST WARM-UP

Ballwork drills should be practiced after the players have warmed up and stretched their muscles. Depending on the desired intensity, there should be one ball for every two or three players and these should remain in play throughout the session.

KEY

- ● Player
- — Player motion
- ○ Ball
- - - - Ball motion
- ▲ Cone

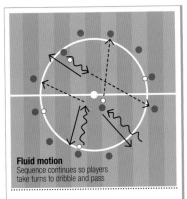

Fluid motion
Sequence continues so players take turns to dribble and pass

DRILL ONE: GIVE AND GO
Each player lines up on the edge of a circle. Those with a ball dribble into the center, pass to a teammate without the ball, and run back.

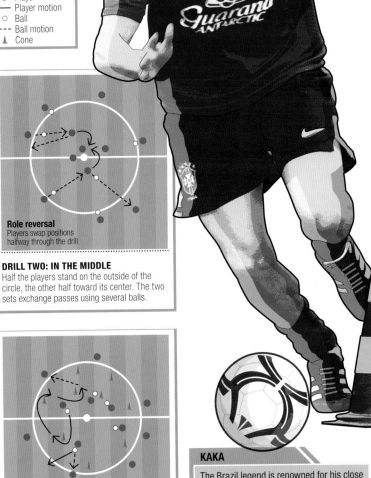

Role reversal
Players swap positions halfway through the drill

DRILL TWO: IN THE MIDDLE
Half the players stand on the outside of the circle, the other half toward its center. The two sets exchange passes using several balls.

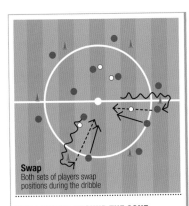

Swap
Both sets of players swap positions during the dribble

DRILL THREE: AROUND THE CONE
Players inside the circle dribble around a cone on the edge, and pass to players who have run to the first player's original starting point.

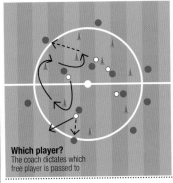

Which player?
The coach dictates which free player is passed to

DRILL FOUR: MORE CONE WORK
Players in the center dribble around cones. When instructed, they pass to a free player on the outside of the circle and swap positions.

KAKA

The Brazil legend is renowned for his close control and ball skills, a talent honed on the training field through his career from junior level. His ability is such that in 2009 British club Manchester City were reportedly willing to pay $157 million (£108 million) to secure his services.

WITHOUT THE BALL

There are two aspects to training without the ball. The first consists of running and building stamina; players recovering from injuries also do strength work in the gym. The second concerns how players look after themselves away from the training ground: diet, rest, and self-discipline are all important (see box below).

BUILDING STAMINA

If a player runs out of energy toward the end of a match, the team is likely to suffer. Soccer players need considerable stamina, and their training should help them to develop it. A typical stamina-building session might consist of three 985-yd (900-m) runs followed by three of 660 yd (600 m) and three of 330 yd (300 m) with a two- to three-minute break between each run.

SPRINT TRAINING

During matches, players sprint in quick bursts and spend the rest of the time jogging or walking. Sprint training is designed to reflect this. Players run flat out for five to ten seconds, then walk back to the start and repeat the procedure. One of the advantages of this kind of training is that it gets the body used to working anaerobically. This means that it is temporarily producing energy without oxygen, which is what happens when a player suddenly has to run flat-out at the end of 90 exhausting minutes. Anaerobic exercise is hard on the body, so it should only be practiced occasionally, perhaps once every two weeks.

COACHING
Top coaches such as Carlos Quieroz help to motivate players during training sessions.

PLYOMETRICS

Players need to run quickly over short distances. Plyometric training is designed to develop the explosive muscle power needed for sudden bursts of acceleration, such as a forward chasing a ball. A good example of this kind of exercise is players jumping over a series of hurdles set narrowly apart.

WE TRAIN ALL WEEK WITH A BALL THAT IS ABOUT...
TWICE THE SIZE!

JUVENTUS DEFENDER **NICOLA LEGROTTAGLIE**
COMPARES THE SIZE OF THE TEAM'S TRAINING BALL TO THE MATCH BALL

FOODS TO EAT, DRINK, AND AVOID

If the wrong kind of fuel is put into a car, it will underperform. The same is true of players with regard to their diets. Players should eat and drink certain types of food to perform at their best on match days.

EAT

Players should consume plenty of carbohydrates (such as potatoes and pasta), as these provide the body with energy; easily digestible proteins such as fish and chicken; and vegetables rich in iron, such as broccoli.

• **AFTER TRAINING**—The body stores energy in the form of a substance called glycogen. Players need to replenish their glycogen levels within two to five hours of exercising. The best way to do this is to eat plenty of carbohydrates.

• **THREE DAYS BEFORE A MATCH**—Players should start "carbohydrate-loading." This means eating meals that are 75 percent complex carbohydrates.

• **MATCH DAY**—An easily digestible meal high in carbohydrates and low in protein and fat should be eaten three to four hours before kick-off. This will optimize the energy available to the player during the game.

DRINK

Soccer players should drink lots of water, particularly before and after training sessions. Players can lose seven pints (four liters) or more of water during a match and will need to rehydrate themselves as quickly as possible. In addition to water, isotonic drinks containing vital nutrients and sugars are particularly easy for the body to absorb. There are several commercial varieties, but a simple version consists of fruit juice and water in equal measures.

AVOID

Players should avoid all caffeine (tea and coffee), alcohol, and junk foods (such as potato chips and deep-fried foodstuffs). Consumption of dairy products and fatty and high-sugar foods should also be limited.

CONTROLLING THE BALL

Possession is the key to controlling a game, and a team can only be said to be in possession when one of its players has the ball under his control. Achieving this is one of the fundamental skills of soccer. No matter how perfectly a pass is delivered, it will be wasted if the receiver fails to control the ball effectively.

FLEXIBILITY AND FIRST TOUCH

Controlling the ball is easiest when it is passed gently to the feet, but players must be prepared for it to reach them at any height, from any angle, and at any speed. The quality of a player's first touch is crucial. The best players are able to put the ball exactly where they want it with the same touch they use to bring it under control, giving them time and space to consider their next move.

SYLVAIN WILTORD

The French international demonstrates the athleticism involved in certain ball control maneuvers. Wiltord has effectively caught the ball at shoulder height with the toe of his boot. Players must have both excellent coordination and suppleness to accomplish this.

HE DOMINATES THE BALL AND HE PLAYS AS IF HE HAS SILK GLOVES... IN EACH BOOT

REAL MADRID LEGEND **ALFREDO DI STEFANO**, ON ZINÉDINE ZIDANE, 2006

USING THE FEET

As with most skills, a player will find it easiest to control the ball with his feet if he gets into position to receive the ball early. The simplest way to practice the art is to kick a ball against a wall at varying heights, strengths, and angles and try to control the rebound. As the player's skills improve, he should ask a friend to rebound the ball for him so that he has to make quick adjustments to cope with the unknown deliveries. Basic foot-trapping techniques involve the sole and inside of the foot. With experience players can move on to the top, outside, and side volley trap.

FOOT TENNIS

One of the best ways to learn ball control is to use a tennis ball. Many of the greatest players in history grew up too poor to afford an actual soccer ball, but honed their skills in this way. If players can master a small bouncy object such as a tennis ball, a regular soccer ball will seem as big as a pumpkin.

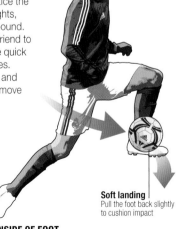

Soft landing
Pull the foot back slightly to cushion impact

INSIDE OF FOOT
This is the easiest way to control the ball. Ideally, the ball will land about a stride ahead of the receiver rather than directly at his feet.

Not too relaxed
Relaxing the leg too much at the moment of impact could result in a jarred knee

OUTSIDE OF FOOT
If the close proximity of opponents precludes using the inside of the favored foot, the player should use the outside of the other foot.

USING THE BODY

If the ball arrives at a player too high for him to control it with his feet, he has three main options: to use his thigh, chest, or head. An excellent way to practice these skills is via a game of "head tennis." Played over a volleyball net, players must keep the ball from touching the ground, and return it over the net by using their head, chest, thigh, and feet. The more frequently a player plays this enjoyable game, the better his skills will become.

SHANKLY'S SWEAT BOX

Liverpool's legendary manager Bill Shankly used an innovative but exhausting device to improve his players' ball control and stamina. Known as the "sweat box," it consisted of an area bounded by four numbered boards, which players shot against, in between controlling the rebounds, corresponding to the number shouted out by the trainer.

Relax
Relax the neck muscles to cushion the ball

Leap
Jump up to anticipate the ball

Lean back
Lean back to take away the ball's momentum

Angle of receipt
The thigh should be about 45 degrees to the ground when the ball arrives

CONTROL WITH THIGH
If a player can "catch" the ball with the upper part of his thigh he can bring it under control very effectively.

CONTROL WITH CHEST
Using the chest to control the ball is easier than it sounds. The receiver must be careful to avoid the ball hitting him too low and winding him.

CONTROL WITH HEAD
This technnique is difficult because the skull is hard, making a degree of bounce inevitable, but sometimes a player will have no alternative.

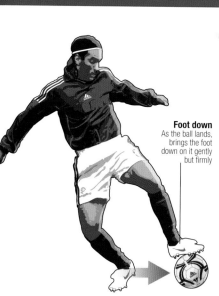

Foot down
As the ball lands, brings the foot down on it gently but firmly

Cushion impact
Bend the knee and cushion the ball on the foot

Pay attention
Pay more attention than usual to the flight of the ball

And relax
Relax the foot as the ball lands on it

SOLE OF FOOT
A ball dropping near the feet of the receiver is best controlled by pinning it to the ground with the underside of the foot.

SIDE VOLLEY TRAP
This is used when the ball arrives too high to trap but too low to chest down. The technique requires flexibility to execute well.

TOP-OF-FOOT CUSHION
An alternative to the trap for controlling a dropping ball, this is difficult to perform correctly, as the player is using the narrowest part of the foot.

PASSING

Passing is the lifeblood of any team and a vital skill for all players to learn, including goalkeepers. There are several reasons why a player might chose to pass—to help his team keep possession, to clear the ball from a danger area, to try to set up a scoring opportunity—but only one "when." The ball should be passed whenever there is a teammate in a better position than the player in possession.

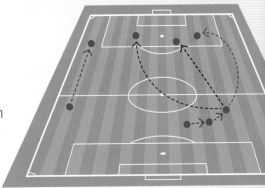

TYPES OF PASS

Players pass in order to develop attacks, or to work the ball away from opponents. These passes can be along the ground or in the air, over short distances or long range. Short passes are the easiest to execute; long-range airborne passes the most difficult. Each type of pass has its advantages and disadvantages.

PASSING OPTIONS
Short passes are sometimes made in tight situations near to the opponent's goal, or laterally between defenders prior to a searching forward pass. Inswinging, outswinging, and driven passes are made over long distances, usually from the player's own half of the field.

KEY	
---	Inswinging pass
---	Outswinging pass
---	Driven pass
---	Short pass
---	Channel pass
●	Player

SHORT PASS

The short pass is the most accurate kind for two reasons: the ball is struck with the side of the foot and any slight miscue is likely to be masked by the small distance the ball has to travel.

WHERE TO STRIKE THE BALL

Standing leg
Place the leg alongside the ball with the toes pointing in direction of travel

Side foot
Strike the ball with the side of the foot for maximum control

Eyes ahead
Watch the ball closely as it heads to its target

1 The player approaches the ball at a 30-degree angle, giving himself room to swing his passing leg.

2 He strikes the ball with the side of his foot and keeps the ball down. The ankle stays firm.

3 The length of follow-through reflects the weight the player wants to give the pass.

MAKING A LONG PASS

Long passes or crosses can be very effective, largely because it is normal for defenders to guard their opponents less thoroughly the further away they are from the action. Accuracy is crucial as any error will be magnified.

WHERE TO STRIKE THE BALL

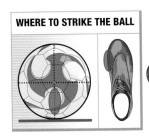

Instep
Strike the ball with the instep at its central point to keep it low

Support
Standing leg should be grounded solidly before the strike

Sweep
Push the foot in the direction of the ball after impact

1 The player should fix his eyes on the ball and approach it at an angle of about 30 degrees.

2 To keep the pass low, he makes sure the knee of his striking leg is over the ball at impact.

3 The player's follow-through is more pronounced than for a short pass.

USING THE CHANNELS

Sometimes a player in possession will have no obvious teammate to pass to. In such cases, he should either run with the ball or pass it into a "safe" channel (usually directly ahead of him—see left) which gives a teammate a realistic chance of winning the race with the defender to receive it.

THE SCIENCE OF SPIN

You don't have to be a physics expert to bend a ball —just a good quality player—but the science behind the ball's movements in the air is fascinating.

Once struck, the ball naturally seeks the path of least resistance, so it will tend to swerve in the direction of the spin—to the right if the ball is spinning clockwise and the left if it is spinning counterclockwise.

SIDEWAYS SPIN

If a ball is spinning through the air sideways, one side of it will be moving in the direction of its flight while the other is moving counter to it. The forward-spinning side develops a greater force than the backward-spinning one. This is called the Magnus force.

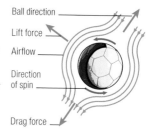

Ball direction

Lift force

Airflow

Direction of spin

Drag force

TOP- AND BACKSPIN

If a ball is rotating forward or backward, the same principle applies but it has different effects. A ball given topspin will move downward faster than it otherwise would, while the reverse is true of a ball given backspin.

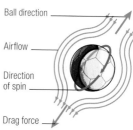

Ball direction

Airflow

Direction of spin

Drag force

ADDING CURVE TO A LONG PASS OR CROSS

Putting curve onto the ball can be useful during attacking moves because the path of a curving ball is much harder to anticipate, and therefore defend, than one that flies straight.

OUTSWINGING PASS OR CROSS
To get the ball to swing left to right, a right-footed player strikes the left side of the ball with the outside of the foot.

INSWINGING PASS OR CROSS
To get the ball to swing right to left, a right-footed player strikes the ball on its right side with his instep.

Strength
Keep the striking foot strong through impact

Ball edge
Strike the right-hand side of the ball

JUAN **RIQUELME**

The Argentinian attacking midfielder is no great athlete but he has the intelligence to let the ball do the work for him. During his career at Barcelona, Villareal, and Boca Juniors, he has proved one of the shrewdest and most incisive passers in world soccer.

WHERE TO STRIKE THE BALL

WHERE TO STRIKE THE BALL

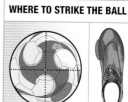

RUNNING WITH THE BALL

Running with the ball under control is known as dribbling. In its basic form the skill involves a player kicking the ball ahead of him, running to catch up with it, kicking it forward again, and so on. In practice, however, players rarely have clear spaces ahead of them for long as opposing defenders arrive to try to check their runs. They therefore need to keep the ball close to their feet and develop a repertoire of skills to avoid would-be tacklers.

BEATING OPPONENTS

Dribblers employ a variety of techniques to get past opponents without checking their runs. One of the most important is the shoulder drop, in which the player lowers the level of one shoulder to fool the defender into thinking he is heading in that direction. Another is having the ability to anticipate tackles and the dexterity to jump over them.

HE... FLOATED OVER THE GROUND LIKE A COCKER SPANIEL CHASING A PIECE OF PAPER...
IN THE WIND

MANCHESTER UNITED MANAGER **SIR ALEX FERGUSON** DESCRIBING THE FIRST TIME HE SAW RYAN GIGGS PLAY

SIR STANLEY **MATTHEWS**

Sir Stanley Matthews (1915–2000) was one of the greatest wingers in history. Famous for his body swerve, the England legend was known as the "Wizard of the Dribble." He continued to play top-class soccer until the age of 50.

HOW TO DRIBBLE

The best dribblers give the impression that the ball is tied to their boots. These players also have the ability to alternate between both feet equally well (using the inside and outside of the feet). A dribble is executed as follows.

Softly softly
Don't kick the ball too hard with either foot

1 Using his left foot, the player gently kicks the ball between 12–19 in (30 and 50 cm) ahead of himself and to the right.

Close range
Keep the ball close by

2 He keeps his eyes on the ball while running forward, occasionally looking up to assess the situation ahead of him.

Look down and up
Keep eyes alternately on the ball and the space ahead

Right foot
Push the ball forward with the right foot

3 When he reaches the ball, he continues his dribble, using his right foot. He repeats this sequence, using left foot then right.

STOP-TURNS WHILE RUNNING

A player dribbling with the ball will often want to change direction, either to develop a different angle of attack, run into space, or to evade the challenge of an incoming defender. There are several means of changing direction with the ball. Among the most popular are the inside and outside hooks and the Puskás turn, also known as the drag back.

THE NUTMEG

The nutmeg is a maneuver in which an attacking player passes the ball through an opponent's legs, weighting it so he can continue his dribble on the other side. Defenders dislike being nutmegged, but if they keep their legs too close together to prevent it, they invite the attacker to kick the ball past them and get around them to the side.

INSIDE HOOK

This hook technique is the easiest of the two hooks. It is used to move inside (to the left for a right-footer) when an opponent is on the player's outside.

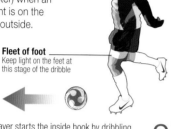

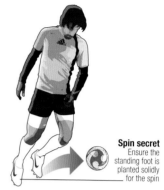

Fleet of foot
Keep light on the feet at this stage of the dribble

Bend it
Twist the foot around the outside of the ball

Spin secret
Ensure the standing foot is planted solidly for the spin

1 The player starts the inside hook by dribbling forward with the ball under close control, attentive to the presence of defenders.

2 The player places one foot slightly ahead of the ball and uses the instep to push the ball back in the direction he wishes to turn.

3 He spins to the left, pushes off his back foot, using his front foot to continue the dribble away from the opponent.

OUTSIDE HOOK

This hooking skill is more demanding than the inside hook because it requires the player to use the outside of his right foot to move 180 degrees to the right (for a right-footer).

Balance
Use the arms to keep steady

Drive
Use the arms to power the run

Turn
Use the outside of the foot

Kick it
Kick the ball to the front

1 As with the inside hook turn, the player starts the maneuver by dribbling forward, feeding the ball between each foot alternately.

2 Using the outside of the foot, the player hooks the ball back in the direction he wishes to go.

3 He turns 180 degrees to the right then pushes off with his back foot and accelerates away using his front foot to continue the dribble.

PUSKÁS TURN

Named after the great Hungarian striker Ferenc Puskás, this trick involves a quarter turn that allows the player in possession to move rapidly at right angles to the direction in which he was originally facing.

Fake kick
Make as if to kick the ball forward

Stop it
Abbreviate the kick and rest the studs on the ball

Drag
Pull the ball back with the studs, then move into space

1 Starting with the ball in line with the center of his body, the player swings one foot as if to kick the ball forward.

2 However, rather than kicking it forward, he moves his foot slightly over the ball and brings his studs into contact with the top of it.

3 Putting his weight on the other foot, the player drags the ball back and then knocks it sideways with the outside of his boot.

STEPOVERS

The stepover, also known as the scissors maneuver, is one of the most visually striking moves in the game. It is used to fool an opponent into thinking the player in possession is about to pass sideways, whereas in fact he just continues his run. Stepovers used to be considered an exotic skill but in recent years, they have become almost commonplace.

TYPES OF STEPOVER

The classic stepover involves the player in possession making to move the ball one way with the outside of one foot, but actually passing the foot over and around the ball (from inside to outside) without touching it before picking it up with the other foot and moving in the opposite direction. There are also two more developed styles of stepover; the double stepover (below) and the Rivelino (opposite).

CRISTIANO **RONALDO**

The Portuguese winger Cristiano Ronaldo is currently the undisputed master of the stepover. Criticized for excessive showmanship early in his career, he is now now held in high regard. In 2008 he netted 42 goals in all competitions, winning the UEFA Golden Shoe Award for the top scorer in a European league.

THE PEDALADA...IS A TRICK I LIKE TO DO...
WITH SPEED

ROBINHO, BRAZIL ATTACKING MIDFIELDER, 2008

DOUBLE STEPOVER

In the double stepover, the player performs the trick twice in quick succession, once with each foot. This is more difficult to master, technically.

THE PEDALADA

In South America, the continent which gave birth to the stepover, it is known as the "pedalada," and was a common skill used by Brazilian legend Pelé.

The eyes
Look straight ahead

Dribble
Dribble forward at a slow pace

1 The player dribbles the ball forward and prepares to set his standing leg.

Drop it
Drop the left shoulder

Swivel
Lift and rotate the right foot through 360 degrees

2 He moves the right foot around and over the ball in a clockwise direction.

3 This brings the player back to the starting point, but further forward than before.

Look
Keep the eyes on the ball

Rotate
Lift the left foot in a circle over the ball

Rolling on
Ball keeps moving forward

4 He performs a second stepover, this time with the left foot and in a counterclockwise direction.

THE RIVELINO

In this variation of the stepover, named after the Brazilian winger, the legs move around the ball in the opposite direction, that is from outside to inside. The Rivelino requires very precise balance.

Eyes peeled
Keep eyes fully focused on the ball to avoid contact with either foot

Shoulder
Raise the right shoulder and move to the left

Hip
Move the left hip forward

Right leg
Place weight on the right side before springing off

Slow
Dribble slowly at first

Foot down
Put the left foot down

1 The player dribbles the ball slowly and precisely toward the defender. He plants his front foot and brings the trailing leg toward the ball.

2 Instead of making contact with the ball, the player brings the trailing leg up and over the ball, placing it on the other side.

3 The player swivels 180 degrees, places his weight on his right foot, then plays the ball with his left.

11 The average number of Cristiano Ronaldo stepovers performed per game during the 2007–08 season

25 The typical amount of space created, in inches (63 cm), by an effective stepover move

6 Number of stepovers Brazil winger Denílson made before evading France midfielder Emmanuel Petit during the 1998 World Cup

3 Number of times Pelé, inventor of the stepover, has won the World Cup

9 Shirt number worn by Brazil's stepover maestro Ronaldo

STEP IT UP

In 2007 Roma's Alessandro Mancini performed a total of six stepovers in rapid succession en route to scoring a goal in a Champions League match against Olympique Lyonnais.

Push off
Spring off from the left side to travel quickly to the right

ROBINHO
Robinho was reportedly once booked for performing too many stepovers while playing for Brazilian club Santos. The referee yellow-carded him for showing disrespect to an opponent.

5 The player is again back to the starting position, but further forward than before.

6 The player knocks the ball forward with his right foot and continues his dribble.

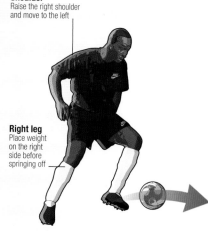

SPINS AND TURNS

Some of the most spectacular moves in soccer involve players spinning or turning in unexpected ways. The skills below are much more technically demanding than the regular turns covered in the dribbling section (see pp.122–23) and often only the world's best known and most skilful players use them successfully in a match situation.

FINDING SPACE

Complex turns require large amounts of practice, but they aren't executed simply to show off (at least not during a match). Making a successful turn is a great way to lose a marker or wrong-foot an opponent, both of which buy the player precious time to run into space or make a considered pass to a teammate. Two of the best maneuvers for achieving this are the Zidane spin and the Cruyff turn.

Balance
Use outstretched arms for balance during the spin and to repel the advances of opponents

JOHAN CRUYFF
The Dutch maestro perfected a move known as the "Cruyff turn" (see right).

THE ZIDANE SPIN

The Zidane spin or turn is a form of pirouette in which a player spins through 360 degrees while keeping the ball under close control. It is almost as difficult to describe as it is to do, but the trick can be broken down into four stages. Zinédine Zidane has performed this technique on many occasions at the highest level. When executed well, it buys the player in possession much-needed time in crowded midfield situations.

Position play
Stop the ball with the favored foot to start the spin

ZINÉDINE ZIDANE
The French international came to worldwide prominence at Juventus in Italy and then Real Madrid in Spain. His personal accolades include being a World Cup winner in 1998, and a three-time FIFA World Player of the Year.

Fleet of foot
Players need to be agile when performing this maneuver

1 The player dribbles forward with the ball as normal, then stops and puts his stronger foot on top of it.

THE CRUYFF TURN

Many famous soccer tricks are named after the players who introduced or perfected them. This silky maneuver, a complex drag back that always leaves defenders behind, is named after the great Ajax and Netherlands forward Johan Cruyff, who first performed it in 1974. When executing the maneuver, the player feigns execution of a long pass or cross but instead spins 180 degrees and continues the dribble.

Fake it Pass the foot over the ball rather than striking it

Solid base Plant the standing foot solidly as this forms a strong base for the move

Drag back Push the ball gently behind you with the right foot

Turn Turn the body 90 degrees

Weight shift Plant the weight on the right side and use this as a springboard

1 The player plants one foot by the ball and makes as if to shoot or hit a long pass with the other leg.

2 He brings the leg toward the ball, but instead of kicking the ball, passes the foot over it.

3 Using the inside of the same foot, he drags the ball back behind him and turns his body.

4 He completes the turn through 180 degrees and runs off with the ball.

THE HALF-PREKI

Predrag Radosavljev began his career with Red Star Belgrade and ended it playing Major League Soccer in the US, where he shortened his name to Preki. In this maneuver, named after him, a dribbling player puts space between himself and an approaching defender by rolling the ball across the front of his body with the sole of his dominant foot. When he lifts his foot to begin the move, there is a good chance that the defender will be fooled into thinking he is going to pass. Another version of the trick starts with a half-Preki and ends with a stepover (see pp.124–25).

[CRUYFF] IS THE BEST PLAYER I HAVE SEEN IN MY... LIFETIME

MICHEL PLATINI, FORMER FRANCE MIDFIELDER

180 degrees Spin counter-clockwise

Foot change Place the weaker foot on the ball after spinning

Turn Complete the spin

Change feet Swap feet again after spinning

Shielding Protect the ball from defenders

Continue Keep dribbling in the same direction as you started the spin

2 He rolls the ball backward, spins 180 degrees around it, then holds it with the weaker foot.

3 He rolls the ball back gently with his weaker foot and turns 180 degrees in the same direction.

4 After completing the full spin, he gets the ball again with the stronger foot.

5 Finally, the player continues his run, leaving the opposition defenders perplexed.

INDIVIDUAL SKILLS

FAKES

Deception is a vital ingredient in top-class soccer. Many of the most effective moves rely on players fooling their opponents into thinking they are going to do one thing and actually doing another. When this works it cons members of the other team into moving out of position and buys crucial time for the team in possession.

TYPES OF FAKE

"Selling" someone a dummy—acting as if to kick the ball but in fact leaving it to run on, usually to a teammate—is one of the most common forms of fakes in soccer. But there are also several others, including shuffles, fake kicks, and "flip-flaps." All have the effect of confusing and wrong-footing the opponent.

PELÉ'S DUMMY

Most dummies involve leaving the ball to run on to another player. Pelé's legendary dummy against Uruguay during the 1970 World Cup was different—he left the ball to run on so he could gather it up himself, and he narrowly missed scoring.

MY GAME IS BASED ON IMPROVISATION... IT IS INSTINCT THAT GIVES THE ORDERS

RONALDINHO,
BRAZILIAN INTERNATIONAL

RONALDINHO

Few players have had as many tricks at their disposal as the Brazilian striker Ronaldinho. Born in Puerto Alegre in 1980, he is a master of deception, using his eyes and a bewildering range of tricks, flicks, and dummies to confuse defenders. "Little Ronaldo," as his name means in Portuguese, is one of the few players who uses freestyle techniques in top-flight matches.

THE BEARDSLEY SHUFFLE

The most famous shuffle in sports, a high-speed shimmy that mesmerized opponents, belonged to Muhammad Ali. The soccer equivalent, essentially an abbreviated stepover (see pp.124–25), was perfected by Peter Beardsley.

PETER BEARDSLEY

One of the most intelligent players of the modern era, Beardsley was a master of close control. Starting his career at Newcastle, he shined for Liverpool, Everton, and England during the late 1980s and '90s.

Balance
Use the arm for balance

Left leg
Plant the left leg on the ground as a brace to start the maneuver

1 Jogging slowly with the ball under close control, the player brings his right leg toward the ball as if feigning to pass it or change direction.

THE FAKE KICK

A player mimes a shot or pass, causing the defenders to flinch, but actually passes his foot over or just to the side of the ball. This affords time and space to turn or deliver a pass.

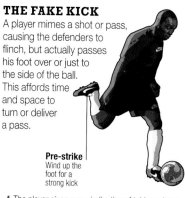

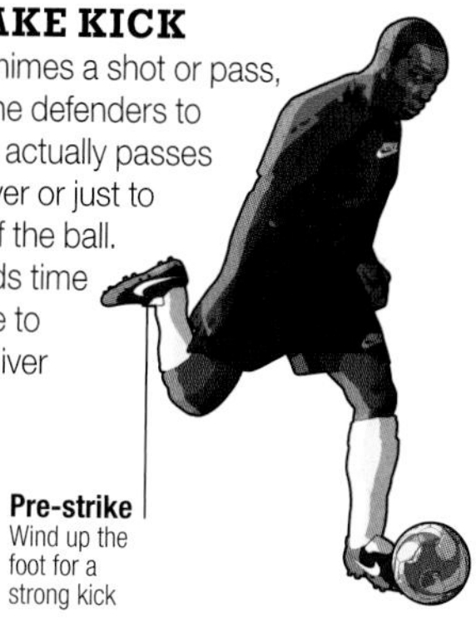
Pre-strike
Wind up the foot for a strong kick

1 The player gives every indication of taking a long-range shot at goal or making a long pass. He draws back his leg in preparation for a strike.

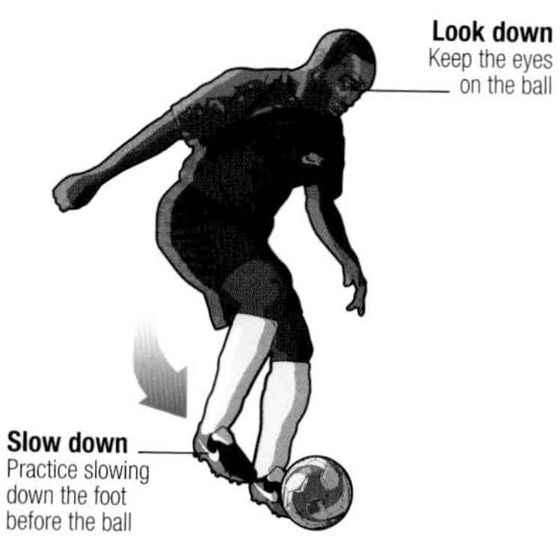
Look down
Keep the eyes on the ball
Slow down
Practice slowing down the foot before the ball

2 He swings his foot down hard, but as it approaches the ball, he slows it down rapidly and passes the foot over the ball.

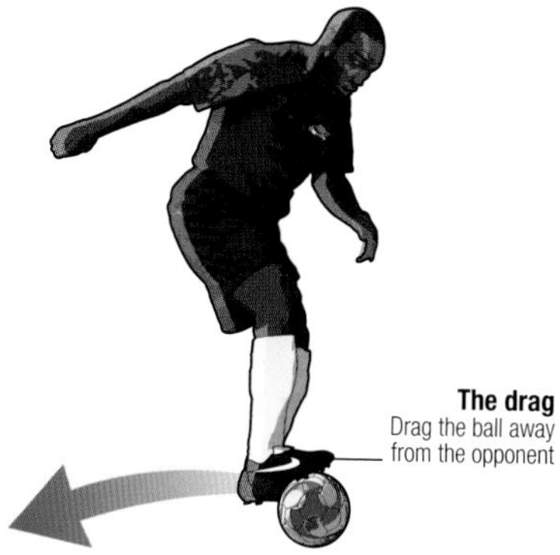
The drag
Drag the ball away from the opponent

3 While his opponent turns away in anticipation of a shot, he places his foot lightly on top of the ball and drags it back quickly.

THE ELASTICO OR FLIP-FLAP

The Brazil striker Ronaldinho is associated particularly with the "elastico" or "flip-flap," which was invented by his fellow countryman Rivelino in the 1970s. The elastico involves the player moving his foot very quickly from right to left while dribbling, keeping the ball in such close proximity that it appears connected to the foot by elastic.

WHY BRAZIL?

Brazilian players are famous for their eye-catching tricks on the field. Why they are so famous is down to their unique soccer philosophy. As well as being tactically astute, Brazilian players like to produce the unexpected, doing simple things with flair and playing for the sheer fun and joy of the game.

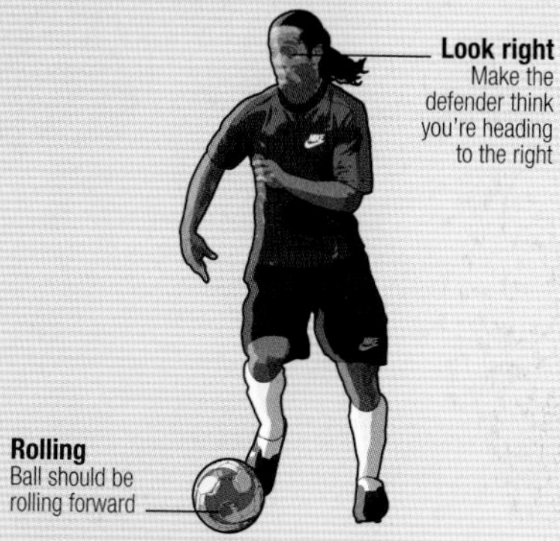
Look right
Make the defender think you're heading to the right
Rolling
Ball should be rolling forward

1 The player prepares for the elastico by looking in the direction he wants the approaching defender to think he is about to play the ball.

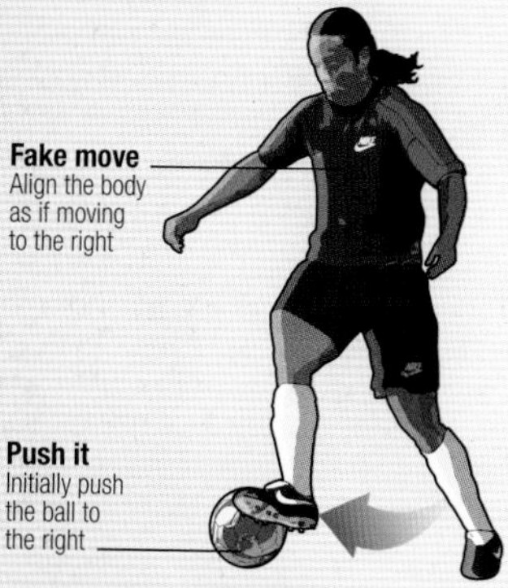
Fake move
Align the body as if moving to the right
Push it
Initially push the ball to the right

2 He pushes the ball with the outside of his right foot as though he is about to dribble to the right.

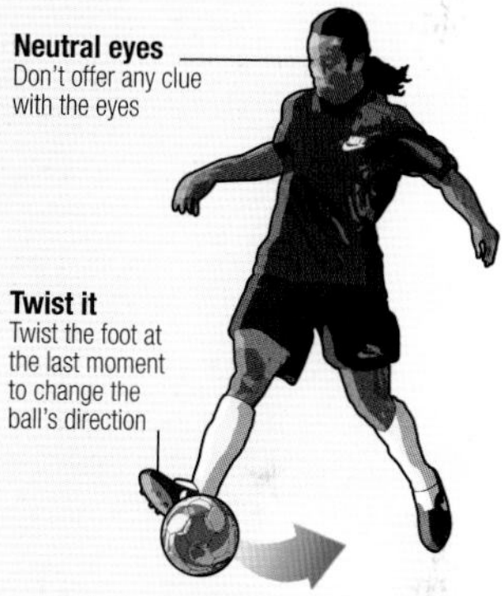
Neutral eyes
Don't offer any clue with the eyes
Twist it
Twist the foot at the last moment to change the ball's direction

3 At the last moment, he gathers the ball in with the instep of the same foot and pulls it back in the other direction, confusing the defender.

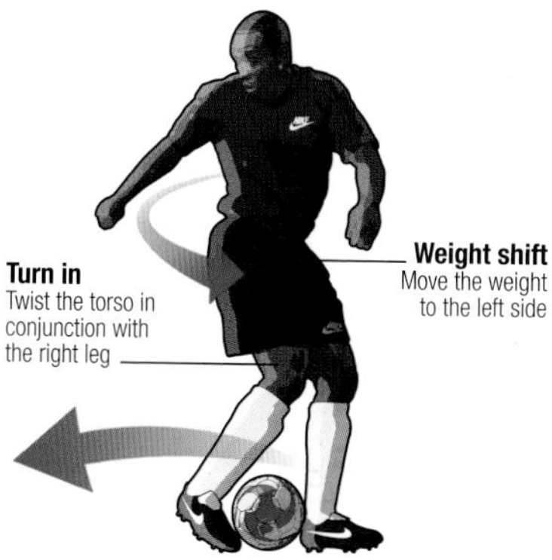
Turn in
Twist the torso in conjunction with the right leg
Weight shift
Move the weight to the left side

2 The player brings his right foot very close to the ball so the defender is convinced he is changing direction.

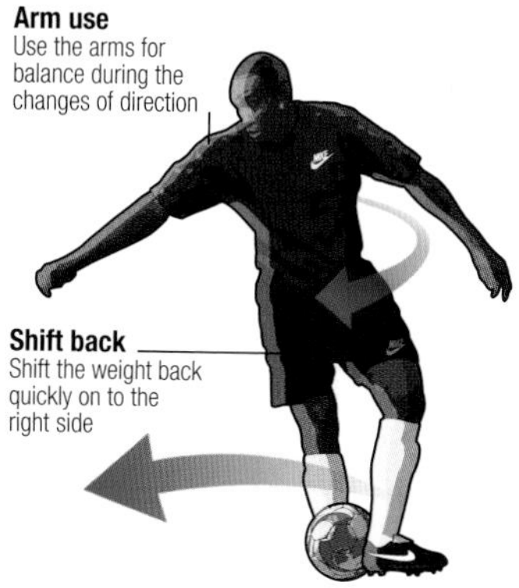
Arm use
Use the arms for balance during the changes of direction
Shift back
Shift the weight back quickly on to the right side

3 In one rapid, fluid movement, he shifts his balance back to the right side, leaving the defender confused as to his chosen path.

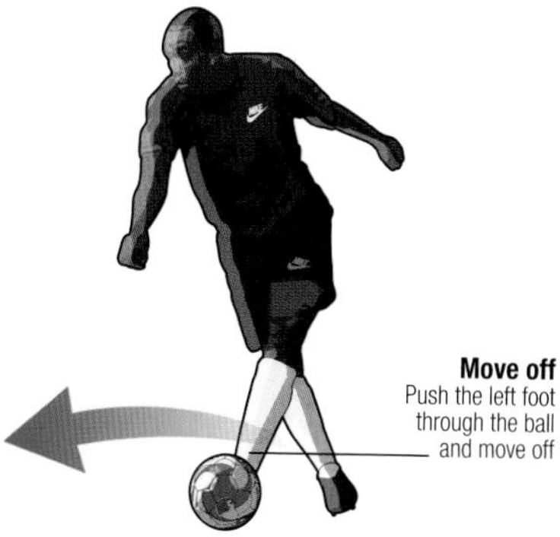
Move off
Push the left foot through the ball and move off

4 The player moves away quickly with the ball in the direction he was traveling in step 1. He will gain precious space as a result.

SHOOTING

Soccer would be nothing without goals. Besides heading the ball or benefiting from an own goal or a lucky deflection, the only way to score is to shoot. This can be done from almost any position on the field (several goals have been scored from the shooter's own half) but the closer a player is to the opponents' goal when he takes a shot, the higher the chances of success.

PLACEMENT OR POWER?

Sometimes the only way to beat the keeper is to strike the ball as hard as possible. At other times, it may be possible to pass the ball into the net. A player should strike the ball as hard as he can without sacrificing accuracy.

THE BASIC SHOT

Certain principles apply whether a shot is long- or short-range, placed or blasted. The shooter should aim the ball either side of the goalkeeper and keep the ball down, so it doesn't fly over the crossbar.

WHERE TO STRIKE THE BALL

MICHAEL OWEN

Michael Owen is an instinctive goalscorer. He scored 118 goals during his time at Liverpool and he has scored goals at an average of almost one for every two games while playing for England.

Sweep
Sweep the striking leg through on a plane consistent with the ball's direction

Open up
Open the leg and strike the ball on the instep

1 The player places his standing foot firmly next to the ball and pointing toward the goal.

2 He makes contact with the center of the ball or a spot slightly below it.

STAT ATTACK

Scoring goals isn't all about power (see above). However, goals scored by hard strikes are spectacular to watch. Ex-England midfielder Bobby Charlton was widely credited with a fierce shot, and in recent years, so was Dutch striker Jimmy Floyd Hasselbaink, but neither of them make this list of soccer's top six hardest strikes.

POWER SHOTS

SOCCER'S HARDEST STRIKES

NAME	MATCH	DATE	SPEED
David Hirst	*Sheffield Wednesday* vs Arsenal	Sep 16, 1996	114 mph (182 kph)
David Beckham	*Man Utd* vs Chelsea	Feb 22, 1997	97.9 mph (156 kph)
David Trezeguet	*Monaco* vs Man Utd	Mar 19, 1998	96 mph (153 kph)
Richie Humphreys	Sheffield Wednesday vs *Aston Villa*	Aug 17, 1996	95.9 mph (153 kph)
Matt Le Tissier	*Southampton* vs Newcastle	Jan 18, 1997	86.8 mph (139 kph)
Alan Shearer	*Newcastle* vs Leicester	Feb 2, 1997	85.8 mph (137 kph)

THE CURVING SHOT

The curving shot is difficult to execute well because it requires a highly precise strike, both in respect of the part of the foot used and the impact position on the ball. For the inswinging strike (see right), connect with the instep on the base of the ball; for the far more difficult outswinger, use the same spot on the outside of the foot (see also p.121).

Ball-watching
Focus on the part of the ball you want to strike

Follow through
Keep the striking leg firm and straight through impact

Solid base
Use the standing foot as a solid base from which to swing the striking leg

Shoe in
Get the toes under the ball for more lofted shots

Lean back
Lean back slightly at impact

WHERE TO STRIKE THE BALL

1. The player approaches the ball and ensures that the standing leg is about 18 in (45 cm) to the side.

2. He sweeps the leg on an in-to-out arc and connects with the bottom right portion of the ball.

3. He follows the path of the ball with the foot to stand a better chance of curving it.

TOP 5: GOAL CELEBRATIONS

Back in the early 20th century, players scoring goals used to be congratulated with a handshake from teammates, but in recent years, the goal celebration has become an art in itself.

BRANDI CHASTAIN
The US women's team defender celebrated scoring the winning penalty in the 1999 Women's World Cup Final by removing her top. She revealed the most photographed sports bra in history.

PAUL GASCOIGNE
Gazza's sensational goal against Scotland at Euro '96 was followed by a reconstruction (using water) of a pre-tournament incident in which England players had been photographed having tequila poured down their throats while sitting in a dentist's chair during late-night revelry.

JULIUS AGHAWOWA
At the 2002 African Nations' Cup, the Nigerian striker celebrated scoring a winning goal against Algeria with a series of six flips and an immaculately executed double somersault.

ROGER MILLA
Cameroon's elder statesman stole the show at the 1990 World Cup with goal celebrations that involved a run to the corner flag and some snake-hipped gyrations to follow.

BEBETO
During the 1994 World Cup, the Brazilian striker's wife gave birth to a son. When he scored in the quarter-final against the Netherlands, Bebeto mimed rocking the baby and his teammates joined in (below).

THE CHIP, LOB, AND SCOOP

When a goalkeeper is off his line, there is a chance of beating him by lofting the ball over his head and weighting the shot so that the ball drops under the crossbar. The three methods by which this can be achieved—the chip, scoop, and lob—are all about touch, timing, and judgment.

Spinning
With backspin the ball gains height quickly

Strike
Strike the ball with finesse on the top of the foot

THE CHIP AND SCOOP
The chip and the scoop are used when the ball is on the ground as the shot is taken. The chip requires back-lift and the scoop doesn't.

THE LOB
The lob is used when the ball arrives at a player full toss or after bouncing. The ball needs to be struck with enough height to clear the goalkeeper.

WOODCOCK WOULD HAVE SCORED, BUT HIS SHOT WAS TOO... PERFECT

RON ATKINSON, COMMENTATING ON AN ENGLAND MATCH IN THE 1980s

INDIVIDUAL SKILLS

VOLLEYING

There are few sights in soccer as satisfying as seeing a cleanly hit volley fly into the net. This technique, which is defined as striking a ball that is in full flight, is also used to make rapid crosses, clearances, and passes. A high level of foot–eye coordination is essential for volleying. When it is executed well, the results can be spectacular.

MARCO VAN **BASTEN**

Marco Van Basten's strike for the Netherlands against the USSR in 1988 was probably the greatest-ever volleyed goal. He received a high cross-field pass on the edge of the six yard box and, from an almost impossible angle, sent a looping volley into the opposite corner of the net.

VOLLEYING STYLES

There are two main styles of volley. The first is the full volley—the most visually arresting— where the ball is struck "on the fly." The second is the half-volley, where the ball is struck very shortly after it has bounced. There is also a third technique, the bicycle (or overhead) kick, but this is normally performed only by experienced, very athletic players.

EVERYONE IS STILL TALKING ABOUT THAT GOAL... IN THE 1988 FINAL

DUTCH MIDFIELDER **RAFAEL VAN DER VAART** ON VAN BASTEN'S WONDER STRIKE, 2008

THE FULL VOLLEY

The full version of the volley is used when the ball arrives at the kicker without touching the ground. It is therefore likely to be traveling quickly, giving the kicker less time to get into the right position to make his strike. The key ingredients for a well-executed volley are timing, composure, and concentration. Repeatedly striking a ball suspended at chest height from a crossbar via a piece of rope is an excellent way to practice this skill.

CHAMPIONS LEAGUE FINAL 2002

In the 44th minute, Real Madrid's Zinédine Zidane was just outside the penalty area, perfectly positioned to receive a high looping cross from Roberto Carlos. Pirouetting exquisitely, his fully outstretched leg hit the ball chest high and sent it blasting into the net. It was a worthy winning goal.

Striking leg
Bend the knee in preparation for the strike

Standing leg
Plant this firmly on the ground to act as a pivot

Impact
Strike the ball with the top of the foot

Swivel hips
Turn the hips quickly toward the ball to generate power

Parallel lines
Keep the leg parallel to the ground during the follow through

Balance
Use the arms for balance during the strike

1 The player keeps his eyes on the ball. He positions himself in its line of flight to have the best chance of making good contact.

2 Starting with the knee, he brings the leg toward the ball and turns the hips. He strikes the ball above center to keep it down.

3 He follows through with the kicking leg parallel to the ground and rotates the hips through the impact area.

BICYCLE KICK

Also known as the overhead kick, the bicycle kick is one of soccer's most spectacular techniques. It was invented in the Peruvian port of Callao during a game between locals and some European sailors in the early 1900s. Residents of the city are known as Chalacos and "Chalaca," the Latin American term for the trick, literally means "from Callao."

DIDIER DROGBA
The Ivorian striker's muscular frame makes him adept at finding space to perform overhead kicks.

MAKING AN OVERHEAD KICK

The bicycle kick is often used when an apparently misplaced cross arrives behind an attacker. Alternatively, a player can "tee" himself up for an overhead kick with his back to the goal by flicking the ball up to strike.

Head and body
Throw the head back to aid lift and the body will follow

Launch
Use the striking leg as a springboard

1 The player launches himself into the air by raising his non-kicking leg and pushing off the ground with the other foot.

Sweep
Sweep the leg toward the ball with controlled pace

2 Once airborne, the player swings his kicking leg beyond the other leg and toward the ball.

Fall
Use the hand to soften the impact of the landing

3 He makes contact with the ball with his back parallel to the ground. Players practice this in training before attempting in a match.

THE HALF-VOLLEY

The half-volley is performed when the ball bounces just before the kicker strikes it. It is therefore sometimes on the rise at the moment of impact. Sometimes a player is able to hit the ball at the exact moment it touches the ground. When this happens, the shot gains more momentum as the ball has lost less energy through not bouncing.

RAW POWER

One of the most memorable half-volleys of recent years was Steven Gerrard's goal for Liverpool against Olympiakos in the 2005 Champions League. He struck the ball sweetly from the edge of the area. Liverpool went on to win the tournament.

Poise
Prepare the body for the dropping ball as timing is everything

Composure
Keep everything smooth through impact

Center strike
Connect with the middle of the ball to control the strike

1 The player watches the ball closely as it drops toward him. He positions his body and pulls back the striking leg before connecting with the ball.

2 He strikes the ball with the top of the foot, either on the rise or as it drops toward the ground heading for a second bounce.

HEADING

Heading the ball is counter-intuitive for any young players learning the game, because they think it will hurt. However, it is an essential skill to master because, in an average match, the ball is in the air for 30 percent of the time.

TYPES OF HEADER

There are many different types of headers—basic, flick, tactical, defensive, and diving. Players need to practice all of them so that they know which one to use in a match situation.

BASIC HEADER

The basic header is used for passing and attempts on goal. It is made with the forehead as this provides the most power and accuracy. It also doesn't hurt, unlike heading the ball with the top (crown) of the head. To get power on a header, the player bends his knees and arches his back as he jumps for the ball, turning himself into the shape of a bow. His head is the "arrow." It is initially tilted back then brought forward rapidly using the neck muscles.

WAYNE ROONEY

England's Wayne Rooney is one of world soccer's most skilful and powerful players. He has extremely powerful neck muscles and knows how to put them to good use.

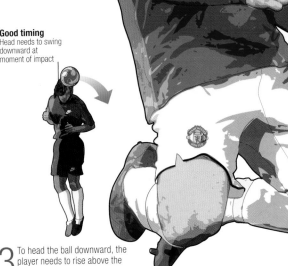

Focus
Keep eyes on the ball

Pull up
Use arms to pull yourself into the air if you're jumping for the ball

Sweet spot
Use the forehead—this provides accuracy and power

Good timing
Head needs to swing downward at moment of impact

1 The player gets into position early and watches the ball onto his head, keeping his eyes open throughout.

2 Without taking his eyes off the ball, he tenses the neck muscles to provide maximum power.

3 To head the ball downward, the player needs to rise above the ball when he jumps.

FLICK PASSES

The flick header is used to head the ball sideways or backward. It is particularly useful in three situations: when a defender facing up-field wants to head the ball back to his goalkeeper; when a midfielder wants to flick the ball back to a defender; or when a forward wants to get the ball into the penalty area from a near post cross or corner without revealing his intentions.

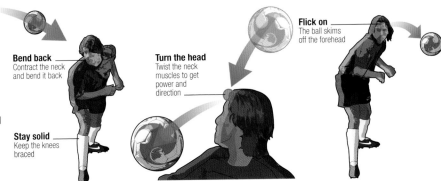

Bend back
Contract the neck and bend it back

Stay solid
Keep the knees braced

Turn the head
Twist the neck muscles to get power and direction

Flick on
The ball skims off the forehead

1 The player has his body arched forward when he makes contact with the ball.

2 He uses the forehead if his neck is supple, otherwise the side of the head.

3 The ball bounces off the player's head and continues on its new path.

The flick header is a staple part of the tactics of most professional teams. It is used on crosses, free kicks, and corners to change the direction of the ball and confuse the opposition defenders.

KEY

- ● Attacker
- ● Defender
- ○ Goalkeeper
- --- Ball motion
- — Player movement

NEAR POST HEADER
A player needs to time his run so that he is in front of his marker when it arrives, then flicks the ball behind him into the area for a teammate.

FAR POST HEADER
A player may need to step backward to lose his marker. He should direct his header back across goal toward the far post.

DEFENSIVE HEADER

The most important thing when making a defensive header is to get good height and distance on the ball. It is usually safer to direct it away from the center of the field.

Timing
Time the jump so you connect with the ball before the attacker does

Air time
Head the ball as high and as far forward as possible

High-headed
Make connect at the very top of the forehead to get height on the ball

Direction
Pass the ball to a teammate if possible

Landing
Be careful when landing

1 The defender needs to get in position early because he will probably be competing with an attacker to get to the ball.

2 Contact should be made with the bottom half of the ball on the very top part of the forehead. The player keeps the neck braced.

3 If the defender approaches the ball from a sideways position, he has less chance of clashing with the attacker.

DIVING HEADER

The player uses his whole body as a battering ram to strike the ball. This skill is not for the faint-hearted—the player stands a risk of getting a kick in the face from a defender—and for that reason it is usually used only to attempt to score. It is an option when the ball arrives in front of a player at a height between his neck and his knee.

LONGEST GOAL

The longest-range goal scored with the head was by Peter Aldis of Aston Villa. In September 1952 he headed the ball into the Sunderland net from an astonishing distance of 35 yds (32 m).

Watch the ball
Pay close attention to the flight of the ball

Watch out
Make sure that the ball doesn't strike the face

Soft landing
Break your fall with the hands

1 Keeping his eyes on the ball, the player launches himself into the air with the foot closest to the goal.

2 When he makes contact with the ball, the player is parallel to the ground. He should head the ball with the top of the forehead.

3 After heading the ball toward goal, the player puts his arms in front of him to protect himself as he falls to the ground.

INDIVIDUAL SKILLS

THROW-INS AND CORNERS

Statistically, corners and throw-ins are the most commonly awarded set pieces (see pp.96–97). A team is likely to make several of each during the course of a game. These can often lead to scoring opportunities—about a third of all goals are scored from set pieces—so coaches make sure that players practice them extensively on the training ground.

RULES ON SCORING

Goals cannot be scored directly from a throw-in. The rules concerning corners are ambiguous, however. FIFA regulations state that "A corner kick falls under the same guidelines as a direct free-kick," implying that such goals are legitimate.

RORY DELAP
Known as the "Delapidator" the Republic of Ireland player terrorizes defenses with his long throws. Delap throws the ball, on average, 86 ft (38 m).

THROW-INS

Throw-ins are used to restart play from the sideline. They can be taken either short or long. The thrower needs to be alert to the movements of his teammates and have a good aim. Throwing onto the field can be risky—if the opponents win possession, they may quickly counter-attack—so the majority of throws are aimed up-field along the sideline, out of harm's way. The exception is the long throw aimed directly into the penalty area. This can be more potent than a corner as the thrown ball is delivered more accurately.

IT'S LIKE A... HUMAN SLING!

EVERTON MANAGER DAVID MOYES **ON RORY DELAP'S THROW-IN STYLE**

TAKING A THROW-IN

Throw-ins awarded in a team's own half are usually taken as a means of getting the ball back in play. But those taken near the opposition's penalty area can be as effective as a free-kick. There are three basic rules for taking throw-ins: the player is permitted a run-up; the ball must be thrown from behind the head with both hands; and both feet must be on the ground at the moment of release.

Grip it
Keep the hands evenly spaced on the ball

Momentum
A short run-up provides momentum

Stay grounded
Both feet must stay on the ground

Follow-through
Arms should follow the path of the ball

Launch
Launch angle is usually about 30 degrees

1 The player holds the ball fully behind the head with both hands. He is permitted to make a short run-up.

2 He brings his arms over his head and whips his body forward as he releases the ball. This generates the power for the throw.

CORNER KICKS

As with free-kicks in general (see pp.138–39), there are several options open to a player taking a corner. Aside from the classic inswinging and outswinging corners, there are five key variations.

FIVE CORNER STYLES

A corner represents a good opportunity to score a goal, so teams always work on these set piece routines. The following corner techniques are all practiced during training sessions: penalty spot, near post, far post, long, and short.

SINIŠA MIHAJLOVIĆ

The former Serbian international was described by manager Roberto Mancini, as "extraordinary at dead-ball situations." His accurate left foot made Mihajlović the perfect corner-taker.

KEY

○ Goalkeeper
● Attackers
--- Ball motion

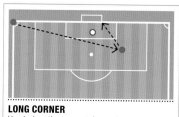

LONG CORNER

Used when the corner-taker notices a teammate hovering unmarked outside the six yard box. A quick pass can set up a strike on goal.

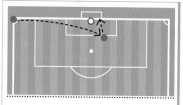

SHORT CORNER

A short-range pass to a teammate creates a different crossing or shooting angle. Defenders have no time to readjust themselves.

PENALTY SPOT CORNER

A corner aimed at the penalty spot may lure the keeper from his goal. The ball must travel fast to reach a teammate before the keeper intercepts it.

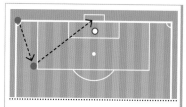

NEAR POST CORNER

The corner is aimed at the near goalpost so that it can be flicked on by a teammate to alter the ball's path and confuse the defenders.

FAR POST CORNER

Usually delivered as an outswinger, the ball will be curving toward the teammate attacking it, helping him to get power into his header.

TAKING A CORNER

The rules of taking a corner are simple: the player is permitted to place the ball anywhere within the segment (the quarter circle between the goal line and the touchline); he is not permitted to remove the corner flag. For more detailed technique on taking a corner, see "Passing" (pp.120–21) and "Free-kicks" (pp.138–39).

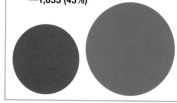

BALL POSITIONING
❶ Right-footed player takes a corner from the left-hand side
❷ Left-footed player takes a corner from the left-hand side

CORNERS PER MATCH

The total number of corners in the English Premier League in 2007/8 is **4,250**.

● Corners awarded to home team
—**2,415 (57%)**
● Corners awarded to away team
—**1,835 (43%)**

Eyes down
Keep the head still and eyes focused on the ball

Standing foot
Plant the non-striking foot firmly next to the ball

Strike
Connect with the ball before the ground

1 Placing the ball anywhere in the segment, the player steps back, picks a target (a teammate in the penalty area), and takes a short run-up.

2 He connects with the bottom of the ball on the right- or left-hand side, depending on the intended curve, if any, and follows through.

THE OLIMPICO

A goal scored directly from a corner with a curving shot is known as an "Olimpico" in South America. The shot is named in honor of Cesáreo Onzari of Uruguay, who scored against Argentina in this manner in 1924 when his team were reigning Olympic champions.

FREE-KICKS

All free-kicks are awarded against the team that has committed some infringement. There are various options open to the player who takes the free-kick. The ball can be struck directly at the goal with force, chipped, curved, or passed to a teammate. Anything, in fact, that catches the opposing team unawares.

Direct free-kick   **Indirect free-kick**

TYPES OF FREE-KICKS

There are two types of free-kicks—direct and indirect. Many direct free-kicks that are taken from the edge of the opposition penalty area give good goalscoring opportunities, while most indirect free-kicks (except those taken from inside the penalty area) are little more than a means of restarting play.

INDIRECT FREE-KICK

An indirect free-kick is awarded against a team for committing a foul other than a penalty foul (for example dangerous play) or for infringing certain technical requirements of the laws (for example offside). An indirect free-kick requires the ball to be touched by more than one player on the same team before it can enter the goal.

HOW TO TELL THE DIFFERENCE

If in doubt about whether a free-kick is direct or indirect, watch the referee. He indicates a direct kick with an outstretched arm (horizontal) and an indirect with a vertical arm position.

THE QUICK FREE-KICK

Usually, a player standing over a free-kick must wait for the referee's whistle before starting play. But the player is permitted to ask the referee if he can take a "quick" kick without the whistle signal, to try to gain an advantage.

YOU REALLY ARE...
CAPTAIN FANTASTIC

ANNOUNCER **MARTIN TYLER** ON DAVID BECKHAM'S FREE-KICK AGAINST GREECE, 2001

AVERAGE SPEEDS

Soccer free-kick—
60–70 mph (96–112 kph)

Baseball pitch—
90–100 mph (144–160 kph)

Tennis 1st serve—
120–140 mph (192–224 kph)

DIRECT FREE-KICK

A direct free-kick is awarded against a team for committing a penalty foul such as kicking a player instead of the ball, pushing, tripping, and similar infringements. If the referee deems the foul to be too malicious or dangerous, he will issue a yellow or red card. Direct free-kicks can be struck directly into the goal without the need for another teammate to touch the ball. The most punitive direct free-kick a team can face is a kick from the penalty spot (see pp.140–41).

THE CURVING FREE-KICK

If the free-kick is awarded close to the goal, the defending team will build a defensive wall (see p.97). If the player taking the free-kick gives the ball enough curve, it will bend around the wall. It will also make it difficult for the goalkeeper to judge its flight. The principles of getting the ball to curve are the same whether the kick is taken from a dead ball situation or on the move (see p.131).

WHERE TO STRIKE THE BALL

Run-up
Approach the ball from an angle of about 45 degrees

Long strides
Make sure the last stride before impact is a long one

Non-striking foot
Plant the standing leg firmly on the ground

It's a wrap
Wrap the instep around the bottom right section of the ball to generate spin

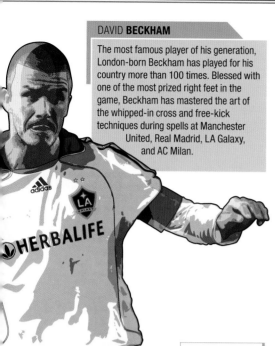

DAVID BECKHAM

The most famous player of his generation, London-born Beckham has played for his country more than 100 times. Blessed with one of the most prized right feet in the game, Beckham has mastered the art of the whipped-in cross and free-kick techniques during spells at Manchester United, Real Madrid, LA Galaxy, and AC Milan.

FREE-KICK OPTIONS

Sometimes the success of a free-kick is down to the skill and ingenuity of one player; on other occasions it is a team effort. Free-kicks are good opportunities to score the goals that win matches, so coaches work on them extensively with players during training.

CURVING SHOT

The art of bending a shot around the wall and away from the dive of the keeper. Curved shots are created by striking the ball on its side and generating spin (see p.121).

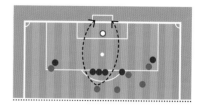

DIPPING SHOT

A challenging skill that requires the player to strike the ball over the wall rather than around it; if struck correctly, the dipping ball drops at the end of its flight.

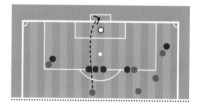

THROUGH THE WALL

The player strikes the ball low so it goes under the players in the wall as they jump; or he strikes directly at a teammate in the wall who jumps out of the way to create a space.

CHIP INTO SPACE

The player dinks the ball into an area 8–10 yd (7–9 m) from the goal, where the goalkeeper cannot easily claim it; the intention is that one of his teammates is then able to shoot or head at goal.

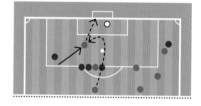

KEY

○ Goalkeeper
● Attacker
● Defender
- - - Ball motion
—— Player motion

BEND IT LIKE BECKHAM

In 2001, David Beckham stepped up to take a free-kick in the 93rd minute of a match against Greece knowing that he had to score to secure England's qualification for the following year's World Cup finals. Sure enough, he hit an unstoppable curving shot from 30 yards (28 m), leaving the Greek keeper helpless. The ball hit the top corner of the net traveling at 42 mph (68 kph). It swerved approximately 9 ft (3 m) during its flight.

KEY

○ Greek keeper
○ England
● Greece
- - - Ball motion

Center point
The kick was taken almost directly in line with the center of the goal

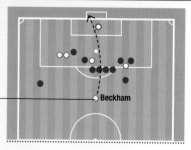

Beckham

Speed
The ball leaves Beckham's foot at 80 mph (130 kph)

On the rise
At this stage the ball is flying slightly to the right from Beckham's perspective, fooling the goalkeeper into making a small move to the left

On the move
The ball has now started to change direction. It swerves above and to the side of the Greek player on the left of the defensive wall

Flight path
The ball is now at its maximum height, curving viciously

Unstoppable
It dips into the top left hand corner with the keeper stranded

30 yd (28 m)

PENALTIES

Penalties provide the most nerve-wracking moments in soccer. They are awarded for fouls committed in the penalty area, such as tripping and pushing. They are taken from the penalty spot, which is located directly between the goalposts, 12 yd (11 m) from the goal line. Scoring from penalties requires composure and skilful ball placement, saving penalties requires agility and anticipation. Goalkeepers are rarely expected to save penalties.

PIRES' POOR PENALTY

In October 2005, Arsenal were awarded a penalty in a match against Manchester City. Instead of shooting, Robert Pires opted for the unorthodox but perfectly legal option of knocking the ball for Thierry Henry to strike. However, Pires' touch was so feeble that the ball failed to move and a defender cleared it.

PENALTY DO'S AND DON'TS	
DO	**DON'T**
KEEP YOUR WEIGHT OVER THE BALL	TAKE TOO LONG A RUN-UP
MAKE A PLAN AND STICK TO IT	LET THE KEEPER PSYCHE YOU OUT
FOOL THE KEEPER WITH YOUR EYES	HIT THE BALL AT CHEST HEIGHT...
STRIKE THE BALL FIRMLY	...OR TOO CLOSE TO THE KEEPER

PENALTY RULES
The penalty is not just a battle of wits between the taker and the keeper, there are various rules and restrictions to be adhered to for other players, too.

PENALTY SHOOTOUTS

Draws are acceptable in some matches (almost all league games), but not in matches where a winner has to be found in order for a tournament to progress or reach a conclusion (cup ties, cup finals, and play-offs). Penalty shootouts are a way of forcing a result when the scores are level at the end of such a game, usually after a period of extra-time.

FINDING A WINNER

Shootouts were introduced by UEFA in 1970 and FIFA in 1976. Each team takes five penalties against the other, with the kicks alternating. The team that's ahead at the end wins the match. If the scores are still level, the match goes into "sudden death." The first team to fall behind when an equal number of penalties has been taken by each side loses. Penalty shootouts are often considered an unsatisfactory way of deciding matches, but no better alternative has yet been found.

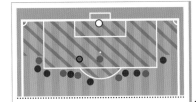

EXCLUSION ZONE
All players bar the taker and the goalkeeper must stay outside the penalty area

- ● Defender
- ● Attacker
- ○ Goalkeeper
- ● Referee

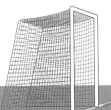

On the move
The keeper will usually calculate that his best chance of saving the kick is to dive early to one side

Second chances
Attackers need to be ready to pounce on any rebounds

On alert
Defenders must be ready to run in to make a clearance if there's a rebound

6 yd (5.5 m) | 12 yd (11 m) | 18 yd (16.5 m)

STAT ATTACK

WORLD CUP HITS AND MISSES

The team shooting first has won 11 of the 20 shootouts (55 percent)

Thirteen players have scored in two separate shootouts, but none in three

Sergio Goycoechea of Argentina has saved five penalties—a record

THE LONGEST

THE LONGEST SHOOTOUTS

TEAMS	YEAR	SCORE
Argentinos Juniors vs Racing Club	1988	20:19
KK Palace vs Civics	2005	17:16
Gençlerbirligi SK vs Galatasaray SK	1996	17:16
Obernai vs Wittelsheim	1996	16:15

...AND THE BEST

THE BEST SHOOTOUT RECORDS

COUNTRY	PEN. TAKEN/ SCORED	%
Germany	18 / 17	94.4%
Brazil	13 / 10	76.9%
France	20 / 15	75.0%
Romania	11 / 8	72.7%
Argentina	18 / 13	72.2%
Italy	20 / 13	65.0%

ALLESSANDRO **DEL PIERO**

The Juventus and Italy striker has a good penalty-taking record. Del Piero often uses delicate chips to outwit the keeper. He was brought on near the end of the 2006 World Cup final against France, in order to take a penalty—which he scored.

WHERE TO SHOOT

Success or failure with the penalty kick is partly determined by the strength of the shot, but if a penalty is poorly placed, the goalkeeper may reach it and its power will be largely irrelevant. So where should a player aim for to guarantee the greatest chance of success?

SCIENTIFIC STUDY

Research carried out at Liverpool University concluded that the perfect penalty was one hit into the top corner of the net. This has a 100 percent success rate but there is a high chance of missing such a kick, hence the conventional advice given by coaches to aim for the bottom of the goal.

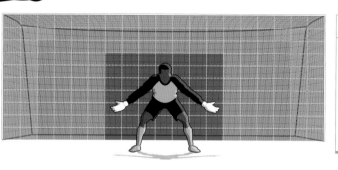

KEY

Goalkeeper will save unless he overcommits

Goalkeeper may save if shot is struck weakly

Goalkeeper is highly unlikely to save

I STUCK IT IN THE CORNER AND IF THE KEEPER WENT THE RIGHT WAY, IT WAS HARD ENOUGH…
TO BEAT HIM

MATT LE TISSIER, OF SOUTHAMPTON AND ENGLAND ON HIS SUCCESS RATE OF 48 FROM 49 PENALTIES

TYPES OF PENALTY

Penalty-takers have three basic options when taking a spot kick: to attempt to pass the ball into the net, to try a chip, or strike the ball very firmly. A penalty struck firmly into the bottom or top corner will register a goal, but there is very little margin for error—the player must be very confident that he will not kick the ball wide.

WOBBLY KNEES

In the 1984 European Cup final penalty shootout, Liverpool goalkeeper Bruce Grobbelaar famously wobbled his legs in mock terror, causing two AS Roma players to miss. Liverpool won the trophy.

PENALTY SCORES

78 penalty kicks were taken in the English Premier League in 2005/6.

● Goal scored—**57 (73%)**

● No goal scored—**21 (27%)**

PENALTY PASS
When a player places a penalty, he effectively passes the ball into the net. This provides accuracy and is a good option if the keeper has dived early.

WHERE TO STRIKE THE BALL

PENALTY CHIP
The most audacious kind of penalty, but extremely risky. The taker relies on the goalkeeper diving before the strike is made.

WHERE TO STRIKE THE BALL

POWER SHOT
The taker sacrifices accuracy for speed with this option and he stands a good chance of success if he doesn't blast the ball wide or high.

WHERE TO STRIKE THE BALL

INDIVIDUAL SKILLS

GOALKEEPING

Goalkeeping is so different from other soccer roles that it almost seems to belong to another sport. All players need agility, bravery, a strong physical presence, and good distribution and decisionmaking abilities, but keepers have to have these characteristics in abundance. The special demands of the position require them to master a set of skills peculiarly their own.

GOAL-FREE MINUTES

- Matos Filho Mazarópi, Vasco de Gama, 1978–79: **1,816**
- Thabet El-Batal, Al-Ahly (Cairo), 1975–76: **1,486**
- Dany Verlinden, Club Brugge, 1990: **1,390**

BASIC TECHNIQUES

The three fundamentals for any aspiring goalkeeper to master are: stance (being "athletically primed"); body positioning (being aware of angles of attack and his position in relation to the goal); and shot-stopping.

STANCE

A keeper needs to be continually alert to the possibility of a shot, leaning slightly forward so that his weight is on his toes rather than his heels. This places him in the optimum position to dive quickly or run toward an attacker if the situation demands it.

BODY POSITIONING

A keeper always needs to know where he and the ball are relative to the goal. As he can't afford to turn around to check, he needs to construct a mental image. One effective way to do this is to imagine a capital "T" with the shaft running through the penalty spot and the cross stroke stretching between the posts.

Fingers and thumbs
When the ball is caught, the thumbs should be almost touching

SHOT-STOPPING

The key task for any goalkeeper is knowing how to catch or stop the ball. There are two differing techniques for this depending on whether the ball is traveling along the ground or in the air—the "W" and the "M" (see left). All saving techniques are based from these two starting points. Whenever possible, a goalkeeper should attempt to use both hands when gathering the ball or making a save. Two hands together are stronger and cover more area than one.

THE "W"

The basic hand position when dealing with a shot close to the body and above the waist forms the letter "W," with the thumbs touching and the fingers pointing upward—a good position to catch the ball.

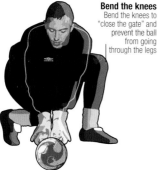

Bend the knees
Bend the knees to "close the gate" and prevent the ball from going through the legs

THE "M"

When dealing with a ball below waist height and close to his body, a goalkeeper should form a downward pointing "M" with his hands, with the four fingers in the middle squeezed together.

DINO **ZOFF**

The great Italian keeper is a role model for anyone who occupies the position. A rock-solid perfectionist, he was still playing first class soccer at the age of 41. Zoff's explanation for his longevity was simple: "I believe it's always possible to make improvements."

MAKE YOURSELF BIG—NARROW THE ANGLE

The closer a goalkeeper is to an attacker running toward him with the ball, the less of the goal the attacker will be able to see. This method is known as "narrowing the angle." When an attacker is running toward the goal with the ball or charging onto a through pass, the keeper needs to decide instantly whether to stay back or run forward. He does not want to be caught in no man's land, where he has run away from the goal but is not close enough to the ball to prevent or block a shot.

THE COLOR [DISTRACTS]... THE STRIKER

CZECH GOALKEEPER **PETR CECH** ON WHY HE WEARS ORANGE

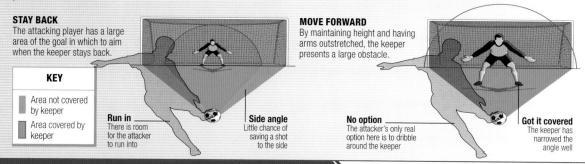

STAY BACK
The attacking player has a large area of the goal in which to aim when the keeper stays back.

KEY
- Area not covered by keeper
- Area covered by keeper

Run in
There is room for the attacker to run into

Side angle
Little chance of saving a shot to the side

MOVE FORWARD
By maintaining height and having arms outstretched, the keeper presents a large obstacle.

No option
The attacker's only real option here is to dribble around the keeper

Got it covered
The keeper has narrowed the angle well

GROUNDING

When a keeper catches a ball but has no chance of staying on his feet, he needs to ground the ball as soon as possible to bring it under control and avoid spilling it into the path of incoming attackers.

A WORD IN YOUR EAR

In the Belgian league in January 2004, Racing Genk's Jan Moons became the first goalkeeper to receive instructions from the bench via an earpiece. His side beat FC Bruges 1–0.

Hands on
Prepare the hands for the catch

Stay straight
Keep the torso fairly rigid during the dive

Weighed down
Focus all upper body weight down onto the ball

1 The player should dive with the hands in the "W" position, watching the ball closely as it approaches.

2 The keeper goes to ground, landing on one knee with the other leg outstretched, and catches the ball slightly above its center.

3 The keeper brings the ball firmly down to the ground, holding it tightly, still with the hands in the "W" position.

DIVING SAVE

The diving save is the most spectacular in a goalkeeper's repertoire. The keys to success are quick reactions, good footwork, and getting into position early.

Eye on the ball
Watch the ball closely to make sure you judge the distance

Lift off
Launch the body toward the ball

Stretch out
Get the fingertips to the ball

1 The player bends the leg closest to the ball and watches its flight. He springs to the side with one arm outstretched and the wrist held firm.

2 He pushes the ball away from the goal to prevent attackers from capitalizing on a rebound, then braces himself for landing.

CATCH OR PUNCH?

A goalkeeper has to decide whether to deal with high balls played into the penalty area by catching them, punching them, or staying on his goal line. He should only do the latter if he believes he has a poor chance of getting to the ball first.

LEV YASHIN

The only keeper to be voted European Player of the Year, Yashin played for Dynamo Moscow. He represented the USSR at three World Cups and was known as "The Black Spider" because he played as though he had eight arms.

Hold on
Keep a grip on the ball as you land on the ground

Challenging
Opposition players jump in front of the keeper

Firm fist
A strong punch gets the ball out of the danger area

Out-jump
The keeper has a height advantage by virtue of being able to use his arms

CATCHING THE BALL
The best option is for the keeper to catch the ball as doing so ends the attack. Whether he can will depend on his ability to reach the ball unimpeded.

PUNCHING THE BALL
The second-best option is for the keeper to punch the ball. This can be done with two arms, but more often, he will only be able to get one to the ball.

DEALING WITH CROSSES

The task of catching a cross or corner is ostensibly a simple one—follow the flight of the ball clearly and time the jump. Complications arise however with the number of players in the penalty area. A keeper must shout loudly to indicate his intentions to the defenders. He must also be strong enough to compete with the opposition's attackers.

DEFENDING A CROSS

The secret of defending a cross is all about organization. Defenders need to pick up the players they're supposed to be marking and the keeper needs to be authoritative.

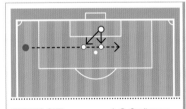

COMING OUT
The keeper comes out to catch crosses in different parts of the penalty area.

O Goalkeeper
● Attacker
-- Ball motion
— Player motion

THE PENALTY IS THE ONE THING KEEPERS DON'T FEAR... IF IT IS SCORED, NO ONE BLAMES HIM. IF HE SAVES IT...

HE'S A HERO

DAVE SEXTON, QUEENS PARK RANGERS MANAGER, 1975

GOALKEEPER'S ROLES

Being a good goalkeeper isn't all about eye-catching saves and a strong physical presence. Keepers have a duty to start attacks by distributing the ball well and being the unofficial captain of the team's defense.

DISTRIBUTION

If a goalkeeper catches or picks up the ball, he has exactly six seconds to put it down again and restart play, otherwise he is at risk of being penalized. His aim should be to launch a speedy counter-attack, so he needs to look up quickly to see where a teammate might be free. There are four methods by which a goalkeeper can start a new attack. Each has its own merits.

DISTRIBUTION DISTANCES

The goalkeeper needs to tailor his distribution method to the player he is trying to reach. Often his target will be on the other side of the halfway line, which will usually necessitate a long punt or a half-volley.

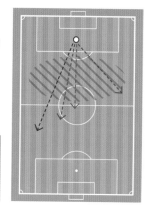

KEY	
--- Punt	--- Roll out
--- Half-volley	O Goalkeeper
--- Long throw	\\\\ Danger area

Good contact
Connect cleanly with the middle part of the foot

Timing
Good timing is paramount with this technique

Serve
Technique is similar to a bowler's action in cricket

Bowling
Technique is similar to 10-pin bowling

THE PUNT
The keeper drops the ball from his hands and volleys it. Long distances are possible with this technique.

THE HALF-VOLLEY
Similar to the punt, but the keeper lets the ball hit the ground a fraction of a second before making contact.

THE OVERARM THROW
Gripping the ball tightly, the throwing arm comes around in an arc over the shoulder to launch the ball upfield.

THE ROLL OUT
Rolling the ball out is a good option over short to medium distances and is extremely accurate.

TOP 5: GOALKEEPING MOMENTS

EL DIVINO'S CIGARS
Spain's Ricardo Zamora first came to public attention at the 1920 Olympics for his excellent goalkeeping and his attempts to smuggle Cuban cigars into the country on the way home, which led to the first of a number of prison sentences.

BERT TRAUTMANN'S NECK
Germany's Trautmann came to England as a prisoner of war and signed for Manchester City in 1949. He secured cult status at Maine Road when it was discovered that he had played most of the 1956 FA Cup Final with a broken neck.

A GUST OF WIND
One of the most famous goalkeeping goals was scored by Tottenham Hotspur's Pat Jennings in the 1967 Charity Shield. His clearance was caught by a gust of wind and sailed past Manchester United's Alex Stepney.

CARELESS HANDS
In a 1967 match away at Liverpool, Leeds United keeper Gary Sprake was about to throw the ball to a teammate, changed his mind, and inadvertently hurled the ball into his own net.

THE SCORPION KICK
Former Colombian keeper René Higuita earned notoriety in September 1995 during a friendly match against England at Wembley. He performed a clearance with the "Scorpion kick," bouncing forward onto his hands, arching his back, and kicking the ball away with his heels (see p.55).

MARSHALING THE DEFENSE

Goalkeepers are the only players able to see the whole game in front of them. They are best placed to organize their defenses for the general benefit of the team.

UNDER ORDERS

A quiet keeper is not doing his job well. He should be extremely vocal in warning his teammates when an opponent is unmarked, and in announcing his intention to clear or catch a ball. A good keeper also barks orders at his defense when setting up defensive walls, as he alone knows where they should stand to give him the best chance of saving a shot.

PETER SCHMEICHEL
The Denmark and Manchester United keeper was a huge physical presence on the field. He is 6 ft 4 in (1.93 m) and wore size XXXL boots.

TACKLING

Tackling is hugely important—it's the principal means of wresting possession from the opposition. It is a skill that every member of a team, including forwards, needs to be prepared to use, coining the phrase "defending from the front."

TYPES OF TACKLES

There are several kinds of tackles, each requiring different techniques, but two principles apply to them all. The first is timing: a good tackler knows exactly when to attempt to win the ball. Lunging in prematurely is likely to result in him missing the ball altogether. The second is safety, not only in terms of avoiding injury, but also in making sure that a clumsy tackle doesn't lead to a free-kick.

IF PLAYERS DON'T WANT TO GET KICKED THEY SHOULD BECOME ACCOUNTANTS

ROBERTO MANCINI FORMER ITALIAN PLAYER AND MANAGER

MOORE STOPS BRAZIL

One of the most famous and elegant tackles in history was made during the "Clash of the Champions"—England's encounter with Brazil in the group stages of the 1970 World Cup in Mexico (see pp.302–303). As Brazil's Jairzinho dribbled menacingly into the box, Bobby Moore slid in with an immaculate tackle. Technically, he used his "wrong" foot (the one further upfield) but he rose majestically and carried the ball out of defense as if the challenge had been merely routine.

BLOCK TACKLE

The block tackle is made when a defending player meets an attacker head on. Both players use the inside of their tackling foot, forceably making contact with the ball. Both players stay on their feet. The block tackle is used more often than any other kind of tackle.

Pivot
Use back leg as a pivot to move sideways during jockeying

1 Before the tackler makes his challenge, he "jockeys" his opponent. This involves standing in front of the other player and denying him room.

Weight shift
Move weight forward into the tackle

2 When the opponent draws his leg back to kick the ball, the defending player brings his tackling foot toward the ball.

Firm ankle
Keep the ankle firm throughout the tackle

3 Once the tackle is engaged, the defending player still has to work hard to control the ball and win possession.

SLIDE TACKLE

Both dramatic and emphatic, this technique should be used only when there are no alternatives. This is because the defender always ends up on the ground and invariably out of the game.

Heading for a fall
The player in possession will fall over the legs of the tackler

Stay up
Stay on your feet until the last possible moment

Knee slide
Slide on the knee of the non-striking leg

1 Approaching from the side, the tackler makes his tackle with the leg furthest forward. He bends his other leg to allow him to slide in.

2 The tackler knocks the ball away, ideally to a teammate. He needs to get back on his feet as soon as possible after making the tackle.

POKE TACKLE

The tackler stays on his feet and pokes or prods the ball away from his opponent into the path of a teammate. It is best used when the ball has bounced up between knee and waist height.

Element of surprise
Player in possession is often unaware challenge is about to be made

Right moment
Wait for the ball to drop before making the move

Find the gap
Aim for the gap between the player's legs

1 The tackler gets himself as close as possible to his opponent before making the tackle and waits for the ball to come into view.

2 Choosing his moment carefully, the tackler flicks his foot out and through the opponent's legs to poke the ball away.

THE "HOOK" TACKLE

This is a variation of the slide tackle in which the tackler "hooks" his foot around the ball. The tackler begins behind the player in possession at an angle of about 45 degrees. He challenges the attacker, hooking his foot around the ball and stealing possession, then passes to a teammate.

Stumble
The attacking player stumbles over the challenge

Support
Use the arm to support the body on the ground

TEAMMATE ANTICS

Mischevious players have been known to tackle their teammates. While playing for Fulham in an FA cup tie against Hereford in the mid-1970s, Rodney Marsh dispossessed his colleague George Best for fun.

RECOVERY TACKLE

Similar in many ways to the sliding tackle, the recovery tackle is not intended to gain possession or set up a pass to a teammate. It's usually made when an attacker has the ball near the touchline and needs to be stopped from advancing. The tackler's best option is to kick the ball into touch.

Get in front
Get the body in front of the player in possession

Clear it
Slide in and kick the ball into touch

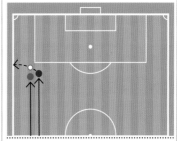

OUT OF PLAY
The recovery tackle is used to dispossess an opponent and put the ball out of play.

● Defender
● Attacker
-- Ball motion
— Player motion

FREESTYLE SKILLS

Most of the skills associated with freestyle soccer (see pp.28–29) are not directly relevant to match play, as they require more space and time on the ball than are ever likely to be available in competitive situations. Nevertheless, they are well worth mastering because they develop ball control and encourage creativity and improvisation. They are also a lot of fun to perform.

MILENE **DOMINGUES**

Known as Ronaldinha, the ex-wife of Brazilian star Ronaldo plays for Italy's Fiamma Monza and is one of the best female players in Europe. With 55,198 touches, she holds the women's record for ball-juggling.

THE MOVES

There are many different moves that an aspiring freestyler can learn and, as with other freestyle sports (such as skateboarding), new tricks are constantly being invented. Tricks usually fall into three main categories: juggling (keeping the ball airborne), flick-ups, and catches.

SHOWING OFF

Sometimes a player uses a freestyle skill during a match. In April 1967, Scotland's Jim Baxter taunted the then World Champions England by juggling the ball near the corner flag during his country's 3–2 victory at Wembley.

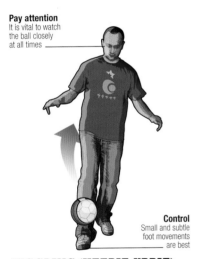

Pay attention
It is vital to watch the ball closely at all times

Control
Small and subtle foot movements are best

Balancing act
Readjust the neck to make head as flat as possible

Poised
Remain agile and light on the feet

JUGGLING (KEEPIE-UPPIE)

In its simplest form, this fundamental freestyle skill involves keeping the ball from touching the ground for as long as possible, usually with the feet and head.

HEAD STALL

This trick involves balancing the ball on the forehead. The performer keeps his eyes on the ball and makes small neck and body adjustments to keep it in place.

PEOPLE ARE ALWAYS KICKING, OLD OR YOUNG. EVEN AN UNBORN BABY IS KICKING

SEPP BLATTER, FIFA SECRETARY GENERAL, 1990

AROUND THE WORLD
With this trick, a player kicks the ball up in the air during juggling session and circles the kicking foot around it before it begins to drop. This must be done smoothly enough to get the foot back in position to continue the juggling at the end of the maneuver. The kicking foot can go around the ball either on the outside (away from the center of the body) or on the inside.

Stay still Keep the head still throughout the trick

Balance Stretch out arms to maintain balance

No contact Keep the foot away from the ball

High kick Strike with a bit more force than usual

1 The player starts by juggling as normal, keeping the ball under close control, then begins the trick by kicking the ball higher than usual.

2 As the ball rises, the player circles his foot over the ball, then controls it and continues juggling as it drops.

24.5 The world record (in hours) for the longest juggling session, held by Nikolai Kutsenko

2 The number of European Freestyle Championships won by Ireland's "Nam the Man"

26¼ The distance in miles (42 km) covered by Dr. Jan Skorkovsky while juggling the ball at the Prague marathon. He ran the race in 7 hours and 18 minutes

THE RAINBOW
In this trick, the player flicks the ball behind him and then back-heels the ball over his head before bringing it under control at the front of his body. The flight of the ball forms an arc over the player's head, hence the trick's name.

Trap it Trap the ball between the heel and toes

Propulsion Drive the heel up and through to propel the ball

1 He places the weaker foot in front of the ball, touching the heel. He rolls the ball a short distance up the back of the ankle with the other foot.

2 When the ball is just above the heel, he hops forward, leading with the stronger foot, and flicks it up over his head with the weaker one.

Anticipate Follow the flight of the ball carefully

3 Concentration and skill is required to anticipate the path of the ball over his head and onto his feet. Then he starts juggling.

TOP 5: MOVIES

ESCAPE TO VICTORY (1981)
A group of Allied prisoners of war, played by most of Ipswich Town FC, Michael Caine, Sylvester Stallone, Ossie Ardilles, Pelé, and Bobby Moore, plan a bid to abscond at half time in a game against their German guards.

ZIDANE: A 21ST CENTURY PORTRAIT (2006)
Seventeen cameras are trained on Zidane in a 2005 La Liga game against Villarreal. Footage of the player is cut with stadium shots and a haunting soundtrack to present a unique and kaleidoscopic picture of the man, the game, and the media.

GINGA: THE SOUL OF BRAZILIAN SOCCER (2006)
Shot like a sportswear commercial, Ginga is a brilliant collection of short soccer stories from Brazil—from the beach, the Amazon, and the favelas (shanty towns). It showcases Brazilian soccer and society in all its guises.

THE MIRACLE OF BERNE (2003)
Sentimental story of soccer-obsessed Matthias whose family, split by World War II and the imprisonment of his father in the Soviet Union, are redeemed by West Germany's victory in the 1954 World Cup.

6:3 (1999)
Soccer-crazed Tutti puts on the shirt of Hungarian legend Hidegkuti and is transported back in time to Budapest on the day of the great game against England in 1953—and he's the only man who knows the score....

SOCCER AND CAPOEIRA
Young urban South Americans have developed a soccer version of Capoeira, the Afro-Brazilian dance-based martial art.

INJURIES

Soccer does not have the frequency of contact injuries sustained in rugby and football. However, players' twists and turns put huge stresses on their joints, and collisions and tackles at high speed can be serious. At the top level, injures are inevitable but can still affect a side's season or even shape a player's entire career.

INJURY RESEARCH

Medical staff at 91 professional clubs examined the number and type of injuries sustained by their players over two seasons, 1997–99. They found more than 3,000 injuries per season, approximately 1.5 per player per year, leading to roughly 24 days a season lost per player.

INJURY FACTS

The most common months for injuries are during pre-season training and the season's early months, when muscles are comparatively untrained. The most common moments in games to get injured are the two 15-minute periods at the end of both halves. Eighty percent of injuries are severe enough to rule players out of at least one match—the average number of matches missed is as high as four.

DJIBRIL **CISSÉ**

Cissé had only played 19 games for Liverpool when in October 2004 a tackle from Blackburn Rovers' Jay McEveley broke two bones in his leg. Then, playing for France against China on June 7, 2006, he suffered another broken leg.

IT IS TOUGH TO HEAR DJIBRIL SCREAM... ## LIKE THAT

THIERRY HENRY ON CISSE'S INJURY IN 2006

STRETCHERED OFF

Stretchers and stretcher-bearers have long been a feature of soccer's touchlines and they are now recognized and required at matches under FIFA regulations. The motorized stretcher or "soccer ambulance" first made its appearance at the 1994 World Cup in the US—the home of the golf cart on which it was modeled. It provides an increased level of comfort for the player prior to him or her receiving further medical attention off the field.

CASUALTY
An injured player leaves the field of play.

TOP CAUSES OF INJURY

Tackling—**25%**
Running—**19%**
Twisting—**9%**
Collision—**8%**
Stretching—**6%**
Landing—**4%**

4 6

19

25 9

8

COMMON SOCCER INJURIES

AREA OF BODY	INJURY/DESCRIPTION
HEAD	CUTS—general abrasions suffered in the course of play CONCUSSION—result of an impact to the head
BACK	MUSCLE STRAIN—caused by excessive spinal stretching SLIPPED DISC—the pain of a vertebrae pushing on a nerve
ARMS	FRACTURE—usually as a result of an awkward fall DISLOCATION—whereby a bone is dislodged from its socket
LEGS (UPPER)	GROIN STRAIN—overstretching of the groin muscles DEAD LEG—loss of feeling of movement from hard blow HAMSTRING STRAIN OR TEAR—usually incurred while running at high speed
KNEES	CRUCIATE LIGAMENT DAMAGE—over-bending or rotation of the knee TORN CARTILAGE—damage to the knee's shock absorbers
LEGS (LOWER)	CALF STRAIN—overstretching of the lower leg SHIN SPLINTS—hard impact to the shin
ANKLES AND FEET	TWISTED OR BROKEN ANKLE—caused by rapid turning or a bad tackle ACHILLES STRAIN—strained tendon in the heel METATARSAL FRACTURE—fractured foot bones

REHABILITATION

When top players get injured, they have a team of medical experts to guide them through the painful process of rehabilitation. In the case of a broken leg, after approximately four weeks in a cast, the player will begin a grueling session of gym work, focused on rebuilding the muscle tissue. Usually the injured body part ends up stronger than it was before the injury.

MEND IT LIKE BECKHAM

In April 2002, David Beckham broke the second metatarsal in his right foot—a long tubular bone in the instep. With just six weeks before the beginning of the World Cup, all England fans (and some of the soccer world) became focused on the complex rehabilitation of bone fractures. While some players have been out for many months, Beckham, albeit treading tentatively, was able to play again quickly.

HYPERBARIC CHAMBER

Studies have proved the recovery period from certain injuries is reduced by 70 percent when players are treated with Hyperbaric Oxygen Therapy—essentially time spent in an oxygen tent.

BIZARRE INJURIES

MATCH INJURIES

SHUT IT:
In 1975, Manchester United goalkeeper Alex Stepney was yelling at his defense so hard that he dislocated his jaw and had to be replaced.

BARKING MAD:
The career of Chick Brodie, Brentford goalkeeper, ended in October 1970. He had collided with a sheepdog that had run onto the field and shattered his kneecap while the dog got the ball.

TRAINING INJURIES

LOOSE MOOSE:
The Norwegian defender Svein Grondalen had to withdraw from an international game in the 1970s after colliding with a moose during his daily run.

PAY ATTENTION:
In 2003, Everton's Richard Wright twisted his ankle falling over a sign that warned players not to warm up in the goalmouth.

INJURIES AT HOME

HOME HELP:
Danish goalkeeper Michael Stensgaard retired in 1999 after suffering an injury to his shoulder while he attempted to fold down an ironing board.

CLOSE SHAVE:
Spanish goalkeeper Santiago Cañizares missed out on the 2002 World Cup when he dropped a bottle of cologne and a shard of glass severed the tendon in his right foot.

WATCH OUT:
In 1998, American goalkeeper Kasey Keller knocked out his front teeth while removing the golf clubs from his car.

AND THE AWARD GOES TO...

WORLD'S GREATEST PLAY-ACTOR

In Brazil's opening round game against Turkey at the 2002 World Cup, Hakan Ünsal kicked the ball at the legs of Brazilian Rivaldo. Rivaldo, standing at the corner flag, grasped his face and fell to the ground, Ünsal was then sent off. FIFA later fined Rivaldo $7,350 for play-acting.

FAKING IT
Brazil's Rivaldo is a brilliantly gifted player, but prone to acts of simulation.

PLANET
SOCCER

FIFA CONFEDERATIONS

The Fédération Internationale de Football Association (FIFA) is the global governing body of soccer. Based in Zurich, Switzerland, it was founded in 1907 by Belgium, Denmark, France, the Netherlands, Spain, Sweden, and Switzerland. The British home nations had turned down an invitation to lead the creation of a global organization five years earlier, but did eventually join the founding seven, only to resign and rejoin twice in the 1920s.

A GLOBAL GIANT

FIFA is the affiliating body for all the major global soccer competitions, first among which is the World Cup, and has acquired more than 200 member countries. These soccer nations are organized into six geographical confederations that each run their own tournaments. FIFA was a small and relatively poorly resourced organization until the 1970s, but under the presidency of Brazilian João Havelange, the World Cup was transformed into the premiere global sporting event. Despite its unique position as the custodian of the world's most popular game, FIFA regularly ranks at the bottom of global surveys on the transparency and accountability of global NGOs.

THE CONFEDERATIONS

The unique geography of planet soccer has seen Israel and Kazakhstan join Europe, Australia leave Oceania for Asia, and South America reduced to its ten largest members with the three minnows of Surinam, Guyana, and French Guyana packed off to the Caribbean.

NORTH AND CENTRAL AMERICA

CONCACAF
Founded: 1961
Headquarters: New York, NY

SOUTH AMERICA

CONMEBOL
Founded: 1916
Headquarters: Asunción, Paraguay

NON-FIFA SOCCER

FIFA may appear to cover the world, but a substantial amount of soccer is played beyond its control. Such teams include those of stateless ethnic groups, such as the Sami of Scandinavia and the European Roma, micro-nations including Vatican City, Monaco, and the Marshall Islands, minorities within bigger states, and regions seeking autonomy, such as Padania in Italy.

STAT ATTACK

FIFA

FÉDÉRATION INTERNATIONALE DE FOOTBALL ASSOCIATION
NUMBER OF MEMBERS: 208
COMPETITIONS:
World Cup, Women's World Cup, Under-16 World Championship, Youth World Championship, Club World Championship, Confederations Cup
AWARDS: FIFA World Player of the Year, FIFA World Team of the Year, FIFA Fair Play Award

MAP KEY

- CONCACAF
- CONMEBOL
- UEFA
- CAF
- AFC
- OFC

CONCACAF

CONFEDERATION OF NORTH, CENTRAL AMERICAN, AND CARIBBEAN ASSOCIATION FOOTBALL
NUMBER OF MEMBERS: 35
COMPETITIONS: CONCACAF Gold Cup, CONCACAF Women's Gold Cup, CONCACAF Champions Cup

CONMEBOL

CONFEDERACIÓN SUDAMERICANA DE FÚTBOL
NUMBER OF MEMBERS: 10
COMPETITIONS: Copa América, Copa Libertadores, Copa Sudamericana

UEFA

UNION DES ASSOCIATIONS EUROPÉENNES DE FOOTBALL
NUMBER OF MEMBERS: 52
COMPETITIONS: European Championship, European Champions League, UEFA Europa League, Intertoto Cup, European Super Cup, European Women's Championship

HE WAS JUST A MASTER OF **POWER**

GUIDO TOGNONI, FIFA EXECUTIVE COMMITTEE
ON JOÃO HAVELANGE, PRESIDENT OF FIFA 1974–98

SEATS ON THE FIFA EXECUTIVE

- UEFA—**8**
- CAF—**4**
- AFC—**4**
- CONMEBOL—**3**
- CONCAF—**3**
- FIFA—**2**
- OFC—**1**

1 2 3 3 4 4 8

EXTRA-TERRESTRIAL SOCCER?

Although the exact number fluctuates from time to time due to political factors, the number of nations in the world is listed by the UN as 192. So where exactly does FIFA get the extra 16 countries? The answer lies in the practice of awarding member status to non-sovereign countries, such as the four principalities of the UK—England, Scotland, Wales, and Northern Ireland.

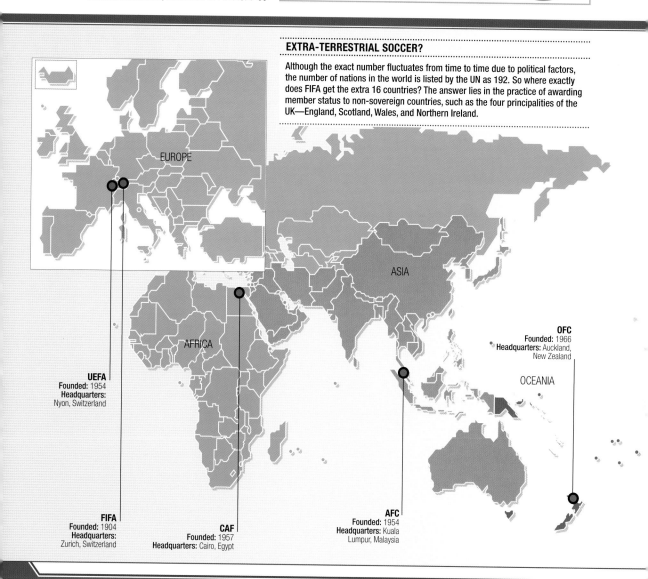

EUROPE

ASIA

OFC
Founded: 1966
Headquarters: Auckland, New Zealand

OCEANIA

AFRICA

UEFA
Founded: 1954
Headquarters:
Nyon, Switzerland

FIFA
Founded: 1904
Headquarters:
Zurich, Switzerland

CAF
Founded: 1957
Headquarters: Cairo, Egypt

AFC
Founded: 1954
Headquarters: Kuala Lumpur, Malaysia

CAF

CONFÉDÉRATION AFRICAINE DE FOOTBALL
NUMBER OF MEMBERS: 52
COMPETITIONS: African Cup of Nations, African Champions League, African Confederations Cup, CAF Super Cup

AFC

ASIAN FOOTBALL CONFEDERATION
NUMBER OF MEMBERS: 44
COMPETITIONS: Asian Cup, Asian Games, Asian Champions League, Asian Women's Championships

OFC

OCEANIA FOOTBALL CONFEDERATION
NUMBER OF MEMBERS: 11
COMPETITIONS: Oceania Nations Cup, OFC Club Championships, Oceania Women's Tournament

EUROPE: UEFA

ENGLAND

HOME   AWAY

POPULATION: 61 MILLION
CAPITAL: LONDON
LICENSED PLAYERS:
MALE: 1.4 MILLION
FEMALE: 42,500
PROFESSIONALS: 6,000
REGISTERED CLUBS: 42,500

English soccer is heavily colored by the fact that it was the birthplace of the professional sport. The strength of the domestic game meant that the nation was slow to pick up on international soccer— England didn't bother to enter the World Cup until 1950. Despite an influx of foreign coaches and players, English soccer is rooted in the Victorian values of hard work.

BOBBY CHARLTON
With a thunderous shot and curious "comb-over" haircut, Charlton was a key member of England's 1966 World Cup winning team.

THE GOOD AND THE BAD

As the "fathers" of soccer and the joint-oldest international team—founded in 1872, the same year as Scotland's team—England play under a huge weight of expectation. Although one of an elite group of only seven nations to have won the World Cup, England is nevertheless prone to buckling under the pressure. Aside from winning the trophy in 1966, the highest achievements have been emotional semi-final penalty defeats to Germany, in both Italia '90 (in which Paul Gascoigne memorably wept) and Euro '96. All in all, England's typical performance—a quarter-final exit—has been about right.

1966 AND ALL THAT

England's finest hour came in 1966 when, as hosts of the eighth World Cup, Alf Ramsey's side triumphed 4–2 over West Germany to lift the Jules Rimet trophy. Geoff Hurst became the first and only player to score a hat-trick in the final, when he scored in the dying seconds of the game.

PAUL GASCOIGNE

Described as "daft as a brush" by England manager Bobby Robson, midfielder Paul Gascoigne was one of England's most talented and charismatic players of the 1980s and '90s.

SOME PEOPLE ARE ON THE PITCH. THEY THINK IT'S ALL OVER...
...IT IS NOW!

KENNETH WOLSTENHOLME
ENGLISH SPORTSCASTER ON ENGLAND'S FINAL GOAL, WORLD CUP FINAL 1966

MANAGER'S WIN RATIO

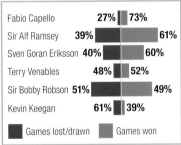

Manager	Games lost/drawn	Games won
Fabio Capello	27%	73%
Sir Alf Ramsey	39%	61%
Sven Goran Eriksson	40%	60%
Terry Venables	48%	52%
Sir Bobby Robson	51%	49%
Kevin Keegan	61%	39%

STAT ATTACK

GOVERNING BODY:
The Football Association
FOUNDED: 1863
NATIONAL STADIUM:
Wembley, London, 90,000
FIRST MATCH: 0–0 vs Scotland, 1882
BIGGEST WIN: 13–0 vs Ireland, 1882
BIGGEST DEFEAT: 1–7 vs Hungary, 1954

THE LEGENDS

MOST CAPPED PLAYERS

Name	From/To	Caps
Peter SHILTON	1970–90	125
David BECKHAM	1996–present	110
Bobby MOORE	1962–73	108
Bobby CHARLTON	1958–70	106
Billy WRIGHT	1946–59	105
Bryan ROBSON	1980–91	90

TOP GOALSCORERS

Name	From/To	Goals
Bobby CHARLTON	1958–70	49
Gary LINEKER	1984–92	48
Jimmy GREAVES	1959–67	44
Michael OWEN	1997–present	40
Tom FINNEY	1946–58	30
Nat LOFTHOUSE	1950–58	30

THE PREMIER LEAGUE

Lured by media mogul Rupert Murdoch's millions, the clubs in the old English top division (Division 1) split from its governing body, the Football League, in 1992 to form the Premier League. It has grown into the most lucrative league in the world, attracting a global television audience and the best players and managers on the planet. It's easy to forget that the Football League has been running since 1888.

WHEN IT ALL GOES WRONG

Following considerable success in the late 1990s, Leeds United borrowed heavily against assumed future revenue from the UEFA Champions League. When they failed to qualify in 2001, everything started to unravel. The best players were sold, the club went into administration, and is now languishing in the lower divisions.

FA CUP MAGIC

The growing importance of qualification for the Champions League has reduced the importance of the FA Cup, but young boys still dream of lifting the trophy at Wembley in May. The world's oldest soccer competition has thrown up legends galore, from the giant-killing exploits of non-league teams to Manchester City keeper Bert Trautmann playing on in the 1956 final with a broken neck.

DAVID **BECKHAM**

Dubbed "Goldenballs," Beckham is a dead-ball expert with a pop-star wife who has become a national icon. He overcame the shame of a red card that led to England's exit from the '98 World Cup to later captain his country.

BORN: **MAY 2, 1975, LONDON, ENGLAND**
HEIGHT: **6FT (1.83M)**
CLUBS: **MANCHESTER UNITED, REAL MADRID, LA GALAXY, AC MILAN**
INTERNATIONAL CAPS: **109**

STAT ATTACK

PREMIER LEAGUE / DIV 1

LEAGUE STRUCTURE: 20 Teams
TOP SCORER: Jimmy Greaves, **357** goals
MOST SUCCESSFUL TEAM: Liverpool, **18** League Titles
BIGGEST WIN: 12–0, West Brom vs Darwen, 1891, and Nottingham Forest vs Leicester Fosse, 1908
HIGHEST ATTENDANCE: 83,260, Manchester United vs Arsenal, 1948 (played at Maine Road)
DIVISIONS BELOW PREMIER LEAGUE: Football League Championship (**24** teams), Leagues One and Two (**24** teams each)

FA CUP

Inaugurated in 1872, the FA Cup is the most prestigious knock-out competition. All clubs from the English League system are eligible, as well as six clubs from the Welsh League.
TOP SCORER: Henry Cursham (Nottingham County), **49** goals
MOST WINS: Manchester United, **11** wins
BIGGEST WIN: 26–0, Preston North End vs Hyde, 1887

LEAGUE CUP

A knock-out competition. 92 clubs can enter —the 20 clubs of the FA Premier League, and the 72 clubs of the Football League.
TOP SCORERS: Ian Rush and Geoff Hurst, **49** goals each
MOST WINS: Liverpool, **7** wins
BIGGEST WINS: 10–0, Liverpool vs Fulham, 1986, and West Ham vs Bury, 1983

13 Paying spectators at Stockport County vs Leicester City in 1921

1,414 Average number of days that England managers have held the job

21 Number of different last names—such as United, City, Rovers, or Villa—of clubs playing in the English Premier and Football Leagues

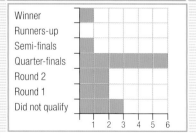

WORLD CUP

	1	2	3	4	5	6
Winner						
Runners-up						
Semi-finals						
Quarter-finals						
Round 2						
Round 1						
Did not qualify						

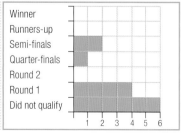

EURO CHAMPIONSHIPS

	1	2	3	4	5	6
Winner						
Runners-up						
Semi-finals						
Quarter-finals						
Round 2						
Round 1						
Did not qualify						

WEMBLEY STADIUM

The old Wembley stadium, built in 1923 for the British Empire Exhibition, had been the home of English soccer for over 80 years. However, despite regular refurbishment, it was tired, dilapidated, and inadequate. In a rare act of boldness, the FA decided to knock it down (including the two iconic towers) and start again. Although plagued by cost and time overruns, the new Wembley opened in 2007 and is one of the largest and most generously appointed soccer stadiums in the world.

WEMBLEY NATIONAL STADIUM

WEMBLEY STADIUM, WEMBLEY, LONDON, HA9 0WS, ENGLAND

OWNER:
THE FOOTBALL ASSOCIATION (THE FA)

ARCHITECTS:
FOSTER AND PARTNERS
HOK SPORT VENUE EVENT

OPENED: 2007

CONSTRUCTION COST:
$1.6 BILLION (£798 MILLION)

CAPACITY: 90,000

HUGE INVESTMENT

The new Wembley stadium is a fitting architectural expression of modern English soccer. Its size and cost are testament to the vast sums of money and waves of euphoria that were surrounding the Premiership and national team. Its funding was complex and international, relying at one point on a German bank for key funds. Ultimately, the stadium's finances rested on selling a significant number of expensive, long-term commercial and hospitality contracts, and using the stadium for other sporting events and rock concerts.

Field dimensions
At 115 x 75 yd (105 x 69 m), the field is slightly narrower than the old Wembley

Roof
The roof covers an area of more than 484,00 sq ft (45,000 sq m), of which 172,000 sq ft (16,000 sq m) is retractable

Foundations
The foundations comprise 4,000 driven piles, up to 115 ft (35 m) deep

FIELD PROBLEMS

Although spectators love the new Wembley for its sightlines and atmosphere, there have been problems with the field—perhaps as a result of its multi-purpose use.

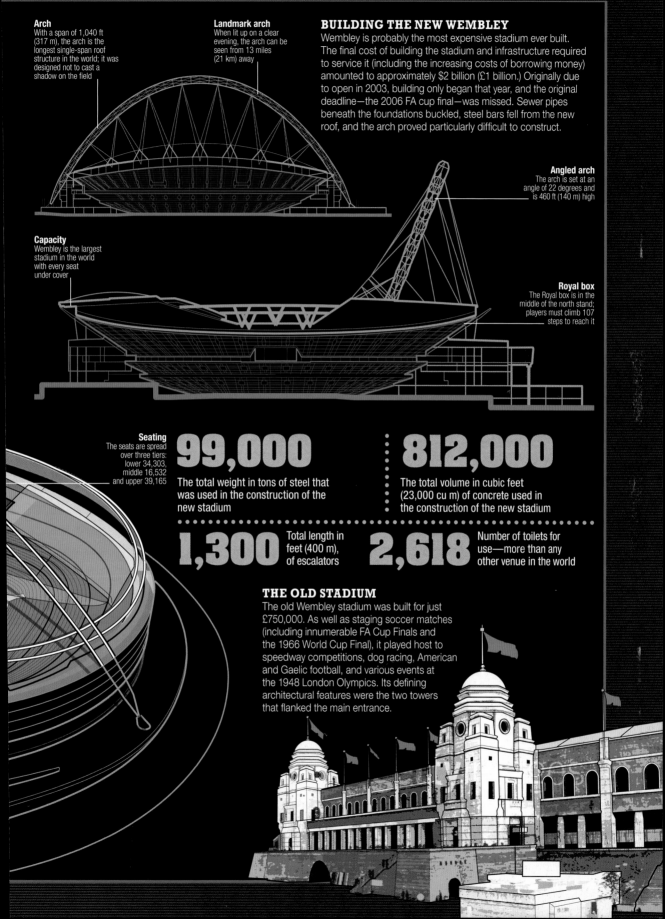

Arch
With a span of 1,040 ft (317 m), the arch is the longest single-span roof structure in the world; it was designed not to cast a shadow on the field

Landmark arch
When lit up on a clear evening, the arch can be seen from 13 miles (21 km) away

BUILDING THE NEW WEMBLEY

Wembley is probably the most expensive stadium ever built. The final cost of building the stadium and infrastructure required to service it (including the increasing costs of borrowing money) amounted to approximately $2 billion (£1 billion.) Originally due to open in 2003, building only began that year, and the original deadline—the 2006 FA cup final—was missed. Sewer pipes beneath the foundations buckled, steel bars fell from the new roof, and the arch proved particularly difficult to construct.

Angled arch
The arch is set at an angle of 22 degrees and is 460 ft (140 m) high

Capacity
Wembley is the largest stadium in the world with every seat under cover

Royal box
The Royal box is in the middle of the north stand; players must climb 107 steps to reach it

Seating
The seats are spread over three tiers: lower 34,303, middle 16,532 and upper 39,165

99,000
The total weight in tons of steel that was used in the construction of the new stadium

812,000
The total volume in cubic feet (23,000 cu m) of concrete used in the construction of the new stadium

1,300
Total length in feet (400 m), of escalators

2,618
Number of toilets for use—more than any other venue in the world

THE OLD STADIUM

The old Wembley stadium was built for just £750,000. As well as staging soccer matches (including innumerable FA Cup Finals and the 1966 World Cup Final), it played host to speedway competitions, dog racing, American and Gaelic football, and various events at the 1948 London Olympics. Its defining architectural features were the two towers that flanked the main entrance.

ENGLAND: THE NORTHERN CLUBS

Soccer was born in the universities and public (private) schools of southern England, but it was in the industrial North that it first became a mass spectator sport. The game remains close to a religion in the urban centers of Merseyside (the Liverpool area), Manchester, Yorkshire, and the Northeast.

NICKNAME: REDS
FOUNDED:
LIVERPOOL, 1892
STADIUM:
ANFIELD, 45,400   HOME
DOMESTIC HONORS:
LEAGUE 18; FA CUP 7
INTERNATIONAL HONORS:
CHAMPIONS LEAGUE 1977, 1978, 1981, 1984, 2006;
UEFA CUP 1973, 1976, 2001

LIVERPOOL FC

The most successful club in the history of English soccer, the Reds enjoyed an unprecedented period of dominance during the 1970s and '80s, winning seven league titles and four European Cups between 1976 and 1984, mostly under Bob Paisley. Since the 1990s, league success has passed to Manchester United, and Liverpool is regarded as a sleeping giant. But by the standards of most clubs, they have been wide awake, winning FA Cups, League Cups, UEFA Cups, and the Champions League.

PEOPLE THINK FOOTBALL IS A MATTER OF LIFE AND DEATH. I ASSURE YOU, IT'S MUCH MORE SERIOUS THAN THAT

BILL SHANKLY, LIVERPOOL MANAGER 1959–74

IAN RUSH
Despite supporting Merseyside rivals Everton as a child, Rush went on to become Liverpool's highest scorer, netting 346 times in 469 games.

HEYSEL AND HILLSBOROUGH
Liverpool fans were involved in two fatal crowd disasters in the 1980s. At the 1985 European Cup Final at the Heysel Stadium in Brussels, Liverpool fans charged the Juventus fans, leading to a wall collapse that killed 39 Italians. Four years later, a policing error prior to the FA Cup semi-final against Nottingham Forest led to thousands of Liverpool fans being diverted into a tiny area of the Hillsborough Stadium. Ninety-six fans were killed.

THE KOP AT ANFIELD

The Kop, or to give it its full name the "Spion Kop," is the most famous field in world soccer. Named after a steeply sloping Boer War battlefield, it is a single-tier structure that once held 28,000 delirious fans. All-seater regulations have reduced capacity to 12,390 seats, but it remains an intimidating place, capable—in the words of Bill Shankly—of "sucking the ball into the net."

BILL SHANKLY
A short, wiry Scotsman, Shankly led Liverpool to two League titles, two FA Cups, and the UEFA Cup. His legacy was a simple but effective "pass and move" philosophy.

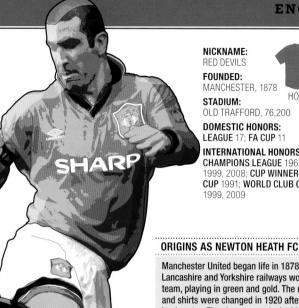

NICKNAME:
RED DEVILS
FOUNDED:
MANCHESTER, 1878
STADIUM:
OLD TRAFFORD, 76,200
DOMESTIC HONORS:
LEAGUE 17; FA CUP 11
INTERNATIONAL HONORS:
CHAMPIONS LEAGUE 1968, 1999, 2008; CUP WINNERS' CUP 1991; WORLD CLUB CUP 1999, 2009

HOME

MANCHESTER UNITED

With the biggest stadium in England and the largest global fan base—estimated at more than five percent of the world's population—United has been by far the most successful club of the 1990s and 2000s, with league titles in double figures, as well as Champions League glory. Manager Sir Alex Ferguson has been at the helm for more than 20 years, and is an unquestioned genius who has won more trophies than any other British manager.

ORIGINS AS NEWTON HEATH FC

Manchester United began life in 1878 as the Lancashire and Yorkshire railways works team, playing in green and gold. The name and shirts were changed in 1920 after near bankruptcy. They have never looked back.

PREMIER LEAGUE WINS

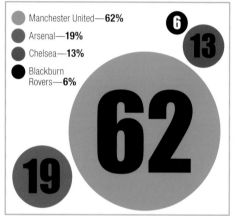

Manchester United—**62%**
Arsenal—**19%**
Chelsea—**13%**
Blackburn Rovers—**6%**

6
13
62
19

THE BUSBY BABES

The man who took Manchester United to greatness once played for Liverpool. Sir Matt Busby became manager in 1945 and began bringing youth players into the first team, the greatest of whom was the wing-half Duncan Edwards. They won the league in 1956 and 1957, and were set to take on Europe when, on February 6, 1958, their plane crashed in Germany. Seven players died, followed a week later by Edwards.

ERIC CANTONA

Ferguson's surprise 1992 signing of Cantona, a maverick French striker with a reputation for trouble, turned out to be an inspired move. More than a decade of domestic dominance was to follow, and Cantona was voted "Greatest United Player of the 20th Century" in 2001.

BORN: **MAY 24, 1966, MARSEILLE, FRANCE**
HEIGHT: **6FT 2IN (1.88M)**
MAIN CLUBS: **AUXERRE, MARSEILLE, NIMES, LEEDS UNITED, MANCHESTER UNITED**
INTERNATIONAL CAPS: **43**

THE TREBLE

In 1968, Sir Matt Busby's second great United team, featuring the talents of George Best, Denis Law, and Bobby Charlton, became the first English side to lift the European Cup. Its achievements were surpassed, however, when the team of 1999 became the first English club to win the treble, winning the Champions League, the Premier League, and the FA Cup in a single season. The victory over Bayern Munich in the Champions League final was particularly memorable. United were a goal down after 90 minutes, but scored twice in stoppage time to win the game.

BEST OF THE REST

EVERTON (1878)
Once the dominant Merseyside team, in modern times Everton have had to stomach Liverpool's success. Their most recent trophy was the FA Cup in 1995.
HONORS: LEAGUE 9, FA CUP 5; CUP WINNERS' CUP 1985

MANCHESTER CITY (1887)
City have lived in the shadow of Manchester United, but recent years have brought new wealth to the club. In 2008, it was bought by the fabulously rich Abu Dhabi Royal Family.
HONORS: LEAGUE 2, FA CUP 4; CUP WINNERS' CUP 1970

BLACKBURN ROVERS (1875)
Blackburn were a force to be reckoned with just before World War I, but had to wait until 1995 for their next league title, which was financed by the investment of local steel magnate Sir Jack Walker.
HONORS: LEAGUE 3, FA CUP 6

LEEDS UNITED (1919)
At the start of the 21st century, Leeds came within a whisker of becoming a top European club. They reached the semi-final of the Champions League in 2001.
HONORS: LEAGUE 3, FA CUP 1; UEFA CUP 1968, 1971

NEWCASTLE UNITED (1881)
"The Toon," as the club is known to its fanatical fans, regularly attracts home crowds of over 52,000. Despite an enviable revenue stream, success has proved elusive in recent years.
HONORS: LEAGUE 4, FA CUP 6; UEFA CUP 1969

PRESTON NORTH END (1881)
Preston secured immortality by winning the first two league titles. Success has been thin on the ground since the 1890s, but the Lancashire club finished as league runners-up in 1953 and 1958.
HONORS: LEAGUE 2, FA CUP 2

ENGLAND: THE SOUTHERN CLUBS

Although London is almost ten times the size of the next biggest city in the UK, it was not until 1931 that the English league title went to the capital. Liverpool alone have won roughly the same number of titles as all of the London teams combined. However, Chelsea or Arsenal won five of the 11 league titles between 1998 and 2008.

NICKNAME:
THE BLUES
FOUNDED:
LONDON, 1905
STADIUM:
STAMFORD BRIDGE, 42,300

HOME

DOMESTIC HONORS:
LEAGUE 3, CUP 4
INTERNATIONAL HONORS:
CHAMPIONS LEAGUE
RUNNERS-UP 2008; CUP
WINNERS' CUP 1971, 1998;
EUROPEAN SUPER CUP 1998

CHELSEA

Arriving late at the top table of English soccer, prior to 2005, Chelsea had won just one league title—in 1955. The club's past is checkered; the 1971 Cup Winners' Cup victory was the high point, and near bankruptcy and hooliganism in the early 1980s were the low points. Bankrolled by the super-wealthy Roman Abramovich since 2003, the sky seems the limit.

KINGS OF THE KING'S ROAD

During the 1960s, London's King's Road became one of the most fashionable streets in the world, and the center of the "swinging" music scene. Stamford Bridge, Chelsea's stadium, is located in the area and became a magnet for celebrities including Steve McQueen, Michael Caine, and Raquel Welch. The Chelsea team of the era played glamorous, stylish soccer, epitomized by talismanic striker Peter Osgood.

THE ITALIAN CONNECTION

Chelsea had already met with recent success by the time Abramovich arrived, having won the FA Cup in 1997 and the Cup Winners' Cup in 1998. Much of this success was the result of the purchase of a series of top-class Italians, notably Gianluca Vialli (who became player-manager in 1998), Roberto di Matteo, and the great Gianfranco Zola.

HE CAME FROM IT-ALY TO PLAY FOR
CHE-ELSEA

CHELSEA FANS SING THEIR APPRECIATION OF **GIANLUCA VIALLI**

THE ABRAMOVICH ERA

In June 2003, Chelsea fans woke to find that their club had become the richest in the world. Wily chairman Ken Bates, who purchased the debt-ridden club for $2 million in the early 1980s, had sold it to Roman Abramovich, a Russian billionaire, for $280 million. Abramovich then spent hundreds of millions of pounds to build one of the strongest teams in world soccer.

GIANFRANCO **ZOLA**

The closest a player has ever come to being a soccer wizard, Zola learned his trade from Diego Maradona while the pair played for Italian champions Napoli. Moving to Chelsea in 1996, he thrilled fans with a wealth of breath-taking ball tricks.

BORN: **JULY 5, 1966, OLIENA, ITALY**
HEIGHT: **5FT 5½IN (1.66M)**
MAIN CLUBS: **TORRES, NAPOLI, PARMA, CHELSEA, CAGLIARI**
INTERNATIONAL CAPS: **35**

NICKNAME:
THE GUNNERS

FOUNDED:
LONDON, 1886

HOME

STADIUM:
THE EMIRATES, 60,000

DOMESTIC HONORS:
LEAGUE 13, CUP 10

INTERNATIONAL HONORS:
CUP WINNERS' CUP 1994; UEFA
CUP 1970

ARSENAL

Founded in 1886 as Dial Square FC, a works team from the Royal Arsenal in Woolwich, Arsenal took their current name in 1914. Their first golden era was under manager Herbert Chapman, who won three league titles and persuaded the authorities to rename the local underground station, Gillespie Road, to Arsenal. Following the arrival of French manager Arsène Wenger, Arsenal shed their defensive, conservative past and emerged as one of the most attractive passing teams in the world.

TONY ADAMS

Adams was made Arsenal captain at the age of just 21 and spent his entire playing career at the club. A tall, gangly defender, he was a courageous, masterful reader of the game. He became an Arsenal legend during his 19-year, 504-game playing career.

BORN: OCTOBER 10, 1966, LONDON, ENGLAND
HEIGHT: 6FT 3IN (1.91M)
MAIN CLUBS: ARSENAL
INTERNATIONAL CAPS: 66

THE NORTH LONDON DERBY

Few local derbies match the intensity of an Arsenal vs Tottenham Hotspur tie. The roots of the rivalry can be traced to 1913, when Arsenal moved to north London from their former south-London home in Woolwich, and 1919, when they joined the top tier. Arsenal, who had finished fifth in Division 2, won a place at the expense of Tottenham, who had come 20th in Division 1.

ONE NIL TO THE ARSENAL

Under manager George Graham (1986–95), Arsenal were known for eking out 1–0 wins with efficient, defensively minded displays. Arsène Wenger, who arrived in 1996, changed things completely, introducing flowing, attacking soccer.

MIDLANDS CLUBS

Clubs from the Midlands, an area of central England known for its industrial heritage, have enjoyed notable success in the past. Aston Villa (see right) won five titles between 1894 and 1900, and Wolverhampton Wanderers won three during the 1950s. Although recent success has been limited, there are usually three or four Midlands clubs in the Premiership, and Villa has recently threatened the dominance of the big four clubs.

BEST OF THE REST

TOTTENHAM HOTSPUR (1882)
Spurs' greatest achievement was winning the Double in 1961. Since then, success has been limited to cup competitions, but the club has a reputation for attractive soccer.
HONORS: LEAGUE 2, CUP 8; CUP WINNERS' CUP 1963; UEFA CUP 1972, 1984

WEST HAM UNITED (1895)
"The Hammers" have won three FA Cups and the Cup Winners' Cup. The club is renowned for producing great players who move on to better things at bigger clubs.
HONORS: CUP 3; CUP WINNERS' CUP 1965

ASTON VILLA (1874)
In the first 12 years of English professional soccer, Villa won 5 league titles and 3 FA Cups. In 1982, the club became the fourth English Club to win the European Cup.
HONORS: LEAGUE 7, CUP 7; EUROPEAN CUP 1982

PORTSMOUTH (1898)
Famed for the "Pompey chimes," a crowd chant that rings out at Fratton Park, Portsmouth is the premier south coast club. It won the league title in 1949 and 1950.
HONORS: LEAGUE 2, CUP 2

IPSWICH TOWN (1878)
Nicknamed "The Tractor Boys," this small East Anglian club punches above its weight. They have supplied England with two great managers—Alf Ramsey and Bobby Robson.
HONORS: LEAGUE 1, CUP 1; UEFA CUP 1981

NOTTINGHAM FOREST (1865)
Nottingham Forest have won as many European Cups as Barcelona and Inter Milan, thanks to the genius of Brian Clough, who led the unfashionable side to greatness in the late 1970s and early '80s.
HONORS: LEAGUE 1, CUP 2; EUROPEAN CUP 1979, 1980

BRIAN CLOUGH
One of the greatest ever English managers, Clough was a true maverick who managed Leeds, Derby, and Nottingham Forest. His nickname of "Old Big 'Ed" was justified; "They say Rome wasn't built in a day, but I wasn't on that job," he once quipped.

EUROPE

HOME

AWAY

POPULATION: 5.1 MILLION
CAPITAL: EDINBURGH
FA: SCOTTISH FOOTBALL ASSOCIATION
LICENSED PLAYERS:
MALE: 374,000
FEMALE: 4,500
PROFESSIONALS: 4,000
REGISTERED CLUBS: 6,500

SCOTLAND

Scotland's contribution to the emergence of professional soccer is on a par with their old rivals, England. The game was played in private schools in Glasgow and Edinburgh in the 1850s, and Queen's Park became the first soccer club to be founded in 1867. By 1875, a network of teams had emerged in Scotland, the first international game had been played against England, and the Scottish FA had been founded.

WORLD CUP WOES

Scotland qualified for five consecutive World Cups from 1974 to 1990, but suffered a series of near misses in the contest. They went out on goal difference in 1974, 1978, and 1982, and their most recent outing at France '98 was no luckier, losing to Brazil thanks to an own goal, and exiting in the first round.

KENNY DALGLISH

The first footballer to score 100 goals in both the English and Scottish leagues, during a playing career that spanned four decades, Dalglish was equally successful as a manager.

BORN: **MARCH 4, 1951, GLASGOW, SCOTLAND**
HEIGHT: **5FT 8IN (1.73M)**
MAIN CLUBS: **CELTIC, LIVERPOOL**
INTERNATIONAL CAPS: **102**

STAT ATTACK

NATIONAL TEAM

NATIONAL STADIUM:
Hampden Park, 52,000
WORLD CUP FINALS:
8 appearances
EUROPEAN CHAMPIONSHIPS:
2 appearances
BIGGEST WIN: 11–0 vs Northern Ireland, 1901
BIGGEST DEFEAT: 0–7 vs Uruguay, 1954
MOST CAPS: Kenny Dalglish, **102**
MOST GOALS: Kenny Dalglish and Denis Law, **30**

SCOTTISH SOCCER FIRSTS

Scotland boasts a number of soccer firsts. The first international match to be played was held at the West of Scotland Cricket Ground, Glasgow, in 1872 against England. The first penalty in an official match was taken by Airdrionians in 1891, and the first stadium disaster occurred at Ibrox in 1902.

THE TARTAN ARMY

Scotland beat England at Wembley to win the 1977 Home Championships, the round-robin tournament between the UK national sides, triggering a huge Scottish field invasion. Since then, Scotland's band of traveling fans has become known as the "Tartan Army," and while English traveling fans became more violent in the 1980s and '90s, the Scottish fans won several UEFA awards for good behavior.

THE SPL

The structure of domestic soccer revolves around the domination of rival Glasgow teams, Celtic and Rangers. The two-division system of the 1970s was deemed too uncompetitive, and shrank in 1976 to a 10-team premier league, a cup, and a league cup. In 1998, the teams of the top tier split from the Scottish FA in a similar move to the English clubs (see p.161), forming the Scottish Premier League (SPL).

25 The number of fatalities at the Ibrox stadium disaster in 1902

The number of copies of "Ally's Tartan Army" sold—a record released for Scotland's 1978 World Cup campaign **360,000**

Attendance at the 1937 Scottish Cup final between Celtic and Aberdeen at Hampden Park—a European record for a club match **146,433**

RANGERS

Rangers is the team of Glasgow's Protestant community, and particularly of the Unionists. By World War I, it had become a major club quietly committed to not signing Catholic players—a ban that held until Mo Johnston joined the club in 1989. The club stands against sectarianism, but tensions can run high, especially when playing Celtic (see below).

NICKNAME: GERS
FOUNDED:
GLASGOW, 1873
STADIUM:
IBROX, 51,000
HOME
DOMESTIC HONORS:
LEAGUE 51, CUP 32
INTERNATIONAL HONORS:
EUROPEAN CUP WINNERS' CUP 1972

ALLY McCOIST
McCoist played for Rangers for 15 seasons, and was the key goal scorer in the side that won nine titles in a row (1989–97).

BARCELONA 1972
Rangers' greatest European night was their victory in the 1972 European Cup Winners' Cup, when they beat Dynamo Moscow 3–2 at the Nou Camp in Barcelona. 2008 also saw them finishing runners-up to Zenith St. Petersburg in the UEFA Cup.

NICKNAME:
THE BHOYS
FOUNDED:
GLASGOW, 1888
HOME
STADIUM:
CELTIC PARK, 60,800
DOMESTIC HONORS:
LEAGUE 42, CUP 34
INTERNATIONAL HONORS:
EUROPEAN CUP 1967; UEFA CUP RUNNERS-UP 2003

CELTIC

Founded in 1888 by a Catholic Brother, Celtic provided soccer and a social club for Irish immigrant boys in the poorest parts of Glasgow. Despite its links with the nationalist cause in Ireland—Irish tricolors are regularly flown by the crowd—the club has never banned Protestants. Jock Stein, manager of the great sides of the 1960s, was himself of Protestant roots.

THE LISBON LIONS
Many Celtic fans claim to have witnessed the club's famous 1967 European Cup final win in Lisbon. Celtic's 2–1 victory over Inter Milan started a tradition of European pilgrimage. When the team played Porto in the UEFA Cup final in 2003, more than 80,000 fans—less than half with tickets—made the trip.

THE OLD FIRM DERBY

Celtic and Rangers are known collectively as "The Old Firm" —as the two largest Scottish clubs, it became clear from an early stage that they would benefit financially from cooperating to ensure huge ticket sales. The Old Firm derby occurs four times a season in the SPL and is historically an intense affair.

HENRIK **LARSSON**

Larsson was a key figure at Celtic for seven seasons. The prolific striker was hugely popular with the crowd as he helped Celtic to four league titles, breaking Rangers' long stranglehold on the championship.

BORN: SEPTEMBER 20, 1971, HELSINGBORG, SWEDEN
HEIGHT: 5FT 10IN (1.78M)
MAIN CLUBS: HELSINGBORG, FEYENOORD, CELTIC, BARCELONA, MANCHESTER UNITED
INTERNATIONAL CAPS: 102

BEST OF THE REST

ABERDEEN (1903)
Alex Ferguson's Aberdeen in the 1980s has been the only real challenge to the Glasgow hegemony, but couldn't dislodge the Old Firm.

HONORS: LEAGUE 4, CUP 7; EUROPEAN CUP WINNERS' CUP 1983

HEART OF MIDLOTHIAN (1874)
The club's name was taken from the Edinburgh dance hall where the club began, and after winning the Scottish Cup in 2006, they had something to dance about.

HONORS: LEAGUE 4, CUP 7

HIBERNIAN (1875)
"Hibs" was the first team to be founded by the Irish immigrant community in Scotland. Recent success has been lacking—fans have been waiting half a century for a title win.

HONORS: LEAGUE 4, CUP 2

HOME

AWAY

POPULATION: 3 MILLION
CAPITAL: CARDIFF
FA: FOOTBALL ASSOCIATION OF WALES
LICENSED PLAYERS:
MALE: 157,500
FEMALE: 16,000
PROFESSIONALS: 550
REGISTERED CLUBS: 1,900

WALES

Soccer took off in north Wales in the late 19th century, then spread to the cities and coal-mining valleys of south Wales. Following World War I, the leading Welsh sides—Cardiff City, Swansea Town, Newport, and Wrexham—joined the English league system and played in the English FA Cup. Although Wales has consistently produced players of the highest caliber, including John Charles, John Toshack, and Ryan Giggs, it has inevitably been with English clubs that they have made their mark.

CROSS-BORDER COMPETITION

The anomalous system of clubs playing in both English and Welsh competitions ended in the 1990s, when the League of Wales (renamed the Welsh Premier League in 2002) and FAW Premier Cup were set up. The Welsh clubs playing in England were excluded.

CARDIFF CITY VS EUROPE

As winners of the Welsh Cup, Cardiff City won a place in the 1968 Cup Winners' Cup, and —amazingly for a team fighting relegation—reached the semi-finals. They met Shamrock Rovers, Dutch side NAC Breda, and traveled deep into the USSR to play Torpedo Moscow in Tashkent, but were beaten 3–2 by Hamburg in the semi-final.

STAT ATTACK

NATIONAL TEAM

NICKNAME: The Dragons
NATIONAL STADIUM:
Millennium Stadium, 74,500
WORLD CUP FINALS: 1 appearance, quarter-finals **1958**
EUROPEAN CHAMPIONSHIPS:
No appearances
BIGGEST WIN: 11–0 vs Northern Ireland, 1888
BIGGEST DEFEAT: 0–9 vs Scotland, 1878
MOST CAPS: Neville Southall, **92**
MOST GOALS: Ian Rush, **28**

1927 FA CUP

Cardiff City's 1–0 victory over Arsenal in the 1927 FA Cup is the only time a Welsh club has won the trophy. The first FA Cup final to be broadcast live by the BBC, it featured one of the worst goalkeeping mistakes ever as Arsenal's Dan Lewis let the ball squirm out of his hands and over the line for an own goal.

WORLD CUP 1958

Wales failed to qualify for the 1958 World Cup. However, FIFA held a ballot of second-placed UEFA teams to decide a play-off opponent to play Israel, after all their group qualifying opponents had refused to play them. Belgium won the lottery but turned it down, so Wales took their chance, beating Israel to book a place at the World Cup finals in Sweden, and making it all the way to the semi-finals.

MAIN DOMESTIC CLUBS

CARDIFF CITY
FOUNDED: Cardiff, 1899
STADIUM: Ninian Park
CAPACITY: 22,000

HOME

INTERNATIONAL HONORS: None
LEAGUE: 0 **CUP:** 1

SWANSEA CITY
FOUNDED: Swansea, 1912
STADIUM: Liberty Stadium
CAPACITY: 20,500

HOME

INTERNATIONAL HONORS: None
LEAGUE: 0 **CUP:** 0

WREXHAM
FOUNDED: Wrexham, 1872
STADIUM: Racecourse Ground
CAPACITY: 15,500

HOME

INTERNATIONAL HONORS: None
LEAGUE: 0 **CUP:** 0

RYAN GIGGS

A lightning-quick left-winger, Giggs has played more games and won more honors for Manchester United than any other player. He made his debut for Wales in 1991 as a 17-year-old and was made captain in 2004.

BORN: NOVEMBER 27, 1973, CARDIFF, WALES
HEIGHT: **5FT 11IN (1.8M)**
MAIN CLUBS: **MANCHESTER UNITED**
INTERNATIONAL CAPS: **64**

NORTHERN IRELAND

Politics and religion have shaped the geography and culture of soccer in Northern Ireland. The game's strongest roots were in industrial Belfast and, following partition from the Republic in 1921, the game was dominated by Unionist teams, such as Linfield, while nationalist teams, such as Belfast Celtic, withdrew.

GEORGE **BEST**

Best was Northern Ireland's greatest player and one of the best, anywhere, ever. He had everything—pace, courage, two equally good feet, superb balance, and an ability, in the words of a Manchester United team mate, to leave opposing defenders with "twisted blood."

BORN: MAY 22, 1946, BELFAST, NORTHERN IRELAND
HEIGHT: **5FT 8IN (1.73M)**
MAIN CLUBS: **MANCHESTER UNITED, LOS ANGELES AZTECS, FULHAM, FORT LAUDERDALE STRIKERS, SAN JOSE EARTHQUAKES**
INTERNATIONAL CAPS: **37**

HOME   AWAY

POPULATION: 1.8 MILLION
CAPITAL: BELFAST
FA: IRISH FOOTBALL ASSOCIATION
REGISTERED PLAYERS:
MALE: 83,000
FEMALE: 9,000
PROFESSIONALS: 220
REGISTERED CLUBS: 820

THE IFA PREMIERSHIP

The top level of competition in Northern Ireland consists of the 12-team IFA Premiership, the Irish Cup, and the Irish League Cup. Attendances are low due to the high level of local support for Scottish rivals Rangers and Celtic, as well as for English Premier League teams. The constant flow of talented young players from Northern Ireland to England and Scotland has also affected the quality of the domestic teams in Northern Ireland.

BELFAST CELTIC

The first nationalist club in Northern Ireland, Belfast Celtic were modeled on their Glasgow namesake. They played in Northern Ireland's Irish League, which led to trouble with Unionist fans. In 1912, a game against Linfield was abandoned after gunfire in the stands. A field invasion following another Linfield tie in 1948 saw many of the team's players badly hurt, and the club withdrew from the Irish League.

THE MAZE

Attempts to build a national stadium in Belfast for soccer, rugby, and Gaelic sports have foundered. Plans to use land formerly occupied by the Maze prison, which held paramilitaries from both sides during the Troubles (the period of violence and protest from the 1960s to late '90s), were blocked by Unionist parties.

STAT ATTACK

NATIONAL TEAM

NICKNAME: "Norn Iron"
NATIONAL STADIUM: Windsor Park, 22,500
WORLD CUP FINALS: 3 appearances, quarter-finals **1958**
EUROPEAN CHAMPIONSHIPS: No appearances
BIGGEST WIN: 7–0 vs Wales, 1930
BIGGEST DEFEAT: 0–13 vs England, 1882
MOST CAPS: Pat Jennings, **119**
MOST GOALS: David Healey, **39**

MAIN DOMESTIC CLUBS

LINFIELD
FOUNDED: Belfast, 1886
STADIUM: Windsor Park
CAPACITY: 20,300
INTERNATIONAL HONORS: None
LEAGUE: 48 **CUP:** 49

HOME

GLENTORAN
FOUNDED: Belfast, 1882
STADIUM: The Oval
CAPACITY: 15,000
INTERNATIONAL HONORS: None
LEAGUE: 22 **CUP:** 20

HOME

CLIFTONVILLE
FOUNDED: Belfast, 1879
STADIUM: Solitude
CAPACITY: 6,000
INTERNATIONAL HONORS: None
LEAGUE: 3 **CUP:** 8

HOME

REPUBLIC OF IRELAND

HOME   AWAY

POPULATION: 4.2 MILLION

CAPITAL: DUBLIN

FA: FOOTBALL ASSOCIATION OF IRELAND

LICENSED PLAYERS:
MALE: 390,000
FEMALE: 31,000

PROFESSIONALS: 500

REGISTERED CLUBS: 5,500

Soccer has always occupied an unusual space in Ireland. The game grew in Dublin under British rule in the 19th century, and a number of teams competed in the all-Ireland cups and leagues. However, the creation of the Gaelic Athletics Association—which aligned nationalism with the revival of Gaelic sports—had the effect of casting soccer as a foreign sport. Further marginalized following Partition in 1921, another 70 years passed before the national team met with any success.

STAT ATTACK

NATIONAL TEAM

NICKNAME: Boys in Green

NATIONAL STADIUM: Croke Park, 82,300

WORLD CUP FINALS: 3 appearances, quarter-finals **1990**

EUROPEAN CHAMPIONSHIPS:
1 appearance

BIGGEST WIN: 8–0 vs Malta, 1983

BIGGEST DEFEAT: 7–0 vs Brazil, 1982

MOST CAPS: Steve Staunton, **102**

MOST GOALS: Robbie Keane, **33**

MAIN DOMESTIC CLUBS

SHAMROCK ROVERS
FOUNDED: Dublin, 1901
STADIUM: Tolka Park
CAPACITY: 9,700   HOME
INTERNATIONAL HONORS: None
LEAGUE: 15 **CUP:** 24

SHELBOURNE
FOUNDED: Dublin, 1895
STADIUM: Tolka Park
CAPACITY: 9,700   HOME
INTERNATIONAL HONORS: None
LEAGUE: 13 **CUP:** 7

BOHEMIANS
FOUNDED: Dublin, 1890
STADIUM: Dalymount Park
CAPACITY: 8,200   HOME
INTERNATIONAL HONORS: None
LEAGUE: 9 **CUP:** 6

THE LEAGUE OF IRELAND

The top-flight FAI League of Ireland contains 12 teams that play each other three times a season. There are also two cup contests, the FAI Cup and League Cup. Attendances are low, especially compared to the sell-out crowds of the national team's games.

SHAMROCK ROVERS

Ireland's biggest club, and the first to play in Europe, Shamrock Rovers has an interesting past. The club spent much of 1967 in the US, playing in the NASL as Boston Rovers. In 1987, the club's stadium was controversially sold to housing developers. In 2005, Rovers were relegated and on the brink of bankruptcy, but re-entered the top flight under fan-ownership.

ROY KEANE

The leading Irish player of the modern era, Keane was an uncompromising midfielder with a volcanic temper and high standards. He became the lynchpin of the hugely successful Manchester United teams of the 1990s.

BORN: **AUGUST 10, 1971, CORK, IRELAND**
HEIGHT: **5FT 10IN (1.78M)**
MAIN CLUBS: **NOTTINGHAM FOREST, MANCHESTER UNITED, CELTIC**
INTERNATIONAL CAPS: **66**

WORLD CUP 1990

The Irish national team finally qualified for a major tournament under manager Jack Charlton, going to the 1988 European Championships and two world Cups—1990 and 1994. Ireland reached the quarter-finals of Italia '90 on the back of vast traveling support, and were the only national team to be granted an audience with the Pope during the contest.

CROKE PARK

Named after a nationalist, anti-soccer Archbishop, Croke Park is the largest stadium in Dublin. Formerly off-limits to soccer, in the new atmosphere of reconciliation following peace in Northern Ireland, Croke Park was made available to the Ireland soccer team in 2007.

BELGIUM

HOME   AWAY

POPULATION: 10.4 MILLION
CAPITAL: BRUSSELS
FA: UNION ROYALE BELGE DES SOCIÉTÉS DE FOOTBALL ASSOCIATION
LICENSED PLAYERS:
MALE: 745,000
FEMALE: 71,300
PROFESSIONALS: 1,500
REGISTERED CLUBS: 2,000

Soccer was played in the English schools of Brussels, and among British textile workers in Antwerp and Liège, as early as the 1870s. As clubs began to emerge in the 1880s, a national association was founded in the 1890s, followed by a Brussels league. The 1970s were marked by professionalization and a short golden age, when Belgian teams won European titles and the national team was a World Cup contender.

WORLD CUP GLORY

The Belgian national team had languished in obscurity until Guy Thys became manager in the late 1970s. They reached the final of the 1980 European Championship, but were beaten by a very late West German goal. The core of this squad, reinforced by midfield playmaker Enzo Scifo, went on to achieve Belgium's finest result —fourth place at the 1986 World Cup after wins over the USSR and Spain, and a semi-final defeat to Argentina.

ENZO **SCIFO**

Midfielder Scifo was the most gifted player of the talented Belgian sides of the 1980s. He came to prominence at the 1986 World Cup, where he won the young player of the tournament award.

BORN: **FEBRUARY 19, 1966, HAINE-SAINT-PAUL, BELGIUM**
HEIGHT: **5FT 10IN (1.78M)**
MAIN CLUBS: **RSC ANDERLECHT, INTER MILAN, AUXERRE, TORINO, AS MONACO**
INTERNATIONAL CAPS: **84**

STAT ATTACK

NATIONAL TEAM

NICKNAME: The Red Devils
NATIONAL STADIUM: King Baudouin, 50,000
WORLD CUP FINALS: 11 appearances, semi-finals **1986**
EUROPEAN CHAMPIONSHIPS: 4 appearances, runners-up **1980**, third place **1972**
BIGGEST WIN: 10–1 vs San Marino, 2001
BIGGEST DEFEAT: 2–11 vs England, 1909
MOST CAPS: Jan Ceulemans, **96**
MOST GOALS: Bernard Voorhoof and Paul van Himst, **30**

DOMESTIC CHALLENGES

The Belgian domestic game has struggled with financial problems and a lack of competition for more than two decades. The big three clubs—Anderlecht, Brugge, and Standard Liège—receive the majority of honors and wealth. Despite local government subsidies and TV revenues, many clubs have been in debt, for which the penalty is relegation, have merged with other clubs, or gone bankrupt and disappeared completely.

1930 WORLD CUP

Belgium's first World Cup appearance was under duress from FIFA, who were intent on increasing the number of teams from Europe. The Belgians lost to the USA in their first game.

MAIN DOMESTIC CLUBS

RSC ANDERLECHT
FOUNDED: Brussels, 1908
STADIUM: Vanden Stock
CAPACITY: 28,100
HOME
INTERNATIONAL HONORS: Cup Winners' Cup **1976** and **1978**; UEFA Cup **1983**
LEAGUE: 29 **CUP:** 9

CLUB BRUGGE
FOUNDED: Brugge, 1891
STADIUM: Jan Breydel
CAPACITY: 29,000
HOME
INTERNATIONAL HONORS: European Cup runners-up **1978**; UEFA Cup runners-up **1976**
LEAGUE: 13 **CUP:** 10

STANDARD LIÈGE
FOUNDED: Liège, 1898
STADIUM: Sclessin
CAPACITY: 30,030
HOME
INTERNATIONAL HONORS: Cup Winners' Cup runners-up **1982**
LEAGUE: 9 **CUP:** 5

MONEY MADNESS

Soccer rarely obeys the laws of economics. When buying players, for example, business people are willing to make far riskier investments than they ever would in their normal dealing lives. For much of soccer's history, owners have had control, imposing maximum wages and ruling the transfer system. Today, however, players and their agents command vast salaries over which owners have little control.

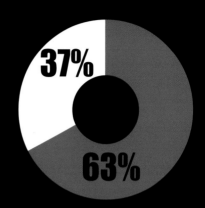

SLICE OF THE PIE
Almost two-thirds of a club's spending is eaten up by players' salaries. The rest goes on operating costs, ground maintenance, and transfer fees.

BOOM TIME
The economics of soccer changed dramatically in the 1990s with the arrival of new forms of pay-per-view TV and sky-high broadcasting rights in the big European leagues. The smaller and lower leagues, however, haven't seen much of this new money—most of which goes to a handful of top-flight clubs.

HOW THE EUROPEAN LEAGUES MAKE MONEY

Legend:
- Match-day revenue
- Broadcasting rights
- Sponsorship deals
- Commercial activities

€ million-billion

- €2.3 b (ENGLAND)
- €1.4 b (GERMANY)
- €1.3 b (SPAIN)
- €1.2 b (ITALY)

WHERE THE MONEY COMES FROM
A club receives most of its income from four main sources—game-day revenue, broadcasting rights, sponsorship deals, and commercial activities (see left). Where necessary, clubs may top-up their coffers with money borrowed from the banks.

IN DEBT
An awful lot of clubs have an awful lot of debt. Many clubs, for example, have been "propped-up" by soft loans from generous owners. Equally, banks with political connections to particular clubs (especially in Spain) have extended huge overdrafts, which have been stretched beyond normal breaking points.

BIG NUMBERS
The English Premier League currently has a three-season broadcasting-rights deal worth $4 billion (£2.7 billion), making it the richest league in the world.

$4,000,00

WHERE THE MONEY GOES

Clubs used to spend less than 40 percent of their income on players' wages, but players are now able to claim a much larger slice of the pie (see left). A club must also pay staff such as coaches and caterers, as well as spend money on maintaining the stadium and training grounds.

TRANSFERS

For the club buying, transfers are a huge drain on resources. UK Premiership clubs spent a combined total of $720 million (£492 million) on players in 2006–07.

INVESTMENTS

Since 1992, UK Premiership clubs have invested a combined total of more than $3.5 billion (£2.4 billion) in new facilities.

PROFITS

In 2007, Manchester United made a profit of $96 million (£66 million)—more than half of the total profit made in the Premier League.

TOP TEN PLAYERS' INCOME FOR 2008 (IN MILLIONS)

David Beckham (LA Galaxy) **$40m (€31m)**

Christiano Ronaldo (Man Utd) **$25.5m (€19.5m)**

Michael Ballack (Chelsea) **$18m (€13.8m)**

Steven Gerrard (Liverpool) **$15.4m (€11.8m)**

Ronaldinho (AC Milan) **$31.5m (€24.1m)**

Thierry Henry (Barcelona) **$22m (€16.8m)**

Ronaldo (Corinthians) **$17.5m (€13.4m)**

Lionel Messi (Barcelona) **$30m (€23m)**

John Terry (Chelsea) **$18m (€13.9m)**

Kaká (AC Milan) **$16.8m (€12.9m)**

TOP FIVE BIGGEST TRANSFER FEES (IN MILLIONS)

Zinédine Zidane: Juventus to Real Madrid— **$68m (£45.6m)**

Luis Figo: Barcelona to Real Madrid— **$54m (£37m)**

Hernan Crespo: Parma to Lazio— **$52m (£35.5m)**

Gianluigi Buffon: Parma to Juventus— **$48m (£32.6m)**

Robinho: Real Madrid to Manchester City— **$47.5m (£32.5m)**

350

The amount in dollars (£240) spent by Leeds United Chairman Peter Risdale on goldfish for his office

350,000

The average cost in dollars (£240,000) of each of the handful of games Thomas Brolin played for Leeds United after his expensive transfer and collapse in form

841

The cost in millions of dollars (£575 million) that Roman Abromavich has put into Chelsea as either soft loans or shares

THE MONEY COMING INTO THE GAME IS INCREDIBLE. BUT... IT COMES IN AND GOES OUT STRAIGHT AWAY

ALAN SUGAR, THEN CHAIRMAN OF TOTTENHAM HOTSPUR

EUROPE

FRANCE

HOME

AWAY

POPULATION: 60.9 MILLION
CAPITAL: PARIS
LICENSED PLAYERS:
MALE: 1.7 MILLION
FEMALE: 49,000
PROFESSIONALS: 2,000
REGISTERED CLUBS: 19,000

After its arrival in France in the late 19th century, soccer jostled for popularity with rugby, and was restricted by the small size of the nation's cities. Nevertheless, a nationwide, professional game was introduced by the 1930s. French soccer has always been marked by stylish passing and a passion for international soccer, which have led to World Cup and European Championship wins.

ZINÉDINE ZIDANE

Of Algerian Berber descent, midfielder Zidane was one of France's greatest players. The key to his brilliance was an astonishing spatial awareness. He delivered perfectly weighted passes time after time, never seeming to look up.

BORN: **JUNE 23, 1972, MARSEILLE, FRANCE**
HEIGHT: **6FT 1IN (1.85M)**
MAIN CLUBS: **CANNES, BORDEAUX, JUVENTUS, REAL MADRID**
INTERNATIONAL CAPS: **108**

A SYMPHONY IN BLUE

The French team's fortunes revived in the early 1980s. Having lost an epic World Cup semi-final to West Germany in 1982, France hosted and won the 1984 European Championships with a midfield of exquisite skill—Jean Tigana, Alain Giresse, Luis Fernández, and Michel Platini. They scored 15 goals in five games and won two games 3–2. At the 1986 World Cup, they beat Brazil in the game of the tournament, only to lose again to West Germany in the semi-final.

MICHEL PLATINI
Considered to be one of the best ever passers of the ball, as a player, manager, and president of UEFA, Platini has lived and breathed soccer.

VIVE LA DIFFERENCE

Under Aimé Jacquet, France's multi-ethnic team—hailing from as far afield as Senegal, Ghana, and New Caledonia—won their first World Cup as hosts in 1998. They beat Croatia in the semi-final after defender Thuram scored his two sole international goals, then triumphed over Brazil in the final, triggering the biggest street-party in Paris since the Liberation in 1944.

A SYMPHONY OF WONDERFUL PASSES ...OF PERFECT THROUGH BALLS

JEAN PIERRE LECLAIRE
ON FRANCE VS BRAZIL, SEVILLA, 1986

STAT ATTACK

GOVERNING BODY:
Fédération Française de Football
FOUNDED: 1919
NATIONAL STADIUM:
Stade de France, Paris, 80,000
FIRST MATCH: 3–3 vs Belgium, **1904**
BIGGEST WIN: 10–0 vs Azerbijan, **1995**
BIGGEST DEFEAT: 1–17 vs Denmark, **1908**

THE LEGENDS

MOST CAPPED PLAYERS

Name	From/To	Caps
Lilian THURAM	1994–2008	142
Marcel DESAILLY	1993–2004	116
Thierry HENRY	1997–present	108
Zinédine ZIDANE	1994–2006	108
Patrick VIEIRA	1997–present	106
Didier DESCHAMPS	1989–2000	103

FRENCH TAXATION

High taxation in France makes attracting the best players financially difficult. To earn an after-tax annual salary of €1.8 million, players must be paid:

- France—**6.1***
- Spain—**5.2***
- England—**4.7***

* € millions

€€€

STAT ATTACK

LIGUE 1

LEAGUE STRUCTURE: 20 teams
TOP SCORER: Delio Onnis, **299** goals
MOST WINS: Saint Étienne, **10** titles
BIGGEST WIN: 12–1, Sochaux vs Valenciennes, 1935–36
HIGHEST ATTENDANCE:
77,840, Lille vs Lyon, 2007–08
DIVISIONS BELOW LIGUE 1:
Ligue 2 (**20** teams), National (**20** teams)

COUPE DE FRANCE

First played in 1918, the Coupe de France is open to every professional and non-professional team in France.
MOST FINAL DEFEATS: Marseille, **7** defeats
MOST WINS: Marseille, **10** wins
BIGGEST WIN: 5–0, Saint Étienne vs Nantes, 1970

COUPE DE LA LIGUE

Introduced in 1994, the Coupe de la Ligue is contested by France's 45 professional clubs, and the winner qualifies for the UEFA Cup.
TOP SCORER: Pauleta, **15**
MOST WINS: Paris Saint-Germain, **3** wins
BIGGEST WIN: 4–1, Monaco vs Sochaux, 2003

LIGUE 1

Established in 1932 as France's first national professional league, La Ligue has been played continuously except during the war years (1939–45). It has 20 teams and a standard three up, three down promotion and relegation format. The first title was won by Olympique Lillois, who later became Lille. The league has a high reputation for administrative competence and tightly monitored finances. Unusually for a national league, one of the teams—Monaco—does not reside on French soil.

COUPE DE FRANCE

First played in 1918, the Coupe de France is the second-most-important competition in French soccer. It was originally named the Coupe Charles Simon after a player who was killed during World War I and, since 1927, the final has been attended by the French President. The cup was played in a restricted format during World War II, but has only been canceled once, due to a stadium disaster in 1992 in which a temporary stand collapsed during a semi-final, killing 18 and injuring thousands, at Bastia's ground in Corsica.

MARCEL DESAILLY
A formidable defender who won almost every honor for both club and country, Desailly also received the dubious distinction of being sent off in a World Cup Final.

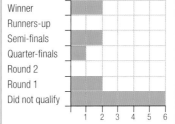

8,008 The population of Guingamp, a Breton administrative region whose team—En Avant Guingamp—topped Ligue 1 in 2002

44 The number of goals scored by Croatian striker Josip Skoblar for Marseilles in the 1970–71 season, a total that is still unbeaten

1922 The year a French Women's XI played the first informal women's international against England in Paris—the score was 1–1

TOP GOALSCORERS

Name	From/To	Goals
Thierry HENRY	1997–present	48
Michel PLATINI	1976–87	41
David TRÉZÉGUET	1998–2008	34
Zinédine ZIDANE	1994–2006	31
Just FONTAINE	1953–60	30
Jean-Pierre PAPIN	1986–95	30

WORLD CUP

Winner, Runners-up, Semi-finals, Quarter-finals, Round 2, Round 1, Did not qualify

EURO CHAMPIONSHIPS

Winner, Runners-up, Semi-finals, Quarter-finals, Round 2, Round 1, Did not qualify

EUROPE

FRENCH CLUBS

French law forbids the sale of soccer clubs, so each one is primarily owned by the amateur clubs and associations from which professional soccer grew. For the past 100 years, this has ensured that no single club can pull too far ahead of the others, and has allowed the very smallest of clubs, such as Auxerre, to triumph occasionally. In addition, French clubs are regulated more closely by the authorities than in most other countries.

SOCCER AS GEOGRAPHY

The soccer clubs of France reflect the country's pattern of dispersed urbanization. Reims and Saint Étienne are small provincial towns, but have been able to support teams at the top of French soccer. Similarly, the island of Corsica is a soccer hotbed with two leading teams—Bastia and Ajaccio.

NICKNAME:
LES GONES
("THE KIDS")

FOUNDED:
LYON, 1950

HOME

STADIUM:
STADE GERLAND, 41,000

DOMESTIC HONORS:
LEAGUE 7, CUP 4

INTERNATIONAL HONORS:
INTERTOTO CUP 1997

OLYMPIQUE LYONNAIS

With just three French Cup wins to their name, Olympique Lyonnais was a small provincial club until 1987, when businessman Jean-Michel Aulas took over the club. Seven consecutive league titles since 2002 followed, as did sell-out crowds, which have given Lyon the financial muscle to dominate French soccer in the 21st century.

DERBY DU RHÔNE

Saint Étienne, located just 25 miles (40km) from Lyon, dominated the French league in the 1970s, just as Olympique Lyonnais has done in the 21st century. The "Derby du Rhône" between the two clubs has become a highlight of the French season.

NICKNAME: L'OM

FOUNDED:
MARSEILLE, 1899

STADIUM: STADE
VELODROME,
60,000

HOME

DOMESTIC HONORS:
LEAGUE 8, CUP 10

INTERNATIONAL HONORS:
CHAMPIONS LEAGUE 1993;
INTERTOTO CUP 2005

OLYMPIQUE DE MARSEILLE

Always a big club, Olympique de Marseille (OM) rose to the top of French soccer under the presidency of the eccentric businessman and politician, Bernard Tapie. Four league titles culminated in the 1993 European Cup, only for the 1993 league title to be stripped and the team demoted after a series of match-fixing allegations were proved true, and financial irregularities were exposed.

ULTRA CULTURE

L'OM has the most voluble fans in France, and their ethnic mix reflects the population of the port city. Different groups inhabit different parts of the Stade Velodrome: the Yankee Nord Marseille, Fanatics, and Dodgers in the north curve, the Commando Ultras 1984 in the south bleachers, the South Winners in the center, and Amis de l'OM in the wings.

ABEDI **PELE**

Legendary Ghanaian international Pele was a pioneering African soccer player in Europe during the 1980s and 1990s. The attacking midfielder enjoyed most success with Marseille, where he won the Champions League in 1993.

BORN: NOVEMBER 5, 1964, DOME, GHANA
HEIGHT: 5FT 8½IN (1.74M)
MAIN CLUBS: **MARSEILLE, LILLE, LYON, TORINO, 1860 MUNICH**
INTERNATIONAL CAPS: **67**

MICHAEL ESSIEN
A central midfielder, Essien made his mark with SC Bastia and Lyon before moving to England. The Ghana international, affectionally known as "The Bison," is the world's most expensive African player.

NICKNAME: PSG
FOUNDED:
PARIS, 1970
STADIUM:
PARC DES
PRINCES, 48,700
HOME
DOMESTIC HONORS:
LEAGUE 2, CUP 7
INTERNATIONAL HONORS:
CUP WINNERS' CUP 1996

PARIS SAINT-GERMAIN

Paris found itself without a major team for the first time in the 1960s, with the demise of Racing Club. A group of some 20,000 Parisians put up the money to buy a small club in 1970, transforming it into Paris Saint-Germain (PSG). Bursts of success have followed, notably in the 1990s, when the club won the Cup Winners' Cup.

PSG VS OM

Since no city can sustain more than one team in the top flight, there are no derby games between neighboring clubs in France. The game between two of the richest clubs and loudest fans—PSG and Marseille—serves as the national derby, pitting Paris and the center against the outlying peripheries, such as Marseille.

BACK FROM THE BRINK

Canal Plus, the giant French TV company, pumped money into PSG after buying the club in 1991. Although they won three French league cups, five French cups, and —under coach Luis Fernández—the European Cup Winners' Cup, the Ligue 1 title eluded them, despite being offered to them in 1993. They had finished second to Marseille, who were stripped of the title for match-fixing, but PSG refused to accept it. In 2006, PSG was bought by a consortium of French and American investors.

CLUBS WILL ALWAYS FIND WAYS TO BREAK THE RULES... ME, I HAVE THREE MILLION WAYS

CLAUDE BEZ
PRESIDENT OF BORDEAUX

ARSÈNE WENGER
The thinking man's manager of choice and Arsenal's most successful manager in terms of silverwear, Wenger cut his teeth with considerable success in Ligue 1 with Monaco.

BEST OF THE REST

SAINT ÉTIENNE (1920)
With seven league titles between 1967 and 1976, Saint Étienne was the first French team to gain national television coverage. The home crowd is nicknamed "Le Cauldron Vert."
HONORS: LEAGUE 10, CUP 8

BORDEAUX (1881)
The biggest French club of the 1980s was funded by president Claude Bez, who was later imprisoned for embezzlement.
HONORS: LEAGUE 5, CUP 3;
INTERTOTO CUP 1995

NANTES (1943)
Nantes is famed for its youth system, which has helped the peripheral Breton side to a series of titles in the 1960s, as well as recent success in the 1990s.
HONORS: LEAGUE 8, CUP 3

AUXERRE (1905)
Small can be beautiful. With a population of less than 40,000, Auxerre won a league title and four French cups under Guy Roux, who was club manager for more than 40 years.
HONORS: LEAGUE 1, CUP 4

SOCHAUX-MONTBÉLIARD (1928)
Founded as the works team of the huge Peugeot factory in Montbéliard, the club had a commercial ethos that led them to become the first professional side in France in 1935.
HONORS: LEAGUE 2, CUP 2

LENS (1906)
The team of France's northern coalfields, Lens' large and stalwart crowds bravely wear the team colors of blood and gold.
HONORS: LEAGUE 1, CUP 0;
INTERTOTO CUP 2005, 2007

MONACO (1924)
The team of the Riviera tax haven, Monaco is backed by the royal Grimaldi family and the Monaco government. Plenty of titles and the top stadium in the country have resulted.
HONORS: LEAGUE 7, CUP 5

EUROPE

NETHERLANDS

HOME

AWAY

POPULATION: 16.5 MILLION
CAPITAL: AMSTERDAM
LICENSED PLAYERS:
MALE: 1.1 MILLION
FEMALE: 84,000
PROFESSIONALS: 1,000
REGISTERED CLUBS: 4,000

Professional soccer came late to the Netherlands. Yet a mere 20 years after its arrival, the national team was unlucky to lose the 1974 World Cup final to West Germany—still a painful memory for Dutch fans. A sparkling win in the 1988 European Championship gave some consolation. The Dutch do not play in the typically high-tempo, tough-tackling northern European style, but are famed for attractive, inventive play. They are widely regarded as the best team never to have won the World Cup.

DUTCH MASTERS

The Dutch national team has produced some of the most sublime moments in international soccer: from the pioneering "total soccer"—featuring Cruyff and Neeksens—of the 1970s to the successive World Cup final defeats in 1974 and 1978, and from Marco van Basten's volley on the way to the 1988 European Championship win to Dennis Bergkamp's amazing goal against Argentina in the 1998 World Cup. When they are good, they are superb.

DENNIS BERGKAMP
An ice-cool, withdrawn striker with a phobia of flying, Bergkamp formed deadly partnerships with Thierry Henry at Arsenal and with Patrick Kluivert in the Dutch national team.

THE DARK SIDE

The Dutch national team are also, on occasions, capable of falling to pieces. This was never more true than at Euro 2000, which they co-hosted with Belgium. In the quarter-finals they decimated a good Yugoslav team 6–1 and Patrick Kluivert scored a hat-trick. But in the semi-finals they seemed to freeze, despite winning two penalties and even though their opponents, Italy, had been reduced to ten men. Italy eventually ground out a 0–0 draw and, in the shootout that followed, scored the first three penalties. The dispirited Dutch scored just one penalty of four.

ORANGE POWER

Wearing the national shirt is almost compulsory for Netherlands fans, and whenever the Dutch team play, the crowd is a sea of orange. The national color is derived from the coat of arms of Prince William of Nassau-Orange (1533–84), the nobleman who instigated the revolt against the ruling Spanish empire that ultimately led to Dutch independence in 1648.

SOCCER IS SIMPLE, BUT THE HARDEST THING IS...
TO PLAY SOCCER IN A SIMPLE WAY

JOHAN CRUYFF
LEGENDARY DUTCH PLAYER AND MANAGER

STAT ATTACK

GOVERNING BODY:
Koninklijke Nederlandse Voetbal Bond (KNVB)
FOUNDED: 1889
NATIONAL STADIUM: None
FIRST MATCH: 4–1 vs Belgium, 1905
BIGGEST WIN: 9–0 vs Finland, 1912, Norway, 1972
BIGGEST DEFEAT: 2–12 vs England, 1907

THE LEGENDS

MOST CAPPED PLAYERS

Name	From/To	Caps
Edwin VAN DER SAR	1995–2008	130
Frank DE BOER	1990–2004	112
Phillip COCU	1996–2006	101
Clarence SEEDORF	1994–present	87
Giovanni VAN BRONCKHORST	1996–present	87

TOP GOALSCORERS

Name	From/To	Goals
Patrick KLUIVERT	1994–2004	40
Dennis BERGKAMP	1990–2000	37
Faas WILKES	1946–61	35
Abe LENSTRA	1940–59	33
Johan CRUYFF	1966–77	33
Ruud VAN NISTELROOY	1998–2008	33

DUTCH COMPETITIONS

The 18 best teams in the Netherlands compete in the Eredivisie ("honorary division"), which began in 1956 and has been dominated by Ajax, PSV Eindhoven, and Feyenoord. Since 1965, they have won every title between them except one—in 1980–81 it was won by AZ Alkmaar. The main knock-out competition is the KNVB Beker, organized by the Royal Netherlands Football Association (KNVB). Also known as the Dutch Cup, it was founded in 1898 and was deliberately modeled on the FA Cup in England. Ajax has won it more times than any other club.

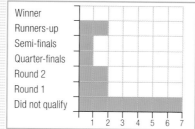

RUUD GULLIT
Few players caught the eye like the dreadlocked Ruud Gullit. Big, athletic, and superbly balanced, he could play in any position and still dominate a match.

STAT ATTACK

EREDIVISIE

LEAGUE STRUCTURE: 18 teams
TOP SCORER: Willy van der Kuijlen, **311** goals
MOST WINS: 21, Ajax
BIGGEST WIN: 12–1, Ajax vs Vitesse Arnhem, 1972
HIGHEST ATTENDANCE: 65,150, Feyenoord vs Ajax, 1970
DIVISIONS BELOW EREDIVISIE: Eerste Divisie (**20** teams)

KNVB BEKER

88 teams participate; every Eredivisie and Eerste Divisie club, the top four from the six third-level leagues, and the remainder from the fourth tier.
MOST WINS: 17, Ajax
BIGGEST WIN: 9–2, Willem II vs Groene Ster, 1943–44

0.51 Average number of goals scored per game by Patrick Kluivert, the Dutch national team's top scorer, in 79 appearances

7 Goals scored by Afonso Alves in Heerenveen's 9–0 thrashing of Heracles Almelo in 2007

73 Percentage of Dutch fans who admit to having hugged or kissed a stranger during a match

111 Eredivisie goals conceded by SHS Den Haag in the 1958–59 season

4 Penalties awarded to PSV Eindhoven in a 2005 Eredivisie match vs RBC Roosendaal. They missed two of them

JOHAN CRUYFF

Cruyff was the most complete player in the Dutch and Ajax teams famous for "total soccer." Nominally a striker, he bamboozled markers by dropping into midfield. His vision and passing skill led to the accolade "Pythagoras in boots."

BORN: **APRIL 25, 1947, AMSTERDAM, NETHERLANDS**
HEIGHT: **5FT 11IN (1.8M)**
MAIN CLUBS: **AJAX, BARCELONA, FEYENOORD**
INTERNATIONAL CAPS: **48**

GULL KICK

During the derby match between Sparta Rotterdam and Feyenoord on November 15, 1970, Feyenoord goalkeeper Eddy Treytel made a long clearance that has gone down in club history. His kick knocked a passing seagull out of the sky, and the unfortunate bird was stuffed and put on display in the club's trophy room. At least that's what Feyenoord fans believe—Sparta fans are not so sure. They were supported by a biologist who stated that the exhibit looks nothing like a gull in its late fall plumage.

WORLD CUP

	1	2	3	4	5	6	7
Winner							
Runners-up		■					
Semi-finals							
Quarter-finals							
Round 2							
Round 1							
Did not qualify							

EURO CHAMPIONSHIPS

	1	2	3	4	5	6
Winner						
Runners-up						
Semi-finals						
Quarter-finals						
Round 2						
Round 1						
Did not qualify						

DUTCH CLUBS: THE BIG THREE

In the early days of soccer in the Netherlands, small clubs like Den Haag and Deventer won titles. However, since the professional era, Dutch soccer has been dominated by three big clubs—Ajax, PSV Eindhoven, and Feyenoord. In the 1960s and 1970s, the game underwent a major period of consolidation and club mergers. Many teams remain reliant on support and subsidy from local and city governments.

NICKNAME:
GODENZONEN ("SONS OF THE GODS")

FOUNDED:
AMSTERDAM, 1900

HOME

STADIUM:
AMSTERDAM ARENA, 51,800

DOMESTIC HONORS:
LEAGUE 29, CUP 1

INTERNATIONAL HONORS:
CHAMPIONS LEAGUE 1971, 1972, 1973, 1995; UEFA CUP 1992; CUP WINNERS' CUP 1987; WORLD CLUB CUP 1972, 1995

AFC AJAX

Ajax is at the center of Dutch soccer. The club has won the European Cup four times, including three consecutive wins between 1971 and 1973, and is one of only five teams to have been awarded the trophy permanently. In the 1960s, Ajax pioneered "total soccer," a revolutionary strategy in which team mates exchanged playing positions rapidly and fluidly.

THE JEWISH CLUB

Amsterdam's complex relationship with its Jewish community is reflected by the Ajax fans, very few of whom are Jewish. Fans have taken to waving the Israeli flag, spray-painting stars of David around the city, and claiming Ajax as a Jewish club.

FRANK RIJKAARD

As a player, Rijkaard was a ferocious midfielder. As a top-flight manager, he is the polar opposite—cool, calm, and collected, but no less successful, as proven by his 2006 Champions League triumph with Barcelona.

BORN: SEPTEMBER 30, 1962, AMSTERDAM, NETHERLANDS
HEIGHT: 6FT 3IN (1.9M)
MAIN CLUBS: AJAX, MILAN
INTERNATIONAL CAPS: 73

NICKNAME:
BOEREN ("FARMERS")

FOUNDED:
EINDHOVEN, 1913

HOME

STADIUM:
PHILLIPS STADION, 36,500

DOMESTIC HONORS:
LEAGUE 21, CUP 8

INTERNATIONAL HONORS:
EUROPEAN CUP 1988; UEFA CUP 1978

PSV EINDHOVEN

In 1913, electronics giant Phillips held a sport day to celebrate the centenary of the Netherlands. It proved so popular that they decided to start a soccer team, which was named Philips Sport Vereniging ("Philips Sports Union") Eindhoven. Considerable sponsorship and solid home support have seen PSV win two European trophies and more than 20 Dutch titles. The Phillips Stadion has often showcased the company's latest products.

RUUD VAN NISTELROOY
A former central defender, van Nistelrooy became a striker at FC den Bosch. He was the Eredivisie's top scorer for two seasons running at PSV, then signed for Manchester United for $36 million in 2001.

VICTORY DRAW
PSV's finest hour was the 1988 European Cup final against Benfica, which they won on penalties after Hans van Brukelen made a crucial save. Amazingly, PSV had failed to win either of the two-leg quarter- and semi-final ties, going through on away goals after drawing both games. The Intercontinental Cup final went the same way later in the year, but PSV lost on penalties after a 2–2 draw with Nacional of Uruguay.

NICKNAME:
DE CLUB VAN HET VOLK ("THE PEOPLE'S CLUB")

FOUNDED:
ROTTERDAM, 1908

HOME

STADIUM:
DE KUIP, 51,200

DOMESTIC HONORS:
LEAGUE 14, CUP 11

INTERNATIONAL HONORS:
EUROPEAN CUP 1970;
UEFA CUP 1974, 2002;
WORLD CLUB CUP 1970

FEYENOORD

Feyenoord was founded in 1908 in the heart of Rotterdam's docks by a group of youths who played outside the Wilhelmina church. The team still play in the area in the newly refurbished De Kuip stadium. Support is drawn from across the region, and although it is the country's second club, Feyenoord was the first Dutch club to win a European title, beating Celtic to take the European Cup in 1970.

THE YEAR OF MAGIC

In 1983–84, Johan Cruyff left Ajax and crossed over to Feyenoord for a single scintillating season. At 37 he played brilliantly, and carried Feyenoord to their most unlikely Dutch league and cup double, dubbed "The Year of Magic."

FEYENOORD FANATICS

The fans of Feyenoord are among the most fervent in European soccer. When the team won the Dutch championship in 1999, more than a quarter of a million people gathered in Rotterdam to celebrate. Ever since more than 3,000 fans traveled by boat to Lisbon to see the team play Benfica in the 1963 European Cup, support at European away matches has been huge. The fans also like their music, and the song "Hand in Hand" has been their unofficial hymn since the 1960s.

DIE KLASSIKER

Whatever the league standings, the games between Ajax and Feyenoord—Die Klassiker—are the biggest of the Dutch season. Ajax hold the lead in this derby and as the country's most successful club attract the ire of not just Feyenoord but much of the rest of the soccer nation. During the 1997–98 season, all fans were banned from the stadium after extensive disorder the previous year.

GIOVANNI VAN BRONKHORST

A gifted, ever-present playmaker who has won league and cup honors in four countries, van Bronkhorst has also appeared in two World Cup and three European Championship finals.

BEST OF THE REST

VITESSE ARNHEM (1892)
The new team of the 1980s, backed with municipal money and recipient of a futuristic stadium, they challenged the big three but were struck by debt and recrimination.
HONORS: LEAGUE 3, CUP 0

SPARTA ROTTERDAM (1888)
An old team from the working-class heart of Rotterdam, Sparta's golden years were before World War I. In recent years, staying in the top flight has been their major ambition.
HONORS: LEAGUE 6, CUP 3

SC HEERENVEEN (1920)
Virtually a village team, Heerenven's youth system has lifted it to the top six of the Dutch league, and even into European competition. Ruud van Nistelrooy began his career here.
HONORS: LEAGUE 1, CUP 0

FC TWENTE (1965)
Formed in Enschede, FC Twente challenged Feyenoord for the league title in 1973 then lost the 1974 UEFA Cup final to Spurs, having already beaten Juventus in the semi-final.
HONORS: LEAGUE 1, CUP 2

FC UTRECHT (1970)
Formed from the fusion of three clubs, FC Utrecht have won two Dutch cups since 2003 and have demonstrated their ambition to challenge for the league title.
HONORS: LEAGUE 1, CUP 2

AZ ALKMAAR (1967)
The team that finally broke the dominance of the big three, Alkmar won the Dutch league in 1981, but have been unable to repeat the performance since.
HONORS: LEAGUE 1, CUP 3

WILLEM II TILBURG (1896)
Named after the 19th-century Dutch King, the team wears the Dutch national colors. Without a title win since 1955, they played in the 1999 Champions League group stage.
HONORS: LEAGUE 3, CUP 2

DIE KLASSIKER RECORD

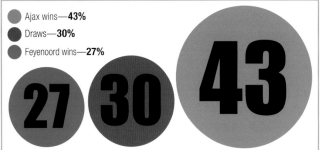

- Ajax wins—**43%**
- Draws—**30%**
- Feyenoord wins—**27%**

27 30 43

EUROPE

HOME | AWAY

POPULATION: 5.5 MILLION
CAPITAL: COPENHAGEN
FA: DANSK BOLDSPIL-UNION
LICENSED PLAYERS:
MALE: 420,000
FEMALE: 91,000
PROFESSIONALS: 1,000
REGISTERED CLUBS: 1,500

DENMARK

Denmark was the first country in continental Europe to embrace soccer, and boasts the oldest national association—one of the seven founding members of FIFA in 1904—outside the UK. Denmark won silver at the 1908 and 1912 Olympics, but further success was limited until the lifting in the early 1980s of a selection ban on players signed to overseas teams.

THE DANISH SUPERLIGA

The Danish national league started in 1913, though it wasn't until the 1950s that a team from outside the capital won it. The league was restricted and reduced to the 12-team Danish Superliga in 1991, in which teams played each other three times a season. The Danish Cup was founded in 1955.

DERBY DAY

Danish soccer has been dominated by the two big Copenhagen teams, who have won more than half the titles since the inception of the Superliga in 1991. Brøndby, from the south of the city, style themselves as the authentic, working-class, community club, whereas uptown FC København are perceived as the brash, nouveau-riche, commercial club.

MICHAEL LAUDRUP
One of the game's most dazzling and creative playmakers, Laudrup's team mates commented "Just run, he will always find a way of passing you the ball."

PETER **SCHMEICHEL**

One of the greatest goalkeepers the game has ever seen, Schmeichel was respected by the opposition and feared by his own defenders, who regularly felt the full "Norse force" when things went wrong. He was not afraid of pressing forward for vital goals, scoring nine times during his career.

BORN: **NOVEMBER 18, 1963, GLADSAXE, DENMARK**
HEIGHT: **6FT 4IN (1.93M)**
MAIN CLUBS: **BRØNDBY, MANCHESTER UNITED, ASTON VILLA, MANCHESTER CITY**
INTERNATIONAL CAPS: **129**

ROOLIGANS

Best translated as "fool-igan" or "fun-igan," Denmark's fans redefined the image of the soccer fan. Colorful, drunken, and friendly, they pioneered the mass-happiness, singing, and odd head-gear that have come to flavor the modern soccer tournament.

EURO '92

Denmark failed to qualify for the 1992 European Championships, and the team was on vacation when it was called up to replace Yugoslavia, who were withdrawn due to the civil war. They scraped through the first round, but made it all the way to the final where, to everyone's amazement, they beat Germany.

STAT ATTACK

NATIONAL TEAM

NICKNAME: Danish Dynamite, Olsen-Banden ("The Olsen Gang")
NATIONAL STADIUM: Parken, 42,000
WORLD CUP FINALS: 3 appearances, quarter-finals **1998**
EUROPEAN CHAMPIONSHIPS: 7 appearances, winners **1992**, semi-finals **1967**, **1984**
BIGGEST WIN: 17–1 vs France, 1908
BIGGEST DEFEAT: 0–8 vs Germany, 1937
MOST CAPS: Peter Schmeichel, **129**
MOST GOALS: Poul Nielson, **52**

MAIN DOMESTIC CLUBS

FC KØBENHAVN
FOUNDED: Copenhagen, 1992
STADIUM: Parken
CAPACITY: 42,000
INTERNATIONAL HONORS: None
LEAGUE: 15 CUP: 1

HOME

BRØNDBY
FOUNDED: Copenhagen, 1964
STADIUM: Brøndby Stadium
CAPACITY: 26,000
INTERNATIONAL HONORS: None
LEAGUE: 10 CUP: 6

HOME

AGF AARHUS
FOUNDED: Aarhus, 1880
STADIUM: NRGi Park
CAPACITY: 21,000
INTERNATIONAL HONORS: None
LEAGUE: 9 CUP: 1

HOME

SWEDEN

HOME   AWAY

POPULATION: 9 MILLION
CAPITAL: STOCKHOLM
FA: SVENSKA FOTBOLLFÖRBUNDET
REGISTERED PLAYERS:
MALE: 791,500
FEMALE: 215,500
PROFESSIONALS: 2,000
REGISTERED CLUBS: 3,000

The first Swedish soccer clubs and leagues were established in the 1890s among the middle and upper classes. Working-class soccer arrived in the early 20th century, and conflict between the two groups was only resolved by the introduction of an amateur code in the 1930s. The national team has challenged for international silverware, though in modern times, the best of Sweden's players have played overseas.

STAT ATTACK

NATIONAL TEAM

NICKNAME: Blåguld ("Blue and Yellow")
NATIONAL STADIUM: Råsunda, 37,300
WORLD CUP FINALS: 11 appearances, runners-up **1958**, semi-finals **1950**, **1994**
EUROPEAN CHAMPIONSHIPS: 4 appearances, semi-finals **1992**, quarter-finals **2004**
BIGGEST WIN: 12–0 vs Latvia, 1927 and vs South Korea, 1948
BIGGEST DEFEAT: 1–12 vs England Amateurs, 1908
MOST CAPS: Thomas Ravelli, **143**
MOST GOALS: Sven Rydell, **49**

MAIN DOMESTIC CLUBS

IFK GÖTEBORG
FOUNDED: Gothenburg, 1904
STADIUM: Ullevi
CAPACITY: 43,200   HOME
INTERNATIONAL HONORS: European Cup semi-finals **1986**; UEFA Cup winners **1982**, **1987**
LEAGUE: 18 **CUP:** 5

MALMÖ FF
FOUNDED: Malmö, 1910
STADIUM: Swedbank Stadion
CAPACITY: 27,500   HOME
INTERNATIONAL HONORS: European Cup runners-up **1979**
LEAGUE: 15 **CUP:** 14

AIK
FOUNDED: Stockholm, 1891
STADIUM: Råsunda
CAPACITY: 37,300   HOME
INTERNATIONAL HONORS: None
LEAGUE: 10 **CUP:** 7

ALLSVENSKAN

The national league was founded in 1900 and was renamed Allsvenskan ("All-Swedish") in 1924. Unusually for a European nation, play-offs between the top teams have been used to determine the winner, most recently from 1982 to 1990. The Swedish league was one of the only leagues in Europe to continue during either of the world wars, and the Swedish cup was actually started during World War II.

HARD TO PLEASE

In 2001, Hammerby IK, a small team from the south of Stockholm, finally managed to win the championship, leading to delirium among the club's long-suffering fans. Nevertheless, the board of the club had already decided to fire the coach Sören Cratz on the grounds that he didn't play attacking soccer.

THE ENGLISH CONNECTION

Both the 1948 Olympic gold-medal winning team and the 1958 World Cup losing finalists were coached by Englishman George Raynor. An ex-professional player, Raynor later managed the Swedish team that beat his home nation 3–2 at Wembley in a 1959 friendly.

ZLATAN **IBRAHIMOVIC**

Ibrahimovic was born of Yugoslav-Bosnian immigrants in the toughest part of Malmö. A sharp-minded striker, he brought an arrogance and invention—honed at Inter Milan—that had been missing from the Swedish team.

BORN: **OCTOBER 3, 1981, MALMÖ, SWEDEN**
HEIGHT: **6FT (1.83M)**
MAIN CLUBS: **MALMÖ, AJAX, JUVENTUS, INTER MILAN**
INTERNATIONAL CAPS: **42**

GRE-NO-LI

Sweden's most famous trio of players—Gunnar Gren, Gunnar Nordahl, and Niels Liedholm—became known as Gre-No-Li. They formed the backbone of Sweden's Olympic gold-medal-winning team in 1948, but were later banned from the national team after signing for clubs in Italy.

0 Games won by Billingsfors IK in 1946–47, their sole season in the Swedish top division

7 Number of goals scored in a single game by IFK Norrköping's Gunnar Nordahl, in 1944

11 Seconds it took for Hjalmar Lorichs to score for Sweden vs Finland in 1912

90 Miles north of the Arctic Circle of the home field of second-division Kiruna FF

HOME   AWAY

POPULATION: 4.6 MILLION
CAPITAL: OSLO
FA: NORGES FOTBALLFORBUND
REGISTERED PLAYERS:
MALE: 409,000
FEMALE: 135,000
PROFESSIONALS: 1,000
REGISTERED CLUBS: 1,800

NORWAY

Norway caught the soccer bug in the late 19th century and took up the sport at once; the national association was founded in 1902, three years before Norway's independence from Sweden. The country's fierce Arctic conditions and national love of skiing initially hindered the growth of the game, but since the Norwegian government began to invest in elite soccer in the early 1990s, the men's and women's national teams have flourished.

WOMEN'S WORLD CUP

Norway is at the forefront of women's soccer, and was one of the first countries in Europe to incorporate the women's game. Norway were runners-up at the first Women's World Cup in 1991, winners in 1995, and Olympic champions in 2000.

THE TIPPELIGAEN

The Norwegian playing season is centered around the summer months, and lasts from mid-March to early November. The top tier was renamed the Tippeligaen ("Premier League") in 1991 and consists of 16 teams. It has been dominated by Rosenborg, who won the title 13 consecutive times between 1992 and 2004. The Norwegian Cup is a knock-out contest open to teams from almost every level of soccer in Norway.

CITY OF KINGS, CLUB OF THE PEOPLE

The Norwegian club that has prospered most from the arrival of professionalism and European money has been Rosenberg. The club was founded in 1917 as a people's team in the city of Trondheim, the seat of the ancient Norwegian kings. After establishing domestic dominance in the 1990s, they went on to win money and games in Europe, and even reached the quarter-finals of the Champion's League in 1996.

BEATING ENGLAND

Norway's first triumph over England came with a 2–1 victory in a 1981 World Cup qualifier. It is remembered in Norway for an extraordinary outburst from radio commentator Bjørge Lillelien: "Lord Nelson, Sir Winston Churchill, Henry Cooper, Lady Diana, we have beaten them all! Maggie Thatcher, can you hear me? Your boys took a hell of a beating!"

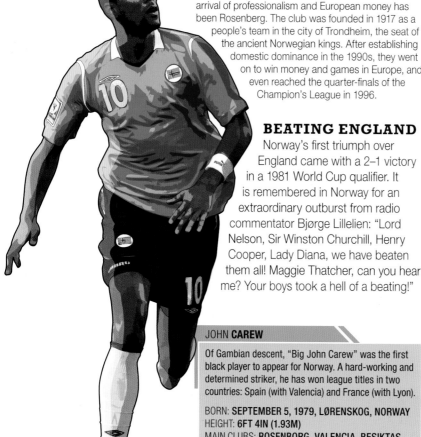

JOHN CAREW

Of Gambian descent, "Big John Carew" was the first black player to appear for Norway. A hard-working and determined striker, he has won league titles in two countries: Spain (with Valencia) and France (with Lyon).

BORN: SEPTEMBER 5, 1979, LØRENSKOG, NORWAY
HEIGHT: 6FT 4IN (1.93M)
MAIN CLUBS: ROSENBORG, VALENCIA, BESIKTAS, LYON, ASTON VILLA
INTERNATIONAL CAPS: 74

STAT ATTACK

NATIONAL TEAM

NICKNAME: Vikingene ("The Vikings")
NATIONAL STADIUM:
Ullevaal Stadion, 25,500
WORLD CUP FINALS:
3 appearances
EUROPEAN CHAMPIONSHIPS:
1 appearance
BIGGEST WIN: 12–0 vs Finland, 1946
BIGGEST DEFEAT: 0–12 vs Denmark, 1917
MOST CAPS: Thorbjørn Svenssen, **104**
MOST GOALS: Jørgen Juve, **33**

MAIN DOMESTIC CLUBS

ROSENBORG BK
FOUNDED: Trondheim, 1917
STADIUM: Lerkendal
CAPACITY: 21,800
HOME
INTERNATIONAL HONORS:
Champions League quarter-finals **1997**
LEAGUE: 20 **CUP:** 9

SK BRANN BERGEN
FOUNDED: Bergen, 1908
STADIUM: Brann Stadion
CAPACITY: 17,800
HOME
INTERNATIONAL HONORS:
Cup Winners' Cup quarter-finals **1996**
LEAGUE: 3 **CUP:** 6

VÅLERENGA IF
FOUNDED: Oslo, 1913
STADIUM: Ullevaal Stadion
CAPACITY: 25,600
HOME
INTERNATIONAL HONORS: None
LEAGUE: 5 **CUP:** 4

HOME

AWAY

POPULATION: 5.2 MILLION
CAPITAL: HELSINKI
FA: SUOMEN PALLOLIITTO
REGISTERED PLAYERS:
MALE: 304,000
FEMALE: 58,500
PROFESSIONALS: 400
REGISTERED CLUBS: 1,000

FINLAND

Soccer may have arrived early in Finland—the first club, Repias Klathi, was set up in 1897 and a Helsinki league soon followed—but soccer has had to compete with the weather, ice-hockey, and ski-jumping ever since. Success for the national team has consisted of a semi-final appearance at the 1912 Olympics. Semi-professionalism arrived in the 1990s, and a few players, including Jari Litamen, Sammi Hypia, and Mikel Forsell moved to the leading leagues of Europe.

THE VEIKKAUSLIGA

Finland's winter is long and harsh, so the playing season runs from late April to early October, and teams in the 12-team Veikkausliga are often forced to play two games a week to fit them all in. The Finnish Cup has been running since 1955, and cup-final day forms a fitting climax to the season in November. During the winter, a more informal league is played indoors.

EUROPEAN HEIGHTS

In 1998, HJK Helsinki qualified for the group stages of the Champions League, becoming the first Finnish side to do so. They beat Benfica but failed to progress from the group stage. Prior to this, the only Finnish success in Europe was a 1987 UEFA Cup-tie win over Inter Milan in the San Siro by Turun Palloseura.

JARI **LITMANEN**

Unusually for a Finn, Litmanen turned down the chance to play ice hockey in favor of being a soccer striker. After blooming in the Finnish league, he moved to Ajax in 1993, where he won a Champions League medal in 1995.

BORN: **FEBRUARY 20, 1971, HOLLOLA, FINLAND**
HEIGHT: **6FT (1.82M)**
MAIN CLUBS: **REIPAS, HJK HELSINKI, MYPA, AJAX, BARCELONA, LIVERPOOL, FC LAHTI, HANSA ROSTOCK**
INTERNATIONAL CAPS: **117**

EAGLE OWLS

The Finnish national team acquired the nickname "Huuhkajat," Finnish for "eagle owl," from a bird named Bubi who lived near the Helsinki Olympic Stadium. His first showing at a match was a 2007 fixture between Finland and Belgium. Finland won 2–0 and Bubi was named Helsinki's Resident of the Year.

STAT ATTACK

NATIONAL TEAM

NICKNAME: Huuhkajat ("Eagle Owls")
NATIONAL STADIUM:
Helsingin Olympiastadion, 40,000
WORLD CUP FINALS: No appearances
EUROPEAN CHAMPIONSHIPS:
No appearances
BIGGEST WIN: 10–2 vs Estonia, 1922
BIGGEST DEFEAT: 0–13 vs Germany, 1940
MOST CAPS: Jari Litmanen, **117**
MOST GOALS: Jari Litmanen, **30**

MAIN DOMESTIC CLUBS

HJK HELSINKI
FOUNDED: Helsinki, 1907
STADIUM: Finnair Stadium
CAPACITY: 10,800   HOME
INTERNATIONAL HONORS: None
LEAGUE: 21 **CUP:** 10

FC HAKA
FOUNDED: Valkeakoski, 1934
STADIUM: Tehtaan Kenttä   HOME
CAPACITY: 3,000
INTERNATIONAL HONORS:
Cup Winners' Cup quarter-finals **1984**
LEAGUE: 9 **CUP:** 12

FOUR NAMES, TWO HOMES, ONE TEAM

Klubi-04 was formerly named Pallo-Kerho-35, PK35, and FC Jokerit, was based in Viipuri until World War II, and is now HJK's reserve team.

19 Number of goals conceded by Reipas Lahti over two legs vs Levski Spartak in the 1976–77 Cup Winners' Cup

2 Number of players in the October 2008 Finland squad who played for a Finnish side

4 Number of newly promoted clubs to have won the Finnish league title

2,900 Average attendance at Veikkausliga (premier division) matches

EUROPE

GERMANY

HOME

AWAY

POPULATION: 82.4 MILLION
CAPITAL: BERLIN
LICENSED PLAYERS:
MALE: 5.4 MILLION
FEMALE: 871,000
PROFESSIONALS: 1,000
REGISTERED CLUBS: 26,000

Soccer was first played in Germany in elite Anglophile circles, but soon spread to white-collar workers in the 1890s. Endorsed by the Kaiser before World War I, the game boomed following the war as it finally spread to the working classes. After World War II, soccer, like everything else, was split between East and West Germany before reunification in 1990.

WORLD BEATERS

Germany's international record is exceptional, winning both the World Cup and European Championships several times and finishing runners-up a total of seven times. Even when playing poorly, the team grinds out results, and is notoriously effective at penalties. The stability and order that have characterized the team were shaped by manager Sepp Herberger, who won the 1954 World Cup and coached the side for nearly 30 years.

JÜRGEN KLINSMANN
Klinsmann's glittering playing career earned him World Cup and European Championship medals. He also managed the German national team to the World Cup semi-finals in 2006.

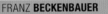
FRANZ **BECKENBAUER**

Known as Der Kaiser ("The Emperor"), Beckenbauer was a midfielder but transformed himself into the definitive modern sweeper, dictating play from the back. He won all the major honors as a player, then managed West Germany to World Cup success in 1990.

BORN: **SEPTEMBER 11, 1945,**
MUNICH, GERMANY
HEIGHT: **5FT 11IN (1.81M)**
CLUBS: **BAYERN MUNICH, NEW**
YORK COSMOS, HAMBURG
INTERNATIONAL CAPS: **103**

SAARLAND

A tiny corner of western Germany, the Saar was an independent soccer nation between 1948 and 1956. Placed under French control after World War II, Saarland entered the 1952 Olympics and 1954 World Cup qualifiers, losing twice to West Germany. In 1957, Saarland was unified with West Germany and the national team disbanded. The Saar was coached by Helmut Schon, who went on to coach the West German national team.

6 Most own goals in Bundesliga, by Manfred Kaltz of Hamburger SV

53 Most Bundesliga goals scored by penalties— also Manfred Kaltz

11 Seconds to score the Bundesliga's fastest goal: Ulf Kirsten (Bayer Leverkusen) against Kaiserslautern in 2002

STAT ATTACK

GOVERNING BODY:
Deutscher Fußball-Bund
FOUNDED: 1900
NATIONAL STADIUM: None
FIRST MATCH: 3–5 vs Switzerland, 1908
BIGGEST WIN: 16–0 vs Russia, 1912
BIGGEST DEFEAT: 0–9 vs England, 1909

THE LEGENDS

MOST CAPPED PLAYERS

Name	From/To	Caps
Lothar MATTHÄUS	1980–2000	150
Jürgen KLINSMANN	1987–98	108
Jürgen KOHLER	1986–98	105
Franz BECKENBAUER	1965–77	103
Thomas HÄSSLER	1988–2000	101
Berti VOGTS	1967–88	96

TOP GOALSCORERS

Name	From/To	Goals
Gerd MÜLLER	1966–74	68
Rudi VÖLLER	1982–94	47
Jürgen KLINSMANN	1987–98	47
Karl-Heinz RUMMENIGGE	1976–86	45
Miroslav KLOSE	2001–present	44
Uwe SEELER	1954–70	43

THE NEXT GAME
IS ALWAYS THE
TOUGHEST ONE...

JOSEF "SEPP" HERBERGER
MANAGER, WEST GERMANY, 1936–64

STAT ATTACK

BUNDESLIGA

LEAGUE STRUCTURE:
18 clubs

TOP SCORER: Gerd Müller, **365** goals

MOST SUCCESSFUL TEAM:
Bayern Munich, **21** league titles

BIGGEST WIN: 12–0, Borussia
Monchengladbach vs Borussia
Dortmund, 1978

HIGHEST ATTENDANCE: 88,075, Hertha
Berlin vs 1FC Köln, 1969

DIVISIONS BELOW BUNDESLIGA:
Bundesliga 2 (**18** teams),
Regionaliga Nord and Sud (**18** teams each)

DFB POKAL

The cup brings the top professional clubs
together with leading semi-professional
and amateur teams of the regional leagues.

HIGHEST SCORING FINAL: 5–2, Bayern
Munich vs VFB Stuttgart, 1986

MOST SUCCESSFUL TEAM:
FC Bayern Munich **14** wins

BIGGEST WIN: 5–0, FC Schalke 04 vs FC
Kaiserslautern, 1972

BUNDESLIGA

The Bundesliga was created as a professional national league in West Germany in 1963, and is operated by the Deutsche Fußball Bund. In 1990, after the reunification of Germany, two leading teams from the former East Germany were admitted to the top division as the old East German leagues were disbanded.

DFB POKAL

First played in 1935, the DFB Pokal is a knock-out tournament cup contest that includes the top professional clubs and the best of the lower league clubs. It was designed to embarrass the big clubs, with single legs decided by shoot-outs. More recently, the top professional clubs have been granted a bye to the later rounds.

EAST GERMAN NOSTALGIA

East Germany and its own particular soccer culture are long gone, but remain legendary. Until the late 1970s, soccer retained a semblance of autonomy from the state. In 1978, Eric Mieleke, head of the Stasi and president of Dynamo Berlin, decided it was time for his team to win. Their turn went on for ten unbroken years. Support for soccer collapsed, and most fans secretly watched the Bundesliga on TV.

AVERAGE ATTENDANCES—EUROPE

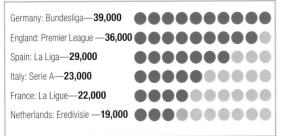

Germany: Bundesliga—**39,000**
England: Premier League —**36,000**
Spain: La Liga—**29,000**
Italy: Serie A—**23,000**
France: La Ligue—**22,000**
Netherlands: Eredivisie —**19,000**

LOTHAR MATTHÄUS
The most capped German player of all time, Matthäus is the only outfield player to appear in five World Cups. Renowned for his hard tackling, imperious passing, and fierce shot, he played for the national side to the age of 39.

RULE 1: SHOW UP

Karlsruhe, favourites for the first German national championship held in 1904, were thrown out at the semi-final stage. They were duped by a fake telegram purporting that the game, against Bohemians of Prague, had been cancelled, so they failed to show up.

WORLD CUP

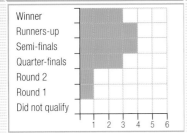

Winner
Runners-up
Semi-finals
Quarter-finals
Round 2
Round 1
Did not qualify
1 2 3 4 5 6

EURO CHAMPIONSHIPS

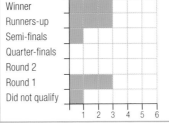

Winner
Runners-up
Semi-finals
Quarter-finals
Round 2
Round 1
Did not qualify
1 2 3 4 5 6

EUROPE

GERMAN CLUBS

Soccer first boomed in Germany in the ports and northern cities of Hamburg, Bremen, and Berlin. While both regions still boast major clubs, the real power-house clubs are in the Ruhr valley, home to Schalke 04 and Borussia Dortmund, and in Munich, home to Bayern as well as TSV München. Many of the leading post-war West German clubs—such as Nürnberg, 1FC Köln, Eintracht Frankfurt, and Kaiserslautern—have struggled since reunification.

MIROSLAV KLOSE
A deadly marksman who has bagged a goal every other game for Germany, Bayern Munich striker Klose was the top scorer in the 2006 World Cup.

NICKNAME: DER FCB, DIE BAYERN ("THE BAVARIANS")
FOUNDED: MUNICH, 1900
HOME
STADIUM: ALLIANZ ARENA, 69,900
DOMESTIC HONORS: LEAGUE 21, CUP 7
INTERNATIONAL HONORS: CHAMPIONS LEAGUE 1974, 1975, 1976, 2001; **CUP WINNERS' CUP** 1967; **UEFA CUP** 1996

BAYERN MUNICH
Known in Germany as FC Hollywood, Bayern is the team everyone loves to hate, but still boasts legions of German fans and more than 1,000 fan clubs outside the country. Founded in 1900 in Schwabig, a working-class district of Munich, the club acquired significant Jewish membership. Despite missing the first year of the Bundesliga in 1973, the club has won more league titles than any other team.

THEY'RE BEHIND YOU
Bayern were caught making a secret TV deal without the other teams in the Bundesliga, but threatened to switch to Serie A —the Italian top tier—if punished.

KINGS OF EUROPE
Bayern Munich won the European Cup three times in a row from 1974 to 1976, with an extraordinary squad that boasted Sepp Maier in goal, Frank Beckenbauer everywhere, and Gerd Müller up front. Bayern went on to lose another three finals in the 1980s and 1990s before winning the trophy for the fourth time in 2001.

NICKNAME: DIE SCHWARZGELBEN ("THE BLACK AND YELLOWS")
FOUNDED: DORTMUND, 1909
HOME
STADIUM: SIGNAL IDUNA PARK, 80,000
DOMESTIC HONORS: LEAGUE 6, CUP 2
INTERNATIONAL HONORS: CHAMPIONS LEAGUE 1997; CUP WINNERS' CUP 1966

BORUSSIA DORTMUND
Founded in 1909 from the fusion of three clubs —Trinity, Rhenania, and Britannia—Borussia Dortmund spent the next fifty years in the shadow of neighboring Schalke 04. That changed in the 1980s and 1990s, when a new commercial strategy made them the Ruhr's biggest club. However, the club has flirted with bankruptcy in recent years.

A GRANDSTAND VIEW
Formerly known as the Westfalenstadion, Borussia Dortmund's huge Signal Iduna Park attracts the biggest regular crowds in Europe. Uniquely for such a large arena, the stadium retains a safe standing section for Bundesliga games only, the Südtribüne. For internationals the section is fitted with temporary seats, reducing the overall capacity to 67,000. During building work ahead of the 2008 European Championships, a 1,000 lb (450 kg) unexploded wartime bomb was discovered buried beneath the halfway line, leading to an evacuation of the surrounding area while the bomb was defused.

MATTHIAS **SAMMER**

Sammer was one of the few East German players to make the transition to the Bundesliga. An adaptable sweeper and midfielder, he was the lynchpin of Borussia Dortmund's European Cup-winning team.

BORN: SEPTEMBER 5, 1967, DRESDEN, GERMANY
HEIGHT: 5FT 11IN (1.8M)
MAIN CLUBS: **DYNAMO DRESDEN, VFB STUTTGART, BORUSSIA DORTMUND**
INTERNATIONAL CAPS: **23 (EAST GERMANY), 51 (GERMANY)**

HAMBURG SV

NICKNAME:
ROTHOSEN
("RED SHORTS")
FOUNDED:
HAMBURG, 1887
HOME
STADIUM:
HSH NORDBANK ARENA, 55,000
DOMESTIC HONORS:
LEAGUE 6, CUP 3
INTERNATIONAL HONORS:
EUROPEAN CUP 1983; CUP
WINNERS' CUP 1977

Uniquely among German clubs, Hamburg's biggest shareholders are the fans, whose representatives sit on the board of directors. However, fan power has yet to return the team to the heady days of the late 1970s and early 1980s, when the club won three league championships, the 1977 Cup Winners' Cup, and the 1983 European Cup.

HAMBURG TO THE CORE

Hamburg is personified by the graft of striker Uwe Seeler, who played 476 league games and scored 404 goals in a club career that spanned three decades. He turned down a lucrative move to Inter Milan in 1961 and went on to play for another ten years, then became club president after retiring.

SOMETIMES YOU LOSE...
SOMETIMES THE OTHERS WIN

OTTO REHHAGEL
BAYERN MUNICH, KAISERSLAUTEN, AND GREECE MANAGER

THE RUHR DERBY

First played in 1925, games between the two Ruhr clubs Schalke 04 and Borussia Dortmund are known as the Revierderby or "District Derby," and attract the biggest crowds of any German league tie. In 2007, on the penultimate weekend of the Bundesliga, Dortmund won the derby and killed off Schalke's best chance to win a league title for almost fifty years.

TORSTEN FRINGS

Despite interest from many of Europe's top clubs, heavy-metal-loving, big-tackling Werder Bremen midfielder Frings has always played in Germany.

CHAMPIONS LEAGUE WINS

- Bayern Munich—**67%**
- Hamburg—**16.5%**
- Borussia Dortmund—**16.5%**
- The rest—**0%**

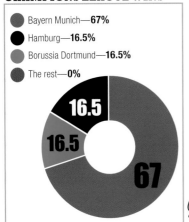

BEST OF THE REST

SCHALKE 04 (1904)
With a huge stadium in the tiny Ruhr town of Gelsenkirchen, Schalke is the worker's club, and won four championships in the 1930s.
HONORS: LEAGUE 7, CUP 4; UEFA CUP 1997

BAYER LEVERKUSEN (1904)
Founded—and still funded—by the Bayer chemical company, Leverkusen has a reputation for choking in the big games.
HONORS: LEAGUE 0, CUP 1; UEFA CUP 1988

HERTHA BERLIN (1892)
Champions in the final years of the Weimar Republic, Hertha spent the Cold War at the Gesundbrune stadium, next to the Berlin Wall.
HONORS: LEAGUE 2, CUP 2; INTERTOTO CUP 2006

BORUSSIA MÖNCHENGLADBACH (1900)
A tiny team from the Ruhr, the club rose to prominence in the 1970s and contested five European finals, winning two of them.
HONORS: LEAGUE 3, CUP 2; UEFA CUP 1975, 1979

WERDER BREMEN (1899)
One of Germany's oldest clubs, Bremen were one of the leading clubs in the 1980s and '90s, winning the Cup Winners' Cup in 1992.
HONORS: LEAGUE 4, CUP 5; CUP WINNERS' CUP 1992

FC NÜRNBERG (1900)
The first great German soccer club, Nürnberg ruled the 1920s and won titles in every decade up to the 1960s, but then won nothing until the DFB-Pokal (see p.187) in 2007.
HONORS: LEAGUE 9, CUP 4

VFB STUTTGART (1893)
Five-time champions Stuttgart are backed by the huge combined powers of local politicians and the German car industry.
HONORS: LEAGUE 5, CUP 3; INTERTOTO CUP 2000, 2002

EUROPE

HOME

AWAY

POPULATION: 8.2 MILLION

CAPITAL: VIENNA

FA: ÖSTERREICHISCHER FUßBALL-BUND

LICENSED PLAYERS:
MALE: 912,600
FEMALE: 55,500

PROFESSIONALS: 900

REGISTERED CLUBS: 2,200

AUSTRIA

The roots of Austrian soccer lie in a match between the Vienna Cricket Club and a team of Scottish gardeners from the Rothschild's estate in 1894. Soccer in Austria never looked back, and the two teams became Weiner Amateur and First Vienna. The national team attracted gates of 60,000 by the 1920s, and reached a peak with the "Wunderteam" that achieved a record run of 14 unbeaten games during the early 1930s. Much of Vienna's soccer culture was wiped out by Germany's Anschluss (annexation) of Austria in 1938.

DOMESTIC STRIFE

The road to establishing a truly domestic game in Austria was marked by turbulence. Teams from Vienna played separately from those in the provinces until 1938, when the Austrian game was absorbed into German soccer. Rapid Vienna went on to win the German title in 1941, while Austria Wien won the German Cup in 1943. A truly national Austrian league—now known as the Bundesliga—has only run since 1949. The Austrian Cup is a minor affair, and even disappeared from the fixture list for most of the 1950s.

THE TANK

Joseph Uridil was the first star of Austrian soccer. A huge, marauding forward affectionately nicknamed "The Tank," he played for Rapid Vienna in the early 1920s. His popularity was marked by a foxtrot, "Urudil Will Play Today," and his face was used to sell soap, underwear, and chocolate.

STAT ATTACK

NATIONAL TEAM

NICKNAME: Das Team, Wunderteam (1930s)
NATIONAL STADIUM: Ernst Happel Stadion, Vienna, 53,008
WORLD CUP FINALS: 7 appearances, 3rd place, **1954**
EUROPEAN CHAMPIONSHIPS: 1 appearance, **2008**
BIGGEST WIN: 9–0 vs Malta, 1977
BIGGEST DEFEAT: 1–11 vs England, 1908
MOST CAPS: Andreas Herzog, **103**
MOST GOALS: Anton Polster, **44**

MAIN DOMESTIC CLUBS

SK RAPID WIEN
FOUNDED: Vienna, 1898
STADIUM: Gerhard Hanappi Stadion
CAPACITY: 18,400
INTERNATIONAL HONORS: Cup Winners' Cup runners-up 1985, 1996
LEAGUE: 32 **CUP:** 14

HOME

FK AUSTRIA WIEN
FOUNDED: Vienna, 1911
STADIUM: Horr Stadion
CAPACITY: 11,800
INTERNATIONAL HONORS: Cup Winners' Cup runners-up 1978
LEAGUE: 23 **CUP:** 26

HOME

FC WACKER INNSBRUCK
FOUNDED: Innsbruck 2002
STADIUM: Tivoli-Neu
CAPACITY: 30,000
INTERNATIONAL HONORS: None
LEAGUE: 10 **CUP:** 7

HOME

MAN OF PAPER

Nicknamed "die Papierene," the man of paper, Matthias Sindelar was the greatest of a great generation of soccer players. Personifying the graceful, intelligent Viennese style, he was described as playing soccer like a grand master played chess. He refused to play for the newly "unified" German team after Austria's annexation by the Nazis.

HAKOAH CHAMPIONS

The first professional Austrian championship was held in 1925 and won by Hakoah ("strength" in Hebrew) Wien, the city's leading Jewish sport club. The team toured the US, playing in front of a crowd of 45,000 at the Polo Fields in New York. Most of the squad enjoyed the tour—and the pay—so much that they stayed in US soccer, and the team never won the league again. After 1938, the club was closed by Nazi Germany and expunged from their records.

DER WUNDERTEAM

The so-called "wonder team," coached by the brilliant Hugo Meisel, was the all-conquering Austrian side that played a mesmerizing passing game that captivated Europe. Between 1931 and 1934, they played 33 games, lost just three, and scored 101 goals. However, their decline was marked by losing to hosts Italy at the 1934 World Cup.

9 Number of goals Austria conceded in a European Championship qualifier against Spain in 1999

1941 Year in which Rapid Vienna won the German league title

10 Number of clubs in the Austrian Bundesliga

10,000 Number of Austrians who signed a petition asking the nation to withdraw as co-hosts with Switzerland of Euro 2008

6 Goals scored by the losing team in the 1924 Austrian Cup Final—the winners scored 8

SWITZERLAND

HOME   AWAY

POPULATION: 7.5 MILLION
CAPTIAL: BERNE
FA: SFV-ASF (SWISS FOOTBALL ASSOCIATION)
LICENSED PLAYERS:
MALE: 507,900
FEMALE: 63,800
PROFESSIONALS: 550
REGISTERED CLUBS: 1,500

Soccer came early to Switzerland, with Geneva Cricket Club playing the game in the 1860s. A league championship was first held in 1895, and Swiss players played for French and Italian teams for the next 20 years. Despite being the home of UEFA and FIFA, hosting the 1954 World Cup, and co-hosting Euro 2008, Switzerland has rarely challenged for international honors.

STAT ATTACK

NATIONAL TEAM

NICKNAME: Nati
NATIONAL STADIUM:
Stade de Suisse, Bern, 32,000
WORLD CUP FINALS: 8 appearances, quarter-finals **1934**, **1938**, **1954**
EUROPEAN CHAMPIONSHIPS:
3 appearances
BIGGEST WIN: 9–0 vs Lithuania, 1924
BIGGEST DEFEAT: 0–9 vs Hungary, 1911
MOST CAPS: Heinz Hermann, 11
MOST GOALS: Alexander Frei, 37

FIXTURE FREEZE

The national league, known as the Super League, has been running since 1933. It consists of ten teams playing each other four times during a year-round 36-game season. During the winter, from the end of November to late February, fans must be content with watching an indoor league.

LATE STARTERS

FC Basel were founded in 1893 (their first captain, Joan Gamper, also founded Barcelona in 1899). They had to wait until 1953 for their first league title. In recent years they have been the most successful Swiss soccer team, and progressed to the second group stage of the Champions League in 2003.

MAIN DOMESTIC CLUBS

GRASSHOPPER-CLUB
FOUNDED: Zurich, 1886
STADIUM: Letzigrund Stadion
CAPACITY: 30,000   HOME
INTERNATIONAL HONORS: None
LEAGUE: 26 **CUP:** 18

FC BASEL
FOUNDED: Basel, 1893
STADIUM: St. Jakob-Park
CAPACITY: 42,500   HOME
INTERNATIONAL HONORS:
1 appearance, Champions League, **2003**
LEAGUE: 12 **CUP:** 9

SERVETTE FC
FOUNDED:
Geneva, 1890
STADIUM: HOME
Stade de Geneve
CAPACITY: 32,000
INTERNATIONAL HONORS: None
LEAGUE: 17 **CUP:** 7

HAKAN **YAKIN**

Attacking midfielder Hakan Yakin, along with his brother Murat, is a key player in the revival of Swiss soccer. Of Turkish descent, he is a public face of Switzerland's real ethnic mix.

BORN: **FEB 22, 1977, BASEL, SWITZERLAND**
HEIGHT: **5FT 11IN (1.8M)**
MAIN CLUBS: **FC BASEL, ST. GALLEN, GRASSHOPPERS, YOUNG BOYS BERN**
INTERNATIONAL CAPS: **64**

GOING, GOING, GONE

Three top clubs, all in French-speaking Switzerland, have gone bankrupt in the last decade. FC Lugano and Lausanne Sports both folded in 2002, then in 2005 Servetee, with its 117-year history and 1999 championship win, collapsed too.

SO MUCH FOR THE CLEAN SHEET

At the 2006 World Cup, Switzerland tied 0–0 with France and then beat South Korea and Togo 2–0 to progress to the second round. They then tied 0–0 with Ukraine and were beaten in a penalty shootout, making them the only team to be knocked out of the World Cup finals without conceding a single goal.

SPAIN

HOME   AWAY

POPULATION: 40.4 MILLION
CAPITAL: MADRID
LICENSED PLAYERS:
MALE: 629,000
FEMALE: 18,000
PROFESSIONALS: 1,300
REGISTERED CLUBS: 18,000

There is one word to describe the Spanish attitude to soccer—"passionate." At both the domestic and national level, the game is heavily influenced by regional identities and past political conflicts within the country. Games between Catalan and Castilian clubs are charged with historical significance, and the nation's ethnic and geographic diversity has produced a fascinating mix of playing styles.

CAUTION TO THE WIND

Prior to 2008, Spain had a reputation as the great underachievers of international soccer. Given the excellence of La Liga and the country's wealth of talent, their poor record was puzzling. Possible explanations included the fact that cautious play was simply not in the Spanish make-up. However, they then set the record straight in style, winning every match en route to taking the 2008 European Championship, and the top slot in the FIFA world rankings.

FERNANDO **HIERRO**

Hierro ("iron" in Spanish) scored more than 100 goals for Real Madrid and 29 for the national team, placing him second on Spain's all-time list of goal-scorers. Remarkable enough for any player, this feat is even more amazing given that Hierro was a central defender.

BORN: **MARCH 23, 1968, VÉLEZ-MÁLAGA, SPAIN**
HEIGHT: **6FT 2IN (1.88M)**
MAIN CLUBS: **REAL VALLADOLID, REAL MADRID, AL RAYYAN, BOLTON WANDERERS**
INTERNATIONAL CAPS: **89**

LUIS SUAREZ
Often described as Spain's greatest ever player, Barcelona midfielder Luis Suárez became the only Spaniard to be voted European Soccer Player of the Year, winning the award in 1960.

REGIONAL TEAMS

Spain is made up of several autonomous regions, three of which field teams of their own. The Catalonian, Basque, and Galician XIs only play friendly games, and their star players also turn out for Spain, but they still have fervent followings in their home provinces. The Catalonian team regularly attracts crowds of 60,000-plus and, in recent years, has played teams as illustrious as Argentina and Brazil. FIFA and UEFA have so far resisted requests to grant them full international status.

69 Percentage of Spanish fans who perform superstitious rituals to help their teams win

14 La Liga titles won by Real Madrid from 1961 to 1980

98,260 Capacity of Barcelona's Nou Camp stadium, the largest soccer stadium in Europe

STAT ATTACK

GOVERNING BODY:
Real Federación Española de Fútbol
FOUNDED: 1913
NATIONAL STADIUM: None
FIRST MATCH: 1–0 vs Denmark, 1920
BIGGEST WIN: 13–0 vs Bulgaria, 1933
BIGGEST DEFEAT: 1–7 vs Italy, 1928, and vs England, 1931

THE LEGENDS

MOST CAPPED

Name	From/To	Caps
Andoni ZUBIZARRETA	1985–98	126
RAÚL	1996–2006	102
Fernando HIERRO	1989–2002	89
Iker CASILLAS	2000–present	88
José Antonio CAMACHO	1975–88	81
Rafael GORDILLO	1977–88	75

TOP GOALSCORERS

Name	From/To	Goals
RAÚL	1996–2006	44
Fernando HIERRO	1989–2002	29
Fernando MORIENTES	1998–2007	27
Emilio BUTRAGUEÑO	1984–92	26
David VILLA	2005–present	24
Alfredo DI STEFANO	1957–61	23

STAT ATTACK

LA LIGA PRIMERA

LEAGUE STRUCTURE: 20 clubs
TOP SCORER: Telmo Zara, **253**
MOST SUCCESSFUL TEAM: Real Madrid, **31** League titles
BIGGEST WIN: 12–1, Athletic Bilbao vs Barcelona, **1931**
HIGHEST ATTENDANCE: 125,000 (maximum past capacity of Real Madrid's Bernabeu Stadium)
DIVISIONS BELOW LA LIGA PRIMERA: Segunda A—**22**, Segunda B—**80** (four groups of 20), Tercera—**360** (18 groups of 20)

COPA DEL REY

First played in 1902 as the Copa del Ayuntamiento de Madrid, the Copa del Rey is a limited-entry knock-out contest.
HIGHEST SCORING FINAL:
6–2, Sevilla vs Rácing Ferrol, 1939
MOST SUCCESSFUL TEAM: Barcelona, **24** wins
BIGGEST WIN: 6–1, Real Madrid vs Castilla CF, **1980**

LA LIGA

La Liga is the name for the professional soccer leagues in Spain. There are two divisions—the Primera and the Segunda. The idea of a national professional league was proposed In 1927, and the first games were played in 1928 with just ten teams. Three of the founding teams—Real Madrid, Barcelona, and Athletic Bilbao—have never been relegated from the Primera.

LA LIGA TITLE WINS

Real Madrid—**43%**
Others—**32%**
Barcelona—**25%**

WHAT DO YOU EXPECT? ...WE'RE SPAIN

WINGER VICENTE
AFTER SPAIN'S EARLY EXIT IN THE 2004 EUROPEAN CHAMPIONSHIP

COPA DEL REY

Known as the Copa de España during the Second Republic (1930s) and the Copa del Generalísimo during the Franco dictatorship (1939–75), the Copa del Rey is Spain's main domestic knock-out competition. All the Primera Division and Segunda A clubs take part, plus around 23 from Segunda B. They are joined by the champions of the Tercera Division, or the runners-up if the champions are the reserve team of a bigger club.

EL PICHICHI

Every year since 1953, the Spanish newspaper *La Marca* has awarded the Trofeo Pichichi ("Pichichi Trophy") to the top scorer in La Liga. It is named after the diminutive Athletic Bilbao striker Rafael Moreno Aranzadi, who was known as "Pichichi" and scored 170 goals in 200 matches before dying of typhus in 1922, aged just 29.

DAVID VILLA
Outstanding Valencia striker David Villa finished top scorer at Euro 2008 despite missing two games through injury.

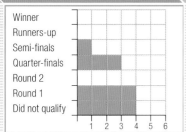

WORLD CUP

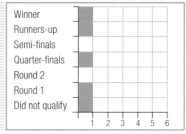

EURO CHAMPIONSHIPS

SPAIN'S BIG TWO

Considering the wealth and success of Real Madrid and Barcelona, La Liga is remarkably competitive—five other clubs have won the title since 1980. The Copa del Rey is even less predictable, and the Big Two do not dominate. The game in Spain has a strong regional character, with the Basque, Catalan, and Galician clubs liking nothing better than victory over the giants from the capital.

NICKNAME:
LOS BLANCOS ("THE WHITES")

FOUNDED:
MADRID, 1902

HOME

STADIUM:
SANTIAGO BERNABÉU, 80,000

DOMESTIC HONORS:
LEAGUE 31; CUP 17

INTERNATIONAL HONORS:
CHAMPIONS LEAGUE 1956–60, 1966, 1998, 2000, 2002; **UEFA CUP** 1985, 1986; **WORLD CLUB CUP** 1960, 1998, 2002

REAL MADRID

Real Madrid consistently tops the global revenue table and the team has won more La Liga titles and European Cups than any other team. Founded in 1902 as Madrid FC, the club were granted the use of the title Real ("royal") by King Alfonso XIII in 1920. Under Santiago Bernabéu (the club president 1945–78), after whom their stadium is named, Real Madrid became the dominant force in Spain and Europe. The fans of Los Blancos expect their team to not only win, but to win with style.

FIVE OUT OF FIVE

Santiago Bernabéu was one of the three men responsible for the creation of the European Cup, so the club's victory in the inaugural tournament in 1956 was singularly appropriate. With the first truly international team of players in soccer history, Real won the competition for the next four years, earning the right to keep the original trophy.

IT WANTS THE TEAM TO WIN FIRST... ## THEN TO PLAY!

ALFREDO DE STEFANO
DESCRIBING THE MADRID CROWD

THE YE-YÉ GENERATION

When former captain Miguel Muñoz became manager in 1959, he ended the policy of buying foreign players. Seven years later, Real won the 1966 European Cup with an all-Spanish side, captained by Francisco Gento. With Beatle-mania in full swing, the victors were christened the Ye-Yé team after the "Yeah yeah yeah" chorus of the band's hit "She Loves You."

ALFREDO DI STEFANO
Legendary Argentinian striker Alfredo di Stefano joined Real Madrid in 1953, winning eight La Liga titles and five European Cups, and scoring 216 goals in his 11 years at the club.

THE GALÁCTICOS

Florentino Pérez, president of Real in 2000, followed up his election pledge of buying Luís Figo from arch-rivals Barcelona by building a team of Galácticos ("superstars"). He bought a world-class player every year, following Figo with Zinédine Zidane (2001), Ronaldo (2002), and David Beckham (2003).

RAÚL

When Raúl González Blanco made his Real Madrid debut in 1994, he became the club's youngest ever player. A prolific striker, he has since gone on to captain Real, and is the Champions League's all-time top scorer.

BORN: **JUNE 27, 1977, MADRID, SPAIN**
HEIGHT: **5FT 11IN (1.8M)**
MAIN CLUBS: **REAL MADRID**
INTERNATIONAL CAPS: **102**

NICKNAME:
BARÇA

FOUNDED:
BARCELONA, 1899

STADIUM:
NOU CAMP, 98,260

HOME

DOMESTIC HONORS:
LEAGUE 18; CUP 24

INTERNATIONAL HONORS:
CHAMPIONS LEAGUE 1992, 2005;
CUP WINNERS' CUP 1979, 1982,
1989, 1997; FAIRS CUP 1958,
1960, 1966

FC BARCELONA

Founded in 1899 by a group of Swiss, English, and Spanish men led by Swiss émigré Joan Gamper (also called Hans Gamper), Barcelona is a symbol of Catalonia, the semi-autonomous Spanish province of which it is the capital. Barcelona (Barça) are co-owned by more than 150,000 fanatical members (known as the "socios"), and they play at the biggest stadium in Europe, the 98,000-capacity Nou Camp. They are Spain's second most successful side, having won fewer La Liga titles but more Spanish Cups than their great rivals Real Madrid.

"MÉS QUE UN CLUB"

Barça's motto, meaning "more than a club," describes the club's symbolism of the Catalan identity, which successive Spanish regimes tried to stamp out. Barça became a center of resistance to the Madrid government. In 1925, the stadium was closed after fans booed the national anthem. General Franco ordered the execution of the club's president in 1936 and banned the Catalan flag and language. While he was dictator, the stadium was one of the few places where Catalan was spoken openly.

MYSTERIOUS TURNAROUND

In the first leg of the semi-final of the 1943 Copa del Generalísimo, as the Copa del Rey was then known, Barcelona beat Real Madrid 3–0. Just before the second leg, General Franco's sinister Director of State Security visited the Catalans' dressing room. Real unexpectedly won 11–1.

THE DREAM TEAM

The team assembled under manager Johan Cruyff featured legends Gheorghe Hagi, Michael Laudrup, Hristo Stoichkov, and the Brazilian goal-machine Romário. Named after the US basketball team of the 1992 Olympics, it won four successive La Liga titles (1991–94), and Barça's first European Cup (1992).

ROMÁRIO

In his first season at Barça, Romário won the La Liga title and the Pichichi, with 30 goals in 33 games. If friendly games are included, the tiny Brazilian's goal tally is well over 1,000.

RONALDINHO

A World Cup winner with Brazil, midfielder Ronaldinho is one of the most gifted players of his generation. Worshipped by many, he frustrates managers and fans with erratic performances, attributed to his party lifestyle.

BORN: MARCH 21, 1980, PORTO ALEGRE, BRAZIL
HEIGHT: 5FT 11½IN (1.82M)
MAIN CLUBS: PARIS SAINT-GERMAIN,
BARCELONA, AC MILAN
INTERNATIONAL CAPS: 84

EL CLÁSICO

Real Madrid and Barcelona embody the opposites of the character of Spain: capital versus provinces, conservative versus liberal, establishment versus the fringe. As a result, any clash between Real and Barça, known as El Clásico, is charged with meaning. It is one of the most-watched sporting events on earth.

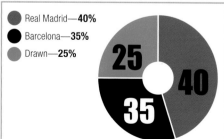

EL CLÁSICO—WINS

- Real Madrid—40%
- Barcelona—35%
- Drawn—25%

25 / 40 / 35

BRAGA STADIUM

Portugal built ten new stadiums when the country hosted Euro 2004 (see p.334), but Braga's municipal stadium is in a league of its own. Sited in space carved out of a disused quarry, the stadium is open at the goal ends, while its two stands form an elegant canyon. At one end the stadium hugs the mountainous rock, while at the other end it is open. The roofs of the stands join over the field and are supported by a thin net of steel cables. The stadium has been approved by UEFA as being of a high enough standard to host a UEFA Europa League final.

ESTÁDIO MUNICIPAL DE BRAGA

PARQUE NORTE, DUME, 4710 BRAGA, PORTUGAL

OWNER:
MUNICIPALITY OF BRAGA

ARCHITECT:
EDUARDO SOUTO DE MOURA

OPENED:
DECEMBER 30, 2003

CONSTRUCTION COST:
$94 MILLION (€83.1 MILLION)

CAPACITY: 30,154

ONE STADIUM, THREE NAMES

In 2007, SC Braga agreed a sponsorship deal with French insurance company AXA, and began referring to the stadium as Estádio AXA. However, the Braga local government has not officially sanctioned the new name. Colloquially, it is known as simply "the quarry."

ROCK BLASTING

A huge amount of rock had to be blasted and removed to build the stadium. A construction cost of $94 million made it the third most-expensive of the ten new stadiums built for Euro 2004. Only the Estádio da Luz in Lisbon (capacity: 65,647) and Estádio do Dragão in Porto (capacity: 52,002) cost more.

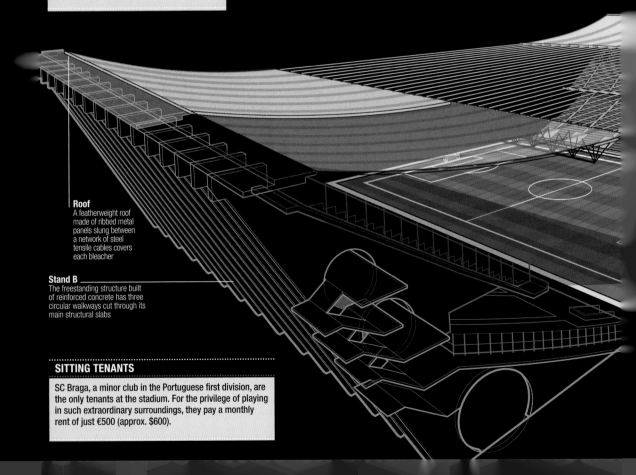

Roof
A featherweight roof made of ribbed metal panels slung between a network of steel tensile cables covers each bleacher

Stand B
The freestanding structure built of reinforced concrete has three circular walkways cut through its main structural slabs

SITTING TENANTS

SC Braga, a minor club in the Portuguese first division, are the only tenants at the stadium. For the privilege of playing in such extraordinary surroundings, they pay a monthly rent of just €500 (approx. $600).

THE SETTING

The stadium was carved out of a quarry called Monte Cristo, which overlooks the city of Braga. It is located to the north of the city and is intended to be the centerpiece of a broader development called Parque Urbano de Braga. The process of removing huge amounts of rock contributed to the total cost of the build. The results, however, were worth the expense—the stadium is often cited as one of the most beautiful in the world.

Exposed rock wall
The area behind one of the goals is exposed granite, which is studded by a series of steel pins to prevent landslides

Bleachers
The bleachers are parallel with the sidelines, rather than behind the goals as is typical at more conventional grounds

Wired for sound
The leading edges of each roof are supported by steel gantries that carry lighting and sound

Entrances
The entrances to the stands are located in the bottom tier of the building

The Plaza
Once inside the stadium, spectators move between stands via an under-field plaza 54,000 sq ft (5,000 sq m) in area

Drainage
Water drains off the roof at two points and runs into freestanding concrete troughs mounted on the granite cliff face. Water runs down the hillside in a snaking open channel

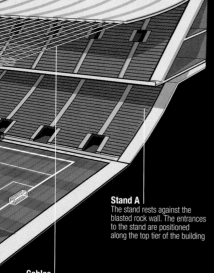

Stand A
The stand rests against the blasted rock wall. The entrances to the stand are positioned along the top tier of the building

Cables
Dozens of steel strings are connected over the field, a design which, according to the architects, was inspired by ancient Inca bridges

ACCORDING TO ME, SOCCER IS WATCHED
...LIKE THIS!

EDUARDO SOUTO DE MOURA, BRAGA'S ARCHITECT
MOVING HIS HAND FROM LEFT TO RIGHT AND BACK AGAIN

EURO 2004
Denmark beat Bulgaria 2–0 at Braga Stadium in the group stage of Euro 2004, although Denmark's coach, Morten Olson, complained that his players couldn't see the goal properly. "Because of that mountain wall," he said, "players found it tough to distinguish the goalposts."

16 The number of vertical concrete slabs that form the spine of Stand A

500 The monthly rent, in euros, paid by SC Braga to play at the stadium

730 The number of days it took to build the Braga stadium

0 The number of full houses SC Braga has attracted since taking occupation of the ground

SPAIN: THE CHASING PACK

While Real Madrid and Barcelona are easily the biggest teams in Spain, a whole pack of other clubs are snapping at their heels, making La Liga more unpredictable than many other big leagues. In recent years both Deportivo la Coruña and Valencia have topped the league and consistent pressure, fueled by regional pride, has come from the leading teams of Andalucia (Betis and Sevilla) and the Basque country (Real Sociedad and Athletic Bilbao).

NICKNAME: LOS COLCHONEROS ("THE MATTRESS MAKERS")

HOME

FOUNDED: MADRID, 1903

STADIUM: VICENTE CLADERON, 54,851

DOMESTIC HONORS: LEAGUE 9; CUP 9

INTERNATIONAL HONORS: CUP WINNERS' CUP 1962; WORLD CLUB CUP 1974

ATLÉTICO MADRID

Founded by Basque students in 1903 as a branch of Athletic Bilbao, Atlético Madrid took off in 1939 after a merger with the Spanish Air Force team Aviaçion Nacional. Although Atlético have won nine La Liga titles, they live in the shadow of Real Madrid. Nevertheless, the club's followers emphasize that they, rather than their famous neighbors, are Madrid's authentic soccer fans.

FERNANDO TORRES
Deadly in front of goal, Torres originally wanted to be a goalkeeper. Thankfully he was persuaded otherwise, joining Atlético Madrid aged 11, where he was always a favorite. He then moved to Liverpool and scored the winning goal for Spain to lift the Euro 2008 title.

JESÚS GIL

Property tycoon, ex-mayor of Marbella, and owner of Atlético Madrid, Gil was one of the most colorful and controversial characters in Spanish soccer. During his 16 years as club president, Gil hired and fired 23 managers, served time in jail for fraud, and outraged the soccer authorities with foul-mouthed verbal attacks. His greatest triumph came in 1996, when Atlético won the league and cup double. Gil upstaged his players at the celebratory parade by riding through the streets of Madrid on horseback. He died in 2004 aged 71.

VICTORY IN THE SHADOWS

For more than a decade, Atlético played in the shadow of Real Madrid, whose dominance included five European Cups. Even when Atlético won the 1962 Cup Winners' Cup, hardly anyone noticed: they drew with Fiorentina in the final, and by the time the replay took place four months later, a new season had started.

FIRING A COACH IS LIKE HAVING A BEER TO ME... I CAN FIRE TWENTY IN A YEAR, EVEN A HUNDRED IF I HAVE TO

JESÚS GIL
PRESIDENT OF ATLÉTICO MADRID , 1987–2003

NICKNAME:
LOS LEONES
("THE LIONS")
FOUNDED:
BILBAO, 1898
HOME
STADIUM: SAN MAMES, 39,750
DOMESTIC HONORS:
LEAGUE 8; CUP 23
INTERNATIONAL HONORS:
NONE

ATHLETIC BILBAO

The most important Basque team in Spain, Athletic Bilbao won two of the first three La Liga titles and went on to win six more. Famed for bringing youth players through the ranks, the club also has a policy of signing only Basque players. Success at the club was largely achieved under manager Javier Clemente, whose tough tackling teams of the 1980s became feared. However, success has recently been hard to find, despite Clemente returning to the club for two further spells in charge.

THROWN TO THE LIONS

Athletic Bilbao's stadium is named after St. Mames, an early Christian who was thrown to the lions in the Colosseum in Rome, but the lions refused to eat him—thus the team's nickname—"the lions" and the stadium's nickname "the cathedral."

ANDONI GOIKOETXEA

Goikoetxea (pronounced "goykochea") was one of the fiercest tacklers of all time. Although he had a distinguished international career, he is most famous for breaking Diego Maradona's ankle in 1983.

BORN: **MAY 23, 1956, ALONSOTEGI, SPAIN**
HEIGHT: **6FT 1IN (1.85M)**
MAIN CLUBS: **ATHLETIC BILBAO, ATLÉTICO MADRID**
INTERNATIONAL CAPS: **39**

NICKNAME:
LOS CHES
("THE LADS")
FOUNDED:
VALENCIA, 1919
HOME
STADIUM: MESTALLA, 55,000
DOMESTIC HONORS:
LEAGUE 6; CUP 7
INTERNATIONAL HONORS:
UEFA 3

VALENCIA

Fourth in the all-time La Liga table, Valencia have won more European competitions than any Spanish club other than Real Madrid and Barcelona. The '80s and '90s were relatively lean times at the Mestalla Stadium, but the club made up for them in the early years of the 21st century, appearing in consecutive Champions League finals under the Argentinean manager Héctor Cúper (2000 and 2001), and winning the UEFA Cup and two La Liga titles under his successor Rafa Benítez.

ECCENTRIC SUPPORT

Valencia is also home to Manuel Cáceres Artesero, better known as Manolo el del Bombo. This infamous, rotund, drum-beating fan sports a distinctive beret, attends every game played by the Spanish national team, and is also a passionate Valencia supporter. He has a bar near the Mestalla stadium.

MARIO KEMPES

Although best remembered for his winning goal in the 1978 World Cup Final, Kempes played some of his best soccer at Valencia, 1977–81. While there he scored an amazing 95 goals in 143 games and was top scorer in the league two years running.

BEST OF THE REST

ESPANYOL (1900)
Barcelona's second team, Espanyol was one of the ten original teams to be included in the first La Liga in 1928, but has never won the league title.
HONORS: CUP 4

SEVILLA (1905)
Although founded by British miners in 1905, Sevilla is wholly Spanish. They won the Copa del Rey in 2007, the first domestic trophy in 60 years and the UEFA cup in 2006 and 2007.
HONORS: LEAGUE 1, CUP 4

DEPORTIVO LA CORUÑA (1906)
Hailing from A Coruña in Galicia, Deportivo is a recent force in Spanish soccer. The club won La Liga in 2000, and finished runner-up in both successive seasons.
HONORS: LEAGUE 1, CUP 2

REAL SOCIEDAD (1909)
Based in the northern city of San Sebastián, Real Sociedad won consecutive league titles in 1981 and '82. It dropped a Basque-only policy in 1989, unlike rivals Athletic Bilbao.
HONORS: LEAGUE 2, CUP 2

VILLARREAL (1923)
With a population of just 48,000, Villarreal is a surprise success story. Promoted to La Liga in 1998, the club came third in 2005, and beat Barcelona to second place in 2008.
HONORS: INTERTOTO CUP 2

REAL BETIS (1907)
The first Andalucian team to play in La Liga, Seville's "other" team won the league title in 1935 and the Copa del Rey in 1997 and 2005. They have also played in the UEFA Cup.
HONORS: LEAGUE 1, CUP 2

REAL ZARAGOZA (1932)
Cup specialists Zaragoza finished runners-up in La Liga in 1975, but have since twice suffered the indignity of relegation, most recently in 2008.
HONORS: CUP 6, CUP WINNERS' CUP 1

PORTUGAL

HOME

AWAY

POPULATION: 10.6 MILLION
CAPITAL: LISBON
LICENSED PLAYERS:
MALE: 489,000
FEMALE: 59,000
PROFESSIONALS: 1,500
REGISTERED CLUBS: 2,500

Portugal's intimate connections with Britain saw soccer played as early as the 1860s. The game really took off in the early 20th century, but it was not until the 1960s that Portugal developed into an international power. After a long fallow period, the 21st century has seen the nation challenge for the European Championships, its clubs win in Europe, and a host of gifted players emerge.

FOOTBALL, FADO, FATIMA

During the long dictatorship (1932–74), "Football, Fatima, and Fado" was commonly heard in Portugal. Football, which was permitted after a defeat to Spain in 1933, the Catholic cult of Fatima, and the melancholy Fado style of music combined to distract the people from politics.

CRISTIANO RONALDO
In 2008, Portugal's dribbling magician Cristiano Ronaldo finished the season as Europe's top scorer—quite an achievement for a winger.

THE GOLDEN GENERATIONS

Portugal won the FIFA World Youth Cup twice in the space of three years (1989 and 1991). The victorious team—including Luís Figo, Nuno Gomes, Rui Costa, Sérgio Conceição, Fernando Couto, Vítor Baía, and Jorge Costa—was dubbed the "Golden Generation" by the Portuguese press. While each of the players went on to successful club careers, Portugal only achieved the expected success (runners-up in Euro 2004 and semi-finalists at the 2006 World Cup) since the emergence of a second golden generation, including Deco, Cristiano Ronaldo, and Ricardo Carvalho.

EURO 2004

When hosting the European Championships in 2004, Portugal put up ten new stadiums that turned out to be the most adventurous and colorful ever built for a major contest (see Braga Stadium, pp.196–97). Perfect weather drew foreign fans in unprecedented numbers; more than 150,000 traveled from England alone. Portugal's steady progress to the final was met by motorcades and parties across the nation's cities. Greece broke up the party by beating the home team twice—first in the opening game, then in the final.

PORTUGAL'S RISE

FIFA ranking (y-axis: 45, 35, 25, 15, 5)
x-axis: Late 1990s — Present

THERE'S NOT ENOUGH BUM
FOR TWO CHAIRS

BÉLA GUTTMAN, BENFICA COACH,
ON WHY THE CLUB COULD NOT WIN THE EUROPEAN CUP
AND PORTUGUESE TITLE IN THE SAME SEASON

STAT ATTACK

GOVERNING BODY:
Federação Portuguesa de Futebol
FOUNDED: 1914
NATIONAL STADIUM: None
FIRST MATCH: 1–3 vs Spain, 1923
BIGGEST WIN: 8–0 vs Lichtenstein, 1994, and vs Kuwait, 2003
BIGGEST DEFEAT: 0–10 vs England, 1947

THE LEGENDS

MOST CAPPED PLAYERS

Name	From/To	Caps
Luís FIGO	1991–2006	127
Fernando COUTO	1990–2004	110
Rui COSTA	1993–2004	94
PAULETA	1997–2006	88
João Vieira PINTO	1991–2002	81
Vítor BAÍA	1990–2002	80

TOP GOALSCORERS

Name	From/To	Goals
PAULETA	1997–2006	47
EUSÉBIO	1961–73	41
Luís FIGO	1991–2001	32
Nuno GOMES	1996–present	29
Rui COSTA	1993–2004	26
João Vieira PINTO	1991–2002	23

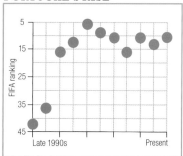

LA LIGA

Founded in 1935 as a national professional league, the top division replaced regional tournaments and a knock-out competition that formerly decided the national title. It was renamed the Portuguese Liga in 1999. Only five clubs have ever won the title, and the big three—Benfica, Sporting Lisbon, and Porto—account for 72 of the 74 title wins since the league's foundation.

CUP COMPETITIONS

Portugal has two major cup competitions. The Taça de Portugal ("Cup of Portugal") is a knock-out contest with amateur teams contesting the first three rounds before the top-flight teams join in. The final is held close to the National Day, June 10. The Taça da Liga ("League Cup") is a more limited knock-out contest that was played for the first time in 2007. Entry is confined to clubs in Portugal's top two divisions.

RUI COSTA
Attacking midfielder Rui Costa was an outstanding player in Portugal's first Golden Generation.

OPERATION GOLDEN WHISTLE

At the end of the 2004 season, the Portuguese police arrested and interviewed more than 60 players, referees, and club presidents— including the president of the Portuguese Liga—over allegations of match-fixing. No cases have been brought to trial.

STAT ATTACK

LA LIGA

LEAGUE STRUCTURE: 16 teams
TOP SCORER: Fernando Peyroteo, **330** goals
MOST WINS: Benfica and Porto, **24** titles
BIGGEST WIN: 14–0, Sporting Lisbon vs Leça, 1941–42
HIGHEST ATTENDANCE: 135,000 Benfica vs Porto, 1987
DIVISIONS BELOW LA LIGA: Liga Vitales (**16** teams)

TAÇA DE PORTUGAL

The nine-round cup is open to all four national divisions, as well as non-league champions.
MOST WINS: Benfica, **27** wins
MOST FINAL DEFEATS: Sporting Lisbon, **16** losses
BIGGEST WIN: 8–0, Benfica vs GD Estoril-Praia, 1944

LUÍS **FIGO**

An incredibly skilful winger, Figo is one of the true greats, but is also no stranger to controversy. His record-breaking $76-million transfer in 2000 from Barcelona to arch-rivals Real Madrid was a source of great ire among the Catalan fans.

BORN: **NOVEMBER 4, 1972, ALMADA, PORTUGAL**
HEIGHT: **5FT 11IN (1.8M)**
MAIN CLUBS: **BARCELONA, REAL MADRID, INTER MILAN**
INTERNATIONAL CAPS: **127**

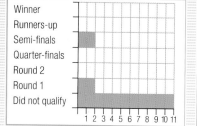

137 The number of Brazilians playing in Portugal's top-tier division in 2008

715 The number of games Eusébio played for Benfica

1875 The year the first club in Portugal—Lisbon FC—was founded

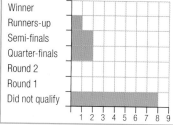

WORLD CUP

	1	2	3	4	5	6	7	8	9	10	11
Winner											
Runners-up											
Semi-finals	■	■									
Quarter-finals											
Round 2											
Round 1	■	■									
Did not qualify											

EURO CHAMPIONSHIPS

	1	2	3	4	5	6	7	8	9
Winner									
Runners-up	■								
Semi-finals	■	■							
Quarter-finals									
Round 2									
Round 1									
Did not qualify	■	■	■	■	■	■	■	■	

PORTUGUESE CLUBS

Portuguese soccer has been dominated by just three clubs since it turned professional in the 1930s—Benfica and Sporting, both from the capital city Lisbon, and Porto, from the great northern city of the same name. The rivalry between Porto and Benfica dramatizes the national divisions between north and south, contrasting hardworking town with hedonistic capital.

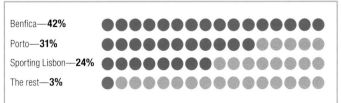

NICKNAME:
O GLORIOS
("THE GLORIOUS")
FOUNDED:
LISBON, 1904
STADIUM:
ESTÁDIO DA LUZ, 65,600
DOMESTIC HONORS:
LEAGUE 31, CUP 27
INTERNATIONAL HONORS:
EUROPEAN CUP 1961, 1962;
UEFA CUP RUNNERS-UP 1983

HOME

BENFICA

The best-resourced and best-supported club in Portugal, Benfica was founded by nationalists who stipulated a ban on foreign players. The club rose to prominence after overturning the ban in the 1960s, signing the Mozambique striker Eusébio, who helped them to win two European Cups. Mismanagement in the 1990s led to a barren period that finally ended with the La Liga title in 2005.

THE GOLDEN ERA

Benfica's golden era began when club president De Brito lured Hungarian coach Béla Guttman away from Porto in 1959. Guttman brought a level of professional organization and tactical sophistication that were new to the club. His squad came of age in 1961 when they won the league and beat Barcelona to win the European Cup, having scored three goals a game in the first four rounds. Eusébio signed the following year, and a league and European Cup double followed.

EUSÉBIO

One of the finest center-forwards the game has ever seen, Eusébio's strike-rate was phenomenal. In 15 years at Benfica, he scored 317 goals in 301 appearances.

BORN: **JANUARY 25, 1942, LOURENÇO MARQUES, MOZAMBIQUE**
HEIGHT: **5FT 9½IN (1.77M)**
MAIN CLUBS: **SPORTING LOURENÇO MARQUES, BENFICA**
INTERNATIONAL CAPS: **64**

NICKNAME:
LEOES ("LIONS")
FOUNDED:
LISBON, 1906
STADIUM:
ESTÁDIO JOSÉ ALVALADE, 52,000
DOMESTIC HONORS:
LEAGUE 18, CUP 19
INTERNATIONAL HONORS:
CUP WINNERS' CUP 1964

HOME

SPORTING LISBON

Sporting was founded in 1906 by disenchanted members of Benfica with the assistance of the Viscount of Alvalade, who gave land for the team's first ground and after whom the club's current stadium, which was built in 1954 and redeveloped in 2004, is named. The 1930s and 1960s—which brought a European Cup Winners' Cup win and three Liga titles—were Sporting's glory days, but despite a focus on nurturing new talent, the club remains the poorer of Portugal's big three clubs.

BY PRESIDENTIAL DECREE

Under coach Bobby Robson, Sporting reached the top of the league at Christmas 1993 and stood an excellent chance of winning the title. New club president José de Sousa Cintra, drawing on his business experience as a mineral water millionaire, decided to fire the coach. Sporting lost the league and Robson went to Porto. He had the last laugh when Porto beat his old club in the Portuguese cup final in the same season.

PORTUGUESE LEAGUE WINS

Benfica—**42%**

Porto—**31%**

Sporting Lisbon—**24%**

The rest—**3%**

NICKNAME:
DRAGÕES
("DRAGONS")

FOUNDED:
PORTO, 1893

HOME

STADIUM:
ESTÁDIO DO DRAGAO, 51,000

DOMESTIC HONORS:
LEAGUE 23, CUP 17

INTERNATIONAL HONORS:
CHAMPIONS LEAGUE 1987,
2004; UEFA CUP 2003

THE CHAMPIONS LEAGUE TROPHY, GOD, AND AFTER GOD... ME

JOSÉ MOURINHO
ON HIS PRIORITIES AT PORTO

PORTO

Although Porto has always been a big club, it was only in the 1990s that the team rose to the top of Portuguese soccer. An unprecedented record since 1995—five consecutive titles (1995–99) and five of six between 2003 and 2008—was capped by the club's first UEFA Cup win in 2003, and its second European Cup in 2004 under then coach Mourinho.

POWER BEHIND PORTO

For most of the modern era, the power behind the throne at Porto has been chairman Jose Pinto da Costa. A brilliant organizer and man of quiet maneuvers, he has overseen the financial and sporting success of the club. Nicknamed Papa—"the Pope"—for his authoritarian infallibility, he was banned from holding office for two years after the 2007 Golden Whistle police investigation into soccer corruption.

PORTO VS BENFICA

The derby between the big clubs of Portugal's major northern and southern cities, Porto and Lisbon, has eclipsed all other games in the fixture list. The Porto vs Benfica game pits urban identities against each other that are economically and culturally at odds. Lisbon is the city of glamor and hedonism, while Porto is the city that gets up and goes to work. The characters of Benfica and Porto are close to these attributes.

JOSÉ MOURINHO
"The Special One" is one of the greatest managers in the modern game. Charismatic and controversial, Mourinho has proved to be as entertaining as his stylish teams.

BEST OF THE REST

BOAVISTA (1903)
Always Porto's second club, Boavista's stadium is packed into the inner-city neighborhood of Bessa. Founded by an Anglo-Portuguese textile firm, the club finally hit the big time in 2001, winning La Liga.
HONORS: LEAGUE 1, CUP 5

OS BELENENSES (1919)
Tucked away in the upper-class Lisbon suburb of Restiro, Belenenses was the only club to break the Liga monopoly of Portugal's three big clubs in the 20th century, with a single title win in 1946.
HONORS: LEAGUE 1, CUP 3

MARITIMO (1910)
Founded by dock workers in Funchal, Maritimo is the biggest team on the Portuguese Madeira islands. With strong foreign support, the team has fan clubs in Brazil, Angola, and Venezuela.
HONORS: LEAGUE 0, CUP 1

BRAGA (1921)
A club on the up, Braga acquired an amazing new stadium carved out of a mountain side for Euro 2004. The club won its first ever European trophy in 2008, the Intertoto Cup.
HONORS: LEAGUE 0, CUP 1;
INTERTOTO CUP 2008

VITORIA SETUBAL (1910)
After a decade of successes in the 1960s, Setubal sank low until the Cup win of 2004. Fans are known as the "Eighth Army" after their 1943 cup-final revelry as the British Eighth Army fought in the Mediterranean.
HONORS: LEAGUE 0, CUP 3

ACADEMICA DE COIMBRA (1876)
Founded by college students in Coimbra in 1876, Academica play in an all-black uniform that mirrors the formal wear of the university scholars. The club's sole success was a 1939 Portuguese Cup win.
HONORS: LEAGUE 0, CUP 1

HOME   AWAY

POPULATION: 58.1 MILLION
CAPITAL: ROME
LICENSED PLAYERS:
MALE: 1.5 MILLION
FEMALE: 16,000
PROFESSIONALS: 3,500
REGISTERED CLUBS: 16,000

ITALY

Soccer plays a huge role in Italian life. Three national newspapers—La Gazzetta dello Sport, Tuttosport, and Corriere dello Sport—are devoted to the game, soccer shows rule the airwaves, and state-controlled pools contests are immensely popular. Fortunately, the nation's teams can justify the devotion. The Azzurri have won four World Cups—more than any country bar Brazil—and Italian clubs have won 28 European trophies.

ANCIENT ORIGINS

Although the modern game was invented in Britain, Italians claim that the violent medieval form, known as Calcio in Italy, came from the Roman ball-sport Harpastum (see pp.14–15).

SAFETY FIRST

The first rule of Italian soccer is "do not concede a goal." Italian teams are typically cautious and defensive, aiming to hit opponents on the break. If they manage to get ahead, their default tactic is to put men behind the ball and "close up shop." At the same time, Italian players are known for their technical excellence. Skill and guile are highly valued, as exemplified by attacking players including Alessandro Del Piero and Roberto Baggio.

SLOW OUT OF THE BLOCKS

Despite their impressive reputation, Italy are notoriously slow starters. They drew all their group matches on the way to World Cup victory in 1982, and reached the final in 1994 despite losing their opening game to Ireland. Meanwhile, every Italian knows the name Pak Do-Ik, the North Korean dentist whose goal sent Italy out of the 1966 World Cup. That said, adversity can bring the best out of the side—Italy won the 1982 and 2006 World Cups despite morale-sapping domestic match-fixing scandals.

SILVIO PIOLA

Famous for his overhead kicks, which he helped pioneer, Piola became the highest scorer in Serie A history, and was the star of Italy's 1938 World Cup winning team.

DINO ZOFF

Zoff once said "If I hadn't been a goalkeeper, I would have used the hands God gave me to be a farm worker or mechanic." Instead, he developed into an unflappable goalkeeper with six Serie A titles, and captained Italy to victory at the 1982 World Cup aged 40.

BORN: FEBRUARY 28, 1942, MARIANO DEL FRIULI, ITALY
HEIGHT: 6FT (1.83M)
MAIN CLUBS: UDINESE, MANTOVA, NAPOLI, JUVENTUS
INTERNATIONAL CAPS: 112

SOCCER IS NOT FOR
BALLERINAS

CLAUDIO GENTILE, HARD-MAN ITALIAN DEFENDER
AFTER SUBDUING MARADONA IN THE 1982 WORLD CUP

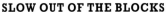

STAT ATTACK

NICKNAME: Azzurri ("Blues")
GOVERNING BODY:
Federazione Italiana Giuoco Calcio
FOUNDED: 1898
NATIONAL STADIUM: None
FIRST MATCH: 6–2 vs France, 1910
BIGGEST WIN: 9–0 vs USA, 1948
BIGGEST DEFEAT: 1–7 vs Hungary, 1924

THE LEGENDS

MOST CAPPED PLAYERS

Name	From/To	Caps
Paolo MALDINI	1988–2002	126
Fabio CANNAVARO	1997–present	121
Dino ZOFF	1968–83	112
Giacinto FACCHETTI	1963–77	94
Alessandro DEL PIERO	1995–present	91
Gianluigi BUFFON	1997–present	91

TOP GOALSCORERS

Name	From/To	Goals
Luigi RIVA	1965–1974	35
Giuseppe MEAZZA	1930–39	33
Silvio PIOLA	1935–52	30
Roberto BAGGIO	1988–2004	27
Alessandro DEL PIERO	1995–present	27
Adolfo BALONCIERI	1920–30	25

SERIE A

A national Italian soccer league was created from pre-existing regional tournaments and national knock-out competitions in 1929. The top division is known as Serie A and the second division as Serie B. The schedule for both leagues pits teams against their opponents once in the first half of the season—the "andata"—and then again in exactly the same order in the second half—"the ritorno"—but switching from home to away and vice versa. Internazionale is the only team to have played continuously in Serie A since its foundation.

PROMOTING THE ITALIAN CUP

The Coppa Italia is usually a low-key affair, with teams regularly fielding their reserve sides and with attendances sometimes half that of Serie A fixtures. In an attempt to raise the profile of the competition, the Italian FA has made a UEFA Cup place available to the winner, and champions are allowed to sport a roundel on their shirt in the Italian tricolor. The two-leg final has been cut to one game and a seeding system put in place.

PLAYERS OF PRIVILEGE

In many parts of the world, soccer is an exclusively working-class sport, but not in Italy. Gianluca Vialli, the former Sampdoria, Juventus, and Chelsea striker and ex-manager of Chelsea and Watford, grew up in a 60-room 15th-century castle outside the city of Cremona in Lombardy. Another Italian player with a wealthy background is AC Milan midfielder Andrea Pirlo, whose father is a steel magnate.

FRANCO BARESI
"Il Capitano" spent his entire career at AC Milan, orchestrating play as sweeper. Baresi's timing and reading of the game were superlative.

STAT ATTACK

SERIE A

LEAGUE STRUCTURE: 20 teams
TOP SCORER: Silvio Piola, **274** goals
MOST WINS: Juventus, **27** titles
BIGGEST WIN: 10–0, Torino vs Alessandria, 1947–48
HIGHEST ATTENDANCE: 89,365 Napoli vs Perugia, 1979–80
DIVISIONS BELOW SERIE A: Serie B (**22** teams), Lega Pro Primera (2 divisions, **18** teams each), Lega Pro Seconda (3 divisions, **18** teams each)

COPPA ITALIA

Entry to the knock-out Coppa Italia was restricted to the 42 Serie A and Serie B clubs from the 2007–08 season onward.
MOST GOALS IN A SEASON: Gianluca Vialli, **13** goals, Sampdoria 1988–89
MOST SUCCESSFUL TEAM: Juventus and Roma, **9** wins
BIGGEST WIN: 6–1 Sampdoria vs Ancona, 2nd-leg tie, 1994

1949 Year in which Italy lost ten first-team players in the Torino air disaster

44 Age at which Lazio goalkeeper Marco Ballotta made his last Serie A appearance, in 2008

6 Goals scored by Italy against France in their first international match, in 1910

88 Percentage of World Cup competitions for which Italy has qualified

WORLD CUP

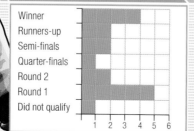

EURO CHAMPIONSHIPS

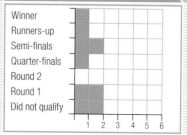

ITALY: JUVENTUS AND INTER

Italian domestic soccer is dominated by teams from the industrial North, with clubs from outside the region having won only seven Serie A titles (*scudetti*) since World War II. Yet *calcio*, as the sport is called in Italy, is an obsession throughout the country. Despite having less money to spend now than in the 1990s, Italian clubs continue to attract a fair proportion of the world's top players.

NICKNAME:
LA VECCHIA SIGNORA ("THE OLD LADY")

FOUNDED:
TURIN, 1897

STADIUM:
STADIO COMUNALE*, 25,400

DOMESTIC HONORS:
LEAGUE 27, CUP 9

INTERNATIONAL HONORS:
CHAMPIONS LEAGUE 1985, 1996; CUP WINNERS' CUP 1984; UEFA CUP 1977, 1990, 1993

* In 2011 Juventus are due to move to a new stadium currently under construction at the site of the Stadio Delle Alpi. The capacity will be 40,200.

HOME

JUVENTUS

Despite a name that means "youth" in Latin, Juventus (or Juve) is widely known as the *La Vecchia Signora* ("The Old Lady"). Some say that the nickname came about because the team's uniform recalls the black clothes and pale faces of the more elderly female members of Italian society. What's not in doubt is that Juventus is the most successful club in Italian soccer, with almost 30 *scudetti* and nine Coppa Italias.

EUROPEAN MILESTONE

In 1985, a goal by Michel Platini gave Juventus a 1–0 victory over Liverpool in the final of the European Cup. It meant that the Italian club became the first team to win all three major European club competitions: the UEFA Cup, European Cup, and European Cup Winners' Cup.

THE TRAPATTONI ERA

Giovanni Trapattoni has had two spells as manager of Juventus. During the first, most successful one, between 1976 and 1986, the team won every major tournament for which it was eligible. Trapattoni built a primarily defensive outfit sprinkled with the creative talent of players like the Irishman Liam Brady and the French genius Michel Platini, who was European Player of the Year three times in succession (1983–85).

THE GIRLFRIEND OF ITALY

While Juve is Italy's best-supported club, average home attendances are lower than those of most other top European teams. The reason is that the majority of the club's fans live elsewhere in Italy, particularly in the South, where local teams have traditionally been weaker and affection for Juventus has been acquired by workers who have migrated north to Turin. As a result of its widely distributed fan base, Juventus is sometimes called *La Fidanzata d'Italia* ("the Girlfriend of Italy").

THE DERBY OF ITALY

Prior to Juve's demotion to Serie B in 2006, the Turin club and Inter were the only teams never to have been relegated from the Italian top flight. Because of this and the fact that the clubs are ranked first and second in the all-time Serie A table, in 1967 a journalist coined the name Derby d'Italia for the intense meetings between the two giants.

ROBERTO **BAGGIO**

One of the few men to have played for each of the Italian Big Three (Juventus, AC Milan, and Inter), ponytailed Buddhist Roberto Baggio was for a time the best player in the world. Small and light, he had great technical ability.

BORN: **FEBRUARY 18, 1967, CALDOGNO, ITALY**
HEIGHT: **5FT 9IN (1.74M)**
MAIN CLUBS: **FIORENTINA, JUVENTUS, AC MILAN, BOLOGNA, INTER**
INTERNATIONAL CAPS: **56**

NICKNAME:
NERAZZURRI
("BLACK-BLUES")

HOME

FOUNDED:
MILAN, 1908

STADIUM:
SAN SIRO (GIUSEPPE MEAZZA),
80,000

DOMESTIC HONORS:
LEAGUE 16, CUP 5

INTERNATIONAL HONORS:
EUROPEAN CUP 1964, 1965;
UEFA CUP 1991, 1994, 1998

INTERNAZIONALE

Inter (or, erroneously, Inter Milan) was formed in 1908 by members of the Milan Cricket and Soccer Club (the forerunner of AC Milan, see p.210) unhappy about its bias toward Italian players. The club has played in the top flight since its formation and only narrowly trails its Milanese rival in terms of accumulated league titles.

LA GRANDE INTER

Helenio Herrera managed Inter from 1960 to 1968, and was given as much credit for his team's performances as the players. He dictated every aspect of his players' lives, from diet to the air that they breathed (he made them inhale pure oxygen the night before games). Herrera's Inter were defensive, ultra-fit, and ruthless. They were also more successful than at any other period in the club's history, winning three Serie A titles and two European Cups in four years. The team of the era is still referred to as La Grande Inter ("The Great Inter").

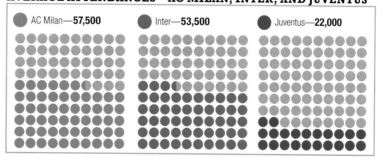

CHRISTIAN VIERI
A powerful, old-fashioned striker, Vieri is one of the few players to have represented each of the principal Milan and Turin teams. He joined Inter in 1999 for a then world-record fee of $46.5 million and scored 103 goals in 144 league matches for the *Nerazzurri*.

THE TWO MILANS

As of fall 2008, Inter and AC Milan had scored and conceded exactly the same number of goals (270) against each other in the three main competitions. The biggest margin of victory between the two clubs came in March 1918, when Milan beat Inter 8–1.

HERRERA WAS THE FIRST MODERN MANAGER... A SUPERSTAR

JOHN FOOT
AUTHOR OF *CALCIO: A HISTORY OF ITALIAN FOOTBALL*

MILANESE GROUND-SHARE

Inter and AC Milan share the 80,000-seat San Siro stadium, or the Stadio Giuseppe Meazza as it is officially called. Traditionally, AC Milan is the team of the working class, with a large contingent of Southern Italian fans, while Inter supporters are more likely to be middle class and local. Two of the most eagerly contested games in the Italian soccer calendar occur when the Milan teams play the Derby della Madonnina, named after the statue of the Virgin Mary on top of the city's cathedral.

AVERAGE ATTENDANCES—AC MILAN, INTER, AND JUVENTUS

AC Milan—**57,500**   Inter—**53,500**   Juventus—**22,000**

AC MILAN vs LIVERPOOL

AC MILAN 3 (PEN 2)	LIVERPOOL 3 (PEN 3)
FORMATION: 5-3-2	**FORMATION:** 5-3-2
MANAGER: CARLO ANCELOTTI	**MANAGER:** RAFAEL BENITEZ

ATATÜRK STADIUM, ISTANBUL, TURKEY
MAY 25, 2005

ATTENDANCE: 70,024

REFEREE: MEJUTO GONZÁLEZ (SPAIN)

"Make us dream," a banner at Anfield had pleaded during the knock out stages of the 2005 Champions League, as Liverpool fought their way to their first final of Europe's biggest club tournament in 20 years. The Reds certainly obliged in Istanbul. In the first half, AC Milan—the favorites, appearing in their second final in three years and 10th overall—were utterly dominant and raced into a three-goal lead. But then Liverpool came back to equalize in six dazzling second-half minutes. Both teams probed for a winning goal in extra time, but ultimately it took a penalty shootout to decide a winner.

Liverpool: 1 Dudek — 2 Finnan, 5 Carragher, 14 Hyypiä, 6 Traoré, 16 Alonso, 17 Gerrard, 4 Luis García, 18 Riise, 10 Baroš, 20 Kewell

AC Milan: 11 Crespo, 16 Shevchenko, 10 Kaká, 14 Seedorf, 7 Gattuso, 12 Pirlo, 2 Maldini, 5 Nesta, 9 Stam, 19 Cafu, 1 Dida

SUBS: 21 Serginho · 21 Rui Costa · 21 Tomasson · 11 Hamann · 19 Smicer · 19 Cissé

00:01

Liverpool start nervously and are immediately punished. Djimi Traoré gives away a needless free-kick on Liverpool's left-hand side and defender Paolo Maldini volleys home Andrea Pirlo's angled cross: 1–0.

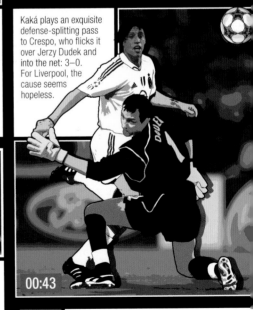

Kaká plays an exquisite defense-splitting pass to Crespo, who flicks it over Jerzy Dudek and into the net: 3–0. For Liverpool, the cause seems hopeless.

00:38

Andrei Shevchenko and Hernán Crespo combine in the area to give AC Milan what already appears to be an unassailable lead, 2–0. AC Milan, as a British announcer states, is now playing soccer out of this world.

00:43

00:45

During the interval, the Liverpool fans sing the club anthem—"You'll Never Walk Alone"—in a way they had never done before. When the teams re-emerge, the AC Milan players are nonplussed, their opponents inspired.

00:54 Liverpool's efforts are rewarded when Steven Gerrard jumps to head home a cross from John Arne Riise: 3–1. The captain windmills his arms as a signal to the Liverpool fans to turn up the volume. Hope is back in their hearts.

00:56 While Kaká ties up his boot laces, perhaps unaware that Liverpool have not yet given up, the ball is played to Vladmir Smicer on the edge of the Italian's penalty area. The Czech midfielder, playing his last match for the Reds, fires home from 20 yards: 3–2.

01:00 Gerrard bursts into the box with unstoppable momentum and Gennaro Gattuso clips his ankles. The referee awards a penalty. Dida saves Xabi Alonso's first effort but the Liverpool player scores on the rebound and is buried under a pile of delirious teammates: 3–3.

01:20+ When Gerrard hoists the Cup, the predominant feeling among Liverpool fans is blissful relief. Their club is back at the top table, European Champions for the fifth time.

01:20 Before the shoot-out, Jamie Carragher encourages Dudek to repeat Bruce Grobbelaar's antics at the 1984 final, when the keeper had put off the Roma penalty takers by wobbling his legs. Serginho blasts the first penalty over the bar. Shevchenko steps up to take Milan's fifth penalty knowing that a miss will mean defeat; his nerves are shot and the Pole denies him. The "Miracle of Istanbul" is complete.

ITALY: AC MILAN AND ROMA

The Juventus–Inter fixture may be known as The Derby of Italy, but from an international perspective the nation's most important club is the last member of Italy's Big Three, AC Milan. Between them, the trio have won approximately 60 percent of the *scudetti* contested to date. However, Italian soccer is much more than a three-horse race—several other teams, including the two principal clubs from Rome, have also risen to the top.

AC MILAN

The Rossoneri ("red-blacks") lag behind Juventus in *scudetto* wins, but in the sphere of international club competitions they are the undisputed aristocrats of Italian soccer. Only Real Madrid can beat AC Milan's haul of seven Champions League titles. The club has also won the Intercontinental Cup a record four times.

NICKNAME:
ROSSONERI ("RED-BLACKS")

FOUNDED:
MILAN, 1899

STADIUM:
SAN SIRO (GIUSEPPE MEAZZA), 80,000

DOMESTIC HONORS:
LEAGUE 17; CUP 5

INTERNATIONAL HONORS:
CHAMPIONS LEAGUE 1963, 1969, 1989, 1990, 1994, 2003, 2007; CUP WINNERS' CUP 1968, 1973

HOME

SILVIO BERLUSCONI

After billionaire media tycoon Silvio Berlusconi purchased AC Milan in 1986, he went on to become Prime Minister of Italy four times and the club secured seven Serie A titles and five Champions League titles. Berlusconi is a controversial figure—when he needed a name for his new political party in 1993, he adapted the words of a Milan chant and came up with "Forza Italia."

GOING DUTCH

The best of several great Milan sides was assembled by manager Arigo Sacchi (1987–91) and built on by his successor Fabio Capello (1991–96). At the heart of the team was a trio of top Dutch players: all-rounder Ruud Gullit, holding midfielder Frank Rijkaard, and striker Marco Van Basten. While they were at the club, Milan won two European Cups and three *scudetti*.

PAOLO MALDINI

An elegant and reliable defender, Paulo Maldini made his debut for Milan as a 16-year-old and was still playing regularly for the club at the age of 40. He has appeared over 1,000 times for Milan and Italy combined, and competed in eight Champions League finals.

BORN: JUNE 26, 1968, MILAN, ITALY
HEIGHT: 6FT 1IN (1.86M)
MAIN CLUBS: AC MILAN
INTERNATIONAL CAPS: 126

EUROPEAN TITLE WINS

AC Milan—14
Juventus—8
Inter—5

5

8

14

NICKNAME:
GIALLOROSSI
("YELLOW-REDS")

HOME

FOUNDED:
ROME, 1927

STADIUM:
STADIO OLIMPICO, 72,700

DOMESTIC HONORS:
LEAGUE 3; CUP 9

INTERNATIONAL HONORS:
FAIRS CUP 1961

ROMA

The Giallorossi ("yellow-reds") have occasionally been good enough to break the stranglehold that Juventus and the two Milan teams have had on the title. The last time Roma did it (in 2002), the cost of mounting the challenge almost bankrupted the club. Roma, who share the Stadio Olimpico with Lazio, hold Francesco Totti as their modern hero.

I LUPI ("THE WOLVES")

As the Eternal City's dominant team, Roma's colors are packed with symbolism. The maroon shirts represent Rome's imperial past, while the orange/yellow trim stands for God (the city is the home of the papacy). The club badge features an image of a she-wolf suckling a pair of infants. According to legend, Rome's twin founders Romulus and Remus were raised by a female wolf who rescued them from the Tiber River.

VOCAL SUPPORT

Roma has two club anthems, both written by local singer Antonello Venditti. The first, *La Roma non si discute, si ama* ("Roma is not to be discussed, it is to be loved") is sung before every home game, while *Grazie Roma* ("Thank you Rome") is played only when the club wins. Venditti has also penned a satirical song about AC Milan owner Silvio Berlusconi.

THEY CALLED ME A FOOL WHEN I SAID THIS TEAM COULD CHALLENGE FOR THE TITLE. NOW THEY CAN THINK AGAIN!

FRANCESCO TOTTI
PRESS INTERVIEW, 2001

FRANCESCO TOTTI
Famous for his passing skills, the Roma captain has scored more goals for the club than any other player. He loves to wind up opposing supporters, particularly Lazio fans.

BEST OF THE REST

LAZIO (1900)
Named after the province in which Rome is situated, Roman club Lazio draws its support from the north of the city. A cash injection after a 1992 buyout led to Lazio winning the Cup Winners' Cup in 1999 and the *scudetto* in 2000.

HONORS: LEAGUE 2 CUP 4; CWC 1999

FIORENTINA (1926)
Only four clubs have spent more seasons in Serie A than Fiorentina. However, in 2002 Florence's premier club went bankrupt. The club was re-established in the lowest division and has since climbed back up to the top flight.

HONORS: LEAGUE 2 CUP 6; CWC 1961

SAMPDORIA (1946)
Genoa's "other" club was formed from the merger of Sampierdarenese and Andrea Doria. Most of its first few decades were spent in Serie B but success came with a Cup Winners' Cup win in 1989 and the *scudetto* in 1991.

HONORS: LEAGUE 1 CUP 4; CWC 1990

TORINO (1906)
Torino was founded in 1906 by a group of defectors from Juventus. Between 1943 and 1949, *Il Grande Torino* was the greatest team in Italy, but most of the squad were tragically killed in a 1949 air disaster.

HONORS: LEAGUE 8 CUP 5

NAPOLI (1904)
Napoli is the only mainland team south of Rome to have won the *scudetto*. True success came after Diego Maradona joined the club for a world record fee in 1984.

HONORS: LEAGUE 2 CUP 3;
UEFA CUP 1989

GENOA (1893)
Genoa Cricket and Soccer Club was founded in 1893, making it one of the oldest outfits in Italy. The club won the first three national championships (1898–1900) but has spent most of the post-World War II period in Serie B.

HONORS: LEAGUE 9 CUP 1

HELLAS VERONA (1903)
Given the prefix Hellas ("Greece") by a classics professor at the university where the club was founded, Verona's biggest claim to fame is winning the 1985 *scudetto* (the last team from outside Rome, Turin, and Milan to do so).

HONORS: LEAGUE 1

EUROPE

GREECE

HOME   AWAY

POPULATION: 10.7 MILLION

CAPITAL: ATHENS

FA: HELLENIC FOOTBALL FEDERATION

LICENSED PLAYERS:
MALE: 705,000
FEMALE: 55,500

PROFESSIONALS: 1,800

REGISTERED CLUBS: 5,500

Soccer was first played in Greece in the late 19th century by British sailors and diplomats, and also featured at the 1896 Athens Olympics. Initially the preserve of the wealthy, who founded Panathinaikos, the game soon spread to the working class, and Olympiakos was born. Greek refugees from Turkey started new clubs in the 1920s, including AEK Athens.

SLOW BEGINNINGS

The Greek Cup was established in 1932, but because intercity communication was poor, it was only in 1960 that the Greeks were able to establish a truly national soccer league. Named the Alpha Ethniki ("First National Division"), it remained an amateur league until 1979, and was replaced by Super League Greece in 2006.

STAT ATTACK

NATIONAL TEAM

NICKNAME:
The Pirate Ship

NATIONAL STADIUM:
OAKA Spiridon Louis, Athens, 70,000

WORLD CUP FINALS:
2 appearances

EUROPEAN CHAMPIONSHIPS:
3 appearances, winner **2004**

BIGGEST WIN: 8–0 vs Syria, 1949

BIGGEST DEFEAT: 1–11 vs Hungary, 1938

MOST CAPS: Theodoros Zagorakis, **120**

MOST GOALS: Nikos Anastopulos, **29**

MAIN DOMESTIC CLUBS

OLYMPIAKOS
FOUNDED: Athens, 1925
STADIUM: Karaiskakis
CAPACITY: 33,000
HOME
INTERNATIONAL HONORS: None
LEAGUE: 36 **CUP:** 23

PANATHINAIKOS
FOUNDED: Athens, 1908
STADIUM: Apostolos Nikoladis
CAPACITY: 16,500
HOME
INTERNATIONAL HONORS: None
LEAGUE: 19 **CUP:** 23

AEK ATHENS
FOUNDED: Athens, 1924
STADIUM: Spiridon Louis
CAPACITY: 70,000
HOME
INTERNATIONAL HONORS: None
LEAGUE: 11 **CUP:** 12

ON A WING AND A PRAYER

In 1971, Panathinaikos made it all the way to the European Cup final—the most successful run in a European club competition by a Greek team. They arrived in London for the final with an array holy Greek Orthodox relics. Sadly, they were beaten 2–0 by Ajax at the Wembley final.

HOW DO THEY DO IT?

The economics of Greek soccer are unfathomable. In 2002, the government reported that the top division had debts of over $180 million and an income of less than $7 million. Little has changed. Olympiakos' domination of the league is bankrolled by its owner, Greek tycoon Socrates Kokkalis.

EURO 2004

After failing to win a point in any previous international competition, Greece won the 2004 European Championships in Portugal under the German coach Otto Rehhagel. Schooled in the no-nonsense Bundesliga, he created a team characterized by tight marking, an exemplary work rate, and drilled set pieces. It proved a potent combination; they beat the hosts in the opening game and the final.

THEODOROS **ZAGORAKIS**

A defensive midfielder who understands how to control a game, Theo's finest hour came when he captained his country to glory in Euro 2004. On top of the shock win, he won the UEFA Player of the Tournament.

BORN: OCTOBER 27, 1971, KEVALA, GREECE
HEIGHT: 5FT 10IN (1.78M)
MAIN CLUBS: KAVALA, PAOK SALONIKA, LEICESTER CITY, AEK ATHENS, BOLOGNA
INTERNATIONAL CAPS: 120

TURKEY

HOME   AWAY

POPULATION: 71.2 MILLION
CAPITAL: ANKARA
FA: TÜRKIYE FUTBOL FEDERASYONU
LICENSED PLAYERS:
MALE: 2,400,000
FEMALE: 345,000
PROFESSIONALS: 4,500
REGISTERED CLUBS: 4,300

Soccer was viewed with suspicion by the last sultan of the Ottoman Empire, and judged to be foreign, dangerous, and illegal. However, after the Turkish revolution of the early 1920s, soccer bloomed. President Kemal Atatürk is claimed by all three of Istanbul's big teams—Galatasaray, Fenerbahçe, and Besiktas—as a supporter.

CAPITAL DOMINATION

Soccer spread rapidly around the country after the Turkish Football Federation was founded in 1923. Only one non-Istanbul club, Trabzonspor, has ever won the the league title. Victory in the Cup, which started in 1963, has been more widely spread.

HAKAN SÜKÜR

Scorer of the fastest ever World Cup goal, during Turkey's third-place play-off in 2002, Sükür has a raft of league titles and cup winners' medals to his name. It's no coincidence that Turkish soccer came of age during Sükür's glittering playing career.

BORN: SEPTEMBER 1, 1971, SAKARYA, TURKEY
HEIGHT: 6FT 3IN (1.91M)
MAIN CLUBS: GALATASARAY, INTER MILAN, PARMA FC, BLACKBURN ROVERS
INTERNATIONAL CAPS: 112

STAT ATTACK

NATIONAL TEAM

NICKNAME: Crescent stars
NATIONAL STADIUM: Atatürk Olympic Stadium, Istanbul, 81,283
WORLD CUP FINALS: 2 appearances
EUROPEAN CHAMPIONSHIPS:
3 appearances, semi-finals **2008**
BIGGEST WIN: 7–0 vs Syria, 1949, and vs South Korea, 1954
BIGGEST DEFEAT: 0–8 vs Poland, 1968, and twice vs England, 1984 and 1987
MOST CAPS: Rüstü Reçber, **118**
MOST GOALS: Hakan Sükür, **51**

MAIN DOMESTIC CLUBS

GALATASARAY
FOUNDED: Istanbul, 1905
STADIUM: Ali Sami Yen
CAPACITY: 23,785   HOME
INTERNATIONAL HONORS: UEFA Cup winners **2000**
LEAGUE: 17 **CUP:** 14

FENERBAHÇE
FOUNDED: Istanbul, 1907
STADIUM: Sükrü Saracoglu
CAPACITY: 50,509   HOME
INTERNATIONAL HONORS: None
LEAGUE: 1 **CUP:** 4

BESIKTAS
FOUNDED: Istanbul, 1903
STADIUM: Inönü Stadi
CAPACITY: 32,750   HOME
INTERNATIONAL HONORS: None
LEAGUE: 10 **CUP:** 7

TURKISH PASSION

Always noisy and exuberant, Turkish crowds have been known to be passionate about their team—visiting fans have been met by flags reading "Welcome to Hell." This applies to the team too—a tunnel-mouth brawl followed Turkey's 2006 World Cup play-off defeat to Switzerland.

LOCAL RIVALRY

Fenerbahçe versus Galatasaray is the most fiercely contested of the nation's derbies, and always begins with the "buruya," a ritual in which every player of each team is called by name to salute their fans, and be saluted in return. Despite the intensity of the occasion, it only rarely boils over, as in 1996 when Graeme Souness, Galatasaray's victorious Scottish manager, planted his club's flag in the center of Fenerbahçe's field.

WORLD CUP 2002

Turkey first went to the World Cup in 1954, but were knocked out after the first round. They failed to qualify for another tournament until Euro '96, then reached the quarter-finals in 2000 and semi-finals in 2008. The national team's greatest achievement was third place at the 2002 World Cup in Japan, after a close-fought semi-final against Brazil. A national holiday was declared on their return.

EUROPE

BULGARIA

HOME   AWAY

Under Ottoman rule, soccer in Bulgaria was subject to official curbs, but the game flourished once the country had achieved independence after the Balkan Wars of 1912 and 1913. Sofia's leading clubs soon emerged: Slavia, founded by intellectuals in 1913; and Levski, started by a group of teenagers in 1914. Following the 1944 communist takeover, the Bulgarian army created CSKA Sofia, which came to dominate the domestic game.

POPULATION: 7.3 MILLION
CAPITAL: SOFIA
FA: BULGARIAN FOOTBALL UNION
LICENSED PLAYERS:
MALE: 289,500
FEMALE: 38,000
PROFESSIONALS: 1,000
REGISTERED CLUBS: 500

SMALL YET MIGHTY

The surprise package of the post-communist era, Litex Lovech is a tiny provincial club that won Bulgaria's top division in 1998 and 1999.

IT'S ALL IN THE NAME

The first truly national league was established in 1949 and has been through various formats, but currently consists of 16 teams. The Bulgarian Cup was established as the Tsars Cup in 1924, and was renamed the Soviet Army Cup following World War II. It took its current name in 1981.

STAT ATTACK

NATIONAL TEAM

NICKNAME: The Lions
NATIONAL STADIUM:
Vasil Levski, 46,500
WORLD CUP FINALS: 7 appearances, 4th place **1994**
EUROPEAN CHAMPIONSHIPS:
2 appearances
BIGGEST WIN: 7–0 vs Norway, 1957, vs Thailand, 1968, and vs Malta, 1982
BIGGEST DEFEAT: 0–13 vs Spain, 1933
MOST CAPS: Borislav Mihailov, **102**
MOST GOALS: Dimitar Berbatov and Christo Bonev, **41**

MAIN DOMESTIC CLUBS

CSKA SOFIA
FOUNDED: Sofia, 1948
STADIUM: Bulgarian Army Stadium   HOME
CAPACITY: 22,015
INTERNATIONAL HONORS: European Cup semi-finals **1967**, **1982**; Cup Winners' Cup semi-finals **1989**
LEAGUE: 31 **CUP*:** 9

LEVSKI SOFIA
FOUNDED: Sofia, 1914
STADIUM:
Georgi Asparuhov   HOME
CAPACITY: 29,980
INTERNATIONAL HONORS: Cup Winners' Cup quarter-finals **1970**, **1977**, **1987**; UEFA Cup quarter-finals **1976**, **2006**
LEAGUE: 25 **CUP*:** 11

* Since 1983, when the Bulgarian Cup became the major knockout tournament

HRISTO **STOICHKOV**

An explosive left-sided attacker, Stoichkov was as famous for his fiery temperament as for his soccer skills. He received an eight-game ban for stamping on a referee's foot, and a lifetime suspension in 1985 (later rescinded).

BORN: **FEBRUARY 8, 1966,**
PLOVDIV, BULGARIA
HEIGHT: **5FT 10IN (1.78M)**
MAIN CLUBS: HEBROS HARMANLI, CSKA SOFIA, FC BARCELONA, PARMA, KASHIWA REYSOL, CHICAGO FIRE
INTERNATIONAL CAPS: 83

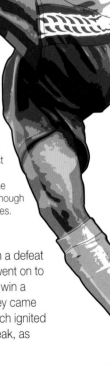

THE UNFINISHED CUP FINAL

The 1985 Bulgarian Cup final between Levski and CSKA Sofia descended into a 22-man fist fight on national television. The game was abandoned, both teams were dissolved on the order of the Politburo, and then renamed—although a year later they reverted to their original names.

WORLD CUP 1994

Bulgaria began the '94 World Cup with a defeat to Nigeria but, contrary to prior form, went on to beat Greece, Argentina, and Mexico to win a quarter-final slot. Led by Stoichkov, they came from behind to beat Germany 2–1, which ignited a national celebration. That was the peak, as they lost to Italy in the semi-final.

HOME   AWAY

POPULATION: 22.3 MILLION
CAPITAL: BUCHAREST
FA: FEDERATIA ROMÂNA DE FOTBAL
LICENSED PLAYERS:
MALE: 929,500
FEMALE: 105,000
PROFESSIONALS: 1,100
REGISTERED CLUBS: 2,800

ROMANIA

An 1888 newspaper report of "two youths running with a ball" in the city of Arad was the first recorded instance of soccer in Romania. A club was founded in Arad in 1899 after students and professionals brought the game from Vienna and Budapest, while employees of British and German oil companies played soccer in Bucharest and Ploesti. King Carol I was a driving force behind the founding of the soccer association in 1909.

CAPITAL DOMINATION

A national league began in 1909 and, aside from a break during World War II, has been played ever since. In 2007, FC Cluj broke a 17-year domination of the domestic championships by the Bucharest trio—Dinamo, Steaua, and Rapid. The Romanian Cup, played since 1953, has been dominated by the same trio.

GHEORGHE **HAGI**

Dubbed the "Maradona of the Carpathians," Hagi was a supremely gifted player and one of only a few to have played for both Barcelona and Real Madrid. His best years arguably came at Galatasaray.

BORN: FEBRUARY 5, 1965, SACELE, ROMANIA
HEIGHT: 5FT 8½IN (1.74 M)
MAIN CLUBS: CONSTANTA, SPORTUL STUDENTESC, STEAUA BUCHAREST, REAL MADRID, BRESCIA CALCIO, BARCELONA, GALATASARAY
INTERNATIONAL CAPS: 125

EUROPEAN CUP TRIUMPH

Steaua Bucharest made it to the 1986 European Cup final in Seville, Spain, and faced Barcelona, who were effectively playing at home. Steaua held out for a draw and won the game on penalties, becoming the first eastern-European team to lift the European Cup. A crowd of 30,000 met them on their return to Bucharest airport, while 40 communist party members who had followed the team to Spain took the opportunity to defect.

TAKING ON THE WORLD

Romania performed well at Italia '90, but at USA '94 they were the most entertaining team around. A 3–2 victory over Argentina was their finest hour, graced by a delicate lob from Hagi, and an amazing full-team counter attack. They lost to Sweden on penalties in the quarter-final.

4 Different names under which Universitatea Cluj have played in their four Romanian Cup final appearances

733 Armchairs at Steaua Stadium, home of Steaua Bucharest

17 Consecutive games won by Dinamo Bucharest, between June and November 1988

STAT ATTACK

NATIONAL TEAM

NICKNAME: Tricolorii ("Three-colored Ones")
NATIONAL STADIUM: Farul, 15,520, to be replaced by the Lia Manoliu, with a capacity of 60,000
WORLD CUP FINALS: 7 appearances, quarter-finals **1994**
EUROPEAN CHAMPIONSHIPS:
4 appearances, quarter-finals **2000**
BIGGEST WIN: 9–0 vs Finland, 1973
BIGGEST DEFEAT: 0–9 vs Hungary, 1948
MOST CAPS: Dorinel Munteanu, **134**
MOST GOALS: Gheorghe Hagi, **35**

GIVE US SOCCER

Under Nicolai Ceausescu's communist regime, soccer was one of the few areas in which attacks on authority were possible. In 1985, when a live transmission of the game between Rapid and Steaua Bucharest was canceled, tens of thousands of disgruntled fans descended upon the stadium, broke through police lines, and entered the stands. At the end of the afternoon there was a pitched battle with the police.

MAIN DOMESTIC CLUBS

STEAUA BUCHAREST
FOUNDED: Bucharest, 1947
STADIUM: Stadionul Steaua
CAPACITY: 27,557
INTERNATIONAL HONORS:
European Cup winners **1986**, runners-up **1989**
LEAGUE: 23 **CUP:** 21

HOME

DINAMO BUCHAREST
FOUNDED: Bucharest, 1948
STADIUM: Stadionul Dinamo
CAPACITY: 15,300
INTERNATIONAL HONORS:
European Cup semi-finals **1984** and Cup Winners' Cup semi-finals **1990**
LEAGUE: 18 **CUP:** 12

HOME

CROATIA

HOME

AWAY

POPULATION: 4.5 MILLION
CAPITAL: ZAGREB
FA: HRVATSKI NOGOMETNI SAVEZ
LICENSED PLAYERS:
MALE: 340,000
FEMALE: 22,500
PROFESSIONALS: 300
REGISTERED CLUBS: 1,500

Soccer came to Zagreb, now capital of Croatia, from other cities in the Austro-Hungarian Empire. The first club, HASK, was founded in 1903, and a Zagreb league was set up before World War I. After the war, Croatian clubs played in Yugoslavia and its later incarnations, finally creating their own league and cup competitions after the independence of Croatia in 1991.

DOMESTIC TRANSITION

The Croat top-flight league, known as the Prva HNL, has been through many formats and numbers of teams. For much of its existence, teams played each other until March and then split into two mini-leagues—one to determine relegation, the other to decide the championship. In 2007, the league shifted to a standard season with the 12 teams playing each other three times. NK Zagreb are the only team to have broken the duopoly of the big two—Dynamo Zagreb and Hadjuk Split.

ZVONIMIR **BOBAN**

In his native country, Zvonimir Boban is loved as much for his patriotism as for his superlative midfield performances for the national team—Croatia have never lost a game in which Boban played.

BORN: **OCTOBER 8, 1968,**
IMOTSKI, CROATIA
HEIGHT: 6FT (1.83M)
MAIN CLUBS: **DYNAMO ZAGREB,**
AC MILAN, AS BARI, CELTA VIGO
INTERNATIONAL CAPS: **8 (YUGOSLAVIA),**
51 (CROATIA)

STAT ATTACK

NATIONAL TEAM

NICKNAME: Vatreni ("Fiery Ones")
NATIONAL STADIUM:
Maksimir, Zagreb, 38,923
WORLD CUP FINALS:
3 appearances, 3rd place **1998**
EUROPEAN CHAMPIONSHIPS:
3 appearances, quarter-finals **1996**, **2008**
BIGGEST WIN: 7–0 vs Australia 1998 and vs Andorra 2006
BIGGEST DEFEAT: 1–5 vs Germany, 1941 and 1942
MOST CAPS: Dario Simic, **100**
MOST GOALS: Davor Suker, **45**

MAIN DOMESTIC CLUBS

DYNAMO ZAGREB
FOUNDED: Zagreb, 1945
STADIUM: Maksimir
CAPACITY: 38,923   HOME
INTERNATIONAL HONORS:
Fairs Cup (now UEFA Cup) winners **1967**, runners-up **1963**
LEAGUE: 10 **CUP:** 9

HAJDUK SPLIT
FOUNDED: Split, 1911
STADIUM: Poljud
CAPACITY: 35,000   HOME
INTERNATIONAL HONORS:
Cup Winners' Cup semi-finals **1973**, UEFA Cup **1984**
LEAGUE: 6 **CUP:** 4

WHAT'S IN A NAME?

After Croatia gained independence, President Franco Tudjman took control of Dynamo Zagreb. The team had been an icon of Croat identity during the Yugoslav era but, against the wishes of the fans, Tudjman renamed the club Croatia Zagreb. After his exit from politics, however, the club reverted to Dynamo.

BOBAN'S KICK

In 1990, Serbian police clashed with Croat fans in Dynamo Zagreb's stadium. Zvonimir Boban, Zagreb's star defender, infamously launched a karate kick at a policeman. The game was abandoned and the civil war began soon after. Relations have remained tense; the 1997 Champions League qualifier between Dynamo Zagreb and Partisan Belgrade was played behind closed doors.

WORLD CUP 1998

In their first appearance in the World Cup—France '98—Croatia made it to the semi-finals. Coached by Miroslav Blasevic, who wore a French police officer's "Kepi" cap for good luck, the exceptional Davos Suker and Robert Prosineki helped the team sweep Germany aside 3–0 in the quarter-final. After losing to France in the semi-finals, they beat Holland to take third place.

CZECH REPUBLIC

HOME   AWAY

POPULATION: 10.3 MILLION
CAPITAL: PRAGUE
FA: CESKOMORAVSKÝ FOTBALOVÝ SVAZ
LICENSED PLAYERS:
MALE: 976,400
FEMALE: 64,000
PROFESSIONALS: 1,500
REGISTERED CLUBS: 4,000

In the late 19th century, soccer came to Prague, and the two dominant teams—Slavia and Sparta—were founded in 1892 and 1893. Adopting a central-European short-passing style, the Czechs—then playing as Czechoslovakia—were good enough to reach two World Cup finals, losing in 1934 and 1962, and to win the European Championships in 1976.

EARLY STARTERS

The popularity of soccer in Prague led to a city-wide league in 1896 and a charity cup in 1906. After World War I, both league and cup became Czechoslovak competitions, and went professional in 1922. The Czech League was first played in 1993, after separation from Slovakia, and consists of 16 teams.

SPARTA VS SLAVIA

Slavia Praha was formed by students and intellectuals, whereas cross-town rivals Sparta attracted working class fans, as reflected by their nickname, "Iron Sparta."

DON'T SCORE FIRST

Czechoslovakia twice took the lead in a World Cup final, and twice finished runners-up. In 1934, against hosts Italy, the Czechs held a one-goal lead for 70 minutes and even hit the woodwork, before losing 2–1. Against Brazil in 1962, an early Czech goal opened the floodgates for three Brazilian goals, and the team lost 3–1.

EURO '76

Czechoslovakia won the 1976 European Championships the hard way, beating an exceptional Dutch team in extra time in the semi-final, then triumphing over world champions West Germany in a penalty shootout.

STAT ATTACK

NATIONAL TEAM

NICKNAME: Locomotiva ("Locomotive")
NATIONAL STADIUM: AXA Arena, Prague, 20,845
WORLD CUP FINALS: 2 appearances, runners-up **1934**, **1962**
EUROPEAN CHAMPIONSHIPS: 4 appearances, winners **1976**, runners-up **1996**
BIGGEST WIN: 8–0 Czechoslovakia vs Thailand, 1968; **8–1** Czech Republic vs Andorra, 2005
BIGGEST DEFEAT: 3–8 Czechoslovakia vs Hungary, 1937
MOST CAPS: Karel Poborsky, **118**
MOST GOALS: Jan Koller, **55**

PAVEL **NEDVED**

Starting out at Sparta Praha, Nedved caught the eye of the world with his midfield displays for the Czech Republic at Euro '96. Incredibly fit and with a remarkable shot, he also won European Soccer Player of the Year in 2003.

BORN: AUGUST 30, 1972, CHEB, CZECHOSLOVAKIA
HEIGHT: **5FT 9IN (1.77M)**
MAIN CLUBS: **DUKLA PRAHA, SPARTA PRAHA, LAZIO, JUVENTUS**
INTERNATIONAL CAPS: **91**

MAIN DOMESTIC CLUBS

SPARTA PRAHA
FOUNDED: Prague, 1893
STADIUM: AXA Arena
CAPACITY: 20,854
INTERNATIONAL HONORS: None
LEAGUE: 10 **CUP:** 5

HOME

SK SLAVIA PRAHA
FOUNDED: Prague, 1892
STADIUM: Eden
CAPACITY: 20,800
INTERNATIONAL HONORS: None
LEAGUE: 2 **CUP:** 3

HOME

SERBIA

In 1896, Hugo Bale, son of a Belgrade tailor, returned home from Vienna with a soccer. The game took off in Belgrade among students, artisans, and the middle class, and then Serb nationalists. While part of Yugoslavia (1919–41 and 1945–91), Belgrade clubs played in Yugoslav leagues; when the country dissolved in 1991, the Serbs set up their own Superliga.

HOME   AWAY

POPULATION: 10.1 MILLION
CAPITAL: BELGRADE
FA: FUDBALSKI SAVEZ SRBIJE
LICENSED PLAYERS:
MALE: 400,800
FEMALE: 40,800
PROFESSIONALS: 1,500
REGISTERED CLUBS: 2,000

STAT ATTACK

NATIONAL TEAM

NICKNAME: Beli Orlovi ("White Eagles")

NATIONAL STADIUM:
Red Star Marakana, Belgrade, 51,500

WORLD CUP FINALS: 10 appearances, semi-finals **1930** and **1962**

EUROPEAN CHAMPIONSHIPS:
5 appearances, runners-up, **1960** and **1968**

BIGGEST WIN: 10–1 Yugoslavia vs India, 1952

BIGGEST DEFEAT: 0–7 Yugoslavia vs Czechoslovakia 1920 and 1925, and Yugoslavia vs Uruguay 1924

MOST CAPS: Savo Milosevic, **101**

MOST GOALS: Stjepan Bobek, **38**

MAIN DOMESTIC CLUBS

RED STAR BELGRADE
FOUNDED: Belgrade, 1945
STADIUM: Red Star Marakana
CAPACITY: 51,328
HOME
INTERNATIONAL HONORS:
European Cup winners **1991**
LEAGUE: 25 **CUP:** 22

PARTIZAN BELGRADE
FOUNDED: Belgrade, 1945
STADIUM: Partizana
CAPACITY: 30,887
HOME
INTERNATIONAL HONORS:
European Cup runners-up **1966**
LEAGUE: 20 **CUP:** 10

RED STAR VS PARTIZAN

Red Star Belgrade was founded in 1945 by the communist party with support from the university, police, and political elite. Partizan Belgrade was created in the same year by the federal, Yugoslav-minded national army. Rivalry between the two teams is intense, and games are known as "the eternal derby."

THE SUPERLIGA

Until 2007, the Serbian Superliga was decided by an end-of-season play-off. This was replaced by a standard league with 12 clubs, cut from 22. The 12 clubs play each other three times per season.

EUROPEAN CUP 1991

In the final year of Yugoslavia's existence, Red Star Belgrade made it to the final of the European Cup. Despite the Serbian affiliation of the fans, the team was resolutely multi-ethnic, including Robert Prosinescki (a Croat), Refik Sabanadzovic (a Bosnian Muslim), and Darko Pancev (a Macedonian). The title was really won in a monumental 4–3 semi-final against Bayern Munich; a disappointing final against Marseilles was decided on penalties.

SAVO **MILOSEVIC**

After bagging 74 goals in 98 games for Partizan, Milosevic moved to Aston Villa in 1995, where he gained the unfortunate moniker "Miss-a-lot-evic" due to his erratic behavior in front of goal. He has played for four national sides as the borders of the Balkans have shifted.

BORN: **SEPTEMBER 2, 1973, BIJELJINA, BOSNIA AND HERZEGOVINA**
HEIGHT: **6FT 1IN (1.87M)**
MAIN CLUBS: **PARTIZAN BELGRADE, ASTON VILLA, REAL ZARAGOZA, PARMA, CA OSASUNA**
INTERNATIONAL CAPS: **85**

YUGOSLAV SOCCER

Both FIFA and the Football Association of Serbia consider Serbia to be the official descendant of both the Yugoslav and Serbian and Montenegran national teams, despite the fact that the Yugoslav team was always multi-ethnic in composition. Yugoslav soccer enjoyed a golden era between the 1950s and 1970s, winning the Gold medal at the 1952 Helsinki Olympics, and contesting four World Cup quarter-finals.

HUNGARY

HOME

AWAY

POPULATION: 9.9 MILLION
CAPITAL: BUDAPEST
FA: MAGYAR LABDARÚGÓ SZÖVETSÉG
LICENSED PLAYERS:
MALE: 477,500
FEMALE: 50,000
PROFESSIONALS: 450
REGISTERED CLUBS: 2,800

Soccer took off in Budapest in the 1890s and clubs soon sprang up—MTK in 1898, Ferencváros in 1899, and Újpest in 1905. The game flourished: club sides competed all over central Europe, the national team made it to the final of the 1938 World Cup, and the remarkable Golden Generation of the 1950s marked the high point of Hungarian soccer.

THE NATIONAL CHAMPIONSHIP

Organizational problems and poor financing of Hungarian soccer in modern times has allowed teams outside the capital, Budapest, to prosper. In recent seasons, the league has been won by tiny provincial teams, such as Debreceni and Zalaegerszegi.

STAT ATTACK

NATIONAL TEAM

NICKNAME: The Magical Magyars (1950s)
NATIONAL STADIUM:
Puskás Ferenc Stadion, Budapest, 68,976
WORLD CUP FINALS: 9 appearances, runners-up, **1938** and **1954**
EUROPEAN CHAMPIONSHIPS:
2 appearances, 3rd place, **1964**
BIGGEST WIN: 13–1 vs France, 1927
BIGGEST DEFEAT: 0–7 vs England, 1908, and vs Germany, 1941
MOST CAPS: József Bozsik, **101**
MOST GOALS: Ferenc Puskás, **84**

MAIN DOMESTIC CLUBS

FERENCVÁROS
FOUNDED: Budapest, 1899
STADIUM: Ülloi Út
CAPACITY: 18,100
INTERNATIONAL HONORS:
Cup Winners' Cup runners-up **1975**
LEAGUE: 28 **CUP:** 20

HOME

MTK HUNGÁRIA
FOUNDED: Budapest, 1888
STADIUM: Hidegkuti Nándor
CAPACITY: 7,702
INTERNATIONAL HONORS:
Cup Winners' Cup runners-up, **1964**
LEAGUE: 23 **CUP:** 12

HOME

WORLD-RECORD RUN

Hungary holds the record for the longest unbeaten run of any national side, with 33 games between May 14, 1950 and July 4 ,1954, when they lost the World Cup final to West Germany.

MTK VS FERENCVÁROS

From its origins, MTK was the team of Budapest's liberals, intellectuals, and Jews. Most of Hungary's Jews perished during World War II and, under the communists, MTK became Red Banner. Ferencváros, named after a city suburb, are the team of the working classes. Favored by the Nazis during World War II, they were punished by the victorious communists, consequently making them the team of the opposition.

GOLDEN GENERATION

The Hungarian team coached by Gustáv Sebes, and boasting the talents of Puskás, Czibor, and Kocsis, combined the best of the traditional passing game with Sebes's tactical innovations. They swept everyone aside in 1952 and 1953, but lost to West Germany in the World Cup final of 1954.

FERENC **PUSKÁS**

A genuine soccer legend, Puskás was one of the greatest strikers of all time. Playing in the Hungarian and Spanish leagues between 1943 and 1966, he scored 514 goals in 529 appearances, a record bettered only by his international career, where he netted in all but one of his 85 outings.

BORN: APRIL 2, 1927, BUDAPEST, HUNGARY
HEIGHT: 5FT 10IN (1.78M)
MAIN CLUBS: KISPEST, AC HONVÉD, REAL MADRID
INTERNATIONAL CAPS: 85

33 Unbeaten games by national team, 1950–54

114 Goals scored by Ferenc Déak of Szentlornic in 64 games between 1945 and 1947

105 Years Ferencváros spent in Hungarian first division before being relegated for financial irregularities in 2006

10 Goals scored vs El Salvador in 1982 World Cup

ENGLAND VS HUNGARY

England's assumption that it was the best team in the world had been knocked by a shock defeat to the USA and an early exit from the 1950 World Cup, but they had never been beaten at home. Meanwhile, the golden generation of Hungarian players had demonstrated to anyone who was watching that Hungary was forging a new and extraordinary form of soccer. Olympic Champions in 1952, they were unbeaten throughout 1953. But England hadn't been paying attention and expected to win with ease. After 90 minutes of exhilarating Hungarian play, world soccer had new stars.

ENGLAND 3	HUNGARY 6
FORMATION: 2-3-5	FORMATION: 4-2-4
MANAGER: WALTER WINTERBOTTOM	MANAGER: GUSTÁV SEBES

WEMBLEY STADIUM, LONDON, ENGLAND
NOVEMBER 25, 1953

ATTENDANCE: 100,000

REFEREE: LEO HORN (HOLLAND)

00:00

England midfielder Billy Wright was taken aback by the appearance of the Hungarian team. "I looked down and noticed that the Hungarians had on these strange, lightweight boots. I turned to big Stan Mortensen and said: 'We should be all right here, Stan, they haven't got the proper gear.'"

Hungary: Grosics; Lóránt, Buzánszky, Zakariás, Lantos; Bozsik, Hidegkuti; Budai, Kocsis, Puskás, Czibor

England: Matthews, Taylor, Mortensen, Sewell, Robb; Wright, Johnston, Dickinson; Ramsey, Eckersley; Merrick

SUBS: 12 Geller (76)

I CAME AWAY WONDERING... WHAT WE HAD BEEN DOING ALL THESE YEARS!

TOM FINNEY ENGLAND STRIKER, 1946–58

TACTICS

England lost the tactical battle completely. The hosts played the standard W-M formation (see p.87), Hungary were playing a flexible 4-2-4 formation. Further confusion resulted from Hidegkuti wearing the No. 9 shirt—always the center forward in England, but Hidegkuti played deep in midfield, and his marker, center half Harry Johnston, was always out of position.

00:02

The Hungarians start the match on the attack. They put together a slalom of one-touch passes from the halfway line to Hidegkuti, who is totally unmarked. He rifles the soaked ball into the net: 1–0.

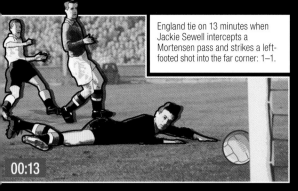

England tie on 13 minutes when Jackie Sewell intercepts a Mortensen pass and strikes a left-footed shot into the far corner: 1–1.

00:13

The situation gets worse for England when Billy Wright totally mistimes a tackle on Puskás, who has dragged the ball back and away from him with his studs. Nonchalantly, Puskás knocks the ball over England goalkeeper Merrick: 3–1. Hungarian announcer György Szepesi demands that a plaque be installed at Wembley to commemorate the drag-back goal.

00:24

00:20

Seven minutes later and Hungary are back in front. Hidegkuti pounces on a loose ball after a series of ricochets: 2–1.

00:27 Puskás diverts a Bozsik free-kick into the net, making it 4–1. Hungary have stamped their authority on the match with less than half an hour played.

00:38 Stan Mortensen scores just on half time, making it 4–2 and giving England the illusion of hope, but the gap between the teams is obvious.

00:50

Hungary have complete control and they finish the job. Bozsik makes it 5–2 five minutes into the second half with a long-range shot, seconds after Puskás has hit the post. Hidegkuti completes his hat-trick on 53 minutes with a half volley from eight yards after a lofted pass from the edge of the area: 6–2.

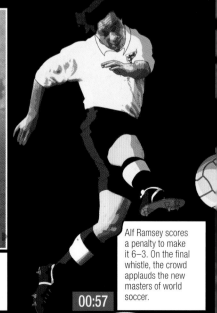

Alf Ramsey scores a penalty to make it 6–3. On the final whistle, the crowd applauds the new masters of world soccer.

00:57

POLAND

HOME

AWAY

POPULATION: 38.5 MILLION
CAPITAL: WARSAW
FA: POLSKI ZWIAZEK PIŁKI NOZNEJ
LICENSED PLAYERS:
MALE: 1.8 MILLION
FEMALE: 182,500
PROFESSIONALS: 1,200
REGISTERED CLUBS: 5,700

Soccer arrived late in Poland, with Krakow becoming the first hotbed. Kracovia and Wisla Krakow were formed by students in 1906, but there was no national team until after World War I. Under communism, success was rare, the exceptions being when they knocked England out of the 1974 World Cup qualifiers, and a 1982 World Cup semi-final place.

THE EKSTRAKLASA

The Polish top flight is the Ekstraklasa ("Top League"), and is a standard 16-team league that was founded in 1927. Dominated by Wisla Krakow from the late 1990s onward, it has suffered a spate of match-fixing scandals in recent years, leading to teams being demoted. In 1993, the title was awarded to third-place Lech Poznan after the top two, Legia Warsaw and LKS Lodz, were penalized for match-fixing.

FIRST-TIME THRILLS

Poland first qualified for the World Cup in 1938, where they played Brazil in the opening round, watched by over 125,000 Polish expatriates. The Poles were losing 3–0, but brought the game back to 4–4 by half time, only to lose 6–5 in the end.

WARSAW RIVALS

Legia Warsaw may be the biggest team in Poland's capital city, but they were not the first team to win a league title. Polonia Warsaw, their smaller neighbors, and the oldest team in the city, emerged from the wreckage of post-war Warsaw and won the league in 1946. Originally the team of the railroad workers and then the city's liberal intelligentsia, Polonia was steadily sidelined by the communist authorities.

ZBIGNIEW **BONIEK**

Renowned as the greatest Polish player ever, Boniek had blistering pace and sublime technique. His hat-trick against Belgium in the 1982 World Cup has been described as the best in the history of the tournament.

BORN: **MARCH 3, 1956,**
BYDGOSZCZ, POLAND
HEIGHT: **5FT 11IN (1.8M)**
MAIN CLUBS: **ZAWISA BYDGOSZCZ,**
WIDZEW LODZ, JUVENTUS, ROMA
INTERNATIONAL CAPS: **80**

THE LAST GAME

The so-called "Last Game" was played on August 27, 1939, four days before World War II broke out. Poland beat one of the best teams of the time —1938 World Cup runners-up, Hungary—4–2 in Warsaw. It is still remembered as the last match before the war, and the biggest win yet for Polish soccer.

STAT ATTACK

NATIONAL TEAM

NICKNAME: Biale Orly ("The White Eagles")
NATIONAL STADIUM:
Silesia Stadium, Chorzow, 47,246
WORLD CUP FINALS: 7 appearances,
3rd place **1974** and **1982**
EUROPEAN CHAMPIONSHIPS:
1 appearance
BIGGEST WIN: 9–0 vs Norway, 1963
BIGGEST DEFEAT: 0–8 vs Denmark, 1948
MOST CAPS: Grzegorz Lato, **100**
MOST GOALS: Wlodzimierz Lubanski, **48**

MAIN DOMESTIC CLUBS

LEGIA WARSAW
FOUNDED: Warsaw, 1916
STADIUM:
Polish Army Stadium
CAPACITY: 13,628,
expanding to 31,800
INTERNATIONAL HONORS:
European Cup semi-final **1970**,
UEFA Cup **1991**
LEAGUE: 8 **CUP:** 13

HOME

WISLA KRAKOW
FOUNDED: Krakow, 1906
STADIUM: Wisla Stadium
CAPACITY: 16,072,
expanding to 34,000
INTERNATIONAL HONORS:
European Cup quarter-final **1979**
LEAGUE: 14 **CUP:** 6

HOME

UKRAINE

HOME   AWAY

POPULATION: 46.3 MILLION
CAPITAL: KIEV
FA: FOOTBALL FEDERATION OF UKRAINE
LICENSED PLAYERS:
MALE: 2 MILLION
FEMALE: 232,000
PROFESSIONALS: 2,500
REGISTERED CLUBS: 68

Soccer was first played in Ukraine under Tsarist rule, prior to World War I. The game grew under the communists and Dynamo Kiev became the first non-Russian team to win the Soviet championships in 1961. Since independence in 1991, Ukraine has struggled internationally, but qualified for the World Cup finals in 2006, where they lost to Italy in the quarter-finals.

THE PREMIER LEAGUE

Founded in 1991, the Ukrainian Premier League consists of 16 teams playing each other twice through the season. However, the season is split by a three-month winter break.

LOBANOVSKY'S DYNAMO KIEV

Dynamo Kiev under coach Valeri Lobanovsky in the 1970s and '80s was notionally Soviet, but became the pride of the Ukraine. With support from the Ukrainian communists, Lobanovsky developed an immaculately planned method of training and playing that was reliant on endless rehearsal. His Dynamo team won six Soviet championships and the European Cup Winners' Cup twice.

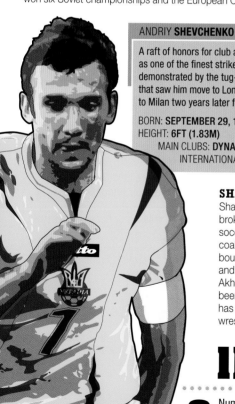

ANDRIY **SHEVCHENKO**

A raft of honors for club and country sets Shevchenko out as one of the finest strikers of his generation. This was demonstrated by the tug-of-war between Chelsea and AC Milan that saw him move to London for $60m in 2006, only to return to Milan two years later for an undisclosed fee.

BORN: **SEPTEMBER 29, 1976, DVIRKIVSCHYNA, SOVIET UNION**
HEIGHT: **6FT (1.83M)**
MAIN CLUBS: **DYNAMO KIEV, AC MILAN, CHELSEA**
INTERNATIONAL CAPS: **85**

SHAKHTAR DONETSK

Shakhtar Donetsk is the club that broke Dynamo Kiev's hold on Ukrainian soccer. Based in the huge Donbas coal and steel region, the club was bought by the area's dominant oligarch and nation's richest man, Rinat Akhmetov. A huge new stadium has been constructed and enough money has been poured in to the team to finally wrest the crown from Kiev in 2002.

11 Ukraine's highest ever FIFA ranking, achieved in February 2007

9 Number of different stadiums in which Ukraine have played their home matches since 1992

18 The percentage of mistakes in moves a team can make and still be unbeatable, according to Valeri Lobanovsky

STAT ATTACK

NATIONAL TEAM

NICKNAME: Zhovto-Blkytni ("Yellow and Blues")
NATIONAL STADIUM: Olympic Stadium, Kiev, 83,450
WORLD CUP FINALS: 1 appearance, quarter-finals **2006**
EUROPEAN CHAMPIONSHIPS: None
BIGGEST WIN: 6–0 vs Azerbaijan, 2006
BIGGEST DEFEAT: 0–4 vs Croatia, 1995, and vs Spain, 2006
MOST CAPS: Andriy Shevchenko, **85**
MOST GOALS: Andriy Shevchenko, **39**

MAIN DOMESTIC CLUBS

DYNAMO KIEV
FOUNDED: Kiev, 1927
STADIUM: Lobanovsky Dynamo
CAPACITY: 16,873
INTERNATIONAL HONORS:
Cup Winners' Cup winners **1975**, **1986**
LEAGUE: 12 **CUP:** 9

HOME

SHAKHTAR DONETSK
FOUNDED: Donetsk, 1936
STADIUM: RSK Olympiyskyi Lokomotyv
CAPACITY: 25,831 moving to Donbas Arena with a 50,000 capacity
INTERNATIONAL HONORS: None
LEAGUE: 4 **CUP:** 6

 HOME

GAME OF DEATH

Kiev was taken by the invading Germans in 1942 and subjected to a brutal occupation. The Luftwaffe and other German regiments played a series of games against the remnants of Dynamo Kiev's players, many of whom ended up in the city's mass graves.

RUSSIA

Soccer was first played in Tsarist Russia by British sailors in Odessa and expatriates in St. Petersburg. The game spread in the big industrial cities and city leagues were formed in Moscow and St. Petersburg. Following the 1917 Russian Revolution, soccer was controlled by the communist state. After the break-up of the USSR, the game boomed as Russian oligarchs invested in their country's league.

HOME   AWAY

POPULATION: 141.4 MILLION
CAPITAL: MOSCOW
FA: RUSSIAN FOOTBALL UNION
LICENSED PLAYERS:
MALE: 5,100,000
FEMALE: 697,500
PROFESSIONALS: 3,500
REGISTERED CLUBS: 14,000

THE RUSSIAN LEAGUE

The 16-team Russian League was founded in 1991, and was dominated by Spartak Moscow for the first decade. In recent years, Spartak have been eclipsed by CSKA Moscow, Lokomotiv Moscow, and Zenit St. Petersburg—funded by the nation's largest company, Gazprom.

THE BOOM PAYS OFF

The Russian soccer boom finally paid off in 2008. Zenit St. Petersburg beat Glasgow Rangers 2–0 to win the UEFA cup in some style. Meanwhile, the Russian national team, coached by Dutchman Guus Hiddink, reached the semi-finals of the European Championships, Russia's best placing since the fall of communism.

THE COMEBACK OF ALL TIME

It's the final 20 minutes of the final of the 1952 Olympics. The Soviet Union are 0–5 down to Tito's Yugoslavia—at that time the bête noire of Stalin. The losing team are facing a long and unpleasant session in the gulag. Miraculously, they manage to find five goals and force a replay, but lose the second game. Despite these superhuman exertions, the CSKA Moscow team, from which most of the Soviet Olympic team were drawn, was disbanded as a punishment.

LEV **YAHSIN**

Known as "The Black Spider" due to his all-black kit and unnatural ability to keep the ball out of the net, Yahsin won five Soviet Championships with Dynamo Moscow, and the 1960 European Championships and Olympic Gold in 1956.

BORN: **OCTOBER 22, 1929, MOSCOW, USSR**
HEIGHT: **6FT 2IN (1.88M)**
MAIN CLUBS: **DYNAMO MOSCOW**
INTERNATIONAL CAPS: **74**

STAT ATTACK

NATIONAL TEAM

NICKNAME: Red Army (USSR team); none for Russian national team
NATIONAL STADIUM: Luzhniki, Moscow, 84,745
WORLD CUP FINALS: **9** appearances, 4th place **1966**
EUROPEAN CHAMPIONSHIPS: 8 appearances, winners **1960**, runners-up **1988**
BIGGEST WIN: 11–1 vs India, **1955**
BIGGEST DEFEAT: 0–16 vs Germany, 1912 (Russian Empire)
MOST CAPS: Viktor Onopko, **109**, Oleg Blokhin, **112** (USSR)
MOST GOALS: Vladimir Beschastnykh, **28**, Oleg Blokhin, **42** (USSR)

MAIN DOMESTIC CLUBS

CSKA MOSCOW
FOUNDED: Moscow, 1911
STADIUM: Dinamo (new 30,000-seat stadium under construction)
CAPACITY: 36,540
INTERNATIONAL HONORS: UEFA Cup winners **2005**
LEAGUE: 10 **CUP:** 9

HOME

SPARTAK MOSCOW
FOUNDED: Moscow, 1922
STADIUM: Luzhniki
CAPACITY: 84,745
INTERNATIONAL HONORS: European Cup semi-finals **1991**, Cup Winners' Cup winners **1993**, and UEFA Cup winners **1998**
LEAGUE: 21 **CUP:** 13

HOME

ZENIT ST. PETERSBURG
FOUNDED: St. Petersburg, 1925
STADIUM: Petrovski
CAPACITY: 21,838
INTERNATIONAL HONORS: UEFA Cup and UEFA Super Cup winners, **2008**

HOME

CAUSE FOR COMPLAINT

The national soccer team was one of the few aspects of Soviet life on which citizens were brave enough to protest. When the USSR capitulated in the quarter-finals of the 1970 World Cup, *Izvetia*—a national paper—received more than 300,000 complaint letters.

ISRAEL

HOME

AWAY

POPULATION: 7.4 MILLION

CAPITAL: TEL AVIV

FA: ISRAEL FOOTBALL ASSOCIATION

LICENSED PLAYERS:
MALE: 251,500
FEMALE: 32,500

PROFESSIONALS: 1,500

REGISTERED CLUBS: 280

Soccer was played in Palestine by Jewish immigrants and Turkish soldiers prior to 1917, but the game took off under the British mandate from 1922. Palestine was FIFA-affiliated in 1929 on the condition that Jews and Arabs would be incorporated. Following the creation of Israel in 1948, the nation entered FIFA and regular league soccer commenced. In recent years, soccer in Arab Israel has become more popular and successful.

ONE AND ONLY

Beating New Zealand and Australia to qualify through the Oceania group, Israel made it to its one and only World Cup finals in 1970 in Mexico. Ties with Sweden and Italy and defeat to Uruguay were not enough to prevent a first-round exit, having scored just one goal.

ISRAELI PREMIER LEAGUE

Founded in 1999, the Israeli Premier League consists of 16 teams which play each other three times in a season. There are also two cup competitions—the Israel State Cup and the pre-season Toto Cup. Although Maccabi Tel Aviv is one of the oldest teams in Israel and boasts the most title wins (20), the most successful teams in the late 1990s and 2000s have been Maccabi Haifa and Beitar Jerusalem. The latter especially is boosted by the lavish funding of their Russian-Israeli billionaire owner Arcadi Gaydamak, although he recently left the country.

HAPPOEL, MACABBI, BEITAR?

Most Israeli clubs bear the prefix Happoel, Maccabi, or Beitar. All three were Zionist organizations committed to the creation of an Israeli state and, among their many social functions, they created sport teams. Happoel clubs were rooted in the trade union movement, the Maccabi clubs represented a more liberal, European Jewish tradition, while Beitar clubs represented Sephardic Jews from Asia and Africa, and were much more militantly right-wing. Official ties between clubs and these organizations have ended, but some of their ethos and attitude remains.

THE LOST CONTINENT

Israel has switched soccer continents three times in its short history. It was initially a member of the Asian Football Confederation but after a series of national federations and teams, such as Iran and Indonesia, refused to play them, FIFA temporarily moved Israel into the Oceania Football Confederation, where they played their World Cup qualifiers from the early 1970s until the late 1980s. The situation was finally resolved when Israel came under European rule in 1992 by joining UEFA.

EUROPEAN ENTRY

Israel's most popular and successful Arab club, Bnei Sakhnin has fielded Jewish players and counts Israeli Jews among its fans. The team was promoted to the Israeli Premier League for the first time in 2003, and went on to win the State Cup in 2004. It subsequently qualified for the UEFA Cup, becoming the first Arab side to play in a European competition.

NATIONAL TEAM

NATIONAL STADIUM:
Ramat Gan, Tel Aviv, 41,583
WORLD CUP FINALS: 1 appearance, **1970**
EUROPEAN CHAMPIONSHIPS: None
BIGGEST WIN: 9–0 vs Chinese Taipei, 1988
BIGGEST DEFEAT: 1–7 vs Egypt, 1934
(as Palestine/Eretz Israel)
MOST CAPS: Arik Benado, **94**
MOST GOALS: Mordechai Spiegler, **24**

MAIN DOMESTIC CLUBS

BEITAR JERUSALEM
FOUNDED: Jerusalem, 1936
STADIUM: Teddy Miacha
CAPACITY: 18,500   HOME
INTERNATIONAL HONORS: None
LEAGUE: 6 **CUP:** 6

MACCABI HAIFA
FOUNDED: Haifa, 1913
STADIUM: Kiryat Eli'ezer
CAPACITY: 17,000   HOME
INTERNATIONAL HONORS:
UEFA Cup quarter-finals **1999**
LEAGUE: 18 **CUP:** 22

HAPOEL TEL AVIV
FOUNDED: Tel Aviv, 1927
STADIUM: Bloomfield
CAPACITY: 15,400   HOME
INTERNATIONAL HONORS:
Asia Champions Cup winners **1967**
LEAGUE: 11 **CUP:** 12

32 Number of Brazilians who have played for Israeli clubs

48 Consecutive league games in which Maccabi Haifa were unbeaten, 1993–94

3 Different continents Israel has been deemed part of for organizational purposes (Asia, Oceania, Europe)

1932 Year British police won the Palestine league title

5 Number of titles won consecutively by Hapoel Petah Tikva, 1958–63

0 Number of points won by Maccabi Nes Tzionia in the 1949–50 season

UEFA MINNOWS

The strange contours of Medieval Europe have left a legacy of small nations, while the break–up of the USSR and Yugoslavia have added to the diversity. Not all of the lesser nations are push-overs—they are playing smarter and making the going harder for the big countries. Some of these minnows have teeth.

LIECHTENSTEIN

The Alpine micro-state of Liechtenstein is a lasting remnant of the Holy Roman Empire. Their best result yet was a 2–2 home draw with Portugal in a 2006 World Cup qualifier.

EUROPE

The European minnows are mainly confined to the principalities dotted around both the north and south of the continent, ranging from Luxembourg to Andorra. The other participants are made up of small or sparsely populated islands such as the Faroe Islands or Iceland. The big countries regard a visit to the smaller ones as a certain win. Traditionally very large scorelines are the norm, placing the minnows at the bottom of all the World Cup and European Championship qualifying groups. However, the smaller countries live in hope that one day they will become giant-killers and pull off a sensational win.

EIDUR GUDJOHNSEN
Iceland's leading player, Gudjohnsen has helped to take the islanders closer to their dream of qualification for a major tournament.

THE COMPETITORS

Europe's peripheries are home to some of the smallest soccer nations on planet soccer, from the desert steppes of Kazakhstan to the icy rocks of the Faroe islands.

Faroe Islands
FA: The Faroe Islands Football Association
Founded: 1979

Iceland
FA: Knattspyrnusamband Íslands
Founded: 1947

Liechtenstein
FA: Liechtensteiner Fussballverband
Founded: 1934

Luxembourg
FA: Fédération Luxembourgeoise de Football
Founded: 1908

Andorra
FA: Federació Andorrana de Fútbol
Founded: 1994

San Marino
FA: Federazione Sammarinese Giuoco Calcio
Founded: 1931

STAT ATTACK

NATIONAL TEAMS

ICELAND
POPULATION: 320,000
CAPITAL: Reykjavik
NATIONAL STADIUM: Laugardalsvöllur, 9,800
BIGGEST WIN: 9–0 vs Faroe Islands, 1985
BIGGEST DEFEAT: 2–14 vs Denmark, 1967
MOST CAPS: 101, Rúnar Kristinsson
MOST GOALS: 22, Eidur Gudjohnsen

FAROE ISLANDS
POPULATION: 48,500
CAPITAL: Tórshavn
NATIONAL STADIUM: Tórsvøllur, 6,000
BIGGEST WIN: 3–0 vs San Marino, 1995
BIGGEST DEFEAT: 0–9 vs Iceland, 1985
MOST CAPS: 83, Óli Johannesen
MOST GOALS: 10, Rógvi Jacobsen

LUXEMBOURG
POPULATION: 480,000
CAPITAL: Luxembourg City
NATIONAL STADIUM: Stade Josy Barthel, 8,100
BIGGEST WIN: 6–0 vs Afghanistan, 1948
BIGGEST DEFEAT: 0–9 vs England, 1960 and 1982
MOST CAPS: 88, Jeff Strasser
MOST GOALS: 16, Léon Mart

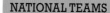

ASIA

Formerly part of the Soviet Union, Kazakhstan was classed as Asian after the collapse of Communism, but joined UEFA in 2002. Soccer in Azerbaijan has been hampered by a 20-year conflict with Armenia, which forced the side to play home games in Turkey in the mid-1990s.

1 Number of competitive games in which Andorra has scored more than one goal

23 Area in square miles (60 square kilometers) of the micro-state of San Marino

1990 Year Faroe Islands won their first competitive game

NATIONAL TEAMS

KAZAKHSTAN
POPULATION: 15.2 million
CAPITAL: Astana
NATIONAL STADIUM: Almaty Central Stadium, 25,000
BIGGEST WIN: 7–0 vs Pakistan, 1997
BIGGEST DEFEAT: 0–6 vs Turkey, 2005 and Russia, 2008
MOST CAPS: 65, Ruslan Baltiyev
MOST GOALS: 12, Viktor Zubarev

MOLDOVA
POPULATION: 4.1 million
CAPITAL: Chisinau
NATIONAL STADIUM:
Zimbru Stadium, 10,500
BIGGEST WIN:
5–0 vs Pakistan, 1992
BIGGEST DEFEAT: 0–6 vs Sweden, 2001
MOST CAPS: 74, Radu Rebeja
MOST GOALS: 11, Serghei Clescenco

AZERBAIJAN
POPULATION: 8.7 million
CAPITAL: Baku
NATIONAL STADIUM: Tofik Bakhramov Stadium, 30,000
BIGGEST WIN: 4–0 vs Liechtenstein, 1999
BIGGEST DEFEAT:
0–10 vs France, 1995
MOST CAPS: 75, Aslan Kerimov
MOST GOALS: 12, Gurban Gurbanov

CYPRUS
POPULATION: 794,600
CAPITAL: Nicosia
NATIONAL STADIUM:
Antonis Papadopoulos Stadium, 9,800
BIGGEST WIN: 5–0 vs Andorra, 2000
BIGGEST DEFEAT:
0–12 vs West Germany, 1969
MOST CAPS: 86, Yiannakis Okkas
MOST GOALS: 25, Michalis Konstandinou

Moldova
FA: Football Association of Moldova
Founded: 1990

Kazakhstan
FA: Football Federation of Kazakhstan
Founded: 1914, switched from AFC to UEFA in 2002

Cyprus
FA: Cyprus Football Association
Founded: 1934

Azerbaijan
FA: Association of Football Federations of Azerbaijan
Founded: 1992

LIECHTENSTEIN
POPULATION: 35,000
CAPITAL: Vaduz
NATIONAL STADIUM:
Rheinpark Stadion, 6,100
BIGGEST WIN: 4–0 vs Luxembourg, 2004
BIGGEST DEFEAT:
1–11 vs FYR Macedonia, 1996
MOST CAPS: 82, Mario Frick
MOST GOALS: 13, Mario Frick

ANDORRA
POPULATION: 72,000
CAPITAL: Andorra La Vella
NATIONAL STADIUM:
Comunal d'Aixovall, 1,500
BIGGEST WIN: 2–0 vs Belarus, 2000, and Albania, 2002
BIGGEST DEFEAT: 1–8 vs Czech Rep., 2005
MOST CAPS: 76, Oscar Sonejee
MOST GOALS: 4, Ildefons Lima

SAN MARINO
POPULATION: 30,000
CAPITAL: San Marino City
NATIONAL STADIUM:
Stadio Olimpico, 7,000
BIGGEST WIN:
1–0 vs Liechtenstein, 2004
BIGGEST DEFEAT: 0–13 vs Germany, 2006
MOST CAPS: 48, Mirco Gennari
MOST GOALS: 8, Andy Selva

SOUTH AMERICA: CONMEBOL

ARGENTINA

HOME   AWAY

POPULATION: 40.3 MILLION
CAPITAL: BUENOS AIRES
LICENSED PLAYERS:
MALE: 2.35 MILLION
FEMALE: 30,900
PROFESSIONALS: 3,500
REGISTERED CLUBS: 3,500

LIONEL MESSI
Tiny but strong and skilful, the midfielder is on course to join Pelé, Maradona, and Zidane as one of the all-time greats.

Soccer has been around in Argentina for a long time—as early as 1867 a group of Englishmen formed the Buenos Aires Football Club. The game really took off when it spread beyond the expatriate community, and by 1907 there were over 300 clubs in the country. It would be fair to describe Argentinians as soccer-crazy—90 percent of the population supports a club, and when the national team plays, the country comes to a halt.

LA NUESTRA ("OUR WAY")

The style of play that has evolved in Argentina is a mixture of South American flair, Anglo-Saxon pragmatism, and *criolla viveza* ("cunning"). Argentinians play to win, and for every super-skilful Lionel Messi there is a no-nonsense hard-man such as Roberto Ayala. The nation has also developed playing positions peculiarly its own, such as the *trequartista* (three-quarter forward). The result of all these combined styles and approaches is extremely effective—Argentina are always formidable opponents.

GOD MAKES ME PLAY WELL... I ALWAYS MAKE THE SIGN OF A CROSS WHEN I WALK ON THE FIELD

DIEGO MARADONA

CROSS-BORDER SKIRMISHES

In 1901, Argentina beat Uruguay 3–2 in the first official international match contested outside the UK. The two have since met in excess of 170 times, more than any other pair of nations. In the early 20th century they sometimes played two matches in a day, one in Buenos Aires and one across the Plate River in Montevideo. The countries are only separated by the width of the river, and Uruguayans sound more like residents of Buenos Aires than the rest of Argentina's citizens.

IGLESIA MARADONIANA

Diego Maradona is often described as being like a god to Argentinians, but some take this quite literally. In 1998, the Iglesia Maradoniana ("Maradonian Church") was founded in Rosario, a city in Santa Fe province that is situated about 186 miles (300 km) northwest of Buenos Aires. The claimed 100,000 church members celebrate Christmas on Maradona's birthday (October 30), worship in the Hand of God chapel, and date their calendars from their idol's year of birth (1960).

STAT ATTACK

GOVERNING BODY: Asociación del Fútbol Argentino (Argentine Football Association)
FOUNDED: 1893
NATIONAL STADIUM:
El Monumental, Buenos Aires, 65,645
FIRST MATCH: 3–2 vs Uruguay, 1901
BIGGEST WIN: 12–0 vs Ecuador, 1942
BIGGEST DEFEAT: 6–1 vs Bolivia, 2009

THE LEGENDS

MOST CAPPED PLAYERS

Name	From/To	Caps
Javier ZANETTI	1994–present	128
Roberto AYALA	1994–2007	115
Diego SIMEONE	1988–2002	106
Oscar RUGGERI	1983–94	97
Diego MARADONA	1977–94	91
Ariel ORTEGA	1993–2003	86

TOP GOALSCORERS

Name	From/To	Goals
Gabriel BATISTUTA	1991–2002	56
Hernán CRESPO	1995–2007	36
Diego MARADONA	1977–94	34
Luis ARTIME	1961–67	24
Leopoldo LUQUE	1975–81	22
Daniel PASSARELLA	1976–86	22

DIEGO **MARADONA**

Arguably the greatest player in history, Diego Maradona's bewitching ball control, strength, speed, and low center of gravity marked him out as unique. His eventful career includes a World Cup win, drug addiction, a heart attack, and becoming manager of Argentina.

BORN: **OCTOBER 30, 1960, LANÚS, ARGENTINA**
HEIGHT: **5FT 5IN (1.65M)**
MAIN CLUBS: **ARGENTINOS JUNIORS, BOCA JUNIORS, BARCELONA, NAPOLI, SEVILLA**
INTERNATIONAL CAPS: **91**

DOMESTIC SET-UP

The structure of Argentinian domestic soccer—particularly the intricacies of relegation and promotion, and qualification for the major South American club tournaments—is very complicated. The formula has been changed several times over the years. Currently, the main features are the absence of a domestic Cup competition—league soccer is everything in Argentina—and the division of the season into two mini-leagues, the Apertura ("Opening") and the Clausura ("Closing"), each with its own champion.

RACING CLUB AND THE BLACK CATS

Black cats are considered extremely unlucky in Argentina. In 1967, fans of the Buenos Aires club Independiente buried seven of them at the stadium of champions Racing Club while their rivals were away beating Scottish club Celtic in the Intercontinental Cup. Racing didn't win another title for 35 years, and only when the seventh cat was exhumed in 2001 did the club's fortunes begin to change.

STAT ATTACK

PRIMERA A

LEAGUE STRUCTURE: 20 teams (Apertura and Clausura)

TOP SCORERS: Arsenio Erico and Ángel Labruna, **293** goals each

MOST SUCCESSFUL TEAM: River Plate, **34** League Titles

BIGGEST WIN: 13–1, Banfield v Puerto Commercial, 1974

DIVISIONS BELOW PREMIER LEAGUE: Primera B Nacional (**20** teams); third tier made up of both Torneo Argentino A (**24** teams) and Primera B Metropolitana (**22** teams)

BARRA BRAVAS

Some clubs have hardcore groups of fans known as the *barra bravas* ("tough gangs"). These organizations have an unhealthy influence on Argentinian soccer—as well as allegedly being hired by would-be club directors to intimidate rival candidates, they also reportedly extort protection money from players and commit acts of violence.

GABRIEL BATISTUTA

A quiet family man away from the field, yet lethal on it, the adored Batistuta is Argentina's all-time top goalscorer.

17 Red cards shown to defender Roberto Trotta during his Primera División career

2 Minutes played by Argentina's Marcelo Trobbiani during the 1986 World Cup tournament

44 Number of penalties it took to decide a 1988 match between Argentinos Juniors and Racing Club

36 League goals scored by Vélez Sarsfield's Paraguayan goalkeeper José Luis Chilavert

WORLD CUP

Rows (top to bottom): Winner, Runners-up, Semi-finals, Quarter-finals, Round 2, Round 1, Did not qualify. Columns: 1, 2, 3, 4.

COPA AMÉRICA

Rows (top to bottom): Winner, Runners-up, Semi-finals, Quarter-finals, Round 2, Round 1, Did not qualify. Columns: 1, 2, 3, 4, 5, 6, 7, 8, 9, 10, 11, 12, 13, 14.

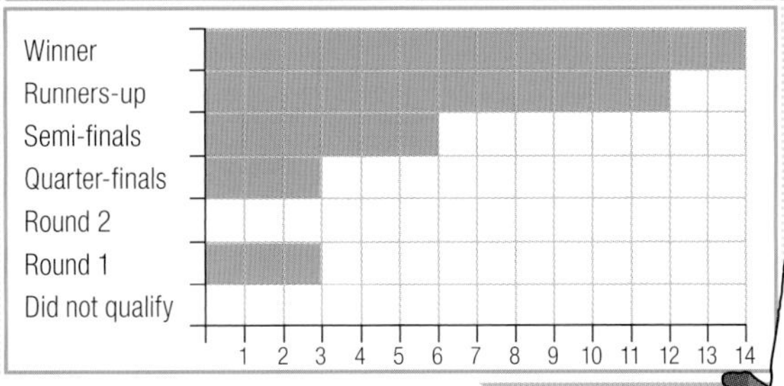

ARGENTINIAN CLUBS

Club soccer in Argentina has always been centered on Buenos Aires. In fact, there were no provincial teams in the national championships until the 1930s, and they still occupy less than half the slots in the top division. *Los Cincos Grandes* ("The Big Five") won every title for nearly 40 years, with Boca Juniors and River Plate way ahead of Racing, San Lorenzo, and Independiente in terms of money and popularity. Smaller clubs such as Argentinos Juniors and Estudiantes have also had periods of success.

EL SUPERCLÁSICO

The Boca-River derby—*El Superclásico*—is a maniacal affair that is often marked by disturbances both inside and outside the stadia. Following Boca's 2–1 defeat of River at the latter's stadium in 2002, the away fans refused to leave and heavy-handed policing precipitated a stadium-wide riot. This was then replicated among the fans of both clubs in provincial cities.

NICKNAME:
LOS XENEIZES ("THE GENOESE")

FOUNDED:
BUENOS AIRES, 1905

HOME

STADIUM:
LA BOMBONERA, 57,400

DOMESTIC HONORS:
LEAGUE 29

INTERNATIONAL HONORS:
COPA LIBERTADORES 1977, 1978, 2000, 2001, 2003, 2007; COPA SUDAMERICAN 2004, 2005; WORLD CLUB CUP 1977, 2000, 2003

BOCA JUNIORS

Though founded by Italian immigrants, Boca took its colors from the Swedish flag—the first flag seen on a ship by early members of this port-side team. Since then, Boca has always seen itself as the team of the people—a fact not lost on former Argentinian leader General Juan Perón, who was a fan. Though the club is currently owned by the Mayor of Buenos Aires, Mauricio Macri, Boca is able to draw on a fan base that is country-wide. Its run of international success is unequalled in Argentinian soccer.

LOS BOSTEROS

Boca's La Bombonera stadium is built on the site of a former horse manure factory. For this reason, supporters of the club are known as Bosteros ("manure handlers"). The name was originally meant as an insult, but Boca fans have embraced it with pride. The team itself is nicknamed Los Xeneizes ("the Genoese"), a reference to the Italian founders of the club.

MARTÍN PALERMO

Despite regular periods out due to injury, Palermo is regarded as a Boca Juniors legend thanks to his deadly finishing. He also makes an appearance in the record books for missing three penalties for Argentina in a single Copa América game against Colombia in 1999.

BORN: NOVEMBER 7, 1973, LA PLATA, ARGENTINA
HEIGHT: 6 FT 1IN (1.87M)
MAIN CLUBS: ESTUDIANTES, BOCA JUNIORS, VILLARREAL, REAL BETIS
INTERNATIONAL CAPS: 7

THE BOMBONERA DOESN'T TREMBLE... ## IT BEATS!

SAYING DERIVED FROM THE FACT THAT THE BOCA JUNIORS STADIUM VIBRATES WHEN ITS FANS JUMP UP AND DOWN

BEST OF THE REST

RACING (1903)
In and out of bankruptcy for many years, Racing is one of the old greats of Argentinian soccer and the team of Eva Perón in the 1940s and '50s.
HONORS: LEAGUE 16; COPA LIBERTADORES 1967

SAN LORENZO (1908)
Formed from a street team in the Almagro barrio of Buenos Aires in 1908, San Lorenzo grew into one of the biggest clubs in the city. Economic problems forced it to relocate in the 1990s.
HONORS: LEAGUE 13

INDEPENDIENTE (1905)
Founded by employees of a British store, it had great success in the Copa Libertadores.
HONORS: LEAGUE 16; COPA LIBERTADORES 1964–65, 1972–75, 1984; WORLD CLUB CUP 1973, 1984

ESTUDIANTES (1905)
The tiny club from La Plata surprised—and then enraged —the world with its brutal version of anti-soccer.
HONORS: LEAGUE 5; COPA LIBERTADORES 1968–70; WORLD CLUB CUP 1968

HOME

RIVER PLATE

Originally based in the Boca area of Buenos Aires, River Plate always had ambition, shifting first to Palermo and then to Nuñez. Boca stayed in the docks, and River Plate became the classy team from the better part of town. In 1931, the club earned its enduring nickname *Los Millionarios* after it went on the first great spending spree in Argentinian professional soccer. River Plate's style of play was defined in the 1940s and '50s by the great *La Maquina*—an elegant passing side that dominated Argentinian soccer for a decade.

FLUCTUATING FORTUNES

Although River Plate is the most successful club in Argentinian soccer history, in recent years it has been in the shadow of arch rivals Boca Juniors. River Plate's inconsistency was highlighted in 2008 when it won the Clausura only to finish bottom of the subsequent Apertura.

LAS GALLINAS

River Plate's title drought from 1957 to 1975 led rival fans to nickname the club *Las Gallinas* ("chickens") for a tendency to lose its head. The team came second in the league 11 times and famously squandered a 2–0 lead in the 1966 Copa Libertadores final to lose 4–2 to Peñarol.

CLAUDIO CANIGGIA
One of the fastest players in the world, *El Pájaro* ("The Bird") once completed 109 yards in 10 seconds. Famously, the striker was not selected for national duty for several years after refusing to cut his flowing locks.

EL SUPERCLÁSICO

- Boca Juniors—**36%**
- River Plate—**33%**
- Drawn—**31%**

31 33 36

VÉLEZ SARSFIELD (1910)
Based in the west of Buenos Aires, Vélez got a new stadium from the Junta in 1978—built on a garbage-filled lagoon.
HONORS: LEAGUE 6; COPA LIBERTADORES 1994; WORLD CLUB CUP 1994

ARGENTINOS JUNIORS (1904)
A small but tough inner-city team, with a following to match. A 15-year-old Diego Maradona got his break into the club's first team.
HONORS: LEAGUE 3; COPA LIBERTADORES 1985

NEWELL'S OLD BOYS (1903)
Formed by students of the English High School in Rosario and named after a British teacher, Isaac Newell. Lost two Copa Libertadores finals during the early 1990s.
HONORS: LEAGUE 5

ROSARIO CENTRAL (1889)
Founded by English railroad workers as the Central Argentine Railroad Athletic Club. Said to receive the nickname *Callanas* ("Scoundrels") after refusing to play a charity match for lepers.
HONORS: LEAGUE 4

BRAZIL

HOME

AWAY

POPULATION: 188.1 MILLION
CAPITAL: BRAZILIA
LICENSED PLAYERS:
MALE: 11.7 MILLION
FEMALE: 190,000
PROFESSIONALS: 16,200
REGISTERED CLUBS: 29,000

British sailors were seen playing soccer on the Rio docks in the 1870s, but it was rich European Brazilians who brought the game home in the 1890s—Charles Miller from Southampton to São Paulo and Oscar Cox from Switzerland to Rio. By the 1920s, the game was especially popular with the then marginalized African-Brazilians. Attempts to exclude them from the professional game were challenged, and Brazilian soccer has never looked back.

SÓCRATES
The midfielder captained Brazil at two World Cups and played for an English non-league team. Appropriately, he has a doctorate in philosophy.

WORLD CUP LEGENDS
Brazil's reputation and global popularity rest on its World Cup performances. The team dazzled at the 1938 World Cup and were favorites at home in 1950, only to lose to Uruguay. Redemption and the famous yellow shirts finally arrived with Pelé in Sweden in 1958 and Garrincha in 1962, and in 1970 the team won for the third time. The drought that followed was broken by the successful 1994 squad.

STATE CHAMPIONSHIPS
In the early months of the year, before the national league starts, there are state championships around the country. Before the league was founded in 1971, these were the principal tournaments, and they remain popular.

PELÉ
Edson Arantes do Nascimento (better known as Pelé) made his debut for Santos at 15 and won the first of three World Cup winners' medals at 17. He scored over 1,000 goals, a milestone celebrated in Brazil.

BORN: **OCTOBER 23, 1940,**
TRÊS CORAÇÕES, BRAZIL
HEIGHT: **5FT 8IN (1.73M)**
MAIN CLUBS: **SANTOS,**
NEW YORK COSMOS
INTERNATIONAL
CAPS: **92**

94 The number of teams in the Brazilian national championship in 1979

19.1 The percentage of Brazilian fans who support Flamengo

7,000 Members of Athletes for Christ —including six players from the 1994 World Cup squad

5 The number of Brazilian high-court judges taken on all-expenses paid trip to the 1994 World Cup Final by the Brazilian FA

STAT ATTACK

GOVERNING BODY:
Confederação Brasileira de Futebol
FOUNDED: 1914
NATIONAL STADIUM: None
FIRST MATCH: 0–3 vs Argentina **1914**
BIGGEST WIN: 14–0 vs Nicragua **1975**
BIGGEST DEFEAT: 0–6 vs Uruguay **1920**

THE LEGENDS

MOST CAPPED PLAYER

Name	From/To	Caps
CAFU	1990–2006	142
Roberto CARLOS	1992–2006	125
Cláudio TAFFAREL	1987–98	101
Djalma SANTOS	1952–68	98
RONALDO	1994–2006	97
GILMAR	1953–69	94

TOP GOALSCORERS

Name	From/To	Goals
PELÉ	1957–71	77
RONALDO	1994–2006	62
ROMÁRIO	1987–2005	55
ZICO	1971–89	52
BEBETO	1985–98	39
RIVALDO	1993–2003	34

JUST THE TICKET

Brazil is so huge and its transportation infastructure so inadequate that no national league could be played before 1970. In 1969, the government started a soccer game lottery to raise money as well as teach some geography—the tickets included games from all over the country. The lottery's popularity pressurized the soccer authorities into creating a national league, resulting in the Campeonato Brasileiro kicking off in 1971.

COPA DO BRASIL

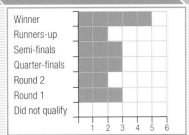

Brazil's premier knock-out competition was introduced in 1989 to give the nation's smaller clubs an opportunity to compete with the big boys. The tournament is contested by 64 teams, most of them qualifying via various state championships. All stages of the cup are over two legs and the away goals rule applies. Any team that wins an away match by two goals or more in the first two rounds automatically goes through to the next round.

THE GAMA AFFAIR

Brazil's big clubs will do almost anything to avoid relegation. In 1996, Fluminese avoided relegation by having the league conveniently expanded by four teams. Three years later, Botofogo was relegated until it persuaded the CBF to reallocate some points on a technicality. This meant that a small team—Gama—was relegated instead, but the club then went to court and was reinstated. The situation was only resolved by creating a complex new one-off tournament made up of 116 clubs.

STAT ATTACK

CAMPEONATO BRASILEIRO

LEAGUE STRUCTURE: 20 teams
TOP SCORER: Roberto Dinamite, **190** goals
MOST SUCCESSFUL TEAM: São Paulo
BIGGEST WIN: 10–1 Corinthians vs Tiradentos PI, 1983
HIGHEST ATTENDANCE: 155,523, Flamengo vs Santos, 1983
DIVISIONS BELOW PREMIER LEAGUE:
Serie B (**20** teams), Serie C (**64** teams), Serie D (**40** teams)

COPA DO BRASIL

The Copa was first contested in 1989. The final is a two-legged affair.
MOST SUCCESSFUL TEAMS:
Gremio and Cruzeiro, **4** wins each
BIGGEST WIN: 5–3, Grêmio vs Corinthians, 2001

IN BRAZIL EVERY KID STARTS PLAYING STREET SOCCER VERY EARLY... IT'S IN OUR BLOOD

RONALDO

WHERE'S THE MONEY?

Despite signing the biggest ever national team deal with a shirt sponsor (Nike paid around $160m in 1996), Brazil's soccer association remained in debt for a decade and grassroots funding remained unchanged. A 2002 investigation by the Senate recommended that 17 leading CBF figures should be prosecuted.

WORLD CUP WINS

Country	Tournaments played	Tournaments won
Brazil	18	5
Italy	16	4
Germany	16	3
Argentina	14	2
Uruguay	10	2
France	12	1
England	12	1

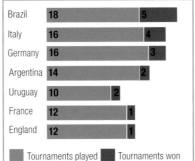

RONALDO
Blessed with lightning feet and a supernatural eye for goal, Ronaldo has scored more times in World Cup finals than any other player.

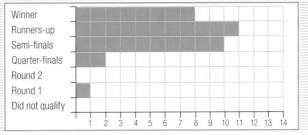

WORLD CUP

Winner
Runners-up
Semi-finals
Quarter-finals
Round 2
Round 1
Did not qualify
1 2 3 4 5 6

COPA AMÉRICA

Winner
Runners-up
Semi-finals
Quarter-finals
Round 2
Round 1
Did not qualify
1 2 3 4 5 6 7 8 9 10 11 12 13 14

BRAZILIAN CLUBS

Until the 1970s, Brazilian soccer was dominated by clubs from Rio and São Paulo. With the arrival of the national championship and the spread of industrialization, teams from the big provincial cities have since challenged them.

ZICO

Zico was among the greatest Brazilians to emerge in the generation after Pelé. He excelled at home with Flamengo and Italy and Japan, boasting an extraordinary shot and miraculous free-kicks.

BORN: **MARCH 3, 1953, RIO DE JANEIRO, BRAZIL**
HEIGHT: **6FT (1.83M)**
MAIN CLUBS: **FLAMENGO, UDINESE**
INTERNATIONAL CAPS: **88**

NICKNAME:
MENGÃO ("BIG MENGO")
FOUNDED:
RIO, 1895
HOME
STADIUM:
PETROBRAS, 30,000
DOMESTIC HONORS:
NATIONAL 5; COPA DO BRASIL 2; STATE LEAGUE 29
INTERNATIONAL HONORS:
COPA LIBERTADORES 1981; COPA MERCOSUR 1999

FLAMENGO

Flamengo is the biggest, best supported, and most chaotic club in Brazil. Founded in 1895 as an elite rowing club, defectors from Fluminense joined in 1911 and began playing soccer at the club. Despite these origins, Flamengo is unashamedly "the people's team," a symbolic tribune of the poor.

NICKNAME:
FLUZÃO ("BIG FLU")
FOUNDED:
RIO, 1902
HOME
STADIUM:
RAULINO DE OLIVERA, 20,000
DOMESTIC HONORS:
NATIONAL 1; COPA DO BRASIL 1; STATE LEAGUE 30

FLUMINENSE

The most unashamedly aristocratic club in the country, Fluminense was founded by Oscar Cox, a Swiss Brazilian from one of the city's richest families. In the early days, the ground's elegant wooden bleachers were filled with Rio's high society, who cheered in English "hip-hip-hooray."

NICKNAME:
GIGANTE DA COLINA ("HILL'S GIANT")
FOUNDED:
RIO, 1898
HOME
STADIUM:
SÃO JANUÁRIO, 35,000
DOMESTIC HONORS:
NATIONAL 4; STATE LEAGUE 22
INTERNATIONAL HONORS:
COPA LIBERTADORES 1998; COPA MERCOSUR 2000

VASCO DA GAMA

Founded as a rowing club for Portuguese immigrants in 1898, the club has always had a less aristocratic and more commercial cast than the other Rio clubs. The second generation of members preferred to play soccer and to win. In the 1920s, Vasco was the first Rio club to field a black player; it was a key force in the emergence of the professional game in Brazil and breaking the color barrier in Rio soccer.

BEST OF THE REST

BOTAFOGO (1904)
Students from the Alfredo Gomez College founded Botafogo in the glamorous neighborhood of the same name, just north of Copacabana beach.

HONORS: NATIONAL 1; COPA DO BRASIL 1; STATE LEAGUE 17; COPA CONMEBOL 1993

INTERNACIONAL (1909)
Formed in opposition to Grêmio, the team's name reflects its open-to-all recruitment policy. Their recent Libertadores and World Club Cup triumphs are a new high for the club.

HONORS: NATIONAL 3; COPA DO BRASIL 1; STATE LEAGUE 38; COPA LIBERTADORES 2006

PALMEIRAS (1914)
The club began life as Palestra Italia, drawing directly on São Paulo's large Italian immigrant community. The name change came when Brazil entered World War II on the side of the Allies.

HONORS: NATIONAL 4; COPA DO BRASIL 3; STATE LEAGUE 22; COPA MERCOSUR 1998

GRÊMIO (1903)
Founded by German immigrants and established merchants, Grêmio achieved great success in the 1980s when managed by Luiz Felipe Scolari.

HONORS: NATIONAL 2; COPA DO BRASIL 4; STATE LEAGUE 34; COPA LIBERTADORES 1983, 1995; WORLD CLUB CUP 1983

RIVELLINO
A World Cup winner in 1970, Rivellino was one of the most elegant midfielders the soccer world has ever seen.

NICKNAME:
TIMÃO ("GRAND TEAM")
FOUNDED:
SÃO PAOLO, 1910
HOME
STADIUM:
PACAEMBU, 37,200
DOMESTIC HONORS:
NATIONAL 4; COPA DO BRASIL 2; STATE LEAGUE 25
INTERNATIONAL HONORS:
WORLD CLUB CUP 2000

CORINTHIANS

Founded by railroad workers in the Bom Retiro district of São Paulo, the club was named after an amateur English side that played in the city. Corinthians has retained its blue collar character and claims almost as many fans across Brazil as Flamengo.

NICKNAME:
O MAIS QUERIDO ("THE MOST LOVED")
FOUNDED:
SÃO PAULO, 1935
HOME
STADIUM:
MORUMBI, 80,000
DOMESTIC HONORS:
NATIONAL 5; STATE LEAGUE 21
INTERNATIONAL HONORS:
COPA LIBERTADORES 1992, 93, 2005; COPA CONMEBOL 1994; WORLD CLUB CUP 1992, 1993

SÃO PAULO

The last of the big clubs from São Paulo, the team emerged from the wreckage of earlier amateur outfits in the west of the city. After living in Corinthians' shadows, it is now the strongest team in the city.

NICKNAME:
PEIXE ("THE FISH")
FOUNDED:
SANTOS, 1912
HOME
STADIUM:
VILLA BELMIRO, 25,100
DOMESTIC HONORS:
NATIONAL 2; COPA DO BRASIL 5; STATE LEAGUE 16
INTERNATIONAL HONORS:
COPA LIBERTADORES 1962, 1963; COPA CONMEBOL 1998; WORLD CLUB CUP 1962, 1963

SANTOS

A short drive south of São Paulo, Santos is the city's port. The club played second fiddle to those in Rio until the arrival of Pelé, who played most of his career here and for a short period in the early 1960s made it the best team in the world.

CARLOS ALBERTO
Defender Carlos Alberto captained the legendary World Cup-winning Brazil team of 1970.

RECORD CROWD

In December 1963, Fluminense played Flamengo in the second leg of the final of the Carioca state championship. As well as 177,656 paying spectators, another 16,947 entered without tickets, to make a grand total of 194,603 fans. The score was 0–0.

BRAZILIAN SUPPORT

The rest—**45%**
Rio Clubs—**30%**
São Paulo Clubs—**25%**

25 **30** **45**

ATLÉTICO MINEIRO (1908)
Won the first national championship in 1971, but corruption and embezzlement by the club's directors saw it drop into the second division in 2006.
HONORS: NATIONAL 1; STATE LEAGUE 38; COPA CONMEBOL 1992, 1997

CRUZEIRO (1921)
Founded by Italian immigrants as Pilestra Mineiro, it originally played in the colors of the Italian flag. During World War II, it changed its name to Cruzeiro.
HONORS: NATIONAL 1; COPA DO BRASIL 5; STATE LEAGUE 34; COPA LIBERTADORES, 1976, 1997

BAHIA (1931)
Bahia is the biggest club in northern Brazil. In recent years, it has suffered calamitous bankruptcies and numerous relegations, but still manages to draw the biggest crowds in all of Brazilian soccer.
HONORS: NATIONAL 1; COPA DO BRASIL 1; STATE LEAGUE 45

RECIFE (1905)
Known locally as "Sport," the club won the chaotically mismanaged 1987 national championship. Recife has recently climbed out of the lower divisions and won the Copa Do Brasil.
HONORS: NATIONAL 1; COPA DO BRASIL 1; STATE LEAGUE 36

GLOBAL MIGRATION

Soccer was introduced to the world by waves of English and Scottish migrants in the 19th century. The earliest non-British clubs, such as Genoa and Milan in Italy or Barcelona in Spain, had a truly cosmopolitan make-up. By the 1930s, Latin American players began to travel across the globe, with African players following suit in the 1940s and '50s. Today the migration patterns of players are truly global and involve virtually every league—from the poorly resourced to the super-rich.

Italy
For decades Italian clubs attracted elite global players, but today they are often out-bid by English and Spanish clubs

Netherlands
A "conveyor belt" of talent has created players that have outgrown their home country

England
Since the arrival of the Premier League, England has become the biggest importer of foreign players

France
A great youth-training system has seen France become a major exporter

Portugal
Portuguese clubs first drew on the talent of the country's African colonies in the 1950s and '60s

Spain
Spain's transfer market once had a ban on foreign players; it now embraces internationalism

West Africa
West African countries, most notably Nigeria, have been supplying talent to Europe since the 1930s

Brazil
Few players left the country during the golden era of the 1950s and '60s, but Brazilians have been heading overseas ever since

Uruguay
With a population of only three million, Uruguay exports more players per capita than anywhere else in the world

Argentina
Argentinians of Italian descent were first enticed to Europe in the 1930s by the promise of huge wages

Mexico
The rising wealth and ambition of Mexican clubs has seen an influx of foreign players to its leagues

Caribbean
Players from Trinidad, Jamaica, and the French-speaking islands have found success in English and French soccer

Colombia, Ecuador, and Peru
As players from Argentina and Brazil have left for Europe, Colombians, Ecuadorians, and Peruvians have stepped into the breach

158 The number of Brazilians playing in top European leagues in 2008

60 The percentage of Premiership squads made up of overseas players in 2008

0 The number of foreign players at Guadalajara and Athletic Bilbao—both have Mexican- and Basque-only policies respectively

400 The amount in millions of dollars (£275 million) spent by UK Premiership clubs on foreign players in 2007

FROM MINNOWS TO MAJORS

NORTHAMPTON TOWN
Until 1961, the small English club had only been promoted out of the bottom league twice. In that year, however, it set out on a roller-coaster ride of success and failure. Promoted in successive years from 1962 to '64, the club reached its zenith in 1965–66, when it played its only season of top-flight soccer. The club was then relegated every year until 1968, when "normal service" was resumed in division four.

COTONSPORT
For years Coton Sport was just the amateur works team of Cameroon's largest cotton company. However, in 1986 it joined the Cameroonian league and, in 1993, was promoted to the top level. The team has been in the top two leagues ever since. Coton Sport played its first African Champions League final in 2008, narrowly losing to Cairo's venerable Al-Ahly.

TSG 1899 HOFFENHEIM
In the late 1990s, TSG 1899 Hoffenheim—an amateur club from the suburbs of small-town Sinsheim in southern Germany—was languishing in the fifth level of German soccer. Dietmar Hopp, founder and owner of the software giant SAP, had played for the club in his youth and it was his financial backing that took them all the way to the Bundesliga in 2008.

The club was at the top of the league by Christmas of the first season, no mean feat given that it was all achieved away from home (Hopp was still building a new 30,000-seat stadium).

SÃO CAETANO
São Caetano is an anonymous suburb of São Paulo, Brazil, and the team was only founded in 1989. In 2000, however, the madness of the Brazilian league saw teams from the second and third divisions play the top teams of the first division for the national title—São Caetano made it to the final. Although the club didn't win, it continued its top-flight run the following year, making it to the finals of the Copa Libertadores.

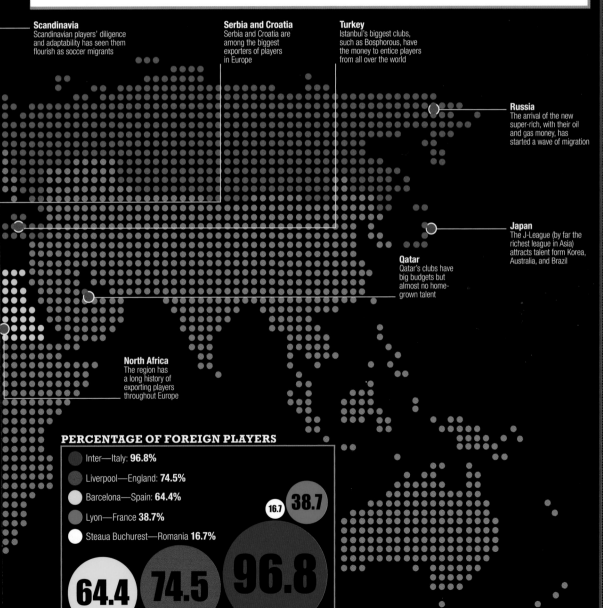

Scandinavia
Scandinavian players' diligence and adaptability has seen them flourish as soccer migrants

Serbia and Croatia
Serbia and Croatia are among the biggest exporters of players in Europe

Turkey
Istanbul's biggest clubs, such as Bosphorous, have the money to entice players from all over the world

Russia
The arrival of the new super-rich, with their oil and gas money, has started a wave of migration

Japan
The J-League (by far the richest league in Asia) attracts talent form Korea, Australia, and Brazil

Qatar
Qatar's clubs have big budgets but almost no home-grown talent

North Africa
The region has a long history of exporting players throughout Europe

PERCENTAGE OF FOREIGN PLAYERS

- Inter—Italy: **96.8%**
- Liverpool—England: **74.5%**
- Barcelona—Spain: **64.4%**
- Lyon—France **38.7%**
- Steaua Buchurest—Romania **16.7%**

16.7   38.7   64.4   74.5   96.8

PARAGUAY

HOME

AWAY

POPULATION: 6.6 MILLION
CAPITAL: ASUNCIÓN
FA: ASOCIACIÓN PARAGUAYA DE FÚTBOL

Soccer arrived in the Paraguayan capital Asunción in the late 1890s with the Dutch teacher William Paats. In 1902, Paats helped found the nation's first club, Olimpia, and in 1903, a second club, Guaraní, was founded to provide some opposition.

COPA AMÉRICA HOST

In 1953, Paraguay had the honor of hosting their first Copa América. However, the state of Paraguay's soccer infrastructure was so poor that despite retaining administrative control of the tournament, the Paraguayan governing body held it in Lima, Peru.

CAPITAL TEAM

Olimpia won three Copa Libertadores under the presidency of Osvaldo Dibbs, a central figure in Paraguayan political life. He is a very successful businessman and married into the family of dictator General Strossner.

NATIONAL TEAM

NICKNAME: La Albirroja ("White and Red")
NATIONAL STADIUM: Estadio Defensores del Chaco, 36,000
WORLD CUP FINALS: 2 appearances
COPA AMÉRICA: Winners **1953**, **1979**; runners-up **1922**, **1929**, **1947**, **1949**, **1963**

MAIN DOMESTIC CLUBS

OLIMPIA
FOUNDED: Asunción, 1902
STADIUM: Manuel Ferriera, 20,000

CERRO PORTENO
FOUNDED: Asunción, 1915
STADIUM: General Pablo Rojas "la Olla," 25,000

LIBERTAD
FOUNDED: Asunción, 1905
STADIUM: Dr. Nicolás Leoz, 16,000

HOME

AWAY

POPULATION: 3.46 MILLION
CAPITAL: MONTEVIDEO
FA: ASOCIACIÓN URUGUAYA DE FÚTBOL

URUGUAY

Soccer came to Montevideo in the 1880s before a Scottish teacher founded the first team in 1893. By the early 20th century, a league had been formed, followed by professionalism in the 1930s. Uruguay has won two World Cups and two Olympic gold medals.

EL MUNDIALITO

In 1980, the ruling military dictatorship decided to promote themselves and celebrate the 50-year anniversary of the first World Cup by staging a mini "world cup" of past champions. England would not go, so the Dutch went instead. Not surprisingly, Uruguay won.

CHAMPIONSHIP COW

For most of the 20th century, all the soccer teams in the Uruguayan top division were from Montevideo. In 1998, a provincial team was finally promoted. Since then places have been allocated to teams from outside of the capital. In 2004, Rochas was the first provincial side to win the league, and celebrated by parading a cow around their field.

ENZO FRANCESCOLI

A graceful striker, Francescoli was a hero for many of the game's greatest players, including Zinédine Zidane, who named one of his sons after him.

NATIONAL TEAM

NICKNAME: Charrúas, La Celeste Olímpica ("Olympic Sky Blue"), La Celeste ("The Sky Blue")
NATIONAL STADIUM: Centenario, 65,000
WORLD CUP FINALS: 9 appearances, winners **1930**, **1950**
COPA AMÉRICA: Winners **1916**, **1917**, **1920**, **1923**, **1924**, **1926**, **1935**, **1942**, **1956**, **1959**, **1967**, **1983**, **1987**, **1995**

MAIN DOMESTIC CLUBS

NACIONAL
FOUNDED: Montevideo, 1899
STADIUM: Parque Central, 20,000

PEÑAROL
FOUNDED: Montevideo, 1891
STADIUM: Centenario, 65,000

UNIVERSITY VS THE RAILROADS

Domestic soccer has been dominated by a century-long struggle between two teams. Nacional play in the national colors and were founded by rich students. Peñarol, founded as a railroad club, is seen as the team of the poor.

CHILE

HOME   AWAY

Soccer arrived in Chile in the late 19th century via British sailors. The first club, Santiago Wanderers, was founded in Valparaíso in 1892. A Santiago league was in place by 1895, although the provincial teams did not join until the 1950s.

POPULATION: 16.1 MILLION
CAPITAL: SANTIAGO
FA: FEDERACIÓN DE FÚTBOL DE CHILE

MIXED HISTORY

In November 1973, two months after General Pinochet's military coup, Chile qualified for the 1974 World Cup by scoring a goal with no opposition on the field. The Soviet Union, their opponents, had refused to play the match because the national stadium was also being used as a prison camp.

BANKRUPTCY BENEFITS

In 2002, Colo Colo, the nation's biggest soccer club, went bankrupt with debts of at least $30 million dollars. The players were forced to arrange friendlies and benefit concerts to raise funds. They were rewarded by larger turnouts than the club had been getting before the collapse.

MARCELO SALAS
One of Chile's most famous soccer sons, Salas is known as *El Matador* ("The Killer") thanks to his lethal left foot and slew of spectacular goals.

STAT ATTACK

NATIONAL TEAM

NICKNAME: La Roja ("The Red One")
NATIONAL STADIUM: El Nacional, 77,000
WORLD CUP FINALS: 7 appearances
COPA AMÉRICA: Runners-up **1955**, **1956**, **1977**, **1987**

MAIN DOMESTIC CLUBS

COLO COLO
FOUNDED: Santiago, 1925
STADIUM: El Monumental, 62,500

UNIVERSIDAD DE CHILE
FOUNDED: Santiago, 1911
STADIUM: El Nacional, 77,000

COBRELOA
FOUNDED: Calama, 1977
STADIUM: El Municipal, 20,200

BOLIVIA

HOME   AWAY

POPULATION: 8.9 MILLION
CAPTIAL: LA PAZ
FA: FEDERACIÓN BOLIVIANA DE FÚTBOL

Bolivian soccer began in 1896 with the formation of Royal Oruro Club using teams of railroad workers. Traditionally, The Strongest and Bolivar from high in the Andes dominate. More recently, the teams from the lowlands such as Jorge Westerman have challenged them.

THE ALTITUDE GAME

In 2007, FIFA banned international matches being played above 9,022 ft (2,750 m), which meant that Bolivia could not play home games in La Paz. A campaign by President Evo Morales saw the ban rescinded a year later.

WORLD CUP GOAL

Bolivia's appearance at the 1994 World Cup tournament was their best yet. They didn't win a match, but they did score in their 3–1 defeat by Spain. In 1930, they lost 4–0 to both Yugoslavia and Brazil, and in 1950 lost 8–0 to Uruguay.

STAT ATTACK

NATIONAL TEAM

NICKNAME: La Verde ("The Green One")
NATIONAL STADIUM: Estadio Hernando Siles, 45,000
WORLD CUP FINALS: 3 appearances
COPA AMÉRICA: Winners **1963**

MAIN DOMESTIC CLUBS

BOLIVAR
FOUNDED: La Paz, 1925
STADIUM: Libertador Bolivar, 25,000

JORGE WISTERMAN
FOUNDED: Cochabamba, 1949
STADIUM: Félix Capriles, 35,000

THE STRONGEST
FOUNDED: La Paz, 1908
STADIUM: Rafael Castellón, 15,000

PERU

HOME   AWAY

POPULATION: 28.7 MILLION
CAPITAL: LIMA
FA: FEDERACIÓN PERUANA DE FÚTBOL

By 1900, the wealthy elite of Lima had adopted soccer from British expatriates. The urban poor were also quick to join in, creating Alianza Lima in 1901 in La Victoria, the working-class area of the capital. Peru peaked with the 1970s side led by Teófilo Cubillas. The side attended two World Cups and won the Copa América, although required the toss of a coin to beat Brazil in the semi-final.

1936 OLYMPICS

Peru's exuberant, multi-racial team beat Austria 4–2 in the quarter-finals of the 1936 Berlin Olympics. The Nazi authorities were desperate for a Germanic team to progress so insisted on a replay due to Peruvian fan celebrations on the field. Peru went home in disgust.

THE ESTADIO NACIONAL DISASTER

Angry scenes among Peru fans at the end of a 1964 Olympic qualifying defeat to Argentina led police to fire tear gas into the crowd at Lima's Estadio Nacional ground. More than 350 people died in the resulting stampede, the highest fatality of any stadium disaster.

STAT ATTACK

NATIONAL TEAM

NATIONAL STADIUM:
Estadio Nacional, 45,500
WORLD CUP FINALS: 4 appearances, quarter-finals **1970**
COPA AMÉRICA: 28 appearances, winner **1939** and **1975**

MAIN DOMESTIC CLUBS

UNIVERSITARIO DE DEPORTES
FOUNDED: Lima, 1924
STADIUM: Teodoro Lolo Fernández

ALIANZA LIMA
FOUNDED: Lima, 1901
STADIUM: Alejandro Villanueva

SPORTING CRISTAL
FOUNDED: Lima, 1922
STADIUM: San Martín de Porres

TEÓFILO **CUBILLAS**

Nicknamed "The Babe," midfielder Cubillas scored in every Peru game at the 1970 World Cup, and won South American Player of the Year in 1972.

BORN: MARCH 8, 1949, LIMA, PERU
HEIGHT: **5FT 8IN (1.73M)**
MAIN CLUBS: **ALIANZA LIMA, PORTO**
INTERNATIONAL CAPS: **81**

STAT ATTACK

NATIONAL TEAM

NATIONAL STADIUM:
Olímpico Atahualpa, 41,000
WORLD CUP FINALS: 2 appearances
COPA AMÉRICA: 24 appearances, semi-finals **1959**, **1993**

MAIN DOMESTIC CLUBS

EL NACIONAL
FOUNDED: Quito, 1964
STADIUM: Olímpico Atahualpa

BARCELONA
FOUNDED: Guayaquil, 1929
STADIUM: Monumental

LDU QUITO
FOUNDED: Quito, 1930
STADIUM: Casa Blanca

ECUADOR

HOME   AWAY

POPULATION: 13.5 MILLION
CAPITAL: QUITO
FA: FEDERACIÓN ECUATORIANA DE FÚTBOL

Soccer came to Ecuador in 1898 with European students in the port of Guayaquil. A city-wide league was in existence by 1908, and the game spread to the capital city, Quito, by the 1930s. Ecuador's international results have improved since 2002.

WORLD CUP 2002

Ecuador has been a minor player for much of its history, but the 21st century has brought a change in fortunes. The national team qualified for the World Cup for the first time in 2002, and reached the second round in 2006.

FOUNDING ORIGINS

Barcelona, Ecuador's leading club, was founded by Catalan immigrants. El Nacional is the team of the Ecuadorian armed forces, while LDU Quito are tied to the city's University.

VENEZUELA

HOME   AWAY

POPULATION: 26 MILLION
CAPITAL: CARACAS
FA: FEDERACIÓN VENEZOLANA DE FÚTBOL

Soccer in Venezuela suffers from competition with baseball, the national sport. The game has improved in the 2000s, though only relatively, with modest World Cup qualifying wins for the national side and first-round victories in the Copa Libertadores.

SLOW STARTERS
Venezuela has been called the Cenicienta ("Cinderella") team of South American soccer, winning just two games in their first 30 years. In 2007, Venezuela hosted the Copa América for the first time and put in their best ever performance, winning their group before losing 4–1 to Uruguay in the quarter-finals.

STAT ATTACK

NATIONAL TEAM

NATIONAL STADIUM: None
WORLD CUP FINALS: No appearances
COPA AMÉRICA: 14 appearances, quarter-finals **2007**

MAIN DOMESTIC CLUBS

CARACAS FC
FOUNDED: Caracas, 1967
STADIUM: Estadio Olímpico

DEPORTIVO TÁCHARIA
FOUNDED: San Cristóbal, 1974
STADIUM: Polideportivo de Pueblo Nuevo

COLOMBIA

HOME   AWAY

POPULATION: 43.6 MILLION
CAPITAL: BOGOTÁ
FA: FEDERACIÓN DE COLUMBIANA DE FÚTBOL

Soccer was slow to gain popularity in Colombia, first catching on in the ports in the early 20th century before spreading to the big cities in the 1930s and 1940s. Ever since the national league was set up in 1948, the domestic game has been plagued by corruption.

INTERNATIONAL SUCCESS
Columbia has been to four World Cups, but has yet to qualify from the group stages. The 2001 Copa América win was wildly celebrated but the country's finest hour was a 5–0 World Cup qualifying win over Argentina in 1993.

DOMESTIC CORRUPTION
Soccer in Columbia has had a history of being tinged by corruption. Opposing teams were controlled by rival drug cartels in the 1970s, and betting scams and intimidation of officials escalated to the extent that Columbia gave up the right to host the 1986 World Cup.

CARLOS **VALDERRAMA**
A great—if inconsistent—player, Valderrama was never one to run if a cultured pass would do. He was instrumental in Colombia's 1990 and 1994 World Cup campaigns.

BORN: SEPTEMBER 2, 1961, SANTA MARTA, COLOMBIA
HEIGHT: **5FT 9IN (1.75M)**
MAIN CLUBS: **INDEPENDIENTE MEDELLÍN, DEPORTIVO CALI**
INTERNATIONAL CAPS: **111**

STAT ATTACK

NATIONAL TEAM

NATIONAL STADIUM: El Campín, 48,600
WORLD CUP FINALS: **4** appearances
COPA AMÉRICA: **18** appearances, winners **2001**; runners-up **1975**; semi-finals **1987**, **1991**, **1993**, **1995**, **2004**

MAIN DOMESTIC CLUBS

MILLONARIOS
FOUNDED: Bogotá, 1946
STADIUM: El Campín

AMÉRICA DE CALI
FOUNDED: Cali**,** 1927
STADIUM: Pascual Guerrero

ATLÉTICO NACIONAL
FOUNDED: Medellín, 1942
STADIUM: Atanasio Girardot

NORTH AND CENTRAL AMERICA AND THE CARIBBEAN: CONCACAF

US

Soccer arrived in the US in the 1870s, by which time (American) football had been invented and baseball was the national sport. Strongest among immigrant communities of European Jews, central Europeans, and Italians, the game acquired an ethnic, working-class identity. Until the MLS in the 1990s, all attempts to kick-start the professional game failed.

HOME   AWAY

POPULATION: 305 MILLION
CAPITAL: WASHINGTON, D.C.
FA: UNITED STATES SOCCER FEDERATION
LICENSED PLAYERS:
MALE: 17.4 MILLION
FEMALE: 7.1 MILLION
PROFESSIONALS: 1,500
REGISTERED CLUBS: 5,000

WORLD CUP AMBITIONS

The US entered the first World Cup in 1930, beating Belgium and Paraguay 3–0 to reach the semi-finals. Their 6–1 loss to Argentina, which FIFA lists as Third Place, remains the team's highest-ever World Cup finish.

STAT ATTACK

NATIONAL TEAM

NICKNAME: Yanks, or Red, White, and Blue
NATIONAL STADIUM: None
WORLD CUP FINALS: 8 appearances, semi-finals **1930**, quarter-finals **2002**
CONCACAF CHAMPIONSHIPS/GOLD CUP: winners **1990, 2002, 2005, 2007**
BIGGEST WIN: 8–1 vs Cayman Islands, 1993
BIGGEST DEFEAT: 0–11 vs Norway, 1948
MOST CAPS: Cobi Jones, **164**
MOST GOALS: Landon Donavan, **36**

MAIN DOMESTIC CLUBS

DC UNITED
FOUNDED: Washington, 1995
STADIUM: RFK Memorial
CAPACITY: 56,600   HOME
INTERNATIONAL HONORS: CONCACAF Club Championship winners **1998**
LEAGUE: 4 **CUP:** 1

LA GALAXY
FOUNDED: Los Angeles, 1995
STADIUM: Home Depot Center
CAPACITY: 27,000   HOME
INTERNATIONAL HONORS: CONCACAF Club Championship winners **2000**
LEAGUE: 2 **CUP:** 2

CHICAGO FIRE
FOUNDED: Chicago, 1997
STADIUM: Soldier Field
CAPACITY: 20,000   HOME
INTERNATIONAL HONORS: CONCACAF Champions League 3rd place **1999, 2004**
LEAGUE: 1 **CUP:** 4

MAJOR LEAGUE SOCCER

Set up in 1996 as a condition of hosting the 1994 World Cup, Major League Soccer (MLS) started small, with just ten sides. It steadily expanded to include 17 teams, the top eight of whom compete in post-season play-offs to determine who wins the championship.

THE SOCCER LEAGUE

The North American Soccer League (NASL) was founded in 1967 to revive the professional game in the US. Early attendance and viewing figures were low, and a number of foreign teams had to be imported and renamed to keep the show on the road. However, after the New York Cosmos signed an ageing Pelé in 1975, the NASL instantly acquired glamor and fans. Pelé stayed for five years, but by 1985, NASL was reduced to an indoor tournament and it ultimately folded.

COBI **JONES**

Starting out at England's Coventry City, Jones was one of the American stars who returned to the US to join the inaugural MLS season in 1996. He became an MLS legend, playing for LA Galaxy for 11 seasons. When he retired in 2007, the club also retired his "13" shirt.

BORN: **JUNE 16, 1970, DETROIT, MICHIGAN**
HEIGHT: **5FT 7IN (1.7M)**
MAIN CLUBS: **COVENTRY CITY, VASCO DA GAMA, LA GALAXY**
INTERNATIONAL CAPS: **164**

WORLD CUP 2002

After a disappointing 1998 World Cup, in which the US team finished 32nd out of 32 teams, the 2002 World Cup was more positive. A 2–0 win over Mexico in the knock-out stages led to a quarter-final against Germany, which ended in a 1–0 defeat. That, and two Gold Cup wins in 2002 and 2005, meant that the US was fourth in the World FIFA ranking in 2006.

1894

The year owners of US baseball franchises tried to run a professional winter soccer league in their ballparks—it lasted a single season

8

The number of goals scored by the New York Cosmos in their 1977 championship play-off victory over Fort Lauderdale—the 77,000-strong crowd at Giants Stadium was also a new record for soccer in the US

CANADA

HOME

AWAY

POPULATION: 33.1 MILLION
CAPITAL: OTTAWA
FA: CANADA SOCCER ASSOCIATION
LICENSED PLAYERS:
MALE: 1.8 MILLION
FEMALE: 86,000
PROFESSIONALS: 150
REGISTERED CLUBS: 7,000

With just one World Cup appearance and no national professional league, Canada remains small in soccer terms. The arrival of European migrants after the World War II enlivened the soccer scene for a time, but ultimately soccer has to compete against established sports such as baseball, basketball, Canadian Football, and ice hockey.

CANADIAN SOCCER LEAGUE

The top-flight division, the Canadian Soccer League, is only semi-professional. It is confined to the east coast and split into two national and international mini-leagues—the latter for teams with an explicit ethnic identity, such as Toronto Croatia, and the former for clubs with an urban affiliation, such as St. Catherine's Wolves.

WHO IS THE CHAMPION?

The three professional clubs in Canada play in the MLS and second-tier USL-1 leagues in the US. As a consequence, there was no Canadian national champion to compete in the CONCACAF championship until 2008, when a round-robin play-off between the three pro teams was started. Montreal emerged victorious, becoming Canada's first representative in 33 years.

INTERNATIONAL PLAYERS

The Canadian national team would possibly do better if more of the best players eligible to join them did so; but the best often seem to have relatives elsewhere. The excellent Jonathan de Guzman, playing with Feyenoord, chose Holland while his brother Julius remained a mainstay of the Canadian midfield. Owen Hargreaves, of Manchester United, chose England.

WORLD CUP 1986

Canada secured their spot at the 1986 World Cup by beating Honduras 2–1 in St. John's, Newfoundland, in 1985. In the final, however, Canada lost their first match 1–0 to France and, after further defeats by 2–0 to both Hungary and the USSR, they went home without gaining a single point or scoring a single goal.

PAUL PESCHISOLIDO

A well-traveled player, Peschisolido has played for several clubs on both sides of the Atlantic. He has scored 12 goals in his 53 appearances for Canada.

BORN: **MAY 25, 1971,**
SCARBOROUGH, ONTARIO, CANADA
HEIGHT: **5FT 7IN (1.7M)**
MAIN CLUBS: **TORONTO BLIZZARD,**
BIRMINGHAM CITY, STOKE CITY, FULHAM,
SHEFFIELD UNITED, DERBY COUNTY
INTERNATIONAL CAPS: 53

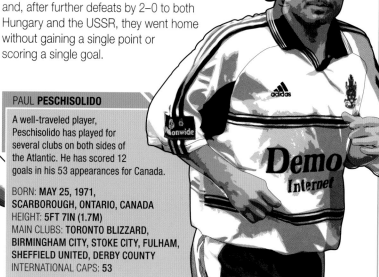

THE FLIP OF A COIN

Canada won the 2000 CONCACAF Gold Cup, beating Columbia 2–0 in the final. However, the victory ultimately rested on the toss of a coin. Having finished level with South Korea in the group stage, a coin had to be flipped to determine who went through to the knock-out stages.

STAT ATTACK

NATIONAL TEAM

NICKNAME: The Canucks, Les Rouges ("The Reds")
NATIONAL STADIUM: none
WORLD CUP FINALS: 1 appearance, **1986**
CONCACAF CHAMPIONSHIPS/GOLD CUP: 6 appearances, winners **2000**
BIGGEST WIN: 7–0 vs USA, 1904
BIGGEST DEFEAT: 0–8 vs Mexico, 1983
MOST CAPS: Randy Samuel, **82**
MOST GOALS: Dale Mitchell, **19**

MAIN DOMESTIC CLUBS

TORONTO FC
FOUNDED: Toronto, 2006
STADIUM: BMO Field
CAPACITY: 20,000
INTERNATIONAL HONORS: None
LEAGUE: 0 **CUP:** 0

MONTREAL IMPACT
FOUNDED: Montreal, 1992
STADIUM: Claude Robillard
CAPACITY: 14,000
INTERNATIONAL HONORS: None
LEAGUE: 2 **CUP:** 7

VANCOUVER WHITE CAPS
FOUNDED: Vancouver, 1986
STADIUM: Swangard
CAPACITY: 6,100
INTERNATIONAL HONORS: None
LEAGUE: 6 **CUP:** 0

MEXICO

HOME   AWAY

Soccer was brought to Mexico City in the late 19th century by British expatriates and French and Spanish immigrants. The first club, Pachuca Athletic, was founded in 1900 by British engineers, and was soon joined by other teams from Mexico City. After the Mexican Revolution of 1920–30, key Mexican teams emerged—América, Atlanta, and Necaxa. UNAM followed in the 1950s, Cruz Arul in the 1970s, and Toros Neza in 1991.

POPULATION: 107.5 MILLION
CAPITAL: MEXICO CITY
FA: FEDERACIÓN MEXICANA DE FÚTBOL ASOCIACIÓN
LICENSED PLAYERS:
MALE: 325,000
FEMALE: 13,000
PROFESSIONALS: 4,500
REGISTERED CLUBS: 311

STAT ATTACK

NATIONAL TEAM

NICKNAME: El Tri ("Three-colored Flag")
NATIONAL STADIUM: Estadio Azteca, 101,000
WORLD CUP FINALS: 11 appearances, quarter-finals 1970 and 1980
CONCACAF CHAMPIONSHIPS: Winners **1965**, **1971**, **1977**, **1993**, **1996**, **1998**, **2003**
BIGGEST WIN: 11–0 vs St. Vincent and the Grenadines, 1992
BIGGEST DEFEAT: 0–8 vs England, 1961
MOST CAPS: Claudio Suárez, 178
MOST GOALS: Jared Borgetti, 46

OLYMPIC PLAYERS

Mexico was absent from the 1990 World Cup following a ban from international competition after fielding over-age players in the qualifiers for the 1988 Olympics under-20 competition.

A NATIONAL LEAGUE

The difficulties of getting teams around Mexico because of its sheer size and the lack of transportation meant there were only regional leagues and cup competitions until a national league was created in 1944. In the 1970s, the league format shifted to its current structure, in which many small groups of teams compete for places in a play-off system to determine the championship. In 1996 the league was split into two separate championships—an *Apertura* ("Opening") and a *Clausura* ("Closing"). The Mexican Cup was discontinued in 1999.

NORTH, SOUTH, OR CENTRAL AMERICA

Mexico's geographical position means teams compete in a variety of continental competitions such as the North-American, the Pan-American, and the Central-American games. Since CONCACAF was formed, Mexico has played in its Gold Cup and club competitions, but regularly attends South American tournaments.

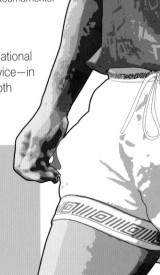

HOSTS BUT NOT CHAMPIONS

Mexico has played well at World Cups it has hosted. The national team has made it to the quarter finals of the tournament twice—in 1970, losing to Italy, and in 1986, losing to Germany. On both occasions they were the host nation.

HUGO **SÁNCHEZ MÁRQUEZ**

The most successful ever Mexican soccer player, Márquez played in Spain for most of his professional career, where he scored more than 200 goals for Real Madrid between 1985 and 1992.

BORN: JULY 11, 1958, MEXICO CITY, MEXICO
HEIGHT: 5FT 9IN (1.75M)
MAIN CLUBS: SAN DIEGO SOCKERS, ATLÉTICO MADRID, REAL MADRID, AMÉRICA, RAYO VALLECANO, ATLANTE, LINZ, DALLAS BURN, ATLÉTICO CELAYA
INTERNATIONAL CAPS: 75

NICKNAME
AZULCREMAS
("BLUE AND CREAMS")

HOME

FOUNDED: MEXICO CITY, 1916

STADIUM: ESTADIO AZTECA, 101,000

DOMESTIC HONORS: LEAGUE: 14 CUP: 6

INTERNATIONAL HONORS: CONCACAF CLUB CHAMPIONSHIP 1977, 1990, 1992, 2006

CF AMÉRICA

For half a century, CF América was the team of the ruling order and its twin pillars, the main political party, the PRI, and Televisia—the main TV station. The giant TV conglomerate Televisia has shaped the landscape of Mexico City's soccer, and for many years, the club received privileged network coverage.

JORGE CAMPOS
Well known for his self-designed garish goalkeeping kits, Campos was sometimes played as striker.

EL CLÁSICO

El Clásico is the derby game between CF América and Guadalajara—the two biggest and best supported teams in Mexico. The competition is all the greater as it is the team from the capital playing the one from the provinces.

EL CLÁSICO

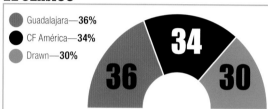

- Guadalajara—**36%**
- CF América—**34%**
- Drawn—**30%**

34
36
30

NICKNAME: LOS
CHIVAS ("THE GOATS")

FOUNDED: GUADALAJARA, 1906 **HOME**

STADIUM: JALISCO, 56,700

DOMESTIC HONORS: LEAGUE: 11 CUP: 2

INTERNATIONAL HONORS: CONCACAF CLUB CHAMPIONSHIP 1962

GUADALAJARA

More commonly known as *Los Chivas* or "the goats," Guadalajara has never been out of the Mexican top flight and they have done so fielding only Mexican-born players—a recruitment policy the club began in 1943. Ironically, Guadalajara began life as Club Union founded by a Belgian and a Frenchman. The club has recently been revitalized by its owner-president, Mexican businessman Jorge Vergara Era—the vitamin king.

1985
The year of the Azteca disaster—ten were killed and 29 injured in a crush at the Mexican Cup Final between UNAM and América

23
The number of different clubs who have won the Mexican national championships

3
The number of Pan-American games titles won by the Mexican national team

107,412
Official attendance at the final of the 1970 World Cup in the famous Estadio Azteca, Mexico City

BEST OF THE REST

CRUZ AZUL (1927)
The team of working class Mexico City, it was founded just outside the city in Jasso in 1927. In 2001 it was first Mexican team to reach the final of the Copa Libertadores.
HONORS: LEAGUE 8, CUP 2; CONCACAF CLUB CHAMPIONSHIP 1969–71, 1996–97

ATLANTE (1916)
Founded in 1916, the club began as Sinaola, switched to Lusitania and U-53 before settling on Atlante. It draws its support from its roots in the inner-city zones of Mexico City.
HONORS: LEAGUE 5, CUP 3; CONCACAF CLUB CHAMPIONSHIP 1983

TOLUCA (1917)
Founded in 1917 Toluca was successful in the 1960s and 1970s. In 2003 this provincial team won the CONCACAF Championship in the first all-Mexican final against Morelia.
HONORS: LEAGUE 8, CUP 2; CONCACAF CLUB CHAMPIONSHIP 1968, 2003

UNAM (1954)
The club was founded as the team of the University of Mexico. No longer run by the university, nor fielding students, it retains its commitment to supporting young players.
HONORS: LEAGUE 5, CUP 1; CONCACAF CLUB CHAMPIONSHIP 1980, 1982, 1989

PACHUCA (1901)
The oldest Mexican club languished in the lower divisions. It reached the top flight in 1998, won the national championship in 1999, and the Copa Sudamericana in 2006.
HONORS: LEAGUE 7, CUP 4; CONCACAF CLUB CHAMPIONSHIP 2002, 2007

NECAXA (1923)
For nearly 80 years, Necaxa was based in Mexico City. They were bought by Televisia and in 2002 were moved north to a town without a top-flight team—Aguascalientes.
HONORS: LEAGUE 15, CUP 5; CONCACAF CLUB CHAMPIONSHIP 1999

DOMESTIC CLUBS

LA GALAXY
The second US team to win an international competition, LA Galaxy have also won two MLS titles. The team was hit hard by the death of general manager Doug Hamilton at the start of the 2006 season. The Galaxy's greatest coup was the signing of David Beckham in 2007, although the talismanic Englishman failed to restore the team to winning ways.

HONORS: LEAGUE 2, **CUP** 2; **CONCACAF CHAMPIONS LEAGUE WINNERS** 2000

DC UNITED
One of the ten founder members of the MLS in 1996, DC United is the most successful club in the league so far, with four domestic titles to their name. In 1998, DC became the first US team to win both the CONCACAF Champions Cup and the Copa Interamerica in the same year, famously beating CONMEBOL team Vasco de Gama of Rio 2–1 in the latter.

HONORS: LEAGUE 4, **CUP** 1; **CONCACAF CHAMPIONS LEAGUE** WINNERS, 1998

MUNICIPAL
Founded by workers of Guatemala City Council, Municipal is the most successful team in Guatemalan soccer. They have never been out of the top division ever since it was founded in 1942, and have won the title a record 26 times. Occasional competitors in CONCACAF contests, Municipal won the Champions Cup in 1974.

HONORS: LEAGUE 26, **CUP** 8; **CONCACAF CHAMPIONS LEAGUE** WINNERS 1974

COMUNICACIONES
Nicknamed Los Cremas ("The Creams"), Comunicaciones is Guatemala City's second team, trailing behind Municipal in the domestic and continental honors tables. That said, they have twice been runners-up in the CONCACAF Champions Cup, and have won 21 domestic league titles. Comunicaciones has always been owned by the Garcia-Granados, a powerful industrial and political family.

HONORS: LEAGUE 21, **CUP** 8

CONCACAF: TOP CLUBS

Mexican clubs, traditionally the strongest in the sides in CONCACAF, viewed the rest of the federation with disdain for many years, even refusing to play in the Champions League. Since reversing this decision, teams from Mexico have regularly won the contest. The next-best clubs are those from the US, Costa Rica, Honduras, El Salvador, Surinam, and Trinidad.

UNITED STATES
Given the dominance of the US over international soccer in the region, the fact that US clubs have yet to stamp their authority on CONCACAF competitions is all the more surprising. Only LA Galaxy and DC United have proved good enough to push the Mexican teams aside and challenge for the CONCACAF Champions League, each winning the trophy on one occasion.

THE LOST WORLD
Surinam is the forgotten powerhouse of CONCACAF club soccer. Robin Hood, the leading team, has played and lost four CONCACAF Champions Cup finals, although the last was in 1982. SV Transvaal, Surinam's second team, has reached six finals of the CONCACAF Champion's Cup and managed to win two of them.

ALEXI LALAS
Lalas was one of the leading US players of his generation, winning 96 caps and playing at the 1994 World Cup.

DOMESTIC CLUBS

CLUB FAS
Club FAS—or to give them their full title, Club Deportivo Futbolistas Asociados Santanecos—is the most successful and best-supported Salvadorian Club. The team's high point was winning the CONCACAF Champions Cup in 1979. Nicknamed Tigrillos ("Tigers"), the club has a long history of importing Argentinean and Brazilian players.

HONORS: LEAGUE 16, **CUP** 0; **CONCACAF CHAMPIONS LEAGUE** WINNERS, 1979

OLIMPIA
The leading club in Honduras, Olimpia is based in the capital city Tegucigalpa. The Leones ("Lions") are the only Honduran club to win two CONCACAF Champions Cups. Olimpia is also notable as the first Honduran club to export a player to a European team, selling striker David Suazo to Italian Serie A side Cagliari in 1999.

HONORS: LEAGUE 21, **CUP** 2; **CONCACAF CHAMPIONS LEAGUE** WINNERS 1973, 1988

MARATHÓN
The second-most-successful team in Honduras, Marathón acquired their name after the founders ordered a soccer ball from a Chicago mail order firm—a football arrived stamped with the name "marathon," which they took for themselves. In 1981, Marathón became the first Honduran team to beat a Mexican team in an official match, defeating Cruz Azul 3–1 in the Champions Cup.

HONORS: LEAGUE 7, **CUP** 1

THE CLUBS

CONCACAF is composed of three distinct regions. Mexican teams—not included on this map—are in a different world, being much richer and better supported than any others in the region. US teams are approaching the success of the Mexicans, but lagging behind both are the Caribbean and Central American clubs.

DC United
Country: United States
Founded:
Washington DC, 1995
Stadium:
RFK Memorial Stadium
Capacity: 56,500

Marathón
Country: Honduras
Founded: San Pedro Sula, 1925
Stadium: Estadio Olímpico
Metropolitano
Capacity: 45,000

Saprissa
Country: Costa Rica
Founded: San Jose, 1935
Stadium: Ricardo Sparissa
Capacity: 21,300

Olimpia
Country: Honduras
Founded:
Tegucigalpa, 1912
Stadium: Estadio
Tiburcio Carias Andino
Capacity: 35,000

LA Galaxy
Country: United States
Founded:
Los Angeles, 1995
Stadium:
Home Depot Center
Capacity: 27,000

Club FAS
Country: El Salvador
Founded: Santa
Anna, 1947
Stadium: Estadio
Oscar Quiteño
Capacity: 15,000

Cartaginés
Country: Costa Rica
Founded: Cartago, 1906
Stadium: Estadio José Rafael
Fello Meza Ivankovich
Capacity: 18,000

Comunicaciones
Country: Guatemala
Founded:
Guatemala City, 1949
Stadium: Estadio
Mateo Flores
Capacity: 30,000

Municipal
Country: Guatemala
Founded: Guatemala City, 1936
Stadium: Estadio Mateo Flores
Capacity: 30,000

Alajuelense
Country: Costa Rica
Founded: Alajuela, 1919
Stadium: Alejandro Morera Soto
Capacity: 22,500

CENTRAL AMERICA

Central America has a wealth of soccer talent, but the sport has suffered from competition from baseball, desperate economic conditions, and even civil war in several countries, which have combined to make the task of creating great clubs even harder. Currently the Costa Rican duo of Saprissa and Alajuelense are the regions' strongest clubs by far.

[AT FIFA] I HAVE NEVER SEEN...
ONE IOTA OF CORRUPTION

JACK WARNER, PRESIDENT OF CONCACAF
REPORTED IN THE TRINIDAD EXPRESS, DECEMBER 12, 2004

DOMESTIC CLUBS

ALAJUELENSE
Starting out as El Once de Abril ("The Eleventh of April"), Alajuelense was formed by a group of friends in the city of Alajuela, Costa Rica. As well as many domestic titles, the club has won two CONCACAF Champions Cups. The club mascot is a lion, but in previous years, it was a mango, in homage to the town of Alajuela, which is nicknamed "The City of Mangoes."

HONORS: LEAGUE 24, CUP 2; CONCACAF CHAMPIONS LEAGUE WINNERS 1986, 2004

SAPRISSA
Based in San José, Costa Rica, Saprissa is nicknamed "The Purple Monster" and their stadium is known as La Cueva del Monstruo ("The Monster's Cave"). They have won numerous domestic titles and three CONCACAF Champions Cups. They went to the World Club Cup in 2005 and came third.

HONORS: LEAGUE 26, CUP 3; CONCACAF CHAMPIONS LEAGUE WINNERS 1993, 1995, 2005

CARTAGINÉS
The oldest club in Costa Rica, Cartaginés is the most recent challenger to the Saprissa-Alajuelense duopoly, winning the CONCACAF Champions Cup in 1994. Their last domestic title was in 1940, and their failure to win another has been ascribed to the curse of a priest at the Basilica de Los Ángles, where players celebrated the 1940 title on horseback.

HONORS: LEAGUE 3, CUP 0; CONCACAF CHAMPIONS LEAGUE WINNERS 1994

AFRICA: CAF

ALGERIA

HOME

AWAY

POPULATION: 32.9 MILLION
CAPITAL: ALGIERS
FA: FÉDÉRATION ALGÉRIENNE DE FOOTBALL

Soccer was popular in Algeria before World War I, with clubs strictly aligned to the French colonists or Algerians. In the 1950s, the Algerian FA became a section of the French FA. Since independence in 1962, Algerian soccer has been a major success.

AMBASSADORS FOR INDEPENDENCE

In 1958, at the height of the Algerian War of Independence, a group of French-Algerian players left France to form a team representing FNL—the the leading force behind the Algerian struggle for independence. This team included Rachid Mekloufi, also a member of the French World Cup squad.

OUTSTANDING SUCCESS

JS Kabylie are the most successful and best-supported team in modern Algerian soccer. From the Berber region of Algeria, they are an icon of ethnic pride and identity. Their recent form in African club cups has been exceptional.

STAT ATTACK

NATIONAL TEAM

NICKNAME: Les Fennecs ("Desert Foxes")
NATIONAL STADIUM: 5 Juillet, 70,000
WORLD CUP FINALS: 2 appearances
AFRICAN CUP OF NATIONS: Winners **1990**

MAIN DOMESTIC CLUBS

JS KABYLIE
FOUNDED: Tizi-Ouzu, 1946
STADIUM: 1er Novembre 1954, 20,000

USM ALGER
FOUNDED: Algiers, 1932
STADIUM: Omar Hamadi, 15,000

MC ALGER
FOUNDED: Algiers, 1921
STADIUM: 5 Juillet, 70,000

EGYPT

HOME

AWAY

POPULATION: 76.1 MILLION
CAPITAL: CAIRO
FA: EGYPTIAN FOOTBALL ASSOCIATION

The British soldiers that occupied Egypt in the late 19th century brought soccer to Cairo. Al-Ahly—the oldest club in Africa—was founded in 1907. A second team, Farouk (later Zamalek)—named after the King of Egypt—was formed soon after. Egypt was the first African team to be represented at the Olympics and the World Cup.

STAT ATTACK

NATIONAL TEAM

NICKNAME: The Pharoahs
NATIONAL STADIUM: Cairo Stadium, 74,100
WORLD CUP FINALS: 2 appearances
AFRICAN CUP OF NATIONS: Winners **1957, 1959, 1986, 1998, 2006, 2008**

MAIN DOMESTIC CLUBS

AL-AHLY
FOUNDED: Cairo, 1907
STADIUM: Cairo Stadium, 74,100

ZAMALEK
FOUNDED: Cairo, 1911
STADIUM: Cairo Stadium, 74,100

FAMOUS YELLOW CARD

Political pressure from the highest levels of the Egyptian government at the 1986 African Cup of Nations saw a yellow card against Egyptian star Tahar Abouzif rescinded. Abouzif had initially been booked for his wild celebrations after scoring a goal in the semi-finals and he was due to miss the final against Cameroon. In the event, Egypt won the final on penalties.

DOMESTIC RIVALRY

Al-Ahly means "the nation." Initially the club founded by wealthy Egyptians attracted elite liberal republicans who were opposed to the conservative royalists grouped around Zamalek. Now both clubs draw support from every level of Egyptian society and between them they have made Egypt the most successful country in African club soccer. The eternal rivalry between the two clubs has dominated Egyptian soccer since they were founded.

HOSSAM HASSAN
Egypt's most capped player and top goalscorer, Hassan became a managerial legend overnight when, in his first job, he saved Egyptian side El-Masry from relegation in 2007–08.

MOROCCO

HOME   AWAY

POPULATION: 33.2 MILLION
CAPITAL: RABAT
FA: FÉDÉRATION ROYALE
MAROCAINE DE FOOTBALL

The French played soccer in Morocco but excluded the locals. The first Arab club, Wydad Casablanca, was founded in 1937 and was joined in 1949 by a workers club, Raja Casablanca. The army team, FAR Rabat, has since joined them at the top of Moroccan soccer.

STAT ATTACK

NATIONAL TEAM

NICKNAME: Lions of the Atlas
NATIONAL STADIUM:
Stade Mohammed V, 60,000
WORLD CUP FINALS: 4 appearances
AFRICAN CUP OF NATIONS:
Winners **1976**

WORLD CUP FIRSTS

Morocco was the first African team to win a group at the World Cup. In 1986, they finished ahead of Portugal, Poland, and England. They were also the first African team to make it to the second round of the tournament. However, in the first match, they lost to a late West German goal.

MAIN DOMESTIC CLUBS

FAR RABAT
FOUNDED: Rabat, 1957
STADIUM: Moulay Abdallah, 60,000

WYDAD CASABLANCA
FOUNDED: Casablanca, 1937
STADIUM: Stade Mohammed V, 60,000

RAJA CASABLANCA
FOUNDED: Casablanca, 1949
STADIUM: Stade Mohammed V, 60,000

ROYAL SUPPORT

King Mohammed IV was such a big fan of Wydad Casablanca that he persuaded the French colonial authorities to install a phone line between his palace and the club's dressing room.

NEW TERRITORIES

The club Jeunesse Sportive Al Massira plays in the Moroccan league, but they are based in Layounne, the capital of the Western Sahara. When Morocco first occupied this territory in 1975, the government sponsored the building of a 30,000-seat sports stadium in an effort to integrate the territory with the rest of country. The soccer club JS Al Massira was founded in 1977.

TUNISIA

HOME   AWAY

POPULATION: 10.28 MILLION
CAPITAL: TUNIS
FA: FÉDÉRATION TUNISIENNE
DE FOOTBALL

The French and Italian colonists played soccer in Tunisia after World War I. Other migrant groups, including the Maltese, Jews, and Greeks, also formed teams. Arab clubs were established alongside these, including Esperance and their great rivals Club Africain.

STAT ATTACK

NATIONAL TEAM

NICKNAME: The Eagles of Carthage
NATIONAL STADIUM:
Stade 7 Novembre, 65,000
WORLD CUP FINALS: 4 appearances
AFRICAN CUP OF NATIONS:
Winners **2004**

AFRICAN TEAM FIRST

Tunisia was the first African team to win a game at a World Cup. In Argentina in 1978, they beat Mexico 3–1 after going 1–0 down to a questionable penalty. Tunisia's coach Chetali remarked "The world has laughed at Africa, but now the mockery is over." In recent years, Tunisian soccer has become among the strongest in Africa with three more World Cup appearances. In 2004, they hosted and won the African Cup of Nations.

PRESIDENT'S TEAM

Espérance Sportive has been the leading team in Tunisian soccer since before the nation achieved independence in 1956. They were the first Arab team to win the national championship in 1941, and have traditionally been the team of the Tunisian President.

MAIN DOMESTIC CLUBS

ESPÉRANCE SPORTIVE
FOUNDED: Tunis, 1919
STADIUM: El Menzah, 40,000

CLUB AFRICAIN
FOUNDED: Tunis, 1920
STADIUM: El Menzah, 40,000

ÉTOILE SPORTIVE DU SHAEL
FOUNDED: Souuse, 1925
STADIUM: Stade Olympique, 35,000

CS SFAXIEN
FOUNDED: Sfax, 1928
STADIUM: Stade Taieb-Mhiri, 25,000

NIGERIA

HOME   AWAY

POPULATION: 135 MILLION
CAPITAL: ABUJA
FA NAME: NIGERIA FOOTBALL ASSOCIATION
LICENSED PLAYERS:
MALE: 35,000
FEMALE: 660
PROFESSIONALS: 1,400
REGISTERED CLUBS: 365

Soccer was first played at a school in Calabar when Englishman Reverend James Luke took up the post of headmaster in 1902, bringing a soccer ball with him. The game's popularity soon spread across the country. In 1960 independence was celebrated in the new national stadium in Lagos, but civil war (1967–70) meant that a league was not established until 1972.

PREMIER LEAGUE

Nigeria runs a 20-team premier league and national cup competition. The majority of top clubs come from the cities of the south, though Kano Pillars' league victory in 2008 was the first for a northern team for over a decade.

SCHOOLBOY VICTORY

The first recorded game In Nigeria was played in June 1904 between the barefoot Nigerian schoolboys of Reverend Luke's Hope Waddell Training Institute in Calabar and the crew of the visiting Royal Navy ship *HMS Thistle*. The schoolboys won the match 3–2.

SUPERSTITION

In 1993, on the advice of a traditional healer, the Nigerian national team refused to shake hands with the Prime Minister and Sports Minister of Ivory Coast before playing a game in Abidjan.

JAY-JAY **OKOCHA**

Nigerian team captain, midfielder Okocha started his career with a local team. He moved to Europe and played for third-division German side Borussia Neunkirchen. Eight years later Paris Saint-Germain paid $24 million for his services.

BORN: **AUGUST 14, 1973, ENUGU, NIGERIA**
HEIGHT: **5FT 8IN (1.73M)**
MAIN CLUBS: **BORUSSIA NEUNKIRCHEN, EINTRACHT FRANKFURT, FENERBAHÇE, PARIS SAINT GERMAIN, BOLTON WANDERERS, QATAR SC, HULL CITY**
INTERNATIONAL CAPS: **75**

STAT ATTACK

NATIONAL TEAM

NICKNAME: Super Eagles
NATIONAL STADIUM: Abuja Stadium, 60,000
WORLD CUP FINALS: 3 appearances, quarter-finals **1994**
AFRICAN CUP OF NATIONS: winners **1980, 1994**
BIGGEST WIN: 8–1 vs Uganda, 1991
BIGGEST DEFEAT: 0–7 vs Ghana, 1955
MOST CAPS: Muda lawal, **86**
MOST GOALS: Rashidi Yekini, **37**

MAIN DOMESTIC CLUBS

SHOOTING STARS
FOUNDED: Ibadan, 1963
STADIUM:
Lekan Salami, 18,000   HOME
INTERNATIONAL HONORS: African Cup Winners Cup **1976**, CAF Cup **1992**
LEAGUE: 5 CUP: 8

ENUGU RANGERS
FOUNDED: Enugu, 1972
STADIUM:
Nnamidi Azikiwe, 25,000   HOME
INTERNATIONAL HONORS:
African Cup Winners Cup, **1977**
LEAGUE: 5 CUP: 5

ENYIMBA
FOUNDED: Aba, 1976
STADIUM:
Enyimba International, 10,000   HOME
INTERNATIONAL HONORS:
African Champions League, **2003, 2004**
LEAGUE: 5 CUP: 1

INTERNATIONAL CLUB COMPETITIONS

Nigeria's turbulence made them late bloomers in international soccer. They hosted and won their first African Cup of Nations in 1980, beating Algeria in the final 3–0 in front of an ecstatic crowd at Surelere Stadium in Lagos. The mid '90s were the Super Eagles' best years. The team won the African Cup of Nations and reached the quarter-finals of the World Cup in 1994, and won Olympic Gold in 1996.

CAMEROON

HOME

AWAY

POPULATION: 17.3 MILLION
CAPITAL: YAOUNDE
FA NAME:
FÉDÉRATION CAMEROUNAISE
DE FOOTBALL
LICENSED PLAYERS:
MALE: 750,500
FEMALE: 36,000
PROFESSIONALS: 540
REGISTERED CLUBS: 220

Soccer was first played in Cameroon by French colonial administrators, but teams formed along ethnic lines by the 1930s, with Beti, Bamilike, and English speakers supporting different sides. In the 1970s, Cameroon clubs began to win major African trophies and in 1982, the national team went to the World Cup. Cameroon has been among the elite of African soccer ever since.

DOMESTIC COMPETITION

Cameroon plays a standard league and cup competition and had a short-lived "super cup" for the winners of the two. Cotton Sport, once a tiny workers' social club from the north, has won six titles in a row.

WORLD CUP 1990

Cameroon earned their nickname—The Indomitable Lions—with three drawn games at the 1982 World Cup. However, at Italia '90 they sparkled, and made it all the way to the quarter-finals—the first African team to do so.

MVF REMEMBERED

Marc-Vivien Foé (MVF) died while playing for Cameroon at the 2003 Confederations Cup. In his honor, the whole team's warm-up kit carried his name in the final of the competition.

SAMUEL ETO'O
Barcelona striker Eto'o is the African Cup of Nations' all-time top-scorer, and the only man to be voted African Player of the Year three times in a row.

STAT ATTACK

NATIONAL TEAM

NICKNAME: The Indomitable Lions
NATIONAL STADIUM: None
WORLD CUP FINALS: 5 appearances, quarter-finals 1990
AFRICAN CUP OF NATIONS: Winners **1984**, **1988**, **2000**, **2002**
BIGGEST WIN: 9–2 vs Somalia, 1960
BIGGEST DEFEAT: 1–6 vs Norway, 1990 and vs Russia, 1994
MOST CAPS: Rigobert Song, **112**
MOST GOALS: Samuel Eto'o, **39**

MAIN DOMESTIC CLUBS

CANON YAOUNDE
FOUNDED: Yaoundé, 1930
STADIUM: Stade Ahmadou, 52,000

HOME
INTERNATIONAL HONORS: African Champions League, **1971**, **1978**, **1980**; African Cup Winners' Cup **1979**
LEAGUE: 10 **CUP:** 12

UNION DOUALA
FOUNDED: Douala, 1957
STADIUM: Stade de la Reunification, 30,000

HOME
INTERNATIONAL HONORS: African Champions League **1979**
LEAGUE: 4 **CUP:** 7

COTTON SPORT
FOUNDED: Garoua, 1986
STADIUM: Omnisport Roumde-Adjia, 22,000

HOME
INTERNATIONAL HONORS: None
LEAGUE: 9 **CUP:** 0

ROGER **MILLA**

Milla toiled in the lower reaches of French soccer for over a decade. But at the age of 38, he came to the world's attention as Cameroon's key goal scorer at Italia '90.

BORN: MAY 29, 1952, YAOUNDÉ, CAMEROON
HEIGHT: 6FT 1IN (1.85M)
MAIN CLUBS: AS MONACO, BASTIA, SAINT-ÉTIENNE, MONTPELLIER, JS SAINT-PIERROISE, TONNERRE YAOUNDÉ, PELITA JAYA
INTERNATIONAL CAPS: 102

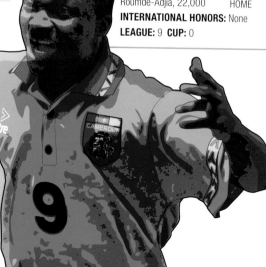

IVORY COAST

HOME   AWAY

POPULATION: 17.6 MILLION

CAPITAL: YAMOUSSOUKRO

FA: FÉDÉRATION IVOIRIENNE DE FOOTBALL

LICENSED PLAYERS:
MALE: 801,500
FEMALE: 0

PROFESSIONALS: 100

REGISTERED CLUBS: 220

Soccer was introduced to the Ivory Coast in the 1920s by French colonial officials and migrants. Locals soon joined in and the first African teams were formed in the 1930s. The national team's greatest success to date was winning the African Cup of Nations in 1992 after a marathon penalty shootout (11–0) against Ghana. In recent years the national team has prospered, but the best of the talent plays in Europe. Domestic soccer suffered because of the civil war.

WORLD-RECORD RUN

Between 1989 and 1994, ASEC Mimosas went a world-record 108 games without defeat. Their run was finally ended in a 2–1 loss to SO Armée. ASEC also has a record of nurturing top players, including Kolo and Yaya Touré.

STAT ATTACK

NATIONAL TEAM

NICKNAME: The Elephants

NATIONAL STADIUM: Stade Félix Houphouët-Boigny, 35,000

WORLD CUP FINALS: 1 appearance

AFRICAN CUP OF NATIONS: Winners **1992**

BIGGEST WIN: 6–0 vs Mali 1985, Botswana 1992, Niger 2000, and Madagascar 2001

BIGGEST DEFEAT: 2–6 vs Ghana, 1971

MOST CAPS: Didier Zokora, **72**

MAIN DOMESTIC CLUBS

ASEC MIMOSAS

FOUNDED: Abidjan, 1948

STADIUM: Stade Félix Houphouët-Boigny, 35,000

 HOME

INTERNATIONAL HONORS: African Champions League **1998**

LEAGUE: 22 **CUP:** 15

AFRICA SPORTS

FOUNDED: Abidjan, 1936

STADIUM: Stade Félix Houphouët-Boigny, 35,000

HOME

INTERNATIONAL HONORS:
Cup Winners Cup **1992**, **1999**

LEAGUE: 15 **CUP:** 13

STADE D'ABIDJAN

FOUNDED: Abidjan, 1936

STADIUM: Municipal, 9,000

HOME

INTERNATIONAL HONORS:
African Champions League **1966**

LEAGUE: 5 **CUP:** 5

DOMESTIC SUCCESS

ASEC Mimosas, or ASEC Abidjan, have been the strongest domestic team, and won the 1998 African Champions Cup—the country's only continental trophy success. They also run the most successful soccer academy in Africa, producing some outstanding players. Since the end of the civil war in 2006 the domestic game has progressed. Africa Sports have taken the top spot by winning league titles in 2007 and 2008.

WORLD CUP 2006

In their first World Cup finals appearance, the Ivory Coast had the misfortune to be placed in the most deadly group yet, containing Argentina, Holland, and Serbia and Montenegro. They lost their two opening games, but the Ivorians were not outclassed. In their final game, an extraordinary second-half rally saw them come back from 2–1 down to beat Serbia 3–2.

DIDIER **DROGBA**

Drogba was only five years old when he left Abidjan to live in France. He played in the lower divisions, initially as a defender, then as a forward. He made his breakthrough at Guingamp.

BORN: **MARCH 11, 1978, ABIDJAN, CÔTE D'IVOIRE**
HEIGHT: **6FT 2IN (1.89M)**
MAIN CLUBS: **LE MANS, GUINGAMP, MARSEILLE, CHELSEA**
INTERNATIONAL CAPS: **55**

GHANA

HOME   AWAY

POPULATION: 22.4 MILLION
CAPITAL: ACCRA
FA: GHANA FOOTBALL ASSOCIATION
LICENSED PLAYERS:
MALE: 27,500
FEMALE: 1,700
PROFESSIONALS: 0
REGISTERED CLUBS: 280

The first recorded game of soccer in Ghana (the Gold Coast)—was played in 1903. Boys at the Ahiimto College were so entranced they created their own side —Cape Coast Excelsior. In 1911 Hearts of Oak, the oldest club in sub-Saharan Africa, was founded. The game was so central to Ghana that independence celebrations in 1957 included a tour by English legend Stanley Mathews. But it took until 2006 to get to the World Cup.

STAT ATTACK
NATIONAL TEAM

NICKNAME: Black Stars
NATIONAL STADIUM:
Essipong, 20,000
WORLD CUP FINALS: 1 appearance
AFRICAN CUP OF NATIONS: Winners
1963, **1965**, **1978**, **1982**
BIGGEST WIN: 9–1 vs Nigeria, 1969
BIGGEST DEFEAT: 2–8 vs Brazil, 1996
MOST CAPS: Abedi Pele, **72**
MOST GOALS: Abedi Pele, **33**

THE BIG CLUBS

Both league and cup are "owned" by the big two clubs in Ghana, Hearts of Oak and Asante Kotoko—no other club has enjoyed the success that these two teams have. The Cup was abandoned in 2001.

REAL REPUBLICANS

The Real Republicans were created in 1962 at the behest of President Nkrumah. They had access to the best players and won five titles, but he wanted them to dominate a continent and win the newly created African Champions Cup—they never did. The team was dissolved after Nkrumah's overthrow.

MAIN DOMESTIC CLUBS

HEARTS OF OAK
FOUNDED: Accra, 1911
STADIUM:
Ohene Djan, 35,000   HOME
INTERNATIONAL HONORS: African Champions League **2000**, CAF Confederations Cup **2005**
LEAGUE: 18 **CUP:** 9

ASANTE KOTOKO
FOUNDED: Kumasi, 1935
STADIUM: Kumasi Sports, 51,500   HOME
INTERNATIONAL HONORS:
African Champions League, **1970**, **1983**
LEAGUE: 20 **CUP:** 8

ACCRA STADIUM DISASTER

On May 9th, 2001, Ghana suffered the worst stadium disaster in African soccer. In the old Accra sports stadium, when a game between Hearts of Oak and Asante Kotoko reached the 91st minute, the police fired tear gas toward the restless Kotoko fans. Many fans were killed or injured in the resulting stampede.

BLACK STARS

The Ghanaian national team is known as the Black Stars. They were given the name by Ghana's first independent president, Kwame Nkrumah, who named them after the Black Star Line, the shipping line set up in 1919 by Marcus Garvey to take black Americans to Africa.

SAMMY **KUFFOUR**

Aged just 15, Kuffour arrived in the European game at Italian side Torino and went on to make his mark at Bayern Munich, where he was a mainstay in their defense for ten seasons. At 18 years and 61 days, he holds the accolade of being the youngest defender to score a goal in the Champions League.

BORN: **SEPTEMBER 3, 1976, KUMASI, GHANA**
HEIGHT: **5FT 10IN (1.78M)**
MAIN CLUBS: **TORINO, BAYERN MUNICH, AS ROMA**
INTERNATIONAL CAPS: **59**

29 Sequence of games in which Ghana scored a goal, from 1963 to 1967

24 The average age of Ghana's squad at the 2006 World Cup —the youngest of any team

1963 The year Ghana beat Italy 5–2 on a European friendly tour

3 The number of times Ghana won the African Cup of Nations, after which they were permitted to keep the Abdelaziz Abdallah Salem Trophy permanently

DR CONGO

HOME AWAY

POPULATION: 65.7 MILLION
CAPITAL: KINSHASA
FA: FÉDÉRATION CONGOLAISE DE FOOTBALL-ASSOCIATION
LICENSED PLAYERS:
MALE: 2.5 MILLION
FEMALE: 0
PROFESSIONALS: 0
REGISTERED CLUBS: 770

Soccer was introduced to the Democratic Republic of Congo (DRC) by Belgian administrators and missionaries after World War I. It spread fastest among the Congolese in the southern mining cities, and mining-company-backed teams played in the 1940s. The national team now suffers from a lack of financial support.

DOMESTIC LEAGUE

The leading teams in the DRC play a national league that in recent years has consisted of a qualifying round of small groups, then a six-team mini-league for the title. The Cup is a more conventional knock-out tournament. Clubs play in regional or city leagues as well.

SHABANI **NONDA**

Nonda is DRC's top-scoring striker—his tally would have been higher, but he exiled himself from international soccer from 2005 to 2007. On his return he scored a hat-trick against Djibouti.

BORN: **MARCH 6, 1977, BUJUMBURA, BURUNDI**
HEIGHT: **5FT 11½IN (1.82M)**
MAIN CLUBS: **FC ZURICH, STADE RENNAIS, AS MONACO, AS ROMA, BLACKBURN ROVERS, GALATASARAY**
INTERNATIONAL CAPS: **49**

STAT ATTACK

NATIONAL TEAM

NICKNAME: The Leopards
NATIONAL STADIUM:
Stade des Martyrs, 80,000
WORLD CUP FINALS: 1 appearance
AFRICAN CUP OF NATIONS: Winners **1968**, **1974**
BIGGEST WIN: 10–1 vs Zambia, 1969
BIGGEST DEFEAT: 0–9 vs Yugoslavia, 1974
MOST CAPS: Shabani Nonda, **49**
MOST GOALS: Shabani Nonda, **32**

PRESIDENT MOBUTO

When President Mobutu took power in 1965 of what was then Zaire, he invested heavily in the team. They won two African Champions Cups and the African Cup of Nations in 1968 and 1974. Mobutu abandoned soccer after their dismissal from the 1974 World Cup.

WORLD CUP 1974

The Leopards, as Mobutu called them, arrived at West Germany 1974 as the first sub-Saharan nation at the tournament. They lost all three games, 2–0 to Scotland, 3–0 to Brazil, and 9–0 to Yugoslavia. When the team returned home, no one met them at the airport.

AFRICAN CUP OF NATIONS

Money was so short for the DRC before the 2004 African Cup of Nations, which was held in Egypt, that members of the Congolese squad were living in hostels in Cairo while training for the games. They were moved to better accomodation thanks to the Egyptian FA. However, in their game against Egypt, the Congolese players were off the field celebrating an equalizer when the Egyptians restarted the game and scored a winning goal.

MAIN DOMESTIC CLUBS

DARING CLUB MOTEMA PEMBE
FOUNDED: Kinshasa, 1936
STADIUM:
Stade des Martyrs, 80,000
INTERNATIONAL HONORS:
Cup Winners' Cup **1994**
LEAGUE: 11 **CUP:** 11

HOME

AS VITA CLUB
FOUNDED:
Kinshasa, 1935
STADIUM:
Stade des Martyrs, 80,000
INTERNATIONAL HONORS:
African Champions League **1973**
LEAGUE: 11 **CUP:** 9

HOME

TOUT PUISSANT MAZEMBE
FOUNDED: Lubumbashi, 1932
STADIUM:
Stade Municipal, 35,000
INTERNATIONAL HONORS: African Champions League **1967**, **1968**, Cup Winners' Cup **1980**
LEAGUE: 10 **CUP:** 5

HOME

SOUTH AFRICA

HOME   AWAY

POPULATION: 42.8 MILLION

CAPITAL: PRETORIA

FA: SOUTH AFRICAN
FOOTBALL ASSOCIATION

LICENSED PLAYERS:
MALE: 1.5 MILLION
FEMALE: 5,000

PROFESSIONALS: 1,000

REGISTERED CLUBS: 450

Soccer began in South Africa in the 1860s among Europeans, and by 1882 a governing body had been set up in Natal along with three clubs. The game spread among Africans working in the mining areas alongside soccer-playing white miners. Later, the apartheid regime banned sports between races. South Africa was expelled from CAF and FIFA, and was not readmitted until 1992.

SOUTH AFRICAN LEAGUE

The Premier League has grown out of the National Professional Soccer League—a black league that merged with its white counterpart in 1978 to create one of the very earliest mixed-race institutions in South Africa. The clubs also play a cup competition and, until recently, a tournament for the top eight teams too.

1996 AFRICAN CUP OF NATIONS

The 1996 African Cup of Nations was due to be hosted by Kenya, but at the last minute, the tournament moved to South Africa. The South African multi-ethnic team made it to the final and won. They took the cup from Nelson Mandela, FW de Klerk, and the Zulu king and celebrated with 100,000 fans in the FNB Stadium.

BENNI McCARTHY

McCarthy made his name with Ajax Cape Town and then moved to Europe. He famously scored two goals in Porto's win against Manchester United on the way to winning the 2004 Champions League.

BORN: NOVEMBER 12, 1977, CAPE TOWN, SOUTH AFRICA
HEIGHT: 6FT (1.83M)
MAIN CLUBS: SEVEN STARS, AJAX CAPE TOWN, AJAX, CELTA VIGO, FC PORTO, BLACKBURN ROVERS
INTERNATIONAL CAPS: 76

SOCCER IN THE TOWNSHIPS

In 1961, a group of independent owners, clubs, and administrators broke from the apartheid soccer authorities. They created their own soccer league in the black townships—the SASL (South African Soccer League), which was led by clubs like Cape Town Ramblers and Moroka Swallows. Their games were a gigantic success and source of great pride to the teams and people of the townships. However, the South African state steadily closed the teams down and dissolved the league in 1966.

STAT ATTACK

NATIONAL TEAM

NICKNAME: Bafana Bafana

NATIONAL STADIUM:
First National Bank (also known as FNB Stadium or Soccer City), 94,700

WORLD CUP FINALS: 1 appearance

AFRICAN CUP OF NATIONS:
Winners **1996**

BIGGEST WIN: 8–0 vs Australia, 1955

BIGGEST DEFEAT: 1–5 vs Australia, 1947

MOST CAPS: Aaron Mokoena, **75**

MOST GOALS: Benni McCarthy, **30**

MAIN DOMESTIC CLUBS

KAISER CHIEFS
FOUNDED: Krugersdorp, 1970
STADIUM:
Amakhosi, 55,000   HOME
INTERNATIONAL HONORS:
Cup Winners' Cup **2001**
LEAGUE: 10 **CUP:** 12

ORLANDO PIRATES
FOUNDED: Johannesburg, 1937
STADIUM: Ellis Park, 55,000   HOME
INTERNATIONAL HONORS:
African Champions League **1995**
LEAGUE: 7 **CUP:** 6

MAMELODI SUNDOWNS
FOUNDED: Pretoria, 1970
STADIUM: Loftus Versfeld, 51,800   HOME

INTERNATIONAL HONORS:
African Champions League runners-up **2001**
LEAGUE: 7 **CUP:** 3

AFRICA: TOP CLUBS

The development of pan-African club competitions in the 1960s enabled a generation of big clubs previously known only at home to shine internationally. Since the 1990s, North African clubs—initially the Egyptian sides, but later the Moroccan, Tunisian, and Algerian teams too—have become more successful and wealthy, although the recent success of Enyimba of Nigeria and Coton Sport of Cameroon show that West African soccer is also thriving.

HAFIA CONAKRY

Once Guinea's biggest and Africa's strongest club, Hafia Conakry was acquired by President Sékou Touré in 1970. With an injection of funds and control of players, the team won three African Champions Cups. After losing the 1976 final to Mouloudi Algiers, Touré sent players to prison for "political re-education."

NORTH AFRICA

North African soccer is so strong that Egypt's third-best team, Ismaily, was actually the first to win a continental trophy. The side has fierce hometown support and has been bankrolled by the powerful Osman family, with links to Egyptian politics and construction. Morocco's leading teams are not far behind: Raja Casablanca, the blue collar team; and FAR Rabat, founded by the late King Hassan II and team of the Moroccan armed forces.

1974 Year in which a Congolese team last won the Champions Cup

9 Algerian club JS Kabylie's rank in CAF's African club of the century poll

0 East African clubs who have won a continental African trophy

MOHAMED ABOUTRIKA
A midfielder for both Al-Ahly and Egypt, Aboutrika is a world-class player who has chosen to play his whole career in Egypt.

WEST AFRICA

The recent rise of Coton Sport from Cameroon is a measure of West Africa's soccer strength. Founded as recently as 1986 as a textile factory's workers team, Coton Sport won the first of their many domestic titles in 1997 and have now made it all the way to the final of the African Champions League.

STAT ATTACK

DOMESTIC TEAMS

JS KABYLIE

The top club in Algeria, JS Kabylie's form in African competitions places the club among the continent's elite. Kabylie come from the city of Tizi-Ouzou in Berber country—an ethnic group distinct from the nation's Arab majority.

HONORS: LEAGUE 14, CUP 4; AFRICAN CHAMPIONS LEAGUE WINNERS 1981, 1990; AFRICAN CUP WINNERS' CUP WINNERS 1995; CAF CONFEDERATIONS CUP WINNERS 2001, 2002, 2003

ETOILE SPORTIVE DU SAHEL

Etoile was founded in 1925 as a multi-sport club for Muslims in the French colonial city of Sousse, in Tunisia. They have won at least one title every decade since independence from France in 1956 and, more recently, have won every African cup competition, demonstrating the strength in depth of Tunisian soccer.

HONORS: LEAGUE 11, CUP 21; AFRICAN CHAMPIONS LEAGUE WINNERS 1993, 1995, 2005

ESPÉRANCE SPORTIVE

The premier team of Tunis, Espérance remains the favored team of the Tunisian nation as a whole. However, the number and quality of domestic challengers is threatening the team's number one status.

HONORS: LEAGUE 13, CUP 7; AFRICAN CHAMPIONS LEAGUE WINNERS 1994; AFRICAN CUP WINNERS' CUP WINNERS 1998; CAF CONFEDERATIONS CUP WINNERS 1997

THE TEAMS

Africa's top teams are clustered in the north and west of the continent. The South Africans, such as Orlando Pirates and the Kaiser Chiefs, have fallen from grace, although Angolan clubs buoyed by oil money are progressing.

JS Kabylie
Country: Algeria
Founded: Tizi-Ouzo, 1946
Stadium: 1er Novembre 1954
Capacity: 20,000

Esperance Sportive
Country: Tunisia
Founded: Tunis, 1919
Stadium: El Menzah
Capacity: 40,000

Al-Ahly
Country: Egypt
Founded: Cairo, 1907
Stadium: Cairo Stadium
Capacity: 74,100

Zamalek
Country: Egypt
Founded: Cairo, 1911
Stadium: Cairo Stadium
Capacity: 74,100

Etoile Sportive du Sahel
Country: Tunisia
Founded: Sousse, 1925
Stadium: Stade Olympique
Capacity: 35,000

Asante Kotoko
Country: Ghana
Founded: Kumasi, 1935
Stadium: Kumasi Sports Stadium
Capacity: 51,500

Enyimba
Country: Nigeria
Founded: Aba, 1976
Stadium: Enyimba International
Capacity: 10,000

Hearts of Oak
Country: Ghana
Founded: Accra, 1911
Stadium: Ohene Djan
Capacity: 35,000

ASEC Mimosas
Country: Ivory Coast
Founded: Abidjan, 1948
Stadium: Houphourt-Boigny
Capacity: 45,000

Canon Yaounde
Country: Cameroon
Founded: Yaounde, 1930
Stadium: Stade Ahmadou Ahidjo
Capacity: 52,000

DOMESTIC TEAMS

ENYIMBA

Founded in 1976, Enyimba means "People's Elephant" in Igbo, and is the nickname for the city of Aba, in which the team is based. The team became the property of the Nigerian government in 1991, and it has recently risen to the top of both Nigerian and African soccer. Enyimba memorably won back-to-back Champions League titles in 2003 and 2004.

HONORS: LEAGUE 5, CUP 1; AFRICAN CHAMPIONS LEAGUE 2003, 2004

CANON YAOUNDE

In its heyday Canon Yaounde was the leading team in Cameroon and among the leading sides in Africa, winning four continental titles between 1971 and 1980. Recent success, however, has been limited to a single domestic league win in 2002.

HONORS: LEAGUE 10, CUP 12 5; AFRICAN CHAMPIONS LEAGUE WINNERS 1971, 1978, 1980, AFRICAN CUP WINNERS CUP WINNERS 1979

HEARTS OF OAK

The oldest club in Sub-Saharan Africa, Ghanaian side Hearts of Oak finally sealed their status among the continent's elite with a Champions Cup victory in 2000. They hit the record books by winning the Ghanaian domestic league six consecutive times between 1997 and 2002.

HONORS: LEAGUE 18, CUP 9; AFRICAN CHAMPIONS LEAGUE WINNERS 2000, CAF CONFEDERATIONS CUP WINNERS 2005

ASANTE KOTOKO

Asante is the main rival to Hearts of Oaks' Ghanaian crown. Founded in the 1930s as Asante United, they acquired the name Kotoko —"porcupine"—in 1935. By this time, the club's patrons and key supporters were the Ashanti mainly elite of northern Ghana, and the club has remained an icon of ethnic identity for supporters in the region.

HONORS: LEAGUE 20, CUP 8; AFRICAN CHAMPIONS LEAGUE WINNERS 1970, 1983

AL-AHLY

Simply the best. Voted by CAF as the top African club of the 20th century, Cairo-based Al-Ahly has continued to be the biggest and most successful African club in the 21st century.

HONORS: LEAGUE 33, CUP 35; AFRICAN CHAMPIONS LEAGUE WINNERS 1982, 1987, 2001, 2005, 2006; AFRICAN CUP WINNERS' CUP WINNERS 1984, 1985, 1986, 1993; CAF SUPER CUP WINNERS 2002, 2006, 2007, 2009

ZAMALEK

In any other country, Cairo-based Zamalek would be the top dog, and their eight African titles make them a potent force in the continental game. But Egyptian soccer also contains the mighty Al-Ahly, in whose shadow Zamalek are forced to toil.

HONORS: LEAGUE 11, CUP 21; AFRICAN CHAMPIONS LEAGUE WINNERS 1984, 1986, 1993, 1995, 2005; CAF SUPER CUP WINNERS 1994, 1997, 2003

ASEC MIMOSAS

Ivory Coast side ASEC Mimosas has a long history and a brilliant domestic record. However, it is best known for its exceptional youth academy, which successfully and profitably sends players to Europe, and is a model to which much of Africa aspires. The export of talent accounts for the fact that they have just a single Champions Cup to their name.

HONORS: LEAGUE 22, CUP 15; AFRICAN CHAMPIONS LEAGUE WINNERS 1998

ASIA AND OCEANIA: AFC AND OFC

HOME   AWAY

POPULATION: 69.7 MILLION
CAPITAL: TEHRAN
FA: ISLAMIC REPUBLIC OF IRAN FOOTBALL FEDERATION

IRAN

Played in Iran since the early 20th century, soccer boomed in the 1960s as oil money flowed in. Iran then won three Asian Cups and competed in the 1978 World Cup just a year before the revolution. Restrictions followed but the game resolutely survived.

STAT ATTACK

NATIONAL TEAM

NATIONAL STADIUM: Azadi, 110,000
WORLD CUP FINALS: 3 appearances
ASIAN CUP: 11 appearances, winners **1968**, **1972**, **1976**

MAIN DOMESTIC CLUBS

ESTEGHLAL
FOUNDED: Tehran, 1945
STADIUM: Azadi Stadium

PIROUZI
FOUNDED: Tehran, 1963
STADIUM: Azadi Stadium

PAS TEHRAN
FOUNDED: Tehran, 1963
STADIUM: Shahid Dastgerdi Stadium

WORLD CUP '98

Iran won its first and only game at a World Cup final in 1998, where the team was placed in the same group as the USA. After almost 20 years of political and rhetorical conflict between the two countries, the Iranians disarmed the world by handing bouquets of white flowers to the US team, who reciprocated with a gift of pennants. Iran won the match 2–1, but lost their remaining two matches and were knocked out of the competition.

THE TEHRAN DERBY

The two biggest clubs in Iranian soccer are Pirouzi, previously known as Persepolis, who have won the top-tier Iran Pro League on eight occasions, and Esteghlal, previously Taj or Crown, who have won the title five times. Under the Shah, Persepolis became the team of the poor, while Taj was the team of the establishment. Games between the two Tehran teams attract huge crowds, with more than 100,000 fans flocking to the teams' shared ground, the Azadi Stadium.

SOCCER AS PROTEST

Soccer has been a lightning rod for politics in Iran, and especially the contentious issue of the place of women in Iranian society. Women have been banned from entering soccer stadiums or, at best, confined to women-only sections. Female fans and activists pressing for women's rights have repeatedly protested over their exclusion by demonstrating outside Iran's national stadium, the Azadi Stadium in Tehran, during the national team's fixtures.

IRAQ

HOME   AWAY

POPULATION: 26.8 MILLION
CAPITAL: BAGHDAD
FA: IRAQI FOOTBALL ASSOCIATION

Soccer came to Iraq with foreign armies and oil workers, above all the British. The game is immensely popular, and the Iraqi team is one of the few institutions to survive the US-led invasion that began in 2003. The team retains the support of most of an otherwise divided nation.

STAT ATTACK

NATIONAL TEAM

NATIONAL STADIUM: Al-Shaab Stadium, 66,000
WORLD CUP FINALS: 1 appearance
ASIAN CUP: 6 appearances, winners **2007**

MAIN DOMESTIC CLUBS

AL-ZAWRA'A
FOUNDED: Baghdad, 1969
STADIUM: Al Zawara'a Stadium

AL-QUWA AL-JAWIYA
FOUNDED: Baghdad, 1931
STADIUM: Al-Quwa Al-Jawiya Stadium

ARBIL FC
FOUNDED: Arbil, 1958
STADIUM: Franso Hariri Stadium

THINGS CAN ONLY GET BETTER

Despite the destabilization caused by the invasion of Iraq, the national team qualified for the 2004 Athens Olympics. Coach Bernt Stange resigned after receiving death threats, but the team reached the semi-finals, which led to celebrations at home. They went one better in 2006, finishing runners-up in the Asian Games, then went on to win the 2007 AFC Asian Cup.

POLITICS BEFORE SOCCER

Al-Zawra'a—previously Police Club—made it to the final of the 1970 Asian Champions Cup, where they faced Israel's Maccabi Tel Aviv. In protest over Israel's national status and oppression of the Palestinians, the Iraqi team boycotted the game, so Tel Aviv were awarded the title.

HOME   AWAY

POPULATION: 27 MILLION
CAPITAL: RIYADH
FA: SAUDI ARABIAN FOOTBALL FEDERATION

SAUDI ARABIA

Despite religious difficulties with the game, the Saudi royal house and nation enthusiastically embraced soccer. The game arrived in the inter-war period with foreign armies and oil workers, and a national FA was founded in 1959.

STAT ATTACK

NATIONAL TEAM

NATIONAL STADIUM: King Fahd, 67,000
WORLD CUP FINALS: 4 appearances
ASIAN CUP: 7 appearances, winners **1984, 1988, 1996;** runners-up **1992, 2000, 2007**

MAIN DOMESTIC CLUBS

AL-HILAL
FOUNDED: Riyadh, 1957
STADIUM: King Fahd Stadium

AL-ITTIHAD
FOUNDED: Jeddah, 1928
STADIUM: Prince Abdullah al-Faisal Stadium

AL-NASR
FOUNDED: Riyadh, 1955
STADIUM: King Fahd Stadium

WORLD CUP HIGHS AND LOWS

After winning the Asian Cup in the 1980s, Saudi Arabia rose to prominence with four consecutive World Cup appearances, starting in 1994. On the first occasion they beat Belgium and Morocco to qualify for the second round, but went home early in 2002 after losing 8–0 to Germany.

CUPS AND KINGS

The presence of the Saudi royal house is felt everywhere in Saudi soccer. The winners of the Prince Faisal Cup, which started in 2008, and the Crown Prince's Cup join six other teams to contest the big-money prize of the Saudi Champions Cup, officially known as the "Custodian of The Two Holy Mosques Champions Cup."

MOHAMED AL-DEAYEA

Goalkeeper for the Saudi Arabia national team for more than eighteen years, Al-Deayea holds the world record for the highest number of international caps.

BORN: AUGUST 2, 1972, TABUK, SAUDI ARABIA
HEIGHT: **6FT 3IN (1.91M)**
MAIN CLUBS: **AL-TA'EE, AL-HILAL**
INTERNATIONAL CAPS: **181**

UAE

HOME   AWAY

POPULATION: 4.4 MILLION
CAPITAL: ABU DHABI
FA: UNITED ARAB EMIRATES FOOTBALL ASSOCIATION

The United Arab Emirates (UAE), a group of seven mini-sheikhdoms in the Gulf, is making its presence felt in world soccer. The 2009 and 2010 FIFA World Club Cups were hosted in Abu Dhabi, and national airline Emirates was the first airline to become a World Cup sponsor.

STAT ATTACK

NATIONAL TEAM

NATIONAL STADIUM:
Sheikh Zayed Stadium, 49,500
WORLD CUP FINALS: 1 appearance
ASIAN CUP: 7 appearances, runners-up **1996**

MAIN DOMESTIC CLUBS

AL-AIN FC
FOUNDED: Al-Ain, 1968
STADIUM: Tahnoun bin Mohamed Stadium

SHARJAH FC
FOUNDED: Sharjah, 1966
STADIUM: Sharjah Stadium

AL-AHLI
FOUNDED: Dubai, 1970
STADIUM: Al-Rashid Stadium

PUNCHING ABOVE ITS WEIGHT

UAE is one of the smallest nations to have played in a World Cup finals, qualifying for Italia '90 but losing all three games. The side also progressed to the final of the 1996 Asian Cup only to lose on penalties, and won the Gulf Cup for the first time in 2007.

AL-AIN FC

Leading side Al-Ain is the only UAE team to have won the Asian Champions League. It has won the top-flight UAE League nine times as well as four UAE Sheikh Cups, partly thanks to direct sponsorship from the Royal Al-Nahyan family since 1968. The club changed its uniform from red and green to the purple of Belgian side Anderlecht, with whom they shared a training camp in 1977.

KING FAHD STADIUM

KING FAHD INTERNATIONAL STADIUM

AL AMIR BANDAR,
BIN ABDUL AZIZ ST.,
RIYADH, SAUDI ARABIA

HOME TEAMS:
SAUDI ARABIAN NATIONAL TEAM,
AL HILAL, AL SHABAB

ARCHITECT:
IAN FRASER, JOHN ROBERTS
AND PARTNERS

OPENED: 1987

CONSTRUCTION COST:
$80 MILLION (£55 MILLION)

CAPACITY: 67,000

Riyadh's extraordinary King Fahd International Stadium is the largest stadium in the Middle East. Completed in 1987, its iconic roof is both functional and symbolic. As well as shielding spectators from the harsh Arabian sun, the roof is redolent of the royal crown of the stadium's patrons and evokes the folds of a Bedouin desert tent—the heart and hearth of traditional Saudi society.

HOME STADIUM

The stadium serves as the home of two Saudi clubs and the national team. Built to the highest FIFA standards, it has hosted a number of international tournaments, including the FIFA World Youth Cup in 1989 and the FIFA Confederations Cup in 1992 and '97.

MULTI-PURPOSE VENUE

No expense was spared by the Saudi royal family in building a national stadium. As well as being a top-class soccer venue, the stadium's athletic track and other facilities allow it to host a variety of international sporting events. Designed as an unbroken ellipse, all seats offer an unimpeded view of the field.

In accordance with Saudi law, women are not allowed into the stadium for events involving men, although foreign women visitors are permitted into a small area near the press stand.

Concourse
A continuous concourse runs around the top of the stands; the VIP areas and press stand are located above it

Running track
The athletics running track was designed to Olympic standards

Roof
The roof covers an area of 506,000 sq ft (47,000 sq m), making it the largest of any soccer stadium in the world

Columns
Twenty-four supporting columns are arranged around a circle, which has a diameter of 810 ft (247 m). A flag pole sits on top of each column, above the roof line

TENTLIKE ROOF

Set in an ocean of parking lots, the King Fahd International Stadium is located on the northeastern edge of Riyadh, the capital city of Saudi Arabia. Widely regarded as one of the most spectacular and beautiful stadia in the world, it is noted for its vast, tentlike roof structure.

SHOOTING MATCH

Although the King Fahd Stadium has an official capacity of 67,000, the biggest games regularly attract larger crowds. When Manchester United played a friendly against Al Hilal in 2008, for example, not only was the stadium full beyond capacity five hours before kick-off, but the game was accompanied by celebratory gunfire.

Ramps
Eight concrete ramps lead fans from the outside ticket booths to the stadium

Seating
Every one of the 70,000 seats is shaded from the sun by the stadium's vast roof

Sightlines
The stadium's design allows for every spectator to enjoy an uninterrupted view

Boxes
The press stand and sumptuous VIP boxes are across from the halfway line

Facilities
There are three levels of support services beneath the stands, which include communications equipment, changing rooms, and catering facilities

Masts
Each of the 24 Teflon-coated masts stand at a height of 190 ft (58 m)

Medical facilities
Medical suites are located under the stands, providing specialist sports medicines and surgical facilities

3 The number of years it took to build the stadium

24 The carat of gold used to make the taps and fittings in the stadium's VIP bathrooms

5,400,000 The total area, in sq ft (500,000 sq m), covered by the King Fahd stadium

506,000 The area in square feet (47,000 sq m) of the membrane roof—making it the largest stadium roof in the world

THE BEAUTY OF KING FAHD STADIUM WILL NOT BE COMPLETED UNLESS THE CROWDS ATTEND... THE SUPPORTERS ARE THE FIRST PLAYER

PRINCE FAHD BIN SALMAN, PRESIDENT OF AL HILAL

HOME   AWAY

INDIA

POPULATION: 1.1 BILLION
CAPITAL: DELHI
FA: ALL INDIA FOOTBALL FEDERATION
LICENSED PLAYERS:
MALE: 19 MILLION
FEMALE: 1.5 MILLION
PROFESSIONALS: 400
REGISTERED CLUBS: 6,500

The first recorded soccer game in India was between British colonialists in 1854, and a Calcutta league existed by the 1870s, composed of British teams. A nationwide federation did not exist until 1936, and the game fared poorly after independence in 1947. The first professional league, the National Football League, was founded in 1996, but became the I-League in 2007.

THE I-LEAGUE

Indian soccer consists of a range of leagues and tournaments. The I-League is the top flight, but all the leading clubs also play in local state divisions. In addition, there are two national tournaments—the Durand Cup, which was established in 1888, and the more recent Federation Cup established in 1999.

THE NEHRU CUP

Set up by the AIFF in 1982, the Nehru Cup is an annual international soccer tournament. It was not held between 1997 and 2007. It took India 25 years to win the trophy, beating Syria 1–0 in the 2007 tournament.

BAICHUNG **BHUTIA**

The leading Indian player of his generation, Bhutia was born in the Himalayas. He played three seasons of English soccer with the Lancashire club, Bury, and is the only player to score a hat-trick in the Calcutta Derby.

BORN: **DECEMBER 15, 1976, TINKITAM, SIKKIM, INDIA**
HEIGHT: **5FT 8IN (1.73M)**
MAIN CLUBS: **EAST BENGAL CLUB, JCT MILLS, MOHUN BAGAN, OHUN BAGAN**
INTERNATIONAL CAPS: **57**

THE GOLDEN AGE

The 1950s and early 1960s were the golden age of Indian international soccer. India won the Asian Games in 1951 and 1962, and came fourth at the 1956 Olympics. They even qualified for the 1950 World Cup, but did not compete due to FIFA's insistence that the team could not play barefoot.

CALCUTTA ALLEGIANCES

The big teams in Calcutta draw support from three groups: Mohun Bagan from Hindu Bengalis, Mohammedan Sporting from the Muslims, and East Bengal from refugee communities from Bangladesh.

MOHUN BAGAN 2, BRITISH EMPIRE 1

The most politically charged game in Indian soccer was in 1911, when Mohun Bagan won the Durand Cup. They beat the East Yorkshire Regiment—and the occupying power—with two late goals. The game drew a crowd of more than 60,000.

STAT ATTACK

NATIONAL TEAM

NICKNAME: The Jalfrezi's, The Wonder Boys
NATIONAL STADIUM: None
WORLD CUP FINALS: 1 appearance
BIGGEST WIN: 7–12 vs Sri Lanka, 1963
BIGGEST DEFEAT: 1–11 vs USSR, 1955
MOST CAPS: Baichung Bhutia, **55**
MOST GOALS: Baichung Bhutia, **55**

MAIN DOMESTIC CLUBS

MOHUN BAGAN
FOUNDED: Calcutta, 1889
STADIUM: Salt Lake Stadium
CAPACITY: 120,000   HOME
INTERNATIONAL HONORS: None
LEAGUE: 3 **FEDERATION CUP:** 12
DURAND CUP: 16

EAST BENGAL
FOUNDED: Calcutta, 1920
STADIUM: Salt Lake Stadium
CAPACITY: 120,000   HOME
INTERNATIONAL HONORS: None
LEAGUE: 3 **FEDERATION CUP:** 5
DURAND CUP: 15

MOHAMMEDAN SPORTING
FOUNDED: Calcutta, 1892
STADIUM: Mohammaden
CAPACITY: 7,000   HOME
INTERNATIONAL HONORS: None
LEAGUE: 0 **FEDERATION CUP:** 2
DURAND CUP: 1

165
India's lowest FIFA world ranking, in 2007

300
Crowd that watched the national team beat Afghanistan 1–0 in Hyderabad, December 2007

7,000,000
The small annual fee, in US dollars, for television broadcast rights, paid by Zee TV to the I-League

HOME   AWAY

POPULATION: 1.3 BILLION
CAPITAL: BEIJING
FA: CHINESE FOOTBALL ASSOCIATION
LICENSED PLAYERS:
MALE: 24.2 MILLION
FEMALE: 1.9 MILLION
PROFESSIONALS: 2,000
REGISTERED CLUBS: 1,500

CHINA

The history of soccer in China has been as turbulent as that of the nation itself. Played in the port enclaves of late-Imperial China, there was sufficient support to send a Chinese team to the 1913 Far East Asian games. However, it wasn't until the establishment of the communist state in 1949 that soccer was organized nationwide. A professional league was set up following the rapid economic growth of the 1990s and 2000s.

CHINESE SUPER LEAGUE

China's first professional league, the Jia A, ran from 1994 to 2003, replacing a collection of national and regional tournaments. This was relaunched and rebranded in 2004 as the Chinese Super League. This consists of 16 teams in a standard league. There is also a knock-out competition, the Chinese FA Cup.

IN OR OUT?

The Chinese FA first joined FIFA in 1931, but left in 1959 in protest at FIFA's recognition of Taiwan. In the 1970s, China began to re-engage with the world, rejoining the AFC in 1974, and FIFA in 1979. The process was crowned with Chinese tours by Pelé's New York Cosmos, and England's West Bromwich Albion.

SUN JIHAI

One of the first Chinese to play for a top European team, Sun moved to Manchester City in 2002. The 2003 tie between City and Everton, who fielded Chinese defender Li Te, attracted a TV audience in China of 150 million.

BORN: **SEPTEMBER 30, 1977, DALIAN, CHINA**
HEIGHT: **6FT (1.83M)**
MAIN CLUBS: **DALIAN WANDA, CRYSTAL PALACE, DALIAN SHIDE, MANCHESTER CITY**
INTERNATIONAL CAPS: **66**

ONE NATION, THREE CHINAS

After the transfer of sovereignty of Hong Kong from the UK in 1997, and Macau from Portugal in 1999, these two special administrative regions have continued to field their own national teams. They play as Hong Kong, China and Macau, China, respectively.

ASIAN CUP 2004

In 2004, China hosted the Asian Cup, its first major soccer tournament. A showcase for China's growing economic success, the Cup was seen as a barometer for the 2008 Olympic Games. China made it to the final but lost an acrimonious game to Japan.

THE MAY 19TH INCIDENT

In May 1985, in Beijing, China were 1–0 up against Hong Kong in a key World Cup qualifier. The team then froze, lost 2–1 and triggered the first ever Chinese soccer riot as exasperated fans smashed windows and burned buses downtown.

STAT ATTACK

NATIONAL TEAM

NICKNAME: Team China
NATIONAL STADIUM: None
WORLD CUP FINALS: 1 appearance
BIGGEST WIN: 19–0 vs Guam, 2000
BIGGEST DEFEAT: 0–5 vs USA, 1992
MOST CAPS: Li Ming, **141**
MOST GOALS: Hao Haidong, **41**

MAIN DOMESTIC CLUBS

LIAONING HONGYUN
FOUNDED: Jinzhou, 1995
STADIUM: Jinzhou City Stadium
CAPACITY: 24,000   HOME
INTERNATIONAL HONORS: Asian Champions League winners **1990**
LEAGUE: 8 **CUP:** 8

DALIAN SHIDE
FOUNDED: Dalian, 1983
STADIUM: Jinzhou Stadium
CAPACITY: 31,000   HOME
INTERNATIONAL HONORS: None
LEAGUE: 8 **CUP:** 3

BEIJING GUOAN
FOUNDED: Beijing, 1992
STADIUM: Workers Stadium
CAPACITY: 33,000   HOME
INTERNATIONAL HONORS: None
LEAGUE: 5 **CUP:** 4

HOME AWAY

POPULATION: 127.5 MILLION
CAPITAL: TOKYO
FA NAME: JAPAN FOOTBALL ASSOCIATION
LICENSED PLAYERS:
MALE: 4.5 MILLION
FEMALE: 304,500
PROFESSIONALS: 976
REGISTERED CLUBS: 1,000

JAPAN

Soccer came to Japan in the 19th century and was initially the preserve of elite university students. A national league was founded in 1965 with teams from major corporations, such as Mitsubishi and Nissan, but there were no full-time professional players. The league was rebranded, professionalized, and relaunched in 1992 as the J-league, with hometown affiliations replacing corporate branding for the teams. Professional soccer culture has now taken root in Japan.

THE J-LEAGUE

Due to Japan's unfamiliarity with the system, the J-League initially used a combination of extra time, the golden goal, and penalty shoot-outs to decide every match. Penalty shoot-outs were dropped in 1999, as was extra time in 2003. Until 2005, the season was divided into two, with the leading teams from each playing each other home and away to decide the champion.

THE NAME GAME

Many of Japan's top sides changed their names to enter the J-League. Verdy Kawasaki became Tokyo Verdy 1969, Mitsibushi Heavy became Industrial Urawa Red Diamonds, and Nissan Motors became Yokohama F. Marinos.

STAT ATTACK

NATIONAL TEAM

NICKNAME: Nippon Daihyo
NATIONAL STADIUM: None
WORLD CUP FINALS: 3 appearances
ASIAN CUP CHAMPIONSHIPS:
5 appearances, winners **1992**, **2000**, **2004**
BIGGEST WIN: **15–0** vs Phillipines, 1966
BIGGEST DEFEAT: **2–15** vs Phillipines, 1917
MOST CAPS: Masami Ihara, **123**
MOST GOALS: Kunishige Kamamoto, **82**

MAIN DOMESTIC CLUBS

TOKYO VERDY 1969
FOUNDED: Tokyo, 1969
STADIUM: Ajinomoto
CAPACITY: 50,000
INTERNATIONAL HONORS: 1
LEAGUE: 7 **CUP:** 5

HOME

YOKOHAMA F. MARINOS
FOUNDED: Yokohama, 1972
STADIUM: International
CAPACITY: 72,400
INTERNATIONAL HONORS: 2
LEAGUE: 5 **CUP:** 6

HOME

URAWA RED DIAMONDS
FOUNDED: Saitama, 1950
STADIUM: Saitama 2002
CAPACITY: 63,700
INTERNATIONAL HONORS: 1
LEAGUE: 5 **CUP:** 5

HOME

ADORING FANS

In the early years of the J-League, it was not unusual to see fans clap for the opposition team and encourage under-performing players, in an atmosphere closer to a pop concert than a soccer match. More conventional forms of fan behavior have had to be learned in Japan, with the fans of Urawa Red Diamonds taking the lead. They were the first to introduce booing, and hummed Elvis's "I can't help falling in love with you" as their team's performances deteriorated in the early 1990s.

BOYS FROM BRAZIL

In the early 20th century, more than a million Japanese peasants migrated to the coffee-fields of Brazil. As a consequence, there have been close links between the two countries. The Japanese national team has been coached by the Brazilian Zico and Brazilian players —such as Dunga—have signed for Japanese teams.

HIDETOSHI **NAKATA**

The most gifted of the modern Japanese players, Nakata's skills were matched by a determination to break with the traditions of Japanese soccer. He left Japan in 1995 for a series of Italian clubs.

BORN: **JANUARY 22, 1977, KOFU, JAPAN**
HEIGHT: **5FT 9IN (1.75M)**
MAIN CLUBS: **BELLMARE HIRATSUKA, PERUGIA, PARMA, FIORENTINA, BOLTON WANDERERS**
INTERNATIONAL CAPS: **77**

SOUTH KOREA

HOME

AWAY

POPULATION: 48.8 MILLION
CAPITAL: SEOUL
FA: KOREA FOOTBALL ASSOCIATION
LICENSED PLAYERS:
MALE: 1 MILLION
FEMALE: 72,500
PROFESSIONALS: 550
REGISTERED CLUBS: 864

South Korean soccer has always faced stiff competition from baseball, due to US influence following the 1949–53 Korean War. The country joined FIFA in 1948, but it was not until the creation of the K-League in 1983 that the game blossomed. The South Korean national side qualified for six consecutive World Cups between 1990 and 2006, even reaching the semi-finals in 2002.

STAT ATTACK

NATIONAL TEAM

NICKNAME: Taegeuk Jeonsa ("Taegeuk Warriors")
NATIONAL STADIUM: None
WORLD CUP FINALS: 7 appearances, semi-finals **2002**
ASIAN CUP CHAMPIONSHIPS: 11 appearances, winners **1956**, **1960**
BIGGEST WIN: 16–0 vs Nepal, 2003
BIGGEST DEFEAT: 0–12 vs Sweden, 1948
MOST CAPS: Hong Myung Bo, **136**
MOST GOALS: Cha Bum Kun, **55**

THE K-LEAGUE

There are two domestic tournaments in South Korea: the 14-club K-League and the Korean FA Cup, which is open to non-professional teams. In the early years of the K-League, there were no home and away games—instead, a circus of teams traveled throughout the country.

MAIN DOMESTIC CLUBS

SEONGNAM ILHWA CHUNMA
FOUNDED: Seongnam, 1989
STADIUM: Seongnam   HOME
CAPACITY: 27,000
INTERNATIONAL HONORS: Asian Champions League winners **1996**
LEAGUE: 7 **CUP:** 1

SUWON SAMSUNG BLUEWINGS
FOUNDED: Suwon, 1996
STADIUM: World Cup   HOME
CAPACITY: 44,047
INTERNATIONAL HONORS: Asian Champions League winners **2001**, **2002**
LEAGUE: 3 **CUP:** 1

BUSAN IPARK
FOUNDED: Busan, 1983
STADIUM: Asiad Main
CAPACITY: 56,000   HOME
INTERNATIONAL HONORS: Asian Champions League winners **1986**
LEAGUE: 4 **CUP:** 3

PARK JI-SUNG

The David Beckham of Asia, Park is a product of the global game. Brought to Dutch club PSV Eindhoven by Guus Hiddink, a line of admirers formed, with Manchester United winning his signature in 2005.

BORN: **FEBRUARY 25, 1981, SEOUL, SOUTH KOREA**
HEIGHT: **5FT 9IN (1.75M)**
MAIN CLUBS: **KYOTO PURPLE SANGA, PSV EINDHOVEN, MANCHESTER UNITED**
INTERNATIONAL CAPS: **75**

THE LORD'S TEAM

Seongnam Ilhwa Chunma, the most successful club in South Korea, is owned by the Unification Church, also known as the "Moonies." Other Christian teams have had success—the first K-League was won by Hallelujah, a Seoul team sponsored by evangelical protestants.

CLEANING UP THE NATION'S ACT

The organizers of the 2002 World Cup left nothing to chance. They exhorted the South Korean people to smile more, organized anti-spitting campaigns, took traditional food stalls off the street, and attempted to close down the "pojangmachas"—the tented drinking clubs normally found in the alleyways of the nation's cities.

WORLD CUP 2002

South Korea's performance at the 2002 World Cup was their best ever. The Korean FA cleared the domestic schedule to allow coach Guus Hiddink and the squad to focus on the tournament. The team displayed an awesome work rate, only matched by their feverish fans. They beat Portugal, Spain, and Italy to reach the semi-finals, only to lose to Germany. No team has ever played so hard in the usually flat play-off for third place.

HOME　　AWAY

POPULATION: 22.4 MILLION
CAPITAL: KUALA LUMPUR
FA: FOOTBALL ASSOCIATION OF MALAYSIA

STAT ATTACK

NATIONAL TEAM

NICKNAME: Harimau Malaya ("Malayan Tiger")
NATIONAL STADIUM: Stadium Nasional Bukit Jalil, 100,000
WORLD CUP FINALS: None

MAIN DOMESTIC CLUBS

SELANGOR
FOUNDED: Selangor, 1936
STADIUM: Shah Alam, 80,000

PERAK
FOUNDED: Ipoh, 1921
STADIUM: Perak,40,000

KEDAH
FOUNDED: Alor Setar, 1935
STADIUM: Darul Amam, 40,000

MALAYSIA

Soccer arrived in Malaysia with the British, and a league was running in Kuala Lumpa by 1905. A national association was set up in 1933, initially based in Singapore. In spite of considerable public and political enthusiasm—the nation's president was head of the FA from 1957–75—Malaysia has yet to make an impact on world soccer. They did qualify for the Olympics in 1972 and 1980.

MERDEKA—HONORING INDEPENDENCE
The Merdeka tournament was first held in 1957 to honor Malaysian Independence day. It is the oldest international tournament in Asia and was an annual invitation event for 30 years. Malaysia have won nine times, although it has also been won by Hamburg SV, Austria's Admiral Wacker, and a Buenos Aires XI. The tournament has been held only seven times since 1988.

M-LEAGUE MATCH-FIXING
In 1996 the Malaysian authorities arrested more than 100 domestic players all linked to systematic match-fixing. The police found that over 90 percent of games in the inaugural season of the M-League were fixed.

SWITCHING OFF THE LIGHTS

In 1999 British police arrested three Malaysians as they attempted to break into Charlton Athletic's Valley stadium in south London. The trio were part of a conspiracy linked to gangs in Malaysia attempting to fix the result of a Charlton game by turning off the floodlights.

VIETNAM

STAT ATTACK

NATIONAL TEAM

NATIONAL STADIUM:
My Đình National, 40,000
WORLD CUP FINALS: None

MAIN DOMESTIC CLUBS

THE CONG (ARMY CLUB)
FOUNDED: Hanoi, 1954
STADIUM: Hang Day, 18,000

CANG SAI GON
FOUNDED: Saigon, 1975
STADIUM: Thong Naht, 25,000

BECAMEX BINH DUONG
FOUNDED: Thu Dau Mot, 2001
STADIUM: Go Dau, 15,000

HOME　　AWAY

POPULATION: 82.7 MILLION
CAPTIAL: HANOI
FA: VIETNAM FOOTBALL FEDERATION

The French administration brought soccer to Saigon in the late 19th century and a league for European ex-patriates was played there before World War I. Subsequent wars have limited progress and interest in the domestic game has plummeted because of corruption.

LEAGUE HISTORY

The Vietnamese were running a league by the 1920s and in 1932 created a league with the Europeans. Soccer, like most things in the country, disappeared during World War II and the wars that followed. Vietnam returned to international competition in 1989 and created a professional V-league in 2000, but it has been plagued by setbacks.

INTERNATIONAL VICTORY
In 2008, Vietnam won their first international tournament in a victory against Thailand and became South East Asian Champions. The win was widely celebrated around the country.

MATCH-FIXING CULTURE
In 1997, players from Ho Chi Minh City Customs were convicted of match-fixing. Their arrest was triggered when a goalkeeper allowed a defender to score an own goal. Song Lam Nghe An lost the 2004 Samsung Cup to the Cong club; players were fined for playing badly.

NORTH KOREA

HOME   AWAY

POPULATION: 22.9 MILLION
CAPITAL: PYONGYANG
FA: DPR KOREA FOOTBALL ASSOCIATION

North Korea first made its mark on the international stage at the 1966 World Cup, where they led Portugal 3–0 but missed out on a quarter-final place after losing 5–3. Clubs have recently begun to compete in Asian contests, despite the Communist regime's isolationist policies.

GIANT KILLERS

North Korea's 1–0 victory over Italy during the 1966 World Cup was one of the biggest upsets in the history of sport, never mind soccer. "The fall of the Roman Empire had nothing on this" the Northern Echo aptly proclaimed in a newspaper article. For many years the North Korean heroes of the match went unrecognized, but in 2001 a British film crew interviewed seven of the surviving players in Pyongyang.

ENFORCED EXILE

Crowd trouble after a 2005 World Cup qualifier against Iran in Pyongyang meant that the team was forced to play its next home game in an empty stadium in Bangkok, Thailand.

NO SONG, NO FLAG, NO WAY

North and South Korea were due to play each other in the qualifiers for the 2010 World Cup. North Korea insisted that the South could not show their flag or play their national anthem. Despite endless negotiations the North Koreans would not give in so FIFA moved the game to Shanghai, China.

STAT ATTACK

NATIONAL TEAM

NICKNAME: Chollima (a mythical horse)
NATIONAL STADIUM:
Kim Il Sung, 70,000
WORLD CUP FINALS: 1 appearance

MAIN DOMESTIC CLUBS

PYONGYANG CITY SPORTS GROUP
FOUNDED: Pyongyang, 1956
STADIUM: Kim Il Sung, 70,000

4:25 (APRIL 25TH)
FOUNDED: Nampo, 1949
STADIUM: Nampo, 30,000

LOCOMOTIVE S.G.
FOUNDED: Sinuiju, 1956
STADIUM: Sinuiju, 17,500

THAILAND

HOME   AWAY

POPULATION: 64.9 MILLION
CAPITAL: BANGKOK
FA: FOOTBALL ASSOCIATION OF THAILAND

The earliest recorded match in Thailand, then called Siam, took place in 1915 between locals and Europeans. A soccer association was founded in 1916. Although Thailand has never made it to the World Cup, they have qualified for the Asian Cup six times.

BETTER TO LOSE THAN TO WIN

When Thailand and Indonesia played their final group game of the 1998 Tiger Cup, both had already qualified for the semi-finals. Winning the game and the group would leave the victor facing Vietnam, and the loser facing Singapore, a weaker team. The game ended 2–2 as both sides stopped defending. Indonesian defender Mursyid Effendi deliberately scored an own goal and both teams were fined for "violating the spirit of the game."

BAD START

Thailand's first official outing in international competition was at the 1956 Olympics. Sadly, they only lasted one game, losing 9–0 to Great Britain.

LOOKING OUTSIDE

Although interest in the Thai Premier League is growing steadily, foreign soccer is incredibly popular. Despite gambling being illegal in Thailand, estimates suggest that five percent of country's GDP was gambled on the 2006 World Cup tournament. Thailand's ex-prime minister Thaksin Shinawatra also bought English club Manchester City, then sold it a year later.

STAT ATTACK

NATIONAL TEAM

NICKNAME: The War Elephants
NATIONAL STADIUM:
Rajamangala, 60,000
WORLD CUP FINALS: None

MAIN DOMESTIC CLUBS

CHONBURI
FOUNDED: Chonburi, 2002
STADIUM: Chonburi Municipality and Princess Sirindhorn, 5,000

KRUNG THAI BANK
FOUNDED: Bangkok, 1977
STADIUM: Chulalongkorn University Sports, 25,000

BEC TERO SASANA
FOUNDED: Bangkok 1992
STADIUM: BEC Tero Sasana Nong Chok, 5,000

ASIA: TOP CLUBS

The sheer size and poor transportation networks of Asia have, until recently, made regular competition between the region's teams—and comparison between them—difficult. The Asian Champions League is an imperfect guide to the elite —the big clubs from Iran, Saudi Arabia, the Gulf, and East Asia are all represented, but some of the biggest teams are not, such as Mohan Bagan of Calcutta, India.

MIDDLE EAST

The clubs of the Middle East used to be also-rans, but in recent years the region's oil money and soccer obsession has produced clubs good enough to join the continents' elite. Al-Ittihad was founded in Jeddah in 1928, making it the oldest surviving club in Saudi Arabia, and is the main rival to Al-Hilal's at the top of Saudi soccer. Al-Arabi is the leading club in Qatar and the first from the country to reach an Asian continental final.

NAKAMURA SHUNSUKE
Starting out at Japanese powerhouse Yokohama Merinos, Nakamura followed the best Asian players by moving to Europe. He joined Reggina (Italy) in 2002 and Celtic (Scotland) in 2005.

THE CLUBS

Asia's top clubs are clustered around the fringes of the continent—the Iranian and Gulf clubs to the west, and the Japanese and South Korean teams to the east. South Asia boasts a number of big clubs, but they have yet to register success beyond their borders.

Esteghlal
Country: Iran
Founded: Tehran, 1945
Stadium: Azadi
Capacity: 110,000

Pirouzi
Country: Iran
Founded: Tehran, 1963
Stadium: Azadi
Capacity: 110,000

Al-Hilal
Country: Saudi Arabia
Founded: Riyadh, 1957
Stadium: Prince Faisal bin Fahd
Capacity: 27,000

Al-Ain FC
Country: UAE
Founded: Dubai, 1968
Stadium: Tahnoun bin Mohamed
Capacity: 10,000

STAT ATTACK

DOMESTIC TEAMS

ESTEGHLAL
Founded by a group of military cycling enthusiasts, Esteghlal was originally named Taj—"Crown" in Persian. After the Islamic Revolution, the name was changed to Esteghlal, which means "Independence." The club forms one half of the Tehran Derby, and has been the most successful Iranian club in Asian club competitions.

HONORS: LEAGUE 6, CUP 5; ASIAN CHAMPIONS LEAGUE WINNERS 1970, 1991

PIROUZI
Founded in 1963 as Persepolis by Ali Abdo, an American-Iranian boxer, the team steadily improved throughout the 1970s and won its first national title in 1973. After the Islamic revolution, the club was renamed Pirouzi ("Victory") but the fans still call it by its old name. In the last decade, Pirouzi has become the leading side in Iran.

HONORS: LEAGUE 9, CUP 3; ASIAN CHAMPIONS LEAGUE WINNERS 1993

AL-HILAL
Founded as Olympic Club, the then-King Saud watched the team play and insisted on changing their name to Al-Hilal. They have since become the Bayern Munich of the Middle East—easily the most successful, if not the most loved, team. They have won two Asian Champions Cups and a host of Arab and Middle Eastern trophies.

HONORS: LEAGUE 11, CUP 2; ASIAN CHAMPIONS LEAGUE WINNERS 1992, 2000; ASIAN CUP WINNERS CUP 1997, 2002

EAST ASIA

Alongside the Japanese and South Korean giants is China's biggest club Dalian Shide, who have won a host of domestic league and cup titles. Life at the once-great Lioaning has not been so kind—despite winning the Asian Champions Cup and seven Chinese titles, they fell on such hard financial times that they were bailed out by stand-up comedian Zhao Benshan, who lent them grounds to train on.

THE RISING GENERATION

A new generation of clubs is rising in Asian soccer to challenge the old guard—Gamba Osaka from Japan came from obscurity to win the Asian Champions League in 2008 and their beaten finalist—Adelaide United—suggest that Australian teams will soon be challenging to match the Asian soccer elite.

DOMESTIC TEAMS

YOKOHAMA F MARINOS
Originally the factory team of Nissan Motors, the club became the Yokohama Marinos when they entered the J-League in 1993, and then took the initial "F" after a merger with cross-town rivals Yokahama Flügels in 1999. They have five J-league titles to their name, and in 2003 became the first team to win both halves of a single season.

HONORS: LEAGUE 5, CUP 6; ASIAN CUP WINNERS CUP 1992, 1993

URAWA RED DIAMONDS
Beginning life in 1950 as Mitsubishi Motors' factory team, Urawa took its current name as a founder member of the J-League in 1993. Despite patchy success, it has the biggest, most consistent, and raucous support in Japan, which was rewarded when Urawa won the J-League in 2006 and the Asian Champions League the following year.

HONORS: LEAGUE 5, CUP 6; ASIAN CHAMPIONS LEAGUE WINNERS 2007

JÚBILO IWATA
Júbilo—"exultation" in Portuguese—have won the Japanese J-League title three times, as well as finishing runners-up on three occasions. The club holds the distinction of being Japan's most successful team in international club soccer, making three successive appearances in the Asian Champions Cup final, winning the title once.

HONORS: LEAGUE 4, CUP 2; ASIAN CHAMPIONS LEAGUE WINNERS 1999

SAMSUNG SUWON BLUEWINGS
With the money of the giant Samsung Chaebol behind them, the Bluewings established themselves as one of Asia's biggest clubs with back-to-back Champions Cup victories in 2001 and 2002. They can also boast some of the largest and most organized crowds and supporters' clubs in the continent—particularly the official club, Grand Bleu.

HONORS: LEAGUE 3, CUP 1; ASIAN CHAMPIONS LEAGUE WINNERS 2001, 2002

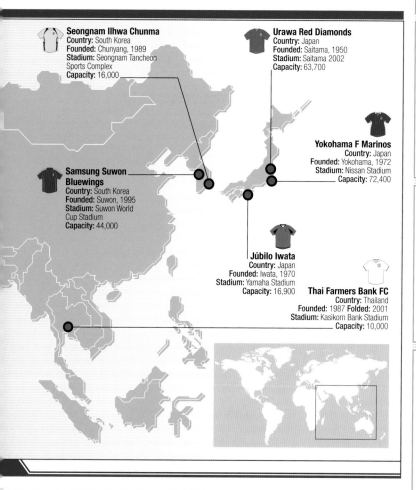

Seongnam Ilhwa Chunma
Country: South Korea
Founded: Chunyang, 1989
Stadium: Seongnam Tancheon Sports Complex
Capacity: 16,000

Urawa Red Diamonds
Country: Japan
Founded: Saitama, 1950
Stadium: Saitama 2002
Capacity: 63,700

Yokohama F Marinos
Country: Japan
Founded: Yokohama, 1972
Stadium: Nissan Stadium
Capacity: 72,400

Samsung Suwon Bluewings
Country: South Korea
Founded: Suwon, 1995
Stadium: Suwon World Cup Stadium
Capacity: 44,000

Júbilo Iwata
Country: Japan
Founded: Iwata, 1970
Stadium: Yamaha Stadium
Capacity: 16,900

Thai Farmers Bank FC
Country: Thailand
Founded: 1987 Folded: 2001
Stadium: Kasikorn Bank Stadium
Capacity: 10,000

AL-AIN
Despite coming from one of the smaller cities of the United Arab Emirates, Al-Ain ("The Spring") is the UAE's leading soccer club, and its only Asian champion. Their uniform has changed several times since their foundation, first from green to red, then to the current purple, inspired by a training match with Belgian side Anderlecht.

HONORS: LEAGUE 9, CUP 4; ASIAN CHAMPIONS LEAGUE WINNERS 2003

THAI FARMERS BANK FC
With two consecutive Asian Champions Cups in 1994 and 1995, Thai Farmers Bank FC was the only Thai side to win the tournament. Unfortunately, the major Asian financial crisis of 1997 led to the club sponsor's stock price collapsing. The club was taken over by foreign investors, finance was withdrawn, and in 2001 the club finally folded.

HONORS: LEAGUE 5, CUP 4; ASIAN CHAMPIONS LEAGUE WINNERS 1994, 1995

SEONGNAM ILHWA CHUNMA
The South Korean club began life as Ilhwa Chunma in Seoul, but was relocated to the provincial city of Cheonon in 1995 by the soccer authorities. Four disastrous seasons followed and the club returned to Seongnam, a satellite town of Seoul. Four K-League titles soon followed and the club returned to the highest levels of Asian competition.

HONORS: LEAGUE 7, CUP 0; ASIAN CHAMPIONS LEAGUE WINNERS 1996

AUSTRALIA

HOME

AWAY

POPULATION: 20.3 MILLION
CAPITAL: CANBERRA
FA: FOOTBALL FEDERATION AUSTRALIA
LICENSED PLAYERS:
MALE: 780,000
FEMALE: 190,000
PROFESSIONALS: 200
REGISTERED CLUBS: 2,300

Association soccer arrived in Australia in the 1870s and faced competition from Australian football, rugby union, and cricket. The game was boosted by Greek, Serb, and Croat immigrants after World War II, but it was not until the 21st century that a wave of Australians playing in the top overseas leagues raised the bar, culminating in qualification for the 2006 World Cup.

WORLD CUP 2006

The Socceroos' trip to Germany in 2006 was their most successful World Cup. They progressed from the group stage only to be knocked out by Italy. A 95th-minute penalty left Australia with the unenviable record of being the first team to be knocked out of a World Cup with the very last kick of the match.

NATIONAL BETRAYAL

Playing for Australia has been passed up by a number of players eligible to play for other nations, including Christian Vieri (Italy); Tony Dorigo and Craig Johnston (England); Joey Didulica, Anthony Šeric, and Josip Šimunic (Croatia); and Saša Ilic and Ivan Ergic (Serbia).

DISASTER IN MELBOURNE

Prior to joining the Asian Football Confederation in 2006, qualification for the World Cup was a tortuous process for Australia, requiring them to win the Oceania group and then enter a play-off with either an Asian or South American team. In 1997, Australia faced Iran in a play-off for a berth at the 1998 World Cup in Frace, and managed a 1–1 draw in Tehran. At home they were 2–0 up when a man notorious for disrupting Australian public events ran onto the field and broke a crossbar. After a long-enforced break, Iran grabbed two late goals to win the place in Paris.

MARK VIDUKA
Captain of the Socceroos at the 2006 World Cup, Viduka is the leading player of his generation, and has played in the top divisions of Croatia, Scotland, and England.

STAT ATTACK

NATIONAL TEAM

NICKNAME: Socceroos
NATIONAL STADIUM: None
WORLD CUP FINALS: 2 appearances
BIGGEST WIN: 31–0 vs American Samoa, 2001
BIGGEST DEFEAT: 0–8 vs South Africa, 1955
MOST CAPS: Alex Tobin, **87**
MOST GOALS: Damian Mori, **29**

A-LEAGUE

ADELAIDE UNITED
CITY: Adelaide, SA
FOUNDED: 2003

HOME
STADIUM: Hindmarsh Stadium
CAPACITY: 16,500
HONORS: ASIAN CHAMPIONS LEAGUE RUNNERS-UP 2008

GOLD COAST UNITED
CITY: Gold Coast, QLD
FOUNDED: 2008

HOME
STADIUM: Skilled Park
CAPACITY: 27,000
HONORS: None

NORTH QUEENSLAND FURY
CITY: Townsville, QLD
FOUNDED: 2008

HOME
STADIUM: Dairy Farmers Stadium
CAPACITY: 25,000
HONORS: None

CENTRAL COAST MARINERS
CITY: Gosford, NSW
FOUNDED: 2004
HOME
STADIUM: Bluetongue Central Coast Stadium
CAPACITY: 20,100
HONORS: None

MELBOURNE VICTORY
CITY: Melbourne, VIC
FOUNDED: 2004

HOME
STADIUM: Telstra Dome
CAPACITY: 56,300
HONORS: A-LEAGUE 2007, 2009

NEWCASTLE JETS
CITY: Newcastle, NSW
FOUNDED: 2000

HOME
STADIUM: Energy Australia Stadium
CAPACITY: 26,100
HONORS: A-LEAGUE 2008

A-LEAGUE

The A-League is the most recent and successful attempt to set Australian professional soccer on a sustainable commercial footing. It was first played in 2005 with eight teams, expanded to ten in 2009, and may expand further. Crowds have been consistent and the league is competitive.

The league imposes a strict salary cap on clubs, but to ensure a sprinkling of minor stars, allows each a marquee player who can be paid above the salary cap. The top two teams in the league qualify for the Asian Champions League.

HARRY KEWELL

The only Australian-born player to win the UEFA Champions League—with Liverpool in 2005—attacking midfielder Kewell made his mark at Leeds United, and has become a favorite at the Turkish club Galatasaray.

BORN: **SEPTEMBER 22, 1978, SYDNEY, AUSTRALIA**
HEIGHT: **5FT 11IN (1.8M)**
MAIN CLUBS: **LEEDS UNITED, LIVERPOOL, GALATASARAY**
INTERNATIONAL CAPS: **38**

THE OLD SCHOOL

Prior to the A-league, Australian soccer was more loosely organized and leagues and clubs regularly rose and fell, although the top-tier National Soccer League (NSL) ran from 1977 to 2004. Shunned by the majority of Australians, the game was rejuvenated by a post-war influx of European migrants. Marconi Stallions and Adelaide City—known as Juventus until the mid-1960s—were Italian clubs, South Melbourne was Greek, and Sydney City began as the Jewish club Sydney Hakoah.

STAT ATTACK
THE OLD SCHOOL

SYDNEY CITY
FOUNDED: Sydney, 1939
STADIUM: Sydney Athletic Field
CAPACITY: Not available
INTERNATIONAL HONORS: None
LEAGUE: 4 CUP: 3

SOUTH MELBOURNE
FOUNDED: Melbourne, 1959
STADIUM: Bob Jane Stadium
CAPACITY: 14,000
INTERNATIONAL HONORS: OCEANIA CLUB CUP 2000
LEAGUE: 4 CUP: 2

ADELAIDE CITY
FOUNDED: Adelaide, 1946
STADIUM: Ram Park
CAPACITY: 3,500
INTERNATIONAL HONORS: OCEANIA CLUB CUP 1987
LEAGUE: 3 CUP: 3

MARCONI STALLIONS
FOUNDED: Sydney, 1956
STADIUM: Marconi Stadium
CAPACITY: 11,000
INTERNATIONAL HONORS: None
LEAGUE: 4 CUP: 1

PERTH GLORY
CITY: Perth, WA
FOUNDED: 1996
 HOME
STADIUM: Members Equity Stadium
CAPACITY: 17,300
HONORS: NSL 2003, 2004

SYDNEY FC
CITY: Sydney, NSW
FOUNDED: 2004
HOME
STADIUM: Sydney Football Stadium
CAPACITY: 45,500
HONORS: A-LEAGUE 2006

QUEENSLAND ROAR
CITY: Perth, WA
FOUNDED: 2005
 HOME
STADIUM: Suncorp Stadium
CAPACITY: 52,500
HONORS: None

WELLINGTON PHOENIX
CITY: Wellington, NZ
YEARS IN COMPETITION: 2007
 HOME
STADIUM: Westpac Stadium
CAPACITY: 36,000
HONORS: None

OCEANIA

Covering the widely dispersed islands of the Pacific, Oceania is a watery region in which soccer was always going to be problematic. The confederation was founded in 1966 by Australia (who left in 2006), New Zealand, and Fiji, and has steadily incorporated most of the Polynesian and Micronesian island chains. It became a full FIFA member in 1996, but World Cup qualification requires a play-off with a South American or Asian team.

NEW ZEALAND

In the last quarter of the 1800s, New Zealand was exposed to the formalized rules of soccer, Gaelic football, Australian Rules football, Rugby League, and Rugby Union. A national FA was established out of the ensuing melee in 1891, and a Glaswegian whiskey merchant created a national competition called the Brown Shield, which was later superceded by the Chatham Cup. The trophy was provided in 1922 by *HMS Chatham*, a passing British naval ship.

THE ALL WHITES

It soon became clear that Rugby Union, above all else, would be the national sport in New Zealand, so soccer was confined to the small industrial and mining towns of the islands. More recently, the economic logic of the sport has led to the expansion of the Australian A-League to include leading New Zealand sides Auckland and Wellington. Despite soccer's minority status in New Zealand, the country did qualify for the 1982 World Cup. The "All Whites" went to Spain where they lost all three group stage games.

RYAN NELSON

One of New Zealand's top soccer exports, Nelsen spent four years playing in Major League Soccer in the US. Signed by Blackburn Rovers in the English Premier League in 2005, Nelsen is a consistent performer for club and country.

CHARLES DEMPSEY

Oceania's biggest moment on the global soccer stage came during the final stages of the 2006 World Cup bid. With Germany and South Africa neck and neck, Dempsey was left with the casting vote but decided to abstain rather than vote for the OFC's choice of South Africa —Germany got the cup.

I CALL ON ALL NATIONS [TO] WORK TOGETHER FOR THE DEVELOPMENT OF SOCCER IN THE SOUTH PACIFIC

SIR WILLIAM WALKLEY
FOUNDING PRESIDENT OF OFC, 1968

STAT ATTACK

NATIONAL TEAMS

NEW ZEALAND
GOVERNING BODY:
New Zealand Football
FOUNDED: 1891
NATIONAL STADIUM:
North Harbour Stadium, 25,000
BIGGEST WIN:
13–0 vs Fiji, 1981
BIGGEST DEFEAT:
0–10 vs Australia, 1936

SOLOMON ISLANDS
GOVERNING BODY:
Solomon Islands Football Federation
FOUNDED: 1979
NATIONAL STADIUM: Lawson Tama Stadium, 15,000
BIGGEST WIN:
17–0 vs Wallis and Futuna Islands, 1991
BIGGEST DEFEAT:
0–18 vs Tahiti, 1963

FIJI
GOVERNING BODY:
Fiji Football association
FOUNDED: 1974
NATIONAL STADIUM:
Post Fiji Stadium, 30,000
BIGGEST WIN:
4–1 vs Tuvalu, 2007
BIGGEST DEFEAT:
0–13 vs New Zealand, 1981

SOLOMON ISLANDS

The Solomon Islands are the rising force in Oceanic soccer. In a tightly contested mini-league to determine an Oceanic play-off for World Cup 2006 qualification, they managed an amazing 2–2 tie with Australia that pushed out New Zealand. However, in the final play-off with Australia, they lost 5–1 and 6–0.

FIJI

Soccer arrived in Fiji at the turn of the 20th century and was initially played by European expatriates. However, Rugby Union became more popular in the 1930s, after which the Indian community of Fiji took up the sport, creating their own Indian soccer association. The game and the association were ethnically broadened in the 1960s.

NEW CALEDONIA

New Caledonia's famous son, Christian Karembeu, won the 1998 World Cup with France. He refused to sing the French national anthem as two of his uncles had been exhibited in a "human zoo" at the 1931 Paris Expo.

VANUATU

What do Vanuatu and Latvia have in common? By 2008, both had produced a team that had won 14 championships in a row—Tafea FC and Skonta Riga.

TONGA

Tonga can boast the services of former Red Star Belgrade and Real Madrid player Milan Jankovic, who took over as the national association's technical director and coach in 2002. His main task was to end the days of losing 22–0.

ASSOCIATE MEMBERS

The OFC includes a number of smaller nations that are classed as Associate Members due to not being full members of FIFA, including Kiribati, Micronesia, Niue, Northern Mariana Islands, Palau, and Tuvalu. They can enter the OFC Nations Cup, but are not eligible to qualify for the World Cup.

AMERICAN SAMOA

American Samoa can claim an international victory—against the Wallis and Futuna Islands in 1983—but FIFA has deemed it unofficial. Consequently the best, if unwanted, soccer record they possess is that in 2001 they suffered the heaviest defeat in competitive international play, losing 0–31 to Australia.

SAMOA

A more technical approach to coaching combined with FIFA investment in infrastructure has ended the days of disastrous results for Samoa. With some professional facilities and the arrival of coach David Brand, Samoa is improving.

PAPUA NEW GUINEA

With a population bigger than New Zealand, there is no shortage of players. But as a developing nation, investment is limited so results remain poor.

TAHITI

Encompassing the whole of French Polynesia, Tahiti achieved an amazing third-place finish at the 2002 OFC Nations Cup after beating Vanuatu 1-0 in the play-off. The country is still the highest-ranked island nation, according to FIFA.

0.5 World Cup Qualifying places allocated to OFC

3,000 Number of licensed soccer officals in the Oceania confederation

2000 Year Tahiti hosted its first Oceania Nations Cup

160 Papua New Guinea's highest place in FIFA World Ranking (2004)

NATIONAL TEAMS

AMERICAN SAMOA
GOVERNING BODY:
Football Federation American Samoa
FOUNDED: 2007
NATIONAL STADIUM:
Veterans Memorial Stadium, 10,000
BIGGEST WIN:
3–0 vs Wallis and Futuna Islands, 1983
BIGGEST DEFEAT:
0–31 vs Australia, 2001

SAMOA
GOVERNING BODY:
Samoa Football Soccer Federation
FOUNDED: 1968
NATIONAL STADIUM: Toleafoa JS Blatter Soccer Stadium, 3,500
BIGGEST WIN:
8–0 vs American Samoa, 2001
BIGGEST DEFEAT:
0–13 vs Tahiti, 1981

PAPUA NEW GUINEA
GOVERNING BODY:
Papua New Guinea Football Association
FOUNDED: 1962
NATIONAL STADIUM:
Hubert Murray Stadium, 15,000
BIGGEST WIN:
20–0 vs American Samoa, 1987
BIGGEST DEFEAT:
2–11 vs Australia, 1980

TAHITI
GOVERNING BODY:
Fédération Tahitienne de Football
FOUNDED: 1989
NATIONAL STADIUM:
Stade Pater Te Hono Nui, 10,000
BIGGEST WIN:
30–0 vs Cook Islands, 1971
BIGGEST DEFEAT:
0–10 vs New Zealand, 2004

NEW CALEDONIA
GOVERNING BODY:
Fédération Calédonienne de Football
FOUNDED: 1928
NATIONAL STADIUM: Stade Numa-Daly Magenta, 16,000
BIGGEST WIN:
18–0 vs Guam, 1991 and Micronesia, 2003
BIGGEST DEFEAT:
0–11 vs Australia 2002

VANUATU
GOVERNING BODY:
Vanuatu Football Federation
FOUNDED: 1934
NATIONAL STADIUM:
Korman Stadium, 5,000
BIGGEST WIN:
18–0 vs Kiribati, 2003
BIGGEST DEFEAT:
0–9 vs New Zealand, 1951

TONGA
GOVERNING BODY:
Tonga Football Association
FOUNDED: 1965
NATIONAL STADIUM:
Teufaiva Sport Stadium, 10,000
BIGGEST WIN:
7–0 vs Micronesia, 2003
BIGGEST DEFEAT:
0–22 vs Australia, 2001

THE
COMPETITIONS

THE WORLD CUP

URUGUAY 1930

When FIFA met in 1929 to decide where to hold the inaugural World Cup, only Uruguay was ready to foot the bill, paid for by its huge beef exports. The government decided to celebrate the centenary of the country's constitution and hold the World Cup at the same time in the great stadium that was specially built for the tournament—the Estadio Centenario.

A GAME OF TWO HALVES

Ahead of the final, the participants argued about which ball to use. They decided to play with Argentina's favored ball in the first half and Uruguay's in the second. The teams picked wisely —both won the half that featured "their" ball.

A HAPHAZARD AFFAIR

The Uruguayan FA wrote to everyone, but not everyone came. The Germans turned down the offer, as did the Scandinavians and the English, Irish, Scottish, and Welsh teams. Jules Rimet insisted that his home team, France, should attend, but the coach stayed home. The Romanians only came because Prince Carol paid for a boat and his mistress persuaded the oil companies that employed most of the team to let them have a month off.

JULES RIMET
With 33 years service, Rimet is FIFA's longest-serving president. The trophy for the winners of the competition he initiated was originally called Victory. In 1946 it was renamed in his honor.

GOALS GALORE
Argentina and Uruguay predictably swept the opposition aside. Yugoslavia were the only Europeans who put up any resistance and the USA made their first and only World Cup semi-final. The game between Romania and Peru recorded what became the lowest ever attendance at a World Cup game —just 300. Remarkably, both semi-finals finished 6–1 and six goals were scored in the final.

JOSÉ LEANDRO ANDRADE
As a mainstay of the dominant Uruguay team of the 1920s, the skilful midfielder was one of the first black players to gain international recognition. He topped his international career during his country's victory in the 1930 final.

SEMI-FINALS		FINAL	
ARGENTINA	6		
USA	1	URUGUAY	4
URUGUAY	6	ARGENTINA	2
YUGOSLAVIA	1		

STAT ATTACK   GROUP STAGE

GROUP 1	W	D	L	PT	GROUP 2	W	D	L	PT	GROUP 3	W	D	L	PT	GROUP 4	W	D	L	PT
Argentina	3	0	0	6*	Yugoslavia	2	0	0	4*	Uruguay	2	0	0	4*	USA	2	0	0	4*
Chile	2	0	1	4	Brazil	1	0	1	2	Romania	1	0	1	2	Paraguay	1	0	1	2
France	1	0	2	2	Bolivia	0	0	2	0	Peru	0	0	2	0	Belgium	0	0	2	0
Mexico	0	0	3	0															

* The top team from each group qualified for the semi-finals

THE FINAL

No one knows exactly how many Argentinians crossed the Plate River from Buenos Aires to Montevideo, but 15,000 is a reasonable guess. Six members of the Argentinian Chamber of Deputies requisitioned a government barge and tugboat to get them there. A fifth of the adult male population of Uruguay watched from the bleachers. The home side trailed 2–1 at half-time, but then came back with three goals in the second half to win the first World Cup.

SUBS: No tactical substitutions at this World Cup

URUGUAY ④	ARGENTINA ②
JULY 30, ESTADIO CENTENARIO: 93,000	
MANAGER: ALBERTO SUPPICI	MANAGERS: FRANCISCO OLAZAR & JUAN JOSÉ TRAMUTOLA
FORMATION: 2-3-5	FORMATION: 2-3-5

OUR FIGHTING SPIRIT OVERWHELMED
THE ARGENTINIANS

JOSÉ NASAZZI
URUGUAY CAPTAIN, 1930

THE VENUES

Uniquely in World Cup history, every match was played in one city – Montevideo. Only three stadiums were used: the Estadio Centenario (ten games), Estadio Pocitos (two games), and Estadio Parque Central (six games). Building work continued at each stadium as the tournament progressed.

GUILLERMO STÁBILE
One of the first globally recognized soccer heroes, Stábile first played for Argentina at the inaugural finals in Uruguay in 1930. He bagged the Golden Boot with an impressive eight goals, including a hat trick on his international debut.

TOP GOALSCORERS

Guillermo STÁBILE	Argentina	8 goals
Pedro CEA	Uruguay	5 goals
Guillermo SUBIABRE	Chile	4 goals
Bert PATENAUDE	USA	4 goals

GOLDEN BALL

José NASAZZI	Uruguay

Estadio Pocitos
Capacity: 20,000

Estadio Parque Central
Capacity: 20,000

Estadio Centenario
Capacity: 100,000

ITALY 1934

By 1934 Uruguay, the first country to host the World Cup and the defending champions, had so little money that they couldn't afford to send a team to defend their title. However, Italy, which was under the control of Benito Mussolini, decided being hosts would be good for national pride. The resulting tournament consequently set the standard for turning sports events into political propaganda.

TWO TROPHIES

After winning the final, the Italian team was presented with two trophies. One was FIFA's Coupe de Jules Rimet and the other was La Coppa del Duce, which Mussolini had specially commissioned. Each player received a gold medal in recognition of the conquest of socccer and a signed photograph of Il Duce.

THE WUNDERTEAM FINALLY LOSE

The Italian government generously paid three-quarters of foreign fans' travel expenses, and transportation within Italy was free. Once again the British decided not to come. The Secretary of the FA, Sir Fredrick Wall, wrote of his invitation, "I have no desire to be a guest of the Italian Football Federation."

The team everyone really wanted to watch were the Austrians, who arrived in Italy on the back of a long, unbroken series of victories. Known as the Wunderteam, they met the hosts in the semi-finals, going down to a single goal bundled over the line on a rain-soaked San Siro field in Milan.

NO GROUP STAGE

The 1934 World Cup seemed especially cruel as there was no group stage, so each team faced elimination after just one game. In the opening match of the tournament, Italy thrashed the USA 7–1. Egypt, the first African team to play at a World Cup finals, gave Hungary a good game. France took the Austrian Wunderteam into extra time—the first World Cup game to do so.

VITTORIO POZZO
As the Italian national coach, Pozzo took his side to World Cup glory, not once but twice during the 1930s. He remains the only manager with a brace of World Cup wins to his name.

1ST ROUND		QUARTER-FINALS		SEMI-FINALS		FINAL	
ITALY	7						
USA	1	ITALY	1 (1)				
SPAIN	3	SPAIN	1 (0)*				
BRAZIL	1			ITALY	1		
HUNGARY	4			AUSTRIA	0		
EGYPT	2	HUNGARY	1				
AUSTRIA	3•	AUSTRIA	2				
FRANCE	2					ITALY	2•
CZECHOSLOVAKIA	2					CZECHOSLOVAKIA	1
ROMANIA	1	CZECHOSLOVAKIA	3				
NETHERLANDS	2	SWITZERLAND	2				
SWITZERLAND	3			CZECHOSLOVAKIA	3		
ARGENTINA	2			GERMANY	1		
SWEDEN	3	SWEDEN	1				
GERMANY	5	GERMANY	2				
BELGIUM	2						

No group stage at the 1934 World Cup   * Replay   • After extra time

GIUSEPPE MEAZZA
The Italian George Best, Meazza was a supremely talented striker whose antics both on and off the field made him the first superstar of the Italian game.

THE VENUES

In 1930 all the matches had been played in one city (Montevideo). The Italians went the other way, using eight widely distributed stadiums for the tournament's 16 games. One, the San Siro in Milan, would eventually be renamed after Guiseppe Meazza, who played in the semi-final that was held there.

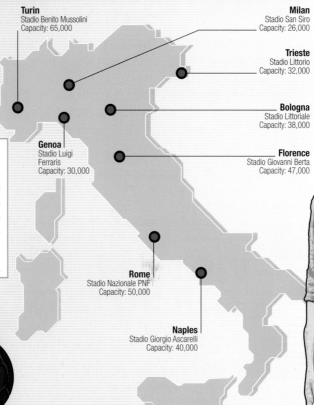

Turin
Stadio Benito Mussolini
Capacity: 65,000

Milan
Stadio San Siro
Capacity: 26,000

Trieste
Stadio Littorio
Capacity: 32,000

Bologna
Stadio Littoriale
Capacity: 38,000

Genoa
Stadio Luigi Ferraris
Capacity: 30,000

Florence
Stadio Giovanni Berta
Capacity: 47,000

Rome
Stadio Nazionale PNF
Capacity: 50,000

Naples
Stadio Giorgio Ascarelli
Capacity: 40,000

TOP GOALSCORERS

Oldrich NEJEDLÝ	Czechoslovakia	5 goals
Edmund CONEN	Germany	4 goals
Angelo SCHIAVIO	Italy	4 goals
Raimundo ORSI	Italy	3 goals
Leopold KIELHOLZ	Switzerland	3 goals

GOLDEN BALL

Giuseppe MEAZZA	Italy

ITALY'S ARGENTINIANS

The spine of Italy's team were Argentinians by birth and were known as the Rempatriato. Luis Monti, Raimondo Orsi, and Enrico Guaita had come to play in the Italian league and, because of their Italian grandparents, played for the national team. Monti had played for Argentina at the 1930 World Cup.

OLDRICH NEJEDLÝ
The Czech striker was nothing short of a goal scoring machine, ending up top scorer at the 1934 finals with five goals. His international career was cut short when he broke his leg during the finals of 1938.

THE FINAL

The only World Cup final to have two goalkeepers as captains—Combi for the Italians and Plánicka for the Czechs—was goalless for 71 minutes. After being taken off and revived with ammonia, the Czech striker Puc returned to the field to score the opening goal just two minutes later. The Italians survived five minutes of panic and recovered their poise when Orsi curled the ball from the edge of the area into the Czech goal. Schiavio's winner came five minutes into extra time.

CZECHOSLOVAKIA ①	ITALY ②
JUNE 10, STADIO NAZIONALE: 45,000	
MANAGER: KAREL PETRU	MANAGER: VITTORIO POZZO
FORMATION: 2-3-5	FORMATION: 2-3-5

GK Combi
DF Monzeglio **DF** Allemandi
MF Ferraris **MF** Monti **MF** Bertolini
FW Guaita **FW** Meazza **FW** Schiavio **FW** Ferrari **FW** Orsi
FW Puc **FW** Nejedlý **FW** Sobotka **FW** Svoboda **FW** Junek
MF Krčil **MF** Čambal **MF** Košťálek
DF Čtyřoký **DF** Ženíšek
GK Plániwka

SUBS: No tactical substitutions at this World Cup

FRANCE 1938

The third World Cup was played in the shadow of World War II. Germany had swallowed Austria, and the Japanese and Chinese were fighting each other. Brazil was the only South American team who could afford to come and the British sent a delegation to watch the games. Italy, the defending champions, were met by large anti-fascist protests, but it didn't bother them as they made it two wins in a row.

ALL ABOUT BRAZIL

The Brazilians gripped the soccer world's imagination. They played an open attacking game against Poland, but their quarter-final against the Czechs was a spiteful draw and the replay a strange, lethargic match. With striker Leônidas injured, however, they lost to Italy in the semi-finals, although they won the third place play-off in some style.

ALFREDO FONI
Foni formed a formidable defensive partnership with Juventus teammate Pietro Rava. Their match-winning performances brought Italy World Cup success.

ATTACKING FLAIR

Brazil brought attacking flair to the World Cup, exemplified by their striker Leônidas—one of only two black players in the squad. Their opening game against Poland in Strasbourg went to extra time with the score at 4–4. Brazil eventually won the game 6–5 on a rain-soaked field. Leônidas scored a hat trick.

VICTORY... OR NOTHING!

BENITO MUSSOLINI
TELEGRAM TO THE NATIONAL TEAM

SOCCER NEW BOYS

Two nations, the Dutch East Indies and Cuba, made their World Cup debut. The former were thrashed by Hungary, losing 6–0, but then nine of the team were winning their first cap and the captain played in glasses. Cuba surprised Romania in a 3–3 tie and then won the replay. The Swedes proved tougher, thrashing Cuba 8–0 in the next round. Switzerland's victory over Germany was popular —they came back from 2–0 down to win 4–2.

1ST ROUND		QUARTER-FINALS		SEMI-FINALS		FINAL	
FRANCE	3						
BELGIUM	1	FRANCE	1				
ITALY	2•	ITALY	3				
NORWAY	1			ITALY	2		
BRAZIL	6•			BRAZIL	1		
POLAND	5	BRAZIL	2*				
CZECHOSLOVAKIA	3•	CZECHOSLOVAKIA	1				
NETHERLANDS	0					HUNGARY	2
GERMANY	2*					ITALY	4
SWITZERLAND	4	SWITZERLAND	0				
HUNGARY	6	HUNGARY	2				
DUTCH EAST INDIES	0			HUNGARY	5		
SWEDEN (WALKOVER)				SWEDEN	1		
AUSTRIA (WITHDREW)		SWEDEN	8				
CUBA	2*	CUBA	0				
ROMANIA	1						

* After replays • After extra time

MEAZZA AND SÁROSI
Captaining their respective countries in the 1938 final, the Italian superstar and versatile Hungarian led their teams in a memorable final. Meazza and teammate Giovanni Ferrari dominated the game, while Sárosi's 70th-minute goal ensured the Italians had to work for their win.

THE VENUES

Ten stadiums in nine different cities were selected for the tournament, but only nine were used. The first-round match between Sweden and Austria in Lyon's Stade Gerland was canceled after Austria withdrew.

Lille
Stade Victor Boucquey
Capacity: 15,000

Reims
Vélodrome Municipal
Capacity: 10,000

Strasbourg
Stade de la Meinau
Capacity: 30,000

Le Havre
Stade Cavée Verte
Capacity: 16,400

Paris
Parc des Princes
Capacity: 60,000

Paris
Stade Olympique de Colombes
Capacity: 60,000

Bordeaux
Parc Lescure
Capacity: 34,000

Toulouse
Stade Chapou
Capacity: 35,000

Antibes
Stade du Fort Carré
Capacity: 7,000

Marseille
Stade Vélodrome
Capacity: 60,000

TOP GOALSCORERS		
LEÔNIDAS	Brazil	7 goals
Gyula ZSENGELLÉR	Hungary	6 goals
György SÁROSI	Hungary	5 goals
Silvio PIOLA	Italy	5 goals

GOLDEN BALL	
LEÔNIDAS	Brazil

LEÔNIDAS
Known as "The Rubber Man," Leônidas was one of the pioneers of the bicycle kick who became top scorer at the 1938 finals.

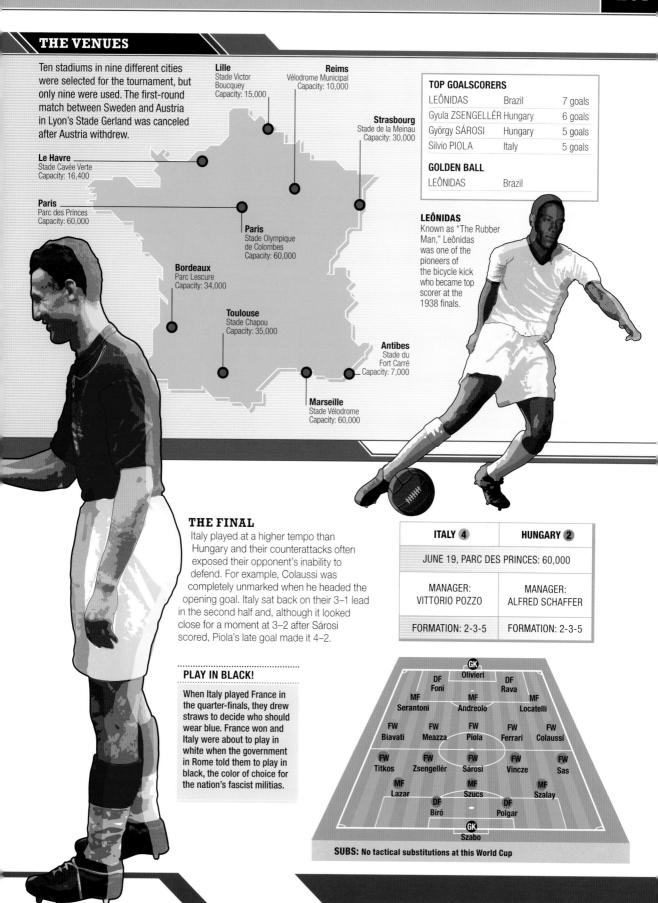

THE FINAL

Italy played at a higher tempo than Hungary and their counterattacks often exposed their opponent's inability to defend. For example, Colaussi was completely unmarked when he headed the opening goal. Italy sat back on their 3–1 lead in the second half and, although it looked close for a moment at 3–2 after Sárosi scored, Piola's late goal made it 4–2.

PLAY IN BLACK!

When Italy played France in the quarter-finals, they drew straws to decide who should wear blue. France won and Italy were about to play in white when the government in Rome told them to play in black, the color of choice for the nation's fascist militias.

ITALY ④	HUNGARY ②
JUNE 19, PARC DES PRINCES: 60,000	
MANAGER: VITTORIO POZZO	MANAGER: ALFRED SCHAFFER
FORMATION: 2-3-5	FORMATION: 2-3-5

GK Olivieri

DF Foni — DF Rava

MF Serantoni — MF Andreolo — MF Locatelli

FW Biavati — FW Meazza — FW Piola — FW Ferrari — FW Colaussi

FW Titkos — FW Zsengellér — FW Sárosi — FW Vincze — FW Sas

MF Lazar — MF Szucs — MF Szalay

DF Biró — DF Polgar

GK Szabo

SUBS: No tactical substitutions at this World Cup

BRAZIL 1950

Brazil was due to host the World Cup 1942, but World War II intervened. It wasn't until 1950 that the world was ready to resume. Domestic soccer was booming in Brazil. The Rio authorities built the world's biggest stadium —the Maracanã—and devoted the Rio Carnival to the World Cup. On the opening day, the Korean War broke out, but nobody in Rio noticed.

BRAZIL ROMP TO THE FINAL

Brazil was the team of the tournament in the opening stages. In their first game, they scored four goals to beat Mexico. They then scored two more against Switzerland and Yugoslavia. In the mini group of four that determined the winner, they beat Sweden 7–1 and Spain 6–1. Uruguay, by contrast, had stuttered through the tournament. Even so, the balance of points meant that the final game between Brazil and Uruguay would determine its outcome.

ENGLAND EMBARRASSED

The big surprise of the group stages was the USA's 1–0 victory over England, who had finally deigned to show up at the World Cup finals. Despite boasting players of the caliber of Tom Finney and Stanley Matthews, England were embarrassingly beaten by a goal from the Haitian-American, Joe Gaetjens. Uruguay were in a group of two—due to Scotland and Turkey pulling out—and thrashed Bolivia 8–0 to progress to the final round.

ZIZINHO
Brazilian legend Pelé says Zizinho was the best player he ever saw. The attacker was lightning fast and very skillful, but is remembered as the figurehead of an outstanding team.

JUAN SCHIAFFINO
Schiaffino, who was known as "Pepe," scored for Uruguay in the 1950 final. His Italian descent later allowed him to be capped for Italy, too.

THE SADNESS WAS SO GREAT... IT SEEMED LIKE THE END OF A WAR WITH BRAZIL THE LOSER

PELÉ
ON LOSING THE FINAL IN 1950

THE MARACANÃ

The Maracanã was the largest and most elegant stadium in the world. With an official capacity of 160,000, it was a double-tiered ellipse with a flat, white, 360-degree roof. Its hidden cantilevers gave unobstructed views from every seat.

STAT ATTACK — GROUP STAGE

GROUP 1	W	D	L	PT	GROUP 2	W	D	L	PT	GROUP 3	W	D	L	PT	GROUP 4	W	D	L	PT
Brazil	2	1	0	5*	Spain	3	0	0	6*	Sweden	1	1	0	3*	Uruguay	1	0	0	2*
Yugoslavia	2	0	1	4	England	1	0	2	2	Italy	1	0	1	2	Bolivia	0	0	1	0
Switzerland	1	1	1	3	Chile	1	0	2	2	Paraguay	0	1	1	1					
Mexico	0	0	3	0	USA	1	0	2	2										

* The top team from each group qualified for the final round

BARBOSA SHUNNED

Brazil's goalkeeper Barbosa and the other black players in the team were made the scapegoats of the great disaster by the press. In later life Barbosa recalled going into a barber shop where a women said to her son, "That's the man that made all Brazil cry" and he was shunned by the Brazilian team at their World Cup training camp in 1994.

THE FINAL

Brazil needed just a point from the final to win the cup. Early in the second half they were 1–0 up in front of the biggest ever crowd at a soccer game. The Uruguayan captain Obdulio Varela picked the ball out of his net and then, in a deliberate act of defiance, walked agonizingly slowly back to the center circle. The crowd turned from cheering to booing to silence. Something broke in Brazil and two late goals from Uruguay made them champions.

URUGUAY ②	BRAZIL ①
JULY 16, MARACANÃ: 199,954	
MANAGER: JUAN LÓPEZ FONTANA	MANAGER: FLÁVIO COSTA
FORMATION: 3-4-3	FORMATION: 3-4-3

GK Máspoli
DF González, M   **DF** Varela   **DF** Tejera
MF Ghiggia   **MF** Gambetta   **MF** Andrade   **MF** Morán
FW Pérez   **FW** Míguez   **FW** Schiaffino

FW Chico   **FW** Ademir   **FW** Friaça
MF Jair   **MF** Danilo   **MF** Zizinho   **MF** Bauer
DF Bigode   **DF** Augusto   **DF** Juvenal
GK Barbosa

SUBS: No tactical substitutions at this World Cup

THE VENUES

Six cities hosted matches in the tournament, all of them on or near the country's Atlantic coastline. Attendances varied wildly. A mere 3,500 spectators turned up to see Switzerland's victory over Mexico in Porto Alegre. Only 1,500 more watched Uruguay thrash Bolivia in Belo Horizonte, but the 199,954 crowd at the final in Rio was the biggest in history.

TOP GOALSCORERS

Ademir	Brazil	8 goals
Estanislao BASORA	Spain	5 goals
Oscar MÍGUEZ	Uruguay	5 goals
CHICO	Brazil	4 goals
ZARRA	Spain	4 goals
Alcides GHIGGIA	Uruguay	4 goals

GOLDEN BALL

ZIZINHO	Brazil

ADEMIR
Nicknamed "Queixada" ("Jaw"), the Brazilian Ademir was the tournament's top scorer, but there is a controversy over whether he scored seven, eight, or nine goals.

Recife
Estádio Ilha do Retiro
Capacity: 35,000

Belo Horizonte
Estádio Sete de Setembro
Capacity: 18,000

Rio de Janeiro
Estádio do Maracanã
Capacity: 200,000

Sao Paulo
Estádio de Pacaembu
Capacity: 60,000

Curitiba
Estádio Durival de Britto
Capacity: 15,000

Porto Alegre
Estádio dos Eucaliptos
Capacity: 20,000

FINAL ROUND

FINAL ROUND	W	D	L	PT
Uruguay	2	1	0	5
Brazil	2	0	1	4
Sweden	1	0	2	2
Spain	0	1	2	1

AN UNCONVENTIONAL HEADER

Yugoslavia began their match against Brazil with only ten men, as Mitic had gashed his head on an exposed girder in the underground passageways of the unfinished Maracana stadium. By the time he had been patched up, Ademir had made it 1–0 and a late goal from Zizinho sealed Brazil's passage to the final round.

SWITZERLAND
1954

No team went to a World Cup as bigger favorites than Hungary in 1954. As the reigning Olympic champions, they had lost just one game in 30 and had twice demolished England. The world waited to crown the kings of modern soccer. All their potential challengers—defending champions Uruguay, and Brazil, Austria, and Yugoslavia—were in decline. West Germany, still barely a nation, had only recently been allowed back into FIFA and were considered rank outsiders.

THE BATTLE OF BERNE

Hungary and Brazil's quarter-final clash was marred by harsh fouls: Hidegkuti stamped on India's calves, Bózsik and Nilton Santos were sent off. The teams started fighting and the police had to clear the field. As the game ended, a free-for-all broke out, continuing in the tunnel and into the changing rooms.

FERENC PUSKÁS
Puskás is also widely regarded as the best finisher the game has ever seen—his lethal left foot claimed 84 goals in 85 appearances for Hungary.

FIRST TELEVISED WORLD CUP

Switzerland was chosen as the host of the 1954 World Cup because no other European country could. Europe was only just beginning to recover economically and psychologically from World War II. In a hint of the technological changes to come, the tournament was the first to be broadcast live on television to viewers across Europe—though few people anywhere had access to sets.

BIZARRE FORMATS

FIFA continued to experiment with bizarre, unfathomable formats in the group stage. This year in each group, two seeded teams played two unseeded teams but did not play each other. Play-offs separated teams that were level on points. Nevertheless, there were plenty of goals. The best action came in Group 2: including the play-off, this group yielded 39 goals in five games.

FRITZ WALTER
When he was a prisoner of war, Walter's life was spared by the Russians after a Hungarian guard recognized him as a soccer player and claimed Walter was Austrian. Later, he captained Germany in the 1954 final where they beat ... Hungary.

QUARTER-FINALS		SEMI-FINALS		FINAL	
BRAZIL	2				
HUNGARY	4	HUNGARY	4		
		URUGUAY	2		
URUGUAY	4				
ENGLAND	2				
				WEST GERMANY	3
				HUNGARY	2
YUGOSLAVIA	0				
WEST GERMANY	2	WEST GERMANY	6		
		AUSTRIA	1		
AUSTRIA	7				
SWITZERLAND	5				

STAT ATTACK   GROUP STAGE

GROUP 1	W	D	L	PT	GROUP 2	W	D	L	PT	GROUP 3	W	D	L	PT	GROUP 4	W	D	L	PT
Brazil	1	1	0	3*	Hungary	2	0	0	4*	Uruguay	2	0	0	4*	England	1	1	0	3*
Yugoslavia	1	1	0	3*	West Germany	1	0	1	2*	Austria	2	0	0	4*	Switzerland	1	0	1	2*
France	1	0	1	2	Turkey	2	0	1	2	Czechoslovakia	0	0	2	0	Italy	1	0	1	2
Mexico	0	0	2	0	Korea	0	0	2	0	Scotland	0	0	2	0	Belgium	0	1	1	1

*The top two teams from each group qualified for the quarter-finals

THE FINAL

The game opened with a frantic exchange of goals. Hungary went two up in eight minutes, but soon West Germany drew level. The next hour saw a relentless Hungarian onslaught in the driving rain. Puskás had a goal disallowed before Rahn, unmarked on the edge of the box, scored the unlikely winner for West Germany with a long low shot.

WEST GERMANY ③	HUNGARY ②
JULY 4, WANKDORFSTADION: 64,000	
MANAGER: SEPP HERBERGER	MANAGER: GUSZTÁV SEBES
FORMATION: 3-2-5	FORMATION: 3-2-5

SUBS: No tactical substitutions at this World Cup

9 The biggest margin of victory in World Cup history achieved by Hungary against Korea. Later equaled when Yugoslavia beat Zaire 9–0 in 1974.

12 The most goals scored in a single World Cup game—Austria 7 Switzerland 5

5.4 Average goals per game by Hungary at the 1954 World Cup—the highest in the competition's history

27 Number of goals scored by Hungary, the most by any team at a single World Cup tournament

THE VENUES

Several new stadiums were built for the occasion and the six venues were evenly distributed between the German-, French-, and Italian-speaking parts of the nation. Despite Switzerland's small size, the average attendance was a healthy 34,211.

TOP GOALSCORERS

Sándor KOCSIS	Hungary	11 goals
Erich PROBST	Austria	6 goals
Max MORLOCK	West Germany	6 goals
Josef HÜGI	Switzerland	6 goals

GOLDEN BALL

Ferenc PUSKÁS	Hungary

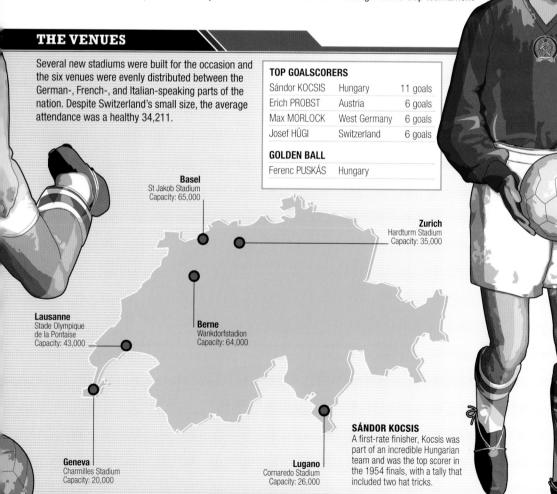

Basel
St Jakob Stadium
Capacity: 65,000

Zurich
Hardturm Stadium
Capacity: 35,000

Lausanne
Stade Olympique
de la Pontaise
Capacity: 43,000

Berne
Wankdorfstadion
Capacity: 64,000

Geneva
Charmilles Stadium
Capacity: 20,000

Lugano
Cornaredo Stadium
Capacity: 26,000

SÁNDOR KOCSIS
A first-rate finisher, Kocsis was part of an incredible Hungarian team and was the top scorer in the 1954 finals, with a tally that included two hat tricks.

SWEDEN 1958

Before it started, Sweden 1958 seemed a very open World Cup. The hosts had a talented but ageing squad. France, Argentina, and Brazil all promised much, yet were untried. The great Hungarians were gone, but the Soviet Union looked strong and, for the first and only time, all four British home nations qualified—England, Scotland, Northern Ireland, and Wales. In the end, however, there was just one team and one player—Brazil and the 17-year-old Pelé.

SCOUTS, SPIES, AND A DENTIST

Brazil was determined to win its first World Cup. The president's office underwrote the squad, which was supported by a team of experts, including a psychologist, a dentist, fitness trainers, and spies who checked up on other teams. The squad had over 300 teeth extracted—most players had never been to a dentist. Twenty-five Swedish locations were scouted before a hotel was chosen and only then when the female staff were replaced by men.

GUNNAR GREN
With Gunnar Nordahl and Nils Liedholm, Gren was one third of Gre-No-Li, a deadly trio of Swedish strikers who scored many times at AC Milan (118 goals in 38 matches) and for their national side.

VARYING FORTUNES

The Brazilian psychologist thought Pelé was "infantile" and considered Garrincha's IQ to be so low that he should not play. Fortunately, his advice was ignored and, alongside Didi and Vavá, they cut a swathe through the tournament.

The other teams showed varying fortunes. The biggest surprise was the decimation of Argentina. Despite their considerable success in South America throughout the 1950s, the team looked slow and unsophisticated against European opponents. France went on a scoring spree (23 goals in the tournament) that began with seven against Paraguay and took them to the semi-finals. Sweden looked comfortable, but Wales needed a play-off victory against Hungary to make the quarter-finals. West Germany won their group.

DANNY BLANCHFLOWER
One of the game's finest passers of the ball, the Tottenham Hotspur legend captained Northern Ireland to a quarter-final against France.

QUARTER-FINALS		SEMI-FINALS		FINAL	
WEST GERMANY	1				
YUGOSLAVIA	0	WEST GERMANY	1		
SWEDEN	2	SWEDEN	3		
USSR	0			SWEDEN	2
FRANCE	4			BRAZIL	5
N. IRELAND	0	FRANCE	2		
BRAZIL	1	BRAZIL	5		
WALES	0				

STAT ATTACK — GROUP STAGE

GROUP 1	W D L PT	GROUP 2	W D L PT	GROUP 3	W D L PT	GROUP 4	W D L PT
West Germany	1 2 0 4*	France	2 0 1 4*	Sweden	2 1 0 5*	Brazil	2 1 0 5*
Northern Ireland	1 1 1 3*	Yugoslavia	1 2 0 4*	Wales	0 3 0 3*	USSR	1 1 1 3*
Czechoslovakia	1 1 1 3	Paraguay	1 1 1 3	Hungary	1 1 1 3	England	0 3 0 3
Argentina	1 0 2 2	Scotland	0 1 2 1	Mexico	0 1 2 1	Austria	0 1 2 1

* The top two teams from each group qualified for the quarter-finals

THE FINAL

The hosts took an early lead when Liedholm scored in the fourth minute, but it didn't bode well. As their English coach George Raynor recalled, "instead of looking dejected, the Brazilians called for the ball to restart the game." His fears were realized. Two goals from Vavá made it 2–1 to Brazil at half-time and in the second half, three more goals followed, two from Pelé. When Pelé broke down in tears on the final whistle, his global stardom had begun.

BRAZIL 5	SWEDEN 2
JUNE 28, RÅSUNDA STADIUM: 51,800	
MANAGER: VICENTE FEOLA	MANAGER: GEORGE RAYNOR
FORMATION: 4-2-4	FORMATION: 2-4-4

WORLD CUP STREAKS

Brazil and Sweden hold the record—seven—for the number of games between two teams in the World Cup finals. When Mexico lost to Sweden, they completed the longest run of consecutive defeats at the World Cup finals—nine games.

3 Gilmar
4 Santos, D **2** Bellini **16** Orlando **12** Santos, N
6 Didi **19** Zito
11 Garrincha **20** Vavá **10** Pelé **7** Zagallo

11 Skoglund **9** Simonsson **8** Gren **7** Hamrin
6 Parling **4** Liedholm **14** Gustavsson **15** Börjesson
3 Axbom **2** Bergmark
1 Svensson

SUBS: No tactical substitutions at this World Cup

GARRINCHA WAS A PHENOMENAL PLAYER. WITHOUT HIM BY MY SIDE... I WOULD NEVER HAVE WON THREE WORLD CUPS

PELÉ
GARRINCHA'S TEAMMATE AT THE 1958 AND 1962 FIFA WORLD CUPS

THE VENUES

The 12 venues used during the tournament were in the south of the country. They varied from the tiny Västerås stadium to the atmospheric Råsunda Stadium in Stockholm, which had been recently expanded.

Sandviken
Jernvallen
Capacity: 20,000

Västerås
Arosvallen
Capacity: 10,000

Eskilstuna
Tunavallen
Capacity: 20,000

Örebro
Eyravallen
Capacity: 13,000

Stockholm
Råsunda Stadium
Capacity: 50,000

Uddevalla
Rimnersvallen
Capacity: 12,000

Norrköping
Idrottsparken
Capacity: 20,000

Halmstad
Örjans Vall
Capacity: 15,000

Helsingborg
Olympia
Capacity: 16,000

Borås
Ryavallen
Capacity: 15,000

Gothenburg
Ullevi
Capacity: 43,200

Malmö
Malmö Stadion
Capacity: 26,500

JUST FONTAINE

The French striker holds the record for most goals scored at a single World Cup. Fontaine's total of 13 included four against the defending champions West Germany. He scored more goals for his country than he had caps.

TOP GOALSCORERS

Just FONTAINE	France	13 goals
PELÉ	Brazil	6 goals
Helmut RAHN	Germany	6 goals
VAVÁ	Brazil	5 goals
Peter McPARLAND	Northern Ireland	5 goals

GOLDEN BALL

DIDI	Brazil

CHILE 1962

In 1960 an earthquake destroyed a third of Chile's buildings and made preparations for the World Cup very difficult. Carlos Dittborn, president of the Chilean Football Federation, called for a major national effort, and everything was ready just in time. Tragically, he died a month before the finals, but the tournament was enlivened by the host's best showing in a World Cup and by the magic of Brazil.

JOSEF MASOPUST
A tremendously skillful midfielder, Masopust was the linchpin of the Czech side and scored the opening goal of the 1962 final.

BRAZIL COME ALIVE

Brazil approached this World Cup with the same organizational discipline they had shown in 1958, including high-altitude training and an inspection of local brothels by the Brazilian FA's technical commission. They had almost the same squad as well. They played within their capabilities during the opening rounds but lost Pelé to a groin strain. However, Brazil came alive in the quarter- and semi-finals, with victories over England and Chile. No one else ever really looked likely to win.

BATTLE OF SANTIAGO

Chile versus Italy became a nasty battle. Bad feeling between the teams before the game were made worse by Ferrini's sending off for retaliating against Chile's Landu. The police had to escort Ferrini away. Then, after being punched by Sanchez, David kicked Sanchez in the neck and was sent off.

GARRINCHA
Manuel Francisco dos Santos—to give Garrincha his proper name—was a fantastic dribbler of the ball. If it wasn't for Pelé, he would probably have been regarded as the world's greatest player.

WE WILL DO EVERYTHING TO REBUILD AND HOST... THE WORLD CUP

CARLOS DITTBORN
PRESIDENT OF THE CHILEAN FOOTBALL FEDERATION, 1960

QUARTER-FINALS		SEMI-FINALS		FINAL	
CHILE	2				
USSR	1	CZECHOSLOVAKIA	3		
CZECHOSLOVAKIA	1	YUGOSLAVIA	1		
HUNGARY	0			BRAZIL	3
BRAZIL	3			CZECHOSLOVAKIA	1
ENGLAND	1	BRAZIL	4		
YUGOSLAVIA	1	CHILE	2		
WEST GERMANY	0				

GOALS DECIDE

In the group stage, teams even on points were separated by their goal average rather than playoffs, replays, or extra time. In the Arica group in the far north (see map opposite), tiny crowds saw the seeded Uruguayans knocked out by the USSR and Yugoslavia. Chile and West Germany also progressed, while Argentina was pushed out by Hungary and England. The eventual finalists, Brazil and Czechoslovakia, faced off in a 0–0 tie, when Pelé was injured.

STAT ATTACK

GROUP STAGE

GROUP 1	W	D	L	PT	GROUP 2	W	D	L	PT	GROUP 3	W	D	L	PT	GROUP 4	W	D	L	PT
USSR	2	1	0	5*	West Germany	2	1	0	5*	Brazil	2	1	0	5*	Hungary	2	1	0	5*
Yugoslavia	2	0	1	4*	Chile	2	0	1	4*	Czechoslovakia	1	1	1	3*	England	1	1	1	3*
Uruguay	1	0	2	2	Italy	1	1	1	3	Mexico	1	0	2	2	Argentina	1	1	1	3
Colombia	0	1	2	1	Switzerland	0	0	3	0	Spain	1	0	2	2	Bulgaria	0	1	2	1

* The top two teams from each group qualified for the quarter-finals

THE FINAL

The Czechs started their second appearance in a World Cup final brilliantly as Josef Masopust hit a low shot to make it 1–0 on 14 minutes. However, Brazil, looking better than ever, struck back. Amarildo made it 1–1 two minutes later, and in the second half engineered a short cross to the unmarked Zito, who made it 2–1. Vavá killed off Czech hopes when he struck home the ball that Czech goalkeeper Shrojf had just let slip from his hands.

1 Gilmar
2 Santos, D   **3** Ramos   **5** Zózimo   **6** Santos, N
4 Zito   **8** Didi
7 Garrincha   **19** Vavá   **20** Amarildo   **21** Zagallo

11 Jelínek   **18** Kadraba   **8** Scherer   **17** Pospíchal
6 Masopust   **19** Kvašnák
4 Novák   **3** Popluhár   **5** Pluskal   **12** Tichý
1 Schrojf

SUBS: No tactical substitutions at this World Cup

BRAZIL **3**	CZECHOSLOVAKIA **①**
JUNE 17, ESTADIO NACIONAL: 68,679	
MANAGER: AYMORE MOREIRA	MANAGER: RUDOLF VYTLACIL
FORMATION: 4-2-4	FORMATION: 4-2-4

THE VENUES

As a result of the 1960 earthquake, only four venues were used, one in Arica in the north, the others around Santiago.

TOP GOALSCORERS

GARRINCHA	Brazil	4 goals
VAVÁ	Brazil	4 goals
Leonel SANCHEZ	Chile	4 goals
Florian ALBERT	Hungary	4 goals
Valentin IVANOV	Soviet Union	4 goals
Drazen JERKOVIC	Yugoslavia	4 goals

GOLDEN BALL

GARRINCHA	Brazil

Arica
Estadio Carlos Dittborn
Capacity: 15,000

Viña del Mar
Estadio Sausalito
Capacity: 18,000

Santiago
Estadio Nacional
Capacity: 67,000

Rancagua
Estadio El Teniente
Capacity: 10,000

GARRINCHA'S BOOKING

Chilean defender Eladio Rojas spent 85 minutes of his team's semi-final clash with Brazil kicking Garrincha. The Brazilian finally snapped, kneeing Rojas from behind. Garrincha was sent off, ruling him out of the final. However, the Chilean referee was persuaded to revoke his decision after discussions involving the Brazilian and Peruvian prime ministers and their ambassadors in Chile. Garrincha was allowed to play in the final.

VAVÁ

Brazilian striker Vavá is the only player to score in the final of two World Cup finals (in 1958 and 1962). He was also one of four players to score three goals in World Cup finals—the others being Hurst, Pelé, and Zidane.

ENGLAND 1966

Soccer returned to its birthplace for the 1966 finals, with FIFA selecting England as host nation to mark the codification of the laws of soccer there just over a century previously. Appropriately enough, Alf Ramsey's "wingless wonders" ended up winning the tournament in what remains the only major international triumph in England's history.

WORLD CUP WILLIE

The 1966 tournament was the first to feature an official mascot. World Cup Willie was a shaggy lion dressed in a Union Jack shirt. Willie featured on all kinds of merchandise and was the subject of a song by the skiffle artist Lonnie Donegan.

SOCCER GOES DEFENSIVE

In many ways 1966 was a transition point between the old and new. Many matches were played in rickety old stadiums and teams could still not make tactical substitutions. A new defensive spirit meant fear of losing often dominated the will to win. The number of goals scored in the group stages was sharply down and cynical fouling was rife.

QUARTER-FINALS		SEMI-FINALS		FINAL	
ENGLAND	1				
ARGENTINA	0	ENGLAND	2		
		PORTUGAL	1		
PORTUGAL	5			ENGLAND	4•
NORTH KOREA	3			WEST GERMANY	2
WEST GERMANY	4				
URUGUAY	0	WEST GERMANY	2		
		USSR	1		
USSR	2				
HUNGARY	1				

• After extra time

BOBBY MOORE

Pelé claimed the West Ham and England captain was the greatest defender he ever played against. The pictures of Moore holding the trophy aloft are among the most iconic soccer images in the world.

A DOG NAMED PICKLES

Four months before the start of the tournament in England in 1966, the World Cup went on display in London and promptly disappeared. After a week of national panic, a black-and-white mutt named Pickles found the Jules Rimet trophy wrapped up in old newspaper at the end of a yard in South London. The dog quickly became an international celebrity.

THRILLS AND SPILLS

The Brazilians were effectively kicked into submission by their opponents and disappointingly went out during the group stage. The behavior of some of the Argentinian players in the quarter-final against England caused England manager Alf Ramsey to brand them "animals." The biggest shock in the group stage came when the North Koreans condemned the mighty Italians to an early exit with a 1–0 victory. A glorious exception to the prevailing negativity was the thrilling quarter-final in which Portugal recovered from a 3–0 deficit to beat North Korea 5–3.

STAT ATTACK — GROUP STAGE

GROUP 1	W	D	L	PT	GROUP 2	W	D	L	PT
England	2	1	0	5*	West Germany	2	1	0	5*
Uruguay	1	2	0	4*	Argentina	2	1	0	5*
Mexico	0	2	1	2	Spain	1	0	2	2
France	0	1	2	1	Switzerland	0	0	3	0

* The top two teams from each group qualified for the quarter-finals

THE VENUES

England's well-developed domestic game meant that the venues were bigger than those of previous World Cups. White City was used for one first round match because Wembley Stadium's owner refused to rearrange a greyhound race meeting.

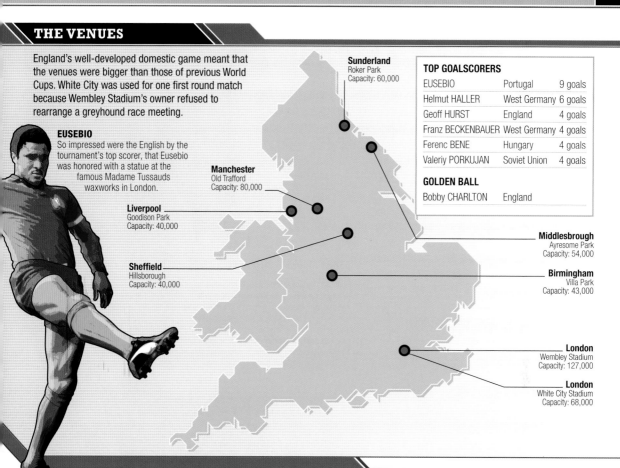

Sunderland
Roker Park
Capacity: 60,000

Manchester
Old Trafford
Capacity: 80,000

Liverpool
Goodison Park
Capacity: 40,000

Sheffield
Hillsborough
Capacity: 40,000

Middlesbrough
Ayresome Park
Capacity: 54,000

Birmingham
Villa Park
Capacity: 43,000

London
Wembley Stadium
Capacity: 127,000

London
White City Stadium
Capacity: 68,000

EUSEBIO
So impressed were the English by the tournament's top scorer, that Eusebio was honored with a statue at the famous Madame Tussauds waxworks in London.

TOP GOALSCORERS

EUSEBIO	Portugal	9 goals
Helmut HALLER	West Germany	6 goals
Geoff HURST	England	4 goals
Franz BECKENBAUER	West Germany	4 goals
Ferenc BENE	Hungary	4 goals
Valeriy PORKUJAN	Soviet Union	4 goals

GOLDEN BALL

Bobby CHARLTON	England

THE FINAL

The defining moment came in the eighth minute of extra time. When Hurst struck a fierce shot against the underside of the crossbar, the Soviet linesman deemed that the rebound had crossed the line. With seconds to go, Hurst became the only player to score a hat trick in a World Cup final.

ENGLAND ④	WEST GERMANY ②
JULY 30, WEMBLEY STADIUM: 98,000	
MANAGER: ALF RAMSEY	MANAGER: HELMUT SCHÖN
FORMATION: 4-3-3	FORMATION: 4-4-2

1 Banks
2 Cohen **5** Charlton, J **6** Moore **3** Wilson
7 Ball **4** Stiles **16** Peters
21 Hunt **9** Charlton, B **10** Hurst

10 Held **9** Seeler
11 Emmerich **12** Overath **4** Beckenbauer **8** Haller
3 Schnellinger **6** Weber **5** Schulz **2** Höttges
1 Tilkowski

SUBS: No tactical substitutions at this World Cup

GROUP STAGE

GROUP 3	W	D	L	PT	GROUP 4	W	D	L	PT
Portugal	3	0	0	6*	USSR	3	0	0	6*
Hungary	2	0	1	4*	Korea DPR	1	1	1	3*
Brazil	1	0	2	2	Italy	1	0	2	2
Bulgaria	0	0	3	0	Chile	0	1	2	1

* The top two teams from each group qualified for the quarter-finals

BOBBY CHARLTON
One of the game's greatest attacking midfielders and a player with the fiercest of finishes, Charlton was one of the stars of the 1966 World Cup. However, he was effectively marked out of the final by a young Franz Beckenbauer.

MEXICO 1970

Mexico 1970 is often regarded as the most exciting tournament in the history of the competition. Much credit for this goes to the Brazilians, who won with a dazzling, free-flowing brand of soccer that was the opposite of the cautious approach that had dominated the previous two finals.

NEW RULES UNDER THE SUN

The conditions in Mexico were tricky. Several matches kicked off at midday to suit European television schedules, exposing players to the intense heat. Three venues were more than 7,000 ft (2,130 m) above sea level, which made oxygen scarce. Luckily, a new rule allowed each team two substitutions per match. Another new rule equipped referees with yellow and red cards to show to players who were booked or dismissed. The scheme came from British referee Ken Anston, who got the idea while waiting at a set of stoplights in London.

JAIRZINHO

A huge star in a team of stars, Jairzinho was a fleet-footed winger who scored in every game Brazil played in the 1970 tournament.

BOBBY MOORE'S BRACELET

England's preparations for the tournament were disrupted by a bizarre incident in South America. Following a warm-up match in Colombia, the cup-holders' normally squeaky-clean captain Bobby Moore was arrested on suspicion of stealing a bracelet from a Bogotá jewelry shop. The charges were eventually dropped.

THE VENUES

Five stadiums in the heart of the country were used for the finals of the Mexico 1970 World Cup. The jewel in the crown was the magnificent Estadio Azteca in Mexico City, which had been built as the centerpiece of the Summer Olympic Games in 1968.

Guadalajara
Estadio Jalisco
Capacity: 73,000

Mexico City
Estadio Azteca
Capacity: 105,000

Puebla
Estadio Cuauhtémoc
Capacity: 47,000

León
Estadio Nou Camp
Capacity: 34,000

Toluca
Estadio Luis Dosal
Capacity: 27,000

GERD MÜLLER

The tournament's top scorer, Müller scored 68 goals in 62 international outings, making him one of the most prolific marksmen of all time.

TOP GOALSCORERS

Gerd MÜLLER	West Germany	10 goals
JAIRZINHO	Brazil	7 goals
Teófilo CUBILLAS	Peru	5 goals
PELÉ	Brazil	4 goals
Anatoliy BYSHOVETS	USSR	4 goals

GOLDEN BALL

PELÉ	Brazil

STAT ATTACK   GROUP STAGE

GROUP 1	W	D	L	PT	GROUP 2	W	D	L	PT	GROUP 3	W	D	L	PT	GROUP 4	W	D	L	PT
USSR	2	1	0	5*	Italy	1	2	0	4*	Brazil	3	0	0	6*	West Germany	3	0	0	6*
Mexico	2	1	0	5*	Uruguay	1	1	1	3*	England	2	0	1	4*	Peru	2	0	1	4*
Belgium	1	0	2	2	Sweden	1	1	1	3	Romania	1	0	2	2	Bulgaria	0	1	2	1
El Salvador	0	0	3	0	Israel	0	2	1	2	Czechoslovakia	0	0	3	0	Morocco	0	1	2	1

* The top two teams from each group qualified for the quarter-finals

REMARKABLE CLASSICS
In a memorable group match between England and Brazil, Gordon Banks denied a downward Pelé header with a seemingly impossible save, but Brazil prevailed with a goal from Jairzinho. The knock-out stages saw some classics. West Germany came from two goals down to beat England, and in their semi-final against Italy, an astonishing five goals were scored in extra time.

In the other semi-final, Brazil finally exorcised the ghosts of their 1950 final defeat to Uruguay. Pelé was in exuberant form, almost scoring with a 50-yard volley and selling the Uruguayan keeper one of the most outrageous dummies of all time.

THE FINAL
Italy reverted to defensive type in the final but was overwhelmed by Brazilian creativity. Player of the tournament Pelé opened the scoring, Gérson canceled out Boninsegna's equalizer, and Jairzinho scored for the sixth match in succession. Finally, Carlos Alberto rifled home a fourth after a sublime move involving eight outfield players.

QUARTER-FINALS		SEMI-FINALS		FINAL	
USSR	0				
URUGUAY	1	URUGUAY	1		
BRAZIL	4	BRAZIL	3		
PERU	2			BRAZIL	4
ITALY	4			ITALY	1
MEXICO	1	ITALY	4●		
WEST GERMANY	3	WEST GERMANY	3		
ENGLAND	2				

● After extra time

I TOLD MYSELF, HE'S MADE LIKE EVERYONE ELSE... BUT I WAS WRONG

TARSICHIO BURNICH
ON MARKING PELÉ IN THE FINAL, 1970

BRAZIL 4	ITALY 1
JUNE 21, ESTADIO AZTECA: 107,412	
MANAGER: MÁRIO ZAGALLO	MANAGER: FERRUCCIO VALCAREGGI
FORMATION: 4-2-4	FORMATION: 4-2-4

PELÉ
Christened Edison Arantes do Nascimento, Pelé is regarded by many as the greatest player of all time. He is the only player to have three World Cup winners medals.

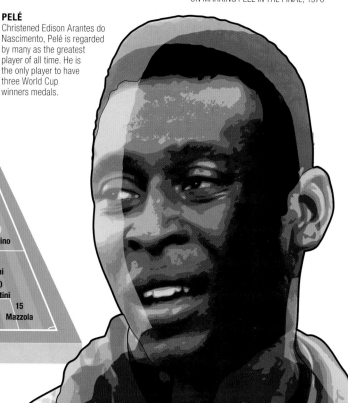

Lineup diagram:

Brazil
1 Félix
4 Alberto — 2 Brito — 3 Piazza — 16 Everaldo
5 Clodoaldo — 8 Gérson
7 Jairzinho — 9 Tostão — 10 Pelé — 11 Rivellino

Italy
11 Riva — 20 Boninsegna — 13 Domenghini
2 Burgnich
16 De Sisti — 10 Bertini
3 Facchetti — 8 Rosato — 5 Cera — 15 Mazzola
1 Albertosi

SUBS: 14 Rivera   18 Juliano

BRAZIL
VS ITALY

The greatest game ever? It was certainly the greatest World Cup final ever. Brazil had already played magnificently against England in the opening round and against Uruguay in the semi-finals. Italy, against form, had beaten West Germany 4–3 in the semi-final with an outstanding display of attacking soccer in extra time. But they were no match in the final for the samba boys.

BRAZIL 4	ITALY 1
FORMATION: 4-3-3	**FORMATION:** 4-3-3
MANAGER: MARIO ZAGALLO	**MANAGER:** FERRUCCIO VALCAREGGI
AZTECA STADIUM, MEXICO CITY, MEXICO JUNE 21, 1970	
ATTENDANCE: 108,000	
REFEREE: RUDI GLOCKNER (EAST GERMANY)	

1 Albertosi
2 Burgnich **5** Cera **8** Rosato **3** Facchetti
10 Bertini **16** De Sisti **11** Riva
13 Domenghini **15** Mazzola **20** Boninsegna
11 Rivelino **9** Tostão **10** Pelé
5 Clodoaldo **6** Gérson **7** Jairzinho
3 Piazza **4** Carlos Alberto **16** Everaldo **2** Brito
1 Felix

SUBS: **18** Juliano (75) **14** Rivera (84)

00:18

Pelé had won the 1958 World Cup, missed most of the 1962 tournament through injury, and left the 1966 tournament after being heavily tackled. In 1970, his last World Cup, he rises majestically to the occasion, opening his account in the 18th minute with a stunning header: 1–0 to Brazil.

BRAZIL'S VICTORY WITH THE BALL COMPARES WITH THE CONQUEST OF THE MOON...
BY THE AMERICANS

JORNAL DO BRASIL, JUNE 1970

00:00

The 1970 World Cup final was the first to be shown live and in color all over the world. The Mexican sun was hot and bright and gave Brazil's shimmering yellow shirts an unforgettable chromatic magic. And when the match kicked off, the Brazilian team played that way too.

00:37

The Italians probe and threaten throughout the first half. When Clodoaldo, the Brazilian defender, makes a mistake with his back-heel pass, Roberto Boninsegna is there to pounce on the loose ball. He slips past Everaldo's sliding tackle and, with the Brazilian goalkeeper out of position, his low left-foot shot makes it 1–1.

01:06

In the second half, Italy reverts to form, playing defensive, cautious soccer, but the steadily rising wave of Brazilian artistry and speed is unstoppable. With just over 20 minutes to go, Brazilian midfielder Gérson breaks the deadlock. Standing outside of the penalty area, he hits a low, left-footed shot: 2–1.

01:17

Brazil's growing dominance of the balance of play finally starts to tell. A long, high left-footed pass from the left wing is headed down in the penalty area by Pelé. A flying Jairzinho gets the loose ball and bundles it over the line. Jairzinho has now scored in every round of the tournament, his seventh goal in all: 3–1.

01:27

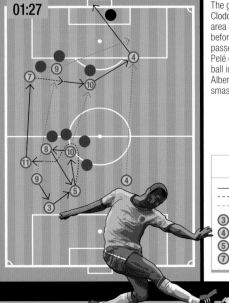

The greatest goal from the greatest final: Clodoaldo picks up the ball near his own area and dribbles past four Italian players before leaving the ball for Rivelino, who passes it to Jairzinho on the wing, then to Pelé on the edge of the box. Pelé rolls the ball into the path of a charging Carlos Alberto who, without breaking stride, smashes the ball low into the goal: 4–1.

KEY

—— Pass/shot
- - - Player move with ball
- - - Player move without ball

③ Piazza
④ Carlos Alberto
⑤ Clodoaldo
⑦ Jairzinho
⑧ Gérson
⑨ Tostão
⑩ Pelé
⑪ Rivelino

01:30

On the final whistle, the field is flooded by thousands of fans. Carlos Alberto is presented with the Jules Rimet trophy. Brazil was allowed to keep it as this was their third World Cup victory. The trophy was later stolen in Rio and probably melted down for its value as gold.

WEST GERMANY
1974

As in the tournament in Switzerland 20 years earlier, when West Germany beat Hungary in the final, the 1974 World Cup is chiefly remembered for the skill and brilliance of the runners-up. The Netherlands, led by the magician Johan Cruyff, entranced spectators with their elegant "total soccer." Just as in 1954, however, West German grit and practicality triumphed and brought the hosts their second World Cup.

JOHAN CRUYFF
A true master of his art, Cruyff was instrumental in ensuring the Dutch cruised all the way to the final, knocking out the reigning champions Brazil on their way. How they didn't win the final is the eternal frustration of all Dutch fans.

GRZEGORZ LATO
Poland's most capped player, Lato was renowned for his blistering pace and lightning acceleration. The striker remains the only Pole to win a World Cup Golden Boot.

A NEW TOURNAMENT STRUCTURE

The tournament was structured in a new way, with a second group stage replacing the standard quarter- and semi-finals. The idea was minimize the lottery element of the old knock-out system by forcing teams that had gotten through the first group stage to play three rather than two of their similarly successful rivals. Highlights of the first group stage included a politically charged clash between West and East Germany (the latter won 1–0). Yugoslavia trounced Zaire 9–0 and Haiti forced Italian keeper Dino Zoff to pick the ball out of his net for the first time in 1,147 minutes of international soccer.

FINAL FLAP

Seconds before the final was due to kick off, English referee Jack Taylor suddenly noticed that something was wrong. There were no corner flags on the field. Amid the excitement of the pre-match ceremony, the official responsible had forgotten to set them up. It took five minutes for the situation to be rectified.

TRICKY DECIDERS

The tournament may have lacked official semi-finals, but the deciding matches in the second group stage amounted to much the same thing. The Netherlands defeated Brazil 2–0 in a strangely violent Group A decider, while the Group B equivalent was played on a field that was almost a swamp, with West Germany edging out Poland 1–0. Only in the 1978 World Cup finals would the pitfalls of a second group phase idea become apparent.

STAT ATTACK — FIRST GROUP STAGE

GROUP 1	W	D	L	PT	GROUP 2	W	D	L	PT	GROUP 3	W	D	L	PT	GROUP 4	W	D	L	PT
East Germany	2	1	0	5*	Yugoslavia	1	2	0	4*	Netherlands	2	1	0	5*	Poland	3	0	0	6*
West Germany	2	0	1	4*	Brazil	1	2	0	4*	Sweden	1	2	0	4*	Argentina	1	1	1	3*
Chile	0	2	1	2	Scotland	1	2	0	4	Bulgaria	0	2	1	2	Italy	1	1	1	3
Australia	0	0	3	1	Zaire	0	0	3	0	Uruguay	0	1	2	1	Haiti	0	0	3	0

* The top two teams from each group qualified for the second group stage

THE FINAL

Holland's Johan Neeskens converted a penalty, the first ever awarded in a World Cup final, before any West German player had even touched the ball. Twenty-five minutes later, the Germans scored a penalty of their own through Breitner. Their lethal striker Gerd Müller slotted home the winner just before half time.

WEST GERMANY ②	NETHERLANDS ①
JULY 7, OLYMPIASTADION: 75,200	
MANAGER: HELMUT SCHÖN	MANAGER: RINUS MICHELS
FORMATION: 4-2-4	FORMATION: 3-4-3

① Maier
② Vogts ⑤ Beckenbauer ④ Schwarzenbeck ③ Breitner
⑯ Bonhof ⑫ Overath
⑨ Grabowski ⑭ Hoeneß ⑬ Müller ⑰ Hölzenbein
⑮ Rensenbrink ⑭ Cruyff ⑯ Rep
③ van Hanegem ⑬ Neeskens ⑰ Rijsbergen ⑥ Jansen
⑫ Krol ② Haan ⑳ Suurbier
⑧ Jongbloed

SUBS: ⑦ de Jong ⑩ van de Kerkhof

THE VENUES

West Germany's economic strength furnished the finals with nine top class venues. The Munich and Berlin stadiums had hosted past Olympic Games and the Parkstadion in Gelsenkirchen was built especially for the tournament. The average match attendance was 46,685.

Hamburg
Volksparkstadion
Capacity: 57,000

Hanover
Niedersachsenstadion
Capacity: 49,000

Dortmund
Westfalenstadion
Capacity: 67,000

Gelsenkirchen
Parkstadion
Capacity: 45,000

Dusseldorf
Rheinstadion
Capacity: 56,000

Frankfurt
Waldstadion
Capacity: 52,000

West Berlin
Olympiastadion
Capacity: 74,000

Stuttgart
Neckarstadion
Capacity: 49,000

Munich
Olympiastadion
Capacity: 69,000

TOP GOALSCORERS		
Grzegorz LATO	Poland	7 goals
Johan NEESKENS	Netherlands	5 goals
Andrzej SZARMACH	Poland	5 goals
Gerd MÜLLER	West Germany	4 goals

GOLDEN BALL
Johan CRUYFF	Netherlands

FRANZ BECKENBAUER
Nicknamed "der Kaiser" (The Emperor) because of his dominance on the field, he was the first captain to lift the new World Cup trophy after Brazil retained the Jules Rimet Trophy four years before.

SECOND GROUP STAGE

GROUP A	W	D	L	PT	GROUP B	W	D	L	PT
Netherlands	3	0	0	6*	West Germany	3	0	0	6*
Brazil	2	0	1	4	Poland	2	0	1	4
East Germany	0	1	2	1	Sweden	1	0	2	2
Argentina	0	1	2	1	Yugoslavia	0	0	3	0

* The top team from each group qualified for the final

ARGENTINA 1978

The staging of the 1978 World Cup in Argentina was highly controversial, because a military junta had recently seized power and the country was in political turmoil. Nevertheless, the tournament went ahead without major incident and, to the delight of its beleaguered citizens, the host nation lifted the cup.

MARIO KEMPES
Despite his wiry exterior, Kempes was strong and skillful. Known as "El Matador," he was as lethal shooting from outside the box as many were in it. He was the only foreign-based player in the side, as he played for Valencia in Spain.

DRAWBACKS OF THE SYSTEM

As in 1974, there were no quarter- or semi-finals. This time, however, the drawbacks of the system became glaringly obvious. When Peru lined up against Argentina in the final game of the second group stage, they had nothing to play for, having already been eliminated. This could not have happened under the knock-out system. Moreover, the scheduling arrangements meant that Argentina's only rivals to win the group, Brazil, had already played their last game and so they knew exactly how many goals they needed.

A SURPRISE AND A CONTROVERSY

In the first group stage, Tunisia were the surprise package, holding reigning champions West Germany to a 0–0 draw and beating Mexico to became the first African nation to win a game at a World Cup tournament. The eventual finalists both finished second in their groups, Argentina behind Italy and the Netherlands behind Peru.

In the second group stage, Group A became relatively straightforward. If either Holland or Italy won their clash they would go through to the final. Group B was another matter. Argentina knew that they had to beat Peru by four goals to eliminate Brazil and duly won 6–0. The Brazilians, however, were convinced that the result had been rigged.

JOHAN NEESKENS
Replacing Johan Cruyff as the Dutch playmaker might seem like mission impossible, but Neeskens proved pivotal in the role as he guided the Dutch to their second World Cup final in a row.

A BARBER'S PERSPECTIVE

The World Cup has witnessed many curious hairstyles, from the blond afro of Carlos Valderama, captain of Colombia in 1990, 1994, and 1998, to Ronaldo's 2002 arrowhead. From a barber's perspective, however, the 1978 World Cup in Argentina was the greatest tournament of all. The Brazilians displayed some bubble perms, but they were all overshadowed by the flowing locks of top scorer Mario Kempes.

STAT ATTACK — FIRST GROUP STAGE

GROUP 1	W	D	L	PT	GROUP 2	W	D	L	PT	GROUP 3	W	D	L	PT	GROUP 4	W	D	L	PT
Italy	3	0	0	6*	Poland	2	1	0	5*	Austria	2	0	1	4*	Peru	2	1	0	5*
Argentina	2	0	1	4*	West Germany	1	2	0	4*	Brazil	1	2	0	4*	Netherlands	1	1	1	3*
France	1	0	2	2	Tunisia	1	1	1	3	Spain	1	1	1	3	Scotland	1	1	1	3
Hungary	0	0	3	0	Mexico	0	0	3	0	Sweden	0	1	2	1	Iran	0	1	2	1

* The top two teams from each group qualified for the second group stage

STAT ATTACK

SECOND GROUP STAGE

GROUP A	W	D	L	PT	GROUP B	W	D	L	PT
Netherlands	2	1	0	5*	Argentina	2	1	0	5*
Italy	1	1	1	3	Brazil	2	1	0	5
West Germany	0	2	1	2	Poland	1	0	2	2
Austria	1	0	2	2	Peru	0	0	3	0

* The top two teams qualified for the final

PAPER SNOWSTORM

The crowd at the final produced one of the most spectacular displays seen at a soccer match. As the Argentinean team ran onto the field, they were greeted by a "blizzard" of torn paper. Clearing it up was impossible so the game was played on a carpet of the stuff.

THE VENUES

The six stadiums in five different cities were used for the finals in Argentina 1978. Three had been newly built: the Chateau Carreras in Córdoba, the Estadio Mar de Plata (later renamed the José María Minella) and the Malvinas Argentinas (later known as the Estadio Ciudad de Mendoza).

Rosario
Estadio Gigante de Arroyito
Capacity: 42,000

Mendoza
Estadio Ciudad de Mendoza
Capacity: 35,000

Córdoba
Estadio Chateau Carreras
Capacity: 46,000

Buenos Aires
Estadio Monumental
Capacity: 76,000

Buenos Aires
Estadio José Amalfitani
Capacity: 50,000

Mar del Plata
Estadio Jose Maria Minella
Capacity: 44,000

TOP GOALSCORERS

Mario KEMPES	Argentina	6 goals
Rob RENSENBRINK	Netherlands	5 goals
Teofilo CUBILLAS	Peru	5 goals
Leopoldo LUQUE	Argentina	4 goals
Hans KRANKL	Austria	4 goals

GOLDEN BALL

Mario KEMPES	Argentina

DANIEL PASSARELLA

A natural leader, the Argentine captain was one of the game's most complete fullbacks. He scored a number of goals, and many with his head, despite being 5 ft 8 in (1.73 m) tall.

THE FINAL

Kick-off was delayed by Argentinian protests about the hard bandaging on René van de Kerkhof's injured arm, which they claimed was dangerous. The match itself was dramatic. Holland had chances to win but Argentina claimed the Cup through Kempes (two goals) and Bertoni who replied to Nanninga's strike for Holland.

ARGENTINA 3	NETHERLANDS 1
JUNE 25, ESTADIO MONUMENTAL: 71,483	
MANAGER: CÉSAR LUIS MENOTTI	MANAGER: ERNST HAPPEL
FORMATION: 4-3-3	FORMATION: 3-4-3

5 Fillol
15 Olguín **7** Galván **19** Passarella **20** Tarantini
6 Gallego **2** Ardiles **10** Kempes
4 Bertoni **14** Luque **16** Ortiz
12 Rensenbrink **16** Rep **10** van de Kerkhof, R
11 van de Kerkhof, W **13** Neeskens **9** Haan **6** Jansen
2 Poortvliet **5** Krol **22** Brandts
8 Jongbleed

SUBS: 12 Larrosa 9 Houseman 18 Nanninga 20 Suurbier

SPAIN 1982

This tournament was graced by the likes of France's Michel Platini, a young Diego Maradona, and a Brazilian team almost as good as its 1970 counterparts. But after overcoming a traditional slow start, it was the Italians who went on to claim their third World Cup.

A GAME OF NUMBERS

To ensure the participation of more African and Asian teams, FIFA had increased the number of finalists to 24, but whittling this down to four for the semi-finals was a logistical challenge. The solution was a first stage consisting of six groups of four teams, followed by four randomly selected groups of three. Unfortunately, the draw for the second stage (see opposite) produced extremely unbalanced groups.

UNSPORTING PLAY

In a farcical first round, West Germany and Austria went into the final match of Group 2 knowing both would go through at Algeria's expense if the Germans won by two goals or fewer. After West Germany had scored, the teams kicked the ball around aimlessly. The crowd was furious; the Algerians livid.

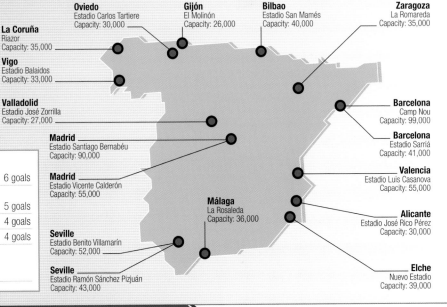

FALCÃO
A sublimely gifted midfielder, Falcão was widely considered to be one of the players of the tournament.

THE VENUES

The increased number of teams meant that 17 stadiums were used in Spain 1982. Three cities —Madrid, Barcelona, and Seville—had two venues each. Average attendance at the matches was the lowest since Chile 1962.

Oviedo
Estadio Carlos Tartiere
Capacity: 30,000

Gijón
El Molinón
Capacity: 26,000

Bilbao
Estadio San Mamés
Capacity: 40,000

Zaragoza
La Romareda
Capacity: 35,000

La Coruña
Riazor
Capacity: 35,000

Vigo
Estadio Balaidos
Capacity: 33,000

Valladolid
Estadio José Zorrilla
Capacity: 27,000

Madrid
Estadio Santiago Bernabéu
Capacity: 90,000

Madrid
Estadio Vicente Calderón
Capacity: 55,000

Málaga
La Rosaleda
Capacity: 36,000

Barcelona
Camp Nou
Capacity: 99,000

Barcelona
Estadio Sarriá
Capacity: 41,000

Valencia
Estadio Luis Casanova
Capacity: 55,000

Alicante
Estadio José Rico Pérez
Capacity: 30,000

Elche
Nuevo Estadio
Capacity: 39,000

Seville
Estadio Benito Villamarín
Capacity: 52,000

Seville
Estadio Ramón Sánchez Pizjuán
Capacity: 43,000

TOP GOAL SCORERS

Paolo ROSSI	Italy	6 goals
Karl-Heinz RUMMENIGGE	Germany	5 goals
ZICO	Brazil	4 goals
Zbigniew BONIEK	Poland	4 goals

GOLDEN BALL

Paolo ROSSI	Italy

STAT ATTACK

FIRST GROUP STAGE

GROUP 1	W	D	L	PT	GROUP 2	W	D	L	PT	GROUP 3	W	D	L	PT	GROUP 4	W	D	L	PT
Poland	1	2	0	4*	West Germany	2	0	1	4*	Belgium	2	1	0	5*	England	3	0	0	6*
Italy	0	3	0	3*	Austria	2	0	1	4*	Argentina	2	0	1	4*	France	1	1	1	3*
Cameroon	0	3	0	3	Algeria	2	0	1	4	Hungary	1	1	1	3	Czechoslovakia	0	2	1	2
Peru	0	2	1	2	Chile	0	0	3	0	El Salvador	0	0	3	0	Kuwait	0	1	2	1

* The top two teams from each group qualified for the second group stage

ROUTE TO THE FINAL

In the first group stage, highlights included Algeria beating West Germany and Northern Ireland defeating the hosts to win their group. Eventual winners Italy only just qualified. In the second stage, there were easy and difficult groups. The Germans won the first "group of death" and the other was decided by an Italy versus Brazil showdown.

The game of the tournament was the France versus West Germany semi-final. When the score was 1–1, the German goalkeeper Schumacher violently fouled Battiston, but went unpunished. After extra time the score was 3–3 and the Germans went on to win the first penalty shoot-out in World Cup final history.

KARL-HEINZ RUMMENIGGE

Many said the striker was Germany's best player in the post-Beckenbauer era. In 1984 Rummenigge's move to Inter made him the world's most expensive player.

THE FINAL

Taking full advantage of West Germany's exhaustion after their epic semi-final victory against France, Italy's Rossi scored the crucial opener, Tardelli followed with a wonder strike, and Altobelli added a third. Breitner's late goal for West Germany didn't trouble the jubilant Italians.

SECOND GROUP STAGE

GROUP A	W	D	L	PT	GROUP B	W	D	L	PT
Poland	1	1	0	3*	West Germany	1	1	0	3*
USSR	1	1	0	3	England	0	2	0	2
Belgium	0	0	2	0	Spain	0	1	1	1
GROUP C	W	D	L	PT	GROUP D	W	D	L	PT
Italy	2	0	0	4*	France	2	0	0	4*
Brazil	1	0	1	2	Austria	0	1	1	1
Argentina	0	0	2	0	Northern Ireland	0	1	1	1

* The top team from each group qualified for the semi-finals

SEMI-FINALS

Italy	2	West Germany	3*
Poland	0	France	3

* West Germany won on penalties

ITALY ③	WEST GERMANY ①
JULY 11, BERNABÉU: 90,000	
MANAGER: ENZO BEARZOT	MANAGER: JUPP DERWALL
FORMATION: 5-3-2	FORMATION: 5-3-2

Zoff ①
4 **Cabrini** · 7 **Scirea** · 2 **Bergomi** · 6 **Gentile** · 5 **Collovati**
13 **Oriali** · 16 **Conti** · 14 **Tardelli**
20 **Rossi** · 19 **Graziani**
8 **Fischer** · 11 **Rummenigge**
6 **Dremmler** · 7 **Littbarski** · 3 **Breitner**
5 **Förster, B** · 4 **Förster, K-H** · 2 **Briegel** · 15 **Stielike** · 20 **Kaltz**
Schumacher ①

SUBS: 15 Causio · 18 Altobelli · 10 Müller · 9 Hrubesch

FIRST GROUP STAGE

GROUP 5	W	D	L	PT	GROUP 6	W	D	L	PT
Northern Ireland	1	2	0	4*	Brazil	3	0	0	6*
Spain	1	1	1	3*	USSR	1	1	1	3*
Yugoslavia	1	1	1	3	Scotland	1	1	1	3
Honduras	0	2	1	2	New Zealand	0	0	3	0

PAOLO ROSSI

The Italian captain is the only player to lead his team to World Cup victory glory as well as win the Golden Boot and the Golden Ball at the same tournament.

MEXICO 1986

Originally scheduled to be held in Colombia, the finals were moved to Mexico when it became apparent that Colombia's stadiums were not up to FIFA standards. Despite a severe earthquake the previous September, the finals went ahead. They belonged to one man: Diego Maradona.

MEXICAN WAVE

During matches, dull passages of play were enlivened by the spectacle of the "Mexican wave." Sections of the crowd stood up, threw their arms in the air, then sat down again. This was the cue for the people on their left to repeat the action. The result was a human "wave" that took about 45 seconds to sweep around a stadium.

MICHEL PLATINI
A devastating midfielder who scored more goals than most strikers, Platini captained France—the reigning European champions—and led them to a second consecutive semi-final against the Germans.

WINNERS AND RUNNERS-UP
Mexico 1986 introduced an improved system in which the top two teams of each group, along with the four best runners-up, make it into the second round. Morocco won the least predictable group while Portugal was eliminated despite having beaten England.

ROUTE TO THE FINAL
Maradona decided the quarter-final between Argentina and England, once with his hand and once with the greatest goal in World Cup history (see pp.314–15). He performed wonders again in the semi-final against Belgium. West Germany beat France 2–0 to reach the final.

2ND ROUND		QUARTER-FINALS		SEMI-FINALS		FINAL	
BRAZIL	4						
POLAND	0	BRAZIL	1				
FRANCE	2	FRANCE	1*				
ITALY	0			FRANCE	0		
MEXICO	2			WEST GERMANY	2		
BULGARIA	0	MEXICO	0				
MOROCCO	0	WEST GERMANY	0*				
WEST GERMANY	1					ARGENTINA	3
ARGENTINA	1					WEST GERMANY	2
URUGUAY	0	ARGENTINA	2				
ENGLAND	3	ENGLAND	1				
PARAGUAY	0			ARGENTINA	2		
USSR	3			BELGIUM	0		
BELGIUM	4•	BELGIUM	1*				
DENMARK	1	SPAIN	1				
SPAIN	5						

* Qualified by penalty shoot-out • After extra time

STAT ATTACK
GROUP STAGE

GROUP A	W	D	L	PT	GROUP B	W	D	L	PT	GROUP C	W	D	L	PT
Argentina	2	1	0	5*	Mexico	2	1	0	5*	USSR	2	1	0	5*
Italy	1	2	0	4*	Paraguay	1	2	0	4*	France	2	1	0	5*
Bulgaria	0	2	1	2*	Belgium	1	1	1	3*	Hungary	1	0	2	2
Korea Republic	0	1	2	1	Iraq	0	0	3	0	Canada	0	0	3	0

* The top two teams from each group qualified for the second round, along with the four best runners-up

THE FINAL

Argentina went into a 2–0 lead, but Germany was strong enough to fight back, scoring two goals through Karl-Heinz Rummenigge and Rudi Völler. However, Maradona sprang into life in the 83rd minute when, with a great pass, he set up Jorge Burruchaga for the winning goal.

ARGENTINA **3**	WEST GERMANY ②
JUNE 29, ESTADIO AZTECA: 114,600	
MANAGER: CARLOS BILARDO	MANAGER: FRANZ BECKENBAUER
FORMATION: 4-5-1	FORMATION: 5-3-2

SUBS: 21 Trobbiani 9 Völler 20 Hoeness

THE VENUES

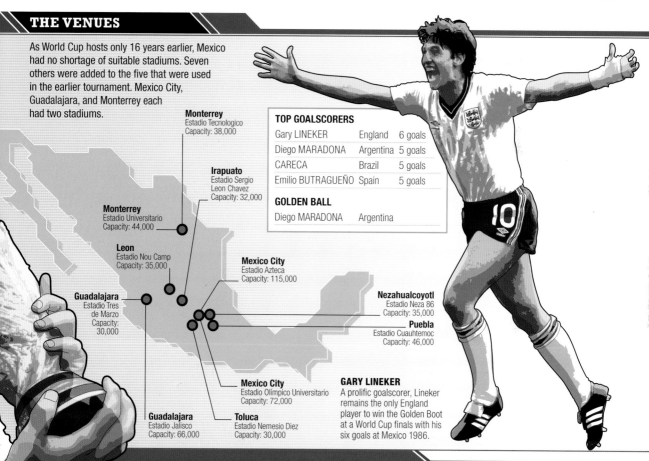

As World Cup hosts only 16 years earlier, Mexico had no shortage of suitable stadiums. Seven others were added to the five that were used in the earlier tournament. Mexico City, Guadalajara, and Monterrey each had two stadiums.

Monterrey
Estadio Tecnologico
Capacity: 38,000

Irapuato
Estadio Sergio Leon Chavez
Capacity: 32,000

Monterrey
Estadio Universitario
Capacity: 44,000

Leon
Estadio Nou Camp
Capacity: 35,000

Guadalajara
Estadio Tres de Marzo
Capacity: 30,000

Mexico City
Estadio Azteca
Capacity: 115,000

Nezahualcoyotl
Estadio Neza 86
Capacity: 35,000

Puebla
Estadio Cuauhtemoc
Capacity: 46,000

Mexico City
Estadio Olímpico Universitario
Capacity: 72,000

Guadalajara
Estadio Jalisco
Capacity: 66,000

Toluca
Estadio Nemesio Diez
Capacity: 30,000

TOP GOALSCORERS

Gary LINEKER	England	6 goals
Diego MARADONA	Argentina	5 goals
CARECA	Brazil	5 goals
Emilio BUTRAGUEÑO	Spain	5 goals

GOLDEN BALL

Diego MARADONA	Argentina

GARY LINEKER

A prolific goalscorer, Lineker remains the only England player to win the Golden Boot at a World Cup finals with his six goals at Mexico 1986.

GROUP STAGE

DIEGO MARADONA
The only player who could top Pelé as the greatest ever was Diego Maradona. His performance during the 1986 tournament secured him global fame—especially the 2–1 win over England, when his dazzling 60-yard run beat six players before scoring the goal of the century.

GROUP D	W	D	L	PT	GROUP E	W	D	L	PT	GROUP F	W	D	L	PT
Brazil	3	0	0	6*	Denmark	3	0	0	6*	Morocco	1	2	0	4*
Spain	2	0	1	4*	West Germany	1	1	1	3*	England	1	1	1	3*
N Ireland	0	1	2	1	Uruguay	0	2	1	2*	Poland	1	1	1	3*
Algeria	0	1	2	1	Scotland	0	1	2	1	Portugal	1	0	2	2

* The top two teams from each group qualified for the second round, along with the four best runners-up

ARGENTINA VS ENGLAND

ENGLAND 1	ARGENTINA 2
FORMATION: 4-4-2	**FORMATION:** 4-5-1
MANAGER: BOBBY ROBSON	**MANAGER:** CARLOS BILARDO
ESTADIO AZTECA, MEXICO CITY, MEXICO JUNE 22, 1986	
ATTENDANCE: 114,580	
REFEREE: ALI BIN NASSER (TUNISIA)	

Argentina went to the 1986 World Cup coached by Carlos Bilardo, whose philosophy of soccer was defensive, cautious, and disciplined. However their jewel was Diego Maradona, one of the most skilful and attack-minded players in world soccer. In the quarter-finals, just four years after the Falklands war between Argentina and the UK, the contest with England offered Maradona a stage on which to secure his canonical status. He scored one of the greatest World Cup goals, but not before netting the most controversial.

Shilton (c)

2 Stevens • 6 Butcher • 14 Fenwick • 5 Sansom
4 Hoddle • 16 Reid • 18 Hodge • 17 Steven
10 Lineker • 20 Beardsley
11 Valdano
16 Olarticoecheav • 14 Giusti • 12 Enrique • 10 Maradona • 7 Burruchaga
2 Batista • 5 Brown • 9 Cuciuffo • 19 Jorge
1 Pumpido

SUBS: 21 Tapia   11 Waddle   19 Barnes

00:51

With the ball on the edge of the England penalty area, Maradona flicks it to the right and finds Valdano. Hodge's leg reaches for the ball and slices it up into the air. Maradona, knees bent and with one fist clenched, punches it into the net. Incredibly the referee awards a goal: 1–0.

Both sides start nervously, but the feel of the game becomes clear when, on eight minutes, Maradona goes on a threatening dribble and is brought down by Terry Fenwick, who receives a yellow card. A few minutes later, Maradona is knocked down by Steve Hodge on the edge of the area. He sends the resulting free-kick just wide of Shilton's left-hand post.

00:08

A LITTLE WITH THE HEAD OF MARADONA AND A LITTLE WITH ...THE HAND OF GOD

DIEGO MARADONA'S EXPLANATION OF HIS CONTROVERSIAL GOAL

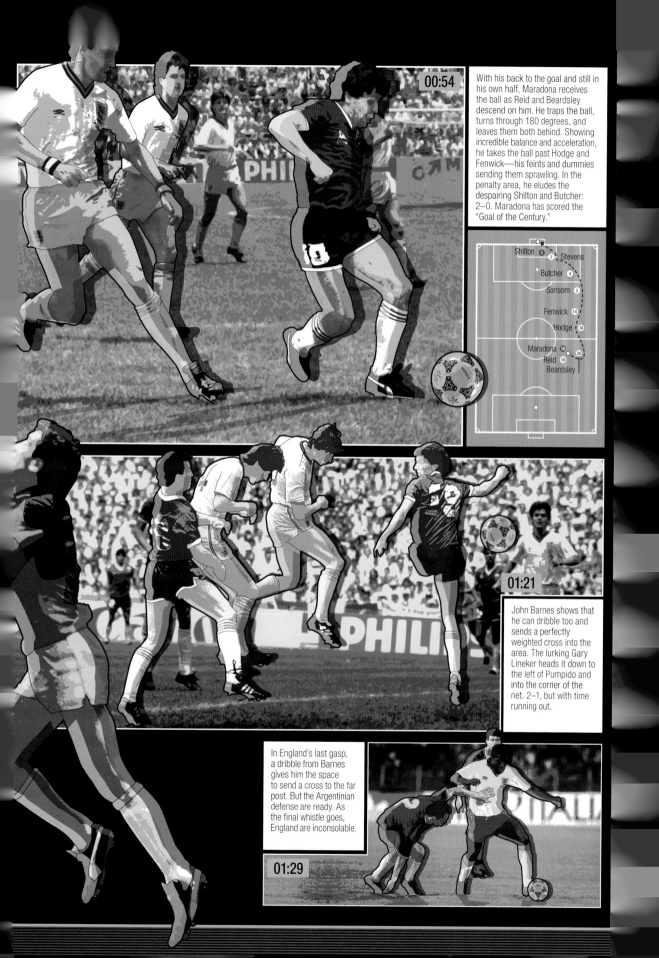

00:54

With his back to the goal and still in his own half, Maradona receives the ball as Reid and Beardsley descend on him. He traps the ball, turns through 180 degrees, and leaves them both behind. Showing incredible balance and acceleration, he takes the ball past Hodge and Fenwick—his feints and dummies sending them sprawling. In the penalty area, he eludes the despairing Shilton and Butcher: 2–0. Maradona has scored the "Goal of the Century."

Shilton **1**
2 Stevens
Butcher **4**
Sansom **5**
Fenwick **14**
Hodge **18**
Maradona **10** **20**
Reid **16**
Beardsley

01:21

John Barnes shows that he can dribble too and sends a perfectly weighted cross into the area. The lurking Gary Lineker heads it down to the left of Pumpido and into the corner of the net. 2–1, but with time running out.

In England's last gasp, a dribble from Barnes gives him the space to send a cross to the far post. But the Argentinian defense are ready. As the final whistle goes, England are inconsolable.

01:29

ITALY 1990

Italia 1990's theme tune was Puccini's "Nessun Dorma," but the tournament was short on operatic drama, with fewer goals per game than in any other World Cup. Still, it yielded some memorable images, including the bulging eyes of Italy's Schillaci and Cameroon's Milla dancing with the corner flag.

THE LUCK OF THE IRISH

Proceedings began with a shock win for nine-man Cameroon against Argentina, England won their group with a single goal difference, and Italy secured three cautious wins. Cameroon and Ireland reached the quarter-finals; the Africans with some style, the Irish without beating anybody, except Romania on penalties.

ROGER MILLA
The 38-year-old Cameroon striker was instrumental in his side's quarter-final finish. The way he danced around the corner flag as a way of celebrating goals also became popular.

ROUTE TO THE FINAL

Argentina, led by a half-fit Maradona, were a shadow of their 1986 selves but progressed via a series of narrow victories, including a 1–0 defeat of Brazil. The eventual winners, West Germany, were one of the few teams to play attacking soccer, beating the Netherlands in a match marred by Rijkaard spitting at Völler. In an epic semi-final against England, the Germans took the lead when Shilton was beaten by a cruelly deflected free-kick. Lineker equalized, Paul Gascoigne cried, and West Germany went through on penalties.

MARADONA'S MESSAGE

Before the semis, Maradona said: "Neapolitans are not considered Italian by people up north. Why should they behave as Italians tomorrow?" As a result the crowd didn't boo the Argentine national anthem.

2ND ROUND		QUARTER-FINALS		SEMI-FINALS		FINAL	
CAMEROON	2•						
COLOMBIA	1	ARGENTINA	0*				
CZECHOSLOVAKIA	4	YUGOSLAVIA	0				
COSTA RICA	1			ARGENTINA	1*		
ARGENTINA	1			ITALY	1		
BRAZIL	0	ITALY	1				
WEST GERMANY	2	REP OF IRELAND	0				
NETHERLANDS	1					WEST GERMANY	1
REP. OF IRELAND	0*					ARGENTINA	0
ROMANIA	0	WEST GERMANY	1				
ITALY	2	CZECHOSLOVAKIA	0				
URUGUAY	0			WEST GERMANY	1*		
SPAIN	1			ENGLAND	1		
YUGOSLAVIA	2•	ENGLAND	3•				
ENGLAND	1•	CAMEROON	2				
BELGIUM	0						

* Qualified by penalty shoot-out • After extra time

STAT ATTACK

GROUP STAGE

LOTHAR MATTHÄUS
The most capped German player of all-time, Matthäus was the archetypal midfield general—a master of the pinpoint pass and the well-timed tackle. He captained Germany in their third consecutive final, against Argentina.

GROUP A	W	D	L	PT	GROUP B	W	D	L	PT
Italy	3	0	0	6*	Cameroon	5	1	4	4*
Czechoslovakia	2	0	1	4*	Romania	1	1	1	3*
Austria	1	0	2	2	Argentina	1	1	1	3*
USA	0	0	3	0	USSR	1	0	2	2

* The top two teams plus the four best runners-up qualified for the second round.

THE VENUES

The distribution of the 12 tournament venues was remarkably even-handed, given that power in Italian soccer is overwhelmingly concentrated in the North. A new stadium was built in Bari and the country's two principal islands, Sicily and Sardinia, also hosted matches.

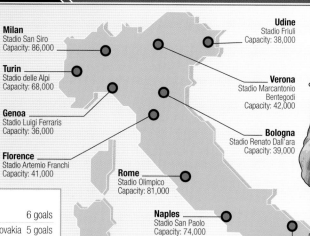

Milan
Stadio San Siro
Capacity: 86,000

Turin
Stadio delle Alpi
Capacity: 68,000

Genoa
Stadio Luigi Ferraris
Capacity: 36,000

Florence
Stadio Artemio Franchi
Capacity: 41,000

Udine
Stadio Friuli
Capacity: 38,000

Verona
Stadio Marcantonio Bentegodi
Capacity: 42,000

Bologna
Stadio Renato Dall'ara
Capacity: 39,000

Rome
Stadio Olimpico
Capacity: 81,000

Naples
Stadio San Paolo
Capacity: 74,000

Cagliari
Stadio Sant'Elia
Capacity: 40,000

Palermo
Stadio La Favorita
Capacity: 36,000

Bari
Stadio San Nicola
Capacity: 56,000

TOP GOALSCORERS

Salvatore SCHILLACI	Italy	6 goals
Tomáš SKUHRAVÝ	Czechoslovakia	5 goals
Roger MILLA	Cameroon	4 goals
Gary LINEKER	England	4 goals
Lothar MATTHÄUS	West Germany	4 goals
MÍCHEL	Spain	4 goals

GOLDEN BALL

Salvatore SCHILLACI Italy

THE FINAL

In a match mainly memorable for its dullness, West Germany's Andy Brehme scored the only goal from a penalty, Pedro Monzon became the first player to be sent off in a World Cup final, and Franz Beckenbauer became the second man to win the World Cup trophy as both a player and a manager.

WEST GERMANY ①	ARGENTINA ⓪
JULY 8, STADIO OLIMPICO: 73,603	
MANAGER: FRANZ BECKENBAUER	MANAGER: CARLOS BILARDO
FORMATION: 5-3-2	FORMATION: 5-4-1

SALVATORE SCHILLACI

Nicknamed "Toto," Schillaci made his debut at the 1990 finals. He landed the Golden Boot with six goals, each as vital to his side's third-place finish as the next.

SUBS: ② Reuter ⑮ Monzon ⑥ Calderon

GROUP STAGE

GROUP C	W	D	L	PT	GROUP D	W	D	L	PT	GROUP E	W	D	L	PT	GROUP F	W	D	L	PT
Brazil	3	0	0	6*	West Germany	2	1	0	5*	Spain	2	1	0	5*	England	1	2	0	4*
Costa Rica	2	0	1	4*	Yugoslavia	2	0	1	4*	Belgium	2	0	1	4*	Rep of Ireland	0	3	0	3*
Scotland	1	0	2	2	Colombia	1	1	1	3*	Uruguay	1	1	1	3*	Netherlands	0	3	0	3*
Sweden	0	0	3	0	UAE	0	0	3	0	Korea Republic	0	0	3	0	Egypt	0	2	1	2

* The top two teams plus the four best runners-up qualified for the second round.

USA 1994

OLEG SALENKO
The Russian striker scored six goals at USA '94, five against a weak team from Cameroon.

Held in the US as part of a concerted effort by FIFA to increase the profile of soccer in North America, this tournament was a mixed success. The majority of Americans were, and still are, lukewarm about the game, but the matches attracted enormous crowds.

ROMÁRIO
Brazilian striker Romário scored in every game at USA '94, except against the hosts in the second round.

A COLORFUL TOURNAMENT

To encourage more attractive play, teams were awarded three points for a win, rather than two, and goalkeepers were no longer permitted to handle back passes. Highlights included a record five goals in one match from Russia's Salenko, Ireland beating Italy, the first ever indoor World Cup match, and Saudi Arabia qualifying for the second round. The biggest story, though, was the ejection of Maradona for taking a banned stimulant.

ROUTE TO THE FINAL

The quarter-finals produced two classics: Bulgaria, who had never won a World Cup finals match, beat reigning champions Germany 2–1, while Brazil beat the Netherlands in a five-goal thriller. In the semi-finals, Italy overcame Bulgaria and the ever-popular Brazil beat Sweden in the teams' second meeting of the tournament, going on to be the victors in the final.

2ND ROUND		QUARTER-FINALS		SEMI-FINALS		FINAL	
NIGERIA	1						
ITALY	2•	ITALY	2				
SPAIN	3	SPAIN	1				
SWITZERLAND	0			ITALY	2		
MEXICO	1*			BULGARIA	1	BRAZIL	0
BULGARIA	1	BULGARIA	2			ITALY	0
GERMANY	3	GERMANY	1			BRAZIL WON 3–2 ON PENALTIES	
BELGIUM	2						
NETHERLANDS	2						
REP OF IRELAND	0	NETHERLANDS	2				
BRAZIL	1	BRAZIL	3				
USA	0			BRAZIL	1	**3RD/4TH PLACE**	
SAUDI ARABIA	1			SWEDEN	0		
SWEDEN	3	SWEDEN	2*			SWEDEN	4
ROMANIA	3	ROMANIA	2			BULGARIA	0
ARGENTINA	2						

* Qualified by penalty shoot-out   • After extra-time

STAT ATTACK

GROUP STAGE

GROUP A	W	D	L	PT	GROUP B	W	D	L	PT	GROUP C	W	D	L	PT
Romania	2	0	1	6*	Brazil	2	1	0	7*	Germany	2	1	0	7*
Switzerland	1	1	1	4*	Sweden	1	2	0	5*	Spain	1	2	0	5*
United States	1	1	1	4*	Russia	1	0	2	3	Korea Republic	0	2	1	2
Colombia	1	0	2	2	Cameroon	0	1	2	1	Bolivia	0	1	2	1

* The top two teams from each group qualified for the second round, along with the four best runners-up

THE FINAL

It may have been a disappointment for 120 scoreless minutes, but this final's penalty shoot-out was suitably dramatic. It began with two misses and ended with Roberto Baggio, Italy's star of the tournament, blasting the ball over the bar. Brazil had become world champions for a record fourth time.

BRAZIL 0	ITALY 0
BRAZIL WON 3–2 ON PENALTIES	
JULY 7, ROSE BOWL: 94,194	
MANAGER: CARLOS ALBERTO PARREIRA	MANAGER: ARRIGO SACCHI
FORMATION: 4-4-2	FORMATION: 4-4-2

SUBS: 14 Cafu 21 Viola 2 Apolloni 17 Evani

THE VENUES

The nine venues were mega-stadiums built for American football. The average attendance was a record-breaking 68,991, despite fears that the matches would not capture local interest.

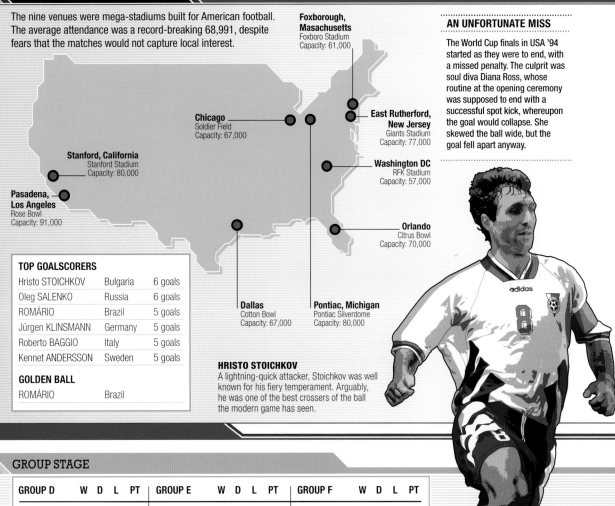

Foxborough, Massachusetts
Foxboro Stadium
Capacity: 61,000

Chicago
Soldier Field
Capacity: 67,000

East Rutherford, New Jersey
Giants Stadium
Capacity: 77,000

Stanford, California
Stanford Stadium
Capacity: 80,000

Washington DC
RFK Stadium
Capacity: 57,000

Pasadena, Los Angeles
Rose Bowl
Capacity: 91,000

Orlando
Citrus Bowl
Capacity: 70,000

Dallas
Cotton Bowl
Capacity: 67,000

Pontiac, Michigan
Pontiac Silverdome
Capacity: 80,000

AN UNFORTUNATE MISS

The World Cup finals in USA '94 started as they were to end, with a missed penalty. The culprit was soul diva Diana Ross, whose routine at the opening ceremony was supposed to end with a successful spot kick, whereupon the goal would collapse. She skewed the ball wide, but the goal fell apart anyway.

TOP GOALSCORERS

Hristo STOICHKOV	Bulgaria	6 goals
Oleg SALENKO	Russia	6 goals
ROMÁRIO	Brazil	5 goals
Jürgen KLINSMANN	Germany	5 goals
Roberto BAGGIO	Italy	5 goals
Kennet ANDERSSON	Sweden	5 goals

GOLDEN BALL

ROMÁRIO	Brazil

HRISTO STOICHKOV

A lightning-quick attacker, Stoichkov was well known for his fiery temperament. Arguably, he was one of the best crossers of the ball the modern game has seen.

GROUP STAGE

GROUP D	W	D	L	PT	GROUP E	W	D	L	PT	GROUP F	W	D	L	PT
Nigeria	2	0	1	6*	Mexico	1	1	1	4*	Netherlands	2	0	1	6*
Bulgaria	2	0	1	6*	Rep of Ireland	1	1	1	4*	Saudi Arabia	2	0	1	6*
Argentina	2	0	1	6*	Italy	1	1	1	4*	Belgium	2	0	1	6*
Greece	0	0	3	0	Norway	1	1	1	4	Morocco	0	0	3	0

* The top two teams from each group qualified for the second round, along with the four best runners-up

FRANCE 1998

For the first time, 32 teams took part in the tournament and "golden goals" reduced the likelihood of penalty shoot-outs. The hosts won the cup without a seasoned striker; Thierry Henry, when he played, was deployed on the wing, and David Trezeguet had yet to flourish.

REVENGE MATCH

The highlight of the second round was England's first encounter with Argentina since the infamous "Hand of God" match in 1986 (see pp.314–315). Eighteen-year-old Michael Owen scored a wonder goal, but the Argentinians went through on penalties.

ROUTE TO THE FINAL

Three of the quarter-finals were high-quality matches. Croatia trounced Germany 3–0, Bergkamp scored an exquisite winner for the Netherlands against Argentina, and Brazil beat Denmark 3–2. The fourth match saw a disappointing 0–0 draw, with France going through on penalties. In the semi-finals, Brazil beat the Netherlands on penalties and France overcame Croatia with a 2–1 win.

DENNIS BERGKAMP

One of the finest poachers of the modern game, Bergkamp punished any team that gave him an inch. His winner for the Netherlands against Argentina in the final minute of their quarter-final is regarded as one of the greatest-ever goals.

A REASON TO RETIRE

One year after the tournament, Argentina's Carlos Roa announced that he was retiring from soccer to devote himself to his religion. Lechuga ("lettuce"), as the vegetarian goalkeeper was known to his teammates, is a devout Seventh Day Adventist who reportedly believed the world was going to end in 2000.

2ND ROUND		QUARTER-FINALS		SEMI-FINALS		FINAL	
FRANCE	1•						
PARAGUAY	0	FRANCE	0*				
ITALY	1	ITALY	0				
NORWAY	0			BRAZIL	1*		
BRAZIL	4			NETHERLANDS 1			
CHILE	1	BRAZIL	3			BRAZIL	0
NIGERIA	1	DENMARK	2			FRANCE	3
DENMARK	4						
NETHERLANDS	2						
YUGOSLAVIA	1	NETHERLANDS	2				
ARGENTINA	2*	ARGENTINA	1				
ENGLAND	2			FRANCE	2	3RD/4TH PLACE	
GERMANY	2			CROATIA	1		
MEXICO	1	GERMANY	0			NETHERLANDS	1
ROMANIA	0	CROATIA	3			CROATIA	2
CROATIA	1						

* Qualified by penalty shoot-out   • After extra-time

DAVOR ŠUKER

With a natural eye for goals, Šuker helped to take Croatia to the brink of the final and became the tournament's top scorer in the process.

STAT ATTACK — GROUP STAGE

GROUP A	W	D	L	PT	GROUP B	W	D	L	PT	GROUP C	W	D	L	PT	GROUP D	W	D	L	PT
Brazil	2	0	1	6*	Italy	2	1	0	7*	France	3	0	0	9*	Nigeria	2	0	1	6*
Norway	1	2	0	5*	Chile	0	3	0	3*	Denmark	1	1	1	4*	Paraguay	1	2	0	5*
Morocco	1	1	1	4	Austria	0	2	1	2	South Africa	0	2	1	2	Spain	1	1	1	4
Scotland	0	1	2	1	Cameroon	0	2	1	2	Saudi Arabia	0	1	2	1	Bulgaria	0	1	2	1

* The top two teams from each group qualified for the second round

THE VENUES

Although the tournament had been expanded to include 32 teams, the organizers managed to fit all the matches into 10 stadiums scattered around the nation. Two were in Paris: the Parc des Princes and the brand new Stade de France.

Lens
Stade Félix Bollaert
Capacity: 42,000

Nantes
Stade de la Beaujoire
Capacity: 39,000

Paris
Stade de France
Capacity: 80,000

Paris
Parc des Princes
Capacity: 49,000

Lyon
Stade de Gerland
Capacity: 41,000

Bordeaux
Parc Lescure
Capacity: 33,000

Saint-Etienne
Stade Geoffroy-Guichard
Capacity: 36,000

Toulouse
Stadium de Toulouse
Capacity: 37,000

Marseille
Stade Vélodrome
Capacity: 60,000

Montpellier
Stade de la Mosson
Capacity: 34,000

TOP GOALSCORERS

Davor ŠUKER	Croatia	6 goals
Gabriel BATISTUTA	Argentina	5 goals
Christian VIERI	Italy	5 goals
RONALDO	Brazil	4 goals
Marcelo SALAS	Chile	4 goals
Luis HERNÁNDEZ	Mexico	4 goals

GOLDEN BALL

RONALDO	Brazil

LILLIAN THURAM

The scorer of both goals that put France into the final, defender Thuram was at the heart of a defense that enabled France to win their first World Cup.

THE FINAL

Ronaldo reportedly suffered a seizure before the final but went on to play. Brazil looked completely shell-shocked by the drama and never really got going. Zinédine Zidane cemented his place as the planet's best player with two goals and Emmanuel Petit added a third in stoppage time.

FRANCE 3	BRAZIL 0
JULY 12, STADE DE FRANCE: 75,000	
MANAGER: AIMÉ JACQUET	MANAGER: MARIO ZAGALLO
FORMATION: 4-1-3-2	FORMATION: 4-4-2

Line-up:
16 Barthez
15 Thuram · 8 Desailly · 7 Leboeuf · 18 · 3 Lizarazu
6 Deschamps
19 Karembeu · 10 Zidane · 17 Petit
Djorkaeff · 9 Guivarc'h

20 Bebeto · 9 Ronaldo
10 Rivaldo · 8 Dunga · 5 Sampaio · 18 Leonardo
6 Carlos · 3 Aldair · 4 Baiano · 2 Cafu
1 Taffarel

SUBS: 14 Boghossian 21 Dugarry 4 Vieira 19 Denilson 21 Edmundo

GROUP STAGE

GROUP E	W	D	L	PT	GROUP F	W	D	L	PT	GROUP G	W	D	L	PT	GROUP H	W	D	L	PT
Netherlands	1	2	0	5*	Germany	2	1	0	7*	Romania	2	1	0	7*	Argentina	3	0	0	9*
Mexico	1	2	0	5*	Yugoslavia	2	1	0	7*	England	2	0	1	6*	Croatia	2	0	1	6*
Belgium	0	3	0	3	Iran	1	0	2	3	Colombia	1	0	2	3	Jamaica	1	0	2	3
Korea Republic	0	1	2	1	USA	0	0	3	0	Tunisia	0	1	2	1	Japan	0	0	3	0

* The top two teams from each group qualified for the second round

SOUTH KOREA & JAPAN 2002

The first World Cup to be held in Asia, and the first to have joint hosts, exceeded expectations. Japan won their group and South Korea reached the semi-final. Brazil won the tournament for a record fifth time and scarcely broke a sweat in the process.

OLIVER KAHN
Despite a costly error in the final, the big Bayern Munich man became the first goalkeeper to collect the Golden Ball for player of the tournament.

EARLY EXITS

Senegal sprung a surprise in the opening match, beating France 1–0. The champions failed to score in any of their three matches and departed. Argentina and Portugal also made embarrassingly early exits, but the real whipping boys were Saudi Arabia, conceding 12 goals without reply. The most eye-catching performances in the second round included the USA's 2–0 defeat of Mexico, Senegal's narrow victory over Sweden, and South Korea's win over Italy.

TRIUMPH AND TROUBLE

Customs police detained the triumphant Brazilian team and their luggage on their return home to Rio airport—a call to President Lula's office was required to pay the huge import duties and get the bags moving.

ROUTE TO THE FINAL

In the quarter-finals, England scored first against Brazil, but saw their chances drain away when keeper David Seaman misjudged a speculative Ronaldinho free kick. Germany defeated a spirited USA, South Korea beat Spain on penalties after a goalless stalemate, and Turkey looked ominously good in a 1–0 victory over Senegal. In the first semi-final, Michael Ballack sent Germany through, despite picking up a yellow card which ruled him out of the final. The Turks lost a closely contested match against Brazil, but they went home with their heads held high after beating the Koreans in the third place play-off.

RONALDO
No one knew what to expect from the great Brazilian striker, but he finished the tournament as top scorer.

2ND ROUND		QUARTER-FINALS		SEMI-FINALS		FINAL	
GERMANY	1						
PARAGUAY	0	GERMANY	1				
MEXICO	0	USA	0				
USA	2			GERMANY	1		
SPAIN*	1			S. KOREA	0		
IRELAND	1	SPAIN	0			GERMANY	0
S. KOREA•	2	S. KOREA*	0			BRAZIL	2
ITALY	1						
JAPAN	0						
TURKEY	1	TURKEY	1				
SWEDEN	1	SENEGAL	0				
SENEGAL•	2			TURKEY	0	3RD/4TH PLACE	
DENMARK	0			BRAZIL	1		
ENGLAND	3	ENGLAND	1			TURKEY	3
BRAZIL	2	BRAZIL	2			S. KOREA	2
BELGIUM	0						

* Qualified by penalty shoot-out   • After extra time

STAT ATTACK — GROUP STAGE

Group A	W	D	L	PT	GROUP B	W	D	L	PT	GROUP C	W	D	L	PT	GROUP D	W	D	L	PT
Denmark	2	1	0	7*	Spain	3	0	0	9*	Brazil	3	0	0	9*	S. Korea	2	1	0	7*
Senegal	1	2	0	5*	Paraguay	1	1	1	4*	Turkey	1	1	1	4*	USA	1	1	1	4*
Uruguay	0	2	1	2	South Africa	1	1	1	4	Costa Rica	1	1	1	4	Portugal	1	0	2	3
France	0	1	2	1	Slovenia	0	0	3	0	China	0	0	3	0	Poland	1	0	2	3

* The top two teams from each group qualified for the second round

THE VENUES

The number of participating teams was the same as France 1998, but twice as many stadiums were used. The host nations each provided 10, most specially built for the tournament. Many of the Korean venues would have been worthy for the final, but Yokohama was chosen for its superb media facilities.

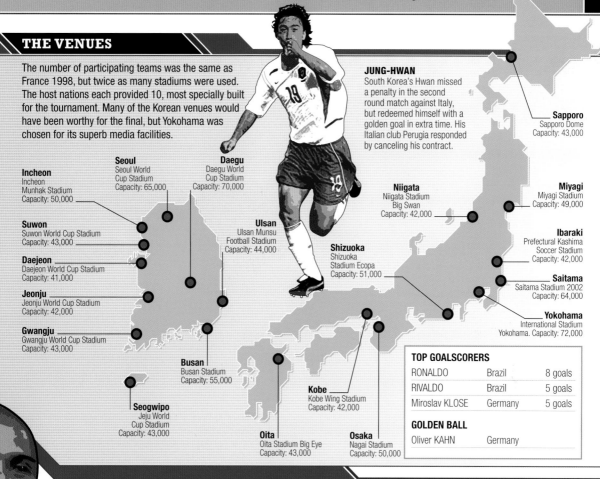

JUNG-HWAN
South Korea's Hwan missed a penalty in the second round match against Italy, but redeemed himself with a golden goal in extra time. His Italian club Perugia responded by canceling his contract.

Sapporo
Sapporo Dome
Capacity: 43,000

Miyagi
Miyagi Stadium
Capacity: 49,000

Niigata
Niigata Stadium
Big Swan
Capacity: 42,000

Ibaraki
Prefectural Kashima
Soccer Stadium
Capacity: 42,000

Seoul
Seoul World
Cup Stadium
Capacity: 65,000

Daegu
Daegu World
Cup Stadium
Capacity: 70,000

Incheon
Incheon
Munhak Stadium
Capacity: 50,000

Ulsan
Ulsan Munsu
Football Stadium
Capacity: 44,000

Shizuoka
Shizuoka
Stadium Ecopa
Capacity: 51,000

Suwon
Suwon World Cup Stadium
Capacity: 43,000

Saitama
Saitama Stadium 2002
Capacity: 64,000

Daejeon
Daejeon World Cup Stadium
Capacity: 41,000

Yokohama
International Stadium
Yokohama. Capacity: 72,000

Jeonju
Jeonju World Cup Stadium
Capacity: 42,000

Gwangju
Gwangju World Cup Stadium
Capacity: 43,000

Busan
Busan Stadium
Capacity: 55,000

Kobe
Kobe Wing Stadium
Capacity: 42,000

Seogwipo
Jeju World
Cup Stadium
Capacity: 43,000

Oita
Oita Stadium Big Eye
Capacity: 43,000

Osaka
Nagai Stadium
Capacity: 50,000

TOP GOALSCORERS		
RONALDO	Brazil	8 goals
RIVALDO	Brazil	5 goals
Miroslav KLOSE	Germany	5 goals

GOLDEN BALL	
Oliver KAHN	Germany

THE FINAL

Amazingly, Brazil and Germany had never faced each other in the World Cup prior to the final. The South Americans won the contest with relative ease. Ronaldo scored both goals, the first after goalkeeper Oliver Kahn uncharacteristically spilled a long range shot and the second after a fantastic dummy by Rivaldo.

BRAZIL 2	GERMANY 0
JUNE 30, INTERNATIONAL STADIUM: 69,029	
MANAGER: LUIZ FELIPE SCOLARI	MANAGER: RUDI VÖLLER
FORMATION: 3-5-2	FORMATION: 3-5-2

BRAZIL
1 Marcos
3 Lucio · 5 Edmilson · 2 Linke
2 Cafu · 15 Kleberson · 11 Ronaldinho · 8 Gilberto · 6 Carlos
9 Ronaldo · 10 Rivaldo

GERMANY
11 Klose · 17 Bode
7 Neuville · 16 Jeremies · 8 Hamann · 19 Schneider · 22 Frings
4 Junior · 5 Ramelow · 21 Metzelder
1 Kahn

SUBS: 19 Juninho 17 Denilson 20 Bierhoff 21 Asamoah 6 Ziege

GROUP STAGE

GROUP E	W	D	L	PT	GROUP F	W	D	L	PT	GROUP G	W	D	L	PT	GROUP H	W	D	L	PT
Germany	2	1	0	7*	Sweden	1	2	0	5*	Mexico	2	1	0	7*	Japan	2	1	0	7*
Ireland	1	2	0	5*	England	1	2	0	5*	Italy	1	1	1	4*	Belgium	1	2	0	5*
Cameroon	1	1	1	4	Argentina	1	1	1	4	Croatia	1	0	2	3	Russia	1	0	2	3
Saudi Arabia	0	0	3	0	Nigeria	0	1	2	1	Ecuador	1	0	2	3	Tunisia	0	1	2	1

* The top two teams from each group qualified for the knock-out stages.

SAPPORO DOME

In 1996, the Sapporo government held a competition to design a stadium for the 2002 World Cup. The requirements were demanding—as well as being a venue for top-flight soccer matches, the stadium had to be able to host baseball games and other sporting and cultural events. In addition, it had to operate in all weathers, including heavy snow, and, to satisfy J-League rules (see p.272), the soccer field had to be made of natural turf.

GREEN, GREEN GRASS

Given that Sapporo's cold climate made it difficult for grass to grow in an enclosed space, the winning architects decided to site the field outside in the sunlight, moving it into the stadium only when matches were being played. This also made it possible to switch the configuration of the stadium from soccer to baseball.

SAPPORO DOME ("HIROBA")

1–3 HITSUJIGAOKA, TOYOHIRA-KU, SAPPORO CITY, JAPAN

HOME TEAM:	CONSADOLE SAPPORO
ARCHITECT:	HIROSHI HARA
OPENED:	3 JUNE 2001
CONSTRUCTION COST:	$442 MILLION
CAPACITY:	53,845

Dome
The aerodynamic dome deflects snow and shelters a vast, column-free space

Stands
The cone-shaped stands accommodate 41,484 fixed seats; the stadium has a capacity of 53,796

Concourse
Encircling the dome is a concourse with a glass curtain wall to afford views of the surrounding countryside

Multiple levels
The construction houses two basement levels and four levels above ground

Baseball field
The baseball field is made from artificial turf, which is rolled away and stored when the soccer field is in use

Sliding wall
Electronically controlled walls slide back to allow the soccer field to be rolled into the stadium

MULTI-PURPOSE STADIUM

Unlike many World Cup stadiums around the globe, the Sapporo Dome is no white elephant. In 2004 the baseball team Nippon Ham Fighters moved in, and, when neither soccer nor baseball games are being played there, the dome hosts a variety of concerts and exhibitions, which have proved highly profitable.

THE DOMED ROOF

Measuring 804 x 745 ft (245 x 227 m), the shell-shaped roof is supported by a series of trusses that transfer the load to a ring of columns around the perimeter of the building. The flat end of the dome opens onto the outdoor stadium. Here an internal "bridge" and a series of tension cables complete the structural loop by channeling loads to either side.

Soft curves
The soft curves of the roof encase an indoor floor with an area of 1,057,296 sq ft (98,226 sq m)

Roof
The shell-shaped, Teflon-coated roof has a total surface area of 570,487 sq ft (53,000 sq m)

Structure
The structure consists of reinforced concrete, ferroconcrete, and a steel framework

Height
The dome rises to a height of 223 ft (68 m) above the arena surface

Inside arena
The closed arena has an area of 155,646 sq ft (14,460 sq m)

Cubic capacity
The inside arena has a volume of 55.8 million cu ft (1.58 million cu m)

262 The height in feet (80 m) of the open-air escalators that take people from the third-floor galleries to the glass-walled concourse that goes out from the roof

27 The precise angle, in degrees, of the incline of the stands

110 The number of pieces of artificial turf that make up the baseball field

3 The number of first-round games played at the dome during the 2002 World Cup: Germany vs Saudi Arabia, Argentina vs England, and Italy vs Ecuador

Soccer field
The mobile natural-turf soccer field measures 131 x 93 yd (120 x 85 m)

FROM BASEBALL TO SOCCER

The world's first "hovering soccer stage" system allows the outdoor soccer field to be moved into the covered arena when baseball is not being played there. The field is rolled on 34 wheels that float on pressurized air 3 in (7.5 cm) above the ground.

1 The baseball field's artificial turf, pitcher's mound, and bases are rolled up and put into storage.

Angled seating
A bank of lower-bowl seats are rotated from their angled baseball position

2 The outfield seats retract, a wall slides open, and the field is rolled into the stadium.

Moveable pitch
As the field slides inside, a set of main-bowl seats at one end of the dome retracts

3 When the field is fully inside the arena, it is rotated through 90 degrees.

Walls
The walls slide closed and the seats re-extend; the change-over is complete

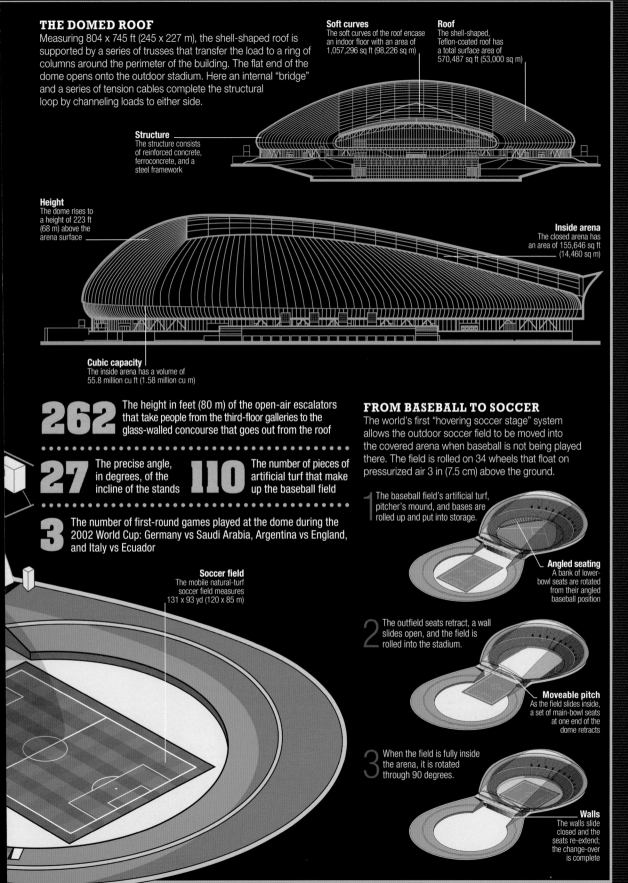

GERMANY 2006

With an uncharacteristic display of patriotism, the Germans unfurled national flags throughout the country. Their underdog team played very well, ousting the excellent Argentinians and pushing the eventual winners Italy to extra time in their semi-final clash.

THREE STRIKES AND YOU'RE OUT

Referee Graham Poll mistakenly showed Croatia's Šimunic three yellow cards in one match. He remembered to dismiss the player after the last booking, but by this stage had already blown for extra time. Luckily the Australians still qualified.

PASSING PLAY

The group stage was fairly predictable, aside from Australia qualifying at the expense of Croatia and Ghana doing likewise to the Czech Republic. Argentina was hugely impressive, with Cambiasso scoring the goal of the tournament at the end of a 24-pass move in a 6-0 destruction of Serbia and Montenegro.

FABIO CANNAVARO

The mainstay of Italy's defense and captain of the team, Cannavaro lifted the coveted trophy on the occasion of his 100th cap. In 690 minutes, the Italians had conceded just two goals.

ROUTE TO THE FINAL

In the second round, France beat perennial underachievers Spain 3–1 and Italy dispatched Australia in the dying seconds. Portugal knocked out the Netherlands in a match that saw the referee hand out a record 16 yellow and four red cards. England scraped through to the quarter-finals but were eliminated by Portugal on penalties. The Germans ran out of luck in their semi-final against the Italians. A Zidane penalty in the other semi-final was enough to get France past Portugal.

ZINÉDINE ZIDANE

Like Cantona before him, Zidane was a flawed genius. This most sublime player picked up both the man of the tournament and a straight red card in the final for his head-butt on Marco Materazzi.

2ND ROUND		QUARTER-FINALS		SEMI-FINALS		FINAL	
GERMANY	2						
SWEDEN	0	GERMANY	1*				
ARGENTINA	2•	ARGENTINA	1				
MEXICO	1			GERMANY	0		
ITALY	1			ITALY	2•		
AUSTRALIA	0	ITALY	3			ITALY	1
SWITZERLAND	0	UKRAINE	0			FRANCE	1
UKRAINE	0*					ITALY WON 5–3	
ENGLAND	1					ON PENALTIES	
ECUADOR	0	ENGLAND	0				
PORTUGAL	1	PORTUGAL	0*				
NETHERLANDS	0			PORTUGAL	0		
BRAZIL	3			FRANCE	1	3RD/4TH PLACE	
GHANA	0	BRAZIL	0			GERMANY	3
SPAIN	1	FRANCE	1			PORTUGAL	1
FRANCE	3						

* Qualified by penalty shoot-out   • After extra-time

STAT ATTACK — GROUP STAGE

GROUP A	W	D	L	PT	GROUP B	W	D	L	PT	GROUP C	W	D	L	PT	GROUP D	W	D	L	PT
Germany	3	0	0	9*	England	2	1	0	7*	Argentina	2	1	0	7*	Portugal	3	0	0	9*
Ecuador	2	0	1	6*	Sweden	1	2	0	5*	Netherlands	2	1	0	7*	Mexico	1	1	1	4*
Poland	1	0	2	3	Paraguay	1	0	2	3	Côte d'Ivoire	1	0	2	3	Angola	0	2	1	2
Costa Rica	0	0	3	0	Trinidad & Tobago	0	1	2	1	Serbia & Montenegro	0	0	3	0	Iran	0	1	2	1

* The top two teams from each group qualified for the second round

MIROSLAV KLOSE
A clinical finisher renowned for his composure in front of goal, Klose was the tournament's top scorer. He is as good with his head as his feet—in the 2002 finals, he scored five headers.

ENTERTAINING THE CROWD

The Ivory Coast's training sessions included an unusual element: dance practice, in which they rehearsed a carefully choreographed goal celebration called the "Elephant Dance". The African team performed well enough in their group matches to treat the world to the ground-stomping routine on five occasions.

THE VENUES

Many of the 13 top-class stadiums in Germany 2006 had to be temporarily renamed because FIFA regulations prohibited the sponsorship of stadiums during the tournament.

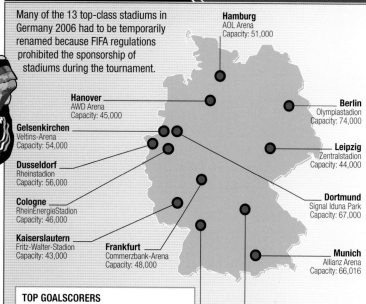

Hamburg
AOL Arena
Capacity: 51,000

Hanover
AWD Arena
Capacity: 45,000

Berlin
Olympiastadion
Capacity: 74,000

Gelsenkirchen
Veltins-Arena
Capacity: 54,000

Leipzig
Zentralstadion
Capacity: 44,000

Dusseldorf
Rheinstadion
Capacity: 56,000

Dortmund
Signal Iduna Park
Capacity: 67,000

Cologne
RheinEnergieStadion
Capacity: 46,000

Kaiserslautern
Fritz-Walter-Stadion
Capacity: 43,000

Frankfurt
Commerzbank-Arena
Capacity: 48,000

Munich
Allianz Arena
Capacity: 66,016

Nuremburg
EasyCredit-Stadion
Capacity: 42,000

Stuttgart
Mercedes Benz Arena
Capacity: 54,000

TOP GOALSCORERS

Miroslav KLOSE	Germany	5 goals
Hernán CRESPO	Argentina	3 goals
Thierry HENRY	France	3 goals

GOLDEN BALL

Zinédine ZIDANE	France

THE FINAL

The final revolved around the unlikely figure of Italian defender Marco Materazzi. He gave away an early penalty, which Zinédine Zidane converted via the crossbar, equalized with a powerful header, and provoked Zidane into head-butting him in extra time. The French genius was sent off and Italy won the game on penalties.

ITALY ①	FRANCE ①
ITALY WON 5–3 ON PENALTIES	
9 JULY, OLYMPIASTADION: 69,000	
MANAGER: MARCELLO LIPPI	MANAGER: ARRIGO SACCHI
FORMATION: 4-4-2	FORMATION: 4-5-1

ITALY
① Buffon
19 Zambrotta · 5 Cannavaro · 23 Materazzi · 3 Grosso
16 Camoranesi · 8 Gattuso · 21 Pirlo · 20 Perrotta
10 Totti · 9 Toni

FRANCE
12 Henry
7 Malouda · 4 Vieira · 10 Zidane · 6 Makélélé · 22 Ribéry
3 Abidal · 5 Gallas · 15 Thuram · 19 Sagnol
① Barthez

SUBS: 4 de Rossi 15 Iaquinta 7 Del Piero 18 Diarra 20 Trezeguet 11 Wiltord

GROUP STAGE

GROUP E	W	D	L	PT	GROUP F	W	D	L	PT	GROUP G	W	D	L	PT	GROUP H	W	D	L	PT
Italy	2	1	0	7*	Brazil	3	0	0	9*	Switzerland	2	1	0	7*	Spain	3	0	0	9*
Ghana	2	0	1	6	Australia	1	1	1	4*	France	1	2	0	5*	Ukraine	2	0	1	6*
Czech Republic	1	0	2	3	Croatia	0	2	1	2	Korea Republic	1	1	1	4	Tunisia	0	1	2	1
USA	0	1	2	1	Japan	0	1	2	1	Togo	0	0	3	0	Saudi Arabia	0	1	2	1

* The top two teams from each group qualified for the second round

SOUTH AFRICA
2010

South Africa has, to its credit, gone out of its way to inject the 2010 World Cup with a pan-African feel, encouraging visiting squads to train and practice in neighboring countries as well as South Africa itself. The organizers have also managed to allocate 100,000 tickets to be given away, as buying one is simply impossible for a large proportion of the nation's population.

BENNI MCARTHY
McCarthy has played in the top leagues of Spain, Portugal, Holland, and England. World Cup 2010 will be the striker's best—and possibly last—chance to shine for the national team.

SECOND TIME LUCKY

After the disappointment of losing the chance to host the 2006 World Cup, South Africa left nothing to chance for its 2010 bid, calling in such luminaries as Nelson Mandela, F.W. De Klerk, and Archbishop Desmond Tutu. However, concerns were expressed over safety, security, and transportation, amid rumors of a FIFA contingency plan in case South Africa proved unable to complete its undertakings.

Nevertheless, the stadium-building program, though fraught with corruption allegations, rose to the task and put South Africa on a perfect footing for hosting the tournament. Given the enormous popularity of soccer in the country and the very low income of many of its people, South Africa reserved special low-price tickets for locals on a small number of seats.

AN ALL-AFRICAN AFFAIR

The competition to host the 2010 World Cup was restricted to African nations. South Africa had hoped to host the 2006 World Cup, but lost out to Germany by a single vote after the Oceania representative abstained. Tunisia and Libya mounted a joint bid, only for FIFA to later rule out sharing the tournament between two nations. Morocco was also a strong contender, but in May 2004, FIFA voted 14–10 in favor of South Africa.

AFRICA'S TIME HAS COME. AFRICA IS CALLING...
COME HOME TO AFRICA IN 2010

THABO MBEKI, THEN-PRESIDENT OF SOUTH AFRICA, AT THE UNVEILING OF THE 2010 WORLD CUP EMBLEM, JULY 7, 2006

PAYING FOR THE PARTY

The South African government is planning to spend 19 billion rand ($2.4 billion) on the tournament—around 1% of GDP. This includes:

- **R17m ($2m)** for festivals and events.
- **R25m ($2.9m)** for the training and preparation of volunteers.
- **R337m ($39m)** for *Leaving a Legacy* projects supporting grassroots sports.
- **R150m ($17.5m)** for the opening and closing ceremonies and arts projects.

INCREASING COSTS

When South Africa first bid for the 2010 World Cup, just two new stadiums were proposed, however, like many others before them, they got carried away and ended up building or refurbishing ten stadiums. Costs on all stadiums, security, and infrastructure have risen to $2.4 billion dollars.

ROAD TO THE FINALS

The 2010 World Cup Finals will be contested by 32 teams. UEFA (Europe) is allocated 13 places while CAF (Africa) receives five, not counting South Africa as hosts. The AFC (Asia) and CONMEBOL (South America) each receive four places plus a play-off place against the top team in the OFC (Oceania) and CONCACAF (North and Central America and the Caribbean) respectively, the latter of which receives three places plus the play-off. While South Africa qualifys as hosts, they still played in the qualifiers because these serve as the qualifying tournament for the 2010 African Cup of Nations.

RECORD PARTICIPATION

While there are only 32 places at the Finals, a record 203 teams from the six FIFA confederations entered the qualification competitions for the 2010 tournament.

AARON MOKOENA

After almost a decade playing in Germany, the Netherlands, and Belgium, South African defender Mokoena now plays in the English Premier League. Known as "Mbazo" —"The Axe"—he is captain of the national side and should be leading the host team's challenge in 2010.

3,000,000 Number of tickets available for World Cup 2010 matches

64 Number of games at World Cup 2010

1,862,319 Requests for tickets in the first phase of World Cup ticket sales

THE VENUES

Some of the usual South African sporting venues will be on display at World Cup 2010, such as downtown Cape Town around the new Green Point Stadium, Soccer City in Soweto, and Ellis Park in Johannesburg. However, World Cup 2010 will take the world to parts of South Africa they are unfamiliar with, such as the new stadium in the industrial city of Port Elizabeth, and provincial towns such as Nelspruit and Polokwane.

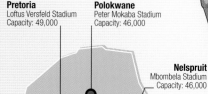

Pretoria
Loftus Versfeld Stadium
Capacity: 49,000

Polokwane
Peter Mokaba Stadium
Capacity: 46,000

Nelspruit
Mbombela Stadium
Capacity: 46,000

Rustenburg
Royal Bafokeng Stadium
Capacity: 42,000

Johannesburg
Soccer City
Capacity: 91,000

Johannesburg
Ellis Park Stadium
Capacity: 62,567

Bloemfontein
Free State Stadium
Capacity: 48,000

Durban
Moses Mabhida Stadium
Capacity: 70,000

Cape Town
Greenpoint Stadium
Capacity: 69,070

Port Elizabeth
Nelson Mandela Bay Stadium
Capacity: 48,000

FANZONES

At the World Cup 2006 in Germany, the attendance at "Fanzones"—viewing areas where live matches were broadcast on huge screens—was six times that of the stadiums. They are central to South Africa 2010—eight are planned for Cape Town alone, while Durban is planning a vast, beachfront Fanzone.

WOMEN'S WORLD CUP

COMPETITION: FIFA WOMEN'S WORLD CUP

FOUNDED: 1991

ORGANIZER: FIFA

NUMBER OF TEAMS: 16

The FIFA Women's World Cup, first held in 1991, is steadily growing in size, public recognition, and status. Now a 16-team tournament held every four years, it is the biggest global showcase for the women's game. Germany and the USA have dominated the fledgling contest, winning four of the first five contests between them.

SHAKY BEGINNINGS

The first forays into a women's world cup were the unaffiliated Mundialato in Italy in 1970, followed by another unofficial tournament in Mexico in 1971. Driven by a fear of losing control of the sport, and a dim recognition that women's soccer was a significant sporting force, FIFA and UEFA finally acted and ordered all their member associations to welcome women's soccer into the "soccer family."

A SLOW START

It took almost two decades to get the Women's World Cup off the ground, and the first tournament was held in China in 1991. The leading teams in the tournament over the years show that women's soccer has three global strongholds: North America, East Asia, and Northern Europe. In the US and China, the relative weakness of the men's game has allowed women's soccer to flourish. In Scandinavia and Germany, the egalitarianism of the social democratic governments has helped to promote the game.

BIRGIT PRINZ
A natural striker, Prinz is the top-scoring player at the Women's World Cup, and has been voted German player of the year for eight years in a row.

WORLD CUP EXPLOITATION

The 1971 Women's World Cup, held in Mexico, was an unofficial tournament backed by South American business interests that was run on crassly sexist, commercial lines. The goal frames were painted pink and some teams were encouraged to wear hot pants rather than shorts. As a prelude to matches there were rodeos, baseball games, and displays by sparsely-clad dancers.

> TRUE CHAMPIONS AREN'T ALWAYS THE ONES THAT WIN, **BUT THOSE WITH THE MOST GUTS**
>
> MIA HAMM
> US SOCCER STAR

STAT ATTACK

MOST APPEARANCES

Name	Country	Goals
Kristine LILLY	USA	30
Julie FOUDY	USA	24
Mia HAMM	USA	23
Bente NORDBY	Norway	22
Bettina WIEGMANN	Germany	22
Birgit PRINZ	Germany	22
Hege RIISE	Norway	22

TOP GOALSCORERS

Name	Country	Goals
Birgit PRINZ	Germany	14
Michelle AKERS	USA	12
Sun WEN	China	11
Bettina WIEGMANN	Germany	11
Ann Kristin AARØNES	Denmark	10
MARTA	Brazil	10
Heidi MOHR	Germany	10

MIA HAMM
With 158 goals in all competitions for the USA, American striker Mia Hamm is the top international goalscorer, male or female, in the history of soccer.

THE TOURNAMENTS

The geography of the Women's World Cup reveals three centers of power—northern Europe, the US, and China. The 2011 tournament will be held in Germany, but as the game grows, the Latin American, Australasian, and African nations are improving.

Norway
Winners: 1995

Sweden
Years Hosted:
1995 ⑫ participants

China
Years Hosted:
1991 ⑯ participants
2007 ⑫ participants

United States
Years Hosted:
1999 ⑯ participants
2003 ⑯ participants
Winners:
1991, 1999

Germany
Winners:
2003, 2007

PULLING POWER

Although it receives a fraction of the coverage of the men's tournament, the Women's World Cup is pulling in the crowds. At the 2007 contest in China, the average crowd was more than 35,000 and the total attendance well over 1.1 million. Rising sponsorship income means that teams were awarded prize money for the first time, with a $1-million prize for the champions.

CONTEST CANCELED

The 2003 Women's World Cup was scheduled to be hosted by China. However the country, and indeed the whole of southeast Asia, experienced an outbreak of the deadly SARS virus, so the contest was rescheduled for the US later in the year.

WORLD CUP POT

World Cup winners' prize money.

⬤ Men 2006—**$29 million**
⬤ Women 2007—**$1 million**

$ $

7,000,000 Number of registered women players in the US—the highest female participation in the world

11 Number of goals Germany scored against Argentina at the 2007 Women's World Cup in China, the most one-sided match of the tournament

100,000 Crowd size at Denmark's win over Mexico in the unofficial 1971 women's world cup final—a record for a women's international

CONTINENTAL COMPETITIONS

EUROPE

EUROPEAN CHAMPIONSHIP

COMPETITION:
UEFA EUROPEAN
FOOTBALL
CHAMPIONSHIP
FOUNDED: 1960
CONFEDERATION:
UEFA
**NUMBER OF
TEAMS:** 52

A European soccer championship was first proposed in the 1920s, but it took until 1960 for the first tournament to be played. The championship has been held every four years since, has grown from just four to 16 teams, and is planned to expand to 24 teams. As the tournament has grown and travel in Europe has become cheaper and easier, fans have come in increasing numbers from a growing range of countries, giving the tournament a truly carnivalesque feel.

OTTO REHAGEL
The German coach of the victorious Greek team at Euro 2004, Rehagal pulled off the impossible and gave the Greek squad tactical nous and a Germanic work rate.

BIRTH OF A DREAM

Henri Delaunay, head of the French FA, first proposed a European nations' tournament in 1927, but at the time, there was no European soccer federation to administer such a contest. It was not until the creation of UEFA in 1954 that Delaunay was able to revive the idea. Delaunay himself died in 1955, but the qualifying rounds of the tournament he had imagined were first played in 1958. In 1960, the USSR won the first final and claimed the Henri Delaunay Trophy.

EURO 2004

Fans came to Portugal for Euro 2004 in numbers never seen before. Swedes, Danes, Germans, the Dutch, and Spanish came in droves, but nobody could match the English for sheer numbers. They even sang the loudest at other teams' games, notably the France vs Greece quarter-final, with chants of "Eng-er-land."

STAT ATTACK

MOST WINS

	1	2	3
Germany			
Spain			
France			

MARCO VAN BASTEN
Dutch striker van Basten scored the tournament's greatest goal—a flying volley from close to the byline on the edge of the penalty area—in the 1988 final, sealing the Netherlands' 2–0 win over the USSR.

MOST APPEARANCES

Name	Country	Games
Liliam THURAM	France	16
Edwin VAN DER SAR	Netherlands	16
Luis FIGO	Portugal	14
Nuno GOMES	Portugal	15
Karel POBORSKÝ	Czech republic	14
Zinédine ZIDANE	France	14

TOP GOALSCORERS

Name	Country	Goals
Michel PLATINI	France	9
Alan SHEARER	England	7
Nuno GOMES	Portugal	6
Thierry HENRY	France	6
Patrick KLUIVERT	Netherlands	6
Ruud VAN NISTELROOY	Netherlands	6

THE COMPETITORS

Western European countries, notably Germany, have dominated the competition since its first tournament in 1960. Sixteen countries now compete and there are plans to expand the competition further to include other nations. As well as this, co-hosting has allowed smaller nations to pool resources and become hosts.

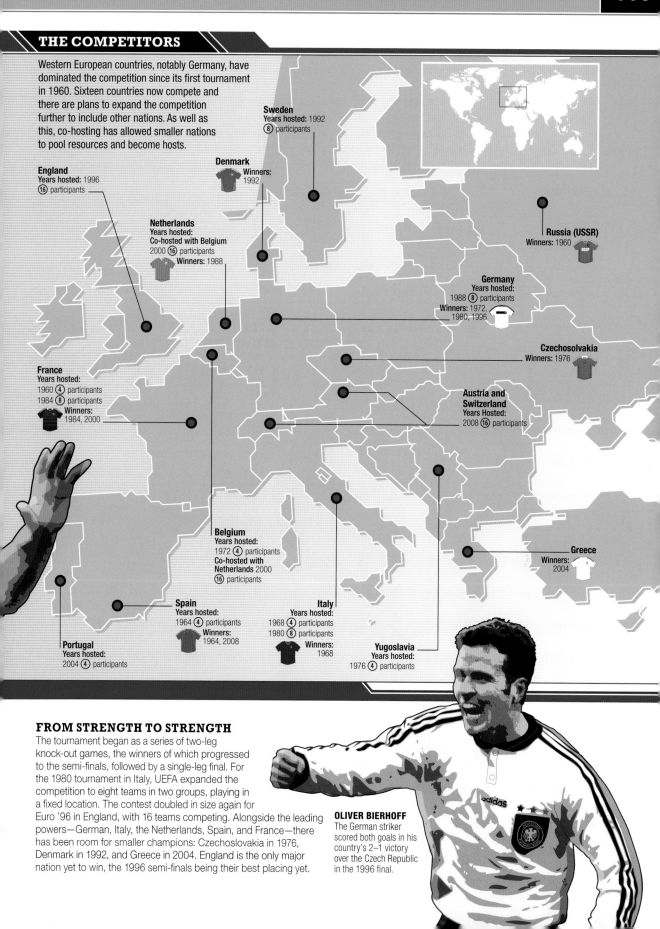

Sweden
Years hosted: 1992
(8) participants

England
Years hosted: 1996
(16) participants

Denmark
Winners:
1992

Netherlands
Years hosted:
Co-hosted with Belgium
2000 (16) participants
Winners: 1988

Russia (USSR)
Winners: 1960

Germany
Years hosted:
1988 (8) participants
Winners: 1972,
1980, 1996

Czechosolvakia
Winners: 1976

France
Years hosted:
1960 (4) participants
1984 (8) participants
Winners:
1984, 2000

**Austria and
Switzerland**
Years Hosted:
2008 (16) participants

Belgium
Years hosted:
1972 (4) participants
Co-hosted with
Netherlands 2000
(16) participants

Greece
Winners:
2004

Spain
Years hosted:
1964 (4) participants
Winners:
1964, 2008

Italy
Years hosted:
1968 (4) participants
1980 (8) participants
Winners:
1968

Portugal
Years hosted:
2004 (4) participants

Yugoslavia
Years hosted:
1976 (4) participants

FROM STRENGTH TO STRENGTH

The tournament began as a series of two-leg knock-out games, the winners of which progressed to the semi-finals, followed by a single-leg final. For the 1980 tournament in Italy, UEFA expanded the competition to eight teams in two groups, playing in a fixed location. The contest doubled in size again for Euro '96 in England, with 16 teams competing. Alongside the leading powers—German, Italy, the Netherlands, Spain, and France—there has been room for smaller champions: Czechoslovakia in 1976, Denmark in 1992, and Greece in 2004. England is the only major nation yet to win, the 1996 semi-finals being their best placing yet.

OLIVER BIERHOFF
The German striker scored both goals in his country's 2–1 victory over the Czech Republic in the 1996 final.

SOVIET CHAMPIONS, EURO '60

The Soviet team that won the first European championships received a bye through the quarter-finals, when Spanish dictator General Franco refused to allow his team to travel to Moscow. Once at the finals, the USSR proved their worth, led by goalkeeping legend Lev Yashin and consisting of the best talent drawn—for once—from more than just the Moscow clubs. Their winner against Yugoslavia in the final in Paris was scored by SKA Rostov-on-Don's Viktor Ponedelnik. Fewer than 18,000 people attended.

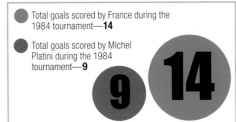

TOTAL GOALS—1984 FRANCE

Total goals scored by France during the 1984 tournament—**14**

Total goals scored by Michel Platini during the 1984 tournament—**9**

9 **14**

BRIAN LAUDRUP
One of two soccer playing brothers, Brian Laudrup was the lynchpin of the Denmark team that won Euro '92. Laudrup brought thoughtful passing and an attacking threat to a team set up to defend.

SPANISH REVENGE, EURO '64

The Soviet Union were fated to defend their title in Spain, who had refused to travel to Moscow in 1960. They met the hosts in the final at the Bernabeu in front of 105,000 people and the entire Spanish political elite. It was 1–1 till the 86th minute, when Marcelino headed home from near the penalty spot. There was no ambiguity about the meaning of the event for the government. Newspaper headlines the following day described the game as a "victory over communism and its fellow travelers."

SOCCER IS NOT ABOUT JUSTICE; WHEN THE REFEREE DECIDES, ## IT IS LIKE HE IS GOD

AUSTRIA COACH JOSEF HICKERSBERGER
ON AUSTRIA'S LAST-MINUTE PENALTY AGAINST POLAND

SEMI-FINAL SHOCK, EURO '84

The home team was fearsome at France 1984 and led for much of the semi-final until Portugal's Rui Jordão scored to take the game into extra-time. He then went one better and scored again to give the Portuguese a shock lead in the 98th minute, but France were up to the challenge and two late goals in a flurry of magnificent attacking play saw them through to the final, which they won against Spain.

DANISH MIRACLE, EURO '92

Denmark failed to qualify for the 1992 European Championships, having trailed to Yugoslavia in their qualifying group. But as the Yugoslav civil war raged, international sanctions saw the Balkan side excluded from the tournament and their place given to the Danes. A solid defense backed by the huge presence of goalkeeper Peter Schmeichel saw Denmark claw their way into the knock-out stages, before Brian Laudrup's sparky play helped them beat the Netherlands, and then Germany in the final. Celebrations in Copenhagen closely followed Denmark's "no" vote in a referendum on the reforming of the European Union. The crowds were the largest to have gathered in the country since the end of World War II.

FRENCH DOUBLE, EURO 2000

The final of Euro 2000 was notable for its open play. Delvecchio gave Italy a 1–0 lead ten minutes into the first half, then rather than putting down the defensive shutters, the Italians took the game to France in a torrid exchange of chances in the second half. France were on the brink of defeat until Sylvan Wiltord squeezed the ball past Italy's Toldo deep into injury time. The momentum switched to France and in the 103rd minute, France's Robert Pires' sharp cut-back from the Italian goal found David Trezeguet, who scored. France became the first team to hold the World Cup and European Championships at the same time.

DAVID TREZEGUET
France striker Trezeguet scored the Golden Goal in the Euro 2000 final that broke the deadlock and gave the French victory over Italy.

YUGOSLAVIA VS SPAIN, 2000

The group match between Yugoslavia and Spain was a pulsating, relentless game in which the Yugoslavs took the lead three times, but each time, Spain found an equalizer. Komljenovic made it 3–2 with just 15 minutes to go, but Mendieta equalized from the spot in the final minute. Deep into injury time, Alfonso fired a searing volley to make it 4–3 to the Spaniards.

16 Most matches played, held by Edwin van der Saar and Lillian Thuram

2 Number of finals won with a golden goal—Germany in 1996 and France in 2000

3 Hosts who have won the title—Spain '64, Italy '68, France '84

18.3 Age of youngest player to appear in the tournament—Enzo Scifo, 1984

65 Number of seconds before Greek player Angelos Charisteas was booked in Greece's 2–0 defeat by Sweden at Euro 2008— it proved to be the fastest yellow card of the tournament

SPANISH DELIGHT, EURO 2008

Euro 2008 was co-hosted by Austria and Switzerland, neither of whom performed well. Defending World Champions Italy were well below par, and the much-touted Dutch and Portuguese fell before the final. Russia, Croatia, and Turkey were the surprise packages and Germany, solid as ever, reached the final, where they met Spain. The Spaniards played with uncommon aplomb and confidence—a 4–1 demolition of Russia in the opening round serving as a demonstration of intent. A close-fought final saw a single, brilliant goal from Fernando Torres give Spain their first international title since 1964.

CESC FABREGAS
Spain's central midfielder was a super-sub at Euro 2008, playing in every game. He scored the winning penalty against Italy in the quarter-final and his goal assists were vital to Spain's final victory.

TURKEY VS CROATIA, EURO 2008

Turkey looked bound for an early exit when they met Croatia in the final group game. They were hit by suspensions and injuries and found themselves 2–0 down after 62 minutes. In a whirlwind of attacking play, however, the Turks seemed to rouse themselves, and the crowd was electrified by Arda's 75th-minute goal. In the final minutes, Nihat struck twice and Turkey won 3–2 to progress to the knock-out stages.

TROPHY CABINET

Pots, mugs, jugs, silverware, and brass—every soccer culture has its own slang for trophies, which reflects the importance of these objects in the professional game. The oldest national cup—the FA Cup—started a trend when the original trophy was stolen and reportedly melted down to make counterfeit coins. The same fate befell the first World Cup trophy too.

1.

2.

3.

4.

5.

6.

7.

1. FIFA WORLD CUP TROPHY

The trophy for this world international competition depicts two human figures holding up the Earth.

2. WOMEN'S WORLD CUP

This world international competition was first played in 1991, but the current trophy was first presented to the USA in 1999.

3. ASIA CUP TROPHY

When the trophy for this Asian international competition was won by Iraq in 2007, it was taken on a nationwide celebratory tour.

4. COPA AMÉRICA

This South American international competition boasts the oldest international soccer trophy in the world.

5. UEFA EUROPEAN CHAMPIONSHIPS TROPHY

This European international competition trophy was named after Henri Delaunay, the first General Secretary of UEFA.

6. GOLD CUP

This international competition is contested by Caribbean and Central and North American countries in the CONCACAF federation.

7. AFRICAN CUP OF NATIONS

This is the trophy for the African international competition, which was first held in 1957 and has been held every two years since 1968.

8. FIFA CONFEDERATIONS CUP

This competition is contested by the winners of the six FIFA championship confederations and the Word Cup winner and host.

9. THE FIFA CLUB WORLD CUP

The trophy for this competition for champion clubs around the world was designed by family-run designers Thomas Fattorini Ltd.

10. UEFA CUP

This tropy is awarded to the winner of the competition held between European clubs and was first contested in 1971.

11. EUROPEAN CHAMPIONS CUP

Contested by elite European clubs, this trophy is nicknamed La Orejona (big ears) in Spanish because of the shape of the handles.

12. COPA LIBERTADORES

Contested by South American clubs, this competition pays homage to the main leaders of independence in South America.

UEFA CHAMPIONS LEAGUE

COMPETITION:
UEFA CHAMPIONS
LEAGUE

TROPHY NAME:
EUROPEAN
CHAMPION
CLUBS' CUP

FOUNDED: 1955

CONFEDERATION:
UEFA

**NUMBER OF
TEAMS:** 77

Although some in South America might disagree, the Champions League is the world's most important club competition. It is contested by the biggest teams and showcases the best players in the world, and attracts TV and sponsorship revenues that dwarf those of the Copa Libertadores. The financial and psychological rewards of victory are enormous—the winning team can expect to get more than $40 million, and no great player feels complete until he has lifted "Old Big Ears."

EUROPEAN IDEALS

Although European club contests were first played as far back as 1897, it was not until 1954 and a proposal by Gabriel Hanot, editor of French soccer magazine L'Équipe, that a regular tournament was taken seriously. UEFA adopted the proposal, creating the European Cup for the 1955–56 season. Entry was restricted to national champions and the previous year's winners.

A LEAGUE APART

The European Cup became the UEFA Champions League in 1992 but its transformation came in 1995. UEFA, following the commercial lines of the FIFA World Cup, reorganized and rebranded the contest, centralizing sponsorship and TV sales, stadium standards, and match officiation. Income rose to over half-a-billion Euros and TV coverage spread to more than a hundred countries.

UNLIKELY BEGINNINGS

The Champions League owes much to Wolverhampton Wanderers, one of the also-rans of English soccer. Wolves beat Hungarian champions Honvéd 3–2 in December 1954, leading manager Stan Cullis to declare them "Champions of the World." Gabriel Hanot disagreed, and persuaded UEFA to introduce a competition to settle the issue.

SIR MATT BUSBY
Manchester United manager Sir Matt Busby assembled a team bound for European glory in the 1950s, only to lose seven players in the Munich air disaster. He recovered to build a side that became the first English club to win the European Cup in 1968.

CLARENCE SEEDORF
Dutch midfielder Seedorf is the only man to win the Champions League with three different clubs—Ajax, Real Madrid, and AC Milan.

STAT ATTACK

MOST APPEARANCES

Name	Club	Played
RAÚL	Real Madrid	128
Roberto CARLOS	Real Madrid, Fenerbahçe	115
Ryan GIGGS	Manchester United	112
Paolo MALDINI	Milan	108
David BECKHAM	Manchester United, Real Madrid	103
Oliver KAHN	Bayern Munich	103
Paul SCHOLES	Manchester United	102

TOP GOALSCORERS

Name	Club	Goals
RAÚL	Real Madrid	65
Ruud VAN NISTELROOY	PSV Eindhoven, Man Utd, Real Madrid	60
Andrei SHEVCHENKO	Dynamo Kiev, AC Milan, Chelsea	56
Alfredo DI STÉFANO	Real Madrid	49
Filippo INZAGHI	Juventus, AC Milan	46

THE WINNERS

The European Cup has been won by Eastern European clubs just twice—Steaua Bucharest of Romania and Red Star Belgrade of Serbia. In the west, the nations who have won it comprise an exclusive club. All but two winners (Celtic and Marseilles) have come from just six nations —England, Germany, Holland, Italy, Spain, and Portugal.

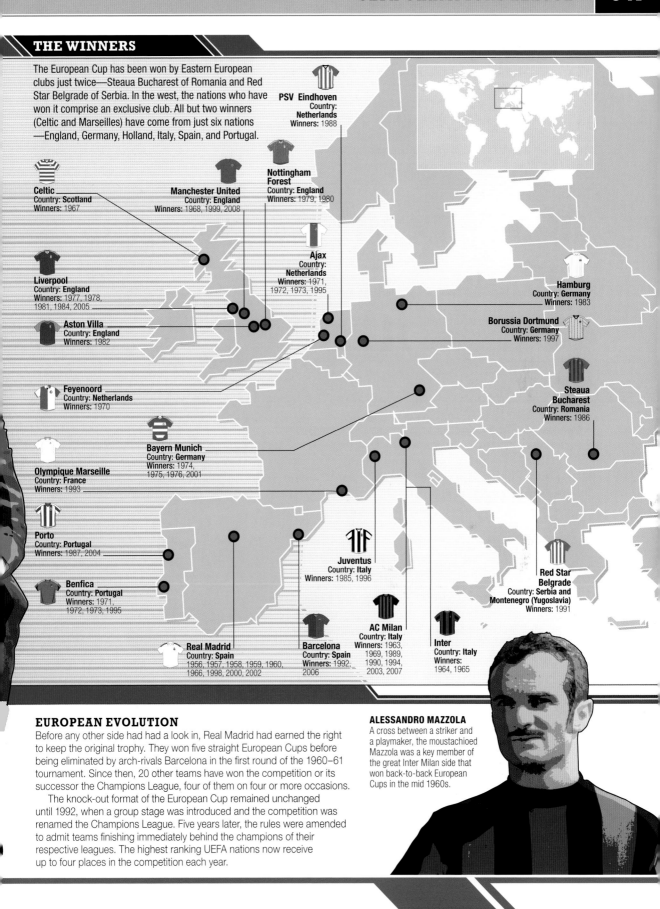

PSV Eindhoven
Country: **Netherlands**
Winners: 1988

Nottingham Forest
Country: **England**
Winners: 1979, 1980

Celtic
Country: **Scotland**
Winners: 1967

Manchester United
Country: **England**
Winners: 1968, 1999, 2008

Ajax
Country: **Netherlands**
Winners: 1971, 1972, 1973, 1995

Hamburg
Country: **Germany**
Winners: 1983

Liverpool
Country: **England**
Winners: 1977, 1978, 1981, 1984, 2005

Borussia Dortmund
Country: **Germany**
Winners: 1997

Aston Villa
Country: **England**
Winners: 1982

Feyenoord
Country: **Netherlands**
Winners: 1970

Steaua Bucharest
Country: **Romania**
Winners: 1986

Bayern Munich
Country: **Germany**
Winners: 1974, 1975, 1976, 2001

Olympique Marseille
Country: **France**
Winners: 1993

Porto
Country: **Portugal**
Winners: 1987, 2004

Juventus
Country: **Italy**
Winners: 1985, 1996

Red Star Belgrade
Country: **Serbia and Montenegro (Yugoslavia)**
Winners: 1991

Benfica
Country: **Portugal**
Winners: 1971, 1972, 1973, 1995

Real Madrid
Country: **Spain**
1956, 1957, 1958, 1959, 1960, 1966, 1998, 2000, 2002

Barcelona
Country: **Spain**
Winners: 1992, 2006

AC Milan
Country: **Italy**
Winners: 1963, 1969, 1989, 1990, 1994, 2003, 2007

Inter
Country: **Italy**
Winners: 1964, 1965

EUROPEAN EVOLUTION

Before any other side had had a look in, Real Madrid had earned the right to keep the original trophy. They won five straight European Cups before being eliminated by arch-rivals Barcelona in the first round of the 1960–61 tournament. Since then, 20 other teams have won the competition or its successor the Champions League, four of them on four or more occasions.

The knock-out format of the European Cup remained unchanged until 1992, when a group stage was introduced and the competition was renamed the Champions League. Five years later, the rules were amended to admit teams finishing immediately behind the champions of their respective leagues. The highest ranking UEFA nations now receive up to four places in the competition each year.

ALESSANDRO MAZZOLA

A cross between a striker and a playmaker, the moustachioed Mazzola was a key member of the great Inter Milan side that won back-to-back European Cups in the mid 1960s.

EUROPE

REAL MADRID

Propelled by the sublime talents of Alfredo di Stéfano and Ferenc Puskás, Real Madrid had a monopoly on the first five European Cups. Although they won the trophy again in 1966, they had to wait another 32 years for their next success. The side that defeated Juventus 1–0 in the 1998 final featured Roberto Carlos, Raúl, and Fernando Morientes and two years later a similar line-up got the better of fellow-Spaniards Valencia. In 2002, Madrid won their third Champions League title in five years and their ninth overall with a superb Zinèdine Zidane volley.

10 Seconds it took Bayern Munich's Roy Makaay to score against Real Madrid in a 2007 tie

20 Unbeaten games in the competition, held by Ajax

136,505 Record attendance at a European Cup match—Celtic vs Leeds United in 1970

40 Romanian fans who defected to the west after Steaua Bucharest won the 1986 final

11 Division One position of Aston Villa the year they won the European Cup

AC MILAN

With four European Cup and three Champions League titles, AC Milan have won the contest more times than any other club except Real Madrid. Their victories have also been more evenly spread out than those of their rivals, making them arguably the most consistent side in the history of the competition. The "Rossoneri" have a tradition of electing to wear their all-white away kit for Champions League finals, having won six out of eight in those colors but only one out of three in their regular red-and-black uniform.

BENFICA 5, REAL MADRID 3

The two Iberian teams who lined up for the 1962 final had won all the previous European Cups between them. The Spanish champions went into the interval 3–2 ahead, courtesy of a hat-trick from the great Ferenc Puskás, but Benfica coach Béla Guttmann transformed the game at half-time by placing a man-marker on the deep-lying Alfredo di Stéfano. This cut off Puskás' supply line and allowed Benfica to take control. The Portuguese equalized through a long-range strike from Coluna and clinched the contest with two goals from a 20-year-old Eusébio.

ROBERTO CARLOS
Famed for his explosive—if erratic—free kicks and seemingly inexhaustible energy, the Brazilian wing back won three Champions League trophies with Real Madrid.

FILIPPO INZAGHI
A busy forward with an uncanny ability to play off the shoulder of the last defender, "Pippo" Inzaghi scored both AC Milan goals in the club's victory over Liverpool in the 2007 final.

AC MILAN 4, BARCELONA 0

Barcelona went into the 1994 final as favorites, having just won La Liga and boasting an awesome strikeforce of Hristo Stoichkov and Romário. Milan, by contrast, were in disarray, with defenders Franco Baresi and Alessandro Costacurta suspended and striker Marco Van Basten out with the ankle injury that ultimately ended his career. Nevertheless, Fabio Capello's team annihilated the Catalans 4–0 in a performance many regard as the greatest in the history of the competition.

LIVERPOOL

The "Reds" won four European Cups between 1977 and 1984, three of them under slipper-wearing manager Bob Paisley. They would almost certainly have won more had their period of domination not ended in tragedy—rioting Liverpool fans caused 39 deaths ahead of the 1985 European Cup final against Juventus at the Heysel Stadium in Brussels, leading UEFA to ban the club from its competitions for seven years. In 2005, Liverpool reached the summit of European soccer once more, overcoming a three goal deficit to beat AC Milan in "The Miracle of Istanbul" (see pp.208–09).

LIVERPOOL WITHOUT EUROPEAN FOOTBALL IS LIKE
...A BANQUET WITHOUT WINE

ROY EVANS
LIVERPOOL DEFENDER (1965–74) AND MANAGER (1994–98)

THE MIRACLE OF ISTANBUL

The comeback of all time, the miracle of belief transmuted into victory; Liverpool's win in the 2005 final offered up every religious and magical metaphor. Utterly outplayed by AC Milan and 3–0 down at half-time, Liverpool appeared shattered, but in an extraordinary 15 minutes clawed their way back to 3–3, held on in extra time, and won a nerve-jangling penalty shoot-out to claim their fifth European Cup (see pp.208–09).

GRAEME SOUNESS
A fiercely competitive midfielder, Souness won three European Cups with Liverpool between 1978 and 1984. A superb passer, he was tough and elegant at the same time.

BAYERN MUNICH

The Bavarian giants swept all before them in the mid-1970s, winning three European Cups in succession. Spearheaded by goal-poacher extraordinaire Gerd Müller, they had quality all over the field and a peerless captain in sweeper Franz Beckenbauer. Bayern fans subsequently had to endure defeats in the 1982, 1987, and 1999 finals, the last particularly heartbreaking as the Germans were beating Manchester United with a minute to go. However, they managed to win Europe's premier club trophy for a fourth time in 2001.

CHAMPIONS LEAGUE WINS BY COUNTRY

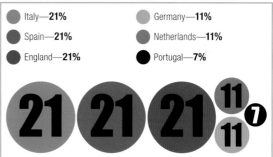

- Italy—**21%**
- Spain—**21%**
- England—**21%**
- Germany—**11%**
- Netherlands—**11%**
- Portugal—**7%**

MOST WINS BY CLUB

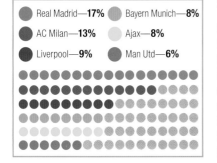

- Real Madrid—**17%**
- AC Milan—**13%**
- Liverpool—**9%**
- Bayern Munich—**8%**
- Ajax—**8%**
- Man Utd—**6%**

AJAX

The Ajax team of the early 1970s supplied the much-loved Netherlands side that narrowly missed out on World Cup glory in 1974 with both its nucleus of players and its "total soccer" philosophy. Unlike the national team, however, the Amsterdam club was able to win when it mattered. In 1973, Ajax beat Juventus 1–0 in the final to become only the second club to win the European Cup three years in succession, with a star-studded team that included all-time greats Johan Cruyff and Johan Neeskens. Ajax have since suffered from a lack of financial muscle, but they won the Champions League with a sparkling young side in 1995, beating AC Milan 1–0 in the final in Vienna.

EINTRACHT FRANKFURT
VS REAL MADRID

Between 1956 and 1960, Real Madrid won the first five European cups, setting a standard of excellence and achievement, a pinnacle of sporting glamor and class, against which all future European triumphs would be measured. Real were not tactical innovators or possessed of a charismatic coach (they went through four in this period) but their squad was peerless and their fight was legendary. The 1960 European Cup final was their peak.

EINTRACHT FRANKFURT 3	REAL MADRID 7

FORMATION: 3-2-5	**FORMATION:** 3-2-5
MANAGER: PAUL OSSWALD	**MANAGER:** MIGEUL MUNOZ
HAMPDEN PARK, GLASGOW, SCOTLAND, MAY 18, 1960	
ATTENDANCE: 134,000	
REFEREE: JOHN MOWAT (SCOTLAND)	

1 Loy
2 Lutz · 5 Eigenbrodt · 3 Hofer
4 Weilbacher · 6 Stinka
7 Kress · 8 Lindner · 9 Stein · 10 Pfaff · 11 Meier

11 Gento · 8 Del Sol · 9 Di Stefano · 10 Puskás · 7 Canario
6 Zarraga · 4 Vidal
3 Pachin · 5 Santamaria · 2 Marquitos
1 Dominguez

SUBS: NONE PERMITTED

00:00

In front of 134,000 supporters, Real Madrid's captain Zarraga (right) exchanges pennants with Eintracht Frankfurt captain Pfaff before the game.

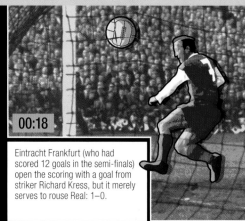

00:18

Eintracht Frankfurt (who had scored 12 goals in the semi-finals) open the scoring with a goal from striker Richard Kress, but it merely serves to rouse Real: 1–0.

Real take the game straight back to Frankfurt and after half an hour, Real center forward Di Stefano ties from short range at the far post after some good work down the right-hand side by Canario: 1–1.

00:30

Three minutes later Real is ahead. Canario's shot, struck with the outside of his foot, spins from the grasp of the Frankfurt keeper Egon Loy, and Di Stefano pounces to fire the ball into the roof of the net: 2–1.

00:33

00:71

Real are now in control and Puskás embarks on 40 minutes of brilliant play that brings four goals. The first of the four comes from a shot fired at a seemingly impossible angle, the second as a result of a controversial penalty. The third is a stooping header after a cross from Gento. Then, in the 71st minute, Puskás sends a rocket of a shot, struck on the turn, inside the post and just under the bar: 6–1.

00:71

Center forward Erwin Stein pulls a goal back for Frankfurt, but Di Stefano responds immediately: a pass from Puskás sees him head straight for goal and he sends the ball flying past Loy: 7–2. A careless back-pass by the Real defense lets Stein in again, but by now it is far too late and Real claim the cup: 7–3.

EUROPE

UEFA EUROPA LEAGUE

COMPETITION:
UEFA EUROPA LEAGUE

NAME OF TROPHY:
THE BERTONI TROPHY

FOUNDED:
1955 (FAIRS CUP),
1971 (UEFA CUP),
2009 (EUROPA LEAGUE)

CONFEDERATION: UEFA

NUMBER OF TEAMS: 100+

Formerly known as the UEFA Cup, Europe's second-most-important cup contest lacks the glamor of the Champions League, but provides vital income for clubs involved. It gives "lesser" teams a shot at European glory, and provides a safety net for clubs eliminated from the Champions League. It can also produce high-quality soccer, particularly in the latter rounds.

DINO BAGGIO
Midfielder Dino Baggio scored in two UEFA Cup finals for two different teams—for Juventus in 1993 and Parma in 1995, against his old club.

EXHIBITIONIST ORIGINS

The UEFA Cup grew out of an esoteric-seeming competition named the Inter-City Fairs Cup, which was first played in the 1950s. It was devised by the Swiss pools magnate Ernst Thommen and was open to teams from cities that hosted international trade fairs. League position was irrelevant and a one-team-per-city rule applied, leading to the entry of artificial sides, such as a London XI.

THE 2001 FINAL

In a rollercoaster classic, Liverpool were two up against Alavés within 16 minutes and 3–1 ahead at half time. The Spanish team pulled the score back to 4–4, but had two men sent off in extra time and conceded a "golden" own goal with penalties just four minutes away.

ONE CUP, MANY NAMES

The first Fairs Cup (1955–58), which was won by Barcelona, was renamed the Runner's Up Cup in 1968, before UEFA took over the tournament in 1971–72. Further changes have included the amalgamation of the contest with the UEFA Cup Winners' Cup in 1999 and the introduction of a group stage in 2004–05.

THE NEW ERA—THE EUROPA LEAGUE

After numerous format changes, the UEFA Cup was renamed the UEFA Europa League from the 2009–10 season. The qualification criteria also changed, with a range of methods of gaining entry. Teams finishing immediately below the qualifiers for the Champions League in their domestic divisions are awarded a place, as are the winners of the main, and in some countries the secondary, domestic cup competition. Three teams that top their domestic Fair Play leagues also gain a place, while clubs eliminated from the Champions League enter the competition in the later stages. Four qualifying rounds are followed by a group stage in which teams play each other twice, followed by four knock-out rounds and a final.

JUANDE RAMOS
In 2007, then-Sevilla manager Juande Ramos became only the second manager to lead his club to a second successive UEFA Cup win.

STAT ATTACK

COUNTRIES WITH MOST WINS

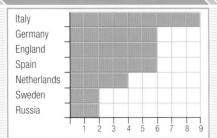

	1	2	3	4	5	6	7	8	9
Italy									
Germany									
England									
Spain									
Netherlands									
Sweden									
Russia									

TOP GOALSCORERS

Name	Club	Goals
Henrik LARSSON	Feyenoord, Celtic, Helsingborgs	37
Walter MACHADO DA SILVA	Valencia	31
Josef HEYNCKES	Borussia Mönchengladbach	29
Dieter MÜLLER	FC Köln, VfB Stuttgart, Girondins Bordeaux	29

THE WINNERS

During the 1980s and 1990s the UEFA Cup seemed to belong to Italy—their clubs won it eight times between 1988 and 1999. More recently, Spain's second-tier clubs and the big teams from new powers Russia and Turkey have become champions.

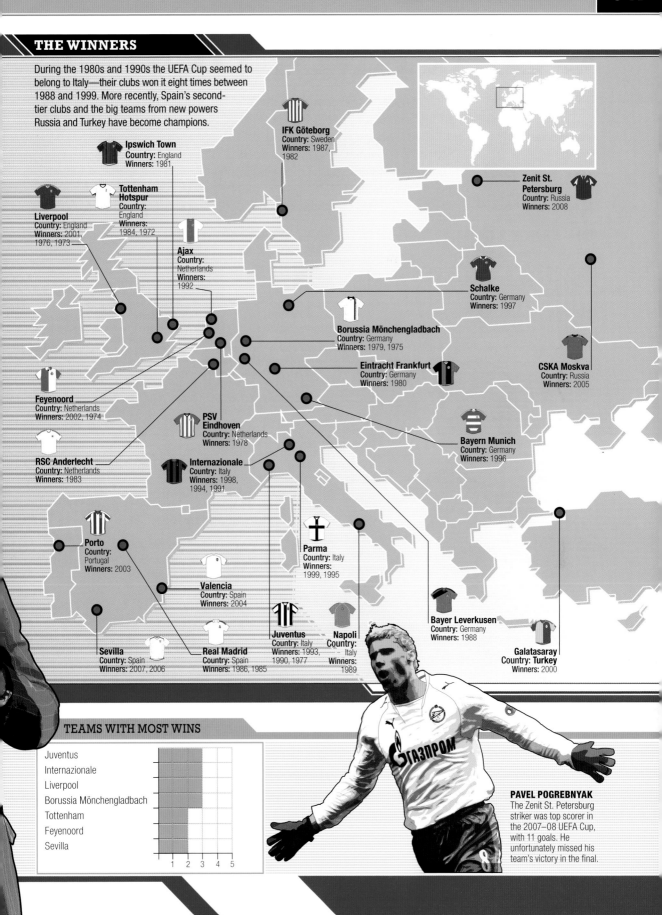

IFK Göteborg
Country: Sweden
Winners: 1987, 1982

Zenit St. Petersburg
Country: Russia
Winners: 2008

Ipswich Town
Country: England
Winners: 1981

Tottenham Hotspur
Country: England
Winners: 1984, 1972

Liverpool
Country: England
Winners: 2001, 1976, 1973

Ajax
Country: Netherlands
Winners: 1992

Schalke
Country: Germany
Winners: 1997

Borussia Mönchengladbach
Country: Germany
Winners: 1979, 1975

Eintracht Frankfurt
Country: Germany
Winners: 1980

CSKA Moskva
Country: Russia
Winners: 2005

Feyenoord
Country: Netherlands
Winners: 2002, 1974

PSV Eindhoven
Country: Netherlands
Winners: 1978

Bayern Munich
Country: Germany
Winners: 1996

RSC Anderlecht
Country: Netherlands
Winners: 1983

Internazionale
Country: Italy
Winners: 1998, 1994, 1991

Porto
Country: Portugal
Winners: 2003

Parma
Country: Italy
Winners: 1999, 1995

Valencia
Country: Spain
Winners: 2004

Bayer Leverkusen
Country: Germany
Winners: 1988

Sevilla
Country: Spain
Winners: 2007, 2006

Real Madrid
Country: Spain
Winners: 1986, 1985

Juventus
Country: Italy
Winners: 1993, 1990, 1977

Napoli
Country: Italy
Winners: 1989

Galatasaray
Country: Turkey
Winners: 2000

TEAMS WITH MOST WINS

	1	2	3	4	5
Juventus					
Internazionale					
Liverpool					
Borussia Mönchengladbach					
Tottenham					
Feyenoord					
Sevilla					

PAVEL POGREBNYAK
The Zenit St. Petersburg striker was top scorer in the 2007–08 UEFA Cup, with 11 goals. He unfortunately missed his team's victory in the final.

COPA AMÉRICA

COMPETITION:
COPA AMÉRICA
FOUNDED: 1910
CONFEDERATION:
CONMEBOL
**NUMBER OF
TEAMS:** 12

International competition in South America was underway as early as 1905, when Argentina and Uruguay competed for the Lipton Cup, donated by English tea merchant Sir Thomas Lipton. In 1910, the Argentine FA invited Uruguay, Chile, and Brazil to the first unofficial Copa América, six years before the continent even had a soccer federation. The first official outing was held in Montevideo in 1917, making it the first continental soccer competition in the world.

THE EARLY YEARS

The Copa América was played on a near-annual basis in the 1920s, but took a six-year break in the 1930s while the sport in South America turned professional. The tournament continued throughout the 1950s and 1960s, but took an eight-year break from 1967 due to Brazil and Argentina taking less interest in the tournament, and their domestic clubs exerting pressure to retain players for the Copa Libertadores. It recommenced in 1975 as a finals-only tournament.

COPA 2007

Venezuela is one of the weaker South American soccer nations, but finally hosted its first Copa América in 2007. Hugo Chávez, the country's president, indulged in a spot of grandstanding, including an on-field kickaround with Diego Maradona and President Morales of Bolivia. But it was steely Brazil, flattening Argentina 3–0 in the final, who stole the limelight.

IVÁN CÓRDOBA

Córdoba was the captain, the rock of the defense, and scorer of the goal that won Columbia the Copa América in 2001. He left South America in 1999 for a decade of success at Internazionale.

THE MODERN ERA

From 1987, the Copa was relaunched with TV broadcasting deals, sponsorship money, and a single host-country every four years. The scheduling problem of having just ten South American teams has been solved with the invitation of two wild-card teams for each contest—such as Mexico, Japan, the USA, or Costa Rica—to make up three groups of four. Group winners, runners-up, and the two best third-place teams qualify for the quarter-finals.

43 Number of minutes of extra time played in the 1919 final before Friedenrich scored the winner for Brazil against Uruguay

34 Most appearances in the Copa América, held jointly by Sergio Livingstone of Chile (1941–53) and Zizinho of Brazil (1942–57)

HOST NATIONS

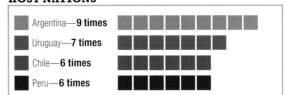

Argentina—**9 times**
Uruguay—**7 times**
Chile—**6 times**
Peru—**6 times**

STAT ATTACK

MOST GAMES WON

Country	Played	Wins
Argentina	173	111
Uruguay	184	103
Brazil	167	95
Paraguay	153	61
Chile	161	54
Peru	132	46
Colombia	99	36

TOP GOALSCORERS

Name	Country	Goals
Norberto MÉNDEZ	Argentina	17
ZIZINHO	Brazil	17
Severino VARELA	Uruguay	15
Teodoro FERNÁNDEZ	Peru	15
Gabriel BATISTUTA	Argentina	13
ADEMIR	Brazil	13
Jair DA ROSA PINTO	Brazil	13

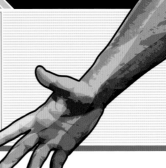

THE COMPETITORS

Since the Copa América was relaunched as a tournament in 1987, the trophy has been well distributed throughout the continent— every CONMEBOL member has either hosted or won the tournament. Brazil, Argentina, and Uruguay are multiple winners and Columbia took a single title, as hosts, in 2004.

THE SPREAD OF COPA AMÉRICA

1 Canada
2 USA
3 Mexico
4 Honduras
5 Costa Rica
6 Japan
7 South Korea

Venezuela
Year hosted: 2007

Colombia
Year hosted: 2001
Winners:
2001

Ecuador
Year hosted: 1993

Bolivia
Year hosted: 1997

Peru
Year hosted:
2004
Winners:
1975

Paraguay
Year hosted:1999
Winners:
1979

Chile
Year hosted: 1991

Argentina
Year hosted: 1987
Winners:
1991, 1993

Brazil
Year hosted: 1989
Winners:
1989, 1997,
1999, 2004,
2007

Paraguay
Year hosted: 1995
Winners:
1983, 1987,
1995

ADRIANO
The temperamental Brazilian striker came to international attention with a flurry of goals that helped to win the Copa América for Brazil in 2004. Sadly, his form has been on the slide ever since.

COPA LIBERTADORES

COMPETITION:
TAÇA LIBERTADORES DA AMÉRICA

FOUNDED: 1960

CONFEDERATION: CONMEBOL

NUMBER OF TEAMS: 38

Originally called the South American Championships, the tournament was renamed the Copa Libertadores in 1960 in honor of the soldier-presidents—such as Simón Bolívar—who fought for independence from Spain in the early 19th century. Just as the ideas of the "Libertadores" have been a huge symbol for the pan-American imagination, so has the cup. It has also proved to be a field on which the continent's bitter rivalries have been staged and fought.

MISSILES INTERRUPT PLAY

The 1962 final saw Brazilian side Santos beat Penarol of Uruguay 2–1 in the first leg. Penarol were 3–2 up late in the second half of the second leg when the referee was knocked unconscious by a stone thrown from the crowd. He resumed the game after waking 40 minutes later, but when the assistant referee was hit by a second stone after a Santos equalizer, the goal was disallowed and the game abandoned. Santos won the play-off.

AN OPEN CONTEST

For most of the Libertadores' history, the cup has been dominated by teams from Brazil and Argentina. The Uruguayan teams – Penarol and Nacional – were powers in the 1960s and 1970s, but have not contested a final since 1988. However, there remains room for smaller teams – Paraguayan champions Olimpia won their third Libertadores title in 2002, Once Caldas, a tiny Colombian provincial club, won in 2004, and LDU Quito from Ecuador triumphed in 2008.

SETTING THE FORMAT

It took almost 30 years for the format of the tournament to be established, with clubs from several nations regularly prevaricating on whether to enter. Brazilian teams asked for extra gate money, while Venezuelan sides were in, then out, then in and out again, and have only recently begun to compete regularly. Mexican clubs were added in the 1990s to raise interest and the standard of the competition. The tournament is currently—after qualifying rounds—a 32-team contest with eight groups of four leading to a knock-out stage of sixteen. All games are played over two legs.

5 Number of finals lost by Colombian player Anthony De Ávila, four with América di Cali and one with Barcelona of Ecuador

26 Most penalties taken in a shoot-out— Newell's Old Boys vs América in the 1992 semi-finals

15 Highest number of consecutive participations in the tournament, by Penarol (1965–79)

STAT ATTACK

MOST CLUB WINS

Independiente
Boca Juniors
Peñarol
São Paulo
Nacional
Olimpia
Estudiantes de La Plata

1 2 3 4 5 6 7 8

TOP GOALSCORERS

Name	Club	Goals
Alberto SPENCER	Peñarol, Barcelona	54
Fernando MORENA	Peñarol	37
Pedro VIRGILIO ROCHA	Peñarol, São Paulo, Palmeiras	36
Daniel ONEGA	River Plate	31
Julio MORALES	Nacional	30

CARLOS TEVEZ
An explosive striker, Tevez hails from the poor barrio of Buenos Aires in Argentina. He made his mark on the soccer world as a teenager, winning the Copa Libertadores with Boca Juniors in 2003.

THE COMPETITORS

Unlike the UEFA Champions League, there still seems to be room for small clubs to win the Copa Libertadores, with Ecuador's LDU winning their first title in 2008, and Paraguay's Olimpia winning for a third time in 2002, but clubs from just four cities—Rio, São Paulo, Montevideo, and Buenos Aires—are the most frequent winners.

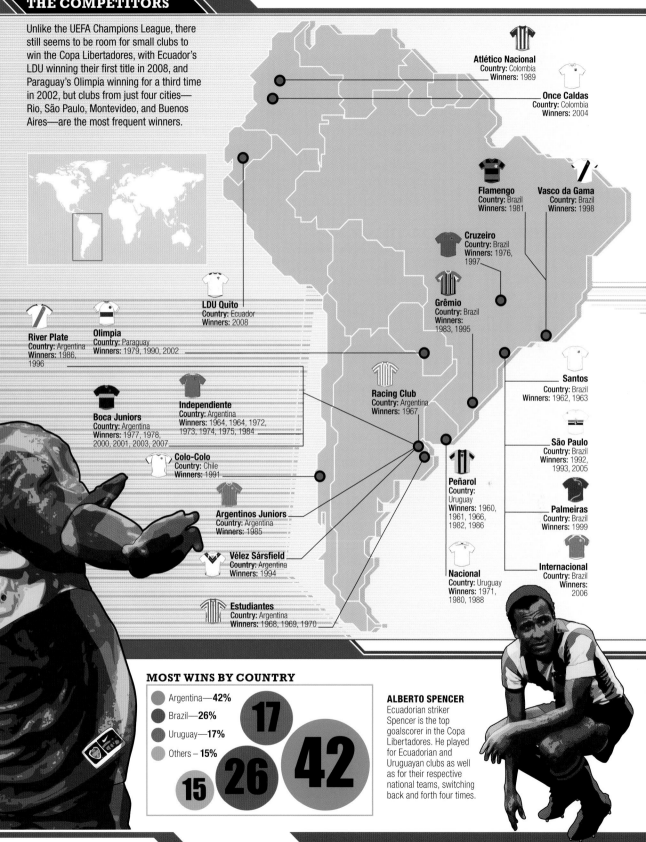

Atlético Nacional
Country: Colombia
Winners: 1989

Once Caldas
Country: Colombia
Winners: 2004

Flamengo
Country: Brazil
Winners: 1981

Vasco da Gama
Country: Brazil
Winners: 1998

Cruzeiro
Country: Brazil
Winners: 1976, 1997

Grêmio
Country: Brazil
Winners: 1983, 1995

LDU Quito
Country: Ecuador
Winners: 2008

River Plate
Country: Argentina
Winners: 1986, 1996

Olimpia
Country: Paraguay
Winners: 1979, 1990, 2002

Santos
Country: Brazil
Winners: 1962, 1963

São Paulo
Country: Brazil
Winners: 1992, 1993, 2005

Boca Juniors
Country: Argentina
Winners: 1977, 1978, 2000, 2001, 2003, 2007

Independiente
Country: Argentina
Winners: 1964, 1964, 1972, 1973, 1974, 1975, 1984

Racing Club
Country: Argentina
Winners: 1967

Peñarol
Country: Uruguay
Winners: 1960, 1961, 1966, 1982, 1986

Palmeiras
Country: Brazil
Winners: 1999

Colo-Colo
Country: Chile
Winners: 1991

Argentinos Juniors
Country: Argentina
Winners: 1985

Vélez Sársfield
Country: Argentina
Winners: 1994

Nacional
Country: Uruguay
Winners: 1971, 1980, 1988

Internacional
Country: Brazil
Winners: 2006

Estudiantes
Country: Argentina
Winners: 1968, 1969, 1970

MOST WINS BY COUNTRY

- Argentina—**42%**
- Brazil—**26%**
- Uruguay—**17%**
- Others – **15%**

17
26
42
15

ALBERTO SPENCER
Ecuadorian striker Spencer is the top goalscorer in the Copa Libertadores. He played for Ecuadorian and Uruguayan clubs as well as for their respective national teams, switching back and forth four times.

CONCACAF

THE GOLD CUP

COMPETITION: GOLD CUP
FOUNDED: 1963
CONFEDERATION: CONCACAF
NUMBER OF TEAMS: 38

Launched by CONCACAF in 1991 as its first truly pan-regional tournament, the Gold Cup has been hosted exclusively by the US, although two contests have been co-hosted with Mexico. It has grown from eight to twelve teams, media coverage and crowds have been good, and since 2003, teams from outside the confederation have no longer been invited to make up the numbers. However, the tournament gains little recognition in the wider world.

ONE REGION, TWO FEDERATIONS

The first international soccer tournament held in the northern half of the Americas was a round of Olympic qualifiers in Havana, Cuba, in 1930. The organizers became the Confederación Centroamericana y del Caribe de Fútbol (CCCF) in 1938, and held their first official tournament in Costa Rica in 1941. It remained a Central American affair—few Caribbean nations could afford to travel, and Mexico, Canada, and the USA played each other irregularly under the North Mexican Football Confederation.

BEGINNER'S LUCK

The tiny Caribbean island of Guadeloupe—a French province with a population of just 450,000—debuted at the 2007 Gold Cup. They got past the group stage by beating Canada, beat Honduras in the quarter-final, and lost to Mexico in the semi-final by a single goal. Had they won the trophy, they would have forfeited the winner's place at the Confederations Cup, as they are not actually a member of FIFA.

LANDON DONOVAN

With eleven goals, Donovan is the USA's leading scorer at the Gold Cup. Four of them came in a single game, when the US beat Cuba 5–0 in 2003. He scored another two against the Cubans in the 2005 tournament too.

0 Number of minutes of live English-language soccer from the Gold Cup broadcast on US television in 2005

3 Number of times Brazil has played in the Gold Cup

1991 Year the first Gold Cup final was settled on penalties—the USA beat Honduras 4–3

2 Times that the Netherlands Antilles reached the CONCACAF Championship semi-finals

STAT ATTACK

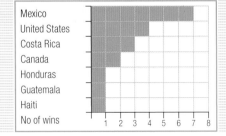

COUNTRIES WITH MOST WINS

Mexico
United States
Costa Rica
Canada
Honduras
Guatemala
Haiti
No of wins   1 2 3 4 5 6 7 8

TOP GOALSCORERS

Name	Country	Goals
ZAGUINHO	Mexico	12
Landon DONOVAN	USA	11
Carlos PAVÓN	Honduras	5
Benjamin GALINDO	Mexico	4
Eric WYNALDA	USA	4
Paulo WANCHOPE	Costa Rica	4
Luis HERNÁNDEZ	Mexico	4

EARLY STAGES

With the creation of CONCACAF in 1963, a regular CONCACAF championship was staged. However, participation and enthusiasm was low, even when the competition was turned into the qualifying rounds for the region's World Cup places between 1973 and 1989.

HOME DISADVANTAGE

Playing at home is normally an advantage, but that wasn't the case for the USA in the 1998 Gold Cup final against Mexico in Los Angeles. The city's Latino community turned out in force to make the final more of a home game for Mexico. Uncharacteristically for games held in the US, the national anthem was booed, and a torrent of bottles and other debris was thrown onto the field. Buoyed by their home-from-home support, Mexico won their third title in a row.

PAULO WANCHOPE

The gangly, flaying legs of Paulo Wanchope may not have been elegant, but they made him Costa Rica's all-time top scorer and a key figure in every World Cup and Gold Cup campaign in which he played.

THE COMPETITORS

CONCACAF's early international competitions were small enough to be held in Central America and even on the larger Caribbean islands, but the advent of the Gold Cup has meant the US and Mexico have a stranglehold on hosting rights.

Canada
Winners: 1985, 2000

United States
Years hosted: 1991–2007 (co-hosted with Mexico in 1993 and 2003)
Winners: 1991, 2002, 2005, 2007

Haiti
Winners: 1973

Guatemala
Year hosted: 1965
Winners: 1967

Mexico
Years hosted: 1993, 2003 (Co-hosted with USA)
Winners: 1965, 1971, 1977, 1993, 1996, 1998, 2003

Honduras
Year hosted: 1967
Winners: 1981

Trinidad and Tobago
Year hosted: 1971

Costa Rica
Year hosted: 1969
Winners: 1963, 1969, 1989

El Salvador
Year hosted: 1963

AFRICA

AFRICAN CUP OF NATIONS

COMPETITION:
AFRICAN CUP OF NATIONS
FOUNDED: 1957
CONFEDERATION: CAF
NUMBER OF TEAMS: 16

The African Cup of Nations is the continent's most celebrated and closely followed sports event. First contested in 1957 by just three teams, it now comprises 16 clubs and is played every two years. It has acquired a high standing in global soccer and offers a window on Africa's extraordinary pool of talent, which European clubs are increasingly exploiting.

THE WEST AFRICAN POWERHOUSES

Although the first three Cup of Nations were won by founder members Egypt and Ethiopia, a change of guard occurred in 1963 when Kwame Nkrumah's Ghana hosted the tournament and won in some style. Ghana went on to win one and lose two more finals in the 1960s and 1970s, first to Zaire and then to Brazzaville-Congo, before winning again in 1982 and 2000. Nigeria soon rose to the fore, winning the trophy in 1980 and 1994, while Cameroon won in 1984, 1988, 2000, and 2002. The Ivory Coast completed the success for West Africa in 1992.

SAMUEL ETO'O
With 16 goals, Cameroon striker Eto'o is the all-time top scorer in the African Cup of Nations. He made his debut in Cameroon's winning squad of 2000, and returned to claim a second trophy in 2002.

CROSSING THE DESERT

The biggest away crowd at the African Cup of Nations was at the 2004 Algeria vs Egypt game in Sousse, Tunisia, when around 20,000 Algerians crossed the Sahara. Algeria went 1–0 up in the opening minutes only for Egypt to equalize, before Algeria had a player sent off. After holding on for most of the game, the Algerians sneaked a last-minute winner, which must have made the long, dusty road home a lot shorter.

1970
Year that the tournament—held in Sudan—was first broadcast on television

21
Number of penalties required to separate the Ivory Coast and Ghana in the 1992 final, which the Ivory Coast won 11–10

NORTH AND SOUTH AFRICA

Although North African nations have not been quite as strong as they have in African club tournaments, Egypt has won the African Cup of Nations six times, making it the tournament's most successful nation. Algeria and Tunisia have both won as hosts, in 1990 and 2004 respectively, while Morocco won in 1976. Southern Africa's only victory came in 1996 when, at short notice, South Africa hosted the event, beating Tunisia 2–0 in the Johannesburg final.

STAT ATTACK

COUNTRIES WITH MOST WINS

Egypt
Ghana
Cameroon
DR Congo
Nigeria
Tunisia
South Africa

1 2 3 4 5 6 7

TOP GOALSCORERS

Player	Country	Goals
Samuel ETO'O	Cameroon	16
Laurent POKOU	Côte d'Ivoire	14
Rashidi YEKINI	Nigeria	13
Hassan EL-SHAZLY	Egypt	12
Hossam HASSAN	Egypt	11
Patrick MBOMA	Cameroon	11
Kalusha BWALYA	Zambia	10

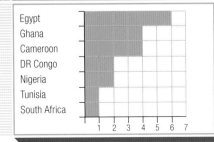

THE COMPETITORS

Winners and hosts have tended to come from West and North Africa, although the tournaments held in Mali and Burkina Faso have shown that CAF is ready to award hosting rights to less-developed nations. The 2010 contest in Angola will be the first Southern African tournament since South Africa in 1996.

Algeria
Years hosted:
1990 (8) participants
Winners: 1990

Tunisia
Years hosted:
1965 (6) participants
1994 (12) participants
2004 (16) participants
Winners: 2004

Egypt
Years hosted:
1959 (3) participants
1974 (8) participants
1986 (8) participants
2006 (16) participants
Winners: 1957,
1959, 1986, 1998,
2006, 2008

Libya
Year hosted:
1982 (8) participants

Morocco
Years hosted:
1998 (8) participants
Winners: 1998

Mali
Year hosted:
2002 (16) participants

Sudan
Years hosted:
1957 (3) participants
1970 (8) participants
Winners: 1957,
1959, 1986, 1998

Senegal
Year hosted:
1992
(12) participants

Burkina Faso
Year hosted:
1998 (16) participants

Ivory Coast
Year hosted:
1984 (8) participants
Winners: 1992

Ghana
Years hosted:
1963 (6) participants
1978 (8) participants
2000 (16) participants
2008 (16) participants
Winners: 1963,
1965, 1978, 1982

**Democratic
Republic of
Congo**
Winners:
1968, 1974
(as Zaire)

Ethiopia
Years hosted:
1962 (4) participants
1968 (8) participants
1976 (8) participants
Winners: 1962

Nigeria
Years hosted:
1980 (8) participants
2000 (16) participants
Winners: 1980,
1994

Cameroon
Year hosted:
1972 (8) participants
Winners: 1984,
1988, 2000, 2002

Congo
Winners: 1972 (as
Congo-Brazzaville)

South Africa
Year hosted:
1996 (16) participants
Winners:
1996

MOST TIMES IN FINAL

	1	2	3	4	5	6	7
Egypt							
Ghana							
Cameroon							
DR Congo							
Nigeria							
Tunisia							

IF AT FIRST YOU DON'T SUCCEED...

CAF's four founding members—Sudan, Egypt, Ethiopia, and South Africa—planned the first Cup of Nations for 1957 in Egypt. The Suez Crisis prevented Egypt from hosting and South Africa was excluded for insisting on either an all-white or an all-black team. The re-jigged contest was held in Sudan and won by Egypt.

**MOHAMED
ABOUTRIKA**
Egypt's talismanic captain, midfielder Aboutrika scored the winning goal in the 1–0 victory over Cameroon in the 2008 Cup of Nations final.

AFRICA

CAF CHAMPIONS LEAGUE

COMPETITION: AFRICAN CHAMPIONS LEAGUE
FOUNDED: 1964
CONFEDERATION: CAF
NUMBER OF TEAMS: 58

The African Champions Cup was first played in 1964, born of the same pan-African ideals that had produced the Cup of Nations. A four-team finals tournament was held in Accra, Ghana, where the Cameroonian champions Oryx Doula beat Stade Malian. Held continuously since 1996, and relaunched with group stages as the African Champions League in 1997, the contest has had to battle against the costs and complexity of intercontinental travel and the poor resources of many clubs—even national champions.

THE EARLY YEARS

During the first 15 years of its existence, the tournament was a West and Central African preserve, with victorious teams hailing from Ghana, Zaire, Cameroon, and Guinea. The first victory for a club outside these regions came in 1981 when JS Kabylie, the Algerian Berber side, swept aside AS Vita of Zaire to announce the arrival of the full force of North African soccer in the tournament.

THIRD TIME UNLUCKY

The 1967 final was played between Asante Kotoko of Ghana and TP Mazembe of Zaire. Drawn after two games and with no provision for penalties, a third match was required. However, the message did not reach Asante Kotoko, who did not show up for the final game. TP Mazembe did, and won the title.

NORTHERN DOMINANCE

Every final—except for Asante Kotoko's victory in 1983—was won by a side from the northern half of Africa until Orlando Pirates, the giants of a newly post-apartheid South Africa, took the title in 1995. South African clubs have generally struggled in the competition ever since. One exception was Mamelodi Sundowns' run to the final in 2001, but Al-Ahly proved too strong for them, winning 4–1 over two legs.

3 Number of back-to-back defenses of the title, by TP Mazembe (1967–68), Enyimba (2003–04), and Al-Ahly (2005–06)

8 Number of times Ghanaian clubs have lost a Champions League final

1,000,000 Amount of prize money received in dollars by the Champions League winner in 2009

HOSSAN HASSAM
Egyptian striker Hassam has, uniquely, won the Champions League with both of the mighty Cairo rivals, Al-Ahly in 1987 and Zamalek in 2002.

STAT ATTACK

PRIZE MONEY

Prize money compared to winners of the 2008 UEFA Champions League.

● Al-Ahly, CAF winners —**$1 million**

● Man Utd, UEFA winners —**$29.5 million**

29.5

1

COUNTRIES WITH MOST WINS

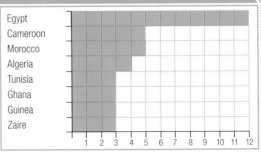

Egypt
Cameroon
Morocco
Algeria
Tunisia
Ghana
Guinea
Zaire

1 2 3 4 5 6 7 8 9 10 11 12

THE MODERN ERA

Since the contest became the African Champions League, there have been wins for West African teams ASEC Abidjan of the Ivory Coast and two for Nigeria's Enyimba. North African and, above all, Egyptian teams remain the dominating force. Al-Ahly made it six in 2008 and, along with Zamalek and Ismaily's victories, took the total for Egyptian sides to 12. The competition has increased its levels of prize money, sponsorship, and television coverage, but suffers in the latter from competition with the UEFA Champions league, where many leading African players are playing, as well as with the Copa Libertadores.

PRESIDENTIAL SELECTION

Hafia Conakry, from the Guinean capital, won the Champions Cup three times (1972, 1975, and 1977). The team was effectively the club of Guinea's populist president Seko Toure, who ensured that the best players stayed with the club. On their return from the 1976 final, which they had lost to Mouloudia d'Algiers, a number of the team members were sent to the infamous Camp Boiro for "political re-education." When they lost the 1978 final to Canon Yaoundé, the increasingly erratic Seko Touré issued a decree that seven of the players should be put in irons.

THE WINNERS

Nearly all of the winners of the Champions League are located on the coast of Africa or on the continent's navigable rivers; even the inland teams are not far from the coast. Only TP Mazembe in the Democratic Republic of Congo is truly from the interior of Africa.

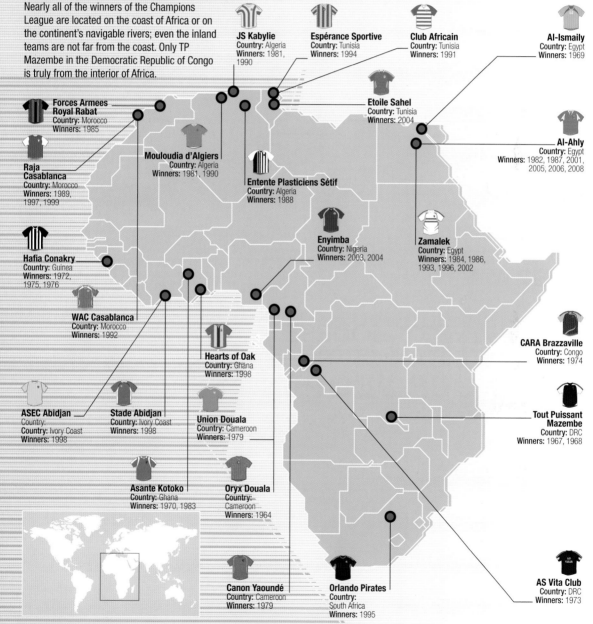

JS Kabylie
Country: Algeria
Winners: 1981, 1990

Espérance Sportive
Country: Tunisia
Winners: 1994

Club Africain
Country: Tunisia
Winners: 1991

Al-Ismaily
Country: Egypt
Winners: 1969

Etoile Sahel
Country: Tunisia
Winners: 2004

Al-Ahly
Country: Egypt
Winners: 1982, 1987, 2001, 2005, 2006, 2008

Forces Armees Royal Rabat
Country: Morocco
Winners: 1985

Mouloudia d'Algiers
Country: Algeria
Winners: 1981, 1990

Entente Plasticiens Sétif
Country: Algeria
Winners: 1988

Raja Casablanca
Country: Morocco
Winners: 1989, 1997, 1999

Enyimba
Country: Nigeria
Winners: 2003, 2004

Zamalek
Country: Egypt
Winners: 1984, 1986, 1993, 1996, 2002

Hafia Conakry
Country: Guinea
Winners: 1972, 1975, 1976

WAC Casablanca
Country: Morocco
Winners: 1992

CARA Brazzaville
Country: Congo
Winners: 1974

Hearts of Oak
Country: Ghana
Winners: 1998

ASEC Abidjan
Country:
Country: Ivory Coast
Winners: 1998

Stade Abidjan
Country: Ivory Coast
Winners: 1998

Union Douala
Country: Cameroon
Winners: 1979

Tout Puissant Mazembe
Country: DRC
Winners: 1967, 1968

Asante Kotoko
Country: Ghana
Winners: 1970, 1983

Oryx Douala
Country: Cameroon
Winners: 1964

AS Vita Club
Country: DRC
Winners: 1973

Canon Yaoundé
Country: Cameroon
Winners: 1979

Orlando Pirates
Country: South Africa
Winners: 1995

ASIAN CUP

COMPETITION: ASIAN CUP
FOUNDED: 1956
CONFEDERATION: AFC
NUMBER OF TEAMS: 16

First held in 1956 as a mini-league of just four teams, the Asian Cup has grown into a 16-team tournament held every four years that attracts ever-bigger Asian TV audiences and sponsorship packages. The tournament has further grabbed the limelight by rescheduling into odd years, and has benefitted hugely from avoiding a clash with the major Olympic, FIFA, and UEFA tournaments.

THE EARLY YEARS

The crown of Asian soccer has been passed around the continent for more than a decade. In the late 1950s and early 1960s, South Korea and Israel shared the laurels, but Iran came on the scene in the late 1960s, winning every game on the way to three tournaments in a row. With Iran consumed by the Islamic revolution and Israel expelled from the AFC, Arab nations came to dominate— Saudi Arabia went on to win three titles.

ALI DAEI
Known simply as "The King" in Iran, Daei is the all-time top scorer in the Asian Cup. However, in three Asian Cups Daei's Iran only made it as far as the semi-finals.

LEBANON 2000

Showing grace under fire, Lebanon managed to host the Asian Cup during a brief interlude between the country's civil wars. Despite the fighting in nearby Gaza and the West Bank, and the kidnapping of Israeli soldiers by Hezbollah on the Israel-Lebanon border, the games went on. The home team departed after the first round while Japan, scoring an amazing 21 goals, romped to victory.

JAPAN

The steady progress of domestic soccer in Japan in the 1990s bore fruit with victories in the Asian Cup in 1992, 2000, and 2004. The victory at the latter tournament, which was held in China, was all the more remarkable for the anti-Japanese vitriol that came from the bleachers in every city in which Japan played. The final was played against China in a hostile Workers Stadium in Beijing, and after Japan triumphed 3–1, the Chinese fans went on an anti-Japanese riot in the aftermath of the defeat.

THIS IS A VERY MODEST THING WE CAN GIVE TO OUR PEOPLE

NOOR SABRI
IRAQI GOALKEEPER ON MAKING THE FINAL OF THE 2007 ASIAN CUP

MOST WINS BY COUNTRY

- Saudi Arabia—**21%**
- Iran—**21%**
- Japan—**21%**
- South Korea—**16%**
- Others—**21%**

STAT ATTACK

COUNTRIES WITH MOST WINS

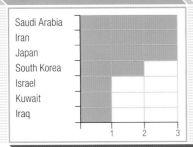

Saudi Arabia
Iran
Japan
South Korea
Israel
Kuwait
Iraq

1 2 3

TOP GOALSCORERS

Player	Country	Goals
Ali DAEI	Iran	14
Lee DONG-GOOK	South Korea	10
Naohiro TAKAHARA	Japan	9
Choi SOON-HO	South Korea	9
Behtash FARIBA	Iran	9
Jassem AL HUWAIDI	Kuwait	8
Behtash FARIBA	Iran	7

THE TOURNAMENTS

The co-hosting of the 2007 Asian Cup by Vietnam, Thailand, Malaysia, and Indonesia greatly enlarged the pool of Asian Cup winners and hosts. Israel is no longer a member of the AFC, having joined UEFA in 2002, while Australia joined the AFC in 2006 and look set to host future tournaments.

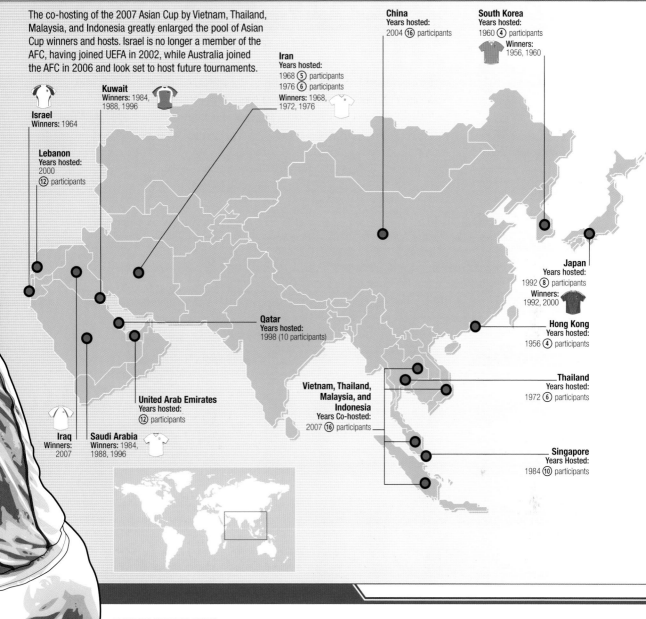

Israel
Winners: 1964

Kuwait
Winners: 1984, 1988, 1996

Lebanon
Years hosted: 2000
(12) participants

Iran
Years hosted: 1968 (5) participants
1976 (6) participants
Winners: 1968, 1972, 1976

China
Years hosted: 2004 (16) participants

South Korea
Years hosted: 1960 (4) participants
Winners: 1956, 1960

Japan
Years hosted: 1992 (8) participants
Winners: 1992, 2000

Qatar
Years hosted: 1998 (10 participants)

Hong Kong
Years hosted: 1956 (4) participants

Vietnam, Thailand, Malaysia, and Indonesia
Years Co-hosted: 2007 (16) participants

Thailand
Years hosted: 1972 (6) participants

United Arab Emirates
Years hosted: (12) participants

Iraq
Winners: 2007

Saudi Arabia
Winners: 1984, 1988, 1996

Singapore
Years Hosted: 1984 (10) participants

ASIAN MINNOWS
The expansion of the Asian Cup to 16 teams has ushered in a host of smaller nations. First-timer nations include Guam, Kazakhstan, Turkmenistan, Uzbekistan, Tajikistan, Kyrgyzstan, Vietnam, Yemen, and the Maldives in 1996; Palestine, Laos, Bhutan, and Mongolia in 2000; and Timor-Leste in 2004.

BITTERSWEET VICTORY
Iraq was the surprise team at the 2007 Asian Cup, beating Australia and South Korea, then Saudi Arabia in the final. Tragically, two bombs exploded in Baghdad during celebrations for the semi-final victory, killing more than 50 people and injuring 150.

500 Number of spectators at Iraq vs Oman in Bangkok at the 2007 tournament

3 Number of Brazilians who have won the Asian Cup as coach—Carlos Alberto Pereira (twice), Zico, and Jorvan Viera

1,020,050 Total attendance at the 2004 Asian Cup in China—a tournament record, with an average attendance of 31,877 per game

1 Number of Asian Cup appearances by Burma (in 1968)

ASIA AND OCEANIA

AFC CHAMPIONS LEAGUE

COMPETITION:
AFC ASIAN CHAMPIONS LEAGUE
FOUNDED: 1967
REGION: AFC
NUMBER OF TEAMS: 32

The Asian Champions League, which was relaunched and reformatted by the AFC in 2002, is the leading competition for club sides in Asia. It has since grown from 16 to 32 clubs and has been dominated by South Korean, Japanese, and Saudi Arabian clubs, who have won all but one title. Ali-Ain of the UAE is the only other team to have won the newly formatted tournament, tasting success in the 2003 contest.

TEETHING PROBLEMS

Gathering together the leading clubs from a continent as vast as Asia proved to be an economic and logistical challenge. The AFC launched the Asian Champion Club Tournament in 1967 with mini-leagues in a single location, but the competition folded four years later after just two contests in Tehran and Bangkok. The 1970 final was abandoned when the Iraqi police team, Al-Shorta, refused to play Israel's Maccabi Tel-Aviv.

THIRD TIME LUCKY

The tournament was relaunched as the Asian Club Championship in 1985 with qualifying rounds and a finals tournament. The first outing was held in Jeddah, Saudi Arabia, and won by South Korea's Daewoo Royals, but the contest still faced two problems—high transportatino costs and a gulf in quality between the clubs. Both were addressed when the third incarnation of the competition was launched—the Asian Champions League—in 2002. Higher sponsorship allowed transportation subsidies, and the bulk of the places in the tournament were allocated to the strongest nations.

HIGHLY ORGANIZED FANS' ORGANIZATION

Urawa Red Diamonds have some of the noisiest—and best-organized—supporters in Asia. The choreography for the second leg of the 2007 Champions League final against Sepahan of Iran was extraordinary, with the entire stadium decked out in red and white stripes and stars—an effect created from the plastic squares left on every seat. Urawa went on to win 2–0 and take the title.

KIM DO-HOON

One of South Korea's most famous players, Kim Do-Hoon was the top scorer in the 2004 Asian Champions League, playing for Seongnam Ilhwa Chunma, and is the competition's joint-top-scorer of all time.

MOST WINS BY COUNTRY

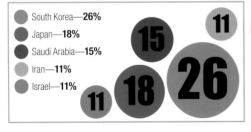

- South Korea—**26%**
- Japan—**18%**
- Saudi Arabia—**15%**
- Iran—**11%**
- Israel—**11%**

STAT ATTACK

TOP GOALSCORERS

Player	Club	Goals
Hao HAIDONG	Dalian Shide	9
Kim DO-HOON	Seongnam Ilhwa Chunma	9
Magno ALVES	Gamba Osaka	9
Nantawat THANSOPA	Krung Thai Bank	9
MOTA	Seongnam Ilhwa Chunma	7

AFC RANKING

Rank	Country	Points
1	Japan	470
2	South Korea	441
3	China	431
4	Saudi Arabia	365
5	UAE	356
6	Australia	343

RINGING THE CASH REGISTERS

The Asian Champions League has become an increasingly business-like affair. The AFC has secured elite corporate sponsorship and increased the annual prize money to $14.5 million, more than three times the prize pot of the African equivalent—though still small compared to Europe and Latin America. Television coverage across the region is also growing since broadcasting is a condition of participation, with major networks carrying the tournament from Beirut to Tokyo and in Adelaide to Melbourne.

AL-HILAL 3, JÚBILO IWATA 2

Saudi Arabian champions Al-Hilal declined the chance to play in the final against Japanese side Yomiuri in the 1988 Champions Cup. In 2000, however, they did show up to play a final against Japan's Júbilo Iwata. The Saudis were 2–1 down for nearly the whole game until their Brazilian striker Ricardo scored a second goal in the final minute of the game, forcing extra-time. He made it a hat-trick in extra-time to secure the title for Al-Hilal.

2003
Year the tournament was canceled due to the SARS virus in Asia, and the Iraq War

1,500,000
Prize money, in dollars, for winning the 2009 Asian Champions League

6
Number of Asian soccer associations that don't participate in the Champions League—Laos, Timor-Leste, Afghanistan, Bhutan, Mongolia, and Chinese Taipei

3
Number of back-to-back defenses of the title: Al-Ittihad (2004–05), Thai Farmers Bank (1984–85), and Suwon Samsung Bluewings (2001–02)

THE WINNERS

The AFC Champions League pits western against eastern Asia. South Asia, where cricket is king, has yet to produce any serious challenger in the tournament. With Israel now in Europe, the western challenge has come from the Gulf and Iran; in the east from Japan, South Korea, and China.

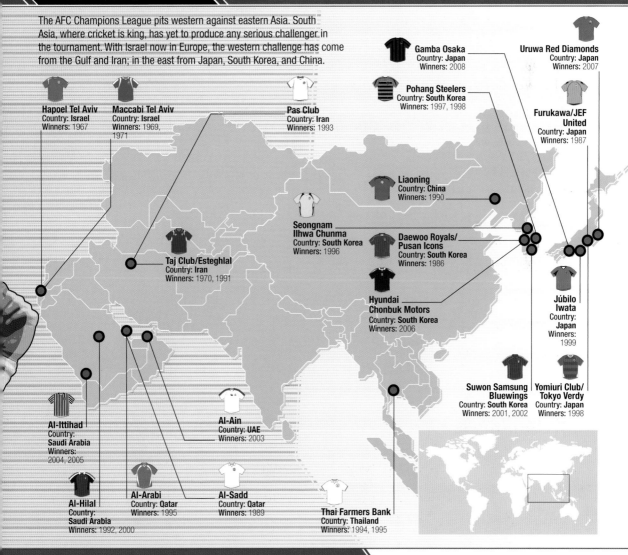

Gamba Osaka
Country: Japan
Winners: 2008

Uruwa Red Diamonds
Country: Japan
Winners: 2007

Pohang Steelers
Country: South Korea
Winners: 1997, 1998

Furukawa/JEF United
Country: Japan
Winners: 1987

Hapoel Tel Aviv
Country: Israel
Winners: 1967

Maccabi Tel Aviv
Country: Israel
Winners: 1969, 1971

Pas Club
Country: Iran
Winners: 1993

Liaoning
Country: China
Winners: 1990

Seongnam Ilhwa Chunma
Country: South Korea
Winners: 1996

Daewoo Royals/Pusan Icons
Country: South Korea
Winners: 1986

Taj Club/Esteghlal
Country: Iran
Winners: 1970, 1991

Hyundai Chonbuk Motors
Country: South Korea
Winners: 2006

Júbilo Iwata
Country: Japan
Winners: 1999

Al-Ittihad
Country: Saudi Arabia
Winners: 2004, 2005

Al-Ain
Country: UAE
Winners: 2003

Suwon Samsung Bluewings
Country: South Korea
Winners: 2001, 2002

Yomiuri Club/Tokyo Verdy
Country: Japan
Winners: 1998

Al-Hilal
Country: Saudi Arabia
Winners: 1992, 2000

Al-Arabi
Country: Qatar
Winners: 1995

Al-Sadd
Country: Qatar
Winners: 1989

Thai Farmers Bank
Country: Thailand
Winners: 1994, 1995

WORLD CLUB CUP

COMPETITION:
WORLD CLUB CUP

FOUNDED:
INTERCONTINENTAL CUP
(1969), WORLD CLUB
CHAMPIONSHIP (2006)

REGION: GLOBAL

**NUMBER OF
TEAMS:** 6

The FIFA World Club Cup is now an annual six-team competition between the winners of each of the Champions Leagues. It grew out of the Intercontinental Cup, created in 1969 as a two-leg tie between the winners of the European Cup and the Copa Libertadores. An experimental World Club Cup was played in 2000 and replaced the Intercontinental Cup in 2004.

GOING INTERCONTINENTAL

Henri Delaunay, general secretary of UEFA, proposed an annual contest in 1958 between the winner of the European Cup and the champions of South America. The Copa Libertadores commenced in 1960, providing a South American champion, and Real Madrid beat Penarol in the first Intercontinental Cup that year.

ALLESANDRO COSTACURTA
Costacurta played more than 450 games for Milan in a 19-year career, winning five European Cups, two Intercontinental Cups, and the World Club Championship.

EUROPEAN WINNERS

Italian clubs have proved the best at following European success with World Championship glory—the big three having won eight titles between them. Guile, patience, and steel was often required to win the title. English clubs, by contrast, have been far less successful.

*World Club Championship winners

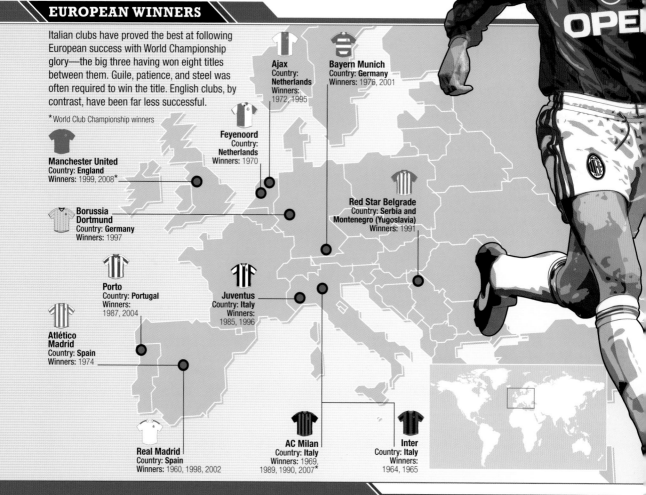

Manchester United
Country: England
Winners: 1999, 2008*

**Borussia
Dortmund**
Country: Germany
Winners: 1997

Porto
Country: Portugal
Winners:
1987, 2004

**Atlético
Madrid**
Country: Spain
Winners: 1974

Real Madrid
Country: Spain
Winners: 1960, 1998, 2002

Ajax
Country:
Netherlands
Winners:
1972, 1995

Feyenoord
Country:
Netherlands
Winners: 1970

Juventus
Country: Italy
Winners:
1985, 1996

AC Milan
Country: Italy
Winners: 1969,
1989, 1990, 2007*

Bayern Munich
Country: Germany
Winners: 1976, 2001

Red Star Belgrade
Country: Serbia and
Montenegro (Yugoslavia)
Winners: 1991

Inter
Country: Italy
Winners:
1964, 1965

2009
The first year that Dubai, UAE hosted the tournament

6
Number of contests played in by Paolo Maldini for AC Milan

3
Record number of wins as a coach—Carlos Bianchi with Vélez Sársfield in 1994, and Boca Juniors in 2000 and 2003

1
Hat tricks in a final, scored by Pelé for Santos

2
Number of Uruguayans who have won the cup as both player and coach—Luis Cubilla (Peñarol in 1961 and Nacional in 1971 as player, then Olimpia Asunción in 1979 as coach) and Juan Mugica (Nacional as player in 1971 and coach in 1980)

INTERCONTINENTAL CUP FINAL, 1967

In the 1967 final, Celtic took a 1–0 lead from the home leg in Scotland to Racing in Buenos Aires. The Argentines denied Celtic a warm-up ball, the Celtic goalkeeper was hit by a stone and substituted, and the referee was cowed by a fanatical crowd. Racing won 2–1 and the subsequent decider in Montevideo, Uruguay, saw five players being sent off. Racing scored once and won.

A TOURNAMENT FOR THE WORLD

The Intercontinental Cup became increasingly fractious in the 1960s and 1970s, leading to a number of European teams declining the invite. In 1980 the fixture, now a single game known as the World Club Championship, was transferred to Japan and sponsored by Toyota.

To accommodate the rising power of world soccer, FIFA initiated an expanded tournament in Brazil in 2000 with other regional champions. The FIFA World Club Cup replaced each of these contests in 2006, creating a six-team tournament. The top clubs from the weaker federations—CAF, CONCACAF, AFC, and OFC—play against each other for a place in the semi-finals against the South American or European champions. No club from outside CONMEBOL or UEFA has yet made the final of the tournament.

WINNERS BY CONTINENT

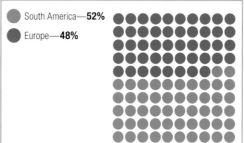

South America—**52%**

Europe—**48%**

SOUTH AMERICAN WINNERS

The Intercontinental Cup was accorded a much higher status in South America than in Europe for most of its history. In a rare opportunity to test their domestic soccer against the "Old World" of Europe, South America's leading clubs proved themselves more than a match. Some of the top sides of Argentina and Brazil have been crowned World Champions since 2000.

GUERILLA SOCCER

Estudiantes built a reputation for anti-soccer across South America, winning three Copa Libertadores. Notoriously rough, cynical, sharp, and tricky, they reached their apogee in the second leg of the 1969 Intercontinental Cup, hosting AC Milan in Buenos Aires. By the time they had lost the tie, they were down to nine men, had broken the collarbone of Milan's Combin, and kicked Rivera to the ground. *El Grafico*, the sports newspaper, reported that "TV took the deformed image of the match and transformed it into urban guerrilla warfare all over the world."

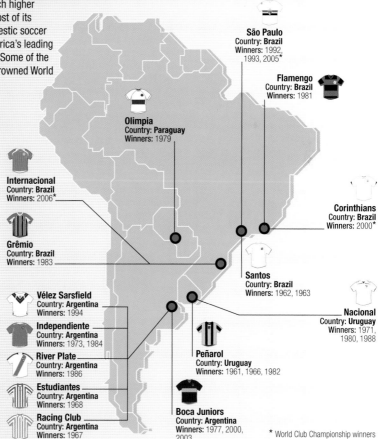

São Paulo
Country: **Brazil**
Winners: 1992, 1993, 2005*

Flamengo
Country: **Brazil**
Winners: 1981

Olimpia
Country: **Paraguay**
Winners: 1979

Corinthians
Country: **Brazil**
Winners: 2000*

Internacional
Country: **Brazil**
Winners: 2006*

Grêmio
Country: **Brazil**
Winners: 1983

Santos
Country: **Brazil**
Winners: 1962, 1963

Nacional
Country: **Uruguay**
Winners: 1971, 1980, 1988

Vélez Sarsfield
Country: **Argentina**
Winners: 1994

Independiente
Country: **Argentina**
Winners: 1973, 1984

River Plate
Country: **Argentina**
Winners: 1986

Estudiantes
Country: **Argentina**
Winners: 1968

Racing Club
Country: **Argentina**
Winners: 1967

Peñarol
Country: **Uruguay**
Winners: 1961, 1966, 1982

Boca Juniors
Country: **Argentina**
Winners: 1977, 2000, 2003

* World Club Championship winners

OLYMPIC GAMES

COMPETITION: OLYMPIC GAMES—MEN'S SOCCER
FOUNDED: 1900
CONFEDERATION: FIFA/IOC
NUMBER OF TEAMS: 16

COMPETITION: OLYMPIC GAMES—WOMEN'S SOCCER
FOUNDED: 1996
CONFEDERATION: FIFA/IOC
NUMBER OF TEAMS: 12

Soccer at the Olympic Games has taken on many forms, from an informal kick-around in the early days to effectively being the championship of the world in the 1920s. With the arrival of the World Cup in 1930, it was demoted to a tournament for the amateurs and state-sponsored athletes of Scandinavia and the Communist Bloc once again. With the addition of a women's tournament in 1996, and the running of the men's competition as a FIFA-administered Under-23 tournament since 1992, interest is rising once again.

HAZY BEGINNINGS

Soccer was an exhibition sport at the earliest Olympic Games. In Athens in 1896, the tournament was contested by teams from Denmark, Athens, and Izmir (a Greek-speaking part of Turkey). The records of the Athenian team have been lost but the Danes thrashed Izmir 15–0. Upton Park FC of East London took on a Paris XI at the 1900 Paris Olympics and won 4–0, and records also mention a match against a team of Belgian students in the Bois de Boulogne, Paris. The first official tournament, held in London in 1908, was won by a Great Britain side against Denmark.

THE 1920 OLYMPICS

When Czech defender Karel Steiner was sent off by English referee John Lewis in the 40th minute of the 1920 Olympic final in Belgium, it was the last straw for the Czech team, who followed him off the field. Belgium was awarded the game by default. The Czechs didn't like the refereeing by 65-year-old Mr. Lewis, especially his awarding of a second Belgian goal, nor the menacing presence of Belgian soldiers in the crowd and the field invasion they led later on. All of the Czech complaints were dismissed.

GROWTH OF THE GAMES

Olympic soccer in the 1920s belonged to Latin America, but with the arrival of professionalism all over the world, the tournament was fought out by the Swedes, Danes, and Eastern Europeans until the 1980s. Since 1992, The men's contest has been an Under-23 tournament with each side permitted to field three older players. Two African gold medals —Nigeria in 1996 and Cameroon in 2000—have boosted TV audiences and crowds.

105,000
Highest attendance for an Olympic game, recorded at the Mexico vs Japan third-place play-off at Estadio Azteca, Mexico City, 1968

1928
Year Domingo Tarasconi scored three consecutive hat-tricks for Argentina

25
Number of own goals in men's Olympic soccer

MASCHERANO
Captain of Argentina, who won Gold at the 2004 and 2008 World Cups, Mascherano is the first male player to win back-to-back Olympic golds since the Uruguay team of 1928.

STAT ATTACK

MEN'S TOP SCORERS

Player	Country	Goals
Ferenc BENE	Hungary	12
Sophus NIELSEN	Denmark	11
Gottfried FUCHS	Germany	10
Domingo TARASCONI	Argentina	9
Kazimierz DEYNA	Poland	9

WOMEN'S TOP SCORERS

Player	Country	Goals
CRISTIANE	Brazil	10
Birgit PRINZ	Germany	5
Ann Kristin AARØNES	Denmark	4
Linda MEDALEN	Denmark	4
PRETINHA	Brazil	4
Sun WEN	China	4

HERE COME THE LADIES

The women's game was finally added to the Olympics in Atlanta in 1996, when the USA beat China in the final. Unlike the men's contest, the women's tournament is for full international teams. The USA has reached every final so far, losing just one of them, to Norway at Sydney 2000. They took gold at both Athens 2004 and Beijing 2008 by beating Brazil in extra-time on both occasions.

THE 1928 OLYMPICS

The Amsterdam Games of 1928 was the peak of Olympic soccer's importance. It was effectively the world championships, and Argentina and Uruguay met in the final. After a 1–1 draw the re-match saw more than a quarter of a million people apply for tickets. Uruguay won the match 2–1, but have failed to qualify for the competition ever since.

THE TOURNAMENTS

More democratic than the World Cup, the map of Olympic soccer reveals hosts or winners on every soccer continent. It is also the only soccer map that shows Great Britain rather than the four home nations—England, Scotland, Wales, and Northern Ireland.

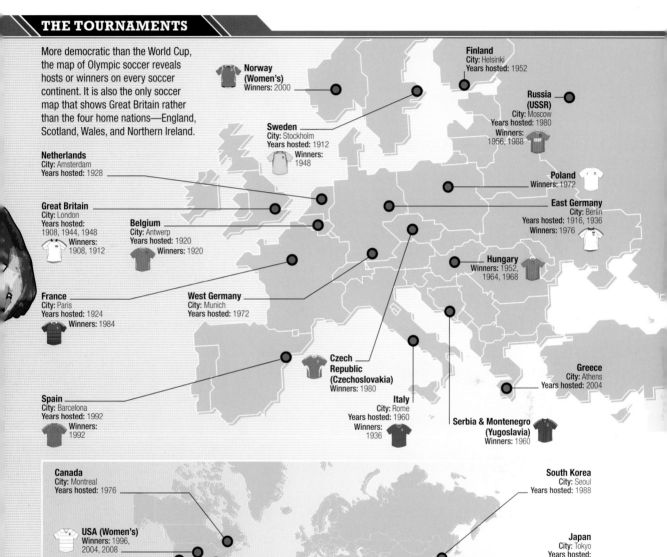

Norway (Women's)
Winners: 2000

Finland
City: Helsinki
Years hosted: 1952

Russia (USSR)
City: Moscow
Years hosted: 1980
Winners: 1956, 1988

Sweden
City: Stockholm
Years hosted: 1912
Winners: 1948

Netherlands
City: Amsterdam
Years hosted: 1928

Poland
Winners: 1972

Great Britain
City: London
Years hosted: 1908, 1944, 1948
Winners: 1908, 1912

Belgium
City: Antwerp
Years hosted: 1920
Winners: 1920

East Germany
City: Berlin
Years hosted: 1916, 1936
Winners: 1976

Hungary
Winners: 1952, 1964, 1968

France
City: Paris
Years hosted: 1924
Winners: 1984

West Germany
City: Munich
Years hosted: 1972

Czech Republic (Czechoslovakia)
Winners: 1980

Greece
City: Athens
Years hosted: 2004

Spain
City: Barcelona
Years hosted: 1992
Winners: 1992

Italy
City: Rome
Years hosted: 1960
Winners: 1936

Serbia & Montenegro (Yugoslavia)
Winners: 1960

Canada
City: Montreal
Years hosted: 1976

South Korea
City: Seoul
Years hosted: 1988

USA (Women's)
Winners: 1996, 2004, 2008

USA
City: Los Angeles
Years hosted: 1932, 1984

Japan
City: Tokyo
Years hosted: 1940, 1964

USA
City: Atlanta
Years hosted: 1996

Mexico
City: Mexico City
Years hosted: 1968

Nigeria
Winners: 1996

Australia
City: Sydney
Years hosted: 2000

Argentina
Winners: 2004, 2008

Uruguay
Winners: 1924, 1928

Cameroon
Winners: 2000

Australia
City: Melbourne
Years hosted: 1956

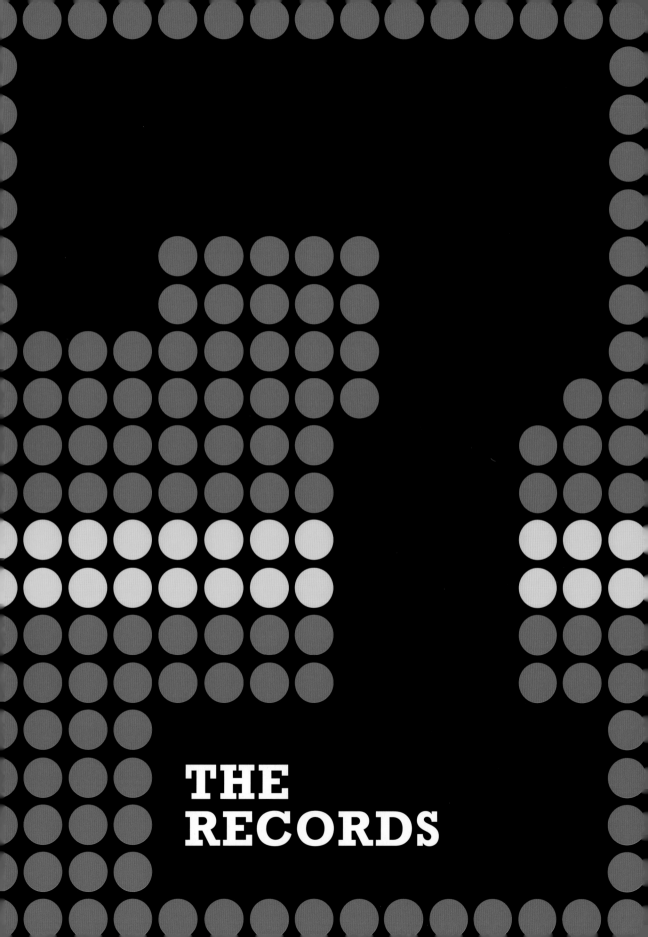

THE
RECORDS

WORLD

INTERNATIONAL AWARDS

FIFA WORLD CUP TOP SCORERS

YEAR	VENUE	WINNER	SCORE	RUNNER UP
1930	Uruguay	**Uruguay**	4–2	Argentina
1934	Italy	**Italy**	2–1	Czechoslovakia*
1938	France	**Italy**	4–2	Hungary
1950	Brazil	**Uruguay**	2–1	Brazil
1954	Switzerland	**West Germany**	3–2	Hungary
1958	Sweden	**Brazil**	5–2	Sweden
1962	Chile	**Brazil**	3–1	Czechoslovakia
1966	England	**England**	4–2	West Germany
1970	Mexico	**Brazil**	4–1	Italy
1974	West Germany	**West Germany**	2–1	Netherlands
1978	Argentina	**Argentina**	3–1*	Netherlands
1982	Spain	**Italy**	3–1	West Germany
1986	Mexico	**Argentina**	3–2	West Germany
1990	Italy	**West Germany**	1–0	Argentina
1994	United States	**Brazil**	0–0	Italy* (3–2)•
1998	France	**France**	3–0	Brazil
2002	South Korea & Japan	**Brazil**	2–0	Germany
2006	Germany	**Italy**	1–1	France* (5–3)•

FIFA WORLD CUP TOP SCORERS

NAME	GOALS	COUNTRY	NAME	GOALS	COUNTRY
Gerd Müller	14	Germany	**Vavá**	9	Brazil
Just Fontaine	13	France	**Uwe Seeler**	9	Germany
Pelé	12	Brazil	**Eusebio**	9	Portugal
Ronaldo	12	Brazil	**Jairzinho**	9	Brazil
Sandor Kocsis	11	Hungary	**Paolo Rossi**	9	Italy
Jürgen Klinsmann	11	Germany	**Roberto Baggio**	9	Italy
Helmut Rahn	10	Germany	**Karlheinz Rummenigge**	9	Germany
Teofilo Cubillas	10	Peru	**Christian Vieri**	9	Italy
Grzegorz Lato	10	Poland	**Stabile**	8	Argentina
Gary Lineker	10	England	**Ademir**	8	Brazil
Gabriel Batistuta	10	Argentina	**Maradona**	8	Argentina
Leonidas	9	Brazil	**Rudi Voeller**	8	Germany
Ademir	9	Brazil	**Rivaldo**	8	Brazil
Juan Schiaffino	9	Uruguay			

*After extra time   •After penalty shootout

FIFA WOMEN'S WORLD CUP WINNERS

YEAR	VENUE	WINNER	SCORE	RUNNER UP
1991	China	**United States**	2–1	Norway
1995	Sweden	**Norway**	2–0	Germany
1999	United States	**United States**	1–0	China*(5–4)•
2003	United States	**Germany**	2–1	Sweden°
2007	China	**Germany**	2–0	Brazil

FIFA WOMEN'S WORLD CUP TOP SCORERS

NAME	GOALS	COUNTRY	NAME	GOALS	COUNTRY
Birgit Prinz	14	Germany	**Hege Riise**	9	Norway
Michelle Akers	12	USA	**Abby Wambach**	9	USA
Sun Wen	11	China	**Liu Ailing**	10	China
Bettina Wiegmann	11	Germany	**Mia Hamm**	8	USA
Ann Kristin Aarønes	10	Norway	**Kristine Lilly**	8	USA
Marta	10	Brazil	**Marianne Pettersen**	8	Norway
Heidi Mohr	10	Germany	**Tiffeny Milbrett**	7	USA
Linda Medalen	9	Norway	**Sissi**	7	Brazil

CLUB AWARDS

TOYOTA CUP

YEAR	WINNER
1980	**Nacional**
1981	**Flamengo**
1982	**Peñarol**
1983	**Grêmio**
1984	**Independiente**
1985	**Juventus**
1986	**River Plate**
1987	**Porto**
1988	**Nacional**
1989	**AC Milan**
1990	**AC Milan**
1991	**Red Star Belgrade**
1992	**São Paulo**
1993	**São Paulo**
1994	**Vélez Sarsfield**
1995	**Ajax**
1996	**Juventus**
1997	**Borussia Dortmund**
1998	**Real Madrid**
1999	**Manchester United**
2000	**Boca Juniors**
2001	**Bayern München**
2002	**Real Madrid**
2003	**Boca Juniors**
2004	**Porto**

INTERNATIONAL CLUB CUP

YEAR	WINNER
1960	**Real Madrid**
1961	**Peñarol**
1962	**Santos**
1963	**Santos**
1964	**Inter**
1965	**Inter**
1966	**Peñarol**
1967	**Racing Club**
1968	**Estudiantes**
1969	**Milan**
1970	**Feyenoord**
1971	**Nacional**
1972	**Ajax**
1973	**Independiente**
1974	**Atlético Madrid**
1975	NOT HELD
1976	**Bayern Munich**
1977	**Boca Juniors**
1978	NOT HELD
1979	**Olimpia**

WORLD CLUB CUP

YEAR	WINNER
2000	**Corinthians**
2001–04	NO COMPETITION
2005	**São Paulo**
2006	**Internacional**
2007	**AC Milan**
2008	**Manchester United**

*After extra time   •After penalty shootout   °Match decided on golden goal

FIFA WORLD PLAYER OF THE YEAR

YEAR	WINNER	COUNTRY	CLUB
1991	**Lothar Matthäus**	Germany	Inter
1992	**Marco van Basten**	Netherlands	AC Milan
1993	**Roberto Baggio**	Italy	Juventus
1994	**Romário**	Brazil	Barcelona
1995	**George Weah**	Liberia	AC Milan
1996	**Ronaldo**	Brazil	PSV Eindhoven & Barcelona
1997	**Ronaldo**	Brazil	Barcelona & Inter
1998	**Zinédine Zidane**	France	Juventus
1999	**Rivaldo**	Brazil	Barcelona
2000	**Zinédine Zidane**	France	Juventus
2001	**Luis Figo**	Portugal	Real Madrid
2002	**Ronaldo**	Brazil	Inter & Real Madrid
2003	**Zinédine Zidane**	France	Real Madrid
2004	**Ronaldinho**	Brazil	Barcelona
2005	**Ronaldinho**	Brazil	Barcelona
2006	**Fabio Cannavaro**	Italy	Juventus & Real Madrid
2007	**Kaká**	Brazil	AC Milan
2008	**Cristiano Ronaldo**	Portugal	Manchester United

FIFA WOMEN'S PLAYER OF THE YEAR

YEAR	WINNER	COUNTRY	CLUB
2001	**Mia Hamm**	USA	Washington Freedom
2002	**Mia Hamm**	USA	Washington Freedom
2003	**Birgit Prinz**	Germany	Carolina Courage
2004	**Birgit Prinz**	Germany	1.FFC Frankfurt
2005	**Birgit Prinz**	Germany	1.FFC Frankfurt
2006	**Marta**	Brazil	Umeå IK
2007	**Marta**	Brazil	Umeå IK
2008	**Marta**	Brazil	Umeå IK

EUROPE: UEFA

INTERNATIONAL AWARDS

UEFA EUROPEAN CHAMPIONSHIPS WINNERS

YEAR	WINNER	SCORE	RUNNER UP
1960	**Soviet Union**	2–1	Yugoslavia*
1964	**Spain**	2–1	Soviet Union
1968	**Italy**	1–1	Yugoslavia* (replay 2–0)
1972	**West Germany**	3–0	Soviet Union
1976	**Czechoslovakia**	2–2	West Germany* (5–3)•
1980	**West Germany**	2–1	Belgium
1984	**France**	2–0	Spain
1988	**Netherlands**	2–0	Soviet Union
1992	**Denmark**	2–0	Germany
1996	**Germany**	2–1	Czech Republic**
2000	**France**	2–1	Italy**
2004	**Greece**	1–0	Portugal
2008	**Spain**	1–0	Germany

UEFA EUROPEAN CHAMPIONSHIPS TOP SCORERS

NAME	GOALS	COUNTRY
Michel Platini	9	France
Alan Shearer	7	England
Patrick Kluivert	7	Netherlands
Nuno Gomes	6	Portugal
Thierry Henry	6	France
Ruud van Nistelrooy	6	Netherlands
Marco van Basten	5	Netherlands
Jürgen Klinsmann	5	Germany
Savo Milosevic	5	Serbia
Zinédine Zidane	5	France
Milan Baros	5	Czech Republic
Dragan Dzajic	4	Yugoslavia
Gerd Müller	4	Germany
Dieter Müller	4	Germany
Rudi Voller	4	Germany
Dennis Bergkamp	4	Netherlands
Vladimir Smicer	4	Czech Republic
Henrik Larsson	4	Sweden
Wayne Rooney	4	England
Angelos Charisteas	4	Greece
Zlatan Ibrahimovic	4	Sweden

**After sudden death extra time   *After extra time   •After penalty shootout

CLUB AWARDS

UEFA CHAMPIONS LEAGUE/EUROPEAN CHAMPIONS CUP WINNERS

YEAR	WINNER	SCORE	RUNNER UP	YEAR	WINNER	SCORE	RUNNER UP
1956	Real Madrid	4–3	Stade Reims	1982	Aston Villa	1–0	Bayern Munich
1957	Real Madrid	2–0	Fiorentina	1983	Hamburg	1–0	Juventus
1958	Real Madrid	3–2	AC Milan*	1984	Liverpool	1–1	Roma* (4–2)•
1959	Real Madrid	2–0	Stade Reims	1985	Juventus	1–0	Liverpool
1960	Real Madrid	7–3	Eintracht Frankfurt	1986	Steaua Bucharest	0–0	Barcelona* (2–0)•
1961	Benfica	3–2	Barcelona	1987	Porto	2–1	Bayern Munich
1962	Benfica	5–3	Real Madrid	1988	PSV Eindhoven	0–0	Benfica* (6–5)•
1963	AC Milan	2–1	Benfica	1989	AC Milan	4–0	Steaua Bucharest
1964	Inter	3–1	Real Madrid	1990	AC Milan	1–0	Benfica
1965	Inter	1–0	Benfica	1991	Red Star Belgrade	0–0	Olympique Marseille* (5–3)•
1966	Real Madrid	2–1	Partizan Belgrade	1992	Barcelona	1–0	Sampdoria*
1967	Celtic	2–1	Inter	1993	Olympique Marseille	1–0	AC Milan
1968	Manchester United	4–1	Benfica*	1994	AC Milan	4–0	Barcelona
1969	AC Milan	4–1	Ajax	1995	Ajax	1–0	AC Milan
1970	Feyenoord	2–1	Celtic*	1996	Juventus	1–1	Ajax* (4–2)•
1972	Ajax	2–0	Panathinaikos	1997	Borussia Dortmund	3–1	Juventus
1973	Ajax	2–0	Inter	1998	Real Madrid	1–0	Juventus
1974	Ajax	1–0	Juventus	1999	Manchester United	2–1	Bayern Munich
1975	Bayern Munich	1–1	Atlético Madrid* (4–0 Replay)	2000	Real Madrid	3–0	Valencia
1975	Bayern Munich	2–0	Leeds United	2001	Bayern Munich	1–1	Valencia* (5–4)•
1976	Bayern Munich	1–0	Saint Etienne	2002	Real Madrid	2–1	Bayer Leverkusen
1977	Liverpool	3–1	Borussia Mönchengladbach	2003	AC Milan	0–0	Juventus* (3–2)•
1978	Liverpool	1–0	FC Brugge	2004	Porto	3–0	Monaco
1979	Nottingham Forest	1–0	Malmö FF	2005	Liverpool	3–3	AC Milan* (3–2)•
1980	Nottingham Forest	1–0	Hamburg	2006	Barcelona	2–1	Arsenal
1981	Liverpool	1–0	Real Madrid	2007	AC Milan	2–1	Liverpool
				2008	Manchester United	1–1	Chelsea* (6–5)•

UEFA CHAMPIONS LEAGUE/EUROPEAN CHAMPIONS CUP TOP SCORERS

NAME	GOALS	COUNTRY	CLUBS
Raúl	64	Spain	Real Madrid
Ruud van Nistelrooy	60	Netherlands	PSV Eindhoven, Manchester United, Real Madrid
Pippo Inzaghi	58	Italy	Juventus, AC Milan
Andrey Shevchenko	58	Ukraine	Dynamo Kiev, AC Milan, Chelsea
Alfredo Di Stéfano	49	Argentina	Real Madrid
Eusébio	47	Portugal	Benfica
Alessandro Del Piero	47	Italy	Juventus
Thierry Henry	46	France	Monaco, Arsenal, Barcelona
Fernando Morientes	39	Spain	Real Madrid, Monaco, Liverpool, Valencia
Ferenc Puskás	36	Hungary	Budapest Honvéd, Real Madrid

*After extra time •After penalty shootout

EUROPA CUP (FORMERLY UEFA CUP) (Aggregate scores)

YEAR	WINNER	SCORE	RUNNER UP
1972	**Tottenham Hotspur**	3–2	Wolverhampton Wanderers
1973	**Liverpool**	3–2	Borussia Mönchengladbach
1974	**Feyenoord**	4–2	Tottenham Hotspur
1975	**FC Twente**	5–1	Borussia Mönchengladbach
1976	**Liverpool**	4–3	FC Brugge
1977	**Juventus**	2–2	Athletic Bilbao
			(Juventus wins on away goals)
1978	**PSV Eindhoven**	3–0	Bastia
1979	**Borussia Mönchengladbach**	2–1	Red Star Belgrade
1980	**Eintracht Frankfurt**	3–3	Borussia Mönchengladbach
1981	**Ipswich Town**	5–4	AZ Alkmaar '67
1982	**IFK Göteborg**	4–0	Hamburg
1983	**Anderlecht**	2–1	Benfica
1984	**Tottenham Hotspur**	2–2	Anderlecht* (4–3)•
1985	**Real Madrid**	3–1	Videoton
1986	**Real Madrid**	5–3	1.FC Köln
1987	**IFK Göteborg**	2–1	Dundee United
1988	**Bayer Leverkusen**	3–3	Español* (3–2)•
1989	**Napoli**	5–4	VfB Stuttgart
1990	**Juventus**	3–1	Fiorentina
1991	**Inter**	2–1	Roma
1992	**Torino**	2–2	Ajax
			(Ajax wins on away goals)
1993	**Juventus**	6–1	Borussia Dortmund
1994	**Inter**	2–0	Austria Salzburg
1995	**Parma**	2–1	Juventus
1996	**Bayern Munich**	5–1	Girondins Bordeaux
1997	**Schalke '04**	1–1	Internazionale* (4–1)•
1998	**Inter**	3–0	Lazio
1999	**Parma**	3–0	Olympique Marseille
2000	**Galatasaray**	0–0	Arsenal* (4–1)•
2001	**Liverpool**	5–4	Alavés**
2002	**Feyenoord**	3–2	Borussia Dortmund
2003	**Porto**	3–2	Celtic*
2004	**Valencia**	2–0	Olympique Marseille
2005	**CSKA Moscow**	3–1	Sporting CP
2006	**Sevilla**	4–0	Middlesbrough
2007	**Sevilla**	2–2	Espanyol* (3–1)•
2008	**Zenit St. Petersburg**	2–0	Rangers

** After sudden death extra time   *After extra time   •After penalty shootout

EUROPEAN PLAYER OF THE YEAR ("BALLON D'OR")

YEAR	NAME	CLUB
1956	**Stanley Matthews** (England)	Blackpool
1957	**Alfredo Di Stéfano** (Spain)	Real Madrid
1958	**Raymond Kopa** (France)	Real Madrid
1959	**Alfredo Di Stéfano*** (Spain)	Real Madrid
1960	**Luis Suárez** (Spain)	Barcelona
1961	**Omar Sivori*** (Italy)	Juventus
1962	**Josef Masopust** (Czech Republic)	Dukla Praha
1963	**Lev Yashin** (Soviet Union)	Dynamo Moscow
1964	**Denis Law** (Scotland)	Manchester United
1965	**Eusébio** (Portugal)	Benfica
1966	**Bobby Charlton** (England)	Manchester United
1967	**Flórián Albert** (Hungary)	Ferencváros
1968	**George Best** (Northern Ireland)	Manchester United
1969	**Gianni Rivera** (Italy)	AC Milan
1970	**Gerd Müller** (Germany)	Bayern Munich
1971	**Johan Cruyff** (Netherlands)	Ajax
1972	**Franz Beckenbauer** (Germany)	Bayern Munich
1973	**Johan Cruyff** (Spain)	Barcelona
1974	**Johan Cruyff** (Spain)	Barcelona
1975	**Oleg Blokhin** (Soviet Union)	Dynamo Kiev
1976	**Franz Beckenbauer** (Germany)	Bayern Munich
1977	**Alan Simonsen** (Germany)	Borussia Mönchengladbach
1978	**Kevin Keegan** (England)	Hamburg
1979	**Kevin Keegan** (England)	Hamburg
1980	**Karl-Heinz Rummenigge** (Germany)	Bayern Munich
1981	**Karl-Heinz Rummenigge** (Germany)	Bayern Munich
1982	**Paolo Rossi** (Italy)	Juventus

YEAR	NAME	CLUB
1983	**Michel Platini** (France)	Juventus
1984	**Michel Platini** (France)	Juventus
1985	**Michel Platini** (France)	Juventus
1986	**Igor Belanov** (Soviet Union)	Dynamo Kiev
1987	**Ruud Gullit** (Netherlands)	AC Milan
1988	**Marco van Basten** (Netherlands)	AC Milan
1989	**Marco van Basten** (Netherlands)	AC Milan
1990	**Lothar Matthäus** (Italy)	Inter
1991	**Jean-Pierre Papin** (France)	Olympique Marseille
1992	**Marco van Basten** (Netherlands)	AC Milan
1993	**Roberto Baggio** (Italy)	Juventus
1994	**Hristo Stoitchkov** (Bulgaria)	Barcelona
1995	**George Weah** (Liberia)	AC Milan
1996	**Matthias Sammer** (Germany)	Borussia Dortmund
1997	**Ronaldo** (Brazil)	Inter
1998	**Zinédine Zidane** (France)	Juventus
1999	**Rivaldo** (Brazil)	Barcelona
2000	**Luis Figo** (Portugal)	Real Madrid
2001	**Michael Owen** (England)	Liverpool
2002	**Ronaldo** (Brazil)	Real Madrid
2003	**Pavel Nedved** (Czech Republic)	Juventus
2004	**Andrey Shevchenko** (Ukraine)	AC Milan
2005	**Ronaldinho** (Spain)	Barcelona
2006	**Fabio Cannavaro** (Italy)	Real Madrid
2007	**Kaká** (Brazil)	AC Milan
2008	**Cristiano Ronaldo** (Portugal)	Manchester United

* Di Stéfano and Sivori were born in Argentina and first played for that country.

SOUTH AMERICA: CONMEBOL

INTERNATIONAL AWARDS

COPA AMÉRICA WINNERS
(NO FINAL MATCH WAS PLAYED UNTIL 1979)

YEAR	VENUE	WINNER	RUNNER UP
1916	Argentina	**Uruguay**	Argentina
1917	Uruguay	**Uruguay**	Argentina
1919	Brazil	**Brazil**	Uruguay
1920	Chile	**Uruguay**	Argentina
1921	Argentina	**Argentina**	Brazil
1922	Brazil	**Brazil**	Paraguay
1923	Uruguay	**Uruguay**	Argentina
1924	Uruguay	**Uruguay**	Argentina
1925	Argentina	**Argentina**	Brazil
1926	Chile	**Uruguay**	Argentina
1927	Peru	**Argentina**	Uruguay
1929	Argentina	**Argentina**	Paraguay
1935	Peru	**Uruguay**	Argentina
1937	Argentina	**Argentina**	Brazil
1939	Peru	**Peru**	Uruguay
1941	Chile	**Argentina**	Uruguay
1942	Uruguay	**Uruguay**	Argentina
1945	Chile	**Argentina**	Brazil
1946	Argentina	**Argentina**	Brazil
1947	Ecuador	**Argentina**	Paraguay
1949	Brazil	**Brazil**	Paraguay
1953	Peru	**Paraguay**	Brazil

YEAR	VENUE	WINNER	RUNNER UP
1955	Chile	**Argentina**	Chile
1956	Uruguay	**Uruguay**	Chile
1957	Peru	**Argentina**	Brazil
1959	Argentina	**Argentina**	Brazil
1959	Ecuador	**Uruguay**	Argentina
1963	Bolivia	**Bolivia**	Paraguay
1967	Uruguay	**Uruguay**	Argentina

YEAR	VENUE	WINNER	SCORE	RUNNER UP
1979	NO FIXED VENUE	**Paraguay** Paraguay wins play-off	3–0/0–1	Chile
1983	NO FIXED VENUE	**Uruguay** Uruguay wins	2–0/1–1	Brazil
1987	Argentina	**Uruguay**	1–0	Chile
1989	Brazil	**Brazil**	1–0	Uruguay
1991	Chile	**Argentina**	3–2	Brazil
1993	Ecuador	**Argentina**	2–1	Mexico
1995	Uruguay	**Uruguay**	1–1	Brazil (5–3)•
1997	Bolivia	**Brazil**	3–1	Bolivia
1999	Paraguay	**Brazil**	3–0	Uruguay
2001	Colombia	**Colombia**	1–0	Mexico
2004	Peru	**Brazil**	2–2	Argentina (4–2)•
2007	Venezuela	**Brazil**	3–0	Argentina

COPA AMÉRICA TOP SCORERS

NAME	GOALS	COUNTRY
Norberto Méndez	17	Argentina
Zizinho	17	Brazil
Severino Varela	15	Uruguay
Teodoro Fernández	15	Peru
Gabriel Batistuta	13	Argentina
Ademir	13	Brazil
Jair da Rosa Pinto	13	Brazil
Héctor Scarone	13	Uruguay
Jose Manuel Moreno	13	Argentina

NAME	GOALS	COUNTRY
Angel Romano	12	Uruguay
Herminio Masantonio	11	Argentina
Victor Ugarte	11	Bolivia
Ronaldo	10	Brazil
Oscar Gómez	10	Peru
Héctor Castro	10	Uruguay
Didi	10	Brazil
Enrique Hormazábal	10	Chile
Arnoldo Iguarán	10	Colombia
Ángel Labruna	10	Argentina

•After penalty shootout

CLUB AWARDS

COPA LIBERTADORES WINNERS
(NO FINAL MATCH WAS PLAYED UNTIL 1988)

YEAR	WINNER	SCORE	RUNNER UP	YEAR	WINNER	SCORE	RUNNER UP
1960	**Peñarol**	N/A	Olimpia	1984	**Independiente**	N/A	Grêmio
1961	**Peñarol**	N/A	Palmeiras	1985	**Argentinos Jnrs**	N/A	América de Cali
1962	**Santos**	N/A	Peñarol	1986	**River Plate**	N/A	América de Cali
1963	**Santos**	N/A	Boca Juniors	1987	**Peñarol**	N/A	América de Cali
1964	**Independiente**	N/A	Nacional	1988	**Nacional**	3–1	Newell's Old Boys
1965	**Independiente**	N/A	Peñarol	1989	**Atlético Nacional**	2–2	Olimpia (5–4)•
1966	**Peñarol**	N/A	River Plate	1990	**Olimpia**	3–1	Barcelona
1967	**Racing Club**	N/A	Nacional	1991	**Colo Colo**	3–0	Olimpia
1968	**Estudiantes**	N/A	Palmeiras	1992	**São Paulo**	1–1	Newell's Old Boys (3–2)•
1969	**Estudiantes**	N/A	Nacional	1993	**São Paulo**	5–3	Universidad Católica
1970	**Estudiantes**	N/A	Peñarol	1994	**Vélez Sarsfield**	1–1	São Paulo　(5–3)•
1971	**Nacional**	N/A	Estudiantes	1995	**Grêmio**	4–2	Atlético Nacional
1972	**Independiente**	N/A	Universitario	1996	**River Plate**	2–1	América de Cali
1973	**Independiente**	N/A	Colo-Colo	1997	**Cruzeiro**	1–0	Sporting Cristal
1974	**Independiente**	N/A	São Paulo	1998	**Vasco da Gama**	4–1	Barcelona
1975	**Independiente**	N/A	Unión Española	1999	**Palmeiras**	2–2	Deportivo Cali (4–3)•
1976	**Cruzeiro**	N/A	River Plate	2000	**Boca Juniors**	2–2	Palmeiras (4–2)•
1977	**Boca Juniors**	N/A	Cruzeiro	2001	**Boca Juniors**	1–1	Cruz Azul (3–1)•
1978	**Boca Juniors**	N/A	Deportivo Cali	2002	**Olimpia**	2–2	São Caetano (4–2)•
1979	**Olimpia**	N/A	Boca Juniors	2003	**Boca Juniors**	5–1	Santos
1980	**Nacional**	N/A	Internacional	2004	**Once Caldas**	1–1	Boca Juniors　(2–0)•
1981	**Flamengo**	N/A	Cobreloa	2005	**São Paulo**	5–1	Atlético Paranaense
1982	**Peñarol**	N/A	Cobreloa	2006	**Internacional**	4–3	São Paulo
1983	**Grêmio**	N/A	Peñarol	2007	**Boca Juniors**	5–0	Grêmio
				2008	**LDU Quito**	5–5	Fluminense (3–1)•

COPA MERCONORTE WINNERS (Aggregate scores)

YEAR	WINNER	SCORE	RUNNER UP
1998	**Atlético Nacional**	4–1	Deportivo Cali
1999	**América de Cali**	2–2	Independiente Santa Fe　(5–3)•
2000	**Millonarios**	1–2	Atlético Nacional
2001	**Millonarios**	2–2	Emelec (3–1)•

•After penalty shootout

COPA MERCOSUR WINNERS

(Aggregate scores where applicable)

YEAR	WINNER	SCORE	RUNNER UP
1998	**Palmeiras**	1–2/3–1	Cruzeiro
		Play-off 1–0	Palmeiras wins
1999	**Flamengo**	7–6	Palmeiras
2000	**Vasco da Gama**	2–0/0–1	Palmeiras
		Play-off 4–3	Vasco da Gama wins
2001	**San Lorenzo**	1–1	Flamengo (3–4)•
2002	**San Lorenzo**	4–0	Atlético Nacional

COPA SUDAMERICANA WINNERS

(Aggregate scores)

YEAR	WINNER	SCORE	RUNNER UP
2003	**Cienciano**	4–3	River Plate
2004	**Boca Juniors**	2–1	Bolívar
2005	**Boca Juniors**	2–2	Pumas UNAM (4–3)•
2006	**Pachuca**	3–2	Colo Colo
2007	**América (Cd. México)**	4–4	Arsenal de Sarandi
	Arsenal de Sarandi wins on away goals		
2008	**Internacional (PA)**	2–1*	Estudiantes (LP)

SOUTH AMERICAN PLAYER OF THE YEAR

By *El Mundo* (Caracas, Venezuela)

YEAR	WINNER	CLUB
1971	**Tostão** (Brazil)	Cruzeiro
1972	**Teófilo Cubillas** (Peru)	Alianza Lima
1973	**Pelé** (Brazil)	Santos
1974	**Elías Figueroa** (Chile)	Internacional
1975	**Elías Figueroa** (Chile)	Internacional
1976	**Elías Figueroa** (Chile)	Internacional
1977	**Zico** (Brazil)	Flamengo
1978	**Mario Kempes** (Argentina)	Valencia
1979	**Diego Maradona** (Argentina)	Argentinos Juniors
1980	**Diego Maradona** (Argentina)	Boca Juniors
1981	**Zico** (Brazil)	Flamengo
1982	**Zico** (Brazil)	Flamengo
1983	**Socrates** (Brazil)	Corinthians
1984	**Enzo Francescoli** (Uruguay)	River Plate
1985	**Julio César Romero** (Brazil)	Fluminense
1986	**Diego Maradona** (Argentina)	Napoli
1987	**Carlos Valderrama** (Columbia)	Deportivo Cali
1988	**Rubén Paz** (Uruguay)	Racing Club
1989	**Diego Maradona** (Argentina)	Napoli
1990	**Diego Maradona** (Argentina)	Napoli
1991	**Gabriel Batistuta** (Argentina)	Boca Juniors
1992	**Diego Maradona** (Argentina)	Sevilla

By *El País* (Montevideo, Uruguay)

YEAR	WINNER	CLUB
1986	**Antonio Alzamendi** (Argentina)	River Plate
1987	**Carlos Valderrama** (Columbia)	Deportivo Cali
1988	**Rubén Paz** (Uruguay)	Racing Club
1989	**Bebeto** (Brazil)	Vasco da Gama
1990	**Raúl Amarilla** (Paraguay)	Olimpia
1991	**Oscar Ruggeri** (Argentina)	Vélez Sarsfield
1992	**Raí** (Brazil)	São Paulo
1993	**Carlos Valderrama** (Columbia)	Atlético Junior
1994	**Cafú** (Brazil)	São Paulo
1995	**Enzo Francescoli** (Uruguay)	River Plate
1996	**José Luis Chilavert** (Paraguay)	Vélez Sarsfield
1997	**Marcelo Salas** (Chile)	River Plate
1998	**Martín Palermo** (Argentina)	Boca Juniors
1999	**Javier Saviola** (Argentina)	River Plate
2000	**Romário** (Brazil)	Vasco da Gama
2001	**Juan Román Riquelme** (Argentina)	Boca Juniors
2002	**José Saturnino Cardozo** (Paraguay)	Club Deportivo Toluca
2003	**Carlos Tévez** (Argentina)	Boca Juniors
2004	**Carlos Tévez** (Argentina)	Boca Juniors
2005	**Carlos Tévez** (Argentina)	Boca Juniors Corinthians
2006	**Matías Fernández** (Chile)	Colo Colo
2007	**Salvador Cabañas** (Paraguay)	C.F. América
2008	**Juan Sebastián Verón** (Argentina)	Estudiantes de La Plata

*After extra time   •After penalty shootout

AFRICA: CAF

INTERNATIONAL AWARDS

AFRICAN CUP OF NATIONS WINNERS

YEAR	VENUE	WINNER	SCORE	RUNNER UP
1957	Sudan	**Egypt**	4–0	Ethiopia
1959	Egypt	**Egypt**	2–1	Sudan
1962	Ethiopia	**Ethiopia**	4–2	Egypt*
1963	Ghana	**Ghana**	3–0	Sudan
1965	Tunisia	**Ghana**	3–2	Tunisia*
1968	Ethiopia	**Congo (Kinshasa)**	1–0	Ghana
1970	Sudan	**Sudan**	1–0	Ghana
1972	Cameroon	**Congo (Brazzaville)**	3–2	Mali
1974	Egypt	**DR Congo**	2–2 (Replay 2–0)	Zambia*
1976	Ethiopia	**Morocco**	1–1 (group format)	Guinea
1978	Ghana	**Ghana**	2–0	Uganda
1980	Nigeria	**Nigeria**	3–0	Algeria
1982	Libya	**Ghana**	1–1 (7–6)•	Libya*
1984	Ivory Coast	**Cameroon**	3–1	Nigeria
1986	Egypt	**Egypt**	0–0 (5–4)•	Cameroon*
1988	Morocco	**Cameroon**	1–0	Nigeria
1990	Algeria	**Algeria**	1–0	Nigeria
1992	Senegal	**Côte D'Ivoire**	0–0 (11–10)•	Ghana*
1994	Tunisia	**Nigeria**	2–1	Zambia
1996	South Africa	**South Africa**	2–0	Tunisia
1998	Burkina Faso	**Egypt**	2–0	South Africa
2000	Nigeria and Ghana	**Cameroon**	2–2 (4–3)•	Nigeria*
2002	Mali	**Cameroon**	0–0 (3–2)•	Senegal*
2004	Tunisia	**Tunisia**	2–1	Morocco
2006	Egypt	**Egypt**	0–0 (4–2)•	Ivory Coast*
2008	Ghana	**Egypt**	1–0	Cameroon

AFRICAN CUP OF NATIONS TOP SCORERS

NAME	GOALS	COUNTRY
Samuel Eto'o	16	Cameroon
Laurent Pokou	14	Ivory Coast
Rashidi Yekini	13	Nigeria
Hassan El-Shazly	12	Egypt
Hossam Hassan	11	Egypt
Patrick Mboma	11	Cameroon
Kalusha Bwalya	10	Zambia
Mulamba Ndaye	10	DR Congo
Francileudo Santos	10	Tunisia
Joel Tiéhi	10	Ivory Coast
Mengistu Worku	10	Ethiopia
Abdoulaye Traoré	9	Ivory Coast
Pascal Feindouno Wilberforce	8	Guinea
Kwadwo Mfum	8	Ghana
Taher Abouzaid	7	Egypt
Ali Abugresha	7	Egypt
Benni McCarthy	7	South Africa
Roger Milla	7	Cameroon
Jay-Jay Okocha	7	Nigeria

*After extra time   •After penalty shootout

CLUB AWARDS

AFRICAN CHAMPIONS LEAGUE WINNERS (Aggregate scores)

YEAR	WINNER	SCORE	RUNNER UP
1964	**Oryx Douala**	2–1	Stade Malien
1966	**Stade Abidjan**	5–4	AS Real Bamako
1967	**Tout Puissant Englebert**	3–3	Asante Kotoko Ghana
	(Cup awarded to Tout Puissant Englebert)		
1968	**Tout Puissant Englebert**	6–4	Etoile Filante
1969	**Ismaili**	5–3	Tout Puissant Englebert
1970	**Asante Kotoko**	3–2	Tout Puissant Englebert
1971	**Asante Kotoko**	3–0	Canon Yaoundé
	Canon Yaoundé	2–0	Asante Kotoko
	Canon Yaoundé	1–0	Asante Kotoko (match abandoned Canon Yaoundé wins)
1972	**Hafia (Conakry)**	7–4	Simba FC
1973	**AS Vita Club**	5–4	Asante Kotoko
1974	**CARA Brazzaville**	6–3	Mehalla Al–Kubra
1975	**Hafia (Conakry)**	3–1	Enugu Rangers
1976	**MC Algiers**	3–3	Hafia (Conakry)* (4–1)•
1977	**Hafia (Conakry)**	4–2	Hearts of Oak
1978	**Canon Yaoundé**	2–0	Hafia (Conakry)
1979	**Union Douala**	1–1	Hearts of Oak* (5–3)•
1980	**Canon Yaoundé**	5–2	AS Bilima
1981	**JE Tizi-Ouzou**	5–0	AS Vita Club
1982	**Al-Ahly (Cairo)**	4–1	Asante Kotoko
1983	**Asante Kotoko**	1–0	Al-Ahly (Cairo)
1984	**Zamalek**	3–0	Shooting Stars
1985	**FAR Rabat**	6–3	AS Bilima
1986	**Zamalek**	2–2	Africa Sports* (4–2)•
1987	**Al-Ahly (Cairo)**	2–0	Al-Hilal
1988	**EP Sétif**	4–1	Iwuanyanwu Owerri
1989	**Raja CA Casablanca**	1–1	Mouloudia Petroliers Oran* (4–2)•
1990	**JS Kabylie**	1–1	Nkana Red Devils* (5–3)•
1991	**Club Africain**	7–3	Nakivubo Villa SC
1992	**Wydad AC Casablanca**	2–0	Al-Hilal
1993	**Zamalek**	0–0	Asante Kotoko* (7–6)•
1994	**Espérance Tunis**	3–1	Zamalek
1995	**Orlando Pirates**	3–2	ASEC (Abidjan)
1996	**Zamalek**	3–3	Shooting Stars* (5–4)•
1997	**Raja CA Casablanca**	1–1	Obuasi Goldfields* (5–4)•
1998	**ASEC (Abidjan)**	4–2	Dynamos
1999	**Raja CA Casablanca**	0–0	Espérance Tunis* (4–3)•
2000	**Hearts of Oak**	5–2	Espérance Tunis

*After extra time   •After penalty shootout

AFRICAN CHAMPIONS LEAGUE WINNERS CONTINUED

YEAR	WINNER	SCORE	RUNNER UP	YEAR	WINNER	SCORE	RUNNER UP
2001	**Al-Ahly (Cairo)**	4–1	Mamelodi Sundowns	2005	**Al-Ahly (Cairo)**	3–0	Etoile du Sahel
2002	**Zamalek**	1–0	Raja CA Casablanca	2006	**Al-Ahly (Cairo)**	2–1	CS Sfaxien
2003	**Enyimba**	2–1	Ismaily	2007	**Etoile du Sahel**	3–1	Al–Ahly (Cairo)
2004	**Enyimba**	3–3	Etoile du Sahel	2008	**Al-Ahly (Cairo)**	4–2	Cotonsport Garoua

AFRICAN CUP WINNERS' CUP WINNERS

YEAR	WINNER	YEAR	WINNER	YEAR	WINNER
1975	**Tonnerre Yaoundé**	1985	**Al-Ahly (Cairo)**	1995	**Jeunesse Sportive Kabylie**
1976	**Shooting Stars**	1986	**Al-Ahly (Cairo)**	1996	**Al-Mokaoulun**
1977	**Enugu Rangers**	1987	**Gor Mahia**	1997	**Etoile du Sahel**
1978	**Horoya AC (Conakry)**	1988	**Club Athlétique Bizerte**	1998	**Espérance Tunis**
1979	**Canon Yaoundé**	1989	**Al-Merreikh**	1999	**Africa Sports**
1980	**Tout Puissant Mazembe**	1990	**BCC Lions**	2000	**Zamalek**
1981	**Union Douala**	1991	**Power Dynamos**	2001	**Kaizer Chiefs**
1982	**Al-Mokaoulun**	1992	**Africa Sports**	2002	**Wydad AC Casablanca**
1983	**Al-Mokaoulun**	1993	**Al-Ahly (Cairo)**	2003	**Etoile du Sahel**
1984	**Al-Ahly (Cairo)**	1994	**Daring Club Motemba Pemba**		

CAF CUP

The CAF Cup merged with the Cup Winners' Cup in 2004 and was renamed the Confederation Cup.

WINNERS

YEAR	CLUB	COUNTRY	YEAR	CLUB	COUNTRY
1992	**Shooting Stars**	Nigeria	1998	**CS Sfaxien**	Tunisia
1993	**Stella Abidjan**	Ivory Coast	1999	**Etoile du Sahel**	Tunisia
1994	**Bendel Insurance**	Nigeria	2000	**JS Kabylie**	Algeria
1995	**Etoile du Sahel**	Tunisia	2001	**JS Kabylie**	Algeria
1996	**Kawkab AC Marrakech**	Morocco	2002	**JS Kabylie**	Algeria
1997	**Espérance Tunis**	Tunisia	2003	**Raja CA Casablanca**	Morocco

CONFEDERATION CUP WINNERS

YEAR	CLUB	COUNTRY
2004	**Hearts of Oak**	Ghana
2005	**FAR Rabat**	Morocco
2006	**Etoile du Sahel**	Tunisia
2007	**CS Sfaxien**	Tunisia
2008	**CS Sfaxien**	Tunisia

AFRICAN PLAYER OF THE YEAR 1970–94

YEAR	PLAYER	CLUB	YEAR	PLAYER	CLUB
1970	**Salif Keita** (Mali)	Saint-Etienne	1982	**Thomas N'kono** (Cameroon)	RCD Español
1971	**Ibrahim Sunday** (Ghana)	Asante Kotoko	1983	**Mahmmoud Al-Khatib** (Egypt)	Al-Ahly
1972	**Chérif Souleymane** (Guinea)	Hafia Conakry	1984	**Téophile Abega** (Cameroon)	Toulouse
1973	**Tshimimu Bwanga** (DR Congo)	TP Mazembe	1985	**Mohammed Timoumi** (Morocco)	FAR Rabat
1974	**Paul Moukila** (Congo)	CARA Brazzaville	1986	**Badou Zaki** (Morocco)	RCD Mallorca
1975	**Ahmed Faras** (Morocco)	SC Chabab Mohammedia	1987	**Rabah Madjer** (Algeria)	Porto
			1988	**Kalusha Bwalya** (Zambia)	Cercle Brugge
1976	**Roger Milla** (Cameroon)	Canon Yaoundé	1989	**George Weah** (Liberia)	Monaco
1977	**Tarak Dhiab** (Tunisia)	Espérance Tunis	1990	**Roger Milla** (Cameroon)	CS Saint Deni
1978	**Abdul Razak** (Ghana)	Asante Kotoko	1991	**Abedi Pelé** (Ghana)	Olympique Marseille
1979	**Thomas N'kono** (Cameroon)	Canon Yaound	1992	**Abedi Pelé** (Ghana)	Olympique Marseille
1980	**Jean Manga-Onguene** (Cameroon)	Canon Yaoundé	1993	**Abedi Pelé** (Ghana)	Olympique Marseille
1981	**Lakhdar Belloumi** (Algeria)	GCR Mascara	1994	**George Weah** (Liberia)	Paris Saint-Germain

CAF'S AFRICAN PLAYER OF THE YEAR 1992–2007

YEAR	PLAYER	CLUB
1992	**Abedi Ayew Pelé** (Ghana)	Olympique Marseille
1993	**Rashidi Yekini** (Nigeria)	Vitória FC Setúbal
1994	**Emmanuel Amunike** (Nigeria)	Sporting CP
1995	**George Weah** (Liberia)	AC Milan
1996	**Nwankwo Kanu** (Nigeria)	Inter
1997	**Victor Ikpeba** (Nigeria)	Monaco
1998	**Mustapha Hadji** (Morocco)	Deportivo La Coruña
1999	**Nwankwo Kanu** (Nigeria)	Arsenal
2000	**Patrick Mboma** (Cameroon)	Parma
2001	**El-Hadji Diouf** (Senegal)	Lens
2002	**El-Hadji Diouf** (Senegal)	Lens / Liverpool FC
2003	**Samuel Eto'o** (Cameroon)	Real Mallorca
2004	**Samuel Eto'o** (Cameroon)	Real Mallorca / Barcelona
2005	**Samuel Eto'o** (Cameroon)	Barcelona
2006	**Didier Drogba** (Ivory Coast)	Chelsea
2007	**Frederic Kanouté** (Mali)	Sevilla

NORTH AND CENTRAL AMERICA AND THE CARIBBEAN: CONCACAF

CCCF AND CONCACAF CHAMPIONSHIPS

The CCCF (Confederación Centroamericana y del Caribe de Fútbol) was founded in 1938 and is the precursor of CONCACAF, which was formed in 1961. The precursors of the current Gold Cup tournament were held under the auspices of the CCCF, then CONCACAF. The last CCCF/CONCACAF Championship was held in 1971; afterward, the winner of the CONCACAF World Cup qualifying zone was considered CCCF champions. Since 1991, the tournament has been revitalized as the Gold Cup.

CCCF WINNERS

YEAR	WINNER
1941	**Costa Rica**
1943	**El Salvador**
1946	**Costa Rica**
1948	**Costa Rica**
1951	**Panama**
1953	**Costa Rica**
1955	**Costa Rica**
1957	**Haiti**
1960	**Costa Rica**
1961	**Costa Rica**

CONCACAF WINNERS

YEAR	WINNER
1963	**Costa Rica**
1965	**Mexico**
1967	**Guatemala**
1969	**Costa Rica**
1971	**Mexico**

WORLD CUP QUALIFYING CONCACAF WINNERS

YEAR	WINNER
1973	**Haiti**
1977	**Mexico**
1981	**Honduras**
1985	**Canada**
1989	**Costa Rica**

GOLD CUP

YEAR	VENUE	WINNER	SCORE	RUNNER UP
1991	USA	**USA**	0–0	Honduras* (4–3)•
1993	Mexico and USA	**Mexico**	4–0	USA
1996	USA	**Mexico**	2–0	Brazil U–23
1998	USA	**Mexico**	1–0	USA
2000	USA	**Canada**	2–0	Colombia
2002	USA	**USA**	2–0	Costa Rica
2003	Mexico and USA	**Mexico**	1–0	Brazil
2005	USA	**USA**	0–0	Panama* (3–1)•
2007	USA	**USA**	2–1	Mexico

*After extra time   •After penalty shootout

CONCACAF CHAMPIONS LEAGUE WINNERS

YEAR	WINNER
1962	**Mexico**
1963	**Haiti**
1964	TOURNAMENT ABANDONED
1965	TOURNAMENT ABANDONED
1966	TOURNAMENT NOT HELD
1967	**Peru**
1968	**Mexico**
1969	**Mexico**
1970	**Mexico**
1971	**Mexico**
1972	**Paraguay**
1973	**Surinam**
1974	**Guatemala**
1975	**Mexico**
1976	**El Salvador**
1977	**Mexico**
1978	**Mexico**
1979	**El Salvador**
1980	**Mexico**
1981	**Surinam**
1982	**Mexico**
1983	**Mexico**
1984	**Haiti**

YEAR	WINNER
1985	**Defence Force Trinidad and Tobago**
1986	**Costa Rica**
1987	**Mexico**
1988	**Paraguay**
1989	**Mexico**
1990	**Mexico**
1991	**Mexico**
1992	**Mexico**
1993	**Costa Rica**
1994	**Costa Rica**
1995	**Costa Rica**
1996	**Mexico**
1997	**Mexico**
1998	**USA**
1999	**Mexico**
2000	**USA**
2001	TOURNAMENT ABANDONED
2002	**Mexico**
2003	**Mexico**
2004	**Costa Rica**
2005	**Costa Rica**
2006	**Mexico**
2007	**Mexico**
2008	**Mexico**

CARIBBEAN NATIONS CUP / CARIBBEAN CHAMPIONSHIP WINNERS

Currently serving biannually as qualifying for the Gold Cup. From 1999 called the Caribbean Nations Cup. From 2008, called the Caribbean Championship.

DATE	WINNER	DATE	WINNER
1989	**Trinidad and Tobago**	1998	**Jamaica**
1990	TOURNAMENT ABANDONED	1999	**Trinidad and Tobago**
1991	**Jamaica**	2000	NOT HELD
1992	**Trinidad and Tobago**	2001	**Trinidad and Tobago**
1993	**Martinique**	2002–04	NOT HELD
1994	**Trinidad and Tobago**	2005	**Jamaica**
1995	**Trinidad and Tobago**	2006	NOT HELD
1996	**Trinidad and Tobago**	2007	**Haiti**
1997	**Trinidad and Tobago**	2008	**Jamaica**

THE RECORDS

ASIA: AFC

INTERNATIONAL AWARDS

ASIAN CUP WINNERS

(Until 1972, no final match was played)

YEAR	WINNERS	SCORE	RUNNER UP
1956	**South Korea**	N/A	Israel
1960	**South Korea**	N/A	Israel
1964	**Israel**	N/A	India
1968	**Iran**	N/A	Burma
1972	**Iran**	2–1	South Korea
1976	**Iran**	1–0	Kuwait
1980	**Kuwait**	3–0	South Korea
1984	**Saudi Arabia**	2–0	China
1988	**Saudi Arabia**	0–0	South Korea* (4–3)●
1992	**Japan**	1–0	Saudi Arabia
1996	**Saudi Arabia**	0–0	United Arab Emirates* (4–2)●
2000	**Japan**	1–0	Saudi Arabia
2004	**Japan**	3–1	China
2007	**Iraq**	1–0	Saudi Arabia
2008			

ASIAN PLAYER OF THE YEAR

YEAR	PLAYER	COUNTRY
1988	**Ahmed Radhi**	Iraq
1989	**Kim Joo-Sung**	South Korea
1990	**Kim Joo-Sung**	South Korea
1991	**KimJoo-Sung**	South Korea
1992	NO AWARD	
1993	**Kazuyoshi Miura**	Japan
1994	**Saeed Al-Owairan**	Saudi Arabia
1995	**Masami Ihara**	Japan
1996	**Khodadad Azizi**	Iran
1997	**Hidetoshi Nakata**	Japan
1998	**Hidetoshi Nakata**	Japan
1999	**Ali Daei**	Iran
2000	**Nawaf Al–Temyat**	Saudi Arabia
2001	**Fan Zhiyi**	China
2002	**Shinji Ono**	Japan
2003	**Mehdi Mahdavikia**	Iran
2004	**Ali Karimi**	Iran
2005	**Hamad Al–Montashari**	Saudi Arabia
2006	**Khalfan Ibrahim**	Qatar
2007	**Yasser Al-Qahtani**	Saudi Arabia
2008	**Server Djeparov**	Uzbekistan

ASIAN CUP TOP SCORERS

NAME	GOALS	COUNTRY
Ali Daei	8	Iran
Behtash Fariba	7	Iran
Choi Soon-Ho	7	South Korea
Lee Dong-Gook	6	South Korea
Hossein Kalani	6	Iran
A'ala Hubail	5	Bahrain Ali
Karimi	5	Iran
Younis Mahmoud	4	Iraq
Yasser Al-Qahtani	4	Saudi Arabia
Naohiro Takahara	4	Japan
Homayoun Behzadi	4	Iran
Giora Spiege	4	Israel
Moshe Romano	4	Israel
Nahum Stelmach	4	Israel
Cho Yoon-Ok	4	South Korea
Fahad Al-Bishi	4	Saudi Arabia
Nasser Nouraei	4	Iran
Gholam Hossein Mazloomi	4	Iran
Fatehi Kamil	4	Kuwait
Jia Xiuquan	4	China
Nasser Mohammadkhani	4	Iran
Shahrokh Baiani	4	Iran
Lee Tae-Ho	3	South Korea
Mordechai Spiegler	2	Israel
Inder Singh	2	India

*After extra time   ●After penalty shootout

CLUB AWARDS

ASIAN CHAMPIONS LEAGUE WINNERS

YEAR	WINNER	SCORE	RUNNER UP
1967	**Hapoel**	2–1	Selangor
1969	**Maccabi**	1–0	Yangzee
1970	**Esteghlal**	2–1	Hapoel
1971	**Maccabi**	WALKOVER	Al–Shourta
1986	**Daewoo Royals**	3–1	Al-Ahly
1987	**Furukawa**	GROUP STAGE WIN	Al-Hilal
1988	**Yomiuri**	WALKOVER	Al-Hilal
1989	**Al-Saad**	3–3	Al-Rasheed
		Al–Saad wins on away goals	
1990	**Liaoning**	3–2	Nissan
1991	**Esteghlal**	2–1	Liaoning
1991	**Al-Hilal**	1–1	Esteghlal* (4–3)•
1993	**Paas**	1–0	Al-Shabab
1994	**Thai Farmers Bank**	2–1	Omani Club
1995	**Thai Farmers Bank**	1–0	Al-Arabi
1995	**Cheonan Ilhwa Chunma**	1–0	Al-Nasr
1997	**Pohang Steelers**	2–1	Cheonan Ilhwa Chunma** (4–3)•
1998	**Pohang Steelers**	0–0	Dalian Wanda
1999	**Jubilo**	2–1	Esteghla
2000	**Al-Hilal**	3–2	Jubilo Iwata
2001	**Suwon Samsung Bluewings**	1–0	Jubilo Iwata
2002	**Suwon Samsung Bluewings**	0–0	Anyang LG Cheetahs** (4–2)•
2003	**Al-Ain**	2–1	BEC Tero Sasana
2004	**Al-Ittihad**	6–3	Seongnam Ilhwa Chunma
2005	**Al-Ittihad**	5–3	Al-Ain
2006	**Chonbuk Hyundai Motors**	3–2	Al-Karama
2007	**Urawa Red Diamonds**	3–1	Sepahan
2008	**Gamba**	5–0	Adelaide

**After sudden death extra time   *After extra time   •After penalty shootout

OCEANIA: OFC

INTERNATIONAL AWARDS

OCEANIAN NATIONS CUP WINNERS

YEAR	WINNER	SCORE	RUNNER UP
1973	**New Zealand**	2–0	Tahiti
1980	**Australia**	4–2	Tahiti
1996	**Australia**	11–0	Tahiti
1998	**New Zealand**	1–0	Australia
2000	**Australia**	2–0	New Zealand
2002	**New Zealand**	1–0	Australia
2004	**Australia**	11–1	Solomon Islands
2008	**New Zealand**	WINS	

CLUB AWARDS

OCEANIA CHAMPIONS' CUP WINNERS

YEAR	WINNER	SCORE	RUNNER UP
1987	**Adelaide City**	1–1	Mount Wellington* (4–1) •
1999	**South Melbourne**	5–1	Nadi
2001	**Wollongong City Wolves**	1–0	Tafea
2005	**Sydney FC**	2–0	AS Magenta
2006	**Auckland City**	3–1	AS Piraé
2007	**Waitakere United**	2–2	Ba
		Waitakere United wins on away goals	
2008	**Waitakere United**	6–3	Kossa

*After extra time   •After penalty shootout

OCEANIAN PLAYER OF THE YEAR

YEAR	PLAYER	COUNTRY	YEAR	PLAYER	COUNTRY
1988	**Frank Farina**	Australia	1998	**Christian Karembeu**	New Caledonia
1989	**Wynton Rufer**	New Zealand	1999	**Harry Kewell**	Australia
1990	**Wynton Rufer**	New Zealand	2000	**Mark Viduka**	Australia
1991	**Robert Slater**	Australia	2001	**Harry Kewell**	Australia
1992	**Wynton Rufer**	New Zealand	2002	**Brett Emerton**	Australia
1993	**Robert Slater**	Australia	2003	**Harry Kewell**	Australia
1994	**Aurelio Vidmar**	Australia	2004	**Tim Cahill**	Australia
1995	**Christian Karembeu**	New Caledonia	2005	**Marama Vahirua**	Tahiti
1996	**Paul Okon**	Australia	2006	**Ryan Nelsen**	New Zealand
1997	**Mark Bosnich**	Australia	2007	**Shane Smeltz**	New Zealand

INDEX

X

Y

Z

W

FURTHER READING

YEARBOOKS AND ENCYCLOPEDIAS

Football Asia, Kuala Lumpur, Asian Football Confederation, annual
Ballard J. and Suff P., **The Dictionary of Football,** Boxtree, Basingstoke, 1999
Creswell P. and Evans S., **European Football: A Fan's Handbook**, Rough Guides, London 1998
Deloitte and Touche Annual Review of Football Finance, Manchester, annual
Il Calcio Italiano Analisi Economico, Deloitte and Touche, Milan, annual
Hammond M. (ed.), **The European Football Yearbook**, Sports Projects, Birmingham, annual
Jelinek R. and Tomes J., **Prvni Fotbalovy Atlas Sveta**, Inforkart, Prague, 2000
Oliver G., **Almanack of World Football**, Harpastum Publishing, London, annual
Oliver G., **The Guinness Book of World Soccer**, 2nd Edition, Guinness, Enfield, 1995
Presti S. (ed.), **Annuario del Calcio Mondiale**, SET, Torino, annual
Radnedge K., **The Complete Encyclopedia of Football**, Carlton Books, London, 1999
Rollin J., **The Rothmans Football Yearbook**, Headline Books, London, annual
FA Premier League National Fan Survey, Sir Norman Chester Centre for Football Research, Leicester, annual survey
Van Hoof S., Parr M., Yamenetti C., **The North and Latin American Football Guide**, Heart Books, Rijmenam, annual

MAGAZINES AND NEWSPAPERS

African Football, AS, A Bola, Calcio 2000, Don Balon, L'Equipe, Football Asia, France Football, Gazetta dello Sport, Guido Sportivo, Kicker, Lance, Marca, Placar, Soccer Analyst, Soccer Investor, Voetbal International, When Saturday Comes, World Soccer. The Daily Telegraph, The Financial Times, The Independent

OVERVIEWS, GLOBAL HISTORIES, COLLECTIONS

Armstrong G. and Giulianotti R. (eds.), **Entering the Field: New Perspectives on World Football,** Berg, Oxford, 1997.
Armstrong G. and Giulianotti R. (eds.), **Football Culture and Identities,** Macmillan, Basingstoke, 1998.
Armstrong G. and Giulianotti R. (eds.), **Fear and Loathing in World Football,** Berg, Oxford, 2001.
Finn G. and Giulianotti R. (eds.), **Football Cultures: Local Conflicts, Global Visions,** Cass, London, 2000.
Giulianotti R., Football: **A Sociology of the Global Game,** Polity Press, Cambridge, 1999.
Glanville B., **The Story of the World Cup**, Faber, London, 2001
Inglis S., **The Football Grounds of England and Wales**, Willow, London, 1983
Inglis, S., **The Football Grounds of Europe**, Willow, London, 1990
Inglis, S., Sightlines: **A Stadium Odyssey**, Yellow Jersey, London, 2000
Kuper S., **Football against the Enemy**, Orion, London, 1994
Murray B., **The World's Game: A History of Soccer**, University of Illinois Press, Urbana, 1994
Sugden J. and Tomlinson A., **Hosts and Champions: Soccer Cultures, National Identities and the USA World Cup**, Arena, Aldershot, 1994
Walvin J., **The People's Game: The History of Football Revisited**, Mainstream, London, 1994
BRAZIL
Bellos, A., **Futbol: the Brazilian Way of Life**, Bloomsbury, London, 2002
Lever J., **Soccer Madness**, University of Chicago Press, Chicago 1983

FRANCE
Ruhn C. (ed.), **Le Foot: the Legends of French Football**, Abacus, London, 2000
Holt R., **Sport and Society in Modern France**, Macmillan, Basingstoke, 1981
ITALY
Manna A. and Gibbs M., **The Day Italian Football Died**, Breedon Books, Derby, 2000
Parks T., **A Season with Verona**, Secker and Warburg, London 2002
JAPAN
Birchall J., **Ultra Nippon: How Japan Reinvented Football**, Headline, London 2000
Moffet S., **Japanese Rules: Why Japan Needed Football and How It Got It**, Yellow Jersey, London 2002
LATIN AMERICA
Mason T., **Passion of the People? Football in South America**, Verso, London, 1995
Taylor C., **The Beautiful Game: A Journey Through Latin American Football**, Phoenix, London, 1998
NETHERLANDS
Winner D., **Brilliant Orange: The Neurotic Genius of Dutch Football**, Bloomsbury, London, 2000
SPAIN
Burns J., Barça, **A People's Passion**, Bloomsbury, London 1999
Hall P., **Morbo: the Story of Spanish Football**, WSC Books Ltd, London
USSR
Edleman R., **Serious Fun: a History of Spectator Sports in the Soviet Union**, Oxford University Press, Oxford, 1993

WEBSITES

www.european-football-statistics.co.uk
www.fifa.com
www.rssf.com
www.theglobalgame.com
www.uefa.com
www.worldstadiums.com

ACKNOWLEDGMENTS

Dorling Kindersley would like to thank the following organizations and people for their help in the prepartion of this book:
Duncan Turner, for the jacket design
Marc Staples, for additional production editorial work
Foster + Partners Ltd, Hiroshi Hara + ATELIER Ø, and Souto Moura Arq. S.A. (Porto)
Shumina Begum, Matt Robbins, Sarah Arnold, Bobby Birchall, Adam Clifton, and Mark Lloyd, for design assistance
Mikhail Sipovich at Colours Of Football and Paul Wootton, for input on the artworks
Ian D. Crane, for the index

For Cooling Brown Ltd
Creative director: Arthur Brown
Design: Tish Jones, Alistair Plumb, Jon Morgan
Editorial: Richard Gilbert, Philip Morgan, Phil Hunt, Jemima Dunne, Dawn Bates
Production: Peter Cooling

PICTURE CREDITS

The publisher would like to thank the following for their kind permission to use their photographs for artists' reference:

(Key: a-above; b-below/bottom; c-center; l-left; r-right; t-top)

Action Images: 113br; **Corbis:** Sandor Bojar/epa 294–295; Geoff Caddick/epa 133t; Christopher Courtois/epa 150–151t; Despotovic Dusko/Corbis Sygma 107; epa 351br; Fiel/yv/EFE 192l; Gary Hershorn/Reuters 314clb; Carmen Jaspersen/epa 126bl; Eddie Keogh/Reuters 209t; Christian Liewig/Tempsport 180r, 214; Leo Mason 128tr; Kai Pfaffenbach/Reuters 212; Stefano Rellandini/Reuters 208cl; Reuters 213, 322–323; Franck Seguin 24–25cr; Franck Seguin/TempSport 235r; Universal/TempSport 301tl; Yossan 94–95; **Getty Images:** AFP 23br, 27bl, 30l, 33, 47b, 49, 52tr, 54cra, 56tl, 67, 97br, 103, 111 (Crouch), 116, 118–119t, 125br, 136l, 140–141, 148–149, 150bl, 175, 176–177, 182r, 186l, 190–191, 200, 204l, 215, 219, 223, 232–233, 233r, 234–235, 240, 257b, 257cl, 258–259, 269b, 270, 271, 272–273, 289r, 291r, 294l, 298tl, 305br, 306tl, 315t, 318tl, 320–321, 328, 334cl, 341br, 348l, 348–349, 350–351, 358–359, 360–361; Bob Thomas 21, 43l, 47t, 101, 111 (Pele), 112l, 128bl, 132tl, 142–143, 159, 162br, 162cl, 163tl, 165b, 166, 169, 171, 176bl, 178–179, 182l, 186tr, 187, 199b, 204–205, 209cl, 230l, 230–231, 236–237, 237tl, 242, 242–243bl, 248, 310, 311b, 312–313, 313r, 314–315, 315br, 315c, 316tr, 318br, 319br, 343; Bongarts 32, 42bl, 54cb, 55b, 58l, 71t, 96–97, 100, 111 (Maradona), 118br, 120br, 120fbr, 165cl, 177bc, 178cl, 183, 188br, 188tl, 189, 195bl, 200–201, 217, 326–327, 327tl, 334–335, 335br, 336, 337l, 353tr; Popperfoto 17, 18, 52bl, 54crb, 55clb, 86, 91l, 91r, 99, 111 (Foulkes), 144bl, 158tr, 161br, 164, 216, 220br, 221bl, 224, 237r, 240–241, 254–255, 286l, 286r, 287, 288l, 292br, 293br, 295r, 296l, 297bc, 298–299, 299br, 301br, 302bl, 302tr, 304bl, 305c, 305tl, 305tr, 307br, 308l, 309r, 321r, 340–341, 342r, 344l, 344–345b, 345br, 345tl, 356; 14, 16, 28, 35, 44, 45, 46bl, 48bl, 48tr, 50tr, 51bl, 51tr, 53, 54ca, 59, 62, 65, 69b, 84, 88, 92r, 93, 98, 102, 104bl, 104r, 110–111, 112r, 113tl, 118bc, 119bc, 119br, 119ca, 120bl, 121br, 121fbr, 121l, 124tr, 130l, 131bl, 134–135, 137t, 145b, 146–147, 151b, 158c, 167l, 167tr, 168, 170, 174bl, 174tr, 179tl, 180bl, 181, 184, 185, 192–193, 193br, 194br, 194l, 195r, 198, 199t, 201t, 202, 205ca, 206–207, 207tr, 208bl, 208br, 209bl, 209br, 209c, 210, 211, 218, 221br, 221cla, 221tl, 221tr, 222, 226, 231br, 234l, 246, 247, 249, 250–251, 256, 259, 260, 261, 267, 272, 276, 278, 279, 280, 290tl, 290–291, 296–297, 300–301b, 303, 306–307, 312tl, 316bl, 317, 320tr, 326tl, 330tr, 330–331, 337t, 340l, 342l, 345c, 345tr, 346tr, 346–347, 347br, 352–353, 354r, 355, 364–365; altrendo images 36–37; Clive Brunskill 64c; Garrett Ellwood / MLS 119cla; Fox Photos 122–123; Keystone 34; Man Utd 43tr, 117, 203; MLS 138–139; National Geographic 304r; Newcastle United 29; Scott Pribyl / MLS 119cra; Andersen Ross 63; Sports Illustrated 61bl, 308–309, 311t; STF / AFP 126tr; **Mirrorpix:** 69t; **PA Photos:** Barrington Coombs/EMPICS Sport 329; EMPICS Sport 55tl; Koji Sasahara/AP 262; **Sky TV:** 105

All images © Dorling Kindersley
For further information see: www.dkimages.com